WITHDRAWN

SKOKIE PUBLIC LIBRARY

3 1232 00523 5389

The Experts Praise
Creative Strategy in Direct and Interactive Marketing

SEP   2011

Creative Strategy in Direct and Interactive Marketing by Susan K. Jones is the one comprehensive guide and handbook that everyone in direct marketing should read and have at their fingertips. Highly recommended and indispensible."

—DAVID FIDELER
Concord Communications and Design

This book is a "must read" for any direct marketing professional. Susan K. Jones combines big-picture thinking with hundreds of examples that bring all of the theories and ideas about creative strategy to life. Whether you are new to direct marketing or a seasoned veteran, you owe it to yourself to read this book from cover to cover. The section on production was especially valuable, and so are the hundreds of relevant examples. Susan covers creative strategy completely and includes the most up-to-date direct marketing techniques and tactics. This book goes directly onto my shelf to be referenced time and again."

—CYNDI W. GREENGLASS
Senior Vice President,
Strategic Solutions,
Diamond Marketing Solutions

The legendary ad man Bill Bernbach once wrote, "Properly practiced creativity can make one ad do the work of ten."* Our business and education challenge becomes: How can powerful creativity be taught, improved and optimized? In this fourth edition, Susan K. Jones brings together her extensive experience as a top DM and digital practitioner with her award-winning college teaching experiences. The result is an easy-to-read, comprehensive guide that covers all of the key elements of effective creative development, from strategy to tactical how-tos. This book is a must-have for any student of advertising, whether in college, in the profession, or an instructor.

—PETER JOHNSON
Professor of Marketing,
Graduate School of Business,
Fordham University

*("Bill Bernbach Said" 1989, DDB Needham)

WITHDRAWN

"If ever there was a perfect time to read *Creative Strategy in Direct & Interactive Marketing—4th Edition,* it is now. At no time in the history of advertising, marketing, or sales promotion have there been so many avenues available to push or pull consumers towards products or services. Knowing the tools, and how and when to use them can make or break the sales goals you set. I have not seen a more clearly laid out set of instructions backed up with background information and advice from professionals in every aspect of the business. If you want to learn how and when to develop a successful direct marketing strategy using modern interactive tools, this book is a must."

—PATRICK KLARECKI
Professor,
Print Media Management,
Ferris State University.

The master of direct creativity, Susan Jones, has now mastered interactive creativity. Learn how to combine, contrast and connect the dots in today's new world of customer-driven interactive marketing for any type of message or messaging designed to deliver results time after time.

—DON E. SCHULTZ
President, Agora
Emeritus, Medill School of Journalism and
Integrated Marketing Communications

For as long as I've been in direct marketing, I've always been impressed with Susan K. Jones' broad understanding of this business, her complete mastery of the craft, and her ability to foresee its future. Her book is important and useful to seasoned practitioners and novices alike. Read it thoroughly and return to it often.

—MARC ZINER
Managing Partner/Creative,
Marketing Highway

Creative Strategy in DIRECT& INTERACTIVE Marketing

FOURTH EDITION

SUSAN K. JONES
Ferris State University
Susan K. Jones & Associates

RĀCOM
COMMUNICATIONS

SKOKIE PUBLIC LIBRARY

Copyright © 2012 Susan K. Jones
Editor and publisher: Richard Hagle

Published by
Racom Communications
150 N. Michigan Ave.
Suite 2800
Chicago, IL 60601
800-247-6553

In conjunction with

The Direct Marketing Association
1120 Avenue of the Americas
New York, NY 10036

All rights reserved. No part of this book may be reproduced, stored in a retrieval system, or transmitted in any form or by any means, electronic, mechanical, photocopying, recording, or otherwise, without the prior permission of Racom Communications.

Catalog-in-Publication data available from the Library of Congress.

Printed in the United States of America

ISBN: 978-1-933199-31-3

This book is dedicated to
Sheridan Doris Jones
"Isn't She Lovely."

Contents

PART THREE

CREATING AND PRODUCING THE WORK   317

Foreword

No matter how many new car models debut each year—sleeker, fancier and highly computerized—one thing doesn't change: the need for four tires. That is creative's role in direct and interactive marketing.

Good creative is the lifeblood of any campaign, online, offline or mobile. In an era when consumers are bombarded with thousands of messages and visuals daily from sunrise to sunset, the right play between word and image can make the difference between success and failure.

Having covered advertising, marketing, media and retail all my working life, the common thread through all the reporting of successful brands and their campaigns was the need to make an emotional connection with the consumer—even more finicky today than in the era known as BI, or Before Internet.

The Talk on Mobile

As currently practiced, digital marketing including online and mobile enables marketers to establish that link between brand and consumer quicker and in a personal manner.

Indeed, mobile marketing has best of all worlds, including the interactivity of online, the directness of mail and email, and the demonstrative qualities of broadcast.

Mobile, in fact, is not a channel, but a medium that encompasses voice, SMS, email, display, content, commerce, video and television, photos, games and social media.

Add to that the convergence between mediums and channels, especially online, mobile and social. Brands couldn't have a more potent marketing and commerce cocktail.

However, the old rules of marketing haven't changed: brands need a good list, great offer and resonating creative. Consumers need to be wooed pre-purchase, while in the process and post-sale.

In other words, old school is cool—no matter how many new students pass through. The principles of marketing are evergreen, regardless of the medium that develops as a result of enhanced technology prowess.

One thing guaranteed from the birth of new marketing mediums to complement the existing channels is the rapid generation of mounds of data. If anything, all advertising and marketing is now database marketing.

New Channels, But Same Principles

Today, mobile and online marketing have captured the hearts and minds of brands, retailers, ad agencies, marketing service providers and publishers. They stand dazzled by applications, mobile sites, new phones and tablets and the winning talk from Apple, Google, Facebook, Microsoft and Amazon.

In their haste to co-opt the new, marketers must not forget that each marketing channel has its place in the consumer-wooing ecosystem.

Direct mail, like email, is push, reminding consumers that the brand or offer needs serious consideration. Catalogs are tactile and portable, bringing a brand to life, adding touch and feel to the shopping equation. Outdoor is a visual reminder. Television is demonstrative. Radio is the audio companion. In-store is in-presence.

So it bears repeating. What underpins good marketing strategy is an understanding of the target audience, tailoring an appropriate permission-based message with the right enticement and delivering it at the time when it will most resonate.

Susan Jones captures this perfectly in the latest edition of "Creative Strategy in Direct & Interactive Marketing." Her knowledge is grounded not just in theory, but also practice. As readers will learn perusing this book, the basic recipe for marketing success remains the same: the right blend of strategy, creative, offer and target. That's as direct as it gets.

Mickey Alam Khan
Editor in chief
Mobile Marketer
Mobile Commerce Daily
Luxury Daily

Preface

The marketing system we "noun" as *direct* is known more for its science—predictive modeling, databases, Customer Relationship Management—than for its art.

In this fourth edition, Susan K. Jones again admonishes us to do better at satisfying the strong appetite for good creative work in direct advertising. Of equal importance, however, she urges us to develop a more clear focus on strategy, especially significant in this era of expanding dialogue between business and customer.

Interactivity has arrived. Direct is two-way.

Advertising still has its way with words. Our world uses *creative*, an adjective everywhere else, as a noun. *Creative* in advertising suggests a person or place. *Creative* is the thing. It paints pictures and forms words that give advertising its punch and its power. The pictures and words we call *the creative* come from a department we call *creative*. The noun *creative* is almost exclusively associated with one department in the advertising agency.

Embedded within the title of her updated classic, however, Susan Jones uses *creative* as an adjective to describe a particular form or type of *strategy,* a double meaning for sure, and one that is ironic. The entirety of the advertising industry, including *direct*, is dependent in all respects—but especially in its strategy—upon creativity. This book is as much dedicated to explicating what defines a creative strategy as it is to describing what defines a strategy as creative.

Creative Strategy in Direct and Interactive Marketing speaks in equal volume to the science and the art of sales campaigning. Susan Jones calls this equilibrium "the profitable balance." At the fulcrum is the force of clever strategy.

The book is as much about strategy as it is about the *creative* upon which effective strategy depends. It is strategy, after all—clear, direct and powerful strategy—that circumscribes the creativity for which the industry is known. Who could have said it better than Ogilvy and Mather *creative* Norman Berry pleading for "the freedom of a tightly defined strategy"?

This book achieves the obvious objective of giving designers and writers a deeper understanding of how creative approach fits into the overall marketing plan. This so achieved in a category of marketing historically defined, if not circumscribed, by an obsession with targets and offers. But the greatest beneficiaries of the book may be the green-eyeshade people—the account executives, media planners, traffic managers, budgeters and financiers who, after its reading, will appreciate, some for the first time, the role visual and verbal artists play in powerful execution of the interactive strategy. They may also appreciate the degree to which a proclivity for creativity is becoming table stakes for anyone who desires a seat at the advertising table.

Susan Jones' opening chapter demonstrates effectively how all "direct and interactive marketing blends art (creativity, talent, and open-ended exploration) with science (research, market testing, segmentation, and measurability)."

Modern *direct* is expanding consumer engagement through a technology-empowered requirement for interaction—creative dialogue, the back-and-forth flow of information.

Speaking to the industry, Susan Jones says: "To become a successful direct and interactive marketer, it is vital to stoke your creative fires: moving beyond the obvious formula and format to discover fresh words and pictures that overcome inertia and incite prospects to action."

As life imitates art, Susan Jones herself is "a profitable balance" of successful marketing consultant and competent academic—part artist and part scientist. Those who might believe that creativity resides within the exclusive domain of those who write words or draw pictures may be disappointed that this book does not reinforce such anachronistic prejudice.

In fact, this book represents quite the opposite position by demonstrating that, if properly inspired, every player on the *direct* team—from the mailer to the board member—is capable of participating in the envisioning, articulation and execution of creative strategy, as they are for the strategy of the creative.

The book is, after all, a recognized creative classic. Someday it may be recognized as a strategy classic as well.

Richard Cole
Professor
Advertising, Public Relations, and Retailing
Michigan State University

PART ONE

Laying the Groundwork

A Profitable Blend of Art and Science

To become a successful direct and interactive marketer, it is vital to stoke your creative fires: moving beyond the obvious formula and format to discover fresh words and pictures that overcome inertia and incite prospects to action. And considering the pervasiveness of predictive modeling, databases, Customer Relationship Management and other analytical elements of today's marketing world, successful copywriters and graphic designers must also hone their expertise in the scientific side of the business.

Indeed, ever since the great copywriter Claude Hopkins coined the term *scientific advertising*, direct and interactive marketers have worked to reach a profitable balance between science and art . . . technique and creativity. At its best, direct and interactive marketing combines the freedom to explore new worlds of creativity with the discipline of measured response . . . the challenge of searching for bright, new ideas and the satisfaction of measuring those ideas' worth in units sold and long-term customer value achieved.

This chapter offers a historical review showing how direct and interactive marketing blends art (creativity, talent, and open-ended exploration) with science (research, market testing, segmentation, and measurability). But first: a brief discussion of direct marketing, Integrated Marketing Communications (IMC), and Multichannel Marketing.

The Definition of Direct Marketing

The late Henry R. "Pete" Hoke, Jr., who was publisher of *Direct Marketing* magazine for many years, defined *direct marketing* as:

> An interactive system of marketing that uses one or more advertising media
> to effect a measurable response and/or transaction at any location, with this
> activity stored on database.

This definition touches on several important points.

1. Direct marketing is a *system of marketing*. That means that it hinges on the marketing concept: creating and promoting products that fill specific consumer and business wants and needs.
2. Direct marketing is *interactive*. It attempts to set up a cause-and-effect relationship with the prospect, asking for a certain response to a call to action, and fostering a dialogue rather than one-way communication.

3. Direct marketing uses *one or more advertising media.* In previous generations, direct marketers delivered most of their messages via space advertising, direct mail, and catalogs. Today, additional media such as telephone, television, radio, the Internet, mobile marketing, and social media may serve as a direct marketer's conduit to customers.

4. Direct marketing produces a *measurable response.* To achieve this, the direct marketing message includes a response device such as a coupon, toll-free or mobile telephone number, e-mail address, Web site, landing page, Web response form, or mail-in address. The direct marketer's call to action is met with an exact number of sales or leads, which then can be measured against objectives.

5. Direct marketing may involve a *transaction at any location.* Thus direct marketers may receive their responses not only via media, but also when customers bring coupons sent by mail or mobile device—or printed out online—to a retail outlet, or when they show up for an advertised sale, or visit a local dealer mentioned in a national ad campaign.

6. Direct marketing activity is *stored on database*. This allows direct marketers to record and manipulate data that helps them to offer customers and prospects the best possible, personalized and customized offers at the optimum times through the most appropriate media.

Interactive Marketing and Customer Empowerment

While interactivity has always been part of the direct marketing definition, today's powerful databases and highly individualized Web sites make the interactive element more crucial than ever before. As Stanford University Professor Ward Hanson defines it, interactivity is "the back-and-forth flow of information. For a Web site, participation plus procedural rules lead to interactivity." When such procedural rules are properly and carefully programmed into a Web site, they allow for real time reactions to customer requests that are sometimes uncanny in their appropriateness and helpfulness. As Ward Hanson explains, "Such a Web site may anticipate user choices and suggest possible alternatives."

This means that when interactive marketing is effectively applied, consumers can get the kind of personalized guidance and shopping assistance online that they can only dream of in today's impersonal, mass-oriented retail environment. Interactive marketing can lead to true customer empowerment, allowing individuals to identify potential product choices and then compare features, benefits, and prices from the comfort of their homes or offices. They can also share their experiences with products and services via social media, and rate those items on Web sites so that other consumers may benefit by their guidance.

The Economic Impact of Direct and Interactive Marketing

Figures provided by The Direct Marketing Association (DMA) put the strength and growth of direct and interactive marketing into perspective as part of the American economy. According to the DMA, annual U.S. sales revenue attributed to consumer direct and interactive marketing topped $1 trillion in 2010, while business-to-business direct and interactive marketing sales amounted to $786.5 billion. Consumer direct and interactive marketing sales are expected to continue to grow at a compound annual rate of 4.9 percent per year through 2014, reaching more than $1.24 trillion. Business-to-business sales are projected to grow at a compound annual rate of 5.4 percent through 2014, to a total of $988.5 billion.

The sales revenue attributed to online media is growing even more dramatically than are offline media sales, according to the DMA. In 2010, total consumer and business-to-business sales resulting from social networking hit $15.9 billion, with an expected compound growth rate of 15.9 percent through 2014. Combined consumer and business-to-business sales resulting from Internet display ads totaled $151.8 billion in 2010, and were expected to grow on by a compound average yearly rate of 8.3 percent through 2014. "Other" Internet-generated sales represented $69.7 billion in 2010, and Internet Search sales were $266.3 billion that same year.

In 2010, according to the DMA, nearly 10 million workers were employed throughout the U.S. economy as a result of direct and interactive marketing activities—representing more than seven percent of the total U.S. work force. Approximately two million of these U.S. employees worked in interactive marketing areas including e-mail, Internet display advertising, Internet search advertising, and social networking.

Characteristics of Direct and Interactive Marketing

The essential character of direct and interactive marketing lies in its *action orientation*. General advertising may inform, persuade, or remind prospects about products or services, but it does not sell. To sell, or to invite a step toward a sale, direct and interactive marketers include a call to immediate action and an easy-to-use response device. Direct and interactive marketers make specific offers: they tell prospects what they're going to get and what they have to do to get it—be it a product in exchange for a price, free information in exchange for a phone call, or some other quid pro quo. In addition to action orientation, direct and interactive marketing has several other important characteristics.

Targeted

Successful direct and interactive marketers develop products and services that will appeal to specific groups of consumers—groups that are *measurable*, *reachable*, and *sizable* enough to ensure meaningful sales volume. Direct and interactive marketers' ability to tailor a list of prospect names combining several characteristics—for instance, proven mail order buyers who own home exercise equipment and take at least two ski vacations a year; or online buyers of both popular novels and infant toys—allows them to carve out new market segments with profit potential.

Personal

Because direct marketers can record so much about their customers' and prospects' buying habits and preferences as well as lifestyle information and Web surfing behavior, they are able to address these people in very specific terms—as tennis enthusiasts, classic movie buffs, or whatever. What's more, today's database and printing applications (including Personalized URLs or PURLs) and "on the fly" Web site responses make possible a broad range of personalization techniques as well as one-to-one customized messages and offers.

Measurable

Because each direct and interactive marketing message carries a call to action, the advertiser is able to measure the effectiveness of mailings, calls, ads, and online offers by tracking the sales, leads, or other responses received. This makes direct and interactive marketers *accountable* for every dollar they spend.

Testable

Because direct and interactive marketers can generate firm numbers that measure the effectiveness of their efforts, it is possible for them to devise accurate head-to-head tests of offers, formats, price, payment terms, creative approach, and much more—all in relatively small and affordable quantities.

Flexible

This is especially true in direct mail, where there are few constraints on size, color, timing, and format. Other than conformance to U.S. Postal Service standards, a direct mail marketer can sell with formats ranging from a post card to a 9″ × 12″ envelope to a three-dimensional package. The mailing date is set by the marketer—not by a publication.

The Role of Direct and Interactive Marketing in Integrated Marketing Communications

The concept of *Integrated Marketing Communications (IMC)* makes absolute sense—so much so that novices in the field may wonder what all the commotion is about. IMC suggests that marketers look at their customer first—his/her preferences, buying patterns, media exposure, and other factors—and then expose that customer to products and services that fit his/her needs via a mix of communication methods the consumer finds attractive and credible.

As Don E. Schultz, Stanley I. Tannenbaum, and Robert F. Lauterborn asserted in their book, *The New Marketing Paradigm*, IMC challenges marketers to "start with the customer and work back to the brand." Why was this revolutionary? Not because it was a new or controversial concept, but because a whole culture of agencies, in-house departments, and consultants once grew up around the notion of separation for advertising, direct marketing, sales promotion, and public relations efforts, rather than the harmonious, customer-centered planning process that IMC requires. What's more, in their haste to get an initial Web site up and running, many companies established their online marketing presence apart from their traditional direct marketing businesses, thereby perpetuating this wall of separation into the new century.

At its worst, this old-style culture leads to arguments among professionals as to how a media budget will be split: how much for general advertising, how much for direct marketing, how much for the Web site, social media and mobile marketing, and so on. Such "turf wars" have very little to do with what the *customer* wants and needs. They rely on chauvinistic notions that "my method is better"—that direct and interactive marketing is inherently superior to sales promotion, for example, or that general advertising is more refined, and therefore more appropriate, than "pushier" direct and interactive marketing techniques.

Because of the paradigm shift required to implement IMC, direct marketers and their counterparts in general advertising, sales promotion, and public relations continue to work to come to grips with this concept. As with other deep cultural changes, intellectual acceptance may long precede the ability to embrace the gains and losses inherent in this new way of doing things. While the evolution continues, this conceptual framework may help creative people to understand IMC and use its tenets to their advantage.

The Evolution That Led to IMC

In their book, Schultz, Tannenbaum, and Lauterborn relate the societal and business changes that led to the need for IMC. They talk about how the propaganda machine of World War II actually heralded IMC with its emphasis on production aimed at victory. This message was imbedded in everything from consumer product ads to current movies. After the war, the IMC concept was lost for a time because of pent-up demand for consumer goods. Mass products could easily be sold by mass media.

What the authors call "demassification" began in the 1970s, however, as economic growth slowed. Since then, mass media have lost much of their punch, and mass messages have—more and more—fallen on deaf ears. In an economy where most product categories are at the maturity stage, many customers are militant or at least wary, and consumers have taken charge of their own media consumption patterns and product ratings. Smart marketers seek integration for their messages as a way to create "a respectful, two-way dialogue."

The Four Elements of IMC

Integrated Marketing Communications encompasses *general advertising*, *sales promotion,* and *public relations* as well as *direct marketing*. In this definition, interactive marketing is combined under the direct marketing banner. Some IMC campaigns feature aspects of all four elements, while others may eliminate one or more elements for strategic reasons. The American Association of Advertising Agencies has defined IMC as follows:

> Integrated Marketing Communications is a concept of marketing communi-
> cations planning that recognizes the added value in a program that integrates
> a variety of strategic disciplines, e.g., general advertising, direct response,
> sales promotion and public relations and combines these disciplines to pro-
> vide clarity, consistency and maximum communications impact.

In an integrated campaign, *general advertising* shines at strengthening brands and brand equity while *direct and interactive marketing* builds relationships and dialogue, and provides the means to close sales. *Public relations*—mainly publicity in this case—offers third-party endorsements and extra reinforcement for the paid advertising messages. *Sales promotion* provides short-term buying incentives for both consumers and the trade. None of the four elements is inherently superior or inferior; they all have important functions in an integrated campaign. The campaign should focus on a "big idea" and a graphic look that threads through all four elements. This maximizes the chances that consumers will get the message and then have the message reinforced and layered in their memories without the "cognitive dissonance" that arises from mixed messages or incongruous graphic-elements.

Multichannel Marketing

Multichannel marketing is the use of multiple media (typically a catalog, a Web site, and a brick-and-mortar retail presence), to effectively reach and serve a targeted customer group. As the IMC concept has evolved, it has increased its focus on this type of multi-faceted communications between buyer and seller—necessitating a sophisticated database integrated across all media and all channels.

Today the Internet has become a vital element in the marketing communications mix, and Internet marketers who lose sight of the importance of integration with other channels and media will do so at their peril. While some firms may choose to present a different message and "look" online, they

Exhibit 1.1. Tiffany Web Site

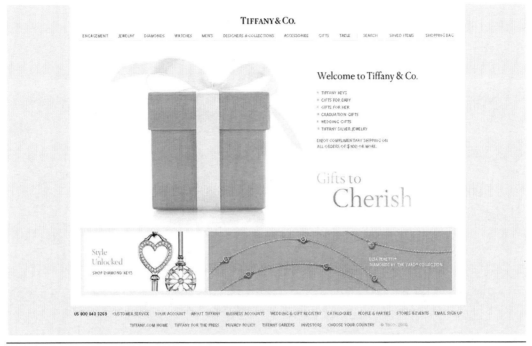

The Web site at www.tiffany.com combines the robin's egg blue color and elegant-yet-streamlined design that also characterize the company's catalog and retail store interiors. Visitors to the site can download and "flip through" Tiffany's several catalogs, and also get directions to their nearest Tiffany store.

Reprinted from the Tiffany Web site at www.tiffany.com.

must make that decision strategically. And most firms will be best served by presenting a Web site that harmonizes with the images and messages of their traditional print and broadcast media. Here are several elements of successful multichannel marketing:

Integrated "Look and Feel"

For a simple example of "total creative integration," leaf through the print catalog of Tiffany & Co., then log on to their Web site at *www.tiffany.com,* and then visit one of their elegant retail stores. Tiffany's catalogs almost always feature the same shiny robin's egg blue cover and white internal pages with minimal copy, lots of negative space (white space), and simple-yet-tasteful product presentation. The Web site displays those same colors, graphics, and type styles—which you'll see echoed again at the retail store where every Tiffany's purchase is presented in a shiny robin's egg blue box with silky white ribbon.

Another fine example is Williams-Sonoma. The firm's catalogs and stores are so well integrated that visiting a Williams-Sonoma store is like stepping into the catalog—and vice-versa. Store visitors may be treated to cooking demonstrations, sampling, and advice on food preparation and presentation. The catalog offers how-to sidebars and recipes, while the Web site *(www.williamssonoma.com)* picks up on the same look and feel with beautiful "lifestyle" photography, recipes, and tips for creative cooks.

Exhibit 1.2. Williams-Sonoma Catalog

The Williams-Sonoma catalog and stores are so well integrated that visiting a Williams-Sonoma store is like stepping into the catalog—and vice-versa. The Web site at www.williamssonoma.com picks up on the same look and feel.

Reprinted with permission of Williams-Sonoma, Inc.

A Strategic Choice for a Unique Online Focus

As much as marketers value the customer knowledge and recognition they gain by integrating their messages, some firms decide to modify their look and feel online for corporate reasons. For example, as pointed out by catalog expert Ed Bjorncrantz, the automotive supplier J. C. Whitney (*www.jcwhitney.com*) has better product presentation and easier search than the firm's catalogs. Bjorncrantz says that's because you can only "cut" a catalog two-dimensionally—by vehicle, by product category, or some simple combination. On a Web site, you can do search by vehicle, keyword, product, or any other method that's helpful to the customer. The Web site is structured to allow the customer to navigate the way they want to do it. You can also create specialty landing pages that help address certain markets that are attracted through e-mails, affiliate programs, banner ads, and the like.

Integrating the Database

At computer and office technology products marketer CDW (*www.cdw.com*), one integrated database covers every transaction and communication, no matter what medium is involved. Account managers can pull up an account and see in a summary system how many times that customer has used the Web site and/or their Extranet, what they've been buying, how many tech support calls have been made, what returns were made, sales this year versus last year, and much more. CDW built its own Customer Relationship Management system in-house, as well as its own order management system."

Let the Customer Buy When and Where They Want

Most direct and interactive marketers agree that if they can entice a customer to buy both online and offline, that customer's long-term value will grow. Yet they also realize the best way to build satisfaction and loyalty is to cater to the customer's buying preferences and habits. Steve Katzman of Steve's Blinds and Wallpaper calls his firm "the Burger King of the home decorating industry—have it your way! Whatever way you want to communicate with us, we'll do it. It costs too much to have a customer consider working with you to shut them down by not facilitating the buying channel they prefer."

This means that every catalog page or spread should include the company's Web site address and toll-free phone number, and that the Web site should allow customers to view the print catalog and access handy functions such as Live Chat or a place to click that will alert customer service to call the customer immediately. What's more, retail stores should be kept up to date about what is featured in catalogs and on the Web so that when customers visit with catalog in hand—or ask about "that item on the front of your Web page," they can help the customer immediately.

Don't Abandon Print When You Go Online

When the World Wide Web first gained prominence in the mid-1990s, some pundits predicted the demise of most every other medium—particularly print. Yet successful online marketers have found that the strategic combination of print and online marketing methods optimizes their efforts. What's more, history shows us that new media do not obliterate old media, they simply sharpen the focus of each medium's function. For example, television's swift rise to ubiquity with strong national networks and exceptional visual qualities did not "kill" radio in the 1950s. Rather, it inspired radio executives to reinvent their medium as a highly segmented, locally focused provider of music and information.

Jim Shanks, formerly of CDW, doesn't believe that the strategic use of multiple media—especially catalogs—will end anytime soon. Noting that CDW mails tens of millions of catalogs every year and that every one of them talks about the Web site, he asks, "How many magazines would you have to take space ads in to get that kind of a circulation?

While online multi-level marketer Amway Global (formerly Quixtar) started as a pure-play Internet company without print support, its executives were quick to add catalogs to the mix. "We realized early on that we couldn't ignore print," says the firm's founding Managing Director, Ken McDonald. John Parker, the firm's founding Vice-President of Sales and Marketing adds, "Out of the gate, not having print support was a mistake, but we responded very quickly. If we had it to do over again, we would have had print right away." Ironically, after McDonald and Parker moved on to other challenges, the next Amway Global marketing team again tried to eliminate the firm's print catalog. Once again, they were quick to reinstate it, realizing that the integration of online and offline media best serves their customer base.

Direct and Interactive Marketing: A Brief History

Social changes and technological advances have fueled major development and growth of direct marketing since the late nineteenth century. Yet even 500 years ago, publishers in Europe used catalogs to attract customers for the new wealth of books available after Johann Gutenberg invented moveable type around 1450. And nurserymen let gardeners know of their wares with seed and plant catalogs issued regularly in England by the late 1700s.

Meanwhile in the American colonies, Benjamin Franklin formed what might be called the first continuity-style book club. Each member paid an entrance fee and dues for the privilege of reading books they selected by catalog. Franklin also published his own bookselling catalog in 1744, boasting nearly 600 titles. In it he pioneered the basic idea of "satisfaction guaranteed or your money back."

During this same period, another major influence of direct marketers came into play: the peddler who sold soaps and patent medicines by means of demonstration, traveling door-to-door or gathering crowds in village squares. Direct marketing masters from Claude Hopkins to Alvin Eicoff have attributed much of their success to techniques learned from these eloquent stand-up salesmen.

Ward and Sears Herald Modern Direct Marketing

Although such enduring American direct marketing firms as Orvis, L. L. Bean, and Tiffany were already well established with catalogs in the early 1800s, the innovations of Montgomery Ward and Sears, Roebuck & Co. are generally considered the beginnings of modern direct marketing in the United States.

As a peddler traveling across the Midwest, Aaron Montgomery Ward developed a unique business strategy idea. It hinged upon the slogan of the powerful farmer's group called the Grange: "Eliminate the Middleman." Ward would sell directly to the consumer and save his customers the money they perceived as going to undeserving intermediaries. Ward started his direct mail business in America's transportation center, Chicago, in 1872. By 1884 his catalog grew to 240 pages.

Many of Ward's brilliant innovations still are used today to good effect by direct and interactive marketers. He guaranteed all products unconditionally, and showed pictures of his employees throughout the catalog to prove that this was indeed a person-to-person operation. His folksy customer service letters matched the tone of friendship in those he received from his isolated rural customers.

Richard Warren Sears first learned the power of direct selling when he peddled a package of watches to his fellow railroad agents in Minnesota. Ads in newspapers followed and by 1887 young Sears was ready to team with Alvah Curtis Roebuck, a watchmaker and printer. Like Ward, Richard Sears and his partner offered money-back guarantees on all products. Hard work and a natural instinct for direct marketing helped Sears, Roebuck & Co. grow to an annual mailing volume of 75 million pieces by 1927. Besides the family Bible, Wards and Sears catalogs were often the only books in the house for America's turn-of-the-century rural families. Some social historians argue that the electric refrigerators and other appliances offered in these wish books provided the concrete evidence farmers needed to understand and support the drive for rural electrification.

Business for both Ward and Sears grew even more once the U.S. Postal Service began Rural Free Delivery in the 1890s and Parcel Post in 1913, making shipping to even remote areas a simple and timely proposition.

Salesmanship in Print

The next generation of advertisers built upon the principles established by Montgomery Ward and Sears, Roebuck & Co. to expand the applications of direct marketing in space advertising and direct mail. Albert Lasker was a fledgling newspaper man who fell in love with advertising and never returned to journalism. He learned two key direct marketing ideas from his enigmatic mentor, copywriter John E. Kennedy. In his reminiscences, first published years ago in *Advertising Age*, Lasker recalled how Kennedy's definition of advertising changed his life and the course of his career.

In those turn-of-the-century days, the main function of an advertising agency was to act as a space ad placement broker for clients. To make their services more attractive, some of these advertising agents offered to create the advertising for their clients. In most cases, their main objective was simply to keep the client's name before the public.

But Kennedy told Lasker that advertising should be much more than that. Effective advertising was *salesmanship in print*. He went on to explain that the key to this salesmanship was "reasons why" copy—writing that convinced the reader that the product was worthy because of its *features* and *benefits*.

Other advertising men of Lasker's and Claude Hopkins's generation were discovering and amplifying the same principles in agencies and companies throughout the East and Midwest. Notable among these were Harry Schermann and Maxwell Sackheim, who launched their "Little Leather Library" in 1916. Unimpressed by the volume of sales they could obtain through retail outlets, the two men began offering their books by mail. At that time, there were few bookstores outside major cities.

Availability of the Library by mail enabled thousands of striving Americans—many of them immigrants—to obtain the books they desired for themselves and their children. The Library's success led Schermann and Sackheim to develop the Book-of-the-Month Club in 1926, paving the way for today's plethora of continuity programs selling books, music, plants and flowers, and food on by-the-month plans.

The Direct Mail Advertising Association (now the Direct Marketing Association) was founded in 1917, and the U.S. Postal Service inaugurated third class bulk mail in 1928. In those days, the first major business-to-business direct marketers emerged, seeking qualified leads for their sales forces. Principal among these were National Cash Register Co. and Burroughs Adding Machine Co.

After World War II, the parents of the "baby boom" generation sought all manner of goods, but often found them in short supply in neighborhood stores. New catalog and direct marketing firms filled the void, including Miles Kimball, Hanover House, and Fingerhut. The 1950s saw the growth of Time-Life, perhaps the first firm to fully understand the potential of a database, recording demographic and psychographic information about customers.

The Growth of Direct Marketing: Social and Technological Change

The 1960s was a decade of profound social change in the United States, as well as a time of many technological advances that spurred the growth of direct marketing. It was during this period that most of the forces that drive the direct marketing boom first emerged.

Advances in Computer Technology

Recording and manipulating a database became feasible when fast and affordable computers penetrated the American business market. The new technology also has allowed for useful innovations in printing and production such as laser, inkjet, and digital personalization techniques as well as digital graphic design, printing and production.

The Emergence of Interactive Marketing

The Internet, originally a tool for the military and universities, found a booming business and consumer market in the 1990s—fueled by user-friendly navigation software, powerful search engines, and high-quality graphics on the World Wide Web. Online services, which had served a small, cult-like audience for years, caught fire in the 1990s as well.

Even though most marketing and IT conferences circa 1997–2000 featured at least one keynoter asserting, "The Internet Changes Everything," the dot.com boom of the late 1990s turned into a bust in the first year or two of the new millennium. But while dot.coms died by the score—and the promise of swift and radical transformation to e-business faded like the Nasdaq's all-time high of 5,132.52—seasoned marketers had expected no less. That dot.com bust represented an inevitable phase in the Internet's life cycle, resulting in the survival of the fittest.

Targeted Media Opportunities

Just as the Sears general catalog has given way to smaller and more specialized books offering narrow product lines like tools, outdoor furniture, supplies for babies and work wear from Sears, the old mass magazines such as *Life* and *Look* have been supplanted by books that define their audiences: *Working Mother*, *Organic Gardening*, and *Men's Health*, just to name a few among hundreds of targeted titles. And the three old-line television networks, with their "all things to all people" programming, lose ground year by year to more targeted networks like Fox and The CW, and to specialized outlets like CNN Headline News, ESPN (all sports), Univision (Spanish), HGTV (Home and Garden Television), and home shopping channels. At the same time, marketers have learned to use broadcast and satellite radio stations geared toward news, talk, classical music, and other defined audiences for direct response offers. What's more, with the unlimited real estate offered by the Web, marketers can develop specialized and targeted sites for sub-sets of their businesses, very cost-effectively.

Growth of Consumer Credit

American Express, Visa, MasterCard, Discover, and other widely distributed credit cards offer consumers the opportunity to make impulse buying decisions, a boon for direct and interactive marketers. Consumer credit works hand-in-hand with telemarketing and online marketing to streamline the buying process: customers can call a toll-free telephone number or fill an online shopping cart, provide their card numbers, and order products from the comfort of home. Credit cards and payment services like PayPal and Bill Me Later also increase the opportunity for trust on both sides of the buying transaction. The marketer is protected against much of the risk of bad credit, and the buyer can call on the credit card or payment firm to help if there is a customer service problem.

Decline in Personal Service

Americans believe that they got better service from retailers in the "good old days." They remember when career salespeople who knew their merchandise well would provide individual service, calling customers by name and showing them deference and respect. Contrast this with today's transient retail sales clerk, often paid a minimum wage and no commission. Add the time-wasting prospect of standing in line only to find that the desired item is out of stock, and it is no wonder that consumers are ripe for the convenience of shopping at home. Vast improvements in direct and interactive marketers' inbound telemarketing systems, their online sales operations, their customer service capabilities, and their inventory and shipping controls have made shopping from home a viable alternative even for those who need merchandise delivered quickly.

Changing Lifestyles

The classic American family, with Dad employed outside the home and Mom staying at home with two or more children, now accounts for only a tiny fraction of American family units. There are more single-parent families and dual-career families than ever before. Women represent about 47 percent of the U.S. work force, and at least one in five working wives makes more money than her husband.

With these changes has come an important alteration in family buying patterns. Today's working woman often has more money than time to invest in shopping. Thus she prefers to complete her buying transactions as quickly and painlessly as possible. Direct and interactive marketers offer ways to do this: catalog; TV home shopping, Internet shopping or even mobile phone purchasing at any hour of day or night; toll-free, 24-hour phone lines for ordering; home or office delivery, including affordable overnight or two-day delivery; liberal guarantees; free-trial privileges; and much more.

Shopping at home also allows customers to remain safe and anonymous in their own "comfort zones"—attributes that are growing in importance to many busy consumers and senior citizens today. Home shoppers need not get dressed up, carry mace spray units on their key chains, or walk through deserted parking lots or garages with their purchases in hand.

In addition, the higher incomes of dual-career families allow them to indulge in hobbies and leisure activities. Special-interest groups like white-water rafters, hunters, movie buffs, and many more offer direct and interactive marketers a fertile field for development of targeted product lines.

A Diverse and Affluent Marketplace

In the United States today, in terms of percentages, the fastest-growing population group is that of Asian-Americans, followed by Hispanics/Latinos, and African-Americans. Sometime in the first half of the twenty-first century, experts project that whites will become a minority in the United States—in other words, people of color will make up 51 percent or more of the American population. While well-heeled consumers who represent visible minority groups may often be forced to purchase products that are promoted using only white faces, music, speech patterns, and culture, their preferences are clear: they appreciate being targeted much more directly.

With media choices broadening, direct marketers can reach specific racial and ethnic groups in magazines and newspapers, and on cable networks like Black Entertainment Television (BET) and Univision (Spanish). Interactive One operates more than 60 Web sites, including social media sites, news sites, and 53 local radio sites, all focused on African-American audiences. Restaurant chains including McDonalds and KFC have reaped considerable financial rewards by tailoring messages and even store decor and menus to the racial and ethnic groups who live and work near specific

Exhibit 1.3. Univision Web Site Capture

The Univision Web site (www.univision.com) and cable television network deliver content and promotions aimed at America's fast-growing and affluent Hispanic community.

Reprinted from the Univision site at www.univision.com.

stores. Automobile companies, cigarette marketers, and sporting goods firms are among many others that have become much more sensitive to the profit potential of better targeting.

While some direct marketers who are personally "steeped in the dominant culture" may initially dismiss such market segmentation as mere political correctness, improvement on the bottom line is the most dramatic business reason for target marketing based on race or ethnicity. Indeed, many direct marketers who do not appreciate and reflect the diversity of their potential customers may be missing business unknowingly.

In recent years, the ability to target individuals by surname has increased marketers' opportunities to address Asians and Hispanics by mail. Since African-American surnames are much less discernible, some marketers have attempted creative methods of identification such as compiling lists from directories of predominately African-American churches.

Segmentation opportunities abound within general ethnic and racial groups as well, as evidenced by the success of Allstate Insurance Company in targeting various specific segments of the Hispanic/ Latino market. Allstate's ads in Spanish featured voice-over announcers with Cuban accents in Miami, Mexican accents in Southern California, and Puerto Rican accents in New York City, for example.

Direct and interactive marketers who recognize the profit potential of sensitively targeting specific racial and ethnic groups will enjoy fertile new fields—especially in a time when many firms are complaining of difficulties in finding untapped markets.

International Opportunities

Large and sophisticated direct marketing companies have long recognized the sales potential in countries beyond the United States. Countries including Japan, France, Germany, the United Kingdom, Taiwan, Italy and Switzerland already represent billions of dollars in direct and interactive marketing sales. Meanwhile, emerging markets including the BRIC nations (Brazil, Russia, India and China) offer huge potential for global direct marketers. Indeed, more than 40 countries boast professional direct marketing clubs and organizations, as discussed in Appendix B. What's more, organizations such as the International Direct Marketing Federation at *http://www.idmf.com* and the Federation of European Direct and Interactive Marketing at *http://www.fedma.org/* provide valuable information for direct marketers with plans for international expansion.

Before the Internet provided immediate potential for global exposure to anyone with a URL, companies had to be intentional about their international efforts. They either set up shop in their targeted countries or hired international agencies to help them deal with myriad differences in language, culture, database availability, postal rules, and so on. Now many companies find international business thrust upon them as their U.S.-based sites are discovered by patrons all over the globe. Some direct and interactive marketing firms admit that their international policies to date are fairly elementary. As Todd Simon of Omaha Steaks comments, "The logistics of shipping our product over borders is so difficult that we do it only on a case-by-case basis." The Omaha Steaks Web site states, "Due to import/export restrictions, we are unable to ship our products outside the United States, Canada, Puerto Rico and the US Virgin Islands." Kevin Giglinto of the Chicago Symphony Orchestra does not actively solicit international orders, but he fulfills them if his regular shipping company is able to deliver the product.

Higher Education Allows for a Longer Story

Although illiteracy is still a major problem in America today, the upscale target prospects of most direct and interactive marketers are better educated than ever before. Thus they are ready and able to read the meaty, benefit-laden copy that helps direct and interactive marketers sell thoroughly and effectively in print media and online.

Challenges for the Direct and Interactive Marketing Community

While direct and interactive marketers enjoy many positive indicators for sustained growth and success, it is essential to recognize and deal with several threats to the industry. These concerns include privacy, the environment, and issues regarding the government and the U.S. Postal Service.

Privacy Issues for Direct Marketers and Interactive Marketers and Their Customers

Responsible direct and interactive marketers see their customer knowledge as a positive way to customize offers and serve individuals better. However, many customers and some activists are concerned about the potential for abuse of personal information direct and interactive marketers may acquire and store on their databases. There are also concerns about what types of lists may be rented, sold, or even obtained on the Internet—including government-recorded data such as vehicle registration and driver's license records. What's more, some buyers are unwilling to let their names be rented to other marketers.

The pressure for search and social marketers like Google, Yahoo, Facebook and Twitter to generate revenue—and these sites' huge potential to gather and leverage information about site users and their friends—has drawn even more attention to this problem.

Direct and interactive marketers are dealing with these concerns in a number of positive ways. First, the Direct Marketing Association and many regional direct marketing groups require their members to adhere to specific codes of conduct. See the Chicago Association of Direct Marketing Code of Ethics in Appendix C of this book for an example, or download The DMA's "Do The Right Thing" ethical guidelines white paper. Second, the DMA's Mail Preference Service (*www.dmachoice.org*) allows consumers to opt out of direct marketing offers—DMA shares these names with direct marketers who eliminate them from their cold lists. Third, responsible direct marketers ensure that they use database information in ways that are perceived as non-intrusive and positive by their customers and prospects.

Another privacy issue has to do with telemarketing. Consumers complain about poorly targeted telemarketing calls that they receive at inopportune times. In addition, while fax marketing is much less prevalent than it was in the past, unsolicited faxes often are considered annoying by both consumers and businesspeople. Self-regulation on the part of direct and interactive marketers can take care of many of these complaints, as can adherence to all applicable federal standards. The Federal Trade Commission/Federal Communications Commission "Do Not Call" laws allow consumers to register their home and cell phone numbers to opt out of many unsolicited calls selling products and services. Telemarketers must adhere to the "Do Not Call" laws or risk very high fines.

Perhaps the thorniest privacy issue in today's marketing world involves unsolicited e-mail marketing, or "spam." Responsible direct and interactive marketers invite their customers and prospects to officially "opt in" to receive e-mail on designated subjects at designated intervals. (The same opt-in standard is applicable to the growing field of mobile marketing.) Because e-mail marketing is relatively inexpensive—and e-mail lists can be culled relatively easily in a number of unauthorized and less-than-ethical ways—some unscrupulous marketers utilize mass e-mail techniques to a maddening extreme. The DMA—long an advocate of self-regulation for the direct and interactive marketing industry—has admitted that government regulation is necessary to control spam.

Environmental Issues

While many direct marketers can make excellent profits with very low response rates, consumers often question how much paper is wasted in the process. To deal with these concerns, many direct marketers have made a conscious effort to use more recycled papers, as well as soy-based printing inks that are less harmful to the environment. Better direct mail targeting can also help cut down complaints on this score. In addition, as more and more transactions are completed online, less paper is needed both for product promotion and consumer communication. In addition, many direct and interactive marketers are inviting their customers to receive invoices and make payments online, thus eliminating both the cost and the paper associated with monthly bills and reminders.

Governmental Concerns

In recent years, federal and state governments have considered imposing a number of restrictions on direct marketing methods, and taxes on direct marketing and online sales. Most concerned direct and interactive marketers work diligently on intelligent self-regulation in concert with the Direct Marketing Association and regional associations and clubs. In addition, these associations expend considerable effort and money in educating legislators, regulators, and consumers about the benefits of direct and interactive marketing and its positive impact on economic development.

Rate and Delivery Issues with the U.S. Postal Service

Even considering the favorable rates available to direct marketers who prepare their mail according to post office standards, the cost of postage has risen substantially over the past few decades. In addition, there are continuing concerns regarding timely and effective delivery in most all mail classes. Looking forward, some experts predict that postal questions eventually will become less pressing, as more and more commercial communication is conducted online. In the meantime, direct marketers seek productive solutions with postal officials, and experiment with alternate methods of delivering both messages and products.

Prospects for Creative People in Direct and Interactive Marketing

With so many factors in its favor, direct and interactive marketing has shown phenomenal growth in recent decades. What's more, Fortune 500 companies and their advertising agencies have come to understand the wisdom of integrating direct response and interactive techniques into a great percentage of their marketing plans.

This growth gives rise to a continuing need for more and better direct and interactive marketing copywriters and graphic designers—including those who specialize in creating e-mail messages, mobile promotions, and content and promotions for Web sites. Experienced direct and interactive marketing creative people with successful track records often command six-figure salaries and lucrative freelance opportunities. But they reach that exalted level only through years of study and practice—usually beginning at subsistence-level salaries. Time was, direct marketers learned strictly through a mentor system. Their craft was handed down from generation to generation. Albert Lasker, for example, staffed about a dozen cubicles at the Lord and Thomas ad agency with fledgling writers whom he schooled in the concepts of "salesmanship in print" and "reasons why" copy. When these men left Lord and Thomas, many of them went on to head some of the most successful advertising agencies of the twentieth century.

Today, direct and interactive marketing has become an academic subject, with at least one course of study available at scores of colleges and universities across the United States. There are centers for direct and/or interactive marketing at Chicago's DePaul University and New York University. Northwestern University offers a master of science degree in integrated marketing communications with a number of specialized courses in direct and interactive marketing.

The Direct Marketing Association and a number of regional direct marketing clubs host frequent how-to seminars—both face-to-face and online—led by seasoned practitioners. The Direct Marketing Educational Foundation, the Chicago Association of Direct Marketing Educational Foundation, and several other regional and local foundations support graduate, undergraduate, professorial, and professional development programs at sites all over the country.

The Chapters Ahead

This book will provide the key information a direct and interactive marketing creative person needs to understand: how to unlock direct and interactive marketing creativity, and discipline it to develop selling propositions that maximize profit potential. This material will help copywriters and graphic designers approach their jobs well-grounded in the hard-won knowledge of their predecessors, and well-armed with strategic knowledge about the latest applications of direct and interactive marketing. What's more, it will enable those who supervise and manage creative people to draw out the best possible work from their writers, artists, and production staff.

Enhance Your Understanding:
The Direct and Interactive Marketing Debate

Consumers enjoy buying by mail, phone, or Internet for a number of reasons: 24-hour convenience; a wide selection of specialized products; the comfort and safety of shopping from home; and the time and energy savings of avoiding crowded malls and shopping centers. Yet critics of direct marketing raise concerns, including: consumer privacy; wasted paper from poorly target mailings; intrusive telemarketing, mobile messages and e-mails; apprehension about not seeing the product before buying, etc. Check the popular press via online search engines or library periodical indices and read some articles about the pros and cons of direct and interactive marketing from the consumer point of view. Are the "pros" for direct and interactive marketing more compelling than the "cons"? What could you do to maximize the "pros" and overcome the "cons" in your creative approach?

2

The Discipline of Direct and Interactive Marketing Creativity

True or false: Either you were born creative, or you weren't. The answer is false! This may come as a surprise to those who think of creativity as a God-given talent rather than a hard-won accomplishment. Yet we all have the same mental resources to harness for creativity.

There are four main ingredients to creativity in direct and interactive marketing:

- Knowledge of proven techniques
- Specific research on the product, target market and competition
- The patience to work through a time-consuming process of discovery
- The courage to put your ideas to the test

Successful direct and interactive marketing creative strategy relies as much on proven techniques as it does on a unique approach to a given situation. Thus most any reader of this book can become a good direct and interactive marketing creative strategist—not just those born with a talent for language or art.

This chapter will discuss the disciplined form of creativity that successful direct and interactive marketers must develop. It will explain how historical perspective can save creative people from reinventing the wheel by considering the many "dos and don'ts" established at great cost by great marketers of the past. It will explore ways in which direct and interactive marketers can prime themselves to become more creative. And it will offer several proven, step-by-step methods of idea generation and applied creativity. By these means anyone can increase his or her potential for creativity in direct and interactive marketing.

Study the Techniques of the Masters

Historians often comment that those who do not learn from the mistakes of the past are destined to repeat them. As direct and interactive marketing creative people, we can gain as much by studying the successes of our predecessors as we can from their failures. Indeed, their successes are much more likely to be discussed in detail in their "how-to" volumes for direct and interactive marketers! Classic books like Claude C. Hopkins's *My Life in Advertising* and *Scientific Advertising*, David Ogilvy's *Confessions of an Advertising Man* and *Ogilvy on Advertising*, Richard V. Benson's *Secrets of Successful Direct Mail* and Gordon White's *John Caples: Adman* offer timeless narratives that are richly laced with information that creative people should keep at their fingertips. Other top direct and interactive marketers and creativity theorists have presented their knowledge in textbook form, enabling fledgling writers and graphic designers to learn from the experience of Bob Stone and Ron Jacobs, Roger von Oech, Mihaly Csikszentmihalyi, Jim Kobs, Katie Muldoon, Ed Nash, Jerry Reitman, Victor Hunter, and scores more. Those who aspire to new heights of direct and interactive marketing creativity should first climb onto the shoulders of the great practitioners of the past and present.

At $20 to $100 per volume (or as little as $9.99 in e-book form!), these books are the greatest bargains a creative marketer ever will find. One "big idea" from each book you read could make or save your firm millions of dollars.

Learn all that books can teach before you begin investing your company's money in mail, e-mail, space ads, the Web, telephone, mobile and broadcast. Trade publications, classes, conventions, Webinars and seminars can also be very beneficial for direct and interactive marketing creative people seeking to increase their knowledge base.

Direct Marketing Formulas and Checklists

In past generations, direct marketers learned their craft by doing. Drawing upon their knowledge of human nature and the techniques of successful one-on-on salespeople, they created and tested direct mail packages and space ads. In this way, they built upon their successes and eliminated their failures. And after some years in the business, they developed formulas and checklists—both as benchmarks for themselves and to use in training new writers and art directors.

Briefly during the late 1990s however, many naïve or arrogant interactive marketers rejected this tried-and-true wisdom. They asserted that the Internet represented an apocalyptic revolution and that the old rules just didn't apply. For example, 17 "New Economy" firms bid the price for a single 30-second Super Bowl ad up to a then-unprecedented $2.5 million in 2000. Of those 17 firms, seven were out of business before the end of the year 2000!

Meanwhile, classically trained direct marketers shook their heads in disbelief as the dot.com upstarts insisted that one or two Super Bowl spots could win them the brand recognition and sustained site traffic necessary to keep them in the limelight all year. These veterans calculated what they could do with $2.5 million in an integrated, highly segmented campaign of direct marketing, public relations, sales promotion, and general advertising! Indeed, Pepsi recently abandoned the Super Bowl in favor of just such an integrated, database-building campaign titled Pepsi Refresh.

What's more, while the Super Bowl has been reclaimed in large measure by traditional, big-name brands, many of them now incorporate interactive marketing methods to draw viewers to the Web for additional content, contests, and relationship building.

With direct and interactive marketing part of most every promotional campaign today, creatives will be wise to add these formulas and checklists to their professional bag of tricks. Read them over and then gather some samples of direct response space ads, direct mail packages, e-commerce sites, e-mails, and perhaps some direct response TV or radio spots. Try to apply one or more of the formulas to each selling message. Determine for yourself where they measure up and where they are lacking. Sometimes an ad or package will not fit any formula, yet still be exceptionally fresh and effective. Take a crack at analyzing why these renegade ads and packages work, and you may develop some new "dos and don'ts" of your own.

Once you have practiced applying the formulas and checklists on other people's work, try using them to develop and critique your own promotions. Eventually, the principles expressed in these lists will become second nature to a seasoned direct and interactive marketing creative person. But a refresher course from time to time will help to keep your work on target.

Famous Direct Marketing Formulas

A-I-D-A

Perhaps the best-known of the direct marketing formula is A-I-D-A. It describes the consumer adoption process:

- A=Attention
- I=Interest
- D=Desire
- A=Action

These are the stages a good ad, Web site, or selling letter will move the consumer through, leading to a positive purchase decision. It is important to remember that the process can end at any point if the marketer's pitch fails to move the consumer along. For direct mail marketers, the result of this failure is all too poignant: packages that fail to generate attention land immediately in the wastebasket. A similar process happens on the Internet when visitors fail to click through on a banner ad, e-mail, or the next level of a Web site.

The Four Ps

Henry Hoke, Sr., past editor of *Direct Marketing* magazine, is credited with another oft-quoted formula that also centers on the process of moving the consumer toward the sale. His "Four Ps" are:

- Picture
- Promise
- Prove
- Push

Hoke suggested beginning with a sizzling word picture, followed by a promise or success story. Then these claims are backed up by proof in the form of testimonials, endorsements, and feature/benefit copy. Finally, the "push" comes with the call to action.

Star-Chain-Hook

Another description of the consumer adoption process came from direct marketing expert Frank Dignan. He called it: Star-Chain-Hook. Dignan suggested "hitching your wagon to a star" with an attention-getting opening, then coming back down to earth with a chain of convincing facts assembled link by link. Finally, the hook is the call to action, moving the consumer toward a buying decision.

While the following formulas are somewhat theoretical, both the late Bob Stone and his co-author Ron Jacobs, and the late Joan Throckmorton offer more specific step-by-step lists. Stone's and Jacobs's appears in their excellent book, *Successful Direct Marketing Methods*, while Throckmorton's is taken from her readable and entertaining volume, *Winning Direct Response Advertising*.

Bob Stone's and Ron Jacobs's Seven-Step Formula for Good Letters

1. Promise a benefit in your headline or first paragraph, your most important benefit.
2. Immediately enlarge on your most important benefit.
3. Tell the reader specifically what he or she is going to get.
4. Back up your statements with proofs and endorsements.
5. Tell the reader what will be lost by not acting.
6. Rephrase your prominent benefits in the closing offer.
7. Incite action now.

Joan Throckmorton's Five Big Rules

1. Establish credibility. Who is the seller and why is he or she qualified to make this offer?
2. Get involvement. This means use the "you" and sing the benefits.
3. Motivate your prospect. Why now, not later?
4. Structure a strong offer. Unless your product is unique, you'll need all the competitive ammunition you can muster.
5. Use common sense. Ask yourself, "Does all this make sense to the prospect?"

Tom Collins's Checklist

One of the most famous checklists for direct marketers is creative and marketing consultant Tom Collins's 28 rules for good direct mail packages. Eliminate the direct mail-specific language, and it can become an effective checklist for other media as well.

28 Rules from Tom Collins

1. Do you have a good proposition?
2. Do you have a good offer?
3. Does your outside envelope select your prospect?
4. Does your outside envelope put your best foot forward?
5. Does your outside envelope provide reading motivation?
6. Does your copy provide instant orientation?
7. Does your mailing visually reinforce the message?
8. Does it employ readable typography?
9. Is it written in readable, concrete language?
10. Is it personal?
11. Does it strike a responsive chord?
12. Is it dramatic?
13. Does it talk in the language of life, not "advertise at"?
14. Is it credible?
15. Is it structured?
16. Does it leave no stone unturned?
17. Does it present an ultimate benefit?
18. Are details presented as advantages?
19. Does it use, if possible, the power of disinterestedness?

20. Does it use, if possible, the power of negative selling?
21. Does it touch on the reader's deepest relevant daydreams?
22. Does it use subtle flattery?
23. Does it prove and dramatize the value?
24. Does it provide strong assurances of satisfaction?
25. Does it repeat key points?
26. Is it backed by authority?
27. Does it give a reason for immediate response?
28. Do you make it easy to order?

Denny Hatch's Seven Key Copy Drivers that Make People Act

In his book, *The Secrets of Emotional, Hot-Button Copywriting*, direct marketing great Denny Hatch provides a list of seven "key copy drivers" that make people act. These were identified by Swedish direct marketing genius Axel Andersson, and Seattle guru, Bob Hacker, who told Denny, "If your copy isn't dripping with one or more of these, tear it up and start over." Here is the list of seven "drivers," with examples from Denny's archives of how each can be turned into a copy appeal.

1. *Fear*—That you're missing out, that you're being kept in the dark, that there's a threat to you or your family, that you may be in financial jeopardy.
2. *Greed*—Ways to get, win or save money, achieve the American Dream, get in on the ground floor.
3. *Guilt*—Assuage your guilt by helping hungry, lonely or oppressed people, providing peace of mind for yourself and your family, saving innocent creatures.
4. *Anger*—Turn your anger into action against political opponents, oppressors of animals and people, defilers of the environment.
5. *Exclusivity*—Be among the few who measure up, be in elite company, be among the first, be accepted for membership.
6. *Salvation*—Get cash to bail you out, find a lucrative and intriguing vocation, gain skills for success, get help from an expert.
7. *Flattery*—Acquire, join or do something that bespeaks your elite status, take advantage of something you've earned.

Can Technique Take the Place of Creativity?

Many a misguided direct and interactive marketer looks askance at those who invest time and money in an involved process of creative discovery. Alas, more than one creative challenge has been "solved" by copying a competitor's positioning and execution right out the window. Some direct and interactive marketers confine their creative process to a matter of sorting through the swipe file or surfing the Internet looking for a likely format to emulate.

On the other hand, even in a strong creative environment, no "high art" mentality will survive in a direct and interactive marketing creative shop. No matter how clever an idea for art or copy, it must advance the selling proposition or be killed. Thus, the pressure to sell with each visual and every line of copy may lead creative types back to the tried and true. In their own minds, direct and interactive marketing creative people often walk a fine line between taking the easy way out and striving for a unique, fresh, and possibly untried approach.

As the late David Ogilvy said, direct and interactive marketers "sell, or else." We need to persuade the reader any way we can. Sometimes the best method is brilliant copy or a striking design. Other times, the very best creative solution is one of those tried-and-true techniques, applied smartly to the current situation. Personalized URLs, scratch-offs, yes-no stickers, bind-in cards, dimensional packages, personalized letters, relevant online pop-ups, timely offers delivered via mobile phone, and other format techniques may raise response rates far more than subtleties of copy and style. But deciding which techniques to use—and how to apply them—requires more time and effort than simply "knocking off" other people's work.

The truth, then, is that technique cannot and should not take the place of creativity. Formulas, checklists, offers, and formats should be studied carefully so that they can be applied where they fill the bill. But technique alone is not enough: copywriters and art directors need to dig deep into their own experiences . . . research the specific product, target market, and selling opportunity at hand . . . and then allow themselves time to develop the best possible solution to each new creative challenge.

What It Takes to be Creative in Direct and Interactive Marketing

Over the past few decades, academicians have devoted considerable time to the study of "how to be creative," and "what makes a person creative." Their lists of creative characteristics sound like every mother's dream profile of her beloved child. Drawn from various sources, these creativity traits include:

Curious	Good imagination
Sense of humor	Energetic
Independent	Hard-working
Observant	Ambitious
Persistent	Visual thinker
Motivated	Original
Eclectic taste	Self-confident
Voracious reader	Sees the "big picture"
Accepts constructive criticism	Detail oriented
Avid researcher	Empathetic

If you have decided to make copywriting or graphic design your life's work, it's a good bet that many of these traits describe you already—at least on your best days. People who do not enjoy reading, imagining things, and thinking visually would be ill-suited to a career in which the main repetitive tasks are studying subjects and database insights, and then writing and illustrating selling messages based on them.

Those who are not hard-working and ambitious would become frustrated quickly with a career that involves little maintenance work: direct and interactive marketing creatives are faced with new challenges, new products, and new clients almost daily. Those who are not self-confident and willing to accept criticism would suffer greatly in a career where their work is scrutinized, critiqued, and subjected to text mining and quantitative response analysis.

There are ways to enhance your creativity characteristics so that you can draw upon them as a direct and interactive marketer. The best method is to groom yourself for greatness, just as an ambitious and indulgent parent might groom the proverbial child "born with a silver spoon in his mouth." Studies of highly creative people show that they often enjoy childhoods of great diversity. They travel, experience different cultures, see plays and movies, visit the ballet and the opera, and enjoy intellectual freedom and stimulation. Their parents ask them questions and give them decisions to make from the time they are toddlers. Yet creative people seldom have lives free from strife: the process of overcoming adversity helps them to develop skills they can bring to bear on creative problem solving.

To remain in top form as a creative person, you must experience the world with a child's innocence and wonder. Make every day a process of discovery. Be the kind of person who reads everything from ketchup bottle labels to *People* magazine to Plato. Listen to music: everything from alternative rock to hip-hop to Bach and classic Beatles. Frequent the theater. Join a Great Books group. Sit on a park bench and make up stories about passersby. Make chance encounters into market research adventures: ask people questions about their lives and opinions and store their answers away in your memory file.

Avoid isolation like the plague. The folly of many direct and interactive marketers is that as soon as they become successful, they move out of the old neighborhood and forget their roots. Market research expert Howard Gordon calls this "confusing yourself with America"—coming to the delusion that everybody thinks and acts just like you. The best way to overcome this problem is to develop your empathy quotient. Plunge into situations with people whose age, race, national origin, religion, socioeconomic status, and world view are very different from your own. Strive to understand their motivations, feelings, hopes, and dreams.

To stay in touch with America, attend church socials in small towns. Accept invitations to wedding receptions in VFW halls. Nurse a soft drink in a booth at a truck stop coffee shop and listen to the drivers as they shoot the breeze. Visit your cousin in rural Tennessee or your great aunt who lives in a Florida mobile home park. Volunteer in a nursing home. Get a part-time job at Christmas, selling seasonal items in a department store. Go to the supermarket at least once a week—all the more important once you're so rich and successful you have a housekeeper to do the shopping.

Watch Black Entertainment Television (BET), Univision, Comedy Central, Bravo, and MTV on cable. Use your TV remote control device to sample all the digital cable or satellite channels and see what's being advertised by direct response. Watch QVC and HSN, and then sit through an infomercial or two. Tune in to network TV and check the latest trends in situation comedies, dramas, and game shows. Listen to all the radio stations on the dial and on Sirius/XM Satellite Radio, not just your favorites. Watch and listen to talk shows.

Surf the Internet regularly—and don't just return to your favorite bookmarked sites. Check out areas marked "new," and type random subjects into your Web browser to broaden your online horizons. Join or "lurk" on social media sites. Follow all kinds of people on Twitter. Read magazines and newspapers—even the *National Enquirer*—to keep current with the interests of different target markets.

Don't confine your creative grooming to these everyday activities: find the time and the means to travel as well. Visit the world's great museums and fabled cities. Look at America through the eyes of Italy or France or Mexico or China. Even as you keep up-to-date with best sellers and hot magazines and music, discipline yourself to read history, classic novels, philosophers, and poets. Increase your word power by using *www.dictionary.com* to look up any new words you come across.

Develop an environment for creativity, too. Familiarize yourself with reference books and Web sites, and gain ready access to research databases online. Familiarize yourself with the best library in your area, and cultivate the librarian so he or she will help you borrow needed "hard copy" research materials from other libraries as well. Attend direct and interactive marketing seminars and luncheons—as much to network with other creative people as to hear the speakers.

Practice various ways of attacking problems, drawing on both qualitative and quantitative skills.

Use analytical thinking to take a problem apart and examine its distinct ingredients. Try synthesis to identify related elements and put the parts back together in a usable whole. Use deductive reasoning to move from general theories to specific applications. Call upon inductive reasoning to draw general conclusions from specific examples and anecdotes.

If all of this seems like too much work, you may be aspiring to the wrong field of endeavor. To the best creative people, these personal development activities come as naturally as breathing. They can't imagine why anyone wouldn't prefer a trip to Asia over a new living room suite. They feel somehow compelled to keep up with the latest music group and the hottest plays and restaurants, just because they want to be "in the know." Instead of shying away from people and situations that are different, they seek them eagerly. Instead of defending their own opinions, they prefer to play devil's advocate, hoping to draw out lots of ideas from people around them. And they enjoy mulling over all that they have learned, drawing connections and conclusions that will serve them well in appealing to various target markets.

What It Takes to Generate and Apply New Ideas for Creative Strategy

The Italian sociologist Vilfredo Pareto said that an idea is merely a new combination of old elements. Take a kaleidoscope, for example. It contains myriad bits of color, forming into many different patterns as the kaleidoscope turns. The pattern is never the same twice, yet it combines all the same ingredients. The Bible says that "there is no new thing under the sun"—only unique ways of relating old elements. Creating an idea, then, is the result of a step-by-step process designed to identify relevant elements and arrange them in new and effective patterns.

When the late Rod MacArthur founded The Bradford Exchange in the early 1970s, he combined existing elements in an unexpected way—thereby developing a direct and interactive marketing business that now spans the globe. MacArthur was offered the opportunity to sell limited-edition collector's plates from France in the United States. He recognized the fact that the product would need a certain mystique to command $15 and up for a simple, decorated porcelain plate. Through extensive research, he learned that there was already a secondary market—albeit fragmented and inefficient—for limited-edition collector's plates. He founded The Bradford Exchange as a sort of stock market for plates, providing a central source for buying and selling.

In developing this combination of elements, MacArthur produced an appealing opportunity for consumers. He could now sell plates with an extra "hook" in addition to their beauty and decor value: the possibility of price appreciation. Once a limited edition of plates was sold out, it would become available only on the secondary market. The Bradford Exchange made buying and selling these scarce plates efficient and accessible. When some plates became so popular that they rose as much as ten times in secondary market price over a few years' time, the resulting excitement helped stimulate the boom in plate collecting. While the secondary market boom in collector's plates has cooled in recent years, there still are millions of plate collectors, a good percentage of whom buy from The Bradford Exchange by mail, or at *www.collectiblestoday.com*.

Rod MacArthur may not have used a written, step-by-step idea generation plan to develop his concept for The Bradford Exchange, but his story exemplifies the process of identifying and implementing new ideas that makes for effective direct and interactive marketing. MacArthur worked for years in the family-owned direct marketing business anchored by Bankers Life & Casualty Co. and founded by his father, John D. MacArthur. He honed his creative skills by selling everything from insurance to banking products to travel clubs and stereo systems by mail. Widely traveled, Rod MacArthur was a former journalist and war correspondent with a French-born wife and an eclectic

Exhibit 2.1. Bradford Plate Ad

"Morning Serenade"
Actual diameter: 8½ inches
© 1989 W. S. George®

A silken vision of one of nature's miracles...
a Bradford Exchange recommendation

Dawn of a warm spring morning. The apple blossoms have just awakened to bask in the rising sun, when suddenly, the melodic song of cardinals soars up to meet the morning light.

Created from artist Lena Liu's original silk painting, "Morning Serenade" is produced in full color under the hallmark of W. S. George Fine China. And like exceptional collector's plates that now command hundreds of dollars on the plate market, "Morning Serenade" appears to have what it takes to go up in value after the edition closes.

Not all plates go up in value; some go down. But the edition of "Morning Serenade" is strictly limited to a maximum of 150 firing days, and demand is expected to be strong. So if you wish to obtain this plate at the $24.50 issue price, the time to act is now. To order your plate—fully backed by our one-year money back guarantee—send no money now, simply complete and mail the coupon at right. ©1989 BGE   BYB-335

Order Form for "Morning Serenade"

The Bradford Exchange
Trading Floor
9345 Milwaukee Avenue
Chicago, IL 60648

Please respond by: May 31,

Please enter my order for "Morning Serenade." I understand I need send no money now. I will be billed $24.50 issue price, plus $3.19 postage and handling, when my plate is shipped. (Limit: one plate per customer.)

X
_____
Signature

_____
Name (Please Print)   (   )
                             Telephone

_____
Address

_____
City   State   Zip

5021-E90001

This collector's plate offering from The Bradford Exchange continues the tradition established in the early 1970s by J. Roderick MacArthur.

Reprinted from the The Bradford Exchange Web site at *www.collectiblestoday.com.*

education. In fact, the reason he was offered the chance to sell Limoges collector plates was because of his fluency in French.

When the collector's plate opportunity presented itself, MacArthur did not content himself with writing an ad or two to see if the product would fly. He immersed himself in the world of collector's plates, making friends with plate dealers and asking them endless questions about why people collect plates, what makes a plate collectible, how the secondary market works, and much more. Only after many weeks of fact-finding did his mission become clear: the creation of The Bradford Exchange as the centerpiece for a direct marketing business selling limited-edition plates.

Creating New Ideas Step-by-Step

In his book, *Flow: The Psychology of Optimal Experience*, Mihaly Csikszentmihalyi helps readers find their way toward the "flow state"—a mental and physical unity that some sports types call "getting into the zone." Csikszentmihalyi maintains that creative people live more fully than others. He notes, "The excitement of the artist at the easel or the scientist in the lab comes close to the ideal fulfillment we all hope to get from life, and so rarely do." He adds that creativity leaves "an outcome that adds to the richness and complexity of the future."

Csikszentmihalyi's "flow state" combines a "seamless sequence of responses" in an experience that is "intrinsically enjoyable," "accompanied by a loss of self-consciousness," and "self-reinforcing." Successful creative people develop patterns of work that help them to reach this state where ideas flow freely. There are as many written creativity formulas for direct and interactive marketers as there are technique checklists for copy and art. Some of these step-by-step processes come from direct and interactive marketing practitioners, while others are advanced by academicians studying the history of ideas. Following are capsulated versions of several helpful creativity formulas that may help you achieve "flow."

A Technique for Producing Ideas by James Webb Young

In this slim volume, which has been printed and reprinted since the 1940s, James Webb Young advances a five-step process for creative thinking.

1. *Gather raw materials.* Young suggests studying both general information about life and events, and specific facts about the product and the target market. He advocates the use of 3″ × 5″ cards, each containing single facts.
2. *Mental digestion.* Young likens this process to putting together a jigsaw puzzle. Using the 3″ × 5″ cards, he suggests arranging and rearranging them to find patterns, contradictions, and relationships among the facts. Some creative people today use sticky notes on the wall instead.
3. *Incubation.* Once the digestion period is over, Young says to drop the subject and forget it—go on to another activity such as music, the movies, exercise, making dinner, or sleeping.
4. *Eureka!* At some point, out of nowhere, an idea will appear, thanks to the work of the subconscious mind.
5. *Testing.* Submit the idea to your own criticism and that of your peers, then refine or reject it.

Eugene B. Colin's How to Create New Ideas

The late Gene Colin, who practiced direct marketing and advertising creativity for over 40 years, offered nine guideposts "to lead you from a blank sheet of paper to a rousing success."

1. *Pick a problem.* Define your problem, in writing. State what's wrong, what needs fixing. State your objective, the end result you seek.
2. *Get knowledge.* Get known facts and new knowledge. Study written references. Experiment. Explore. Research deeply and broadly. Talk with informed people. Check your findings. Put them in writing.
3. *Organize knowledge.* Put your information into understandable form; sort it, organize it, write it.
4. *Refine knowledge.* Screen knowledge for relationships and principles. Match fact against fact. Look for similarities. Differences. Analogies. Cause and effect. Combinations. Patterns.
5. *Digest.* Let the conscious mind get its second wind. Put the subconscious mind to work. Relax, take up another problem, work at a hobby, or enjoy some mild diversion until refreshed.
6. *Produce ideas* with total freedom and speed, or concentrate anew on your problem until ideas begin to emerge. As they occur, write them down. Don't stop to judge them. Produce and write and build up as many as you can.
7. *Rework ideas.* Check your new ideas for flaws. Examine each new idea objectively. Question it, challenge it, test it, rework it, improve it, follow it through.
8. *Put ideas to work.* If the approval and acceptance of others are required, sell your ideas. Plan each sale. Allow enough time. Get participation. Use samples.
9. *Repeat the process* until it becomes a natural habit.

10 Steps to Personal Creativity from Susan K. Jones

Your author has developed this creativity process over the course of a 30+ year writing career.

1. *Block out the time.* Don't try to create a breakthrough layout or copy outline in a half-hour between meetings. Carve out a period of an hour or more—preferably much more—in which you can devote yourself totally to the question at hand. For those who work in distracting surroundings, this may well call for early-morning, late-night, or at-home work sessions.
2. *Get comfortable.* My favorite outfit for creative work is a sweat suit in winter, shorts and T-shirt in summer. Your corporate environment may not allow for this, but make sure that your waistband doesn't bind and your shoes don't hurt. Such distractions keep you from concentrating.
3. *Eat something healthy.* To be creative, you need to have your energy level at a peak. Have a bran muffin or bagel with fruit, or your own equivalent of a healthy snack. My colleague Judy Finerty swears by chocolate as a jump-start for the brain.
4. *Soak up lots of background—then do something else.* Quiz the client like a journalist writing a story about the product—who, what, where, when, why, how. Read every bit of background you can get your hands on, and use or at least go and see the product if at all possible. Check the competitive files.

Then give it a rest—do something else or call it a day. Let what you've learned roll around in your subconscious. Don't try to work with it right away.

5. *Experience the world*. When you are looking for a breakthrough, let the world around you serve as inspiration. Signs over storefronts, packaging in the supermarket, TV ads, You Tube videos, school classrooms, popular music, and many other seemingly unrelated sights and sounds can provide a spark that leads you to a fresh layout or piece of copy. Get away from the desk and soak things up if you're running dry.

6. *Be ready when the ideas strike*. Some of my best ideas have come to me in the shower, driving alone in the car, or walking around the neighborhood. Thus I keep a pencil and paper handy at all times—by the bedside, too. That idea you thought of in the middle of the night is guaranteed to be gone in the morning unless you write it down.

7. *Have a dancing hat*. The "dancing hat" is a leftover from my college days. Living in a sorority house, each of us had one article of clothing that we would wear as a signal when we needed to be left alone to study. Yours doesn't have to be a hat—just something you put on to tell yourself and others that you're working in an intense manner and shouldn't be disturbed for mundane matters. Putting it on sends signals to others—and will begin to have a Pavlovian effect on you, too.

8. *For blue-sky projects, have a glass of wine*. After reading all the background material and taking a break, pour yourself a glass of wine and start sketching or writing down ideas. Some of the ideas may not pass muster the next day, but by lowering your inhibitions you just may come up with a germ of a breakthrough idea.

9. *Let your work rest before evaluation*. Once you've done a rough layout or copy draft, let it sit at least overnight before you begin to touch it up. Looking at it fresh will help you see where it can be improved. More important, the next day you'll have the energy to pull it apart and start over if necessary—not just do a patch job.

10. *Enjoy the process*. Remember that we creative types are lucky. People pay us to learn about things and then share what we have learned with others to stimulate a sale. What we do for a living keeps our minds alive—and there is always a new challenge. So enjoy it: many people envy our freedom to create!

A quick read through these idea-generating formulas shows that the basic process follows a predictable pattern:

- Outlining the problem
- Gathering information
- Evaluating information
- Walking away from the problem to let the mind do its work
- Enjoying one moment when ideas strike
- Weighing the pros and cons of various ideas
- Implementing the best idea

The process begins with ambiguity and generality and proceeds to a concrete and specific plan of action. When set forth in these terms, creativity no longer seems a mysterious concept. Yet few of us reach our full creative potential because of stumbling blocks imposed by our upbringing, ourselves, and our society.

Roger von Oech, author of the popular books *A Whack on the Side of the Head* and *A Kick in the Seat of the Pants*—as well as *the Creative Whack Pack® iPhone app* and *card deck*—is noted for his humor. He pokes fun at the "shoulds" and "givens" in our lives, and challenges us to overcome them. He suggests that the American educational system is more concerned with putting youngsters into pigeonholes than nurturing their individual creative powers.

As von Oech says, "Children enter school as question marks and leave as periods." The result is that American adults live by guidelines that serve as roadblocks to creativity: rules such as "there's only one right answer," "be practical," "be logical," "don't be ambiguous," and "don't be foolish." Marketers who find that such ingrained rules are inhibiting their ability to create may find new freedom by reading von Oech's books.

Other factors that keep us from achieving our maximum creativity include poor health, lack of encouragement, narrow mindedness, fear of failure, and plain old-fashioned laziness. Indeed, in his book, *The Care and Feeding of Ideas*, James L. Adams asserts that "the most common reason for lack of individual creative accomplishment is simply unwillingness to allocate the resources."

Brainstorm Your Way to a Breakthrough Idea

One of the most effective resources for idea generation is brainstorming. While it's possible to "brainstorm with yourself," most creative experts agree it's not preferable. Working with others lets you benefit from different perspectives, experiences, and thought processes, and also builds excitement and enjoyment. Here is a step-by-step plan for effective brainstorming.

1. *Identify a specific question* that brainstorming will attempt to answer, based on a problem or opportunity you're facing. A good way to frame the question is to begin it with, "In what ways can we . . . "
2. *Select a neutral and non-judgmental facilitator* who will draw out all participants and keep the most verbal and forceful individuals from dominating the process. Make sure the facilitator records all ideas, or has a recorder in place to do so.
3. *Gain agreement* that participants are to consider each other equals during brainstorming—no pecking order of job title or seniority allowed.
4. *Shake things up.* Change the lighting in the room, and arrange chairs in a circle, semi-circle, or other pattern that breaks the norm. Go outside if the weather is nice. Play some mood music to start. Do a warm-up exercise—for example, see how fast the group can think of 20 or more alternate uses for a common object like a paper clip or ball point pen.
5. *State your "in what ways" question to the group* and begin brainstorming. Have people call out their ideas randomly, one by one. Suspend judgment—no criticism or praise allowed at this point. Record all ideas without stopping to evaluate them. Quantity of ideas is the goal.
6. *Encourage participants to build on the ideas of others*, and to throw out wild ideas. There will be time later to "reel in" these ideas and make them more practical.

7. *Use the resulting "laundry list" of ideas* for a later refinement process. Set criteria that may include budget, logistics, timing, uniqueness, target market, and other factors. Select the best idea or ideas to pursue based on these criteria. But don't discard the "laundry list"—there may be some gems in there that can be used later.

Becoming a "creative person" requires a major investment of time, dedication, and diligence. Yet the rewards are well worth the effort: indeed, the exhilaration of the "aha" or "Eureka" moment is all the greater because it follows a long period of careful and disciplined work. What's more, careful planning at the initial stages will help ensure the development of a strategy and execution that attracts and motivates your target market.

Creatives as Chameleons or How Creatives Get to Know the Audience

by Judy Finerty, President, Finerty & Wolfe Advertising

Successful direct response creatives have the ability to get inside the skin of the people who are the audience. Read what they read. Find out what they enjoy and then discover its pleasures for yourself. It's hard to be isolated from an audience when you make the effort to live their lives. That way you can start thinking like them and identifying with them.

   Become a chameleon. Role-play the part of people from your audience. If you're affluent and they're not (or if you're not affluent and they are), how would that affect the way you think and act? If they have kids and you don't (or vice-versa) how does that change your life . . . your thinking . . . your attitudes? This ability to assume different personalities is critical to the direct response creative person. At one time, it may have been considered a mental defect and the people were locked away in asylums! Today, they're merely put in direct response creative positions.

Judy Finerty's Rules for Working Smarter

1. *Test reality.* Don't just rely on input to tell you about the product or service. Try it out for yourself. If you're selling clothing, wear it around. If you're selling food, be sure you eat it. If you're selling insurance, be sure to read a policy yourself rather than trust what someone else tells you is in it.
2. *Keep your own time logs.* Time is money. Keep track of how long it actually takes you to create a certain type of letter, direct mail package, TV commercial, or space ad. That gives you a better handle on how realistic your schedules are. Creatives will usually try to do the best job they can in the time allowed, but the client should be aware of time and performance trade-offs, if any.
3. *Develop your own "idea starter" file.* Save things you love or that attracted your attention. Tape TV commercials you love and rerun them for yourself to discover why. Keep any advertising that makes you stop or makes you say "I wish I created that." Keep formats you've fallen in love with. Hang on to short stories, magazine articles, funny pictures, records/CDs, art that moves you or

inspires you. When you need to start a new project and can't get going, browse through your file of dynamite stuff to jump-start your motor. But never steal.

4. *Go ahead and panic.* Abject fear can be a part of the creative process. If creatives were football players, we'd be putting on our game faces and slamming ourselves into lockers to get ourselves up for the big game. It's a way to help psych yourself up to do something that's hard.

5. *Start with more than you need and then cut back if you need to.* When you're roughing out ideas, put everything in you think you need to make that sale or get that lead. Add the bells and whistles if you think it's right. It's easier to cut back than to try and add an important element after your concepts are done.

6. *Let your subconscious do some of the heavy lifting.* Once you know the assignment and have studied the product or service, distance yourself from the work for a while to let the information percolate. Often, you'll find ideas "pop" into your head when your brain is on neutral for a time. Can't let it go overnight? Even a judicious trip to the "facilities" or a walk around the block can help.

Enhance Your Understanding: Create Ideas Step-by-Step

Read over the step-by-step "creativity formulas" in this chapter and choose the one that intrigues you most. Then select a real or hypothetical creativity challenge, and work through the process to develop ideas. Do your research, study and manipulate your data, go through a conscious period of incubation, and then be ready for the ideas when they come. How does this analytical process differ from the way you have worked in the past? What can you do to fortify yourself for enhanced success in idea generation and creativity?

If you need help with a subject for this process, here are several:

1. Choose an everyday object like a nail file, apple, or men's tie. Pretend that the world has never seen this object before—it's just been discovered or developed. Generate a list of ideas for potential uses of this item as well as the benefits users would gain.

2. Your rich aunt has died and left you $300,000 in her will. There is one catch: the money must be used to purchase a house, condominium, or co-op. You've never owned a home before and haven't given home ownership much thought. Generate a list of criteria you'd use in selecting a home—and a list of the potential benefits and drawbacks of home ownership.

3. You've been called back for a second interview at a top agency or company where you'd love to work. Here's the catch: 19 other individuals also have received call-backs, and there's only one job to be had. Generate a list of reasons why you should be selected for the job, and ways you could effectively demonstrate your unique qualifications.

3

Research in Direct and Interactive Marketing

Howard Gordon, of the Chicago-based market research firm GRFI Ltd., points out a paradox in the way general advertisers and direct and interactive marketers treat marketing research. General advertisers, he says, spend considerable time, effort and money in discovering and pretesting creative ideas. Then they sometimes dilute the effectiveness of their work by broadcasting these creative ideas via mass marketing—network television, general-interest magazines and the like. Although more and more general advertisers are customizing messages based on the medium, they are less likely than direct and interactive marketers to acknowledge the subtle differences between typical readers of *Fortune* and *Forbes*, or even the very real differences between typical readers of *Rolling Stone* and *Atlantic Monthly*. With more and more segmentation possibilities available via cable television and specialized publications—let alone the "customization on the fly" that can be accomplished online—it is all the more important that general advertisers recognize the extra impact they may obtain through targeted marketing.

Indeed, one of the greatest strengths of direct and interactive marketing is the ability to test different creative concepts against each other, and obtain a readable, actionable result. Yet because direct and interactive marketers are such sophisticated database managers, they sometimes focus more attention on *how* to test than on *what* to test.

While our general advertising counterparts invest money on focus group interviews, creative pretesting and other costly research methods, some direct and interactive marketers still hammer out their creative concepts in a vacuum. Then they place their ideas head-to-head in space ads, direct mail, on television, or online, and wait to see whether Concept A or Concept B sells best. But the nagging question remains: might there be a Concept C, D, or E, yet to be discovered, that would sell even better?

It's true that direct and interactive marketers are experts at targeting messages. They are able to segment lists they mail to and call individuals out by name as "owner of a 2012 Buick LaCrosse," "parent of a 'SpongeBob SquarePants' fan" and so on. Yet they are sometimes reluctant to take advantage of even the least costly and time-consuming research methods that could ensure the messages they send these people are as effective as they could be.

Careful marketing research will help you strengthen and improve your creative strategy. This chapter will discuss the most useful methods of research for direct and interactive marketers and how they impact creative strategy decisions. It will focus first on general topics such as consumer behavior, lifestyle trends and popular culture, and then on means of standard or customized research to develop a creative concept for a particular product or service.

What Research Can Do for Direct and Interactive Marketers

Although the term "marketing research" may conjure up visions of complex and costly programs that only Ph.D.s can understand, its real purpose is simple and straightforward. Marketing research offers a way to find out how people think and feel about products and services, and how they go about buying them. It allows direct and interactive marketers to gain direction on basic questions such as:

- Who is our market for this product or service?
- What are some possible, undiscovered additional market segments?
- What are the characteristics of our prospects?
- What should we tell the prospects in each market segment about this product or service? Which benefits do they consider the most important and unique?
- How should we tell them about the product? What words, what tone, what format and graphic style, what medium should we use? Which offer (price, payment terms, add-on features, etc.) will work best?
- What media are the best to reach our target market—and what are some "wild card" media to test based on combinations of characteristics (for example, if buyers of sports-theme décor items also play golf in large numbers)?

Research cannot answer these questions conclusively, but it can point direct and interactive marketers in the most promising directions for testing. It may not be able to predict creative winners, but it can save a great deal of time, effort, and cost by weeding out creative losers.

Barriers Direct and Interactive Marketers Erect Against Research

Today, many of the largest and most sophisticated marketing firms have recognized the cost-effectiveness of marketing research. In addition, packaged goods companies with vast experience in general advertising and marketing research are integrating direct and interactive marketing. Yet creative people may still find barriers to marketing research in a number of traditional direct marketing firms.

First, some old-school marketers consider direct mail, space, or television testing a perfectly effective research tool. Indeed, once the test is complete, they *will* know which test cell won. But will they know *why* it won? Research could help them find out. What's more, even the most ambitious testing programs are limited as to how many concepts can be tried. Marketing research allows actual prospects to help select the top three or top five creative ideas for testing.

Another barrier is financial. A single focus group may easily cost $2,500 or much more, and a full-scale program of quantitative and qualitative research can easily run $50,000 and up. Some marketers consider the expenditure frivolous. They are used to receiving orders when they test, so they're making money even as they discover the best way to sell. But with the average direct-mail package costing $500 to $1,000 per thousand, it makes good sense to refine the selling message as much as possible to maximize sales, even at the testing stage.

A third barrier is lack of understanding. Many direct and interactive marketers understand testing, but they don't understand research. They consider it mumbo-jumbo, and they don't trust it. Howard Gordon recommends that creative marketers approach these decision-makers without ever using the term "marketing research." He says they take much more kindly to this request: "We want to go out and ask some people what they think about X."

Types of Direct and Interactive Marketing Research

Direct and interactive marketing creative people should ground their research work with a general understanding of *consumer behavior*: how people think, make decisions, and react to the world around them. Then when faced with specific selling propositions to perfect, marketers may engage in *secondary* research, which comes from standard reference sources or other organizations' findings, or *primary* research, which is customized to answer certain questions about a specific topic. They may choose to do *quantitative* research, which provides numerical information reflecting the prevalence of various characteristics, attitudes, and behavior; or *qualitative* research, which provides concepts and ideas but cannot be projected statistically. Direct and interactive marketers may develop *pretests,* which help them determine exactly who they should address and what they should say, or *post-tests*, which help ascertain why buyers bought and non-buyers did not.

Consumer Behavior: From Theory to Zip Code-Based Lifestyle Data to Individual Household and Buyer Information

Until the past decade or two, the study of consumer behavior was a theoretical exercise. Academics and market researchers would observe and interview groups of people and then publish their conclusions. Marketers could use this data to develop products and offers aimed at reflecting consumers' wants and needs. However, all they could do was sell "on the average." Today we have specific consumer behavior data available that is much more actionable. Tied to lifestyle data keyed by zip codes, this information helps marketers identify clusters of prospects that are likely to share certain demographic, behavioral, and attitudinal characteristics. What's more, many direct and interactive marketers now record, analyze, and act upon data at the individual and household level, allowing them to completely customize the timing, offer, and media used for communication and persuasion. Even though we now can be much more analytical about consumer data, it is helpful for creative people to understand the underpinnings of consumer behavior theory. This helps ensure that direct and interactive marketers will keep searching for new insights on why consumers do what they do—and how to motivate them toward specific buying actions.

Classic Consumer Behavior Theories

The study of consumer behavior in the United States is largely a twentieth- and twenty-first-century phenomenon, although Alexis de Tocqueville did a skillful job of analyzing the emerging American character in *Democracy in America*, published in 1835. There he pointed out how Americans lack the sense of belonging that strict class systems traditionally provide to Europeans. Thus, Americans seek out other means of affiliation by joining groups. Some of these groups are organized and structured, such as unions, fraternities, clubs, and societies. Other groups are completely unstructured—they are simply labels applied to people who appear to exemplify certain traits. Examples from various time periods include groups that were dubbed as "empty nesters," "hippies," "yuppies," "slackers," "highbrows," or "jet setters."

To enhance their sense of belonging to either the structured or unstructured groups, Americans may make buying decisions that echo these groups' values. Some such decisions are blatant: purchasing a hat or jacket with a union logo, for example, or proudly swinging a keychain decorated with the logo of a BMW automobile. Others are more subtle or even unconscious: for instance, a consumer might choose to purchase the same brand of designer handbag she saw worn by a leader of a neighborhood social enclave she wishes to join.

Of course, not all consumers are sufficiently safe and secure to invest their time and money feeding the desire for affiliation. From Abraham Maslow's classic Hierarchy of Needs, we learn that humans move along a continuum of concerns, ranging from food, clothes, shelter, and safety at the lower levels to affiliation, self-esteem, and finally self-actualization. Once a need is met, an individual is free to move up to the next level of concern. If a problem occurs, he or she may slide back down to a lower level. Direct and interactive marketers who can pinpoint the psychological "need level" of their target markets will be in a better position to tailor products, services, and selling messages to fulfill the desires of their prospects.

At the turn of the twentieth century, Thorstein Veblen advanced the concept of "conspicuous consumption," whereby consumers make many of their purchase decisions based on what they see others doing around them—also known as "keeping up with the Joneses." Some years later, John Kenneth Galbraith decried materialism, a term that describes American consumers' interest in more and better houses, cars, clothes, and personal playthings at the expense of cultural and social values. To help explain why consumers do what they do, Ernest Dichter developed motivational research. By means of long and intensive interviews, Dichter was able to discover hidden reasons for certain buying behaviors.

In 1966, Dr. Steuart Henderson Britt of Northwestern University introduced a book entitled *Consumer Behavior and the Behavioral Sciences—Theories and Applications*. His goal was to bridge the gap between the behavioral sciences and marketing—to help marketers apply what they learned about consumers to develop products and selling messages that touch consumers where they live.

How Consumers Make Buying Decisions

Over the past five decades, many advertising agencies and research firms have built upon Dr. Britt's concept, conducting rigorous scientific testing and then applying the results to advertising and direct and interactive marketing. Knowing how individuals make decisions, for instance, allows marketers to facilitate this decision-making process via their selling messages. As a professor at Northwestern University and contemporary of Dr. Britt's, Dr. John Maloney introduced this step-by-step process of decision-making based upon the classic stimulus/response model:

1. New information enters the consumer's field of vision.
2. Interest/curiosity level determine whether—and to what extent—the consumer pays attention.
3. Socialization, prior learning, and memory combine to help determine the consumer's attitude toward the information.
4. The consumer reaches a decision regarding the information.
5. The consumer either stores the decision for later reference, or acts upon the decision.

This process corresponds to classic advertising decision-making models like the Hierarchy of Effects (Attention-Interest-Desire-Action or Attention-Knowledge-Liking-Preference-Conviction-Trial/Purchase). The decision can be short-circuited at any point if the consumer does not proceed to the next level. Curiosity and prior positive associations with similar information are helpful to the process. Boredom, distractions, or negative associations can end the process.

Direct and interactive marketers can enhance positive decision-making in their selling messages. According to decision researchers, they may:

- *Associate the product offer with something/someone consumers know and trust.*
  Your offer may be foreign to the person's experience, but if you relate it to a

comfortable person or idea, the consumer may well make the "mental leap" along with you. For example, a senior citizen may find the idea of buying insulin supplies via direct response intimidating or even potentially dangerous. But when a known and trusted spokesperson, actor Wilford Brimley, vouches for Liberty Medical, the transaction becomes less threatening. Presenting Katy Perry and other celebrities as real-life users of Proactiv offers credibility to potential teen and young adult users of the acne product.

- *Make positive statements.* Decisions are hampered by mental negativism. Remember the old question about whether the cup is half-full or half-empty? Be optimistic in copy. Say that "90 percent of those who used this product lost weight," not "our failure rate is only 10 percent."

- *Set up a flattering comparison.* A marketer of figurines planned to sell a new product for $19.95. Then a focus group of experienced dealers told the firm that the price was too low for the market—the product had a perceived value of $29.95. The firm positioned the figurines as "a $29.95 value, available to preferred customers at only $24.95," and tested that concept head-to-head with the $19.95 price point. The $24.95 price point won—probably because it had been compared with a higher yet believable number and thus was perceived as a bargain.

- *Overcome disbelief at the time of product sale or delivery.* Consumers must trust the seller in order to make a purchase by mail, phone, or online. A solid guarantee, testimonials, and discussion of the firm's long and exemplary track record for customer satisfaction are some of the things you may test as ways to cultivate consumers' trust and help move them toward a buying decision and satisfaction with their purchase. Testimonials and user ratings can be helpful here as well.

- *Avoid raising concerns too early in a two-step process.* John Stanphill, an expert in selling big-ticket educational and business products using a two-step process, notes that pushing guarantees can hurt response in the lead generation process. As he says, "When someone is getting ready to respond for the first time, they're not thinking that your product or service is not going to work. When I was in the distance learning business, we tried a huge guarantee flyer in our fulfillment literature and it hurt response. What we ended up doing was sending the guarantee with the sales contract. We kept it very low-key."

Social Classes and Lifestyles in America

Until the emergence of zip code-based data and other modeling methods, marketers often had to rely on generalizations about groups they targeted—and books such as *The Nine American Lifestyles* by Arnold Mitchell were helpful. As a result of Mitchell's work, Americans were classified in three main lifestyle groups with eight subgroups: Need-Driven (with two subgroups called survivors and sustainers), Outer-Directed (with three subgroups called belongers, emulators, and achievers), and Inner-Directed (with three subgroups called I-am-me, experiential, societally conscious). The ninth lifestyle subgroup was called "integrated"—those few who are psychologically mature, tolerant, understanding, and flexible.

Mitchell furthered his research, called "VALS™," to develop a framework of eight VALS types:

1. Innovators
2. Thinkers
3. Achievers
4. Experiencers
5. Believers
6. Strivers
7. Makers
8. Survivors

According to the Strategic Business Insights Web site, "VALS assigns individuals a VALS type on the basis of their responses to questions in the VALS Survey. VALS-typing populations of interest, such as customers or constituents, is the first step in a VALS approach to achieving strategic marketing and communication goals."

In another revealing book, *Class: A Guide Through the American Status System*, Paul Fussell made fun of the American social class structure. In so doing, the curmudgeonly author pointed out a number of telling characteristics that marketers should remember when writing copy and designing ads. Fussell divides Americans into nine social classes:

1. Top-out-of-sight
2. Upper
3. Upper-middle
4. Middle
5. High-proletarian
6. Mid-proletarian
7. Low-proletarian
8. Destitute
9. Bottom-out-of-sight

He discusses class differences based upon patterns of speech, manner of dress, home decor, occupation, social life, and intellectual life.

Patterns of speech are especially telling for copywriters, who often find themselves pitching to upper-middle-class executives one day and blue-collar workers the next. For instance, Fussell's research indicates the following class differences in announcing a family tragedy:

Upper class: "Grandfather died"
Middle class: "Grandfather passed away"
Lower class: "Grandfather was taken to Jesus"

A warning: some readers find Fussell's work offensive because he spares nothing in his description of class quirks and inanities. However, he is just as scathing in his discussion of every class—except for the exalted X-class (not to be confused with Generation X), people who have risen above all class stereotypes and are unashamedly and uniquely themselves. Your author finds frequent re-readings of *Class* an indispensable aid to switching class mindsets. For instance, intensive study of Fussell's writings on the upper-middle group is helpful in writing upscale giftware catalog copy. On the other hand, for an assignment selling accidental death and dismemberment insurance by mail, a quick review of proletarian characteristics and speech patterns is vital.

Relating Consumer Behavior to Specific Target Groups with PRIZM NE

With database products like PRIZM NE from Nielsen Claritas, direct and interactive marketers can learn more about the lifestyle and product choices of small groups of consumers. PRIZM NE begins with census data, used as a starting point for neighborhood clusters based on geography, demographics, and behavioral data. These geographic units cover census block groups of 250 to 550 households, evaluated according to six categories of demographic and lifestyle variables: 1) social rank; 2) household composition; 3) mobility; 4) ethnicity; 5) urbanization; and 6) housing. This results in a PRIZM NE description for every U.S neighborhood in terms of 66 distinct lifestyle types with colorful descriptors like "Money and Brains," "Winner's Circle," or "Bedrock America."

For creative people, PRIZM data provide a host of insights into our target markets. We can help select likely initial target groups based on short descriptions provided by these products' promotional literature. Once we've zeroed in on a small group of likely segments, we can read a description of several pages that provides a wonderful picture of each group's characteristics that can help with relatable copy and graphic design.

Data from PRIZM NE allows marketers to identify top candidates for focus group research as well. For example, the media company Lee Enterprises selected a segment called "Settled In" for a test aimed at attracting new subscribers for its newspapers in several cities. The firm identified households in the "Settled In" segment, then called to make sure that they fit the segment's profile for age, income, education, etc. Qualified individuals then were invited to a focus group to discuss their media consumption habits. The results were very helpful in structuring copy to fit the perceptions and predispositions of the target market. What's more, it was much easier to choose models for the direct mail piece after seeing a group of individuals that "fit the profile" at the focus group session.

One-to-One Direct and Interactive Marketing

Today some of the most sophisticated direct marketers—and most Web marketers—are moving past cluster groups of PRIZM NE to develop data on a household-by-household or individual-by-individual basis. This is especially true for firms that sell big-ticket items and/or that have large potential lifetime values for their customers—supermarket chains (easily averaging $5,000+ per year for an affluent young family), car and truck manufacturers (close to $500,000 total lifetime value per new-car customer), and so on. Web marketers can glean a great deal of insight into their customers and prospects by analyzing individual data gathered through Web visitors' online actions and comments, and customizing responses and offers to customers "on the fly."

As we move toward more one-to-one communications, direct and interactive marketers will need to balance consumers' privacy concerns with their ability to record and act upon more specifics about individual customers and prospects. See Chapter 4 for more on privacy and ethics in marketing.

Basics About the Direct Response Buyer

In the past, direct and interactive marketers concentrated on learning why people choose to buy via direct-response media. But today, much time and effort is channeled into finding out why certain people choose *not* to buy through these means—and how they can be convinced to enter the ranks of direct response buyers. If the field of direct and interactive marketing in general—and individual firms in specific—are to continue to grow during the 21st century, it is essential that they find ways of serving direct-responsive buyers more effectively—and cultivating non-buyers as well. Three reasons why people buy by mail, phone, or online are cited most often:

- *Convenience*. Busy dual-career and single-parent families have little time to brave crowded shopping malls, especially during typical business hours. They have no patience with the ill-trained, transient sales clerks found in many of today's department stores. They prefer to shop from home, and enjoy direct and interactive marketers' 24-hour-a-day service, toll-free telephone numbers, home delivery, liberal guarantees, and free-trial privileges.
- *Target marketing*. Few can resist the lure of slick offers targeted directly to them: the fly-fisherman, the career woman in need of a wardrobe, the amateur interior decorator, the concerned money manager, and so on. As the world expands and retail stores become more and more impersonal, consumers delight in the cozy, me-to-you friendliness of custom-tailored direct marketing and online offers.
- *Uniqueness and selection*. When most every chain store carries the same narrow range of merchandise, consumers enjoy shopping through direct-response channels that offer products not available on local store shelves. The items they select by mail or online may be unique, or simply available in more depth: for instance, Martex towels in all 22 colors and the four quality levels Martex manufactures rather than the ten colors and two quality levels offered by a department store.

In recent years, another reason for consumers to buy via direct and interactive marketing methods has come to light.

- *Safety concerns*. With stories about mall gang violence and parking lot muggings reported in suburban and urban areas alike—not to mention a more cautious American public ever since the tragedies of 9/11/2001—many shoppers find it less nerve-wracking to stay home and call, mail, or place their orders online for home delivery—even for groceries. And although malls and shopping areas have beefed up security and taken steps to eliminate security problems, more and more consumers are citing personal safety and security as reasons for using direct and interactive marketing channels for buying.

The most often-quoted reason why people choose *not* to buy via direct response is *lack of credibility*. Since direct marketing began as a mail-order version of the patent medicine "pitch men," many direct-mail, space, and television offers still rely on "such a deal" techniques. Exaggerated claims and starbursts do sell products to many Americans, but they are one of the top complaints of those who do not currently buy via direct-response channels. These non-buyers find such low-class selling methods less than credible. In addition, credibility suffers at the hands of some direct and interactive marketers whose customer service records are less than pristine.

Secondary Research

The preparation for a particular creative assignment often includes some secondary research. Here are some typical sources for secondary research material.

- *Federal, State, and Local Governments*—Census data, labor statistics, health statistics, etc. Much of the general government information is now available on the Internet.
- *Competitive Information*—Gathered via observation, decoying, trade groups, visiting competitors' point of sale and Web sites, and so on.
- *Associations and Groups*—Surveys, statistical data, staff library resources.
- *Database Marketing Firms*—Information compiled from telephone directories, census figures, auto and boat registrations, real estate records, purchase histories, Nielsen data, surveys, etc.
- *Libraries*—Public, private, university sources. The Internet brings library resources from around the world to your desktop.
- *Online and Offline Trade Publications*—Case histories, articles, and surveys.

Primary Research

Although direct and interactive marketers may do some of their primary research directly, many times they call upon specialized market research firms for this work. Joseph Castelli, then of Ogilvy & Mather Direct in New York, pointed out several criteria for the selection of a market research firm in his article on research methods for *The Direct Marketing Handbook*, edited by Ed Nash. Castelli suggested that marketers should select a firm that:

- Has a broad range of experience and a proven track record of helping other companies.
- Is problem-oriented rather than technique-oriented. Good researchers will be sure they understand the problem before they offer a solution. They have no vested interest in using a particular research technique.
- Has a staff that can communicate well. The most brilliant research study will be of little value unless the results and implications can be clearly communicated.
- Is concerned with quality control. Choose a firm that pretests the questionnaire as a standard practice and provides a series of controls throughout the research process.
- Is marketing-oriented. Their conclusions and recommendations should be specific and practical.

Castelli offered this advice to direct and interactive marketers on how to get the best work from their research firms:

- Confide in them. Tell them what your problems are. Give them all the background they need to fully understand the situation.
- Trust them. Rely on them to determine whether research can be helpful, and if so, how the research should be done.
- Don't be penny wise and pound foolish. If they recommend research that you regard to be too expensive, consider the value of the information. It may well be worth the cost.

What Market Research Firms Can Do for Direct and Interactive Marketers

Research firms can conduct both quantitative and qualitative tests for direct and interactive marketers. Here are several examples of the type of work they may be engaged to do.

Traditional Methods for Interviews and Surveys

Whether conducted face-to-face, by telephone, mail, or online, traditional interviews and surveys may be useful in determining information about a particular group such as:

- Demographics—Age, sex, income, residence, point in the family life cycle.
- Psychographics—Lifestyle and attitudes.
- Buying behavior—Decision process and action.
- Preferences—In products, ways of buying, frequency of buying, services, etc.

Online and mail surveys are the least costly to conduct, and the least labor intensive. However, unless the recipient has a vested interest in the sponsoring firm or the product category, response percentages are likely to be low. Many direct marketing firms use mail surveys of their customers, club members, or other affiliated individuals to add valuable information to their databases. Online surveys on Web sites and phone surveys offer a middle ground in cost between mail and person-to-person surveys. In the article at the end of this chapter, Jerry Kaup, President of the e-mail ad agency, offers an overview of the pros, cons, uses for, and methods of doing online marketing research.

On the phone, market researchers face the same challenges as telemarketers: individuals who are wary of any non-personal phone call, screening via voicemail or answering machine; non-published numbers, etc.

The most expensive method of individual interview or survey research is face-to-face. It allows the interviewer to probe for deeper answers and to seek answers to "why" questions—not just straight behavioral data.

Physiological/Emotional Tests

Although only the most sophisticated direct and interactive marketers use physiological and emotional tests today, general advertisers find them especially meaningful because they are free from the self-censorship imposed by consumers when they answer verbally. Brain-wave tests, pupil dilation, voice pitch, and other measures show whether a consumer reacts to a given selling message. A strong reaction may mean repulsion or attraction—and therefore is not conclusive without further testing. No reaction to a particular selling message means it has no impact, however, and thus can be discarded.

Focus Groups. A focus group includes between six and 12 consumers interacting under the leadership of a trained moderator who uses a prepared discussion outline. For maximum effectiveness, direct and interactive marketing focus groups generally should include only proven direct response buyers. Other qualifying factors will depend on the subject of the focus group. For example, a focus group sponsored by a book club might require that each attendee had bought at least six nonfiction books during the previous year, and be a current or former member of at least two direct-response book clubs.

Ideally, the focus group's sponsor observes the group from behind a two-way mirror or via closed-circuit television. In addition, the group should be video recorded or at least audio recorded for future reference. After completion, in most cases the moderator will prepare a written interpretation of each focus group's findings.

The best focus groups are those in which consumers are allowed to function as consumers—making choices and evaluations just as they would in the marketplace. Focus group participants should not be allowed to act as amateur marketing consultants. For example, they should not be shown a creative concept and asked, "What do you think of this copy and layout?" Rather, they might be shown an ad and asked, "What kind of person would buy the product presented here?"

Focus groups may be used to help direct and interactive marketers find the right words to use in communicating with a target market of consumers. They may help marketers discover how certain types of consumers think, and how they become motivated to buy particular products. Some direct and interactive marketers use a series of focus groups in a step-by-step process. First they show a group a number of rough creative concepts, eliminating those that draw indifferent or negative responses. Then they proceed to copy and layout on the most promising concepts, and show these to focus groups at various points in the creative process, seeking more and more refinement.

Online marketers may benefit greatly from "usability testing" of their Web sites, either done in a focus group setting with multiple moderators, or one-one-one. While participants' surfing patterns are captured online for later analysis, moderators can ask them to discuss what they are doing, what they like, what they find difficult to use, and so on. Market research experts caution direct and interactive marketers not to expect direction from a single focus group. Two, four, or even more sessions may be necessary to cover a particular topic adequately. Cost per session may range from several thousand dollars on up, which may or may not include the cost of the written report.

Focus Groups Using Perception Analyzer Technology. Erard Moore Associates (EMA) of Riverside, Connecticut, is among the market research firms who have offered direct and interactive marketers the same type of "perception analyzer" technology used by American presidential candidates and television networks to determine reactions to concepts, words, and images on the screen.

Erard Moore calls this product "DRTV Scope" and explains how marketers can use it to receive consumer reaction to TV spots, videos, or information frame by frame, and word by word:

1. Each participant receives an 11-number (0–10) dial.
2. While the video materials are played, participants turn the dial clockwise to indicate a positive reaction or counterclockwise to indicate a negative reaction.
3. The EMA computer cumulates the scored reactions for each participant instantaneously and creates a moving horizontal line graph (with "peaks" and "valleys" for high and low scoring reactions). The graph can also be segmented by male and female reactions, by age groups reactions, etc.
4. The client observes this graph (on the client monitor) overlaid on the commercial, infomercial, or video being tested. Participants do not see the aggregate score graph on the monitor they are viewing.
5. After the rating process, participants are exposed to the combined score graph and video and are probed as to why they favored/did not favor certain copy or visual elements.

Another firm offering a similar market research tool is DialSmith of Portland, Oregon. They call their product The Perception Analyzer (PA) and present it as a method that can "elicit instant, honest and unbiased feedback from a group through the use of wireless hand-held dials." DialSmith notes that this method gives everyone in a group an equal and anonymous voice and thus helps eliminate "group think" where some participants influence the stated opinions of others. What's more, results are recorded for immediate viewing as well as deeper "post-group analytics."

Benefit Tests

Perhaps the most immediately useful and cost-effective marketing research tool for creative people is the benefit test. To develop a benefit test, a copywriter prepares a list of possible benefit statements pertaining to a product or service. These statements may be drawn from comments at focus groups, consumer interviews, or brainstorming sessions. Each benefit should be stated individually, in sentence form, on a card. In private interviews, qualified prospects should be shown the cards, one after the other, and asked to rate the importance of each in the product purchase decision on a scale of 1 to 10. Then the consumer should look at each card again, this time rating the same benefits as to their uniqueness. In addition, consumers should be asked if they can identify other important benefits that were not mentioned as part of the test. To evaluate a benefit test, determine which benefits are considered both important and unique by prospects. These are the most promising benefits to use in developing creative concepts.

Buyer/Non-buyer Surveys

Post-testing often takes the form of a buyer/non-buyer survey. The objective is to learn the differences between prospects who responded to an offer, and those who did not. Such a survey should focus on demographic information, general attitudes, and specific reactions to the selling message received. A well-done buyer/non-buyer survey may point the way toward new creative approaches that reinforce buyers' positive attitudes and find new ways to increase appeal and believability to those who failed to respond in the past.

The Future of Research in Direct and Interactive Marketing Creative Strategy

Over the past several decades, much progress has been made in establishing direct and interactive marketing as an academic subject. A number of professors at universities and colleges have selected direct and interactive marketing as a research specialty, and direct and interactive marketing courses, concentrations, and majors are now available at many schools—both at the undergraduate and graduate levels.

The Direct Marketing Educational Foundation (DMEF) supports the development of such programs through numerous grants and activities, notably its annual Research Summit in conjunction with the Direct Marketing Association fall convention. At this conference, professors from around the world present their academic research findings on a host of topics, including creative strategy.

DMEF and the Chicago Association of Direct Marketing Educational Foundation (CADMEF) also have provided support for Case Writers' Workshops in conjunction with the annual Research Summits, where professors are linked with successful companies and agencies to develop cases that illustrate direct and interactive marketing concepts and challenges.

An agenda has been set for direct and interactive marketing research—with strong emphasis on the development of more effective means of pretesting creative concepts. As more students earn degrees or concentrations in direct and interactive marketing and set their sights on the academic advancement of the field, there is growing potential for creative strategy research breakthroughs in the years to come.

Using Online Surveys for Effective, Easy, Economical Marketing Research

by Jerry Kaup, President, the e-mail ad agency

Developing products and services *well aligned with customers' needs* is essential to increase the value delivered. And now, browser-based E-surveys provide a low-cost, fast, and easy way to gain actionable insight into customer needs and preferences. E-surveys, or surveys viewed on the Internet with any Web browser, offer many advantages over traditional survey methods, including:

- Lower overall cost, minimum cost-per-response
- Access to real-time results
- Elimination of human bias (interviewer)
- Improved data; responses to open-ended questions are more extensive and legible
- Able to direct survey respondents to a specific Web page once they've completed the survey
- Limit each participant to a single response
- Allow book-marking to complete the survey in more than one visit
- Immediately display aggregate survey results to participants, with individual response kept private
- Track responses to individual e-mail address, thus allowing for profiling of individual preferences
- Can include graphics, audio, and video content

HOW IT WORKS

E-surveys are simply Web pages that present questions and easy response elements (check boxes, buttons, text boxes, and so on). An e-mail invitation is sent to a list of customers or prospects, and contains a link to the survey. Survey responses are captured in digital form for further tabulation.

While E-surveys offer many advantages, be aware of a possible significant limitation to this approach: online bias. This is the difference in feedback you receive from an online survey versus a mail survey. If you have e-mail addresses for a large percentage of your prospects, however, this should not be a factor.

What's more, even for those with Internet access, a small percentage may not be able to view all elements of your survey. While this factor is so small that it will not bias results, it can result in customer service calls from those few having difficulty with old browsers.

EIGHT SURVEY TIPS

To maximize actionable feedback, consider these ideas:

1. **Start with the end in mind.** Ask, "What decisions will we make that will benefit from information provided from the survey?" The goal of the survey is to gather the accurate information that helps you make those

decisions. Keep the focus on your main topic, asking no more than 20 to 25 questions.

2. **Offer Incentives.** Highlight any incentives for responding in the introduction. Use incentives to increase response when possible. Special content on a Web site can be an excellent incentive. Another motivator can be the privilege of viewing a tabulation of all responses to the survey. This can be a strong incentive when the data provides valuable information. Discounts, coupons and special offers can also work well.

3. **Survey Format.** *Introduction*—The survey introduction for e-mail surveys should include your logo and any other immediately identifiable branding, and a message explaining why you are asking these questions, and how their feedback will be used. A mention of the number of questions and time estimate to complete the survey will help response.

   Page Layout—The first question immediately follows the introduction. Each question is numbered, and white space between questions is provided to avoid a crowded or busy feeling. The page background color should provide contrast so that white text boxes, check boxes, and other important response elements stand out. Start with easy-to-answer check box questions. Place more extensive "open-ended" questions later in the survey to be answered after the recipient gets involved.

4. **Question Format.** Here are some guidelines on formulating questions to produce the accurate information you seek:

   • Ask questions that will provide descriptive, diagnostic, and predictive information. Descriptive questions are commonly used to identify the segment of the member for cross-tabulation purposes, and may include other demographic information, past buying, or usage behavior (recency, frequency, dollar value). Diagnostic questions will ask the member for judgments and rankings about past experiences. Predictive questions will ask about future usage plans and reactions to "what if" scenarios.

   • Make sure questions are easily understood. Don't use terms or jargon that only some prospects may understand. Be careful of internal, company-only vernacular or acronyms that you understand well but may be a mystery to outsiders. Test questions with others before your survey goes live.

   • Open-ended questions are crucial for better understanding the satisfaction of customers. For instance, if a question allows a high or low ranking, allow an open-ended text box to give the member a chance to explain why the rank was high or low. However, too many open-ended questions can wear down participants, leading to unanswered questions and incomplete surveys. Since it's a delicate balance, test your surveys before going live.

   • For ranking questions, provide additional blank text boxes so members can add, and rank, any items they feel are important, but have not been included in your list of items.

   • Avoid "double-barreled" questions like "The seminar was helpful and convenient" or "The presenter was knowledgeable and articulate." By including two criteria in a single question, it is not clear exactly what the response evaluates.

5. **Gather and/or confirm demographic information as you ask questions.** Not only is this a good way to align benefits with core prospect segments, but you also may discover more about segments than you knew prior to the survey.

6. **Pretest the survey on a small sample: 10 percent of the list.** When you tabulate (and for some questions cross-tabulate) results, you may see ways to revise questions to make them more meaningful.

7. **Increase response by sending multiple waves of the e-mail invitation.** Exclude those who have already responded.

8. **The timing of e-mail surveys can make a big difference in response.** Try to avoid sending them on Monday mornings or Friday afternoons. Generally, sending them to arrive in the morning is the best approach, since it gives busy individuals all day to respond.

With the ease and low cost of online surveys, think in terms of creating an ongoing dialogue with prospects and customers to better understand their needs and preferences on an ongoing basis. Using online surveys can make it easier than ever to insure that your offers are aligned with their needs.

Enhance Your Understanding: The Benefit Test

Try conducting your own basic benefit test. Choose a product or service you know little about and a viable target market that is very different from yourself in terms of demographics and psychographics. Research the product/service and make a list of potential benefits for it—then follow the step-by-step benefit test format described in this chapter. Conclude each interview with an open-ended question such as, "What else would you see as a benefit of product/service XYZ? Analyze your results. What did you discover about the product/service and the target market—just by conducting this simple test—that you would not have learned otherwise?

4

Databases, Privacy, Ethics, and Customer Relationship Management

Databases have become so essential to direct and interactive marketers that the terms "direct marketing" and "database marketing" are used interchangeably. Yet as marketers become ever more sophisticated about what they can collect and how they can cross-reference that information with other sources of data, concerns about privacy, ethics, and the effectiveness of customer relationship management inevitably arise.

Indeed, as Emily Yellin reported in her book, *Your Call Is (Not That) Important to Us*, the Customer Rage Study (sponsored by Customer Care Measurement and Coaching, and Arizona State University), 68 percent of customers had experienced "customer rage" in the previous year. Yellin noted that according to this study, 90 percent of "enraged customers" shared their stories with other consumers, and 77 percent complained to the company that caused the problem. As a result of that customer complaint, 57 percent decided never to do business with the company again, while 28 percent "yelled or raised their voice" at a company employee, 8 percent "cursed," and 8 percent "threatened legal action." Later studies showed that 15 percent of complaining customers "wanted revenge" against the offending company, while only 1 percent reported ever getting it. The chief conclusion of the report is that "U.S. companies are driving their customers crazy."

All direct and interactive marketing involves the use or creation of a database, or store of information about customers and prospects. Some direct marketing media, such as direct mail, e-mail, mobile marketing, and outbound telephone marketing, require a database of customers and/or prospects who will receive mail, e-mail, texts, or phone calls. Other media, such as magazines, newspapers, radio, television, and the Web, rely upon prospects to identify themselves when they see or hear about offers that appeal to them. Once these prospects have "raised their hands" by inquiring or making a purchase, their names, addresses, and other vital information are added to the database. From that point on, the database can be enhanced and enriched as customer actions and preferences are layered on from both internal and external sources.

But considering the results of the Customer Rage Study, it is crystal clear that all of this must be done with customer satisfaction and customer privacy concerns firmly in mind. Customers appreciate what they perceive as respectful suggestions on the part of marketers. They like the fact that companies recognize them as individuals and can pull up or provide helpful information for them or about them at every touch point (online, phone, face-to-face, etc.). They do not appreciate the "creepy sense" that marketers are recording and reacting to their every move, online and offline. Customers will answer questions about themselves when they perceive that the marketer will use that information to serve them better. They do not enjoy answering question after question when the process seems needlessly intrusive or tedious.

This chapter will explain how databases are constructed, enhanced, and used. It will also discuss how responsible marketers are dealing with consumer and business concerns about privacy and ethics, and how today's Customer Relationship Management systems can benefit both buyers and sellers when properly constructed and used.

Harnessing the Power of the Database

Top direct and interactive marketing consultant Ashleigh Groce Sawdon defines database marketing as:

> An automated system to be used to identify people—both customers and prospects—by name, and to use quantifiable information about these people to define the best possible purchasers and prospects for a given offer at a given point in time.

Delete the word "automated" from this definition and such a system could apply to some of the oldest marketing concepts in the world: what went on at the corner grocer, the old-fashioned hardware store, or even the general store of America's pioneer days. Herein lies a fascinating paradox for direct and interactive marketers: the more sophisticated our futuristic database technology becomes, the more it allows us to treat customers just as individually as the corner merchant did generations ago. But by the same token, we have to make sure we gather and use this knowledge respectfully and helpfully—not as an intrusion or invasion of privacy.

The Corner Merchant's Selling Method

Once upon a time, the local grocer knew the name of every member of his customers' families. He could even tell you their birthdays: after all, he helped Mother pick out the makings for each birthday cake! The butcher could tell you which families ate pork chops every Wednesday—and he'd put the choice chops aside for them. The neighborhood druggist sympathized with folks who had asthma attacks, and he could tell you just by the way the wind was blowing when Mr. Smith would stop by for his hay fever medicine.

Let's say you are a ten-year-old from a previous generation who has been sent to the grocer's for a quart of milk. If Mr. Jones, the proprietor, had just received the spring's first shipment of strawberries, he'd be likely to give you a sample and send a few berries home with you along with a note to your Mom saying, "Berries are in." And say Mr. Jones knew it was your parents' twentieth wedding anniversary tomorrow. Since your family had shopped with him for years, he'd probably provide an extra-fancy gift box of cookies with his best wishes for the happy couple. Back then, Jones the grocer made it his business to know your likes and dislikes—what you could afford to buy, the types of things you splurged on, and places where you economized. He found ways to say "thank you" and "I value your business," and "try this—I think you'll like it." But eventually, Jones's family grocery store faced a formidable competitor: a shiny new supermarket with greater selection and lower prices. Many families stayed with their friend Mr. Jones until the bitter end, but eventually they watched him go out of business, a victim of the supermarket's volume buying power. There are still a number of retailers who pride themselves on the personal touch. But today's largest firms—the Walmarts of the world—are more likely to offer unmanned self-service aisles than to model the individual attention style of yesteryear. In an attempt to add a personal touch to their shopping environments, stores of this type have added "greeters" at the door and encouraged their customer service personnel to be warm and welcoming. Yet as friendly as they may be, the "greeters" are equipped to do little more than give customers a cart and point them toward the correct aisle for the product category they seek.

How Database Marketing Helps Marketers Sell One-to-One

More than ever in today's world, consumers wish to assert their individual identities. There's not much satisfaction—other than saving money—in being another one of the nameless, faceless customers at Walmart. It's even more disheartening to pay large mark-ups in major department stores and still find yourself being waited on by transient clerks who don't know much about their merchandise—or you.

That's where direct and interactive marketing come in. It provides that personal, "I know you" feeling we used to get at the corner store. And it fits in with today's busy lifestyles, since few people have time to chat with a storekeeper anyway. Direct and interactive marketing allows firms to talk one-on-one with customers, keying in to known factors about them: age, family size and stage, interests, hobbies, travel preferences, purchasing behaviors, products owned, services used, and much more. Yet these communications can go on thousands or even millions at a time—making this form of personalized selling very cost effective.

How to Develop and Use a Database

The most important concept to remember in establishing and building a database is to keep the customer as the focus. Don't become so fascinated by statistics that you forget to look at things from the motivational side. Strive to understand why consumers do what they do. To return to the corner store analogy, a database is essentially a sophisticated version of the old-fashioned retailer's "data retrieval system." The corner grocer probably kept all of his data in his head. And he had few enough customers that he could keep it all straight. But today's successful personal sales executive is likely to have a computerized database of his or her own on a computer or PDA. Those very few remaining technophobes have—at the very least—a Rolodex with cards about each customer.

The insurance salesperson knows size of family, ages, disabilities and health problems, whether any family members smoke or indulge in dangerous hobbies, who travels extensively, and even whether his customers exercise regularly. The real estate star knows when each customer last changed houses, how much they spent for that house, what kind of financing they arranged, and when they're likely to be in the market again. Real estate agents also keep track of family size and changes in status—for instance, when the last child goes off to college—because these factors have a great deal to do with when a customer might be in the market to buy or sell. The designer clothing salesperson knows each customer's sizes, her favorite labels, and her preference for suits, separates, dresses, knits, evening wear, and so on. She makes it her business to know whether this customer goes South for the winter or stays in the North—this has to do with the weights of clothing the customer will wish to own, and whether she'll be in the market for resort wear.

The idea is this: as direct and interactive marketers develop their databases, they should think about what they'd like to have on an imaginary Rolodex card or in file folders about each of their customers. The database is basically the same thing—the only difference is that since it's captured in a computerized form, it's much easier to call upon in volume. What's more, with the regression analysis, predictive modeling, and other highly specialized database applications affordable for high-volume marketers, it's possible to "psych out" customers with much more sophistication than the grocer ever dreamed of. As Richard Hren, of Euro RSCG Worldwide explains, predictive applications "discover what customers want and predict what they will do . . . and apply this knowledge to create more profitable customer relationships."

Even if you're working with a very basic database, you can take advantage of profitable segmentation opportunities. Instead of communicating with one customer at a time, you can go after *all* of your tennis buffs, *all* of your new empty-nesters, or *all* the ladies who head South for the winter right after Christmas. Even so, you will be wise to use database technology to customize one-to-one messages as much as possible—keeping specifics and preferences on file that set individual customers apart, and using them to enhance your relationship.

Such information may be captured in several ways. For example, it may come as a result of inferences made based on products or services purchases, and the timing of such purchases. It may be recorded on the basis of customer questionnaires. It could come from lifestyle data based on nine-digit customer zip codes or compiled by firms like Acxiom or Equifax Marketing Services.

Essentially, database marketing allows direct and interactive marketers to move beyond quantitative, demographic measures such as age, sex, and geographic area. Now they can draw knowledge about subtler differences of customers' attitudes and lifestyles. Ultimately, both demographic and psychographic information helps marketers target their audiences and refine their selling and relationship-building messages better than ever before.

Record What You Need to Know and What the Customer Wants You to Know

When setting up a database, it is tempting for marketers to think simply in terms of what they want and need to know about their customers and prospects. But it is just as important to find out what your customers want you to know about them so that you can serve them better. Here are some examples of each type of information.

Capture the Information You Need to Serve the Customer. The following are some of the basic elements you will want to record on your database. To serve your customers best, you may need to add other elements based on availability of information and your experience.

- Prefix, name, and address
- Titles (business) and family relationships (consumer)
- Phone (day and evening), e-mail, fax (if still relevant for your target group)
- Original source of customer or prospect (what mailing, ad, etc.)
- Original purchase
- Purchase history, continually updated (what, how much, and when)
- Yearly or seasonal purchase volume
- Credit risk history
- Customer service history (i.e., how often is merchandise returned; how often have we been unable to meet this customer's needs)
- For consumers: Lifestyle information (by ZIP+four or individual household data)
- For business databases: Company sales volume, number of employees, home office location, and other indicators of the customer's overall potential and needs

Capture the Information the Customer Wants You to Have. Customers will be generous in sharing their preferences with you if there is something attractive in it for them such as time savings, special opportunities, or pampering. They will also share data with you if you promise to offer them needed reminders. You can also learn much from "market basket analysis"—who buys what at what times of year or days of the week, in what combinations. Here are just a few examples of things your customer would probably like for you to know—some from the direct and interactive marketing field and some that combine direct mail with retail. Use these as idea-starters for your own field and customer base.

Customer Preferences:

- *Airline*—Seating choices, Frequent Flyer number, food choices for overseas trips
- *Hotel*—Bed size, newspaper preference, high or low floor, view preferred, smoking/non-smoking where applicable
- *Clothing catalog*—Favorite labels, sizes, wardrobe color scheme

Customer Reminders:

- *Online florist and catalog food sellers*—Significant others' birthdays, Mother's Day, and so forth
- *Quick oil change outlet*—Mail reminders of when oil change is due based on your personal driving patterns, not the average
- *Veterinarian*—Mail reminders about annual check-ups, shots, heartworm medicine time, bird wing clipping; all pets covered to avoid multiple trips to the vet

Learning About Customers Online

When prospects and customers visit your Web site, you have a golden opportunity to glean information about them for your database. Your site can identify each unique visitor through a cookie—a small amount of text data given to a Web browser by a Web server. This cookie data is stored on the user's hard drive and is returned to the specific Web server each time the browser requests a page from that server. While some customers will "disable cookies" on their browsers, a large percentage will "allow cookies," because they enjoy the benefits of site customization you provide based on their activities and buying patterns on your site.

When you are tracking your site visitors, you'll be able to gather data about where they enter your site, what pages and products they view, how long they stay on each page and in total, what they put in the shopping cart, and what (if anything) they end up purchasing. You'll have the opportunity to record this information and use it to add dimension to that customer's profile on your database, integrating the customer's online behavioral and buying patterns with his or her offline activities and demographics. What's more, using the Web analysis tools offered through Google Analytics or other third parties, you can create a dynamic Dashboard that will present rich information about your site's visitors in chart and numerical form.

Use the Full Power of Your Database to Segment Your Market and Serve Your Customers

With an effective and user-friendly database at their disposal, direct and interactive marketers can play "what if" games to their heart's content, devising possible tests of products, offers, incentives, and other opportunities that may increase the productivity of customer files—and/or enhance the relationship with each customer and prospect. These qualitative methods may seem "quick and dirty" compared to regression analysis, neural networking, predictive modeling, and other, higher math techniques used by sophisticated database operations. But for many firms, this type of intuitive brainstorming can be quite helpful in developing worthy test concepts. Here are some ideas on how this can be done:

- *Develop logical product offerings to obtain more "share of customer."* You may increase your "share of customer" (also known as "share of wallet") either by getting a customer to purchase additional types of products/services from you, or by enticing them to purchase more of the same. In the first case, let's say your database reveals that you have a substantial number of customers who have purchased both luggage/travel accessories and tennis supplies from your firm. How about offering them something new: a premium-priced trip to the U.S. Open tournament hosted by your well-known company president? In the second case, what if your database shows significant numbers of individuals who buy food products from you fairly regularly, but only as gifts for others. Could you come up with a "treat yourself" concept that would give these folks an incentive to purchase a continuity plan with special goodies arriving at their homes each month? Web sites offer an opportunity to make additional product offerings like this on an instant basis—either alongside items site visitors click to view, or in the shopping cart area as add-ons.
- *Offer different gifts and incentives by segment.* Many firms make the mistake of looking at customers in one dimension only. They fall in love with the 80/20 rule (80 percent of your sales often come from as few as 20 percent of your best customers). But they look at that golden 20 percent as a group, offering them all the same incentives and gifts. With a good database, it's possible to segment your best customers with much more precision, and then tailor offers to them that fit their wants and needs. For example, some of your "golden 20 percent" may have gotten into that category with one big purchase: your top-of-the-line music system, a diamond ring, a computer and accessories, etc. Others may have reached the exalted level through a series of much smaller purchases that cut across many categories in your product line. It doesn't make much sense to offer an individual who spent $2,000 on one item the same next-purchase incentive as someone who spent $2,000 on a total of 20 different purchases. Nor does it make sense to offer the same incentive to a $2,000-a-year women's clothing buyer that you offer to a computer software buyer at the same level. Think from the customer's point of view: what would best motivate each type of buyer to buy again?
- *Make sure your incentives offer an appropriate challenge.* Frequent traveler clubs provide an excellent example for this point. Many such clubs try to offer the same incentive to everyone: for example, fly six segments between x-time and x-time and get so many bonus miles; stay ten nights at XYZ hotels by December 31 and get two weekend nights free. Incentives are much more likely to be productive if they are keyed to individual customers' records. For instance, it's no challenge for someone who travels 100 nights a year to rack up six segments and ten nights. It would be better to offer that individual a challenge based on increasing his/her usage of your airline or hotel (say, up from 50,000 miles flown to 100,000 miles flown in a year; up from 25 nights a year to 40

nights a year) and provide a suitably powerful incentive. On the other hand, if your records indicate that an individual only flew two segments with you in an entire calendar year, it may not be realistic to think that they have the travel schedule and lifestyle to purchase six quick segments on *any* airline. Try offering that individual a more achievable goal with appropriate incentive, and then offer greater incentives after the first goal has been met. This concept also holds true for product purchasers: try initially upgrading the $100 customer to $200 a year, not $2,000.

- *Identify new product, market, and business opportunities.* The more you know about the demographics and psychographics of your customers, the more likely you are to be able to identify new opportunities that will be especially intriguing to them, and potentially profitable for you. In the catalog and online world, examples of this concept abound. For example, Lands' End has expanded from its original sportswear catalog to offer books focused on home products, corporate attire, school uniforms, plus sizes, and other categories. With its unlimited online "real estate," the Lands' End Web site (*www.landsend.com*) allows visitors to click immediately on these and many more product subsets. Williams-Sonoma offers a catalog and Web site of kitchen products (*www.williamssonoma.com*) as well as print and online versions of home furniture and lifestyle marketer Pottery Barn, and Pottery Barn spin-offs West Elm, Pottery Barn Teen and Pottery Barn Kids. Visit *www.williams-sonomainc.com* to click on any of these Williams-Sonoma properties.

- *Use retail, direct mail, and online databases in segmentation.* If your firm sells through direct marketing, retail outlets, and online, the potential for each can be optimized by sharing database information. Knowing that a customer never buys women's clothing online but that she is a heavy retail clothing buyer offers intriguing possibilities. On the other hand, what if a catalog shopper purchases considerable kitchen equipment by mail but has no record of kitchen purchases at retail? The parent company would be well served to invite such an individual to local in-store cooking demonstrations, but without the shared database, such opportunities often are lost.

- *Understand your customer so copy and design are personal and "you oriented."* For creative people, knowing all they can about the customers they serve is essential. And when markets are sharply segmented, the copywriter and graphic designer need to know the basis for segmentation so that they can reflect it just as sharply in their words and pictures. Sometimes writers and designers are kept at arm's length from database information, and sometimes they shy away from such data fearing that it is "only for number crunchers." But these apprehensions need to be overcome. With many of today's desktop database systems and online Web analysis data, anyone who has enough technological prowess to use Microsoft Word or InDesign is fully capable of manipulating data and playing database "what-if" games of their own. Writers and designers who take the time to learn their firm's database capabilities and find out all they can about the demographics and psychographics of each target group will be well on their way to developing a compelling creative product.

Privacy and Ethics

As marketers become capable of increasingly detailed data collection and database enhancement, consumers and privacy advocates focus more concern on what information companies collect, and how they use and share it. Indeed, ever since Louis Brandeis and Samuel Warren wrote *The Right to Privacy* in 1890, the subject has concerned government, business, and individuals alike. According to media attorney Charulata B. Pagar of Virtual Law Partners LLP, early legal discussion of privacy was a response to the technology of Brandeis's and Warren's era: photography, transatlantic cables and other "modern devices for rewording or reproducing scenes and sounds." Brandeis and Warren argued that the complexity of life necessitated some retreat from the world, and man . . . "so that solitude and privacy have become more essential to the individual; but modern enterprise and invention have, through invasions upon his privacy, subjected him to mental pain and distress, far greater than could be inflicted by mere bodily injury."

If the relatively impersonal media named by Brandeis and Warren were cause for concern, consider today's Web sites that are capable of tracking individuals' every mouse click and relating that data to individual-specific demographic, lifestyle, and behavioral information. Consumers are aware of this "intimate tracking ability" on the part of Web marketers, and it has them concerned. Indeed, a 2008 poll from the Consumer Reports National Research Center reported that "72 percent are concerned that their online behaviors were being tracked and profiled by companies." The poll also revealed that this uneasiness has led 35 percent of Americans to use alternate e-mail addresses to avoid providing real information. What's more, about a quarter of consumers have used software to hide their identity online, and about the same number have provided fake information to access a Web site.

It is little wonder that consumer privacy is considered one of the most vital issues facing today's direct and interactive marketers—and that they struggle with the ethics of balancing what they are capable of doing with what is right and proper. From the collective wisdom of some of today's top experts on marketing privacy and ethics, here is some advice for creative marketers:

- **Use the resources of the Direct Marketing Association and other trade groups**. For example, the DMA's Web site (*www.the-dma.org*) includes a robust, regularly updated section on corporate responsibility and ethics. The DMA also publishes a booklet of "Guidelines for Ethical Business Practices" and a "Privacy Policy Generator" for marketers.
- **Do not relegate privacy concerns solely to your firm's chief privacy officer**. Copywriters and graphic designers will be wise to educate themselves and help influence decisions balancing consumer privacy protection with effective database marketing.
- **Put customers' and prospects' concerns first**. Sheila Colclasure, Business Leader for Privacy Practices and Solutions at Axiom Corporation, suggests that marketers adhere to Best Practices including:
  - ‣ **Compliance** with all federal, state, and international privacy laws
  - ‣ **Education** for all internal and external stakeholders
  - ‣ **Public Relations** to effectively manage messages to all your firm's publics
  - ‣ **Disaster Recovery**—responding swiftly and effectively when issues develop
  - ‣ **Leadership**—promoting best privacy practices in your industry

▸ **Commitment**—making sure the entire company is committed to the privacy effort
▸ **Respect** for the consumer
▸ **Value**—being able to articulate the value you bring to consumers based on the information you collect about them

- **Be forthright and specific in opt-in and opt-out methodology.** Ask consumers how they would like to hear from you, how often, and for what types of information. Allow them to specifically opt-out of direct mail and e-mail list rental, and to specifically opt-in for newsletters, informational e-mails, text messages, and the like.
- **Continue the ethical collection and use of information about consumers.** When done properly and respectfully, it provides a win-win for marketers and customers alike.

Customer Relationship Management

Customer Relationship Management, or CRM, has become a major buzz term in the direct and interactive world. According to John White, Senior Vice-President, Product Management, at Nuveen Investments, much of the focus on CRM is due to the proliferation of software "solutions" that allow for the integration of database information across various customer contact points such as mail, phone, online, retail outlets, and personal sales. Richard Hren says that the essence of CRM is "Leveraging data to understand better the wants, needs, and behaviors of customers to enable the development of highly differentiated customer experiences." For creatives, the heart of CRM lies not in technology but in a very straightforward concept. As Melinda Nykamp, author of *The Customer Differential: The Complete Guide to Implementing Customer Relationship Management,* explains, CRM focuses on the proposition that if we maximize the value of our business to a customer, that customer will reciprocate. Nykamp suggests that CRM efforts focus on three main goals: 1) increasing revenues; 2) decreasing costs; and 3) increasing competitive differentiation to build loyalty.

Nykamp observes that CRM challenges marketers because it requires the active cooperation of sales, service, and marketing personnel—departments that often have resisted integration in the past. CRM also changes the focus for traditional direct marketers who concern themselves more with programs than with individual customer relationships. Rather than look at the overall results of an ad, mailing or e-mail campaign, CRM emphasizes finding ways to interact with and understand individuals—thus allowing for the development of customized offers that deliver increased value. What's more, companies implementing CRM must balance their ability to use robust software and provide personalized offers and communications with concerns about customer privacy.

The Corner Merchant's Method Comes Full Circle: Tesco Serves Individual Customer Needs with Its Clubcard

The more things change, the more they stay the same—or perhaps better stated in this case, the more they change back to the way they used to be. In today's world of grocery marketing, many of the corner merchant's methods are being revisited in an effort to appropriately serve big-ticket customers. The Bureau of Labor Statistics reports that the average American family spends about ten percent of income—about $6,500 a year—on food. The Office of National Statistics in the United Kingdom says that British consumers allocated 15 percent of their budgets for food and non-alcoholic beverages. Modestly estimating $100 a week for groceries and home supplies purchased at the supermarket, even an average middle-class family has a grocery "wallet" worth $5,000 or more per year. Yet, when a customer enters many grocery stores, there is little to differentiate the one-time $50 buyer from the individual who already spends thousands of dollars a year with this grocer—or could do so, if properly motivated.

To combat this problem, many grocery chains (as well as drug stores like CVS Pharmacy and other retail chains) have implemented "values" or "valued customer" database programs. Shoppers are encouraged to sign up as a "valued customer" in a simple application process. They are immediately issued a plastic, bar-coded card that identifies them by individual or family. Sometimes there are multiple cards: one in credit card shape and another that slips onto the customer's key ring for easy access. Upon each visit, the checkout clerk asks the individual for this card, and it's swiped across the bar-code reader along with all purchases. This allows the grocer to build a database that indicates how much each customer buys, what they buy, and when and where they buy it.

One of the pioneers in this arena was the British supermarket chain Tesco, which has offered its Clubcard since 1995. To encourage sign-ups, Tesco promotes its Clubcard program as a way to save money and gain access to special opportunities and rewards. Their Web site (*www.tesco.com*) notes:

> Clubcard is our way of saying thank you for shopping with us.
> *You collect Clubcard points every time you shop with us.*
> You now get 2 points for every £1 you spend in-store or online on your groceries, DVDs, CDs and Books from tesco.com, and at Tesco direct. You also collect 1 point for every £1 you spend on Petrol, Mobile phone top up and many other places.

It's clear that the Clubcard program offers an opportunity to treat each of its customers with some of the same individual care as that shown by the old-fashioned corner grocer. Marketing communications to Clubcard members are highly segmented based on "market basket analysis" that determines each customer's "unique DNA profile," according to Professor Martin Block of Northwestern University. Segments are determined by what individual members buy, when and where they buy it, and in what combination. By studying this information it is easy to discern the presence of children and pets, wine aficionados, and single shoppers versus family shoppers, as well as brand preferences.

According to Professor Block, a long-time consultant for Tesco, "Our image of customers is built from seven pieces: lifestage, profitability, primary channel (supermarket, express, online, petrol), basket typology (vegetarian, organic, etc.), promotional promiscuity (those who cherry-pick price deals and load up on specials), shopping habits, and brand advocacy (participation in Baby Club, Wine Club, and Tesco.com)."

To avoid criticism on privacy grounds, U.S.-based valued customer programs, like Tesco's Clubcard, have built certain limits into the program. Typically, they do not sell or give customers' names and addresses to any outside packaged goods companies. They do not rent the participant list, and they do not target people individually. Rather, such firms may query the database for "all heavy buyers of Coca-Cola," using certain parameters, or "all pet food buyers spending more than X-dollars last year." Card holders receive offers in groups, not one-by-one.

Another function of such U.S.-based programs is to reward customers based on their volume of purchases with the store. For example, at Thanksgiving, the best customers could be mailed a coupon for a free turkey. The next-best group could receive a $10-off turkey coupon, and another

Exhibit 4.1. Tesco Clubcard

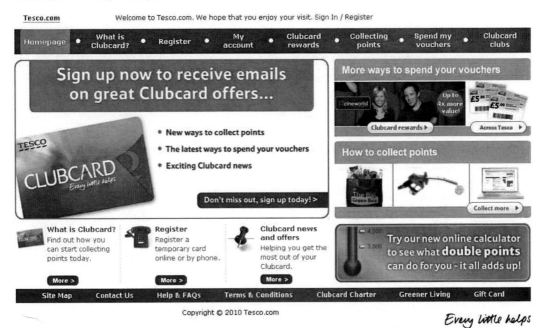

Tesco's Clubcard program has enabled the company to leap ahead of its traditional British grocery store rival, Sainsbury's, and maintain a strong position as England's number-one grocery store chain with a market share in the 30 percent range.

Reprinted from the Tesco Web site at *www.tesco.com*.

group could get a $5-off coupon. At Easter or Christmas, a similar promotion could be offered for hams or other traditional main-course meats.

These valued customer programs rely on bar codes, both on the card and on products purchased, to capture relevant information. In the near future, however, programs of this type may be further enhanced by pinpoint-sized computer chips and tiny antennae that may be cost-effectively packaged with products. According to the Associated Press, in the decades to come, "the miniscule transmitters are expected to replace the familiar bar codes." Called "radio frequency identification" (RFID), this technology provides convenience for marketers and customers alike, although it does raise concerns about privacy.

These little chips also can alert marketers when products are spoiled or compromised in the store. But if they are not disabled before the customer leaves with them, they open the potential for spying. As this technology develops, direct and interactive marketers will be wise to monitor its potential uses as well as consumer perceptions.

CRM and Data Management

By Robert Galka, Executive in Residence, DePaul University (Excerpted from *The IMC Handbook: Readings and Cases in Integrated Marketing Communications.*)

Creating a single accurate view of a customer is a key to CRM success. It is probably the most difficult CRM-related task a company must undertake, but if not done optimally, it can inhibit the best CRM strategy. It is extremely time consuming, very complex and very detailed work. It takes a certain discipline to create an optimal, data-integrated environment. The steps necessary to perform this methodology are:

1. *Touch-point identification*—This is the process of identifying every location within the organization as well as within the value chain that a customer can interact with the respective organization or its value chain partners. B2C examples would be point of sale, phone, web, customer service, survey, promotion response, and distribution. B2B examples may include procurement, sales, and technical support. These sample lists are of course not all inclusive of the various interaction touch-points.

2. *Define how data is collected*—i.e., human, technology, self-reported or generated versus two-way exchange.

3. *Establish data collection rules*—This is the process of setting priorities for data variable collection from each touch-point.

4. *Define the data collection process*—Specific process steps, timing, and security.

5. *Place data in similar formats (optional)*—Some software that will work with the collected data requires it to be in the same or similar formats.

6. *Split data into two areas: linkage and non-linkage*—Linkage data is any set of variables that can be used to identify the customer. Non-linkage data is everything else. Name and address or customer loyalty card numbers are examples of linkage variables. Products purchased would be non-linkage data. Non-linkage data can contain an extremely large number of variables. A unique number can be assigned to both so that both parts of the customer data, linkage and non-linkage, can be connected together later. Splitting data is not always necessary, but in many instances it improves the efficiency of the processing of linkage data— through those steps necessary to enhance customer matching across multiple interactions and transactions.

7. *Standardize and correct linkage data*—Commercial software is used to correct errors in any addressable variable (e.g., street name, zip code, e-mail address)

8. *Postal processing*—Ensures that the most current customer address will be used as well as improve mailing efficiency. There are multiple processes in this step and the USPS website (*www.usps.com*) is a good source for information on what is involved with this process.

9. *Linkage identification*—This step is sometimes referred to as de-duplication or Merge/Purge. It identifies each appearance of a customer's multiple set of interactions or transactions and links them together. This is a critical step as it helps build a centric view of the customer, a critical success factor for CRM.

10. *Data enhancement*—Secondary sources of information are added to the customer information to enhance the view of the customer (e.g., demographic variables, secondary sources).

11. *Data suppression*—Use data captured about customers to suppress from a variety of activities such as: reduced or eliminated marketing efforts to non-profitable customers; adherence to customer request for non-interaction; and legal and ethical conformance (children, prisons, deceased, military, and fraud detection).

12. *Consolidate data*—Link data together.

13. *Prepare data for respective database update process.*

These steps have been listed as a serial process. They can be executed in real time and in part or in whole, depending upon the requirements and resources, both technical and financial. The data integration process is a key success factor as it creates a single—and hopefully accurate—view of the customer at a point in time.

Enhance Your Understanding: Adding Value to the Tesco Club Card

Read over the description of the Tesco Clubcard program in this chapter, visit the company's Web site at *www.tesco.com*, and then consider the material covered here about building a database, privacy, ethics, and CRM. Already, the Clubcard gathers a host of data that Tesco wants to know in order to serve its customers better and provide them with buying incentives. Yet beyond the fact that customers have a Clubcard in hand, Tesco's in-store personnel may know very little about the individuals they serve: their preferences, needs, wants, etc. Could the Clubcard concept be expanded to better use the rich mine of information Tesco has about where, when and what customers buy? Keeping ethical concerns in mind, how could the Clubcard program be enhanced to include additional customer preferences, offer customer reminders, or even create a sense of community among customers who have something in common—as evidenced by their buying patterns—such as parents of small children or pet owners?

How Creative Strategy Fits into the Direct and Interactive Marketing Plan

As much as direct and interactive marketing creative people would like to consider their work the central focus of any marketing campaign, the fact is that creative strategy and execution represent only part of the overall marketing plan. What's more, the conventional wisdom is that in direct and interactive marketing, the most vital element is the precise choice of target market and the media used to reach them—usually called the "list." After that, most experts attribute 30 to 40 percent of success to the "offer" being made—what the customer or prospect will get and what they have to do to get it. This means only the remaining 20 to 30 percent is due to the creative approach—about half attributed to art and half to copy.

This is not to say that creative involvement in direct marketing programs has a finite beginning and end. On the contrary, the best way to develop successful creative campaigns is to become involved in each marketing venture as early as possible, and see it through evaluation.

This chapter will provide a general outline for a comprehensive direct and interactive marketing plan. It will show how creative strategy fits in as part of the overall plan. In addition, it will focus on the important role of the direct and interactive marketing creative person at all stages of the marketing plan.

The Direct and Interactive Marketing Plan

Direct and interactive marketing plans are complex selling methods that require careful orchestration of market evaluation, research, product development, marketing strategy, and execution. The functions of a direct and interactive marketing plan are to assess the situation, lay groundwork, set a step-by-step course for timely action, and provide a control document to measure and evaluate results. Such a plan helps everyone involved to retain their marketing orientation, and to orchestrate their actions to bring about a desired outcome.

For best results, the direct and interactive marketing plan should be written as an extension of a strategic plan encompassing the overall business's internal *Strengths* and *Weaknesses* and its external *Opportunities* and *Threats* (SWOT analysis). For more on strategic business planning, see Chapter 2 of Bob Stone's and Ron Jacobs's Eighth Edition of *Successful Direct Marketing Methods* or a good business management textbook. The basic format illustrated in Exhibit 5.1 may serve as a guide in the preparation of a direct marketing plan.

The Creative Person's Role in Marketing Planning and Execution

In the marketing plan in Exhibit 5.1, creative objectives and strategies are listed specifically under Marketing Strategies. However, copywriters and graphic designers will not maximize their effectiveness in developing words and pictures that sell if they jump directly to this part of the plan. First they must help develop, understand, and implement other parts of the marketing plan.

Direct and Interactive Marketing Review

As part of their overall research efforts, creative people should make sure that they have access to all materials used in writing the review section of the marketing plan. Creatives should study competitors' products and marketing techniques, get on competitors' mailing lists, surf competitors' Web sites and sign up for personalized treatment there, and decoy competitors' products to receive at home. Competitive ad samples look one way in a stack with other samples, and another way altogether when juxtaposed with one's own electric bill and personal letters in the family mail box.

There also is a world of difference between watching a competitor's direct response TV ad on a tape in the office, and happening upon it while "channel surfing" at home. The same is true about seeing an e-mail pop up in your own "in" box, or a mobile message appear on your own smart phone. Once creative people have considered competitive promotions and products in light of the challenge at hand, they should share their insights with general marketing types. Indeed, the creative perspective may be invaluable to the marketer who is struggling with issues regarding the offer—pricing, premiums, guarantees, etc. In addition, creative people may turn up unique product advantages—or ways to turn possible disadvantages into selling pluses.

Marketing Objectives

Creative people need to understand the scope of the challenge they are involved with. If the marketing plan calls for an ultimate sales volume of $50 million and the generation of a million new customer names, the perspective is quite different than if the strategy outlines an initial test of three or four small-space ads and banner ads to determine the product's basic viability. Sadly, some creative people fail to gain this kind of perspective. When this occurs, they may find themselves suggesting a full-scale, jumbo, spectacular mailing package costing $1,000 per thousand in quantities of a million or more to an entrepreneur with an initial testing budget of less than $50,000 and hopes of confining most of his efforts to affordable media like e-mail and Google Ad Words.

Marketing Strategies

The copywriter or graphic designer who shows active interest at this stage of the game is much less likely to be "force-fed" a formula plan. Do you believe that a postcard mailer combined with an e-mail campaign is a better alternative than a traditional envelope mailing for this proposition? Do you think this marketing plan should include online promotions, broadcast advertising, social media, or mobile marketing, even though use of these media in this scenario might be considered unorthodox? It is essential that you state your views and back them up with precedents, projections, and creative concepts at this level, before plans are approved and budgets are set.

Operations Guidelines

On the surface, it might seem that the creative person has little to do with the nuts and bolts of order processing and fulfillment. But unfortunately, many a "front-end" program is allowed to lose its vital marketing orientation when it reaches the "back end." For best results, creative people should dig in

Exhibit 5.1. The Direct and Interactive Marketing Plan

I. *Direct and Interactive Marketing Review*—Provides the assessment and groundwork that are necessary before new plans can be initiated.
  A. Description of Your Product or Service
    1. Features—Product attributes
    2. Benefits—Product advantages
    3. Possible Alternates/Variables
  B. Description of the Market for Your Product or Service
    1. Size and Scope
    2. Market Trends and Stage of the Product Life Cycle (i.e., introduction, growth, maturity, decline)
    3. Evidence of Demand
    4. Distribution Patterns
      a) Direct and Interactive Marketing Channels
      b) Other Distribution Channels (retail, personal sales, etc.)
  C. Description of Competitive Facts
    1. Share of Market—Yours and Competitors'
    2. Competitors' Product/Service Descriptions—Quality, Price, Features/Benefits
      a) Your Product's Advantages
      b) Your Product's Disadvantages
      c) Competitors' Advantages
      d) Competitors' Disadvantages
      e) Your Product's Point(s) of Differentiation from Competitors' Products
    3. Competitors' Marketing Efforts
      a) Media
      b) Creative
      c) Offer(s) (what the customer will get, and what they have to do to get it)
  D. Positioning—Synthesize knowledge of product, market, and competition as well as knowledge gleaned from predictive analysis of your database to develop a target market segment, or segments, that fits your product's strengths and weaknesses and maximizes chances for success considering competitors' known strategies. (Market segmentation + product differentiation = positioning)
II. *Marketing Objectives*—Make these as specific and measurable as possible. The objectives may be expressed in one or more of these ways:
  A. Total Sales Volume
  B. Percentage Share of Market
  C. Number of and Projected Lifetime Value of New Customers
  D. Amount of Increase in "Share of Customer" for Existing Customers
III. *Marketing Strategies*
  A. Media Objectives by Medium—E-mail, Direct Mail, Space, Web Site, Social Media, etc.
    1. Overall Projected Results (Leads, Sales)
    2. Projected Response Levels by Vehicle (List, Magazine Insertion, E-mail Campaign, Mobile Marketing, etc.)
  B. Media Strategies
    1. Direct Mail and/or E-mail Testing Plan—For example, begin with eight lists of 5,000 rented names each to be followed by validations and roll-out promotions.
    2. Testing Plan for Each Medium—Similar projections for space ads, online advertising, broadcast, mobile, etc.
  C. Creative Objectives—Typical objectives could be:
    1. Sales or Leads at Specific Volume Levels
    2. Heightened Awareness of Company or Product
    3. Relationship Building to Gain a Larger Share of Customer

    D. Preliminary Creative Strategy Input

      1. Features and Benefits in Order of Importance to the Target Market

      2. Changes of Emphasis for Various Market Segments

      3. Creative Plan

        a) Assignments—Creation of e-mails, direct mail package, ad(s), Web site updates and landing pages, etc.

        b) Preliminary Guidelines for Graphics and Copy

        c) Needed Collateral Materials for Back End—E-mail acknowledgments, package inserts, etc.

IV. *Operations Guidelines*

    A. Program-Specific Instructions for Departments

      1. Order-Processing

      2. Data-Processing

      3. Fulfillment

      4. Customer Service

      5. Online Marketing Requirements

    B. Master Timetable—Beginning with mail date or day materials are due to the publisher or to be posted online or e-mailed, and working back

V. *Budget Summary*—A chart listing projected expenditures for media, list rentals, production, postage, etc.—every cost that is not considered a part of the firm's overhead.

VI. *Special Activities*—Research, public relations, sales promotion, special events, social media, general advertising, or other related activities that will impact this direct/interactive marketing plan.

VII. *Evaluation*—Each marketing plan should include a mechanism for evaluating results and using what has been learned as input for the next plan's Direct and Interactive Marketing Review.

---

and find out every detail about how each order or lead will be handled when it reaches the firm. For example:

- Will appropriate landing pages and/or QR codes be created to coordinate with space ads, direct mail packages, and e-mail solicitation, including possible use of Personalized URLs (PURLs)?
- Will the Web site be updated in a timely manner to correspond with the offers and promotional methods being used in other media?
- What kind of order acknowledgments will be sent by e-mail or snail mail? Who will write them?
- Who is in charge of creating the legally required notices that will be sent to customers in case their product shipments are delayed?
- How will the product be packaged?
- What kind of collateral materials will accompany the shipment?
- Does the customer service department have a good, marketing-oriented set of standard e-mails and letters to use in responding to customer complaints and requests?

If you do not have sufficient clout to find out the answers to these questions from inside your firm, do a little investigation on your own. Order from your own firm, and have several friends or relatives do the same. Respond to Web offers, e-mails, space ads, direct mail and other media deployed by your firm. Find out how you are treated as a customer, and document the results. Handled with tact and care, such information can provide the ammunition you need to improve the marketing orientation of the firm's operations.

Such care is needed because many firms routinely send out e-mails and letters to hard-won customers that read as if robots had written them. And many a customer *service* department comes across instead as a group of customer *discipline* specialists, because their communications are production oriented—aimed at internal goals rather than customer satisfaction.

The need for such vigilance in customer care is obvious, since according to marketing and sales expert Murray Raphel, "The average business in the United States spends five times as much money for a new customer than it does on the customers it already has." Help your firm to maximize the long-term value of each new, hard-won customer, and your creative contributions to the marketing plan will add to the bottom line as well.

Budget Summary

The creative person's concern here is similar to that expressed under objectives: an understanding of available dollars helps creatives keep their plans and ideas in proportion with budget reality.

Special Activities

Based on their research and analysis of competitors and knowledge of the marketplace, creative people may well be able to suggest public relations ventures, sales promotion ideas, online partnerships, viral marketing campaigns, or events that would integrate the communications message and amplify the impact of direct and interactive marketing programs. Preparing their proposals at the marketing plan stage ensures that the necessary time and budget can be allocated if these ideas are approved.

Evaluation

The creative person who spends the necessary time to study campaign evaluations in depth can become an invaluable resource to the firm. Analysis of individual rental list and media results, results from segments of the internal database, Web site statistics, creative testing, formats and offers are important—but even more vital is the ability to develop logical hypotheses for future testing based on market research and the synthesis of various prior results.

Developing a Creative Strategy or Creative Brief

Before the first word is written or a single line placed on the computer screen, the copywriter and graphic designer should accept and understand the Creative Strategy Statement (also known as a Creative Brief) for the job they've undertaken. This format (shown in Exhibit 5.2) is from Ron Jacobs, President of the Chicago-based, multichannel direct/digital marketing agency, Jacobs & Clevenger and co-author of *Successful Direct Marketing Methods*. It provides good, basic direction for the creation of a multichannel campaign that might include some combination of direct mail, space ads, television, a Web presence, mobile marketing, public relations, and/or sales promotion.

A comprehensive creative strategy statement like Ron Jacobs's is useful to ensure that both company and agency—or creative people and marketing types—are in agreement before copy and art are developed. An informal creative strategy statement can be used at a minimum, by setting down a sentence or two each to describe:

Exhibit 5.2. Creative Strategy Statement

CREATIVE WORK PLAN

Client:

Project title:

Date:

Job no.:

Prepared by:

Key fact
Single most important fact relevant to preparing this advertising.

Consumer problem this advertising must solve
Related to KEY FACT. State in consumer terms. Not what the brand or product needs . . . what the consumer needs.

Advertising objective
How this advertising proposes to solve the problem stated above.

Creative strategy
Prospect profile: *Portrait of the best prospects, list key demographics, psychographics, product usage facts.*
Competition: *Not a list of brands: what we must replace in order to attract consumers to our offer.*
Promise: *The single most important consumer benefit. The basis upon which this advertising will be built.*
Reason why: *Most important single reason we can give the consumer to believe the promise above.*

Legal or policy considerations/mandatory factors

Source: Ron Jacobs, President, Jacobs & Clevenger.

- The target market (described in terms of demographics and psychographics)
- The number-one benefit you'll be demonstrating to that market, along with proof of that benefit
- The objective of your advertising (inform, persuade, remind, generate leads, sell directly)

Discipline yourself to agree with your creative partners, clients, and/or account people on at least these three concepts, and you'll stand an excellent chance of delivering creative work that all agree is "on strategy" the first time around.

Enhance Your Understanding: Decoy Assignment

The Direct and Interactive Marketing Review section of this chapter emphasizes the importance of "decoying"—getting on competitors' databases to see what offers they make, what formats they use, how often they mail, e-mail and phone, and what tests they undertake. Here's a simple assignment that will help you study positioning and fulfillment in space advertising and direct mail/telephone/e-mail/mobile promotion.

Select several magazine space ads in one category of products (tennis supplies, women's clothing, kitchen equipment, etc.), each offering a catalog or information package to respondents. Use the Reader's Service Card (bingo card) if available to request information. If no bingo card is available, fill out a coupon or bind-in card and mail it in, or call the toll-free number, or e-mail, or use a Web response form. Provide your e-mail address and opt in to receive information from the firm. If you are asked for your mobile (cell phone) number, and if you are willing, provide that as well.

Record the date you make your request. Then watch your mail and keep alert for phone follow-up, e-mails, and mobile alerts. Make a chart—compare and contrast how the various competitors communicate with you as a prospect. Buy an item from each firm and keep track of how you are treated during the buying process . . . how long it takes for your purchase to arrive . . . how it's packaged . . . what kind of follow-up mailings, phone calls, e-mails and texts you receive, etc.

When you do this to track all known competitors in a real-world situation, this process will provide you with vital, current information on what your competitors do well and where there's room for you to fill empty niches or make improvements.

6

A Creative Person's View of Direct and Interactive Marketing Media

Direct and interactive marketing media may include any channel of communication that invites a direct response. Even skywriting can be considered direct marketing if it includes a call to action and a telephone number or address. Marketers have enthusiastically integrated the Internet, e-mail, and, more recently, mobile marketing and social networking sites into their media options. That said, smart marketers still make frequent use of the tried and true: various forms of direct mail, print advertising, telephone, broadcast, or interactive media.

Every good direct and interactive marketing plan calls for an outline of media objectives and strategy. Creative people can be of great help in determining appropriate media for a given marketing plan, based upon the creative advantages, disadvantages, and budgetary impact of various media alternatives. This chapter discusses the basic pros, cons, and relative costs of entry for the most frequently used direct and interactive marketing media.

Direct Mail

Creative Advantages

- Almost unlimited format opportunities: size, looks, colors, paper, use of gimmicks, extent of copy, three-dimensional packages, pop-ups, etc.
- Extremely well targeted if market segmentation is done correctly.
- Allows for personalization and relatively private communications. As direct marketing expert Denny Hatch notes, "What makes direct mail different is that it goes to an individual person and has a letter. It's the only place in advertising where one person can make an emotional connection with a reader in his or her home."
- You may utilize all technological advances as they hit the market—you needn't wait for the medium to catch up, as you often do in dealing with space advertising vehicles and many Web sites.
- Ability to take advantage of database management and computer applications to reach highly defined markets with highly targeted messages—even individually targeted messages using variable data printing.
- Helps you learn in a controlled environment. You can develop test cells you

want, not be at the mercy of a publication or broadcast medium, or limited by their ability to do A/B splits, geographic and lifestyle splits, etc.

- Highly responsive; only properly executed telephone marketing has higher response rates among direct marketing media.
- Allows you to use inexpensive formats like postcards, double postcards, or self-mailers to draw timely attention to an offer or opportunity on a Web site or landing page.

Creative Disadvantages

- Expense may bar entry. Space ads can be placed much more cheaply to test viability of a concept. Direct mail packages routinely cost $600 per thousand to $1,000 per thousand or more, even in large quantities.
- May be difficult to discover and reach a wide enough audience to meet volume goals, given limited universes and "list burn-out," a phenomenon in which good outside lists are barraged with so many offers that their value declines rapidly—especially if not replenished constantly with fresh names.
- Post office restrictions must be followed to the letter. Risks include paying extra postage and producing packages that cannot be mailed.
- The post office is less reliable on timing of delivery than broadcast and most print media. In addition, horror stories persist about non-delivery of significant amounts of standard mail.
- Direct mail is very complex and requires coordination of lists, creative production, and mailing. Other media are much easier to prepare for.
- Most direct mail does not come "invited into the home" the way ads do as part of a magazine, newspaper, Web site, or TV show selected and often paid for by the prospect.

Magazines

Creative Advantages

- Ability to reach mass markets with magazines like *Better Homes and Gardens* and *National Geographic*, or very carefully segmented markets with magazines like *Golf Digest, Popular Mechanics, Prevention, Maxim, Working Mother*, etc.
- Rising costs of direct mail and dearth of good lists in many market segments make magazine advertising cost effective where it wasn't years ago.
- Mass magazines offer larger circulations than many lists, providing more exposure.
- Magazines come invited into the home, unlike much direct mail. This facilitates trust among readers, and a predisposition to feel positive about advertised products.
- No barrier to entry: 1/6- or 1/12-page black-and-white ads in mail-order sections of mass publications can be had for as little as a few thousand dollars; even less in highly targeted magazines with small circulation.
- Excellent color reproduction capability.
- More format options are available than in the past: pre-prints, bind-ins, tip-ons,

promotional items enclosed with the publication in see-through mailers, personalization, scents, samples, etc.

- Generally much easier to produce and less to coordinate than with direct mail.
- A/B splits and regional editions are sometimes available. Testing can be done fairly inexpensively.

Creative Disadvantages

- Limited format possibilities due to page sizes and advertising configurations.
- Long lead time. Closing dates can be months ahead of cover dates.
- Lack of control over position. Some publications bunch ads together, creating ad "ghettos" without surrounding editorial. Response may vary a great deal between far-forward and far-back ad positions.
- Relatively slow response and a long shelf life make magazines hard to evaluate and react to for further testing.
- Relatively impersonal medium. Although personalization and customization are possible in some magazines, relatively few offer this option, or if available it may be limited to high-volume advertisers only.

Newspapers

Creative Advantages

- Immediate, authoritative, and newsy.
- A good medium for quick testing. Newspapers have late closing dates and yield quick response, so results are available fast.
- Fairly broad local coverage of a mature, literate audience.
- National newspapers like *The Wall Street Journal* and *U.S.A. Today* offer broad reach; excellent regional testing possibilities at affordable cost.
- Comes invited into the home by subscribers—and read in many households almost immediately upon receipt.
- Editorial-style ads let you trade on the publication's franchise as a respected source of news.
- Inexpensive to test. Many publications will even provide layout and typesetting so a concept can be tested in small papers for a few thousand dollars, then expanded as warranted.
- A/B split testing available in some local papers as well as zoned editions, splits by ZIP+four designation, etc., in some markets.
- Some segmentation can be achieved by advertising in specialized sections such as home and garden, lifestyle, sports, autos, entertainment, etc.

Creative Disadvantages

- Poor color reproduction in many cases; poor photo fidelity.
- Impersonal medium.
- Position and format limitations abound.

- A mass medium with little selectivity except by city and suburban zones in many cities.
- Can be a complex media procedure to create a national campaign using local newspapers.
- Local events and conditions can affect ad response, jeopardizing projectability of results.
- Sharply declining readership among younger consumers make this medium problematic for many attractive target markets.

Free-Standing Newspaper Inserts and Weekend Magazines

Creative Advantages

- Many of the same advantages as direct mail: format flexibility, good color reproduction, control of production.
- A plus over direct mail: exact timing, since your ad or insert arrives in a specific day's paper rather than whenever the standard mail happens to be delivered.
- Huge and concentrated reach. For example, *Parade* magazine has a circulation of over 32 million and a readership of 74 million each Sunday, with most all of the reading done in a 48-hour time period.
- Co-op inserts like those of Valassis and News America (Smart Source) allow for cost-effective testing in a small number of markets, and roll-out potential in the tens of millions.
- Advertising in newspaper-circulated magazines such as *Parade* and *USAWeekend* provide good testing possibilities and mass roll-out quantities.

Creative Disadvantages

- In some markets there is a great deal of clutter among free-standing inserts (FSIs). In addition, studies show that certain market segments almost never read FSIs.
- This is a mass medium with relatively little opportunity to target prospects. It may be effective only for relatively low-end, mass-appeal products and services. Individual FSIs can be nearly as costly as direct mail, yet response is considerably less than direct mail.
- Format opportunities for FSIs are constrained by what newspapers will accept and can insert.

Billing Inserts/Package Inserts/Co-Ops/Card Decks

Creative Advantages

- Extends reach for direct marketing programs that have proved effective in mail and/or space.
- Affordable: may cost only a tenth to a fourth as much as direct mail (because the costs are shared with other advertisers), with results proportionately lower.

- Ability to control your own color quality and production within the confines of size and format restrictions.

Creative Disadvantages

- Format and size constraints, especially in card decks and co-ops.
- Usually not considered a stand-alone medium—most often used to extend the reach of successful, proven programs.
- Must be controlled to ensure your offer is being promoted in a compatible medium. Co-ops range from mass-market coupon envelopes to the exclusive ranks of executive card decks.

Telephone

Creative Advantages

- Immediate, personal, selective, and very flexible. Allows for spur-of-the-moment up-selling and cross-selling to customers.
- Allows you to ask specific questions to gain market research information while selling or reinforcing sales.
- Highest response medium when done appropriately; also most costly per prospect contact.
- May be used as a primary selling medium or a follow-up for continuity sales.
- Works best with established customers, for following up qualified leads, for business-to-business pitches, for proactive customer service, or when you have specific questions to ask.

Creative Disadvantages

- More consumers consider outbound telemarketing an invasion of privacy than any other main direct marketing medium; indeed, about 80 percent of Americans have signed up for the federal Do Not Call list.
- Creatives must adhere to the specific and strict telemarketing regulations of the Federal Trade Commission regarding disclosures, prizes, misrepresentations, etc. The Direct Marketing Association provides information that outlines these rules in detail.
- Does not allow for visuals.
- Even a well-written script will not come across well unless the representative delivering it has been well trained, speaks clearly, and speaks with enthusiasm.
- Expensive on a per-call basis, although a small test may be designed at a reasonable rate to test viability.
- Many consumers are virtually unreachable by phone because of government Do Not Call lists, long work hours, unlisted numbers, and screening calls on caller I.D. systems.

E-Mail

Creative Advantages

- Immediate: messages arrive in the recipient's mailbox seconds or minutes after they are sent, and usually are dealt with relatively promptly on receipt.
- Outstanding testing flexibility. Testing of lists, offers, sender names, subject lines, and creative approaches can be done very readily with very quick results.
- Attractive, interactive, and colorful HTML e-mails have largely replaced less appealing text formats as more and more customers enjoy broadband service.
- Much lower cost than most any other medium, with the best return on investment of any medium ever invented (more than $40 for each dollar invested, per the Direct Marketing Association).
- Excellent for verification of orders, shipment alerts, and other customer service functions that normally are welcomed by buyers.
- High penetration among literate, affluent customers both at home and at work.
- Exceptional ability to customize e-mail delivery schedules and messages based on customer or prospect input and interests.

Creative Disadvantages

- The broad-brush connotation of "spam" has tarnished the image of e-mail as a promotional medium.
- Potential for deletion of promotional e-mails, even among opted-in customers, is very high.
- E-mail messages and delivery plans must be developed with great care since responsible e-mailers offer customers and prospects the opportunity to opt-out in response to any message. An annoying or poorly targeted message, or too-frequent communications, may have dire consequences for your e-mail list.
- Even an HTML e-mail is quite limited in appropriate format and length.
- Not as cost-effective as the phone for customer service purposes.

Mobile Marketing

Creative Advantages

- Immediate and timely—great for limited-time offers and opportunities that customers and prospects can take advantage of immediately, while out and about in the marketplace.
- A very personal and "always on" medium—many people are "joined at the fingertip" to their mobile devices.
- Pinpoint targeting of customer/prospect and exact location are possible.
- Very trackable with great database-building opportunities.
- Great for impulse purchases as consumers can pay with a few clicks on their mobile devices.
- Potential to create easily updatable "apps" that build brands, build relationships with customers, and/or become profit centers.

Creative Disadvantages

- Perceived by many as intrusive, unwelcome, a possible privacy invasion and, in the case of immediate geographically-targeted offers, even somewhat creepy.
- The challenge is to make an offer that is integrated with your larger campaign, and is more than simply a price appeal.
- Under scrutiny by the Federal Communications Commission with potential limitations coming on use and release of mobile customer data.
- Limited target market in the United States currently due to relatively low penetration of smart phones, and the need for consumer opt-in for respectful mobile marketing.
- Fragmentation due to a wide range of carriers and devices in use.

Social Networking Sites (including Blogs)

Creative Advantages

- The ultimate mass media of the twenty-first century with top sites boasting tens of millions of participants.
- Incredible opportunities for pinpoint targeting based on what consumers reveal about themselves and what they talk about on social sites.
- Ability to reach younger consumers and others who spend little time with traditional media.
- "Natural relevance" for ads and offers—for example, ads that appear at the bottom of YouTube videos that offer more information about the brand or product featured in the video.
- Ability to establish a very human, accessible brand personality.
- Ability to build brand loyalty through fan pages, people who "like" your product or site, and bloggers who report positive experiences with your products or services.
- Site visitor analytics, consumer reviews, and comments provide inexpensive yet valuable market research information.
- Highly inexpensive from the point of view of media cost.

Creative Disadvantages

- Consumer control is paramount in social media: consumers and bloggers may say negative things about your product or service in the social space.
- It is very time-consuming to keep social media sites updated and monitored on a continuous basis.
- Results of ads on social media sites can be measured in terms of click-throughs, requests for information, purchases and time on site, but the ROI of social media sites and fan pages can be difficult to measure.
- High noise level and much competition for attention to your message.

Television

Creative Advantages

- Best medium for demonstration.
- Endless possibilities for formats and forms: drama, slice of life, pitch man, testimonial, celebrity spokesperson, or some combination—in studio or on location.
- More and more targeting is possible with digital cable and satellite options, as well as niche cable networks with shows catering to specific demographic groups.
- Versatile medium—may be used for sales, lead generation, integration with or support of other media.
- Growing options for digital editing allow for easier and much less costly customization or editing of TV spots.
- Quick responses: you can get an initial read on a commercial in minutes as customers call the toll-free number or log on to a landing page on the Internet.
- By their very length, many direct marketing commercials eliminate clutter. At 90 to 120 seconds, they may consume much of the time allotted to a commercial break period.
- Infomercials—entire 30-minute shows with an advertising message—offer the luxury of time to explain, demonstrate, and sell a product or service in an atmosphere that seems more like a show than a commercial.

Creative Disadvantages

- Very expensive: often takes $100,000 or more for production and media to perform even a simple test. High costs make this the realm of large and sophisticated direct-marketing firms—or start-ups with deep pockets.
- Finite amount of television time available on desirable networks and cable channels. Time is especially scarce in the year's second and fourth quarters, when general advertisers beef up their broadcast buys.
- The woes of general advertisers on television hold true for direct marketers: more consumers are "zapping" commercials of all kinds, eliminating them from digital video recordings and using remote control devices to sample other shows while commercials are on the air.
- A fleeting medium: unless you can move the consumer to action in 120 seconds or less (or 30 minutes in the case of an infomercial), you have lost your opportunity since nothing is written down.

Radio

Creative Advantages

- Stations with specific formats allow for considerable targeting to businesspeople, country music fans, classical music buffs, sports fanatics, and so on.
- Inexpensive to test on a local basis; most rates are open for bargaining.
- Radio networks and satellite radio allow for considerable nationwide reach.

- Timely and newsy.
- A good medium for fantasy and humor.
- Ability to go on the air almost immediately—copy can be written one minute and read by an announcer the next. Even studio-produced spots take little time to prepare.
- Creative direct marketers have found that they may use the strength of radio personalities to help sell their products: Sean Hannity touts LifeLock as protection against identity theft; money expert Dave Ramsey gains leads for mortgage brokers and term life insurance sales agents.

Creative Disadvantages

- Much the same as television: a fleeting medium with nothing written down; listeners may switch stations during commercial breaks.
- Except for satellite radio, a few networks and syndicated programs, it is a difficult and complex job to obtain national reach via radio.
- No visuals; no response device.
- Radio is often used by listeners as background noise; thus getting their attention with an ad may be difficult.
- Reports of listening audience may be exaggerated since many use radio as background noise at home or at work.
- The number of people who do most of their listening in cars cuts down potential response, since they may not have access to phone or paper and pencil. Near-universal penetration of cell phones helps cut down this problem, especially for drive-time pitches to businesspeople.

Internet and Other Interactive Media

Creative Advantages

- A "hot" medium, especially with younger and more affluent audiences.
- Many site visitors are willing to provide database information in exchange for samples, insider information, and specially tailored responses from you. This information also allows you to customize your presentation to each visitor upon his or her return or even "on the fly"—making one-to-one marketing a reality.
- Your presentation can (and should) be changed often to attract prospects and customers back again and again.
- Ideal for the integration of sales promotion techniques like contests or online voting.
- Non-linear medium allows browsers to delve deeper into parts of your presentation that interest them most.
- You can tell what interests visitors and what stops them short by analyzing the data from their visits.
- Advancing technology and broadband penetration in homes and offices allows for excellent color, motion, sound, videos, and so on.
- Excellent for building public relations and providing wanted services to customers at very low cost to the provider—such as FedEx online package tracking.

- Relatively low financial barriers to entry for a basic Web presence, although effective e-commerce requires a considerable investment. A small firm with a good Web designer can afford to appear much larger and more sophisticated than it can in other media.
- Nearly unlimited potential reach and frequency if you can attract visitors to your site and intrigue them to return.

Creative Disadvantages

- Because best practices for Web site design and copy are so different from those in print media, it requires acquisition of a whole new set of skills on the part of seasoned creatives.
- Site visitors expect constant updates. Done right, this is a high-maintenance medium.
- Leading sites like Amazon and eBay provide streamlined and highly customized experiences for their clients, and customers quickly come to expect similar state-of-the-art applications and customer service features from every site.
- While colors online are vibrant and varied, the ability to produce a picture of a product with fidelity and clarity is limited.
- The downside of a non-linear medium is that customers who "click onto" a hyperlink or banner ad on your site may never come back to see your selling message unfold.
- Actual purchasing online can be frustrating and time-consuming even on the most user-friendly sites.
- Concerns (rational or not) persist about security of credit card information and other personal information online.
- Designers must balance their desire for a dramatic and exciting site with the reality of some site visitors' limited computer systems. It is frustrating for consumers to wait many minutes for a picture to appear or a video to become available—no matter how delightful the finished product. Indeed, some experts say that the average Web viewer will become frustrated after just eight seconds if the page does not load.
- At least parts of your site will most likely be open to access by all: competitors, "enemies," etc., and your mistakes can be heralded throughout cyberspace by disgruntled customers—an opportunity not easily available to them in any other medium.

How to Choose the Media Mix

For best results, start testing a new marketing concept in the medium where you have had the most previous success. If your firm or client is new, track the media buys of competitors for clues as to where the most fertile customer base might be. In most cases, direct mail, space advertising, e-mail and the Web will be your best bets for initial testing. Indeed, testing offers, pricing, products, and creative elements via e-mail or on a Web site can be inexpensive and quick. In some cases, firms may choose to begin with telephone marketing since they can obtain direct feedback from customers—not only on whether they will buy, but also on why or why not. If tests prove successful, then consider expanding to additional media such as television, radio, social media, mobile marketing, co-ops, and package inserts.

In evaluating any media selection, be sure that results are tracked not only on initial responsiveness, but also on continued performance levels. In most cases, your ultimate goal is to obtain customers with maximum value over time—not just individuals who have a high front-end response rate.

Enhance Your Understanding: Preliminary Media Plans

Your direct and interactive marketing agency has been assigned to develop preliminary media plans for two new products. *Product #1* is a collectible doll inspired by the heroine of the latest animated Disney feature. It will sell for $49.95, and there are several more character dolls from the same film that can be used as follow-up products. The client is a collectibles direct/ interactive marketer with an extensive database, and the goal is to use this product to acquire new customers. *Product #2* is a downloadable software package (also available on a CD/ROM) for financial planning aimed at baby boomers facing retirement. It will sell for $99.95. The client is a magazine publisher with little past experience in software sales. Their goal is to find customers for the new software package beyond their current subscriber lists.

Develop a media plan for each product including first-round test media and then one or more phases of additional testing if the initial media choices prove successful. Consider the following in creating each media plan: target markets, price points, need for demonstration, need for good color fidelity, relative cost and financial risk, track record of similar past products, and other criteria you deem important.

7

Who Should Do the Creative Work and What Do They Need to Know?

If you visit direct and interactive marketing agencies and companies with the best track records for bottom-line performance, you will sense a special energy in the air. That energy springs from a staff that works in a healthy, creative environment built on respect for employees as partners in producing sales and profits.

In this chapter, both managers and creative practitioners will learn ways to develop such an environment in their own firms and agencies. Once the atmosphere for creative thinking is established, direct and interactive marketers must develop a system for gathering and sharing background information for creative assignments. This chapter provides a guide for managers on what the creative team needs to know, and some hints to creatives on how to draw out this essential material from clients.

The discussion of the human element in marketing concludes with some pros and cons for managers deciding whether to have creative work produced by a large outside agency, in-house staff, individual freelancers, or a small "virtual agency." There are also some pointers for creative people considering whether to work for an agency or company, or to hang out a freelancer's shingle.

How Managers Can Nurture the Creative Person in Direct and Interactive Marketing

During the 1960s and 1970s, the prevailing image of the advertising creative person was wild, undisciplined, and free spirited. Creative offices were decorated in bold colors, with accessories ranging from slinky toys to sofas in the shape of huge red lips. People envisioned copywriters and graphic designers roller skating down the halls and standing on their heads—ostensibly in search of that breakthrough idea.

Some of this was true, particularly during the dot.com boom of the late 1990s—but in the direct marketing field, very little of this creativity window dressing ever occurred. The main reason direct marketing creative people have always appeared and acted more businesslike than their general advertising counterparts is rooted in the quantitative measurement of direct marketing success. Few direct and interactive marketers consider an ad, Web site or direct mail package "creative" if it does not generate leads or sales at acceptable levels.

General advertising creative people often fill their résumés with the lists of creative awards they have won. But in direct and interactive marketing circles, even the creative awards competitions ask very specific questions about a campaign's performance against quantitative objectives. Even so, it is important not to envision the direct and interactive marketing creative person as a nuts-and-bolts numbers cruncher. Traditionally, some of the most successful heads of direct and interactive marketing agencies and companies have also been excellent writers or artists: the late David Ogilvy, the late Bob Stone, Joe Sugarman, and the late Rod MacArthur, just to name a few.

In this chapter, those who want to work effectively with copywriters and graphic designers will learn some of the typical characteristics of these creative types. Such traits and tendencies may make "creatives" exasperating to deal with at times. But the manager who understands the artistic mindset and handles creative people accordingly can look forward to top performance from them—and in many cases a resulting boost to the bottom line. Here, then, are some essentials about direct and interactive marketing creative people.

The Creative Person Loves to Write or to Create Art

The first quirk of the creative person is that he or she does not necessarily love business. In fact, he or she may be one of business's harshest critics. But working in advertising or direct and interactive marketing allows the creative person to write or create art for a living, with some job security and a fairly predictable income.

Get to know copywriters and graphic designers, and you will learn that most of them have some less commercial ambition for their talent. Many of them do these things part-time already: creating novels, poems or short stories, fine art canvases, plays or movies that may or may not ever be produced.

Others keep this higher ambition on the back burner for years. Believing that some day they will make movies or write novels or poetry—or paint landscapes instead of layouts—keeps these people relatively content in the work-a-day world of direct and interactive marketing. The point behind this discussion is a simple matter of motivation. You won't motivate most creative people by rhapsodizing about business and how their latest ad is going to improve the bottom line. You will reap much greater rewards by focusing on the creative product and how to make it the best it can be—while still fulfilling marketing objectives.

Many managers become impatient with discussions involving subtle nuances of photographic lighting, choice of one adjective over another, or the difference between PMS color 178 and 179. But if you show a creative person that you care about her craft, and that you're willing to take the extra time to make the ad a source of pride for her and for you—you will win her everlasting loyalty.

Creative People are Sensitive; They Always Take Their Work Personally

Good copywriters and graphic designers nurture their projects like children. In fact, the late Joan Throckmorton actually referred to her hypothetical direct mail package as "Baby" and "the kid" in her fine book, *Winning Direct Response Advertising*.

With this level of care invested, the creative person is extraordinarily sensitive to criticism—just as parents are when relatives or teachers start picking on their beloved offspring. Yet toning down the creative person's emotional involvement might well lead to a less effective product. Thus the smart direct and interactive marketing manager keeps the creative person's point of view firmly in mind when critiquing copy and layout. Doing so is not only a good investment in human relations, it's also a guaranteed way to save money, time, and aggravation.

Most every creative person can tell a horror story or two about insensitive clients and account executives whose ideas of constructive criticism include marginal notes such as "yuck," "ugh," or "this stinks—fix it by Friday *or else*!" Obviously, such statements are counterproductive because they give no specific direction for improvement. But more destructive is the fact that pejorative terms are interpreted as personal attacks on the creative person. The resulting anger and insecurity lead inevitably to lower productivity. In his book *The Inner Game of Tennis*, Tim Gallwey explained that "the safer you make a situation, the higher you can raise the challenge." When managers help their staff feel supported and worthy, they can raise the creativity stakes higher and higher. When worry or lack of trust are part of the prevailing atmosphere, creativity plummets.

Creative People Need Time to Think— They Can't Always Do What Looks Like Work to You

According to legend, Wolfgang Amadeus Mozart wrote some of his most brilliant musical pieces as fast as he could place the notes on paper. Samuel Taylor Coleridge's famous poem *Kubla Khan* is said to have come to him word for word in a dream. Nashville's country music museums and Cleveland's Rock and Roll Hall of Fame display the originals of some of the world's most popular music scribbled longhand on envelopes, napkins, or other paper scraps. Yet for every piece of creative work that seizes its author or artist all at once, there are hundreds that develop only by means of painstaking effort, word by word and image by image.

Businesspeople who are used to assigning specific time limits for jobs may be appalled to find that it is impossible to stop-watch creative work. A faster writer is not necessarily a better writer. A graphic designer who always delivers on time may be following predictable patterns to meet deadlines rather than striving for a creative breakthrough. Schedules are a fact of life in direct and interactive marketing, and successful creative people learn to keep them firmly in mind. Mike McCarthy, for many years the creative director at Chicago's MARCOA direct marketing agency, used to say to clients and account executives, "We'll give you the best job we can in the time we're allowed." He knew that a little more time usually meant a much better product because the creative people had the opportunity to play out a number of ideas searching for the best. It is essential to build enough days into the schedule to allow the creative process to work. Research, time to digest background material, freedom to make false starts and to reach for the best possible approach will yield a much better product. What's more, your creative people will appreciate your respect for the intricacies of their craft.

Creative People Thrive on Recognition and Opportunities for Growth

It costs the manager very little in time or effort to reward good ideas with recognition. Team spirit is healthy and constructive, but if one person's germ of an idea becomes the centerpiece of a winning campaign, make sure that person is recognized and publicly congratulated. Creative people greatly appreciate memos of commendation, especially those which the boss and the rest of the staff see as well. Encouraging copywriters and graphic designers to enter creative awards competitions is another positive step. Even though direct and interactive marketing results are ultimately measured on the bottom line, the recognition of peers provides a powerful tonic to most creative people.

Make sure copywriters and graphic designers are not cloistered away from clients and the marketing world at large. Encourage them to attend client meetings, both to soak up background information and to receive face-to-face recognition for their work. Trips to direct and interactive marketing workshops, seminars, and conventions help provide the outside stimulation that keeps creative people sharp and open to new concepts. Memberships in special interest groups such as the Creative Exchange of the Chicago Association of Direct Marketing enable copywriters and graphic designers to compare notes with their peers, learn new techniques, and develop valuable networks of contacts.

How Creatives Can Contribute to a Business Environment Where Ideas Flourish

Marketing managers and account executives can do a great deal to help foster a positive atmosphere for creativity. But copywriters and graphic designers must do their part as well, harnessing their creative powers to conquer specific marketing problems. Here are several tips for creative people on how to work better with businesspeople.

In Direct and Interactive Marketing, Creativity Is a Means to an End

If your business associates are smart, they will value you for your creative flair—your ability to develop unique ways of highlighting product features and benefits and motivating prospects to buy. But as a copywriter or graphic designer you must remember that *all* of your talents must be aimed at meeting marketing goals, not satisfying your personal creative muse.

Many direct and interactive marketing creative people complain about having to produce the same old stuff over and over. They lobby for the opportunity to do four-color work when test results have proved conclusively that two-color pieces are most cost effective for the offer at hand. They yearn for the chance to start from scratch and create a package, Web page or ad that ignores hard-won direct and interactive marketing principles. Yet most breakthrough ideas in direct and interactive marketing are built upon principles, dos and don'ts developed through decades of careful testing. Remember that before Pablo Picasso broke new ground with his unique artistic vision, he spent years studying the Old Masters. Direct marketing creative types should do the same.

Read the works of creative giants like John Caples, Herschell Gordon Lewis, and Dick Hodgson. Study direct mail, broadcast, Web and space ad samples diligently and learn all you can about their results and analytics.

Do your homework on each product or service, investing the time you need to fully understand its attributes and drawbacks. Become as much of a *marketer* as you are a creative person, so that you can understand the numbers side of the business. And above all, remember that in direct and interactive marketing, the ultimate creativity of a campaign is in direct proportion to its sales and bottom line performance. As author and direct marketing veteran Bob Stone once noted, "If you ever grow weary of caressing order blanks and checks, it's time for you to leave the direct-response business." In today's world those orders are more likely to come in online via credit card rather than by mail via check, but the point still holds true: make it your business to monitor results on a daily basis, no matter what media you are using.

Understand and Accept the Marketing Concept of "Sunk Costs"

Businesspeople often warn of "throwing good money after bad." They advise others to cut their losses and abandon a floundering product line or sell a stock that's falling in price rather than follow it to the bitter end. Their business training makes it easier for marketers to abandon impractical advertising campaigns than it is for the creative types who developed them. Businesspeople are interested in the *commercial* value of any given idea. If its commercial value plummets, the idea is no longer any good to them. Money that has been invested in such an idea is considered "sunk costs" to be written off and forgotten as soon as possible.

As a creative person, ideas are your stock in trade. Even though an idea no longer fits strategy, you may have difficulty abandoning it. But don't fight for it just because you have time, blood, sweat, and tears tied up in it. Remember that it's just the *idea* that's being abandoned, not the talent that developed it. Keep your eye on the marketing plan and the bottom line. Be sure to save that abandoned idea in your personal files, though—it might be perfect for another project or client down the line.

Park Your Creative Ego at the Door, and Watch the Gamesmanship Stop

Many times when a creative person and a businessperson try to work together, their value systems, personality styles, and conflicts take over the conversation. The project they're trying to complete languishes while the two egos fight head to head.

Creative types often fan such a fire by becoming defensive about their work, accusing the manager or account executive of insensitivity or lack of discernment. Yet they can easily turn the conversation into a productive dialogue with a simple change of attitude.

Instead of setting up an adversarial, head-to-head encounter, try standing or sitting side by side with the person you're working with. Figuratively, you're placing yourself on the same team with that person, looking out toward the project and its possible solutions from the same vantage point. You're a partnership ganging up on the project, not on each other. In this way, you'll place the emphasis where it should be: on the job itself, not the power struggle within the relationship.

Strive to Work Well with Your Creative Counterparts

Even direct and interactive marketers who claim that copy is king must admit that there is considerable difference in reader perception between an ill-designed direct mail piece, Web site or ad and a masterful job by a graphic designer. Better to proclaim that the *product* is king, and that both copywriters and graphic designers should work to enhance it, forsaking "art for art's sake."

Unfortunately, in many cases copywriters and graphic designers may seem to be natural adversaries, like cats and dogs. The copywriter fights for another paragraph of copy space and complains that the graphic designer really didn't try to arrange the location shots that would have been perfect for a particular brochure or Web page. The graphic designer complains about long copy—in his mind, anything over 30 words—and insists on breaking up a block of type that needs to be read in sequence because it looks better his way. But if the copywriter and graphic designer respect each other's work and understand how much each can do to make the other look good, their cooperative efforts can be a joy to behold—and their working relationship can become one of work's greatest pleasures.

In practice, you will find many situations where the copywriter receives completed layouts to write from, and never even sees the graphic designer face to face. Or the writer may prepare rough layouts and send them off into a void for production. But having the writer and artist work together from start to finish is the ideal that creative people should strive for.

Now that e-commerce, mobile marketing, and social media command an impressive share of many direct and interactive marketing budgets, the traditional team of writer and designer may well be expanded to include a Web expert, a social media maven, and other specialists. For true integration of strategy and message, it's essential that all of these players are consulted and included from the beginning of the creative process.

What the Creative Team Needs to Know

Marketing professors teach that there are three main types of client-agency relationships: client dominant, agency dominant, and partnership. In the *client-dominant model,* the agency or freelancer is given a strict set of instructions and a specific, encapsulated assignment. In the *agency-dominant model,* the client turns over the marketing reins to the advertising specialists and participates very little in the creative process. While both of these relationships have worked fairly well for some firms and their agencies, they are generally far inferior to the partnership model. Based upon mutual respect, a *client/agency partnership* encourages open communication and sharing of ideas at all stages of the creative process.

As a manager striving for partnership, you must do your homework before meeting with the copywriter and graphic designer. You will either have to provide the type of information described below, or point your creative people in the direction in which to obtain it. Keep in mind that the more digging you expect them to do, the more the assignment is likely to cost in time and money.

If the creative team has worked with you before, they may already know about the company, product, and market. But even so, you will need to talk specifically about objectives, copy points, and the plans that have been made for this particular promotion.

Here, then, is a checklist of information creative people should have to begin a direct and interactive marketing project. Both managers and creatives can use this list to ensure they have compiled and shared all necessary material. It might also be helpful to set up a creative input sheet that includes the basic information in boilerplate form (or instructions on how to find this information on your corporate Web site), as well as fill-in blanks for information that changes from project to project.

What Is the Company Behind Your Product?

- Has your firm been involved in direct and interactive marketing before?
- How long has it been in business?
- What is its reputation?
- What kind of people and businesses form its present customer base?

What Is the Competitive Environment for This Product?

- Who are your competitors—both direct (same product category) and indirect (fulfills same or similar need)?
- How does your product fit into the competitive frame—i.e., market leader, middle market share, small market share, new entry?
- How do the competitors' products differ from yours?
- What features of your product, if any, excel theirs?
- Do you have a lower price or better overall benefit package?
- How have the competitors been promoting their products as compared to your efforts?

What Is the Product?

- Provide a product sample for the copywriter and designer, and encourage them to use it.
- If you are selling a service, allow the creative team to participate in the service as a consumer and/or as a provider of the service.
- Provide all collateral materials that come with your product or service.
- Put the writer in touch with the buyer or developer of the product, if someone other than yourself.
- Let the writer and designer visit the production site if possible.

- Answer the creative people's questions about how the product works and what it can do for the customer.
- Provide library research, Web site references, articles, books, or anything else that will help the creative people understand the product and its benefits.
- Point the creative people toward any social media sites that you sponsor, or that others have developed to talk about your product or service.

Who Is the Customer?

- Describe the likely buyer of your product, by segment.
- Include known demographics such as age, sex, income level, family size, region in which he or she lives, education level.
- Include known psychographics such as lifestyle factors, buying patterns, media consumption patterns, etc.
- For new products, share plans for list or media testing to provide ideas about likely buyers.
- Include testimonials from users of this or similar products.

How Will We Sell This Product?

- Share the media plan—direct mail, space, broadcast, telemarketing, online, mobile, social media, viral marketing, etc.
- Explain reasons for using these media and solicit ideas from creatives for more media concepts.
- Explain budgetary restrictions.

How Have We Sold the Product in the Past?

- One of the best sources of research for creatives is studying past efforts for a product.
- Don't mention only the winners. As much can be learned from what did not work as from what did.
- If the product is new, provide samples of past efforts on your other products. This can be supplemented by competitors' advertising samples.

What Are the Objectives for This Product?

- Lead generation, sales campaign, renewal, relationship building, fund-raising?
- Specific numbers—percentage response, orders per thousand, and so forth.
- Are you looking for loose leads (people who are interested but not committed) or tight leads (people who are already somewhat prequalified)?
- For retail campaigns, are you looking to generate traffic, sales by direct mail, Web, and phone/mobile, or some combination?

What Are the Copy Points for This Product?

- Work with the copywriter to develop this set of points.
- Make a list of what you want the advertising to get across starting with the chief product benefit and working down.
- Discuss product perception in the marketplace—how the target market and others feel about the product.
- Include important specifications such as price, size, shipping information, guarantee, etc.

What Other Creative Work Has Been Done So Far for the Product?

- If rough or comprehensive layouts are done, share them with the copywriter and provide the layouts themselves or photocopies.
- If you have rough copy, share it with the graphic designer.
- Get copywriter and graphic designer together as a team if at all possible.

What Are Your Preferences as to Creative Tone and Look?

- If this direct and interactive marketing effort is to be part of a multichannel marketing campaign, share the "big idea" and "look" of that overall campaign.
- Share information about the overall impression you wish to make: friendly, upscale, snobby, down-to-earth, sporty, etc.
- Provide samples of direct and interactive marketing you admire, and explain what you like about it.

What Is the Immediate Assignment?

- Outlines and thumbnail sketches or simple storyboards?
- Rough layouts with headings and a concept piece attached?
- Full-copy treatment plus comprehensive layouts?
- Deadline information and overall critical date schedule.

Few clients are organized and experienced enough to provide all—or even part—of this information on their own. Creative people must learn to dig for it by asking these questions themselves, sometimes over a period of days or weeks to avoid overwhelming the client.

In the meantime, they can prepare for assignments to come by doing general research on the client's product category, visiting retail outlets where such products are sold, or even taking on a sales shift or two at such a retail store. They can study the client's Web site in depth—corporate Web sites often provide a wealth of background information on the company, its history, founders and present leadership, product lines, and so on. They can visit the factory where the product is made, accompany field salespeople, and sit in on focus groups—or watch the video/read the results of such events. They can check out the social media associated with this product and category and read what people are saying on Facebook, Twitter, and other such sites. Marketers who encourage this detailed research on the part of their creative staff will reap extraordinary benefits in the resulting copy and layouts.

Who Should Do the Creative Work: A Full-Service Agency, In-House Staff, Freelancers, or a "Virtual Agency"?

The array of direct and interactive marketing creative service options can be confusing to the novice. Should you hire a large full-service agency or a specialist agency, or develop an in-house creative staff? Is freelance help the best option for you due to budgetary concerns, need for highly specialized help, or seasonal ups and downs in your creative needs? Should you forge an alliance with one or more of today's smaller "virtual agencies"? Or should you invest the time to learn the ropes of direct and interactive marketing creative work yourself, and go it alone? Here are some of the basic pros and cons of each option.

Benefits of Working With a Large Full-Service Agency

- *A full staff of personnel to meet your needs.* You can assume the role of manager and supervisor of your campaigns, meanwhile delegating a great deal of the creative and production work without giving up the decision-making function.
- *Direct and interactive marketing experience.* Even if you are somewhat seasoned in direct and interactive marketing, you probably don't have the broad background that the staff of an agency can offer you, including knowledge about what works and what doesn't, and experience in getting mailings, ads, Web site updates, and other promotions done on time and effectively.
- *Unbiased feedback.* The agency is an outsider, with the ability to give you a fresh view of your objectives, your product, your promotions, and your results. You don't have to work in a vacuum or rely strictly on the opinions of your own staff.
- *A constant idea supply.* Assuming you have found a good agency, you won't be stuck in a rut in terms of your product, promotions or media options. The stimulation of seeing what works and what "bombs" for other clients will keep your agency alive to new creative and media possibilities for you.

Benefits of Working With a Specialist Agency

You may choose to work with an agency that specializes in areas such as creative, search engine optimization and sponsored search, social media, or media placement. Here are some reasons why this may make sense for you.

- *Deep knowledge in a specialized area.* Your general agency may be able to provide you with specialized services, but chances are, they won't have the top experts in fields like search engine optimization and sponsored search on their staffs.
- *Pay for the services you want and need.* Specialist agencies serve a specific niche for clients—you won't be paying part of the overhead for services that your firm does not access.
- *Cutting-edge ideas.* Specialist agencies stay on the cutting edge—sometimes even the "bleeding edge"—of what can be done in their area of expertise. Their innovations may encourage you to test new ideas well before your competitors.

Why Some Direct and Interactive Marketers Don't Like Agencies

Here are some of the negative aspects of working with a full-service agency.

- *Expense.* The bigger the agency, the bigger its overhead. Whether you use them or not, you'll be helping to support the agency's media department, production staff, and other facilities right along with the creative department whose help you really need. So think hard about going with a full-service agency unless you need all or most of its services.
- *Ongoing costs.* Most full-service marketing agencies want to work on a retainer basis only; very few will do more than a single introductory job on a project basis. This makes sense from the agencies' viewpoint, since the time and energy they must invest to win a new client and learn the business is considerable. But you must ask yourself if your business is year-round and constant enough to justify the payment of a monthly retainer. Perhaps you'd be better off calling in a consultant when you need help, with no strings attached.
- *The education process.* If your product, proposition, or way of doing business is quite complex, you may be better off training people to do your direct and interactive marketing work for you—at least the marketing planning and creative work—on an in-house basis. With an agency you run the risk of getting the agency copywriter "where you want him" in terms of product knowledge, and suddenly have him transferred to another client or account group.
- *Your size/their size.* Perhaps you've read about some of the agency giants of the direct and interactive marketing field and would like to have one of them work for you. If you're a division of a *Fortune 500* company with a sizable budget, you may have no problem getting this. But if you're beginning with more enthusiasm than money, you may have a problem finding even a small agency that's willing to gamble the time it will take to get your fledgling program off the ground.

The In-House Creative Staff: Pros and Cons

A number of direct and interactive marketers, large and small, prefer to develop an in-house staff to handle all or most of their promotional needs. There are three main pluses of such an arrangement.

- *The in-house agency can develop experts and keep them.* If the product is complex or the method of selling unique, it may be easier for a firm to develop its own creative talent than to teach its business over and over again to outsiders.
- *Work can be turned around quickly.* Since the in-house writers and designers seldom have clients other than the parent firm and its divisions, they can meet the firm's creative priorities on a daily basis. Often an outside agency can get away with longer lead times simply because the advertiser is not fully aware of the mechanics of getting a job done. With the in-house staff, these mechanics are much more open to scrutiny, and built-in contingency time is therefore harder to obtain.
- *The advertiser has more control.* For an in-house creative staff, company philosophies are easier to get across and keep in mind. There is more day-to-day

supervision of the creative work, and more give and take between creative people and the firm's other personnel.

There are, however, some harsh critics of the in-house creative shop. Here are a few of the negative comments.

- *Work from an in-house agency tends to lose freshness.* Agency people benefit from the stimulation of working on a variety of accounts, and seeing new and different marketing strategies succeed. The in-house writers and artists may turn out less innovative work than outsiders would.
- *The firm with an in-house staff takes on a good deal of overhead.* Rather than treating creative help as an expense, the in-house agency owner must pay advertising support costs as a part of the regular corporate payroll. This continuing cost of doing business must be warranted by the results.
- *Bureaucracy or inner-directed thinking.* In-house creative people are often less sales oriented than their outside agency counterparts. They consider themselves a service department in the same mode as computer services or accounting. Thus these creatives tend to become more inner-directed, concerned with office politics and corporate problems rather than finding the best ways to intrigue customers.

Working with Freelancers

If you do not hire a direct and interactive marketing agency or develop your own in-house staff, you will have to find your own copywriter, graphic designer, Web designer, and/or social media expert. If you already have a database marketing consultant, market researcher, or other consultant whom you trust, you can ask them to refer you to creative people. You might also discuss your requirements with colleagues who do direct and interactive marketing, to see if they know a freelancer who may suit your needs. Checking the classified ads in online or offline trade publications is a third option. And if you are a member of a local or regional marketing organization, its roster should provide you with a list of the creative services in your area.

Once you've located a likely candidate, call him or her and introduce yourself. Explain the kinds of products you're going to be marketing and any ideas you have about media or themes for your campaign. If the information is confidential, say so right away. Direct and interactive marketing freelancers who expect to stay in business know that confidentiality is nearly as important in their profession as it is for the clergy and for doctors.

Listen carefully for the reactions of the prospective freelancer to your product and your ideas. Does the person sound enthusiastic about your proposition? Does he or she know what you're talking about, or does your field seem foreign to that person's experience? If a freelancer has heard of your firm and starts mentioning your previous efforts and those of your competitors in a knowledgeable way, you may have found yourself a gem. But you might also ask for verification of experience in your own or a related area. Some direct and interactive marketers have sufficiently broad backgrounds and interests to sell almost any type of product if they get complete input, while others choose to specialize in consumer or industrial goods, retail clients, or even something as specific as fashion or financial services.

Don't talk only about the product. Make sure the creative person knows whether you are considering a mail program or space advertising, television, business-to-business, a new or revamped Web site, telephone campaign, social media, or mobile marketing. It's a rare creative who is equally proficient in all of these areas, and an honest one will tell you where his or her specialties lie. A well-connected writer or graphic designer may be able to help you find a colleague who can do television scripting, a social media campaign or Web site design for you, while handling your direct mail packages, space ads, and catalog work personally.

If the phone contact goes well, invite the creative to send you a URL with some work samples posted online, or to visit you and show his or her portfolio. Keep in mind, however, that some creative people have been turned off by unscrupulous "prospective clients" who send for non-returnable samples and use them to get free ideas—never intending to hire them or any other writer or graphic designer. You may yield better results by asking for a résumé of experience and perhaps one or two photocopied samples. That said, many creative people today have robust portfolios of work available to view on their Web sites, either open to the public or behind a password they may choose to give you if they believe you are serious.

The promptness of the response and presentation of materials you receive will be good indicators of the way in which this person will handle your account. Are the samples or examples keyed in to your expressed interests in terms of product and media? Or do they look liked a canned package that would be provided to any prospective client? When introducing the work, does the creative person talk about target markets, strategy, and results, or seem more concerned with pretty pictures and nice turns of phrase? Is the copy meaty and specific, or vague and general? Is the layout clear and easy to follow? Do your best to separate the graphics presentation from the copy, however, since the writer often has no say about the work of the graphic designer, and vice versa, especially when they are freelancers.

Once you have evaluated the samples, a face-to-face meeting is the next step. A meeting by phone can sometimes be sufficient if your first-choice creative source is too far away for cost-effective "face time." However, to establish the best working relationship, at least one face-to-face meeting is preferable. Make sure you have an advance understanding of whether the meeting will be held on a speculative basis or whether you will be charged for this consultation time and/or for travel expenses.

A good way to get started is to give the creative person a straightforward, simple assignment like a one-column space ad, a direct mail flyer, a simple e-mail promotion, or a storyboard. But to indoctrinate the person, you will have to provide plenty of the background information discussed earlier. Before giving the creative person an initial assignment, keep in mind that you are asking him or her to do research on your firm and its products that will continue to pay off if you give that person more work to do in the future. A flat fee is probably safer than an hourly rate at this point, because creative people work at greatly varying speeds. But do inquire about the person's usual rates and payment terms.

To establish trust from the beginning, you should provide your new freelancer with a purchase order (P.O.) number. Also state your policy about payment (net within 30 days, payment on receipt, payment when your material appears in print, or whatever). Clients who are candid about their payment arrangements and keep their word are rewarded with loyal and swift service by grateful freelancers.

An Additional Option: The Smaller "Virtual Agency"

In recent years, technological advances and an era of "downsizing" and "rightsizing" have created a climate that is very hospitable to what Judy Finerty, President of Finerty & Wolfe in Chicago, calls the "virtual direct and interactive marketing agency." As she explains, "This type of small, full-service agency strikes a balance between the large full-service agency and freelance talent.

Sometimes it's four or five people who've worked together at other agencies. They've banded together to be a mini-agency because they like working together and believe they do good work together. Other times, it's an affiliation among several different people—a few creatives, a marketing person, a media person, and a database person, for instance. They all maintain their separate offices (often out of their homes) but come together as a 'virtual agency' for specific clients or assignments."

Clients are drawn to "virtual agencies" for several reasons. First, they usually cost less than large direct and interactive marketing agencies because they have much less overhead. Second, they are more likely to be open to project work instead of seeking a retainer arrangement with every client. Third, because the "partners" are not formally aligned in an ongoing agency structure, they can configure a set of services that fit a client's specific needs and budget: creative and media placement but no database services, for example. Fourth, "virtual agencies" often include highly talented and experienced specialists whose individual work would be billed at much higher rates in an agency environment.

On the other hand, "virtual agencies" generally provide less hands-on service than larger, formalized agencies do. In addition, since virtual agencies lack the strict hierarchy and structure of larger firms, clients may have concerns about who is accountable for quality control, meeting time schedules, and dealing with problems.

If You Decide to Create your Own Direct and Interactive Marketing Promotions

Most firms and individuals who hope to grow smoothly and quickly in the direct and interactive marketing field feel more confident with expert creative help right from the beginning. But teaching yourself the ropes is not an impossible task, assuming you have a measure of talent for writing and design and an ability to soak up knowledge and put it to work. This book and those listed in Appendix A should be your first sources of information. You'll learn hard-won facts about what works in direct marketing and what doesn't.

Attending seminars, online and offline classes, and direct and interactive marketing certificate programs, trading experiences with direct and interactive marketing professionals, and reading trade publications and white papers as well as books may help you—if you are also smart and lucky—to build a lucrative and successful business on the basis of your own creative skills.

Decisions for Creatives: Agency, In-House, or Freelance?

For direct and interactive marketing creative people, the grass always seems to be greener on the other side of the business. Agency creatives believe that a position on the client side would be less pressured. They imagine working 9 to 5 and concentrating on just one product line instead of the ever-changing array of assignments that is part of agency life.

In-house creative people imagine work in an agency as more glamorous. They dream of building their portfolios with a wide variety of projects in consumer markets, business-to-business, catalog, broadcast, and interactive media. They wonder if agency people make more money than they do, and fantasize about living in Chicago, New York, Hong Kong, or London instead of direct and interactive marketing "company towns" like Freeport, Maine or Emmaus, Pennsylvania.

Both agency and in-house people have been known to consider the freelance route, envying the independent writer or artist his ability to make his own hours, demand high fees, and travel at will. On the other hand, freelancers may well covet the employed person's regular paycheck, health insurance, 401K plan, expense account, and team identity. They sometimes find being on their own unsettling and lonely. This is one reason for the growth of "virtual agencies," which enable freelancers to work—at least some of the time—with other specialists in a team environment.

If you are a creative person considering these various employment options, ponder these pros and cons carefully. If you are wise, your decision will combine factors of personal temperament, your age and the stage of your career, areas of expertise, supervisory ability and aspirations, personal and family considerations, and much more.

In general, *agency creatives* need to thrive on pressure. They must be able to juggle several clients' needs at one time, and to express their ideas well in meetings. As their careers progress, agency creatives often move into supervisory roles, charting the strategic course for clients and watching over other creative peoples' work. Necessarily, they do less and less writing or graphic design on their own as they move up this supervisory ladder. For someone whose stock-in-trade has been rolling up her sleeves and developing words and pictures from scratch, achieving a supervisory position (even with its greater salary and perquisites) may feel like a hollow victory. Many an agency or in-house Creative V.P. has quit the corporate world to hang out a shingle and get back to the hands-on work of writing or designing as a freelancer—or as a partner in a small consultancy.

On the other hand, *in-house creatives* must be able to sustain curiosity about and interest in the same product or service category for months or even years at a time. They must be willing and able to become experts in their company's product line, actually considering themselves as much insurance people or office products people as they are direct marketers. They must strive for fresh ways of looking at the same old thing, and inspire this attitude in those they work with. In general, their jobs may be less stressful than those of agency creatives, but some in-house agencies are more pressured than New York's or Chicago's hottest direct and interactive marketing shops.

Freelance creatives must combine their talents for writing or art with salesmanship. They must be accomplished enough to convince companies and agencies to use their services, and to pay them hefty rates for the privilege. Even more than those who are employed, they must be deadline oriented and disciplined. Since many of them work at home, they must be able to separate their work lives from their personal lives. They must have the business sense to strive for one or more monthly retainers to avoid complete uncertainty about income. They must accept responsibility for their own well-being and future, which includes putting money aside for slow periods and for taxes, obtaining appropriate health and disability insurance, and saving independently for retirement. They must also have the energy to work extremely long hours when business is good, and the nerve to stay strong when the inevitable dips in workload occur. In these low periods, they must resist the temptation to panic, and instead use the time to update their knowledge and skills, prospect for new clients, and experience the world to build a "creativity base" for the next crunch period. On the plus side, the best freelancers enjoy a great deal of flexibility in timing their work and selecting their clients.

As creative people consider these options, they should keep in mind that in a career spanning 40 years or more, many writers and artists sample each of these alternatives: large agency, in-house, and freelance—with or without a "virtual agency" team. Each opportunity provides some of the ingredients for a well-rounded career in the creative arena of direct and interactive marketing.

An Account-Side View of Working with Creatives

by Susan Johnson, Marketing & Communications, Spectrum Health, Grand Rapids, Michigan

I quickly discovered as an account executive that I was instinctively "mistrusted" by the creatives. What ultimately gained their respect was my willingness to "get into their heads" to understand what they were trying to accomplish via their concepts and ideas. This also (not surprisingly) made me a stronger AE—more viable to clients, who'd perceive that "she really seems to believe in what she's trying to sell me."

Anyway, I became known among the creatives as an "AE who can sell creative almost as well as we can ourselves." And one of my prized possessions is a big piece of layout paper with a huge "9.5" written on it . . . given to me when I was involved in a tricky sell over the phone at the agency. The creative staff was eavesdropping, and I did ultimately sell the idea.

As for dealing with insensitive clients, I remember receiving a piece of copy back from a client on a job we thought was going to be a winner—not just the "same-old, same-old" furniture brochure. Emblazoned across the top of the front page were the words, "Overall, too casual in tone."

Well, you can imagine the copywriter's indignation. We'd deliberately written the piece in a friendly, conversational tone, so we all assumed the entire piece would need rewriting. I took it upon myself to call the client to discuss his comment. As he hedged around, unable to give me anything concrete, I suggested we take it sentence by sentence. He agreed (luckily it was a six-pager, not 50!), and I ultimately discovered that what made him make that comment was the one phrase, "Just plug 'em in." Moral is: Sometimes clients can't readily communicate what it is that bothers them, and it could be worth a deeper probe.

Regarding scheduling sufficient time for creativity, I feel compelled to point out that there's a quid pro quo attached. I always try to give the creative team ample amounts of time to create, but *they* need to appreciate that meeting client deadlines is essential to agency credibility. Here's an example of what I mean.

When working with a particular creative team on a project for a brand-new client, I was livid to find that *nothing* was done on the day before a scheduled presentation. Fearing the worst, I showed up the following morning to the sight of two bedraggled, scruffy (and, yes, smelly) creatives who'd stayed up all night to prepare. Upon reviewing the layouts, and discovering lots of "holes" based on the input we were given, I decided that I wasn't presenting the work. However, since I don't cancel meetings at the last minute (and, frankly, I wanted to teach these guys a lesson), I said one of them had to come with me and make the presentation. To make a long story (of squirming in front of the client) short, I *never* had that problem with these two again. (Yes, he *did* shower and change before the meeting.)

Finally, I agree that creatives should never abandon an idea just because it doesn't fit one specific need. When I was with J. D. Thomas Company in Grand Rapids, we instituted an "Idea Bank" for "lost" ideas. Sometimes we "withdrew" an idea that didn't work for one client (but was a terrific idea) for another for whom it worked. Also, during down time, we encouraged development of "outside the lines" ideas for existing clients. When the situation warranted, we presented the ideas to the clients with no strings attached. If the client bought the idea, it was "withdrawn" from the bank and paid for. My favorite example of this was a TV commercial for Metro Health's Family Doctor Referral Service. The spot went on to win awards, and with our help, they sold a generic version of it to referral services around the country and more than made up their cost!

Enhance Your Understanding: Agency/Client Relations

As discussed in this chapter, there are three main types of relationships that exist between direct and interactive marketing agencies and their clients. In the *client-dominant* model, the agency has little or no input on strategy, planning, or execution. The agency creates and produces creative work and media plans according to strict guidelines set and enforced by the client. In the *agency-dominant* model, the client is expected to place his/her marketing efforts completely in the hands of the agency for strategy, planning, execution, and evaluation. In the *partnership model*, agency and client work together at all stages in a climate of mutual respect and sharing. Which model(s) have you experienced? Which model(s) do you consider most effective? Can you see a rationale for the other model(s) in certain circumstances?

8

The Offer in Direct and Interactive Marketing

As Robert Bly explained in his fine book *Business-to-Business Direct Marketing*, an offer is "what you are going to get, and what you have to do to get it." Second only to the list or media in importance for direct and interactive marketing success, a clear and specific offer must be agreed upon before the creative team writes a word or a line on the layout pad or computer.

An offer consists of a set of tangible and intangible "deliverables" (what you are going to get) and a set of requirements (what you have to do to get it). Examples of deliverables might be an actual product, a premium, a warranty or guarantee, and/or a carrying case or other accessory. Or, "what you are going to get" might be more information, a free booklet, an estimate, or other intermediate step before a purchase. Examples of requirements might include the price, payment terms, and/or information you are asked to share about yourself—things like your address, e-mail address, mobile phone number, or occupation.

If you work with an established, well-organized firm or agency, you may be lucky enough to receive a succinct statement of the offer at the outset of your project. Better yet, the copywriter and graphic designer may be invited to help hammer out the details of product, price, place, and promotion. If such an offer statement is not forthcoming, it may be up to the writer and artist to work with the company or client to establish one, using the structure outlined in this chapter.

The marketing mix—product/price/place/promotion—must be addressed fully to ensure that your prospective customer receives a clear picture of the proposition at hand in your direct mail package, ad, e-mail, or other communication. What's more, even a slight adjustment in one or more of these factors has been known to affect response quite dramatically. For instance, some careful testing to determine the maximum acceptable price for an item may greatly increase profitability at roll-out time. The introduction of a premium, strengthening of a guarantee, offer of a free trial period, or addition of a split-payment option may all have significant impact on response as well.

Designing a package of product/price/place/promotion cannot be done in a vacuum. Before the terms of the offer are set, it is essential for direct and interactive marketers to analyze the target market carefully. It is also important to focus on the long-term goals of the promotion at hand—obtaining a list of good customers for future promotions, for example, or maximizing the "share of wallet" we get from each customer, or obtaining qualified leads for a sales force to follow up—not just making an initial sale.

As Bob Stone said in one of the early editions of *Successful Direct Marketing Methods*, the most important objective in designing any offer is to *overcome inertia* on the part of the prospect. Every detail of the offer and its presentation must be considered from the point of view of the prospect.

What will spur him on to phone in an order or place one online? What will deter her from completing the Web response form or making a decision?

The financial services industry offers many examples of marketers keying in very specifically to the target market's wants and needs. The proliferation of credit card competition and the profit potential of loyal, long-term credit card customers are just two reasons why banks and other financial firms compete harder than ever for customer loyalty. To fine-tune their offers, through scientific testing they find out from the customers themselves what would make a good credit offer: no annual fee, a more favorable interest rate, or a longer grace period before interest is charged.

These three examples represent a simple manipulation of standard parts of the offer, but financial service marketers have become much more creative in recent years. They have learned that consumers resist filling out long applications, so they offer pre-approved credit, requiring only a few pieces of information to apply. To differentiate one Visa or MasterCard from hundreds of others, marketers have developed affinity programs whereby individuals can carry credit cards that indicate their affiliation with an institution or charitable group—and each purchase nets a small donation to

Exhibit 8.1. Discover CardBuilder

This Web page allows new Discover Card holders to customize their card based on elements such as credit history, payment preferences, rewards and terms, and a choice of 28 vanity card designs.

Reprinted from the Discover Card Web site at *www.discovercard.com.*

that group. Other affinity cards gain their users a personal benefit, such as a mile credited on an airline's frequent flyer account for each dollar spent. American Express offers a host of investment and travel-related services as part of its various annual membership programs. Discover Card offers cash back to the card holder on every charge as well as the choice of segmented cards that fit the customer's lifestyle, and interests. The CardBuilder function at *www.discovercard.com* allows the consumer to customize his or her credit card based on credit history, payment preferences, rewards and terms, and a choice of 28 vanity card designs.

Whatever your product or service may be, the example of the financial service marketers provides an excellent guide. In structuring an offer, consider first the usual possibilities for manipulation: modifying the product, testing the price, establishing a stronger guarantee, etc. But also spend the time and effort necessary to talk with customers—informally or in focus groups—to get ideas for creative enhancements that would strongly entice them to buy. Validate your findings through scientific testing, because people's actions are always better indicators than their stated intentions or attitudes.

This chapter presents the specifics on how to build an offer based upon the four "Ps" of the marketing mix: product, price, place, and promotion. The following pages contain idea-starters on how to structure each aspect for maximum customer interest value, short-term sales gains, and long-term customer loyalty. There is also information on how to develop direct and interactive marketing offers for the generation of qualified sales leads.

The Product

The product or service you sell via direct and interactive marketing must be differentiated in some way from items consumers can pick up at any store near home. You must make prospects perceive that your product is unique . . . more exclusive . . . easier to buy . . . or more economical. Remember also that in any sales proposition, it is important to focus on results, not just the product itself; on benefits, not simply product features. Products most likely to succeed in direct and interactive marketing are those that can be demonstrated or dramatized by means of illustrations, descriptions, and well-written selling copy. To overcome inertia, and to combat the prospect's natural resistance to buying "here and now," you must convince him or her that you have the best product or service of this type, and that buying it directly from you is the best available option. Here are some techniques to help you develop and present your product in the most effective way.

Market Segmentation

You may segment a market and provide an appropriate product by catering to a region or state, to psychographics and personality elements, to past or predicted buying patterns, or to statistical measures like gender, income, or age. Study packaged goods marketers for excellent examples of effective market segmentation. There are beers aimed at party-minded young men, urban African-Americans, and the calorie-conscious dieter. There are cereals targeted at health-minded adults, nutrition-concerned parents, and at children seeking out the latest breakfast fad.

Among direct and interactive marketers, those who sell clothing offer excellent examples of segmentation. The same basic garments are modified and marketed with subtle differences in color, construction, and presentation by old-line sporting goods firms like Orvis and L. L. Bean, and by sportswear firms exhibiting a more timely fashion flair, like J. Crew.

Direct and interactive marketers of music and books also do a superb job with segmentation. Check out Pandora (*www.pandora.com*) for the opportunity to customize your own channels based on favorite artists or genres—each complete with low-key but highly targeted advertising. Book Movement (*http://www.bookmovement.com*) is an affiliate of Amazon.com that caters specifically the members of more than 20,000 book clubs. Doubleday Book Club (*www.doubledaybookclub.com*) serves niches including African-American, Biographies and Memoirs, Children's, Christian, Cooking and Entertaining, Fiction, Mysteries, Real-life Drama and Romantic Reads.

To gain new customers for market segments like these, a judicious choice of mailing and e-mail lists, banner ads and online affiliations, space ads and social media can help you reach the prospects who feel most at home with each clearly defined product concept.

Product Differentiation

Marketing textbooks often tell the stories of Lucky Strike and Wonder Bread to illustrate product differentiation. Contrary to the fictional account in the first season of the TV program "Mad Men"— showing Don Draper presenting this campaign in 1960—it was 1916 when Claude Hopkins's classic Lucky Strike cigarette ad and packaging first presented the two-word slogan, "It's toasted." This evocative phrase won converts from among smokers who liked the idea of smoking toasted tobacco. The fact is that all cigarette tobacco is toasted in its processing, but it took a smart marketer like Claude Hopkins to visit the Lucky Strike factory and discover this intriguing point. The same concept holds true for Wonder Bread's classic slogan, "It builds strong bodies 12 ways." The 12 nutritional points applied equally to all enriched breads, but since Wonder Bread carved them out as a factor of differentiation, consumers perceived that this brand was unique. If your product does not carry inherent differences from the competition that you can point out to win favor, consider how you could differentiate it enough to make ordering from you an attractive alternative. Perhaps you could negotiate with manufacturers for exclusive items, or items emblazoned with your company name or a designer's name. Or, say that a number of firms offer a popular handbag designed with special pouches for wallet, make-up, smart phone, keys, etc.—but it is available only in vinyl. If you can offer the same design in fine-quality leather, customers may perceive this as a positive differentiation worthy of special attention.

Brand Name

At holiday time, dozens of firms sell popcorn and pretzels in gift tins—but only Neiman-Marcus can sell these snack items in a tin emblazoned with the famous N-M logo. Scores of companies sell cotton turtlenecks, but only Lands' End can trade upon its hard-won reputation for the utmost value for the money, emphasized by double-page catalog spreads that have explained the turtleneck's attributes and improvements over the years.

Promoting a strong brand name is a tried-and-true way to overcome inertia on the part of a prospect—especially if the branded item is available only by direct response, and only through you. Direct and interactive marketers with strong brand names may find that they are able to sell otherwise parity products successfully—perhaps even at a premium price—by emphasizing that this is a Bloomingdale's night shirt or a Godiva chocolate gift box, not just a generic product.

Demonstration

Some products require little or no demonstration to sell, but the interest value of most products can be enhanced by carefully crafted copy and appropriate illustrations. Your competition selling home music systems or down comforters in a retail store has a salesperson available to point out the item's features and benefits. In direct and interactive marketing, it is up to the writer and artist to grab the prospect's attention and maintain interest by explaining the product's attributes and what it could do

Exhibit 8.2. Doubleday Book Club

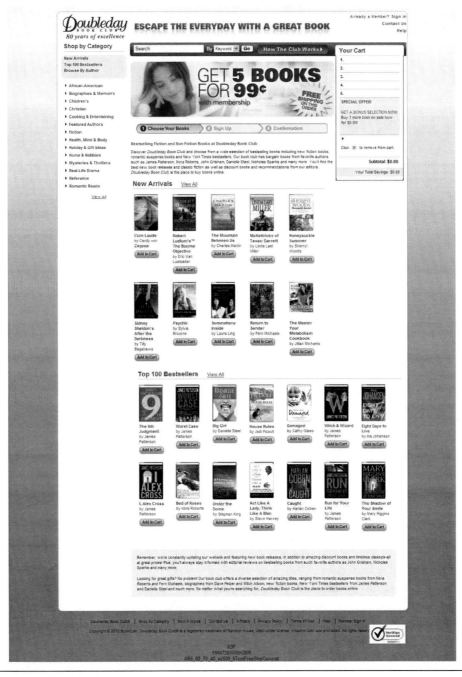

The Doubleday Book Club represent an excellent example of market segmentation, with club niches for African-American readers, lovers of mysteries, those who like biographies and memoirs, and many more targeted groups.

Reprinted from the Doubleday Book Club Web site at *www.doubledaybookclub.com*.

Exhibit 8.3. Neiman-Marcus Popcorn Tin

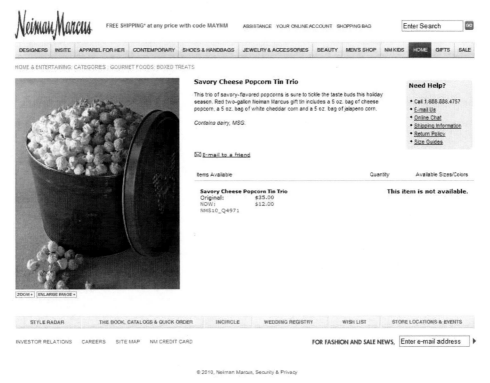

Popcorn in a plain tin can hardly command a premium price, but popcorn presented in a gift tin with the Neiman-Marcus logo provides a powerful brand name edge. While this holiday-decorated tin of popcorn was discounted sharply in the months after Christmas, it was priced at $35.00 for just 15 ounces of product in the pre-holiday gift-buying season.

Reprinted from the Neiman-Marcus Web site at *www.neimanmarcus.com*.

to enhance its owner's life. Brochures and Web sites provide the perfect opportunity to introduce cross-sections, large illustrations with call-outs describing product benefits, testimonials discussing the product's attributes in use, etc. Short videos on Web sites can also demonstrate the product in use, show how it works, how to install it, and so on. In direct mail, send along a sample of the product to enhance demonstration: a sample CD-ROM or Personalized URL to exhibit the quality of a series of teaching software, for instance, or perhaps a sample magazine issue or fabric sample, just to mention a few possibilities.

Product Presentation

Order the same type of product from an assortment of direct and interactive marketing companies, and you will be fascinated by the range of ways in which products are presented at the time of shipment. Some marketers merely shove the product into the proverbial plain brown wrapper and ship it off as is. At the other end of the spectrum is Tiffany, which presents most every item in a shiny robin's egg blue gift box with fine white grosgrain ribbon at no additional charge.

Naturally, the care and money which you invest in packaging your product will depend upon its price tag. But no matter what price level of product you are selling, it pays to keep the recipient's probable reaction in mind. When your package arrives via mail, FedEx, or U.P.S., there is no sales-person on hand to thank the customer or reinforce the wisdom of this buying decision. At the very least, your product presentation should handle this function with a "thank you" communiqué of some sort, and a tasteful and protective product wrapper.

Product Assortment

You may be able to increase your average order size and do your customer a favor at the same time if you offer helpful advice about the proper assortment that should be purchased for a given family situation, occasion, or gift. Study marketers of food for some excellent examples of how this is done. Many food marketers offer "fruit-of-the-month" plans, or similar selections that feature monthly gifts of nuts, coffees, desserts, or even English muffins. Firms selling steaks and other fine meats put together "executive assortments" and "surf and turf dinners," while some food catalogs provide hol-iday gifts in typical price ranges such as $25, $50, $100, and up.

You can do this with other product lines and even with intangible products and services. Life in-surance marketers, for instance, often offer the customer a chance to choose coverage in the $20,000, $50,000, $100,000 range or more, and within these ranges, to select a program for the indi-vidual, or for the entire family. Consider a wardrobe assortment—a week's worth of men's dress shirts at a special price, for instance—or groupings of toys selected especially for two-year-olds, four-year-olds, etc. Whatever your product or service, brainstorm ways to combine it into a package deal that prospects will find appealing and/or convenient. A well-designed Web site offers wonderful opportunities to quiz your site visitor and then immediately present the ideal assortment to fit his or her stated needs. In addition, Web sites can be set up to offer such simple-but-effective options as "customers who bought this item also bought these other items" or "you may also be interested in this product" (i.e., a sport coat that looks well with the slacks being considered).

Preselected Kits

Just as customers enjoy an expert's advice on how many shirts to buy or how to select the right amount of insurance, prospects also find it helpful to be offered a preassembled package that accom-plishes a goal of theirs. Examples might include an all-in-one home entertainment center, or a pre-chosen baby nursery decor including bedding, accessories, and wallpaper. This is especially true in today's climate of serve-yourself retailing, when very little expert help may be forthcoming for the customer in a store.

Copy for such a presentation should explain why this particular kit or outfit was selected, and point out the features and benefits that set it apart from alternative products or packages. Illustrations and call-outs can help explain how the elements of the kit work together, and help the prospect visu-alize the package as it would appear and function in the home.

Customer Involvement in Product Parameters

Consider letting the customer choose the unit of sale or help in the design of the product. Magazine publishers increase customer involvement by allowing prospects to select the exact number of issues of a publication they would like to receive, at a certain per-copy price. This lets the prospect choose his or her own comfort level as to length of subscription term and dollars spent. As for product de-sign, personalization is one form of this phenomenon. Also, some clothiers show outfits made up in various materials and colors and then offer many other color and fabric options. This is especially

Exhibit 8.4. One Step Ahead

A. Create a Colorful Nursery with Farm Yard Bedding

Adorable Boynton Barn Yard Animals make fun bedtime companions in this bright ensemble from the winner of the famed Children's Choice Award. ONE STEP AHEAD offers ALL accessory pieces as well as the basics to make decorating your child's nursery a breeze. 100% cotton for comfort! Complete the look with wallpaper border that matches bumper panel design. 9" wide, pre-pasted vinyl, 15 ft. per roll.
#426 Crib Comforter $56.95
#427 Crib Bumper Panel $49.95
#429 Crib Pillow $23.95
#430 Crib Dust Ruffle $33.95
#428 Crib Sheet $16.95
#252 5 pc. Set SPECIAL Save $14 $167.75
Accessories:
#433 Wall Hanging $31.95
#432 Diaper Stacker $25.95
#431 84" Pr. curtains $48.95
#434 Lightweight Quilt $28.95
#630 Wallpaper Border $22.95

The "One Step Ahead" catalog offers new parents several fully merchandised sets of crib bedding, such as this "Barn Yard Animals" ensemble. A number of accessories are included as well as standard pieces. Such a wide range of coordinated items is seldom available at a retail store, which gives the catalog a competitive advantage.

Reprinted with permission of Chelsea & Scott.

appealing today, when very few stores offer custom tailoring or even alterations. Direct and interactive marketers of furniture and home accessories may offer options for fabric, wood finish, brass or chrome accents, etc. Using mass customization, each Dell computer customer can create a computer online that suits his needs perfectly. Auto makers provide the same type of service online, letting buyers choose color, upholstery, options and the like, and then delivering the finished car in a matter of days or weeks to the dealer for pick-up.

Timing of Product Delivery

Try to find a way in which you can serve the customer with timely delivery and increase your own volume, revenue, and sales bookings at the same time. Perhaps you could arrange to send a corporate executive woman a half-dozen new pairs of her favorite pantyhose monthly, or a month's supply of a special pet food to a dog owner or cat fancier. Or maybe you could offer to fulfill all of a customer's gift-giving needs throughout the year—sending preselected products on the appropriate dates. Online marketer Amway Global has perfected this technique with a program called Ditto Delivery, which sends everything from shampoo to nutritional supplements direct to the customer's front door on a customized and easily altered schedule.

Good, Better, Best

In the days when Chicago-based catalog firms like Alden's, Spiegel, Montgomery Ward, and Sears dominated the direct marketing scene, many merchandising departments were structured around the trade-up concept, or "good, better, best." Direct and interactive marketing are ideal media for this type of comparison shopping, since similar products can be shown together on a brochure, catalog page, or Web page, and their features and benefits can be displayed head-to-head.

The classic catalog trade-up begins with a picture and selling description of the basic model. Then the more expensive items are discussed one by one, balancing their additional features and benefits with their higher prices. In this way, the customer gets the positive feeling of being involved in an informed decision-making process. Online, this concept can get much more sophisticated. For example, at the CDW site, customers can list the type of product they are interested in and then view examples presented head-to-head and sorted by shipping availability, group, brand, or price.

The Club Concept

People enjoy affiliating with clubs that bring them benefits such as savings, special opportunities, information on favorite topics, or strength to fight for a cause. Book and music clubs provide the savings concept with many variations of an offer like this: "Choose six books now for just $1 and buy six more over the next year at below-publisher's rates." Collectibles clubs and societies offer members the chance for affiliation with others who collect Lladro, Hummel, or Swarovski products, and also the opportunity to purchase special, "members-only" figurines and participate in "members only" tours and travel opportunities.

Groups like the American Association of Retired Persons (AARP) may begin as a springboard for the sale of products or services, but when millions of like-minded individuals band together, such organizations may become powerful lobbyists or even activists for the rights of elderly people, environmental causes, etc. When structured with the consumer's interests in mind, such clubs may provide substantial services to their members—while still offering an ideal opportunity for selling merchandise, trips, insurance, and other services. Auto clubs sponsored by firms such as AAA and Allstate are prominent examples; study their literature for ideas on club member benefits. In its simplest form, the club concept may only represent an appealing way of justifying frequent communications or payments. Car wash clubs offer their members discounts on weekly washes, for instance, and bank Christmas clubs are simply savings accounts in which individuals deposit a certain amount each week of the year.

Accessories to Enhance a Product or Increase a Sale

Adding related accessories to your product offer may make it more unique and appealing. At the same time, the purchase of such accessories may increase your average order size dramatically. What's more, you may be able to achieve a higher mark-up on appealing accessories because of their nature as an add-on to a particular product.

For example, say that one of your bread-and-butter products is a boy's hooded snowsuit in navy blue with bright green trim. If you can develop a stocking cap and mitten set in the same navy blue and green, many customers may pick up the set as an impulse item, increasing your sales. At the same time, offering the hat and mittens makes the snowsuit more appealing because now it is an out-

Exhibit 8.5. CDW Head-to-Head Comparison

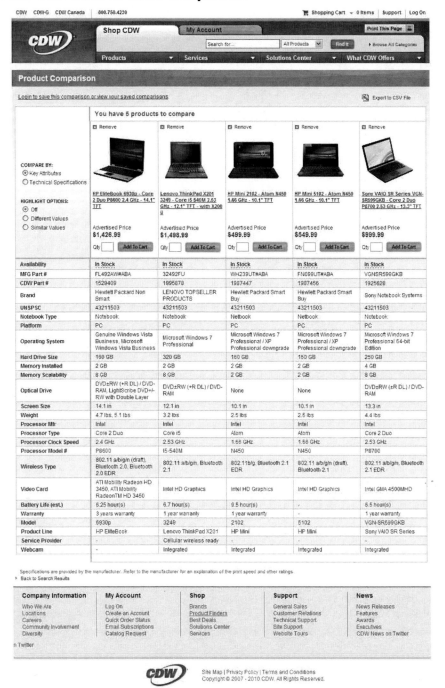

CDW (*www.cdw.com*) allows site visitors to compare products head-to-head and ranked by price, availability, and other factors, with just a few keystrokes on its Web site.

Reprinted from the CDW Web site at *www.cdw.com*.

fit, not just a generic snowsuit. In such a case, you might push the outfit concept even further by selling the snowsuit plus cap/mitten set together at a savings of a few dollars over the individual prices.

Sometimes your accessory sale may be perceived as a helpful service by the customer. For instance, if you sell a product that requires batteries, try selling the proper batteries as a separate item. This increases customer convenience, which may help overcome inertia and make the sale. What's more, if you offer the batteries at a good mark-up, their sale may become a small but helpful source of extra revenue.

The Price

Some direct and interactive marketers determine their prices solely according to a set of internal parameters. Others look strictly at what the market will bear, as indicated by their competitors' price structure. The best way to set price is by considering both internal and external factors, and then taking advantage of the direct and interactive marketer's considerable ability to test.

Catalog marketers who purchase their products from outside sources often must live with a two-time mark-up—what retailers call a 50 percent mark-up. This means that a product that wholesales for $20 will be sold for about $40 in a direct-mail catalog. Direct and interactive marketers who develop and produce their own products rather than going through a wholesaler may achieve a three- or even a four-time mark-up on their cost of goods.

When considering whether to offer a particular product, first decide how much price flexibility your firm has. Then find out what price level customers consider appropriate for this product. Some inexpensive testing in space ads or on your Web site may show you that your target market is happy to pay $34.95 per pair for corduroy slacks, but that they balk at a $39.95 price for the same merchandise.

Even though consumers have their own built-in comfort levels where price is concerned, they may be won over by appeals of exclusivity or outstanding quality. The Squire's Choice, an upscale nut and coffee company, ran an ad in *The New Yorker* with the headline, "Sample the Largest Nuts in the World For Just $9.95." The ad listed the nuts' regular price at $16.95 per pound, but offered this special sample offer at "just" $9.95. If a group of consumers had been asked the question, "How much is too much to pay for a pound of nuts," many of them might have given an answer considerably lower than $9.95. But when the $9.95 price was juxtaposed against the true, regular price of $16.95—and the nuts were characterized with the superlative, "largest in the world"—consumers almost began to see these nuts as a bargain.

The choice of a price point for any given product also must be made with the promotion's objectives in mind. In the case of the "largest nuts" ad, the firm was interested in generating a list of gourmet nut buyers. Therefore, The Squire's Choice was willing to sell nuts at a discounted price on a one-time basis to get their product into the hands of consumers they hoped would become regular buyers. Other promotions may be intended to make the biggest possible profit, in which case the highest volume might not meet the stated objective.

A glance at retailers' prices shows that many stores—especially those catering to bargain shoppers—offer prices that end in odd numbers such as $29.99 instead of $30.00. The concept is that at the consumer's first glance, $29.99 appears to be a price in the $20.00 range instead of the $30.00 price it essentially is. Direct and interactive marketers must weigh the possible psychological benefits of odd-number pricing against the consumer's perception that this is a bargain-basement pricing system. To combat this perception, consider a price like $29.50 instead of a typical promotional number like $29.99. Once you determine the best base price for a given product and promotion, further testing may help prove the value of some of the following price strategies or payment terms.

Exhibit 8.6. Squire's Choice

The Squire's Choice attracted new customers for its catalog by means of a 1/6-page ad offering a pound of the "largest nuts in the world" for $9.95—a $7.00 savings over the regular price of $16.95 per pound.

Reprinted with permission of The Squire's Choice.

Price Strategies

Quantity Price. Sometimes you do not even have to offer a comparison along with a "two-for" or "three-for" price: the mere mention of a quantity price may imply a savings to the customer. Catalog marketers sometimes offer items only in quantities of two, three, or more when the one-item price is too low to offer cost-effectively.

More typically, a quantity price involves a savings comparison, such as "$12 each; two for $20." Or you might offer even greater savings with a "per-case" price on products like office paper or wine. Another way to offer a volume price is to allow the quantity to accumulate over time, thus encouraging customer loyalty. In this case, you might provide a ten percent rebate once the customer's total purchases reach a certain level. Or, once they have purchased ten printer ink cartridges, for example, they might receive one of the same cartridges for free.

Discounts for Order Size. Instead of—or in addition to—offering a "two-for" or "three-for" price, some direct and interactive marketers encourage an increase in the customer's order size by offering a discount if the total order reaches a certain level. One way to structure such an offer is to place the target order level for the discount just above the firm's average order size, thereby trading off the discount to achieve a higher average order. For example, if your firm's average order size is $70, you might try offering a five or ten percent discount for any order over $75. If your database allows for more customization, you might structure discounts so that they incentivize each individual customer to move from their past buying level to a new, higher one. Free shipping is another attractive incentive to offer once an order gets to a profitable level—indeed, free shipping has proven in many tests to be the most attractive offer for e-mail promotions.

Introductory Price. When packaged goods firms introduce a new toothpaste, soap, or cereal, many are quick to provide coupons and samples aimed at getting the product into the consumer's hands. In direct and interactive marketing, magazines often make introductory offers for new subscribers, while renewals may be asked to pay a higher rate. This strategy, however, may well upset your best customers—the renewers—when they see brand-new customers offered a better rate than they can acquire.

Conventional wisdom in direct and interactive marketing is that it is better to offer either an introductory sample or a coupon for dollars-off the retail price than to offer a discounted price. In this way, the consumer understands what the regular retail price for the merchandise will be.

Refund with Initial Purchase. Catalog marketers often use this technique to qualify inquiries, asking individuals to pay anything from $1 to $10 or more to receive the firm's catalog. Then, with the first purchase from the catalog, the initial fee is refunded. Another idea is to offer double the initial catalog price as a discount off the first purchase. This method not only qualifies the prospect, but also provides an added incentive to buy.

Discount Based upon a Relationship. Sometimes marketers will offer a special price on an item only to established customers, and charge the regular price to new customers. For instance, the issue price for a collector's plate might be set at $30, but those who have already purchased works by the same artist could be offered the plate for $25.

Seasonal Discount. Some products are ideally suited to seasonal discounts: Christmas merchandise sold in January, for instance, or lawn furniture offered in late winter or at the end of the outdoor season. Another concept is to maximize volume by discounting your product at the height of its season—thereby attracting attention to your firm when the consumer's mind is focused on your type of product. If you try this type of offer, however, be sure that you have sufficient available inventory to fulfill orders immediately: a 15 percent discount on fresh fir Christmas wreaths offered in November will win you customer loyalty only if you deliver in time for holiday display.

Sale Prices. Sales may be used to clear out overstocked inventory, to level out buying patterns on seasonal goods, or to provide a special opportunity for loyal customers or hot new prospects. Some direct and interactive marketers create special sale literature or Web site sections, often becoming a bit more promotional in copy and graphics than they would for a regular mailing. Other firms rely on their standard presentations, and modify these materials with inexpensive methods like catalog wrap-arounds, "10 percent off all merchandise" banners, special sale-focused e-mails and sale letters, or special price lists.

Loss Leaders. Retail stores often draw traffic by promoting a small number of universally appealing items at a deeply discounted price. Direct and interactive marketers may do the same, calling such an item an "order starter" because it helps the customer make the decision to order and begin filling a shopping cart online or dialing the toll-free number. Once the decision to order is made, the customer may then browse around the catalog, mailing, or Web site to see if there is anything else worth buying. Thus the "order starter" serves the same function as the quart of milk that sends consumers to the grocery store—only to emerge with a sack full of impulse items.

Comparative Pricing. Giving customers a point of reference for your pricing may help them decide that your offer makes financial sense. For decades, the old Sears general catalog used this comparative technique to show customers how long it had been since prices were this low. For instance, they might headline a featured line of men's underwear with this claim: "Our lowest price for Covington briefs since 1995." Or they might have promoted a DVD player this way: "Our lowest price ever for a portable DVD player." It is important to research such price claims carefully: if you are incorrect, your customers may well take you to task. You may elect to compare your price favorably with that of a competitor, but be careful: selling strictly on the basis of price can lead to a price-cutting war—and that can end up being costly to every marketer in your field, including you.

Payment Terms

What your prospect considers a fair price for a given offer may vary depending on how you ask him or her to pay for the product or service. The more you can reduce the customer's perception of risk and increase ease in payment, the more likely you are to make and keep a sale. On the other hand, it is important to build in protection for your firm to ensure that payments will be made according to agreed-upon terms.

Although it is important to keep the terms of your offer simple and understandable, direct and interactive marketing experts agree that a range of payment options often rewards you with increased sales. Here are some of the payment plans you may consider or test, from the least to the most restrictive.

Free Trial. When a customer visits a retail store, he or she often has the opportunity to try on clothing, listen to stereo equipment, sample food products, and compare colors with swatches of fabric brought from home. Because mail order and online buyers must take a "leap of faith" and trust that the products they buy will match the description and photos in sales literature or on the computer screen, their perception of risk may be lessened with the offer of a free trial period.

When structuring a free trial offer, base the time limit on the type of product you are promoting. It may take only ten days for a consumer to make a decision about a book or DVD. But if you are offering a vitamin supplement program that claims to increase vigor and strength over a 30-day period, the free trial needs to encompass that time span. Whatever time period you select, be very clear about the parameters of your offer on the reply device. Does the item have to be returned within ten days, or can the return be postmarked on the tenth day and still be acceptable? Does the ten-day period begin when you ship the item, or when the item is received by the customer?

Some direct and interactive marketers offer free trial options only to lists of customers who have been prescreened for credit worthiness. Others do a quick credit check once the free trial request is received, and grant the trial only to those whose credit is good.

If you offer free trial, be sure to promote it strongly in each ad, spot, Web page, or direct mail package. Some marketers become so used to the free trial concept that they begin to take it for granted and soft-pedal it in their presentations. Since a free trial can be a powerful inducement to buy, its availability should figure prominently in your copy.

When the product is shipped according to a free trial offer, you may elect to send the invoice along with the product, calling for payment or return of the product within the free trial period. Or you may send the invoice separately at the time the free trial period ends, along with a letter thanking the customer again for the purchase. If payment is not made and the product is not returned during the free trial period, most direct and interactive marketers follow up with a short series of increasingly urgent reminders.

Direct and interactive marketers who use free trial offers report that although this concept usually yields more orders than a cash-up-front offer would, it also tends to result in more returns. However, in most cases the net result is an improvement in sales, even accounting for the administrative cost of returns and of tracking down late payments. If you cannot make the free trial option work for you, consider polling some of the customers who returned your product to learn why they found fault with it.

Bill Me Later. Some customers may be intrigued by the opportunity to purchase merchandise now and pay for it at a more convenient time. For instance, you might offer to send Christmas gift merchandise in December, but not bill the customer or his or her credit card until January or February. Or you might sell the customer a complete school wardrobe for a family of children in July, but wait until the school year begins after Labor Day to enter the bill. This option is safest for the seller if the billing is to be done on a major credit card rather than direct bill to the customer. Or you might consider offering this option only to established customers.

There is also a service called "Bill Me Later," part of the eBay/Paypal organization. This firm acts as a third-party payment service for direct and interactive marketers. As the "Bill Me Later" Web site explains, "Seamlessly integrated into your checkout experience, Bill Me Later offers valuable customer convenience, deferred billing options and extra buying power at the point of sale."

Reservation Options. The reservation concept offers the prospect ease in responding, and provides increased security for the seller. At the time the purchase decision is made, the buyer only has to return a simple form stating the quantity of the purchase and preferred payment terms. But unlike the free trial option, in which the seller ships the product without any payment up front from the buyer, reservation customers may be asked to pay for all or part of their merchandise before it is shipped.

When the pre-shipment invoice is received by reservation customers, some of them will change their minds and neglect to pay, thereby canceling their orders. However, for many marketers the reservation option results in a net increase in sales, even considering its administrative and time costs.

An added benefit of the reservation option is that it can help marketers determine the extent of demand for a product that they are not yet able to ship. By taking reservations instead of up-front payments, they avoid upsetting customers whose money might otherwise be tied up until the product is ready for shipment.

Money-Back Guarantee. With this offer, the customer pays all or part of the cost of the product before it is shipped. But if the product is unsatisfactory in any way upon receipt, the customer may return it within a specified time period for a full refund or credit. To lower the prospect's fear of risk, such guarantees should be played up to the fullest. In copy, be sure that the guarantee is worded as positively as possible, emphasizing that no questions will be asked if a product is returned. In layout, call attention to the guarantee by boxing it, setting it in large type, and/or surrounding it with a "value border."

Mention the guarantee on each piece of selling literature in a direct mail package: letter, brochure, order card, and elsewhere if applicable. Be sure to set out the terms of the guarantee in every detail. For instance, will you refund the customer's original shipping and handling charge as well as the price of the product? Will you reimburse the customer for insurance and shipping the product back to you? How long does the guarantee period last: 10 days, 30 days, a full year, or forever? Some stalwart direct marketing firms like L. L. Bean guarantee their merchandise for the life of the product. Here are several of the most famous—and liberal—guarantees in the direct and interactive marketing business:

- **L. L. Bean:** "Our products are guaranteed to give 100% satisfaction in every way. Return anything purchased from us at any time if it proves otherwise. We do not want you to have anything from L. L. Bean that is not completely satisfactory."
- **Lands' End:** "Everything we sell is Guaranteed. Period.® If you're not completely satisfied with any item, simply return it to us at any time for an exchange or refund of its purchase price.
- **Quill Corporation:** "If at any time you are not completely satisfied with the performance of any Quill Brand® product, we will replace the item or refund your money."

Split Payment. Offer a customer a diamond necklace at $1,100 and the price may seem staggering. But offer that same customer the opportunity to purchase the necklace for $100 per month at no interest, and the proposition suddenly becomes more realistic. Firms with their own credit cards—like American Express and many retailers—can offer the option of adding one-half, one-twelfth, or some other agreed-upon percentage of an item's cost to an established customer's bill each month. With split payments, customers can enjoy the immediate gratification of the products they want, without paying interest on their debts.

Many firms handle split payments without involving credit card programs, simply by sending the customer a series of bills by mail or online. On a four-way payment for a work of art, for instance, the buyer might pay one-fourth before the item is shipped, one-fourth upon shipment, and one-fourth in each of the next two months after the item is received.

"House" Charge Account. Some direct and interactive marketing firms establish their own charge-account systems in order to facilitate long-term payments and offer customers a service. To decide whether this is warranted, consider the administrative work and debt collection that may be involved. These costs may outweigh your potential interest income and the goodwill of a house charge option. In general, unless direct and interactive marketing firms are already in the credit card business (American Express, Discover, etc.), relatively few offer their own charge accounts to customers. Instead, they accept major credit cards as well as checks and money orders.

Credit Card Option. Even very small business ventures today are welcomed by banks to set up MasterCard and Visa charging systems for their customers. Medium-to-large firms usually take American Express as well, and often they add Discover to the mix. You pay a small percentage of your receipts to the credit card company to cover its costs for processing your orders. In turn, the credit card company pays you for each purchase, and your customers pay the credit card company. Because so many consumers today use credit cards regularly, the credit card option is very likely to justify its cost—indeed, it is all but mandatory for selling online. Not only does it increase customer goodwill, but it may also contribute to impulse buying and larger sales. In addition, the risk of dealing with your firm is lessened for new customers when they know there is a buffer—the credit card company—to help them resolve any billing or shipping problems that may arise.

Cash Up Front. Asking customers to pay the entire amount due by debit card, check, or money order before product shipment affords maximum security to the marketer. Some firms even wait for the check to clear before processing the order and shipping merchandise. Some customers prefer to make their payments up front, but others may need an incentive to do so. You may consider offering free shipping and handling or some other benefit for advance payment.

Online Payment Options. Today's sophisticated online buyers may well expect you to offer e-payment options. Paypal.com, owned by eBay, has been a leader in this area—allowing registered users to send a payment to anyone with an e-mail address simply by writing a dollar amount into an online form. Offering customers the opportunity to set up an "e-wallet," such as Amazon.com's exceptionally easy 1-Click option, is another way of streamlining payments online for buyer and seller alike.

The Place

In marketing terms, "place" is shorthand for distribution system. For retailers, place has to do with store location, ambiance, and service. Since direct and interactive marketers operate through the mail and by phone, e-mail, or Web site, their customers' concerns about place have to do with the way buyers are treated in written and online communications, over the telephone, at the time of shipment, and in dealing with customer service. These factors of place are crucial to the direct and interactive marketing mix, since customers who are poorly treated in the act of purchasing have many other options—including dealing with retailers or other direct and interactive marketers. Here are some of the place considerations marketers should focus upon in creating their offers.

Method of Customer Response

By Mail, E-mail, or Online Shopping Cart. In arranging for a purchase by mail, e-mail, or online shopping cart, the customer deals with an order form rather than a salesperson. In addition to order form design issues, which are discussed in Chapter 10, consumers are concerned with nuts and bolts such as shipping and handling, time of delivery, and sales tax. It is important to make clear how shipping and handling charges are determined. Some firms allocate these charges on an item-by-item basis, determined by weight and method of shipment. Others use a chart to determine shipping charges for a given order based on total price or total weight. Still others expect the customer to determine shipping charges based on geographic zone. Some firms build the shipping and handling charge into the merchandise price. In today's competitive marketplace, many firms offer free shipping once an order reaches a certain threshold. There is no one right way to proceed on this score, except to ensure that the customer considers your shipping and handling charges fair and easy to calculate.

Sales tax is another issue which consumers must deal with in filling out an order form. This is a hot issue for direct and interactive marketers, who continuously lobby to avoid having to make sales tax payments to states other than those where their facilities are located. Even so, sales tax always must be collected in one or more states where your firm has a business presence, so the direct and interactive marketer should strive to make the amount due as easy to determine as possible.

By Telephone. Direct and interactive marketers have a set of important decisions to make in arranging to serve customers by telephone. While most firms employ toll-free numbers, some few require the customer to pay for all calls. Most firms now provide toll-free customer service lines, while some allow for toll-free ordering but expect the customer to pay for inquiry and complaint calls. While some ordering numbers operate only during business hours, many direct marketers have taken advantage of the fact that their "place" can be available 24 hours a day, with phone lines open at all times.

The level of telephone service is another issue for direct and interactive marketers to consider. Some firms hire an outside service to perform a strict order-taking function, while others keep all telephone communications in house, and train their personnel to be customer advocates. Such trained telephone salespeople can assist customers in determining sizes and colors, and find out immediately if an item is in stock or will have to be backordered. They can also be trained to offer customers add-on items to enhance their purchases—or at the very least to discuss daily specials available at special prices. In addition, they may ask a few simple questions that help build the database on this customer, or help answer market research concerns. Once again, there is no one right answer for all direct and interactive marketers offering telephone service. However, it is important to weigh the options available against competitors' services, the wants and needs of your customers, and the size and sophistication of your firm.

By Mobile Phone. Companies like Amazon.com have led the way with easy-to-use mobile "apps" that allow customers to purchase products with just a few clicks on their hand-held smart phones. Banks are also in the forefront of mobile marketing, offering their customers a convenient "place" for bill-paying, transfer of funds, paying bills, and even paying the babysitter from the mobile using a PayPal application. Optimizing your site for mobile users is an important first step here.

Delivery Systems. Another aspect of place for direct and interactive marketers has to do with the delivery of goods. Retailers typically deliver goods right into the customer's hands, or ship items locally by U.P.S. or delivery truck. Direct and interactive marketers today may offer a number of options aimed at streamlining the customer's purchase, ensuring prompt delivery, and maximizing the customer's ease in receiving merchandise. Some firms ask the customer what means of shipment is preferred: U.S. mail, U.P.S., or FedEx (the last often at an extra charge). Others offer just one service, such as U.P.S., but will send merchandise using that firm's one or two-day services at an extra charge if requested.

With broadband Internet service already penetrating about two-thirds of U.S. households, certain products and services can also be delivered digitally. These include books for eBook readers, magazines via services such as Zinio, movies direct to the desktop or television from Netflix, Webinars both for consumers and business markets, informational videos on YouTube, business white papers, and bills and statements. Digital delivery can provide cost savings to both buyer and seller, and it also offers instant gratification for the buyer. Indeed, there is considerable competition in today's market to deliver direct response-bought goods as promptly as possible. Firms that keep products readily available and ship reliably and immediately upon receipt of orders gain a definite edge in the consumer's mind.

The Promotion

Offers may be sweetened by many tried-and-true means of sales promotion including premiums and add-ons, sweepstakes and contests, special conditions of sale, and strong guarantees. This section will survey some of the promotional methods that direct and interactive marketers have found effective in overcoming customer inertia.

Premiums and Add-Ons

A free gift may well provide the extra incentive a prospect needs to send for more information, try your product, or purchase it outright. The terms of your premium offer have a great deal to do with its success—and its effect on your bottom line.

At one extreme, you may find it profitable to provide a free gift to everyone who indicates an interest in your product by sending for more information. Other marketing plans call for the shipment of the premium only after the customer has purchased and paid for the item in question. Another concept allows the prospect to keep the premium that is shipped with a product purchase, even if the product is returned for a refund.

In continuity programs, a premium may be offered at the outset, but not shipped until a certain amount of product has been purchased. For instance, a set of figurines might have a custom-designed display case available at no extra charge to series subscribers. If the average series buyer purchases five of eight figurines, the marketer might ship the premium right before this average is reached. This will encourage the buyer to purchase more figurines, with the incentive of filling up the attractive new display device.

There is no one right way to offer a premium: in fact, you may wish to test the structure of your premium offer as well as the premium itself. You may also be wise to test different premiums to distinct market segments. It is essential in any case, however, to spell out to your customer exactly what he or she must do to earn the premium.

When testing premium offers, some direct mailers opt for the easy course and simply throw in a premium slip describing the free gift and how it may be obtained. For a fair test, however, the premium and terms of its receipt should be a part of each main component of the direct mail package: letter, brochure, and order form. It should be mentioned prominently in conjunction with the offer in broadcast media or online, as well. Otherwise you cannot be sure that your prospect is aware of the premium as an integral part of your offer.

Types of Premiums. Some marketers boast excellent results offering premiums that are directly related to their products: a display stand for a collector's plate, for instance, or book ends for a set of illustrated volumes. Other firms—including large publishers who buy their premiums in volume—swear by unrelated products that are perceived to have maximum value. Successful mass magazine premiums, for instance, have included tote bags and topical DVDs not available in stores. Conventional wisdom is that a non-related premium brings less committed respondents, so weigh this factor in considering the potential lifetime value of customers attracted by premiums.

Certain premiums are offered continuously—a customer newsletter, for instance, or a regular free gift for every $100 of merchandise purchased. If your continuous or regular premium is attractive enough, it will encourage customers to keep up their level of buying with your firm. A prime example of a continuous premium is the airline frequent-flyer club, which strives to build brand loyalty among customers who might otherwise simply choose the airline with the best fare or most convenient flight time.

While many premiums are considered part of advertising cost, others are self-liquidating. This means that they are sold to the customer at your cost. Examples of items that might be offered as self-liquidating premiums would be carrying cases or accessories for items purchased at retail price.

Ways of Using Premiums. In addition to a classic premium-with-purchase offer, you might test offering gifts at certain order levels to encourage a larger average order size. For instance, if your average order is $45, consider offering a free gift for every order of $50 or more in hopes of boosting the average. Some companies swear by offering several small free gifts instead of one big one. Other companies have good results with add-on offers such as free gift boxes or gift wrapping.

Books and music clubs are among the marketers who use successful "member-get-a-member" premium plans. They entice members with a certain amount of free merchandise or credit for each new person they can get to commit to a certain level of purchasing.

Sweepstakes and Contests

Sweepstakes and other games of chance have become extremely profitable customer incentives for Publishers Clearing House and many other mailers. Head-to-head tests show that the lure of such contests can substantially increase or even double response for some propositions. In successful sweepstakes promotions, the fantasy of winning a bright red sports car, a dream house, or $10,000,000 in cash translates into excitement that surrounds your product. And although sweepstakes rules must allow non-customers to enter on equal terms with customers, prospects tend to perceive that they'll have a better chance of winning if they buy something.

When considering a sweepstakes or contest proposition, learn from the masters: study the colorful and complex packages from major magazine sellers for ideas on package design, TV support, and prize selection. With regard to prizes, testing over the years has shown that fantasy/dream prizes and cash consistently win out over more practical awards like kitchen remodeling. Online contests of all kinds have proliferated in recent years as well, with the immediacy and interactivity of the medium adding excitement for participants.

Most important of all, engage the services of a firm that specializes in contest management. The rules, regulations, and laws in this area are too specialized to handle safely on your own. For smaller firms with limited budgets, a full-scale sweepstakes may well be too costly and complex to be viable. In this case, however, you may be able to become a partner in a group sweepstakes, where a number of firms promote the same prizes and pool entries for one set of awards.

A word to the wise: for some years now, sweepstakes have come under close scrutiny by attorneys general and other regulators. Make sure your sweepstakes and contests are not deceptive in any way or you may find yourself enduring negative publicity or worse.

Special Conditions of Sale

By emphasizing the urgency of a prompt response, or by setting special terms for the frequency or conditions of shipment and payment, marketers may enhance response and improve their profits. Here are some conditions of sale to consider testing in your solicitations.

Exhibit 8.7. Publishers Clearing House

Many direct and interactive marketers test sweepstakes as a means of stimulating response to subscription drives and product offers. This Web solicitation from Publishers Clearing House offers the chance to win a prize of up to $10,000,000.

Reprinted from the Publishers Clearing House Web site at *www.pch.com.*

Urgency. Every direct response presentation requires a call to action—a message which replaces the personal sales "close" and helps convince the customer to buy right away. There are several typical ways in which the urgency of a prompt response is stressed, encouraging the customer to mail, call, or go online to place an order immediately instead of putting the sales piece aside or logging off the computer.

A *time limit* requires prompt action, but for credibility, it should be accompanied by a reason such as seasonal cut-offs or limited production time. Many direct mailers and e-mailers have excellent success in *re-mailing* an offer to the better segments of their house or outside lists, reminding the customer that time is running out. The best timing for a postal re-mail is approximately two weeks after the original mailing. The simplest form of a re-mail is the original package, sometimes enhanced by a stamp effect on the outer envelope and order form saying "Last Chance" or similar wording. A pseudo handwritten note on the original letter or a photocopy of the original letter might remind the prospect of the final date for orders, or emphasize urgency in other credible ways. Other marketers create a special "last chance" re-mail letter with urgency woven into the entire presentation. When combined with a reduced price, many publications limit their offers to a certain *subscription period*. This same concept—also known as a "subscription block"—has been used to enhance urgency for collectibles, financial services, and other investment-related appeals.

Another way to encourage immediate ordering is to offer a *charter membership* or *subscription* to those who respond by a certain date. The charter designation might afford these customers special offers or privileges in the future. A limited edition may feature a cut-off by the number of items made, a time period, or similar limitation. This strategy is widely used in the art, collectibles, and book fields.

Finally, the announcement of an *upcoming price increase* may stimulate customers to buy immediately.

Frequency and Terms. A wide range of offer structures has been devised and tested by firms selling music, books, collectibles, and other related groups of products that are shipped over a long period of time. Some of these concepts may enhance the attractiveness of other product series you sell. The *negative-option* concept calls for the customer to agree to take shipment of products as they are made available, unless he or she specifically indicates otherwise. Negative-option plans usually consist of a mailing at monthly or other regular intervals, in which a featured selection is promoted—often along with a wide range of alternate selections. Unless the customer returns the enclosed card asking for no shipment or an alternate shipment, the regular selection will be sent along with an invoice for payment.

It is important that the wording of the initial negative-option agreement be specific and complete enough to be binding: check promotions from long-established music and book clubs for pointers. You will also want to note that the initial incentive for customers to agree to a negative-option program is usually a free or reduced-price offer: for example, get three books for $1 when you agree to buy three additional books at the regular club price over the next year.

In a *positive-option* plan, the customer receives regular offerings of product, but must return a card in order to be sent items. Thus no merchandise is shipped unless it is specifically ordered. In general, it will be easier to get a commitment to a positive-option plan than a negative-option plan, but fewer guaranteed, regular sales will result. However, the amount of merchandise returned should be less with this scheme: in a negative-option plan the customer may refuse merchandise on arrival if he or she simply neglected to return the card in time asking that it not be shipped.

To lower shipping costs and get the customer to make a commitment for an entire series of merchandise, many marketers utilize a *load-up* plan. Some firms make the load-up a regular feature of their offer, while others make it an option. The marketer must balance the bad-debt potential of shipping merchandise in bulk before it is paid for against the high shipping costs of month-by-month delivery. Once the load-up is sent, the customer may be given the option of paying for all the merchandise at once, perhaps with a premium or discount for doing so. Or the customer may take the option of continuing to pay by the month, in which case the firm may send out monthly invoices via mail or e-mail, or provide a booklet of payment coupons.

When you are selling a product that requires regular replenishment—vitamins or gourmet coffee, for example—a *ship-'til-forbid* plan may maximize regular sales for you and enhance convenience for your customers. The customer agrees to receive and pay for a regular shipment at intervals, unless and until he or she notifies the marketer to cancel.

Unlike ship-'til-forbid plans that continue indefinitely, a *continuity* plan typically offers the customer a set number of related items to be purchased at monthly or other regular intervals. Some continuity plans obligate the customer to purchase every item, while others allow customers to terminate at any time, or to pick and choose among the items as they are introduced. If you are designing a club program, charging a *membership fee* helps distinguish those who are eager to affiliate with the group from those who are merely curious. In exchange for the membership fee, the marketer should devise a set of benefits that members perceive as worth their dues. Collectibles clubs offer "members only" purchase options, trips and newsletters, and advance notification of new product introductions or limited editions that are closing. Travel clubs provide a certain amount of free service such as trip planning, as well as discounts on lodging and car rentals, and availability of members-only insurance plans. Some memberships must be renewed yearly, while others require only a one-time fee—or a lifetime membership may be offered for a substantially higher fee than yearly dues.

When setting the parameters for any of these plans, consider encouraging your customer to permit you to charge each new item as it is introduced, using a credit card number they supply. This simplifies payment for the customer, and also helps ensure you of smooth and regular sales. When the customer pays item by item, the introduction of each new product constitutes another buying decision that requires you to overcome his or her inertia.

Types of Guarantees

Because of the trust inherent in a transaction by mail, phone, or online, it is important for direct and interactive marketers to offer a standard guarantee of satisfaction. Typically, such a guarantee allows the customer to return merchandise within a given period of time such as 30 days, and receive a complete refund with no questions asked. Sometimes the refund also includes initial shipping and handling fees and reimbursement for the cost of returning the item. Some firms allow the customer to call a toll-free number or go online and arrange for a free U.P.S or FedEx pick-up of unsatisfactory merchandise. Whatever the terms of your guarantee, be sure that they are spelled out in detail in your front-end promotion.

For ideas in structuring the wording of your guarantee, gather the promotional materials of seasoned marketing firms in your line of business, or check their Web sites, and study their guarantee terms. Just as important in print campaigns is the way the guarantee is emphasized throughout their literature: in the letter, on the order form, in a box as part of the brochure, and perhaps even in the lift letter or other extra selling piece. On TV, the guarantee should be prominently mentioned and shown on the screen to ensure that prospects are fully aware of it. Online, the main menu may have a special link to the guarantee. Beyond the guarantee of satisfaction, direct and interactive marketers may make a wide range of promises to enhance the prospective customer's level of trust in responding. Here are several examples.

Guarantee of Acceptance. Insurance marketers use this tool to streamline the prospect's application process and provide a benefit that may not be available with policies purchased direct from agents. Individuals with a history of medical problems or obesity, or people who consider themselves too busy to take an insurance medical exam, may be won over by this simplified application process.

The guarantee of acceptance states that, within a given range of age and for a given value of insurance, the prospect cannot be turned down and will not be asked medical questions.

Guarantee of Performance. Marketers selling educational programs leading to licensing or SAT/ACT test performance may use this type of guarantee. The firm sets out minimum standards which the purchaser must meet: so much study time, etc. Then if the customer fails to pass the exam or perform at a certain level, the firm may provide a refund if it is requested within a certain set time period after purchase. A similar guarantee might be devised to cover a do-it-yourself project where the buyer is guaranteed to be able to complete the project by following the instructions and materials provided.

Guarantee of Quality. When a prospect has not had the opportunity to examine an item before purchase, a quality guarantee may enhance trust. This guarantee may come from the manufacturer, from the marketer, or from a third-party source like Good Housekeeping magazine or Underwriter's Laboratory.

Guarantee of Repair or Replacement. Some prospective direct response buyers may hesitate to purchase because they fear they will not have recourse if the product they buy is defective or needs repair. A guarantee that the item will be repaired free of charge within a given time period may help cut down buyer resistance. Likewise, a promise of replacement for defective merchandise reinforces the customer's buying decision.

Attracting Qualified Sales Leads

When a product or service carries a high price, or when the ultimate sale is to be closed in person, the direct and interactive marketer's goal may be to generate names of individuals who are interested in the offer and are qualified to purchase. Such names acquired for a two-step sales process are called inquiries or leads—and even if they do not purchase the initial item that is offered to them, they may well be excellent prospects for later buying opportunities.

Some lead-generation offers may be so attractive that no premium or other incentive is necessary to bring in a large number of names. But in most cases, the offer of a brochure, catalog, premium, product prototype, or other information will enhance the response of prospects. Here are some of the typical free items that win positive response from prospects:

- Free information/facts
- Free book/catalog/booklet/white paper
- Free analysis/estimate/demonstration/sample or prototype
- Free meal or trip
- Free evaluation of talent
- Free seminar

With all of these offers, be sure to stress that there is no obligation to the prospect. When sending follow-up materials by mail or e-mail, it is important to overcome clutter by flagging your materials with wording such as "Here is the Information You Requested." As part of the package, a letter—personalized if possible—would refresh the prospect's memory about his or her request and what is being sent in reply.

Response devices for lead-generation campaigns can serve as a valuable source of database information. For instance, automotive firms offer coupons, bind-in cards, toll-free numbers and Web URLs with landing pages in magazines like *Car and Driver* or *Road and Track*. Banner ads or sponsorships on the Web may be used to seek qualified leads as well. Respondents are asked for their ages, occupations, current vehicle ownership, and time frames for the next automobile purchase. This information helps the company determine the mix of product brochures to send the prospect—and to plan for a contact close to the time of the customer's buying decision. Leads may be followed up by a direct mail package, e-mail, telephone call, personal sales call, or staged combination of two or three of these methods.

Tight and Loose Leads

For some propositions, your goal is to attract as many leads as possible—even if some of them are only mildly interested in your offer. Direct and interactive marketers call these "loose" leads. In other cases, you may wish to qualify each lead in advance as to eligibility and degree of interest. Such well-qualified leads are called "tight" leads.

To *"loosen" the leads you will attract,* make it easier to respond. Provide a stamped envelope or a Business Reply Envelope or Reply Card. Use bind-in cards in magazine ads. Provide toll-free numbers for calling and faxing, a special URL that leads to a landing page with a simple online response form, or a pre-labeled card that the prospect can drop in the mail. Some card decks help participants obtain as many leads as possible by enclosing pre-printed, pressure-sensitive labels in the deck: the respondent simply attaches one of the labels with his or her name and address to the reply cards representing offers of special interest.

Offering a premium also helps to loosen leads. The less the premium is related to the offer itself, the looser the lead may be. Premiums with high perceived value may also help attract more—albeit marginally qualified—leads. Emphasizing the "no obligation" aspect of your offer should result in more leads. And from the copy perspective, remember the age-old advice to sell the sizzle, not the steak. Tell the customer about all the product's benefits, but save the nuts and bolts—and even the price—for the follow-up contact.

To *"tighten" the leads you will attract,* be forthright about the price and payment terms of your offer. State that a salesperson will call or will deliver the promised, free materials. Charge money for the information or service rather than making it free. Eliminate post-paid cards and envelopes, and instead require the prospect to use his or her own postage—or even to write a letter, card, or e-mail to request the information. Finally, from the copy perspective, talk about how the product works and why it does what it does. Don't stop with the benefits—delve into the nuts and bolts of the product. Customers who express interest after reading this specific information should be excellent prospects for a sale.

Defining a Winning Offer:
Ferris State University's Residential Life Scholarship

Around the turn of the new century, Ferris State University found itself with multiple challenges to keep enrollment stable and attract a student body with good potential for academic achievement. For most of its 100-plus year history, the Big Rapids, Michigan, public university had simply opened the doors for applications each year, with resulting annual growth in the student population.

Then the "baby bust" generation reached their late teen years and the number of high school graduates in Michigan dipped to only about half the number who graduated in the "baby boom" years. What's more, a growing number of Michigan high school graduates chose to attend lower-cost, local community colleges instead of beginning their college careers at four-year schools like Ferris State. Combine these external factors with Ferris's transition from quarters to semesters, a change in top administrative leadership, and a well-publicized contract fight, and Ferris State found itself losing enrollment at an unacceptable rate.

While Ferris State continued to attract a small cadre of top students with ACT scores over 25, the school found itself losing out on too many of what its admissions officials called "mid-range" students: those with ACTs in the 20 to 25 range. Another problem at Ferris State was empty dorm rooms: with lower enrollment and plenty of affordable housing surrounding the campus, the residence halls needed an influx of new residents. Ferris State Marketing Professor Eric Panitz studied the situation and made a strategic suggestion for an offer that would attract mid-range students and solve the "empty housing" problem at the same time. *What the incoming students would get* would be a "Residential Life Scholarship" worth $2,000 per academic year. *What they would have to do to get it* was deliver an ACT score of 21 or higher, and a high school grade point average

Exhibit 8.8. Residential Life Scholarship Program

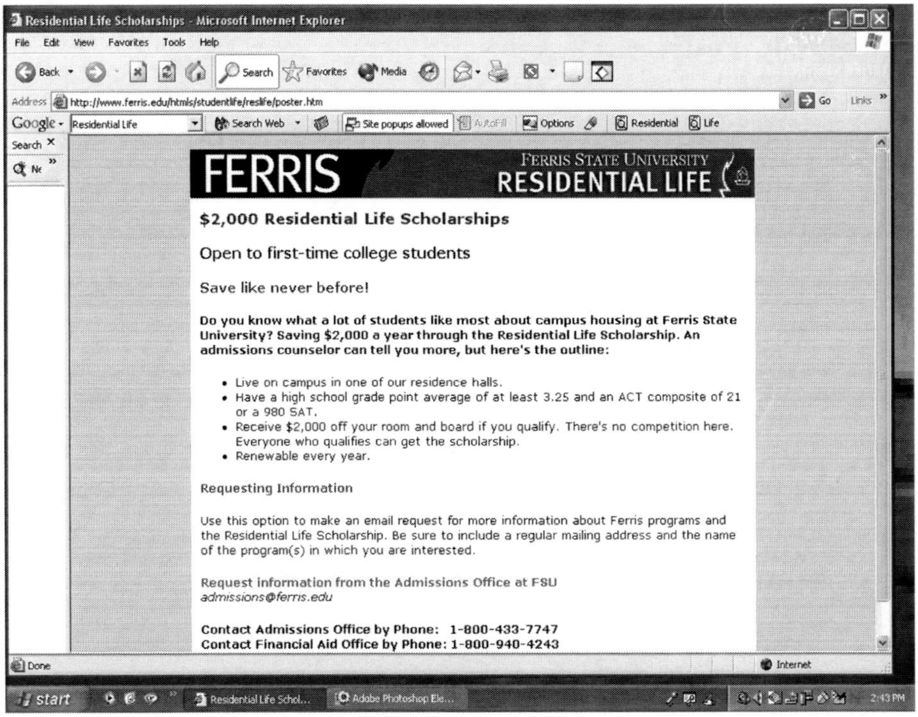

Ferris State University's Residential Life Scholarship appeals to an under-served college market segment. The scholarship pays $2,000 toward annual housing expense for any incoming student with a score of 21 or better on the ACT test and a high school grade point average of 3.25 or better on a 4.0 scale.

Reprinted from the Ferris State University Web site at *www.ferris.edu*.

of 3.25 or higher. What's more, the $2,000 was good only to defray the cost of living in a residence hall on Ferris State's Big Rapids campus.

Ferris State's advertising agency at the time, Davison Dietsch and McCarthy of Grand Rapids, prepared materials about the Residential Life Scholarship for use in media communications to likely students, at college nights, and for public relations activities. The scholarship was promoted on the school's Web site as well (*www.ferris.edu*). The Residential Life Scholarship program was profiled on National Public Radio and received immediate attention from students and parents alike: indeed, the first year it was implemented, it showed an immediate uptick in new Ferris State students with ACTs in the 21 to 25 range.

The key to Dr. Panitz's offer was that it richly served an unmet need. Students with grade points above 3.5 and high ACT scores often receive numerous offers for academic-based scholarships, but the mid-range student is virtually ignored by many schools. The Residential Life Scholarship brings pride to both students and parents for the student's academic achievement and promise, and it provides Ferris State with students who have a demonstrated capacity to learn and achieve. What's more, it improves the quality of student life with well-populated on-campus residence halls. More than a decade after its initial implementation, the Residential Life Scholarship program is still going strong.

Enhance Your Understanding: Ideas for Offers

You are developing an offer for a new club concept called "Wine and Cheese of the Month." Your client looks to you for guidance on all aspects of offer creation: product, price, place, and promotion. Make a list of at least five variables you might consider for each aspect of the offer. Here are a couple of ideas in each category to get you started.

WINE-AND-CHEESE-OF-THE-MONTH CLUB

Product Variables

Example A: Will there be product choices, or one standard wine and cheese each month?
Example B: How will the products be packaged?

    1.
    2.
    3.
    4.
    5.

Price Variables

Example A: Will cheese and wine be priced together, or separately?
Examples B: Will there be discounts for quantity orders?

    1.
    2.
    3.
    4.
    5.

Place Variables

Example A: How will the wine and cheese be delivered?
Example B: Will the club be available by direct response only, or will there be party plans and retail outlets as well?

    1.
    2.
    3.
    4.
    5.

Promotion Variables

Example A: Will the club utilize a negative option, positive option, or ship 'til forbid plan?
Example B: What type of guarantee(s) will we offer?

    1.
    2.
    3.
    4.
    5.

9

The Science of Creative Testing

The late John Caples explained the value of testing in his book *Tested Advertising Methods* when he said it "enables you to keep your finger on the public pulse . . . . to sense trends in advance." He added, "Regardless of what method of testing you use, the important thing is to have some method of testing. Testing enables you to throw opinions overboard and get down to facts." Caples continued by explaining what he meant about opinion in advertising. "Testing enables you to guard against an advertising manager whose pet ideas may be hurting your advertising. Testing enables you to guard against an advertising agency whose idea of agency service is merely to turn out pretty layouts and stereotyped copy. Testing enables you to guard against mistaken ideas you yourself may have in regard to advertising."

A well-designed, ongoing program of creative testing can reap thousands of dollars in extra profit even for small-volume direct and interactive marketers. More impressive yet: a valid test yielding as little as a one-half percent increase in response can mean millions of dollars in extra sales when rollout quantities or media potentials are large. With a firm understanding of the most successful direct and interactive marketing offers under your belt, you are now ready to learn how to develop your own creative tests. This chapter will explain the importance of testing as a way of life in direct and interactive marketing. You will also learn what elements are worth testing and how to frame a testing program aimed at establishing or beating the control. And you will learn several ways to test creative concepts inexpensively before launching a full-blown marketing program.

Why Direct and Interactive Marketers Test

Even seasoned creative professionals are often amazed at their own test results. A plain outer envelope may outpull one with a teaser line the copywriter swore was irresistible. The graphic designer's pet 9″×12″ four-color envelope may be shown up by a plain #10. A 60-second direct response TV spot may outpull the longer 120-second version, much to the amazement of the writer. Yet the long and involving copy of a four-page letter may beat a simple one-page letter when they're tested head-to-head. On the other hand, there have been cases where a simple picture of the product outpulled an elaborate brochure. But in just as many cases, the opposite proved true.

Creative testing is not an exact science, because each new product is offered to a constantly changing audience of consumers. The consumers themselves are affected by the season, the weather, the economic news, happenings in their personal lives, and the other advertising messages they've seen recently, or in conjunction with your message. There are no absolute rules for creative testers, therefore, except "keep testing."

Copy great Tom Brady called testing "the R&D of direct marketing." Considering the thousands—even millions—of dollars many firms pour into research and development, the costs of testing direct mail packages, ads, Web page elements, e-mails, and TV spots may be easier to justify in this light. Indeed, direct and interactive marketing experts agree that the test phase of a promotion should not have making money as its goal. Professor Julian Simon called testing "a way of buying information." It's an investment that can end up saving you a great deal of money—and produce additional profit in later phases of mailing or media placement.

As customer relationship management expert Melinda Nykamp points out, the overall purpose of direct and interactive marketing testing is to determine the most effective and efficient means of meeting your objectives—be they making the most profit, increasing the number of customers, lowering customer acquisition costs, etc. To do this, direct and interactive marketers may test factors having to do with lists, databases, and media as well as creative elements like offers, formats, and copy and art presentation.

The specific purpose of *creative* testing is to determine the desires of the customer or prospect. Do they want your product or service? On what terms will they buy or respond? Which creative approach will attract the most qualified prospects? An understanding of potential testing elements will help you frame a test that can answer these questions.

Determine What Creative Elements to Test

When you begin to market a product or service for the first time, you are testing one very specific thing: its viability, or ultimate profit potential. The first time in the marketplace, you are testing multiple elements of necessity, simply because you have no control package, product presentation, ad, or spot to use as a benchmark.

You will position your product to be as appealing as possible, based upon any market research, focus groups, or other sampling techniques you have used. You will choose the best possible lists and media, develop the most appealing offer you can, and create the words and pictures that put your product in the most attractive light.

If your initial test fails, you have a choice of abandoning the program or continuing to test, focusing on improving the area or areas you believe are responsible for the test's problematic results. You may choose to leave the creative product alone and test different lists, media, or database segments. Or you may elect to test a new positioning, a different offer, or new copy and/or layout. *If your initial test succeeds* by meeting the criteria you have established for viability, then you can focus additional testing efforts on improving the success of your program. You do this most effectively by focusing on one element at a time including lists, offer, positioning, copy, and/or layout.

Ensure That Your Tests Make a Profitable Difference

Direct mailers have been known to get bogged down in testing subtle changes such as light blue versus light gray letterhead, or #6-3/4 versus #9 Business Reply Envelope. Before scheduling such a test, ask yourself, "What will I do with the knowledge I gain, and how much money could it save me/make me?" Honest answers to these questions will help you avoid wasting precious test cells with frivolous concepts. Conventional direct and interactive marketing wisdom states that the list, database, or ad medium is responsible for 40 percent of success, so considerable time should be devoted to developing refinements and tests in this area. To determine what else could be tested, consider these standard creative test ideas:

1. *Offer*—Test different combinations of "what will I get" and "what do I have to do to get it"
2. *Product positioning*—Strive to learn what principle benefit or "bundle of benefits" will prove most appealing to a specific target market
3. *Format*—Size, length, envelope mailing versus self mailer, graphic "look," and so forth
4. *Copy*—Style, tone, length, density, emphasis on certain features or benefits
5. *Price and payment terms*—Assortments, premium prices, volume prices, methods of payment and billing, split payments, and so forth
6. *Timing/Seasonality*—How often to mail or run ads or send e-mails; how often to re-mail, re-e-mail, or re-run ads; best times of year, times of week, times of day, and so forth
7. *Premiums/Bonuses/Discounts*—Types, value levels, ways of describing, etc.

All seven of these test concepts offer the potential for an outstanding increase in sales and profit. Read through the chapters in this book on offers, direct mail, print ads, catalogs, broadcast, interactive, other media, copywriting, and graphic design to spark ideas on how these test concepts might be developed for any given proposition.

How to Test in Direct Mail

There are two main schools of thought about testing creative concepts in direct mail. Although some direct marketers use one method exclusively, both have an important place in an overall testing plan.

Test One New Element Against the Control

Once a marketer has an established control package, the most exacting way to work toward improving the control is to select one element at a time that could be modified for a possible lift in results. This does not mean that only one test can take place per mailing: your test matrix might include any number of separate element tests, each to be measured against the performance of the control. Your in-house database expert, database consultant, or computer service bureau can help you develop viable test cells of names for this purpose. Exhibit 9.1 shows how a simple version of such a testing matrix might look. In this six-way test, the mailer puts half of the 100,000 names in the control cell, using the package which has proven most effective in the past. This allows the mailer a cushion against which to invest in some carefully thought-out tests, element by element: a more expensive letter, a less expensive brochure, the addition of an extra element, trying a higher price, and experimenting with payment due upon shipment instead of with the order.

The test cells contain 10,000 names each. If the cells are prepared properly, on a random-name basis, test cells of this size are large enough to yield a valid test for most direct mail offers. Direct mail guru Bob Stone used to say that any test cell needed at least 30 responses for a statistically readable result. To obtain this, some mailers are able to work with cells as small as 5,000 names—even less on a responsive house list—while others need larger cells to obtain sufficient orders or inquiries for a readable test. Today, however, some statistical experts, including Dr. Robert Dwyer of the University of Cincinnati, contend that much smaller sample sizes can produce readable results. Element testing works best for mailers who have already established a serviceable control package. This scientific approach seldom results in "breakthrough" response increases. Rather, it allows a mailer to steer a good direct mail package toward greatness by fine-tuning one element at a time.

Exhibit 9.1. Direct Mail Testing Matrix

TEST CELL	PACKAGE ELEMENTS	QUANTITY MAILED
A	CONTROL—#10 outer envelope, 2-page letter, 11" x 17" four-color brochure, 8-1/2" x 3-3/8" order form, BRE, $40 product price	50,000
B	LETTER TEST—Use control package but substitute 4-page letter	10,000
C	BROCHURE TEST—Use control package but substitute 8-1/2" x 11" two-color brochure	10,000
D	LIFT LETTER TEST—Use control package but add a short letter answering prospect's objections	10,000
E	PRICE TEST—Use control package but substitute $50 price for $40 price	10,000
F	OFFER TEST—Use control package but substitute "no money now" for payment required with order	10,000

Test a Whole New Approach

Sometimes called "breakthrough" testing, this method is riskier than element testing, but it also stands to yield much greater rewards. It calls for the creative team to put any existing control packages aside and develop a whole new way to sell a product or service from scratch.

Whereas element testing is often executed in-house by staffers who live and breathe the control package, some direct marketers like to open up their breakthrough testing programs to outside creative resources that bring fewer preconceived notions to the project. A more clinical approach may also lead to a breakthrough positioning or offer. One or more members of the creative team may take the control package apart, paragraph by paragraph, listing the points it makes and considering their relative emphases. Text mining software from SPSS or other firms may also be used for insights into what the copy stresses. These "outlining and mining" techniques allows creative people to consider, point by point, what is good about the control package and what could be improved. They can pull out written points or visual features that could be played up to better advantage. At the same time, production experts can suggest various formats, personalization methods, printing and paper ideas, and other technical innovations that might help sell the product more effectively.

The negative aspect of testing completely different packages against the control is that when a package emerges as a winner, the mailer never knows precisely why. Another problem is that an untried package is just as likely to result in a costly failure as it is in a profitable breakthrough. Over a period of time, however, direct mailers will do well to mix the exacting, step-by-step science of element testing with some risk-taking breakthrough testing to maximize profit potential.

Tips for Profitable Direct Mail Testing

From the combined wisdom of successful marketers, here are some points to keep in mind when developing direct mail tests:

- *Make sure that your entire test is mailed at the same time.* If parts of your test mailing are dropped even two days apart, the readability of your results may be compromised by changes caused by news reports, competitive mailings, and other uncontrollable factors. If your mailing is so large that it cannot be mailed all in one day from one lettershop, find a lettershop or group of lettershops with more capacity. If any part of the mailing must be dropped earlier, make it the far-flung zip codes—i.e., California and New England if you are in the Midwest. These may require more time for delivery.

- *You need a difference of about 15 percent in results between two test segments to consider the results meaningful.* If, for instance, you have a 5,000 name control cell that yielded 40 orders and a 5,000 name test cell that yielded 44 orders, the 44-order cell has only ten percent more orders than the 40-order cell. In this case, you would need at least 46 orders in the test cell to consider it measurably better than the control.

- *When you find a test element that makes a measurable improvement in results, retest it against the control.* Make sure it isn't a fluke before you establish it as part of the new control.

- *Track the long-term profit and loss consequences of any test, not just its short-term results.* It is much easier to produce "loose" leads—people who have indicated a modicum of interest in a product in order to get a free premium, for example—than it is to develop "tight" leads who are expecting a salesperson to call on them. Make sure that your "loose" lead program converts sales at a level high enough to make it more profitable than the "tight" lead program before you pronounce it the winner. The same concept holds true in continuity programs. You may bring in more "starters" with a free book offer, but will they convert into long-term subscribers as well as those who pay $14.95 for their first book?

- *Keep careful records of what you are testing and what results you receive.* The first date you receive orders, and the number of orders received for each test cell on a daily basis, are essential pieces of information. Later on they will help you establish benchmarks for your firm's mailings so that you can estimate total responses and begin planning roll-out mailings earlier. Make sure each test cell is coded on the reply device so that you can track its source. When you accept orders via media other than mail, such as phone or online, make sure the code must be provided when the order is placed.

- *Test each concept for yourself.* Some mailers track the testing of their competitors and then wait to see which kits or ads show up later at the roll-out stage. This knowledge can raise questions to be answered by your own testing plan, but it cannot provide specific answers for your program. You would have to know all of your competitors' objectives and financials to draw absolute conclusions from their testing—and even then, their results would provide specific direction for you only if your situation were identical to theirs.

- *Keep testing.* The marketplace changes constantly due to customers' attitudes, economic factors, product life cycles, and your competitors' offers in the mail. Just because you proved that a two-page letter was better than a four-page letter five years ago doesn't mean that this is still the case. Test some of the same things you tested in the past—and keep looking for new ideas to test. Look beyond your direct competitors for testing ideas—try to adapt the ideas of top marketers in many fields to your situation.

- *It is beyond the scope of this book to discuss further specifics of direct marketing statistics and testing design.* Those interested in learning more about planning statistically significant, readable, and meaningful tests and roll-out mailings will find excellent chapters in many general direct marketing books including *Successful Direct Marketing Methods* by Bob Stone and Ron Jacobs and *Contemporary Database Marketing* by Martin Baier, Kurtis M. Ruf, and Goutam Chakroborty.

- *Keep in mind that many experts say list testing is even more essential than creative testing to the success of a direct mail program.* Working with a good list broker, database consultant, and/or computer house, the marketer can develop mailings whereby both lists and creative concepts are tested at the same time, utilizing state-of-the-art database and merge/purge techniques.

Simple Pretests for Creative Ideas

At a Case Writers' Workshop at DePaul University, database marketing expert Ashleigh Groce Sawdon noted that more and more direct and interactive marketers are allocating time and dollars for focus group research. Creatives should embrace and foster this trend, since well-done focus groups can yield a bounty of background on the target market's hopes, fears, likes and dislikes, the tone of copy they'd be most likely to respond to, best product benefits, and much more.

In this light, academic and market researchers may frown upon some of the quick and dirty methods employed by direct and interactive marketers in search of direction for their creative testing. Yet many successful writers swear by these simple and inexpensive techniques. So while professional research and focus groups are preferable, here are some basic methods you may use as a fallback position or as supplementary research.

Have "The Person on the Street" Read Your Copy

Show your masterpiece to a disinterested party and ask him or her to read it. Ask the reader to share the main idea with you—what did he or she come to understand from reading the piece of copy? If the idea that is played back does not fit with your strategy, it's back to the computer. Or perhaps the reader will come up with a new twist you hadn't thought of—a benefit you might be able to amplify by rewording the copy.

Do Some Unscientific Opinion Testing

You can get general direction on the viability of various offers, prices, and terms by showing your product to groups of people in your target market, either in formal focus groups or informal gatherings. Some marketers have remarkable success determining the appeal and perceived value of products just by approaching people in office buildings and shopping malls. Market researchers might scoff at this unscientific methodology, but simply getting the reactions of people who have not seen the product before can spark new creative ideas.

Poll Your Current Customers

Your loyal clientele may be thrilled to be singled out for their opinions about your new product offerings. Find out from them what they think of your offer, price, and terms. Mail or e-mail them a product description and ask them questions about it. Is it a fair value for the money? Is it an appealing product?

How likely would they be to buy it? To cut down on "yea-saying," the customers' wish to please you by answering "yes" to most questions, ask them to rate the relative appeal of various products and offers—not just one. You may also consider using social media sites like Facebook to get customer reactions to your new products and offers, but keep in mind that a very large number of people—including some who may be less than friendly to you and your company—will see your concepts this way. Only do this if you are willing to tip your hand to the marketplace at large.

Use the Telephone

Some quick calls to a random sample of your house list can provide an even faster reading of a product's viability. This is an inexpensive way to test the waters before putting your offer in print. Again, be sure to call only customers and only those who have indicated a willingness to receive phone calls from you.

Use Your Web Site

You're probably already looking for methods of engaging your Web site visitors in a dialogue. Asking visitors' opinions about products and services can involve them and may benefit you. Keep in mind, though, that while polling customers via mail or phone is something of a "stealth method" of quick research, your Web site is open to world view—including the scrutiny of your competition—unless you require some type of access code available only to customers.

Consider a Dry Test

Perfected by publishers, this technique allows you to make an offer of a product or service that does not yet exist. If the response is good enough, continue with further promotions and produce and deliver your product. If the response is disappointing, notify respondents that you cannot deliver, sending your apologies and an explanation of technical difficulties. Dry testing is considered allowable by the Federal Trade Commission as long as you adhere to certain disclosure guidelines. For instance, you may not imply that the product already exists, and you must communicate promptly with customers if you cancel the program. It is best to use a "send no money now" offer in dry testing to avoid having to refund customers' monies you've held for a time, in case the program fails.

Direct Response Testing in Other Media

While many of the direct mail testing parameters established here can be applied to other major direct response media, there are modifications that must be made to fit each medium's constraints and opportunities.

Print Ad Testing

Dramatic increases in response often can be achieved by expanding from a one-page print ad to a page plus bind-in card. Keep in mind, however, that the bind-in card is costly, and test carefully to make sure it is paying for itself and that the respondents have equal long-term value to those who respond from a page ad alone. Bind-in cards may be enhanced by adding a bind-in envelope that al-

Exhibit 9.2. Hamilton Ads

Testing provides direct marketers with the opportunity to prove out innovative formats like this one used in space advertising by The Hamilton Collection. This format consists of two facing one-page ads for Hamilton products, united by a bind-in card offering both products.

Reprinted with permission from The Hamilton CollectionThe Hamilton Collection.

lows the customer to respond more privately, and even to send along a check or credit card number with confidence. Again, balance any additional responses against the additional cost.

The next step up from a page plus bind-in card is a double-page spread plus bind-in card. Some marketers have invested in advertising sections that go on for four or even eight pages. Keep in mind that package goods companies may use such spectacular set-ups partially as brand builders—a costly luxury which many traditional direct marketers will not allow themselves unless that particular format pays out on its own.

Technological advances now allow for a host of personalization options in space advertising, although not all publications have this capability. What's more, the opportunity to use personalization may be reserved for a publication's most loyal and lucrative advertisers. In theory, a personalized bind-in card should lift response as it makes it easier for the customer to respond. Again, balance the extra cost against results.

Classic print ad tests often revolve around headline testing or the manipulation of other creative elements, price, payment terms, etc., in publications that allow A/B splits. It is worthy of note that few marketers can make ads of a page or larger pay out when seeking inquiries rather than sales. Most cost-effective inquiry ads are less than a page in size and may be as small as a 1/12 page—or even smaller in the classified section.

There are rules of thumb about seasonality in print advertising, with the August through November and January through March periods proven most responsive for general-interest product. However, it may prove helpful to test relative response in various months for yourself, considering your product's seasonal uses and appeal.

Broadcast Ad Testing

Scientific offer testing is not feasible using most current television and radio technology, although it may be possible on television in the near future. Marketers today are able to get a read on the viability of various offers, formats, etc., by comparing results in similar markets, or results in the same market from different test spots run at different times. Nuts-and-bolts TV and radio tests include: length of spot; use of celebrity presenter versus non-celebrity announcer; use of one celebrity versus another; offer variations; and so on. Ideas for various formats to test can be found in Chapter 13 of this book.

Using sophisticated focus group research, creators of direct response broadcast spots can learn which spokespeople and themes—and even what key words—pique the interest and attention of people in the target market. Then spots can be reworked to highlight the most effective elements, and tested to prove their viability in the marketplace.

In recent years, many direct response television marketers have tested the viability of half-hour infomercials versus 60-second spots, 120-second spots, or other short formats. There are infomercials of various lengths on radio as well, often in the guise of regular shows—but paid for by advertisers. The infomercial format does not guarantee success, even though it offers the advertiser the luxury of telling the story in great detail, and making the selling pitch several times in its entirety. The problem is that infomercials are much more costly to produce and place than are the shorter, traditional commercials. It is important to track results carefully to ensure that infomercials perform and convert for your offer at an acceptable cost. Even if you are buying broadcast time on a "per-inquiry" basis, it will behoove you to refine your creative product to yield the most sales or leads possible each time your spots are aired. What's more, if a cable network or local station has a choice of "per-inquiry" infomercials to air, those with the highest production values and best chance of success will likely win the available time.

E-mail Testing

E-mail offers many of the positive attributes of direct mail testing plus incredible affordability and much quicker response times. What's more, an e-mail campaign can be stopped and started at will, whereas at a certain point with direct mail, the die is cast for the whole mailing. As Cody Heiderer, President of Chicago-based Marketing Economics says, "You can imagine the laughter you would hear if you called the Post Office and asked them to stop your direct mail half-way through." In a matter of days you can test to determine the viability of many different campaign elements, and then roll out without any of the delays inherent in direct mail implementation. Elements to test in e-mail campaigns include:

- *Lists*—What's the response from various segments of your own house list of opted-in names, and from names on various opt-in rental lists?
- *Timing*—What days of the week and times of day engender the best response for your product lines and offers?
- *Sender names*—What works best: an e-mail from the company CEO, a listing of the company name by itself, the name of a celebrity endorser, or other sender name?
- *Subject lines*—Does a price-related subject line work better than a product-related subject line? How about mention of time-limited special offers, savings, free shipping, premiums, sweepstakes, or contests?
- *E-mail format*—Does a simple, plain text message work better than an HTML image that may download slowly for some—or be deleted by others for fear of an embedded virus? What copy approach, length, and tone works best?
- *Multiple offers or one offer only*—Should each e-mail focus on one simple concept and offer, or will you gain more total sales by making multiple offers with click-through options for multiple landing pages in one targeted e-mail?
- *Landing pages*—Once the e-mail recipient clicks through, what product(s) should be displayed and how many product(s) should there be? Will average order size improve if suggestions are made about accessories or add-ons to the main product shown?
- *Transition to main Web site*—Should visitors to the landing page be ushered quickly to the main site, or offered transport there only after they purchase something from landing page?

Testing on the Web

The World Wide Web offers the potential for what Professor Emeritus Ted Spiegel of Northwestern University calls "speed-of-light testing"—the ability to go online in a matter of hours with various products, offers, and creative approaches and then read the results in real time. Marketers can eliminate poor-performing tests right away, or modify what's on the site if anything proves to be misleading or disadvantageous. They can also use online testing to help weed out products and offers so that only those with the most potential are moved to "slower" print media like direct mail and catalogs. Online testing elements may include:

- Product versus product
- Sales per user session
- Promotions
- Layouts
- Headlines
- Offers
- Creative look and feel
- Banner ads for the company's own specials
- Price or percentage-off coupons

Ed Bjorncrantz, President of Bjorncrantz & Associates, Inc., and former executive with J.C. Whitney and Sears, says that online marketers have the ability to do A/B split testing, to deliver alternating presentations, and track conversion, average order size, and so on. The alternates can be every-other visit, every-other hour, or another parameter. However, he believes that few Internet marketers are optimizing their testing opportunities. As he comments, "I don't think anybody does enough testing on the Web just like they don't in print media."

The Importance of a Written Testing Plan

Real estate agents teach their customers that there are three important attributes of a house: location, location, and location. Direct and interactive marketers have a similar statement when asked for their three basic rules: test, test, test. But it is important that each creative test be a part of a well-conceived, written testing plan. The discipline of such a plan will help marketers ensure that each creative test they execute will provide valuable information that can help lead to maximum potential profit.

Enhance Your Understanding: Test Concepts

You work for the in-house marketing department of a major insurance company that sells via direct response media. The volumes your firm mails are so large than an increase of 1/10th of 1 percent in front-end response could net millions of dollars of "lifetime value" to the bottom line. You are charged with developing test concepts to sell Accidental Death and Dismemberment policies. Your firm has sold such policies for decades and you have considerable testing history at your disposal. Would you advocate testing one element at a time against the control, or testing whole new approaches? Why? Would your answer be different if you were promoting a brand-new policy type with no testing history to study? Would you test using other media besides direct mail? If so, what media would you use, and why?

PART TWO

Creative Direct Marketing

10

Direct Mail Marketing

Millennial Generation students often express skepticism about the continued viability of direct mail. "I don't get any—except maybe credit card offers," they say—not realizing that their nomadic existence and often-meager budgets make them unlikely targets for many direct-sold products and services. Their eyes grow wide when they see a basketful of recently received consumer direct mail packages from just one baby boomer household—scores of offers from publications, non-profits, insurance companies, clubs, travel companies, and financial services firms, among others. Then the Millennials are a bit more accepting of the fact that there were nearly *100 billion* advertising mail pieces delivered by the U.S. Postal Service in a recent year.

Indeed, because direct mail offers a host of benefits to marketers and to customers, it has long reigned as the centerpiece of most direct response campaigns. Even today, with increased interactive media opportunities and concerns about postal rates and deliverability, direct mail serves a number of functions that other media are hard-pressed to duplicate. It combines flexibility of format with unsurpassed targeting and personalization opportunities. And while much direct mail does not come "invited to the home" as magazines, newspapers, and broadcast media do, consumers do not consider it as intrusive as telemarketing or unsolicited e-mail. Direct mail arrives regularly along with vital communications such as bills, checks, governmental notices (the Census and IRS correspondence are conducted by snail mail—not by e-mail) and personal letters, which helps ensure it will be considered (even if rejected) on a fairly timely basis. Just as important, it serves as a private method of communication between a marketer and an established customer: an ideal way to build a strong and personal relationship.

Another plus for direct mail is its ability to directly and effectively simulate a customer's retail store experience. The classic direct mail package includes four elements, each of which has a specific retail correlate:

Direct Mail Package Element	Related Retail Element
Outer Envelope	Store Window
Sales Letter	Personal Sales
Brochure	In-Store Display/Demonstration
Reply Device	Closing the Sale

When a customer walks through a downtown shopping district or mall, he or she may window shop: deciding whether to enter shops based on what each store window advertises. Some stores reveal little: they seem to say to the customer, "If you don't already know what we sell inside, you probably can't afford it." The direct mail correlate of this type of retailer might be an elegant, closed-faced envelope made of textured stock, offering no teaser copy or return address. The goal is to intrigue the recipient by the richness of the presentation to open the envelope (walk into the store). Many other retail stores are specific and inviting with their window displays. They show off their most attractive, timely merchandise and indicate something about their store's image and character. They do their best to entice passersby to walk in with news about sales, special events, and the like. These store windows can be correlated to direct mail envelopes with teaser copy—offering enough targeted "sizzle" to get the envelope opened.

A good retail store has salespeople who know their merchandise and their clientele well. Such salespeople use a combination of information sharing, service, and sales techniques to move the customer smoothly toward a purchase. A good direct mail letter does the same thing—and often today direct marketers have the opportunity to do a much better job than the transient retail clerks in many stores. By drawing information from our databases as well as primary and secondary research, we can hone in on the benefits that our prospective customers will find most compelling in a selling letter.

Successful retailers display their products attractively and offer demonstrations such as food tastings, vacuum cleaner performance tests, and fashion shows. Direct marketers can derive many of the same advantages by creating brochures that not only show off the product, but also highlight its uniqueness and all its features and benefits.

Finally, a skilled salesperson knows how to move gracefully toward closing a sale by answering objections and offering assurances and guarantees of satisfaction. Direct mail packages do the same through the reply device, which summarizes the offer and motivates the prospect to respond.

This chapter provides a survey of successful direct mail formats, but it is intended only as an idea starter. Because proven direct mail buyers may receive several selling messages in the mail on any given day, the onus is on marketers to continue the search for breakthrough design and copy concepts that cut through the clutter and earn the attention of the prospect.

Variety of Formats

The classic direct mail package described above offers a basic template for creative people. However, there are many other options to choose from. The format you select for any direct mail sales presentation should serve as a visible and active statement of the strategy put forth in your marketing plan. Like the strategy itself, your format should be based on what you know about your target market and your competitors, the company image you wish to project, and the amount you can safely spend to make a sale, gain an inquiry, or enhance a customer relationship.

Just as the function of a direct mail offer is to overcome inertia, the job of a direct mail format is to stimulate action on the part of the prospect. When designing any piece of your direct mail package, consider how it can be used to help lead the prospect toward the desired action stated in your marketing plan: a purchase, inquiry, or visit to your place of business.

Selecting a format for a direct mail presentation can be as challenging as choosing an ice cream cone at a store with 33 flavors. While television and radio formats are constrained by time, and print media ads must conform to the parameters of the publisher, direct mail marketers enjoy considerable freedom and control over their packages' dimensions, materials, and involvement devices.

Two important constraints must figure into each direct mail design decision: current U.S. postal rules and budgetary considerations. Some firms use only standard formats with outer envelope sizes like #10, 6″ × 9″or 9″ × 12″—and find them very effective in bringing about action.

Most successful marketers, however, continually test a wide range of other formats and supplementary enclosures.

Sources of Format Ideas

Direct mail graphic designers do not have to work in a vacuum: sources of format inspiration are readily available.

Maintain Sample Files

First, and most basic of all, become an avid direct mail consumer yourself. This need not be costly, if you get into the habit of making as many necessary personal purchases as possible via the mail. Order products from companies in all price ranges selling clothing, home items, electronics, sporting goods, food, office supplies, and other goods frequently sold by mail. Answer inquiry ads for high-ticket items like automobiles, and for intangibles like insurance and mutual funds. Join book and music clubs, and sign up for a continuity series of collectibles. Subscribe to a wide variety of publications: specialized subscriber lists often are rented to firms with direct mail offers. When you do so, mail will roll in from all over the country—not just from the firms you patronize, but from the companies that rent their mailing lists. Perhaps your company or agency already cultivates an organized file of competitive materials, commonly called a swipe file. If not, start your own, and categorize it by product type or format—whatever you find most helpful.

Talk with Vendors

Involving those who sell you paper, both sheet-fed and Web printing, and computer and lettershop services should yield you a constant source of format ideas. As these vendors add new equipment and applications to their plants, they will enthusiastically share the news with you. They should also be eager to show you innovative packages and concepts that they have completed for others, once they are in the mail and in the public domain. Remember also the benefit of showing your vendors your new concepts before the exact size and specifications are set. By shaving a fraction of an inch here and there, or changing the materials slightly, vendors may be able to save you enough money to make a radical new idea cost effective.

Read Books and Trade Publications, Look Online, and Attend Shows

Books such as this one will give you an overall understanding of the basic direct mail formats, and some ideas for additional sizes, enclosures, and refinements you might consider. Online and print trade publications offer news about production methods and successful packages that may fuel your creativity. Many publications also highlight award-winning packages. And since most direct marketing awards are given for bottom-line performance rather than pure creativity, such noteworthy applications may be well worth considering.

Many freelance copywriters and graphic designers maintain Web sites where they showcase their direct mail success stories, including visuals of the formats and copy and sometimes even specific results. If you meet—or read an article written by—a creative you admire, check to see if they have a Web site you can learn from. Finally, visits to international, national, and regional direct marketing shows may help stimulate your creativity as you chat with vendors in their display booths and attend talks on creative and production- related topics.

Update your Software Knowledge

As direct marketing creative expert Marc Ziner notes, "Because our field has skewed so dramatically toward electronic and computer-based production, creative people will be wise to seek training in systems software, word processing, and graphics applications." Knowing and using the latest software programs will help make copywriters and graphic designers more open to new techniques and formats for direct mail, and quicker to understand how technology can be applied for creative breakthroughs and cost savings.

The Outer Envelope

Studies show that your prospect may consider your direct mail package for only a second or two before deciding whether to read it immediately, save it for later, or dispose of it. Your choice of size, paper, graphics, and message will help the prospect make a decision on whether to open the envelope. Check the Web site of Mackay Envelope Corporation (*www.mackayenvelope.com*) for a good overview of technical considerations and terminology for direct mail envelopes. Here are some of the factors to consider in designing an outer envelope.

Standard or Custom Sizing

The most common direct mail envelopes are #10 (standard business outer envelope size), 6″ × 9″ or 9″ × 12″, but many other sizes are acceptable to the post office: square, oversized, European-sized, monarch, invitation-look, etc. Larger sizes like 9″ × 12″ often require extra postage, however: keep abreast of postal regulations to avoid a surprise upcharge. Selecting a common-sized envelope generally saves money: always check with your envelope vendor when designing a custom piece to make sure it can be manufactured at an acceptable cost. Odd-sized envelopes may prove to attract more attention than predictable-looking ones, and sometimes an outer envelope is chosen to complement the sizes of pieces that will fit inside. It may well be worth a test, however, to see if a unique envelope with a premium price justifies its cost compared to a standard-sized envelope and package with the same graphics and message.

Materials

Because most direct marketers have their envelopes manufactured from scratch, they have the same wide range of paper and print options that are available for brochures or letters. For last-minute or small-quantity jobs, you may choose to overprint a stock envelope, which will limit your selection of papers and your ability to decorate the envelope. Paper availability often is an issue, so to maximize your options for envelope paper and printing, work with experienced envelope vendors and plan to order early. Check your sample files for an overview of the types of envelope materials available: everything from simple wove and kraft paper stocks to elegant parchment and laid finishes, coated papers for four-color printing, foils for attention-getting effects, and even see-through plastics. Considering environmental factors, many direct marketers are opting for recycled envelope stocks printed with soy-based inks—both for their own corporate citizenship and to make a positive impression on customers.

Closed Face or Window

The traditional direct mail envelope usually featured a window showing through to an addressed letter or reply card. This method made it possible to both address and personalize the mailing with only

Exhibit 10.1. American Express Envelope

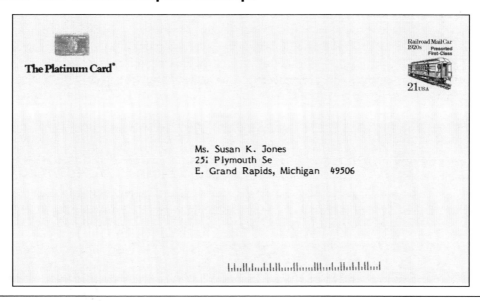

This closed-face envelope from American Express features an actual postage stamp and a "typed" address. Top-quality textured stock completes the impression of a personal invitation that is well worth opening.

Reprinted with permission of American Express.

one piece in the direct mail package having a label or computerized address. It was, however, an immediate "tip-off" to consumers that they had received a commercial direct mail offer.

With today's many options for computer personalization of multiple pieces in the same direct mail package, many marketers are opting for closed-face packages that more closely simulate personal business correspondence. If you invest in a closed-face package, be sure that the other elements of the envelope maintain this personalized one-to-one look: use a stamp or postage meter instead of a printed indicia, and avoid promotional teasers or graphics.

Teasers Versus Plain Outers

While many direct marketers swear by colorful, decorated envelopes and envelope teasers that entice the prospect to look inside, others point to test results that show the same or better performance from packages with plain outer envelopes. A teaser tells the prospect that this is a direct mail offer. It should help lure the prospect inside with the promise of a special offer, free gift, intriguing information, or the answer to a question or group of questions. Sometimes a teaser makes a statement and then trails off, enticing the reader to look inside for the rest of the message. Some marketers have tried beginning the letter on the outside of the envelope, then continuing the story inside. Resist the temptation to disclose too much with your teaser: this may prompt the prospect to make a decision on your offer without even looking inside.

Not all teasers require words. Sometimes it is enough to place a logo or motif on the outer enve-

Exhibit 10.2. Time-Life Books Outer Envelope

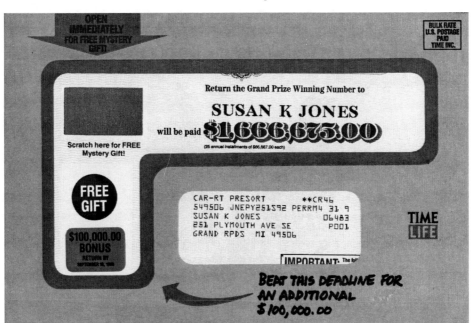

Stickers and a scratch-off involvement device show through the window of this sweepstakes offer from Time-Life Books. Stickers may also be affixed to the outside of an envelope. In either case, the intent is to motivate the prospect to open the package and find out more about the offer inside.

Reprinted with permission of Time-Life Books.

lope. The prestige of a designer's logo, or that of a European sports car, might be sufficient to entice aficionados inside an envelope. Cat lovers will probably open an envelope that features a feline. A single or secondary teaser could be a window with a die cut that shows through to a picture of the product or a premium.

Involvement Devices on Envelopes

If your budget permits, you may consider testing yes/no/maybe stickers or other involvement devices on the outside of the envelope instead of inside on the reply form or letter. Another interesting test is to tip the lift letter onto the back of a 9″ × 12″ envelope instead of inserting it inside: this serves to summarize the offer and challenge the reader to look inside, asking "what have you got to lose?"

Corner Card

The corner card is the return address that appears at the upper left of the front of your envelope. The return address may also appear at the upper middle of the envelope's back. Usually this will be your own return address, but you might also consider having the corner card list an endorsing organiza-

Exhibit 10.3. Rodale Prevention Package

↓ **INSIDE** ↓

SECRETS
THAT CAN
SAVE YOUR LIFE

PREVENTION.
America's Leading Health Magazine

Dear Friend,

Recent scientific studies prove that what you eat has a dramatic effect on your body's ability to fight and prevent illness. In fact, top medical researchers have found that eating certain foods can help you lower your cholesterol level, reduce your risk of heart disease and enable you to enjoy many other health benefits.

Now you can take advantage of these exciting discoveries in a important new book from Prevention magazine. THE HEALING POWER OF NUTRITION is yours free--just for mailing the enclosed card.

You'll learn:

*Four anti-aging nutrients that may help protect you against cataracts, respiratory disease, senility--even cancer! (Page 7)

*How to pump up the iron content of your spaghetti sauce to more than 8 times the RDA. (Page 13)

*How eating more of this versatile entree can help cool the fiery pain of arthritis. (Page 20)

*Delicious foods that "sneak" extra calories out of your body. (Page 27)

*How to lower your cholesterol level up to 30 points in 30 days. (Page 25)

*The detoxifying nutrient you absolutely cannot live without! (Page 36)

*50 top anti-cancer foods you may already have in your kitchen. (Page 18)

To get your free copy of THE HEALING POWER OF NUTRITION, mail the enclosed card today!

Sincerely,

Mark Bricklin
Editor

On page 13: A shortage of these two minerals can be life-threatening! Here are delicious ways to make sure you get enough of both.

On page 27: Tired of oat bran? Substitute this tasty dish and enjoy the same cholesterol-lowering benefit.

On page 4: 10 smart tricks to help you get the most nutrition for the least amount of money.

On page 12: How to double your absorption of iron by making this simple dietary addition.

On page 10: The powerhouse vitamin that may help reduce your cholesterol level.

THE **HEALING POWER** OF **NUTRITION**
From Prevention Magazine

PLUS
• 9 mealtime strategies to help you lower your blood pressure and build stronger bones.
• 12 ways to boost your fiber intake deliciously.
• 14 slimming foods that let you eat well and lose weight.
• And much more!

Printed in U.S.A.   B9732

Rodale Press tips a lift letter onto the outside of a mailing package to stimulate interest in the book inside.

Reprinted with permission of Rodale Press, Inc.

tion or an individual. This has been done successfully in fund-raising efforts with packages that appear to come directly from celebrities or political figures.

Indicia or Postage

An easy and cost-effective way to affix presorted standard postage is to preprint the indicia right on the envelope, but this is a dead give-away of a direct mail solicitation. As an alternative, consider using a postage meter, which gives the look of a regular business mailing even if it displays the presorted standard postage amount. There are also presorted standard rate stamps, which may be costly to affix, but provide a personal-letter look. Recipients probably won't look closely enough to note that the amount of postage on the stamp is less than the first class rate. To speed your mailing and provide the ultimate in the appearance of personal mail, however, consider testing first class mail to see if the extra postage costs are justified for some very well-targeted offers.

The Letter

Because it takes the place of the face-to-face salesperson, the letter is the most essential piece in any direct mail package. Unlike a brochure or reply device, the letter can sometimes stand alone and still make the sale. So important is the sales letter that Richard S. Hodgson wrote what is now a classic book on the subject: *The Greatest Direct Mail Sales Letters of All Time.* Hodgson suggested using this book as an idea source to see how top writers tackle challenging assignments.

The book contains some of the most famous and responsive letters in the history of direct marketing, as well as tips from renowned letter writers including Bob Stone, Victor O. Schwab, Ray W. Jutkins, Herschell Gordon Lewis (who wrote his own helpful how-to book called *Sales Letters That Sizzle*), Don Kanter, and Hodgson himself. The Hodgson book also contains scores of examples from the "pros" on ways to start and close letters effectively. This volume is highly recommended as a how-to guide for new direct marketing writers and designers, and as a source of reference and inspiration for veterans.

The key to successful letter writing is in creating a personal "me-to-you" communication. Thus the writer and designer of any direct mail letter must immerse themselves not only in product background, but also in knowledge and understanding of the target audience. You must know their hopes, fears, and aspirations . . . what kinds of messages stir their emotions and entice them to buy. To get on the right track, study psychographics, material from the database, and customer service communications with your firm. Read the comments customers make on your Web site about your products and services, and check out what's being said about your products and services on blogs and via social media. Find out what magazines your target market reads . . . what television shows they watch . . . what Web sites they frequent. . . whom they admire. Walk in the shoes of your target market to prepare yourself for effective communications. Read over past letters that have been the biggest sales winners with the same target audience. Once this careful preparation is done, you will be ready to consider specific elements such as these in the development of your direct mail letter format.

Characteristics of Successful Direct Mail Letters

A Showcase for Benefits. In a typical direct mail solicitation, the selling letter sets up the product features and benefits that are demonstrated in the accompanying brochure. The letter works to persuade the prospect that this product or service will uniquely and personally benefit him or her. It then

Exhibit 10.4. New Yorker Letter

This direct mail letter by Judith Hannah Weiss for The New Yorker is highly readable because of its conversational style and short paragraphs.

Reprinted with permission of The New Yorker.

creates a sense of urgency that should lead the prospect to respond promptly by mail, phone, Web site, or person-to-person visit.

"You" Orientation. The word "you" is used or implied frequently in most good direct mail letters, focusing on the prospect's wants, needs, triumphs, home, family, interests, and comfort. A good selling letter points out product benefits in a very personalized way, assisting the prospect to visualize having and using this product and thereby enhancing his or her quality of life. Creating these mental pictures helps move the prospect from the attention stage through interest, desire, and finally to action—just as a skillful salesperson does in a retail store or on a showroom floor.

The Letter May Be Lengthy. Some fledgling direct marketers are skeptical about the length of typical direct mail letters: two, four, or even eight or more pages in some cases. But an involving and readable four-page letter can be far more appealing to a prospect than a one-page communiqué with long sentences, 20-line paragraphs, and no subheads. While some clients and production types like to "button down" the letter length well before it is written—calling for a two-page or four-page letter and asking the writer to oblige—it is usually wiser to let the letter run to the length that is necessary to tell the story effectively.

The Letter Should Be Readable. As a rule, direct mail letters feature short sentences, short paragraphs, lots of indentation, and subheads. All of these elements help make letters readable and appealing. Some direct mail letters feature the use of second or even third colors, handwritten "call outs," illustrations and photographs, underlining or highlighting of important points, and headlines before the salutation.

Promotional or Straightforward: Either May Work. Purists and those new to direct marketing may question the wisdom of using promotional ploys like handwriting, illustrations, and headlines in a letter that purports to be a one-to-one communication. The effectiveness of these methods has been proven over the years through extensive testing, however, and they work because they engage the attention of readers. This is not to say that a more straightforward letter will not pull well: indeed, some effective letters to consumers—especially those making upscale offers or requesting political contributions—may appear as businesslike as correspondence from a Fortune 500 company. As in all direct marketing efforts, the key to success in developing a letter format is to test, test, test.

Elements of a Direct Mail Letter

The Letterhead. The letterhead you select should reflect the image of the product or of the firm that sells it: economical or upscale, modern or traditional, liberal or conservative, sporty or elegant. Some firms add a list of advisors or board members to the letterhead to reflect status, or the historical, religious, or authoritative nature of the company and its products. Most direct mail letters are printed on 8-1/2″ × 11″ letterhead, using both sides. Monarch-sized stationery may be used for a more personal look. This smaller size often is used for an endorsement letter or other supplementary note. Sometimes an unusual paper stock is used to attract attention or make a visual point: parchment for an old-time historical look, or lined paper for an informal appearance. Marc Ziner notes that today many consumers look for the recycled logo on a letterhead as an indicator of the sender's environmental responsibility. For ideas on types of letterheads to try, imagine the personal stationery of someone in your target market. Would they use elegant, monogrammed notecards, business letterhead, informal notepaper with pictures of flowers or kittens on it, or a piece of notebook paper? Try testing a similar paper stock for your selling messages.

The Salutation. While many direct mail letters—especially those with a promotional tone—have no salutation at all, others use general wordings such as "Dear Friend," "Dear Collector," or "Dear Preferred Client." In recent years, however, personalization and variable data printing have become cost-effective enough that many letters can be personalized with "Dear Mary Smith" or "Dear Mrs. Smith" as a salutation. Because the novelty of personalization has long since worn off—and direct marketers have realized that customers and prospects are not necessarily impressed with letters that have their addresses and names peppered here and there throughout the body—most letters are personalized only in the salutation.

The Signer. In most cases, the letter in a direct mail package comes from the president or other high official of the firm presenting the selling message. Sometimes, when the letter comes from a family-owned firm and the concept is to create a "down home" atmosphere, the letter may be signed by the owner's spouse, mother, or key employee. In other cases, the main selling letter appears over the signature of a third party, someone whose credentials qualify him or her to describe and endorse the product or service being offered. Marc Ziner notes that a "peer-to-peer" letter is likely to be read: homemaker to homemaker, or Little League coach to Little League coach, for example.

The Typeface. It is important to remember that the letter should uphold the illusion that this is a personal communication from one person to another, written especially for its recipient. In general, tests show and conventional wisdom dictates that effective direct mail letters are presented in conventional serif fonts. Headlines, subheads, and other enhancements may be printed in another font to add emphasis. Underlining may be done via regular word processor underlining, or by simulating hand-underlining. To further the appearance of a personal letter, the second color for hand-underlining, handwritten notes, and signatures is typically medium-dark blue—the same color as a pen's ink.

The Tone. Depending upon the market segment they are intended to reach, effective direct-mail letters may come across as folksy, friendly, high-toned, or strictly factual. It is important to create a scenario for the letter: who is the writer, who is the recipient, and what are we trying to get across. Envisioning the target market as one typical recipient will help in this process: for instance, are you writing to your Aunt Martha the needlepoint hobbyist, or your multi-millionaire boss who is looking for a real-estate tax shelter?

The Opening. The beginning of your letter must be an attention-getter, or you will lose the prospect before you even get started. Typical opening gambits include telling a story, asking a question, identifying the prospect as a certain type of individual, or extending an invitation. Chapter 2 of this book offers Bob Stone's and Ron Jacobs's benefit-oriented seven-step formula for good letters. Become a connoisseur of the direct mail letters you receive, and save those that capture your imagination as idea-starters.

The Johnson Box Opener. Some direct mail letters begin with a Johnson Box: an indented, introductory copy block (with or without an actual box) that may preview the offer, provide a teaser about the offer, or set the stage for the letter itself. In an interesting twist, some direct marketers use the Johnson Box to offer a short endorsement statement from a third party, commending the offer in the letter to the prospect's attention.

The Body. The body of the letter performs the essential job of selling. It refers to the product features and benefits as shown in the accompanying brochure, and explains to the prospect why this product or service will benefit him or her personally. The body of the letter also may include testimonials, evidence to back up sales claims, and other "reasons to buy" copy. In addition, the body of the letter should contain all the nuts and bolts of the offer: price, payment terms, premiums, conditions of sale, and guarantee.

The Close. The end of a direct mail letter serves the function of a sales close. It requires a reinforcement of the "reasons to buy" copy combined with urgency based on time pressure, limited quantities, putting the product's benefits to work right away, or even a subtle version of the old "be the first on your block" pitch.

The P.S. Studies of direct mail readers tell us that when they pick up a letter, prospects look first at the signature and next at the P.S. Thus the P.S. provides such a vital selling opportunity that most every direct mail letter includes one. The P.S. may be used to restate the prime product benefit; highlight the urgency of the offer; refer the reader to the brochure, order form, testimonials, or other component of the package; remind the prospect about the premium; offer a toll-free number or Web address for ease in ordering; or emphasize the no-risk nature of the offer due to Free Trial or Money-Back Guarantee. It is not a good idea to introduce a new concept in the P.S.

Letter Variations

Letter Versions to Suit Prospect Groups. Printing different letter versions is one of the least expensive ways of tailoring a direct mail package to target different market segments. For example, you may use the same brochure for both previous buyers of the product and new prospects, and acknowledge the status of the recipient in the letter. If you rent a list of people who are all travel club members, you might acknowledge this in a special letter and use a different letter for a group of people who are all personal computer owners. You may also use your database to tailor offers and incentives for specific groups of previous buyers—or even use variable data printing to customize your offer to the individual—showcasing these unique opportunities in versions of the same letter.

Endorsement Letters. If you are able to obtain an endorsement for your product by a respected or authoritative group or individual, or the executives of a club or organization whose members will then be more likely to want to buy, one of the best ways to utilize this endorsement is by means of a special letter to be included along with the main selling letter. Such letters are usually signed by the president of the endorsing organization. In it, the president will mention some of the product's features and benefits from the organization's point of view, and recommend the product to your prospects.

Publisher's Letters or Lift Notes. In personal sales, one of the most important aspects of closing the deal is overcoming the prospect's objections. In direct mail, many marketers use a "publisher's letter" or "lift note" to do the same thing. Such a supplementary letter is customarily folded, or contained in a separate envelope. On the outside it might say something like "Please do not open this note unless you have already decided not to respond to this offer." Few readers can resist opening such a note, especially when they have been told not to. The note brings up common objections to the product and politely refutes them before offering an urgent message to respond.

Next-Day Delivery Letters and Simulated Formats. One way to enhance the urgency of your message is to replace the usual business-type letter with a next-day delivery letter sent by the U.S. Postal Service, FedEx, or another quick delivery service. Since such services are quite expensive, you might create a package that has the same look of urgency but is sent by standard or first-class mail. If you go this route, use the various courier services' next-day packaging as inspiration, but make sure your design is sufficiently different from those of actual overnight delivery services to avoid copyright infringement or deceiving the reader.

The Brochure

The brochure displays the features and demonstrates the benefits of the product or service being sold. Also called a circular, flyer, folder, or booklet, the brochure illustrates the product, demonstrates its use, and provides interesting background information about it. Just as a good direct mail letter contains all the main sales points about a product or service, so does a good direct mail brochure.

Select the Format

Some direct mail researchers say that the brochure should contain all points of the offer on a single surface, so that the prospect can take it all in at one time without flipping pages or switching from the letter to the brochure. Many successful direct mail brochures, however, have been done in booklet form with various points of the offer explored page by page. Whatever your format, make sure that the brochure copy includes a phone number, Web landing page, and mailing address for responding, and that it ends with an urgency statement: don't leave your prospect hanging with a mere recitation of facts.

Consider a Range of Sizes and Folds

Of all the pieces in your direct mail package, the brochure generally provides the copywriter and graphic designer with the greatest range of possibilities where sizes and folds are concerned. One standard brochure is the 8-1/2″ × 11″ sheet folded twice into a "C-fold" flyer. Many brochures look like booklets and may be stitched or stapled to keep their pages together. If you want your prospect to keep and carry your brochure, consider making it pocket size. If you want to make a big splash, design a broadside brochure that opens up to a flat size of 17″ × 22″ or more. You may also add shorter, folded panels for detail shots, guarantee boxes, and the like. Save brochures with sizes and folds you like and consider how they may be adaptable to your products and offers, but don't make a commitment without checking with a trusted printer or two.

This will help you avoid paper waste and extra bindery charges. Also remember that any brochure you design for machine insertion into an envelope must have a closed edge for the inserting machine to grab. This will save you costly and time-consuming hand insertion.

Fit the Brochure to the Product

When their budgets permit, many direct mailers are tempted to create brochures that are pleasing to their own egos—colorful, expensive, splashy, and impressive. For high-ticket, status items this may be the right alternative. But the best way to develop your brochure's look is to consider the target market and characteristics of the product. A brochure selling flower bulbs at 100 for $19.95 does not require an eight-page color piece on 100-pound coated stock. By the same token, a brochure sent to prospective customers for a $70,000 foreign luxury car cannot convey the proper message if it is printed in black and white on limp offset paper. Gather the brochures your competitors use or those in similar fields for ideas on paper sizes and stocks, the use of color, and supplementary illustrations. And study brochures used in other fields as well: they may provide fresh ideas on ways to display your product or service.

The Brochure Must Relate to the Package

Make sure your brochure fits with the other items in your package. An expensive, slick brochure should be complemented by a tasteful letterhead and a well-designed order form on good-quality stock. By contrast, a two-color flyer on offset stock looks fine with an inexpensive letter and order form. The graphic look of all the pieces should be considered as well. They may all be coordinated in color scheme, typeface, and stock, or some elements may be intentionally designed to stand out in the package.

Color Can Increase Response

Head-to-head tests show that a full-color brochure usually can out-pull the same brochure printed in black and white. This is especially true if color is one of the product's strongest attributes, as is the case with clothing and home furnishings. While few direct mail brochures are done in black and white, some firms use this one-color approach for a homey or small-company look. Other companies use black and white for sale supplements only. Most brochures feature at least two colors, and the majority are done in four colors. However, a black-and-white brochure printed on fine-quality stock can be very dramatic for certain products such as white bisque figurines.

The Reply Device

Once your customer has made the decision to take advantage of your offer, he or she needs to be eased through the actual buying process. Many firms offer toll-free numbers or step-by-step online guides for this purpose. However, not all customers want to use the phone or Web to order—and you may be unable to offer phone or Web ordering for some products and services. In this case, it is essential that your reply device breeze the customer through the act of buying, and reinforce the wisdom of doing so. A reply card that is confusing, complex, or intimidating can easily terminate the sale. Marc Ziner notes, "The reply device/order form is often the most neglected component of an otherwise well crafted package. Spend time tailoring this most important element to be as appealing and user-friendly as possible."

A Summary of the Offer

There should be nothing new included in your reply device, no announcement of a premium, sale price, or other terms and conditions that have not been discussed in the letter and/or brochure. The reply device should summarize all the elements of your offer presented elsewhere in the mailing package. At the same time, it should be able to function on its own as a free-standing sales piece. Some customers save only the reply card and put it aside for a later decision: they should be able to use the card to refresh their memories, regain excitement about the offer, and return an order with confidence. Thus the reply card should comfort the buyer with a restatement of the guarantee or other risk-reducing elements of the offer. It is also a good idea to picture the product on the reply card.

Names Other than "Order Form"

Many direct marketers believe that the term "order form" sounds too much like a request for money and a discussion of the mechanics of ordering. They prefer terms that focus more on benefits and less on nuts and bolts. Thus you might name your card an "Invitation," "Preferred Reservation Card," "Free Information Card," or "Membership Application," if these terms are appropriate.

Make It Easy to Fill Out the Form

When a reply card is printed with the prospect's name and address, it streamlines the process of responding. If you design the reply card so that the label shows through a window in the outer envelope, it will serve as the means of addressing the piece as well. If you must ask the customer to fill in his or her name and address on the reply form, make sure there is ample space in which to do so. Try it yourself on a photocopy of the final artwork before you release the form for printing. Make sure that the paper stock you use is easy to write on: get a sample and try this for yourself as well. Some coated stocks do not take well to pens or pencils of any kind. And use a light-colored stock so

Exhibit 10.5. History Book Club

RETURN THE ATTACHED CARD TO GET 3 BOOKS FOR $1 EACH, PLUS A 4th AT THE MEMBERS' PRICE, WITH NO OBLIGATION TO BUY MORE.

Write the titles of the 4 books you have chosen below. Then detach and retain this stub for your records:

Price	Title
$1	_____
$1	_____
$1	_____

Member's $:_____

History unfolds here.

Return this card to get 3 books for $1 each, plus a 4th at the Members' Price, with no obligation to buy more—and to begin your exploration of all that history has to offer.

YES. Please enroll me in History Book Club. Send me the 4 books I've indicated below. Bill me $1 each for the first three, Members' Price for the one on the bottom, plus shipping and handling. I understand that I have no obligation to buy more. However, if I choose not to buy at least one book in any six-month period, you reserve the right to review my membership. A shipping and handling charge is added to each shipment.

Indicate by number the 4 books you want. Then return this portion in the envelope provided.

```
                      CAR-RT SORT    **CR46
         I08-07-0    611006 221046
         SUSAN K JONES
         251 PLYMOUTH AVE SE
         GRAND RPDS   MI   49506
```

0-13   All orders subject to approval.   (See other side for facts about membership.)
                                                                                        H790/0

The History Book Club suggests that its prospective members save the tear-off stub as a reminder of the four books they have chosen. With the stub removed, the order form is the right size to fit easily into a standard 6-3/4 Business Reply Envelope.

Courtesy History Book Club. ©2006.

that any color of pen or pencil will show up. Also, make sure that you specifically request all the information you need to fill the order: name, street address, apartment number, city, state, zip code, and perhaps day and evening phone numbers and e-mail address.

When to Use a BRC Versus a BRE

When your prospect is returning only an inquiry or reservation, and no payment is required, you may opt for a postage-paid Business Reply Card (BRC) that the prospect can simply drop in the mail. But if you are asking for any confidential information on the card—a credit card number or the prospect's age, for example—a Business Reply Envelope (BRE) may ease your prospect's mind and make him or her more likely to respond. Of course, if you are asking for a check or money order in payment, or if the offer is one the prospect might want to keep confidential, a BRE is warranted as well.

Tear-off Stubs Serve a Dual Purpose

The customer-oriented purpose of a tear-off stub on an order form is to allow the prospect to save a record of his response for future reference. The stub should have your firm's address and phone and/or Web address on it, and allow room for the customer to record what he or she ordered, the date it was ordered, what payment method was used, and when delivery is expected. A statement on this stub of any applicable guarantee is also a good idea, and the stub provides another, more practical benefit: you may design your card so that removing the stub makes it just the right size for one of the standard Business Reply Envelopes. If the card were sized this small in the first place, it would float around too much in the outer envelope. This means that if you are using an outer envelope with a window, the address label would not show properly through the window.

Exhibit 10.6. Allstate Motor Club

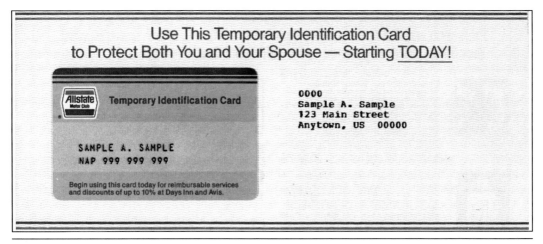

Allstate Motor Club used a Temporary Identification Card that resembles a regular membership card to interest prospects. The card shows through the envelope window to reinforce the offer of a 30-day free trial membership.

Reprinted with permission of Allstate Motor Club.

Combining Order Form and Letter Facilitates Personalization

One widely used format has the order form attached to the sales letter, and perforated for easy removal. In this way, two benefits are achieved. First, the order form and letter can be personalized at the same time. Second, the letter's appeal for urgency is easy to act upon since the prospect does not have to sift through the package looking for the reply device.

Action and Involvement Devices Stimulate Replies

To incite action with a reply card, many marketers use involvement devices. Here are several variations:

- *Stickers or stamps*—Products, prizes, or premiums may be depicted on pressure-sensitive or lick-and-stick stamps. The prospect affixes the appropriate stamps to the reply form.
- *Yes/no/maybe*—To stimulate action, some marketers ask prospects to respond whether their answer is yes or no. Sometimes a "maybe" option is given, possibly to indicate that the prospect would like to take advantage of a free trial period with no obligation. Stamps with the words YES, NO, and MAYBE are made available on the outer envelope, order form stub, or letter. The prospect chooses the appropriate one to affix to the reply portion of the form.
- *Membership card*—To give the prospect the feeling of "immediate belonging," some marketers attach a temporary membership card to the reply device, which the prospect can remove and keep before sending in dues or other payment. In its simplest form, such a card could be made of the same stock as the reply form

and perforated for removal. However, many marketers have had success using plastic cards similar to credit cards in appearance and weight.

- *Postage stamp*—While the majority of direct mail offers include a prepaid reply envelope or card, the inclusion of a "live" postage stamp adds more urgency to a request for response—especially if it must be transferred from an order form to the proper place on the reply card or envelope. Keep in mind that this method is considerably more expensive than Business Reply Mail, in which you pay postage only for those envelopes that come back to you.

Business Reply Envelopes Encourage Response

Repeated tests show that the cost of providing a Business Reply Envelope is justified in that it encourages a greater level of response. The customer finds it much easier to return an order in a postage-paid, self-addressed envelope than to search around for a plain envelope and stamp. Business Reply Envelopes also serve an excellent purpose for the direct marketer: they may be coded by color, size, or other means to allow for a quick and dirty way to visually estimate daily mail response—even before the orders are input. To use a Business Reply Envelope, you need a permit from the local post office. To get this you will fill out a form, pay a yearly fee, and receive a reply number to use on your envelopes. You will pay the current first class rate plus a small surcharge for all BREs that are returned to you. Provide the post office with money in advance, which it may draw against as mail arrives, and keep that account replenished; this will help avoid delays in receiving your mail.

Business Reply Envelopes must be designed and sized in accordance with post office rules. The specifications for Business Reply Envelopes and Cards are available at your post office or online at *www.usps.com*. Graphic designers and production specialists need to be very familiar with these rules, as violations waste time and money. There are standard sizes for Business Reply Envelopes, the most common being sizes 6-3/4 and #9. You may use other sizes within post office guidelines, but they may be more costly if they must be custom ordered from your envelope house. Make sure that the Business Reply Envelope you select fits easily into your outer mailing envelope, and that the reply form fits easily into the reply envelope, preferably without folding.

Other Inserts and Formats

Mailers have tested and proved the effectiveness of a wide range of additional pieces and special formats that increase response to direct mail offers. For fresh ideas on this score, sift through a wide range of direct mail samples and keep in contact with marketing-oriented printers and other suppliers. Here are a few of the most commonly used inserts and special formats.

Testimonial Flyers

If you have or can obtain flattering and believable testimonials from satisfied users of your product, a flyer containing these testimonials may make a good addition to your package. Optionally, you may highlight one or more testimonials in your letter, or put them on a panel of your brochure. Good testimonials offer specific examples of benefits received, performance, or other positive virtues of using your product or service. Users of established products or services may send you excellent, unsolicited testimonials: keep in touch with your customer service department to make sure you receive them. In the case of new products, you may solicit testimonials from customers who purchase the product as a result of a test mailing. Or you may send the new product to some of your established customers, and ask them to use it and respond with their opinions. Before using any testimonial, you should obtain written permission from the individual who will be quoted.

Premium Slips

The customer who barely skims your mailing may not realize that you are offering a premium unless you devote a special piece to it. The premium slip should discuss the features and benefits of the premium, its dollar value if impressive, and what the prospect must do to obtain the premium. Also mention if the prospect is able to keep the premium even if the product is returned for a refund.

Buckslip Reminders

These small flyers are most often used to simulate last-minute news. A buckslip might be inserted to tell the prospect that a certain item being offered is now sold out, thus stimulating urgency for buying other items offered. Such a piece might highlight your toll-free number and Web address, or the buckslip might explain a recent improvement in the product or the offer. It should cover the offer thoroughly enough to make sense to a reader who has not read your promotion package.

Article or Ad Reprints

These pieces add credibility to your offer by including statements from "independent" articles or ads. In many cases such articles are written specifically for the direct mail package and never appear in any publication, but only look as if they had. Where ads are concerned, the marketer might obtain reprints of an ad run in a particular publication and overprint a message such as, "In case you missed our ad in XYZ magazine . . . ." For more impact, have the message printed on a sticky note and affixed to the article or ad reprint.

Questions and Answers

A question-and-answer piece gives you the opportunity to restate your offer and the attributes of the product in a new and simple-to-understand form. For example, one question might be, "What makes the new Smith Widget better than the widget I've been buying for years?" The answer would point out the most outstanding and unique benefits of the product.

Samples

If your product is inexpensive and easy enough to send, you might include a sample of it in your mailing. Products frequently sampled in this way include ad specialties, stationery, and perfume. Swatches of fabric may be enclosed in clothing or home furnishings offers as well.

CD-ROMs

Direct marketers of high-ticket items sometimes test sending CD-ROMs instead of—or in addition to—brochures or booklets as lead generation devices. Sales of a computer software series may be enhanced when an introductory CD-ROM is included with a direct mail package or follow-up to an inquiry. The CD-ROM might highlight the benefits of the software being sold and allow the prospect to sample some of its applications. Testing such an enclosure on the front end may be warranted when the database of prospects is highly targeted—say, a list of PC owners who have a demonstrated interest in personal finance. Directing the customer to a download of the same material online may prove to be a more cost-effective method, but the CD-ROM carries perceived value, so don't make this assumption without a test.

Exhibit 10.7. Hamilton Article

Today's Doll Collectors Delight in the Variety of Exquisitely Appealing Editions

by Collectibles Writer, Cheryl Monahan

For whatever reason you choose a particular doll for your collection, you're bound to be pleased if you've made a good investment—if you purchased at issue price and within a relatively short time, demand for your doll results in secondary market appreciation.

Congratulations are in order for the collector who makes the "right" decisions. Aside from pure appeal, keep an eye out for artist exclusives from the highly regarded collectibles companies. Though designed by the very same artists whose personally crafted originals can cost several hundreds, even thousands of dollars, "collectible house" editions can be had for a fraction of the price—and because you needn't sacrifice quality, their secondary market potential can be most impressive.

The Hamilton Collection
A Rare Friend Indeed

Through the years, The Hamilton Collection of Jacksonville, Florida, has become one of collectors' greatest friends, commissioning works from super-star artists as well as new discoveries—all with the talent to draw the eye and touch the heart. The 1990s, in particular are enjoying unrivaled success, with several closed editions that are rapidly climbing to the top of the charts.

Connie Walser Derek's first-ever doll for Hamilton, "Jessica," made waves the moment she was unveiled to an adoring public. In 1990 the picture-perfect baby was issued for $155. Since then, the edition has been closed, the molds broken, and the secondary market price has more than tripled!

Another great story is told by the figures posted for Helen Kish's dazzling "Ashley." She sashayed onto the scene in 1991 for just $135, and the music is still playing with bids up to a heady $300.

Some of Hamilton's most darling successes are inspired by portraits created by the great illustrators of the past. Among them, Bessie Pease Gutmann, one of America's most celebrated child-subject artists during the 1920s

and 1930s, and Maud Humphrey Bogart, whose renowned actor son made his public debut at a tender age in portraits painted by his gifted and distinguished mother.

"Love is Blind," re-born as the premiere issue in Hamilton's *Bessie Pease Gutmann* Doll Collection, has appreciated to $220 since 1989. "Playing Bride," a lavishly ruffled and laced Maud Humphrey Victorian doll, issued in the same year, is quoted at $225.

A Delightful New Blond Takes Center Stage at Hamilton

With so many gifted artists under Hamilton's nurturing wing, the question is not if, but when the newest success will debut to an adoring public. And the answer is, "right now."

Internationally acclaimed artist, Virginia Ehrlich Turner, has created a new work exclusively for Hamilton. If past history is any indication of things to come, "Johnny on the Spot" promises to become one of Hamilton's most coveted dolls of the year.

Winner of several of the doll world's most prestigious awards, including a 1991 "Dolls Awards of Excellence" for "Hannah," one of her biggest sellers ever, Virginia Turner seems to have the "golden" touch that eludes so many others—an extraordinary number of her dolls are currently sold out, including "Michelle," her darling first work commissioned by Hamilton in 1992. It seems this artist can do no wrong! The proof is in "Johnny on the Spot," an adorable little firefighter with head, hands and feet sculpted of fine, hand-painted bisque porcelain.

"Johnny" takes his responsibility very seriously. When the alarm sounds, he's the first to grab his fire truck—along with the mascot, "Spot." Posed on one bended knee, "Johnny" is incredibly lifelike as he holds the nozzle in both hands and bravely puts out a "fire" as "Spot" barks his encouragement.

The heartwarming realism that is the signature of all Virginia Ehrlich Turner collector dolls is beautifully reflected in "Johnny on the Spot," her latest creation for The Hamilton Collection.

Besides the true-to-life quality that is Virginia Ehrlich Turner's trademark, collectors will also appreciate the attention to detail given to the doll's costuming. The yellow vinyl jacket and matching boots make "Johnny" look every inch a firefighter, as does the big red hat that covers his blond hair. Underneath his protective gear he wears a red shirt and blue denim pants. For realistic display in your home, "Johnny" comes with a plastic fire hose and, of course, his plush Dalmatian puppy, "Spot."

As your assurance of authenticity, "Johnny on the Spot" will be inscribed with Virginia Ehrlich Turner's signature. With your hand-numbered doll, you will also receive a same-numbered Certificate of Authenticity. Interested collectors are strongly urged to contact The Hamilton Collection in Jacksonville, Florida at their earliest convenience.

© 1996 Monahan Creative. Reprinted with author's permission. Price quotes taken from the Collectors' Information Bureau's Collectibles Price Guide & Directory to Secondary Market Dealers, Sixth Edition, 1996.

\4391

Cheryl Monahan's life-long appreciation for the arts, enhanced by an education in theater, dance, and art history, has culminated in a decade-long career as director of her own collectibles consulting company.

The Hamilton Collection has used informative articles like this one about doll collecting to provide additional background information for prospective customers. The article format provides the appearance of an independent endorsement.

Reprinted with permission from The Hamilton Collection The Hamilton Collection.

Exhibit 10.8. Boys Town

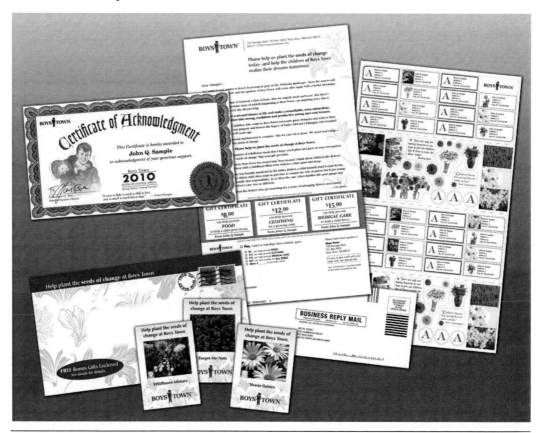

This innovative direct mail package was designed as a test against a long-standing, existing control for Boys Town. Boys Town has had an Easter-themed appeal since the 1940s, and the mail dates for the calendar year are based on when Easter falls (anywhere from mid-March to mid-April). The new package allowed for more consistency with mail dates and plans for the first half of the calendar year. The package size allows for maximum postal savings, but it is filled with response-boosting components. The package mailed in late February and was in home for early Spring. The "freemium" of three seed packages was selected to emphasize the "promise of spring," while reinforcing the "seeds of change" theme. Donors are literally planting seeds that will turn into new life, while their donations have the power to change the lives of children. Other components of the package included a Certificate of Appreciation, and a personal story lift note. This package was tested against the winning Easter Renewal control. The control garnered a 5.89 percent response rate, and this test package achieved a 9.81 percent response rate.

Reprinted with permission of Boys Town.

Exhibit 10.9. The University of Iowa Foundation

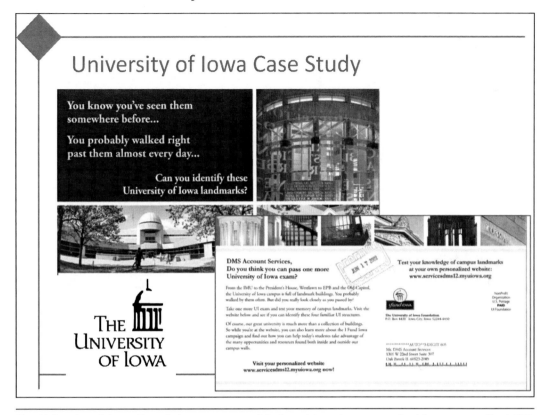

The University of Iowa Foundation sent potential donor/alumni a postcard with a personalized URL (PURL), inviting them to visit their own Web site to take a quiz on campus landmarks. When the respondent visited his/her Web site, they were invited to take the quiz and get instant results, forward the quiz to friends and fellow alumni, and donate to the Foundation. The Foundation derived extra benefit by tracking the viral marketing "forwards," and picking up new, potential supporters.

Reprinted with permission of The University of Iowa Foundation.

DVDs

Some complex and/or high-ticket products have been sold effectively with the enclosure of a DVD that highlights product benefits. Once again, the potential effectiveness of such a costly promotion depends upon your ability to use the database to prequalify prospects as to their sales potential. DVDs are more likely to be used in a fulfillment package sent to qualified inquiries. And as with CD-ROMs, it may prove more cost-effective to direct your customer to a Web site or landing page where they can view the same video content online.

Gimmicks

To induce a response, some marketers send their prospects actual checks for small amounts of money, which the customer may endorse and cash for responding to or even for simply receiving the mailing. Or the recipient may be told that if they cash the check, this will be taken as permission to start the service or send the product. The marketer may send a penny or other coin or coins to create interest value, with a line such as, "A penny for your thoughts." Advertising specialties firms can provide a wide range of gimmick items that may be enclosed or tipped onto your promotional pieces. Examples of these might be a packet of instant coffee, a lapel button, or a bumper sticker.

Follow-Ups

In a series of mailings, varying your formats may inspire fresh interest from your prospects. You might, for example, send what looks like a photocopy of your original letter, with a handwritten note saying, "In case you missed this special offer the first time around . . . ." Using different outer envelope sizes will encourage prospects to read mailings sent later in a series, as will printing a two-color brochure in a different color combination.

Postcards

Some mailers find that they can sell products via a toll-free number or draw traffic to a Web site simply by sending a postcard to their prospects. Many magazines use multi-panel postcards for cost-efficient renewal efforts. Other firms use postcards as up-front "teaser" mailings, alerting the prospect to a package they will receive soon and including appropriate benefit-oriented language about its contents. To draw prospects to a Web site or landing page, the postcard should be "more sizzle than steak," talking about premiums or exceptionally good deals. The "steak," leading the customer to actually buy the product, send for a catalog, or take other specific action, can be presented online. This method can save considerable money over a full-scale direct mail package or catalog mailing, and also may expose prospects to the full range of products, services, and features available on your Web site.

Self-Mailers

While the standard direct mailing includes various separate pieces enclosed in an envelope, self-contained mailers come in a number of attractive formats. A self-mailer may be as simple as an offset-printed sheet with an ordering device separated from a letter by a dotted line, or it may be a complex format with ingenious folds, perforations, and combinations of paper stocks to provide a brochure, letter, order form, and pre-formed Business Reply Envelope all in one.

In general, mailers find that they get a better response to envelope mailings than to self-mailers. But people are more likely to pass a self-mailer along to a friend or associate than they are an envelope mailing. So if your offering appeals to a cult audience or special interest group, the self-mailer may work beautifully for you. And because some self-mailers cost less than envelope mailings, the cost per order with the self-mailer may be less, even if you get fewer total orders. Often the self-mailer concept is worth a test against a successful control direct mail package. Work with an experienced printer to find a cost-efficient format, and try it against your standard envelope mailing.

Enhance Your Understanding: Direct Mail = Retail Store

To be effective, a direct mail package must take the place of the complete retail store experience at its best: attracting the prospect, demonstrating the product or service, relating to the prospect in a one-to-one way, closing the sale, and making the customer feel good about the purchase. A good direct mail package can be related directly to the retail store experience, piece by piece. In other words:

Outer Envelope equals Store Window
Sales Letter equals Personal Sales
Brochure equals In-Store Display/Demonstration
Reply Device equals Closing the Sale

Take a direct mail package from your mail or swipe file and see how it stacks up according to this model. Does each piece do its part to attract, sell, demonstrate, or close the sale? Are there additional pieces in this package? What are their functions? Are there pieces missing? Is this a problem, or does the package do the job effectively anyway?

11

How to Create Effective Direct Response Print Ads

With the great advances in database technology for direct mail and online applications, it might appear that the print medium is no longer competitive. On the contrary, many consumer and business-to-business direct and interactive marketers still consider magazine and (to a lesser extent) newspaper advertising essential as a primary source of leads, sales, members, or subscribers. In some fields, direct mail lists of likely prospects have become saturated over time, so print advertising has evolved into a cost-effective means of soliciting new customers. Other firms use print media to reach groups of customers that cannot be targeted or reached by mail, broadcast, or other means. Since only about half to two-thirds of American adults are considered true direct response buyers, print media may expand a marketer's reach. Still other companies find print ads an excellent source of incremental business, or a means to support and amplify their efforts in television or mail. Finally, print advertising offers a relatively quick and inexpensive way to test the viability of a product or offer.

What's more, while some pundits once predicted that the Internet might severely curtail the use of print ad media, the reality is quite different. Web sites are very passive—they need to have customers' attention drawn to them—and space ads provide one of the many viable ways of attracting "eyeballs" to a Web site or landing page cost-effectively.

"Print is not dead," asserts John Kennerty, Director of Marketing for the Sinclair Institute in Chapel Hill, NC. "In fact, we recently ran a single ad in *AARP* magazine that generated more than 8,000 orders and over $300,000 in sales."

Kennerty says that while online media get much of the attention these days, "For a lot of people ages 45 and older, print publications are still legitimate. These people are comfortable with print. They like their magazines and newspapers to be transportable. They find the content believable. These people grew up with print, and they still consider it meaningful and compelling. They're not going to let their subscriptions go. These are the people who like to have their magazines and newspapers delivered to the house. They'll take the *Wall Street Journal* out with them for coffee in the morning."

Kennerty notes that those who are still subscribing to print publications are a special breed. "People who have stuck around are very interested in the content they're receiving. That means that the advertising in these publications is going to be of more value as well. So for many firms like ours, you can still do very well with direct response print."

The pure-play dot.com companies have actually started using print for some applications, Kennerty notes. "Zappos has used print to push people online, for example. Online advertisers also are using catalogs to supplement their marketing efforts, sending catalogs to their better customers or prospects. It's a good way to remind your online buyers that it's time to shop again."

Learning from the Masters

In the decades before database management made it possible to pinpoint market segments for targeted mailings, direct marketers looked to magazines and newspapers to attract most of their new customers. The field's legendary mail-order writers—Tom Collins, David Ogilvy, John Caples, and many more—cut their teeth on space advertising.

Back then, segmentation had to be achieved in the ad itself. A compelling headline and carefully chosen photograph or drawing could grab the right readers and draw them into the body copy. Compact classified ads with one- or two-word headlines did the trick for other firms, with every word carefully chosen to attract prospects and inspire them to action.

In his book *A Whack on the Side of the Head*, Roger von Oech states that the surprise value of studying concepts outside of their familiar context can make the ideas more accessible. Thus a look back at some classic direct advertisements from decades ago can help clarify the enduring principles they exemplify. Clothing styles, buzz words, and status symbols may change, but the appeals that were "grabbers" in decades past can still win a prospect's attention. Julian Lewis Watkins assembled a priceless archive of ads in his classic book, *The 100 Greatest Advertisements—Who Wrote Them and What They Did*. The book includes print ads from the turn of the century through the 1940s, with a supplement of ads that first appeared in the 1950s.

Famed direct mail copywriters whose works Watkins celebrates include Max Sackheim ("Do You Make These Mistakes in English?"); Victor O. Schwab ("How to Win Friends and Influence People"); John Caples ("They Laughed When I Sat Down At the Piano But When I Started to Play!"); and David Ogilvy ("At 60 miles an hour the loudest noise in this new Rolls-Royce comes from the electric clock.").

Today's print ad writers owe a great debt to creative geniuses such as these. For in addition to leaving us the legacy of their ads, they also took the time to share the concepts behind them. The "old masters" of print combined a thorough study of human nature with an understanding of the necessity to "test, test, test"—then record their test results, draw conclusions, and build upon them.

The general principles they established are as useful today as they were generations ago. From the collective wisdom of the marketing greats of yesterday and today, here are some basic creative concepts behind successful print advertising.

Newspapers as a Direct Response Medium

The decline of newspaper circulation and ad revenues is a much-discussed topic in the media today. Newspapers are losing readers and advertisers for several reasons. First is the "24/7/365" news cycle on the Internet and cable TV news networks, which makes it difficult for the one-issue-per-day newspaper to deliver any "new news" to its readers. Second, the rise of Craig's List and other online substitutes for classified advertising in print has curtailed one of the most profitable ad revenue streams for newspapers. Third, the newspaper-reading population is aging fast, and young people show few signs that they will ever adopt their parents' and grandparents' habit of daily newspaper reading.

That said, there are still a number of reasons why direct response marketers consider the newspaper a viable medium for many offers—especially when their target market is middle-aged or older. For one thing, the newspaper provides the most immediate means of testing a proposition in print.

Newspapers accept advertising until a few days or even a few hours before publication, while magazines may require up to three months' lead time. Readers consider the offers newspapers contain to be newsy and time-urgent, so if they decide to respond, they are likely to do so quickly. Newspapers are an excellent medium for local or regional offers. Some direct marketers also use them to heavy-up their coverage of high-potential areas. Such multi-media programs may add newspaper to direct mail and/or television.

Newspapers have been open to new ad formats in recent years, including various types of wrap-arounds and inserts that are ideal for direct response offers. In addition, many newspapers now accept peel-off, sticky note-type ads that can be placed on the front page of the newspaper. These are ideal for direct response offers because they are hard to miss, and because they can be removed and saved for follow-up by phone or online. The Kennedy Group (*www.kennedygrp.com*) offers a front page sticky-note ad program that coordinates 450 newspapers reaching 35 million consumers in a single ad purchase.

The "mass" medium of newspapers may be segmented somewhat by placing ads in specific sections: retirement village ads near the obituaries, men's products in the sports section, or furniture ads in the home section. In recent years, some newspapers have developed more sophisticated zoned editions based on segmentation factors as well as geography. What's more, newspapers have become markedly more sensitive to the advertiser's wish for segmentation—often running weekly sections or pages devoted to gardening, fitness, home decor, automobiles, the online world, and other specialized interests.

Running a national direct response campaign via newspaper may prove to be an administrative nightmare, since complete coverage requires securing space in hundreds of publications. On the other hand, national papers such as the *U.S.A. Today*, and *The Wall Street Journal* offer both immediacy and broad reach. What's more, they can be tested in regional editions before a commitment to national roll-out is necessary. Also available nationwide, but delivered with the local newspaper, are Sunday supplements like *Parade*. Such ride-along magazines provide better color reproduction than newsprint, a magazine environment for ads with the immediacy of newspapers, and mass circulation in the tens of millions weekly. Regional test programs and affordable remnant-space buys make *Parade* and its competitors appealing to many direct marketers.

Free-Standing Newspaper Inserts

When they were a novelty decades ago, Free-Standing Inserts (FSIs) represented a very cost-effective way of reaching prospects via newspaper. In recent years, FSIs have suffered from a "clutter" problem similar to that on network television. On television, two-minute commercial breaks once included only two 60-second ads. Now commercial breaks on cable networks—where many direct marketers buy most of their time—are stretching to three minutes, four minutes, or more, and splintered into six or more spots. At one time, the average Sunday newspaper contained only one or two extra inserts, whereas today's weekend edition may be stuffed with retail offers, coupon co-ops, flyers from local aluminum siding companies, and fast-food sales promotion pitches.

At least one FSI format has been successfully copyrighted, making it essential to clear the format you wish to use with a knowledgeable production expert before final plans are made. Even so, the FSI offers several advantages worth considering by marketers of mass-appeal products and services. *First*, it offers a free-standing, visible advertising medium that does not require page turning for the prospect to find it. *Second*, it gives the direct marketer control over size, paper selection, color reproduction, and format. *Third*, it allows for a post-paid reply card or envelope, which lets the prospect respond quickly and conveniently. *Fourth*, many newspapers are able to deliver local FSIs selectively by zone or segment, eliminating some of the medium's inherent waste. *Fifth*, FSIs can offer a total national circulation in the tens of millions. *Sixth*, advertisers may place ads in co-op FSIs at an exceptionally favorable cost per thousand.

Magazines as a Direct Response Medium

In recent years the magazine medium has begun to focus more and more on publications that cater to narrow interest groups such as runners, crafts enthusiasts, or people who keep pet birds. These magazines allow marketers to target space ads to specific market segments, much as they do via direct mail lists. Even among the larger-circulation publications, direct marketers may take advantage of segmentation opportunities to help target their ads. These include:

- Regional editions
- Market or metro editions
- Editorial sections providing ad environments for special interests such as:
  - ▶ Travel
  - ▶ Pet owners
  - ▶ Decorating
  - ▶ Parenting
- Demographic-based editions providing audiences representing groups such as:
  - ▶ Doctors
  - ▶ Students
  - ▶ High-income families
  - ▶ Women

Although magazines require a longer ad lead time than newspapers, they offer several advantages that newspapers do not. For instance, the life of a magazine ad is considerably longer, since magazines generally are kept in the home for at least a short period—not swept out with the day's recycling like newspapers. Magazines offer pass-along value as well: they often are shared with family members, neighbors, friends or co-workers. Color reproduction and paper quality in magazines are generally superior to those of newspapers.

Another important factor is the "implied endorsement" of the magazine when a direct marketer runs an ad there. Since most consumer magazines—and many business publications—are sent mainly to paid subscribers, advertisers can assume that the magazine's readers generally feel somewhat positive toward its editorial material. This positive feeling may carry over to the ads that appear in the magazine as well, bestowing upon them an unstated "seal of approval" from a respected source of information.

Some magazines are considered especially fertile fields for direct response prospecting. While this media list changes frequently, certain publications carry many more direct response ads than others. When ads from the same respected marketers appear repeatedly in these magazines, their relative effectiveness is confirmed. Generally accepted good direct response books include but are not limited to:

- *AARP The Magazine*
- *Smithsonian*
- *Parade*
- *Good Housekeeping*

Exhibit 11.1. Lands' End Ad

While many catalog firms use modest 1/6 or 1/12 black and white page ads to prospect for new customers, Lands' End took a more dramatic route with a full-color, double-page-spread coupon ad in national publications.

Reprinted with permission from Lands' End.

- *Ladies Home Journal*
- *Family Circle*
- *Woman's Day*
- *Redbook*

In addition, various "shelter books"—those dealing with home and decor—are excellent sources of direct mail prospects. Music clubs, book clubs, and major marketers of collectibles run frequent ads in a much broader range of publications. Financial services and investment firms find fertile fields in publications like *Money* and *Smart Money*. This list should be used only as a general guideline. Indeed, media experts suggest that direct marketers with a new offer begin their print prospecting with the most narrowly targeted publication possible and work "outward" to more general books. Thus a fledgling marketer of custom-made dog beds might study the results of an ad in *Dog World* before trying the pet section of a general, family-oriented, higher circulation shelter publication like *Better Homes and Gardens*.

The Elements of a Direct Response Ad

Observe people flipping through newspapers and magazines and one thing becomes readily apparent: each article or ad has only a split second in which to engage the prospect's attention. Thus every word and picture must be selected with exceptional care.

There are four main elements of a good direct response advertisement: the headline, illustration, body copy, and response device. Here are some guidelines to use in preparing and combining them in an effective presentation.

Select and Entice the Audience with Headlines

One classic way to train for direct response headline writing was to spend time on what used to be called the horseshoe desk of a daily newspaper. While headline writing is now done online, the example still holds true. Story after story arrives at the headline writer's desk or screen along with the city editor's specifications for exact headline length. Clarity and brevity are essential, for each headline has to fulfill two main criteria in just a few words: to summarize the story, and to pique the readers' interest enough to make them read on.

By the same token, a good direct response headline flags down qualified prospects and lures them into the body copy. It is considered the most important element of a print advertisement. Thus, a smart copywriter will invest all the time and care necessary to make each headline irresistible. Journalists are taught to answer six questions in each news presentation:

WHO?	WHEN?
WHAT?	WHY?
WHERE?	HOW?

These are the questions people want answered immediately about most any situation or opportunity—and thus they are powerful idea-starters for direct response headlines. Yet because journalists are supposed to remain unbiased, newspaper headlines seldom fall into the "irresistible" category. To make a headline compelling, direct marketers have developed some attractive headline "buzz words" of their own, including these suggested by William A. Cohen in his book, *Building a Mail-Order Business—A Complete Manual for Success:*

advice to	important	remarkable
amazing	improvement	revolutionary
announcing	introducing	secret
at last	it's here	sensational
bargain	just arrived	startling
challenge	last chance	success
compare	magic	suddenly
easy	miracle	wanted
found	new	when
free	now	which
how	power	who else
how to	powerful	why
hurry	quick	

But when we're faced with our own blank piece of paper or computer screen, how should we put these words together to capture the attention of the prospect? In his brilliant book, *Tested Advertis-*

ing Methods, the late John Caples said that irresistible headlines do one or more of the following things:

Appeal to the Prospect's Self-Interest
Example:
"We Guarantee to End Your Foot Pain . . . and We'll Prove It to You . . . Risk-Free!"

Give News
Example:
"Finally, a waxless, shaveless, creamless, painless method of hair removal. Finally Free."

Arouse Curiosity
Example:
"What's this woman doing?"

Offer a Quick, Easy Way
Example:
"If you can sew on a button you can create a rose."

An even better headline may result when two or more of these key elements are combined. John Caples stated that of the four main headline appeals, self-interest is by far the most powerful. If we wish to appeal, above all, to the prospect's self-interest, we need to know what people are interested in. We can start by asserting that people are *not* inherently interested in products and services. They are interested in *results*—what products and services can do for them.

They are attracted by the *sizzle,* not the steak. They want to know about benefits (what's in it for me?), not just product features (attributes that may or may not seem important to the prospect). While preparing to write headlines for a product or service, ask yourself what would make you want to buy it. If you are not a member of the prime target market for the product, find some people who are, and learn what motivates them. Try to determine their overall hopes, dreams, and aspirations—this can often prove much more helpful than a detailed discussion of their thoughts about insurance, lawn service, or kitchen appliances.

Here are some of the basic human interests, needs, and aspirations that well-written headlines may address:

- Money—Making it, saving it, investing it for the future, using it to buy possessions, getting it easily (greed).
- Security—Health, financial, family.
- Saving Time—Ending drudgery, having more leisure, relaxing more, getting more done at work, being more organized.
- Self-improvement—Career advancement, better looks, fitting in socially, impressing loved ones and friends, gaining power, increasing pride.
- Enjoyment—Travel, escape, excitement, freedom, novelty.

When you sit down to write headlines for an ad, don't stop at one or two. Write all the headlines you can, branching out in different directions. Create some headlines that focus on the main product benefit. Try some others aimed at a different benefit—it just might turn out to be the key to the product's initial appeal. Set the scene for a psychological reward. Work on some testimonial headlines.

Keep at it until you have a wide range of options. Then if you think several are equally promising, consider testing them head-to-head to see which ad produces sales or leads most effectively.

Avoid writing headlines that are merely labels such as "New Spring Fashions from Macy's" or "The Prudential Life Insurance Plan." Most effective headlines contain verbs, often vivid ones such as the classic, "How to Win Friends and Influence People."

In general, it is best to avoid negative headlines, although sometimes a warning not to do something "unless" or "until" may entice the prospect to read on. Cute or funny headlines may amuse their writer, but they seldom gain the attention of the right readers. Above all, make sure your headlines are concise and clear.

Keep in mind that today's climate of law and regulation may call for increased temperance in headline writing—especially when it comes to claims regarding money and product performance. It is wise to make your company's or client's attorney your ally to ensure that your copy combines the most compelling claims compatible with a solid legal position.

Smooth the Decision-Making Process with Body Copy

If your headline is effective, it has accomplished one of two things: set up a problem to be solved, or teased with an opportunity to be grasped. Now a reader with some interest in your proposition is poised at the brink of the body copy. It is time to continue with a clear, simple, and straightforward presentation. You may opt to begin your body copy in many different ways. Here are several examples:

- Tell a story.
- Give a testimonial.
- Explain the product's problem-solving or opportunity-grasping potential straight out.
- Compare your product favorably with the competition.
- Use an editorial format.
- Let a spokesperson do the talking.
- Tell of the marvelous results, then flash back to the problem and how it was solved.

Don't use your first paragraph for "warm-up." Jump right in with a strong follow-up to the headline. Many writers find that their strongest lead paragraph is the second or third one they write. By moving the clearest statement of the product's benefits to the forefront, they strengthen their copy. Once you have shown how your product or service does what you say it does, move on to strike the bargain with the prospect. Explain and justify the price, and emphasize your guarantee to ensure the buyer of no risk.

Create urgency—the need to respond right away. Urgency can be explained in terms of limited quantities, limited edition, offer of a premium for quick response, or the immediate need of the prospect to put the product's benefits to work

Ask for the order, and take the prospect by the hand to make sure he or she responds. Tell them to return the coupon, make the telephone call, send in the inquiry, or go online to respond.

To maximize response, don't ask the prospect to make too many choices. The more choices of size, price, color, etc., the prospect has to make, the more difficult it will be to respond.

As for copy length, in general the more you expect the prospect to do or spend at this stage of the game, the more copy you need. Lead-generation ads may be quite short, and all sizzle. Ads signing up a prospect for a book or music club require much more copy for selling, provisions of the agreement, and reassurance. When you use long copy, break it up with action-oriented subheads.

How to Design an Ad for Maximum Impact

The way your ad should look depends upon your target market, the medium in which the ad will appear, and the product's attributes. A direct response ad in a fashion publication like *Vogue*, aimed at upscale women, might well make use of a full-color bleed presentation with an avant-garde typestyle for headlines. An ad in the *National Enquirer*, aimed at lower-to-middle-income women, might be black and white, set in a newspaper-like typeface that is compatible with that used by the publication itself. Clothing, home decor items, and other fashionable products call for color so that they can be displayed to maximum effect. Other products—notably financial services—can be presented quite effectively in black and white.

Many successful direct marketing ad campaigns have utilized "editorial ads"—pieces crafted to look as much like an article in the publication as possible. This ploy helps capitalize on the credibility of the publication itself in the eyes of its readers. What's more, it implies the unbiased "news value" of the information in the ad. Keep in mind that some publications may refuse ads that look too much like their editorial material, or place the word "advertisement" at the top of such ads as a disclosure to readers.

On the other hand, in his book *Direct Marketing: Strategy, Planning, Execution,* Ed Nash asserts that a well-designed ad stands out from the other ads in its medium. If you are not striving for an editorial look, find some way to make your ad a "stopper" when people are turning pages. Make the product dominate the page . . . emphasize key words in the headline . . . use a color or a readable typeface that's seldom seen in the particular publication.

A good way to check in advance how your ad will appear in its editorial environment is this: make up a dummy that is as close to the real thing as possible, and then insert it randomly in a copy of the magazine where it will appear. Have various people flip through the magazine and test their reactions to learn if your ad stands out or blends in, and why.

Choosing the Size of Your Ad. Standard sizes for newspaper ads may vary greatly depending upon the publication: see SRDS's *Newspaper Advertising Source* to check on the newspaper of your choice. As for magazines, Standard Rate and Data Service's *Consumer Media Advertising Source* and *Business Media Advertising Source* will help you determine specifications. Standard sizes for magazines display ads include:

- 1 Page
- 2/3 Page
- 1/2 Page
- 1/3 Page
- 1/6 Page
- 1/12 Page

In addition, you may opt for a double-page spread, one or two pages with bind-in card, or a special insert which you may supply if the magazine agrees.

When testing a new offer, larger firms tend to begin with full-page ads and then test smaller to see if they can gain the same number of sales or inquiries in less space. If a one-page ad works well, many marketers also "test up" to a page plus bind-in card, or double-page spread. Even though bind-in cards and double-page spreads are highly likely to bring in more sales and leads than one-page

Exhibit 11.2. Gevalia

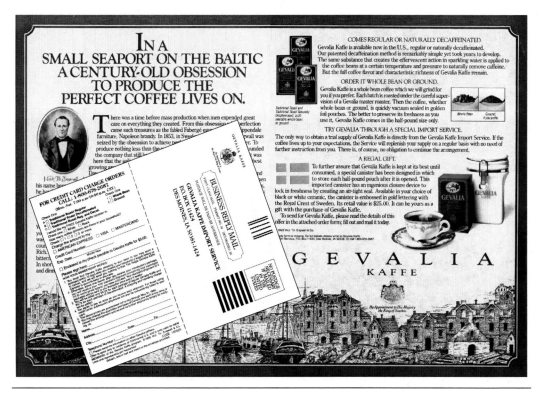

Gevalia Kaffee Import Services went the bind-in card one better with a bind-in Business Reply Envelope and tear-off reply form. Rather than place a coupon on the face of its handsome, full-color ad, the firm provides contact information for prospects to use if the form is missing.

Reprinted with permission from General Foods (now Kraft).

ads, they are also more costly. Thus, conventional wisdom is to start with the less expensive one-page ad, and then move on to test more expensive media buys with proven offers only. What's more, in their book, *Successful Direct Marketing Methods*, Bob Stone and Ron Jacobs say that the first test "up" from a full page should be to a page plus bind-in card rather than a two-page spread: it is more likely to pay off.

Pros and Cons of Bind-In Cards. Bind-in cards offer several advantages to space advertisers. They add bulk to the magazine and pop up, so it is likely that the book will fall open to the page where your ad appears. They allow for post-paid reply cards on a stock heavy enough to return in the mail, thus making it easier for prospects to reply. For these reasons, they have traditionally brought anywhere from three to ten times as many replies as an on-page coupon or toll-free number alone.

On the other hand, they cost twice to two and a half times as much as a one-page ad, and thus they need to generate many more responses for break-even. In addition, because bind-in cards make it easier for prospects to respond, the names received on bind-ins represent less committed customers than those received on cut-out coupons where the sender pays for the postage. What's more, for many target markets, replying online is considered easier and quicker than replying by mail. An intermediate step to test is the bind-in card without business reply postage. Making the customer pay postage will likely draw less responses than the post-paid card, but these respondents may prove to be more qualified and more valuable in the long run.

Color or Black-and-White? In general, a four-color ad will out-pull a black-and-white—but not necessarily enough to justify its extra cost. This can be tested on an A/B split in some publications. Use black- and-white or full color only: two-color or three-color ads seldom bump the response at all. Bleed ads are generally more attractive than those with white borders, but they are more costly, and not guaranteed to pay out. Test bleed versus non-bleed if you have a product that might benefit by the artistic advantage of a bleed ad.

Choice of Typestyle. Direct response print ads must be easy to read, and thus serif typefaces are recommended over sans serif. Some graphic designers try to "sell" the story that sans serif is easier to read. If they pull this on you, ask them to show you a daily newspaper or national magazine with body copy printed in sans serif type—this usually settles the issue. The reason why serif faces make for easy reading has to do with the tiny hooks and squiggles on their letters—they are more soothing to the eyes than the straight lines of sans serif type. Stylish typefaces may be used for headlines if this contributes positively to the overall effectiveness of the ad.

When working with a graphic designer who is not a direct response "pro," one other "don't" should be kept in mind. Although reverse type is quite dramatic, it is difficult to read, and should be used sparingly if at all in direct response ads.

Photos and Drawings. When a photograph and a drawing are tested head-to-head, the photograph will almost always win. Using captions under photographs in direct response ads boosts readership, and therefore response. When choosing photography for your ads, remember to make the product the star. You may be able to borrow attention with an intriguing photo that has little to do with your sales pitch, but you won't be able to sustain it long enough to close the sale.

Surefire attention getters are pictures of animals and people, so consider using them if they relate directly to your product. Psychologists say that men look more closely at pictures of other men, and women look more closely at pictures of other women. Keep this in mind if your product is being marketed to one sex or the other.

Don't underestimate the power of before-and-after shots. But if you must choose only one photo, make it the "after," never the "before." An upbeat, positive, aspirational approach is best.

General advertisers make frequent use of symbolic photographs and drawings in their image-building ads. This is seldom advisable for direct response pitches. Print ad illustration types most often used effectively by direct marketers include: product, product in use, results of using the product, and product in setting with people.

Coupons versus Toll-Free Numbers and Landing Pages. Some fledgling print advertisers rebel against the concept of a coupon. They believe it takes away from the streamlined look of the ad, and they prefer to use only a toll-free number or Web address for responses. Indeed, many general advertisers are now adding Web addresses and landing pages to their ads, believing that this small gesture toward direct response may make their ad dollars work harder. The toll-free number and/or landing page may be appropriate for many consumer audiences, but for older audiences, marketers will be wise to test adding a coupon before rejecting the idea.

This way you can determine the most cost-effective means of obtaining responses—then track respondents to see if coupon or toll-free call or Web customers are most valuable in the long run.

Designing the Coupon. Coupons are a tried-and-true means of soliciting response, but some coupons are much more effective than others. Here are some tips for creating the best possible coupon:

- Make sure the coupon can stand alone, spelling out the basics of the offer, and including the full address of your company. Many consumers clip only the coupon and put it aside for later action. Don't risk losing a sale by providing them with a less-than-complete means of doing so.
- Put your address and the basics of the offer, including the price, elsewhere in your ad as well. This way, pass-along readers will be able to respond even if the coupon is missing.
- When using a bind-in card, the addition of an on-page coupon provides two means for convenient customer response.
- Resist the temptation to "liven up" your ad with a coupon that is placed sideways, fashioned in an exotic shape, or screened with a color or pattern. A rectangle at the bottom right corner, printed in black on white with readable, serif type, is still your best bet. Some graphic designers have actually presented coupon layouts indicating type reversed out of black. Unless you plan to provide a pen with white ink to each prospect, beware of this mistake!
- Make it as easy as possible for the prospect to fill out the coupon. Provide four lines if possible: Name, Address, City, and State/Zip. Asking prospects to "Please Print" will help eliminate problems in adding names to the database when responses are received.
- Take a photocopy of your print-ready coupon and sit down to fill it out for yourself. Make sure the lines are long enough and tall enough to be filled out comfortably.
- Add a friendly note of urgency to the coupon, such as "Clip Here and Mail Today." Dots or dashes to mark the coupon border facilitate easy clipping.
- Make sure to add a source code to every coupon so that each customer's origin can be discerned. Depending upon the sophistication and requirements of your database, you might do one of the following:
  - ▸ Add a department number to your address, such as 123 Main Street, Dept. BHG-612 (for *Better Homes and Gardens,* June, 2012).
  - ▸ Place a similar code in the corner of the coupon.
  - ▸ Assign a number of three or more digits which is coded in your database system to indicate publication and date.

Classified Magazine Ads

Although many direct and interactive marketers today invest millions of dollars in start-up campaigns, there are still many success stories about kitchen-table entrepreneurs who begin their direct

Exhibit 11.3. Sinclair Institute

Sinclair Institute combines a toll-free number, a landing page, and a coupon for maximum response flexibility in its ads aimed at middle-aged adults.

Reprinted from *AARP The Magazine*.

response businesses very small and build up to impressive levels over time. The least expensive way to start prospecting in print is by means of classified ads—the short attention-getters that appear in special "shopping sections" at the back of many national magazines. Yet, amateurs fall by the wayside if they underestimate the difficulty of writing an effective classified ad. Every word counts in a piece that may measure only one column inch in length. A classified ad with a strong headline may bring ten times the orders received from another ad with a headline that does not capture the prospect's attention.

The best way to prepare to write classified ads is to study the best ads in the marketplace. Tear out the ads that appear again and again and keep them to study. Be on the alert for headline tests, and then track to see which headlines show up later, and which are abandoned. If there is competition for your product already in the marketplace, study their ads carefully. Find a way to do a better job in classifieds than they do, perhaps drawing upon the appeals used in other product categories.

When you begin to write your classified ad, don't worry about length right away. Write the best ad you can—even if it's two pages long. Then hone and cut and combine. Eliminate flowery language and extra adjectives. Use action verbs. Pull out the most important product benefit and ruthlessly cut out secondary messages. Write a number of headlines and be prepared to test them head-to-head.

Consider price and offer tests. Consider testing various lengths for your classifieds. Test using a small coupon versus name and address only with toll-free-number and landing page. Investigate opportunities for editorial coverage offered by many shopping sections. If you offer a catalog, look for catalog inserts with bingo cards (better known as Readers' Service Cards or information cards to magazine readers) that appear on a seasonal basis. Keep in mind that initial response alone is not enough to track on bingo card offers. How many of those loose leads actually turn into buyers and then long-term customers for you?

Using Ads to Generate Leads

There are a number of situations in which it is more effective for print advertisers to develop a two-step approach. Step number one involves the solicitation of a lead, while step number two includes a follow-up by mail, e-mail, telephone, or personal visit to close the sale. Here are some examples of propositions that may pay out better in the long run with a two-step approach up front:

- For club or continuity offers that involve a long-term commitment—Offer the prospect a premium or inexpensive way to sample the product before deciding.
- For catalogs—Offer the catalog-only as an alternative to selling a product from the catalog and then following up with a catalog mailing.
- For big-ticket or complex items—Sell the "sizzle" in the step-one ad. Then send a detailed package that introduces the "steak" only to those prospects who have indicated a certain level of interest.
- For business-to-business offers—Identify quality prospects to be followed up by mail or e-mail, phone, a sales call, or some combination.

When soliciting leads, it is important to set objectives for the quality and quantity of names you wish to obtain. In some cases, you may wish to maximize the number of loose leads you acquire, and then worry about converting them into buyers later on. In other cases, you may wish to qualify your prospects considerably, obtaining only a limited number of tight leads who are predisposed to buy. Exhibit 11.4 gives some pointers to use in structuring your offer to obtain tight versus loose leads.

Exhibit 11.6. Tight Leads vs. Loose Leads

To Obtain Tight Leads	To Obtain Loose Leads
Charge money for information or catalog	Provide free information
Do not offer a premium	Offer a premium
Offer a product-related premium	Offer a highly appealing premium unrelated to the product
Include address only—make the prospect do the work in responding	Use coupon or bind-in card to minimize work the prospect must do to respond
No phone number or no toll-free number	Provide a toll-free number
Indicate that a salesperson will call	Indicate that there is no obligation and that no salesperson will call
Ask questions on the coupon as qualifiers—such as age, phone number, income, when the prospect plans to buy, size of business, number of employees, title and responsibilities	Simple coupon—asking name and address only
For business offers—insist that the prospect reply on company letterhead	Provide coupon or place no restrictions on method of response
Talk specifically about price	No talk of price
Do not participate in bingo card offers—or do participate, but charge for information	Participate in bingo card offers, and offer information free of charge

Final Advice About Print Advertising

In recent years, general advertisers have pushed the boundaries of print advertising with advertorial sections, pop-up inserts, samples of scent and eye shadow, and tip-on samples and premiums. All of these advances and more can be considered for tests by direct marketers.

What's more, all the foregoing points in this chapter should be kept in mind—the best advice for direct response print advertisers still echoes from the writings of the "old masters": To write successful ads, learn first about human nature. Then research the product, the market and the print medium, write your ads with care, and "test, test, test"!

Enhance Your Understanding: Write Powerful Headlines

Flip through a consumer magazine until you find a direct response ad that catches your eye. Study its headline and identify whether it appeals to self-interest, gives news, arouses curiosity, or offers a quick, easy way. If it's a self-interest headline, does its appeal hinge upon money, security, saving time, self-improvement, or enjoyment? Now study the body copy, the offer, and the response device. Then put yourself in the place of the copywriter and write ten more headlines that could be used to sell this product. Make some of them self-interest, some newsy, some curiosity building, and some offering a quick, easy way. Edit your headlines to make sure they are meaty, compelling, and specific.

Catalogs and Multichannel Marketing

When *Catalog Age* changed its name to *Multichannel Merchant* several years back, the publication's editors explained the change with these comments: "Once upon a time, catalogers sold through catalogs, and retailers sold through stores. But most companies are now channel-agnostic. They realize that they must go well beyond their core channel to reach the largest pool of potential buyers." The renamed publication was intended to "serve catalog companies, online merchants, retailers, manufacturers and wholesale/distributors who sell via print catalogs and/or transactional Web sites."

Times certainly have changed since Montgomery Ward and Sears, Roebuck & Co. reigned supreme in the world of American catalogs. A century ago, their thick "wish books" served the purpose of a general store by mail. Reaching deep into the nation's heartland via Rural Free Delivery, the catalogs offered general merchandise to fill the needs of families that might live hundreds of miles from the nearest store. But as Americans gained mobility, and suburbs spilled into what had been remote farmland, many more shoppers were able to visit cities, towns, and outlying malls to make their purchases in person. Thus catalog merchandisers were forced to find new reasons for being, based on the needs of a changing culture.

Many catalog marketers have struck a positive chord with consumers through unique selection, ease of shopping from home, and other factors. Indeed, while some pundits claimed that the Web would make print catalogs obsolete, the Direct Marketing Association reports that there were more than 13.5 *billion* catalogs mailed in a recent year. That said, according to The National Directory of Catalogs, 84 percent of the 12,524 catalogs it lists have companion Web sites. It is clear that for buyer and sellers alike, the combination of paper catalog, Web site, and sometimes brick-and-mortar retail outlets as well, makes for powerful synergy.

Meanwhile, according to Epsilon Targeting's 2009 Multichannel Trend Report, online purchasing "continues on a steady growth path while sales from the retail channel remain relatively flat" and the direct mail/call center channels declined (in 2009) for the fourth consecutive year. Smart marketers realize, of course, that the drop in mailed-in or called-in orders relates back to those "channel agnostic" consumers identified by *Multichannel Merchant*: customers enjoy the flexibility of flipping through a paper catalog and then ordering however they choose on any given day: online, by phone, in a retail store, or—less often these days—by means of a mail-in order form.

Here are some additional facts about catalogs: The DMA reports that consumer catalog sales hit $75.8 billion in 2010, while business-to-business catalog sales clocked in at $38.3 billion. Consumer catalog sales are projected to grow by 4 percent per year through 2014, while business-to-business catalog sales are expected to increase by 4.4 percent yearly in that same period. Even so, the swift rise and fall of many shiny new catalogs proves again and again that the market isn't magic: each book must carve out its own "reason for being" and support its positioning with top-quality, well-targeted merchandise, a crisp creative product, and excellent customer service.

What's more, the days of overnight success for the "kitchen table" catalog entrepreneur are all but over. Fierce competition has driven down the average response rate of both direct mail and space prospecting for new customers, and online banner ads and sponsored search are far from inexpensive. A peek into the mailbox of an inveterate catalog shopper reveals that five, ten, or more different books may arrive daily between Labor Day and the end of October. This pre-holiday catalog glut rivals even the worst advertising clutter on cable television. The situation in space advertising is little better, with catalog shopping guides and small-space ads for catalogs filling the back pages of nearly every likely fall publication. And while Web sites are part of most every catalog's multichannel presence today, this medium is often less than effective in attracting new customers without the integration of a strong print presence.

This chapter will provide a step-by-step guide for creative people charged with positioning and creating a catalog and its companion Web site. It includes ideas that graphic designers and copywriters may use to make their creative product as appealing and "user friendly" as possible. It offers proven ways to increase average order size, reader involvement, customer loyalty, and impulse purchasing. And it concludes with some hints to help keep the day-to-day output of catalog writers and designers from getting predictable and stale.

Catalog Positioning

In the age of "niche marketing," the most exciting aspect of catalog creativity is *positioning*. It is not enough to choose a general merchandise category like women's clothing, food, or children's toys. All of these categories abound with catalogs that have already established an image and a basis of trust with consumers. Rather, the catalog marketer must embark on a period of research to identify a unique and viable target market for each new book and companion Web site.

The Target Market

To succeed in the competitive catalog realm, each firm must discover and fulfill one or more unmet needs of a target group of consumers. Equally important, the target group must be *reachable* by some cost-effective combination of direct mail lists, space advertising, e-mail, mobile marketing, sponsored search and social media. What's more, the market must be *sizable* enough to result in a business with sufficient volume to meet the goals of its sponsoring organization.

Fulfilling an Unmet Need

Some firms are able to translate their successful retail sales concepts to catalog and Web marketing. For example, the Crate and Barrel catalog and Web site both echo the spare, contemporary good looks of the tabletop, cookware, furniture, and linens stores that preceded it. Other organizations approach the marketplace with only a rough idea of the product category they wish to enter.

A number of large firms have recognized the potential of catalog and Web marketing as a new profit center. As wholesalers, these producers of products like clothing, food products, or dinnerware miss out on the large percentage of mark-up that retailers enjoy. Thus they may wish to develop catalog and Web concepts around the general merchandise categories they can supply.

As an example, Hanes sells its Hanes, Bali, Playtex, Champion and Wonderbra brands through various retailers' outlets. There is also the One Hanes Place catalog as well as a Web site (*www.one-*

hanesplace.com) that sells all these brands in a broad range of sizes, styles, and qualities (regular or irregular) at a discount. American Spoon Foods sells its jarred fruits, jams, salsas, and sauces in up-scale grocery stores and its own retail outlets in Michigan resort towns, but broadens its reach with a colorful American Spoon catalog and a Web site at *www.spoon.com.*

How to Find a "Niche"

The discovery of a unique multichannel marketing selling proposition begins with two forms of research. The first entails studying the existing catalog and Web competition, while the second involves consumer research to determine the viability of unmet needs you may discover.

Multichannel Marketing Research. To begin the research process, gather as many competitive catalogs as possible, and also take a look at their companion Web sites. If they have retail stores as part of the mix, visit one or more of those brick-and-mortar outlets as well. To gather your catalogs, answer their ads in publications, call the firm to request a catalog, or ask for one through the company's Web site. You can get an overview of what catalogs are available at *www.catalogs.com.* Also take a look at *www.catalogcity.com*, which offers access to international catalogs as well as thousands based in the United States. Don't stop with a handful of catalogs: in general categories such as women's clothing or food, you should end up with several shopping bags full.

Next, identify the creative team that will be working on developing the catalog positioning. This team might consist of a marketing person, a top-notch copywriter, and an equally experienced graphic designer. Each member of the creative team should be allowed the time necessary to leaf through/surf through all the competitive catalogs and Web sites for a general impression of the existing market. Then each member may begin conceptualizing in his or her own area. For instance, the marketing person might create a matrix of some of the best and most sharply defined companies in the product category.

Placing orders with a number of these firms is also a good idea, so that their response times and quality of customer service can be noted on the matrix. Exhibit 12.1 shows how a portion of such a matrix for the women's clothing category might look. While the matrix is under construction, the copywriter and art director can pull examples of distinctive layout, copy, photography, typeface selection, and other items of interest from the catalogs, Web sites and retail stores they are studying.

By sharing what they have found, all members of the creative team begin the process of narrowing down their options, considering the competitive environment and the capabilities of the firm that will publish the catalog. For example, suppose that a leading textiles firm has determined that it wishes to enter the field with a catalog of women's clothing. This textile company can make most any type of clothing: trendy, classic, inexpensive, or more finely crafted and costly. They have no facilities to make undergarments, shoes, purses, or other accessories. Thus the creative team will be looking for an area of unmet need that can be fulfilled with a catalog that is anchored by women's clothing products. These are the items that can be sold at attractive margins, since they will be manufactured by the textile firm with no middleman to cut into profits.

Upon completion of their catalog research, the creative team might agree upon three, four, or even ten possible areas of unmet need in the women's clothing realm. They then begin to shape these general ideas into catalog concepts including a working title, merchandising mix, price range, layout and copy concept, and extra factors such as specialized customer service or Web site features. In rough form, these catalog concepts might appear as shown in Exhibit 12.2.

Exhibit 12.1. Catalog Research Matrix

CATALOG NAME	MERCHANDISE MIX	COPY/ART	FULFILLMENT "LOOK"
J. Crew	Close-cropped, trendy clothing for young, fashion-conscious women. Reasonable prices.	Plain back-. grounds; few settings, locations, or props. Simple copy set in serif type.	Ordered online 7/15; arrived UPS 7/21. One backorder. No payment due until October under special promotion.
Austin Reed	Tailored, business-like clothing for working executives or "ladies who lunch." Mid-range prices.	Liberal use of elegant settings; models from young to mature; simple, descriptive copy.	Phone order 7/15. They called 7/16 to verify size; order arrived 7/18 via Second Day Air.
Chico's	Easy-fitting clothing with lots of shiny fabrics, bright colors, tweeds, textures. More casual than Austin Reed.	Cover sets the tone for exotic locales inside; spreads echo that look with models to appeal to middle-aged women's market	Faxed order 7/15. Received a card by mail 7/21 stating item is back-ordered to 9/1. Called to cancel 7/22.

Consumer Research. After the creative team and the prospective catalog firm come to an initial agreement on some unmet needs it may wish to fill, it is essential to do some groundwork aimed at determining the feasibility, size, and reachability of each prospective "niche." List and space advertising brokers can be of great help at this stage, assuming that your firm or agency has sufficient clout to command their work on a speculative basis. If not, your own careful research with the SRDS Web sites for consumer lists and magazines may suffice. Look for lists of proven mail order and e-mail buyers who would be likely prospects for each "niche" you have identified. Can you reach successful career women via list rentals? How about young mothers? Sportswomen? Women who travel? How large is the universe of likely lists in each category you are considering?

Look for space advertising opportunities that will put you in touch with each target market you are considering. Are these magazines known as good direct response books? How large are their circulations? Next, you need to determine whether the rough creative concepts you have developed have sufficient appeal in the marketplace. Demographic and psychographic research from secondary sources—the work of Faith Popcorn (*www.faithpopcorn.com*) for instance—can help identify trends. An example: a trend toward mothers leaving the work force to stay home and raise their children might be a positive indicator for the "Mom's Wear" catalog concept.

Focus group research can provide consumer reaction to your rough ideas and may well help you eliminate some and add depth to others. You might also consider testing the catalog concept in space and Web advertising—perhaps with a representative product offering that you can fulfill. If you choose to "dry test" the catalog concept, do not ask for money. Make it a free catalog offer. Then all

Exhibit 12.2. Catalog Concepts

Unmet Need in the Women's Clothing Catalog Realm—Clothes for career women who want to go right from the office to evening galas or casual events.

Rough Creative Concept—"DAY FOR NIGHT"

A catalog of outfits that can be worn as serious career clothes and then transformed into evening or casual wear. For instance: a black wool dress has turn-back cuffs and collar that can open to reveal black sequins and a low V-neckline. Or with the change of a belt from snakeskin to hand-tooled leather, and the change of a scarf from silk to challis, a tan gabardine skirt and beige cotton blouse goes from work to a casual sporting event in perfect style. Price range would be from $175 to $350 per outfit—for the successful career woman. Layout would be lavish with thick paper stock and copy and photography that amplify the outfits' versatility. Copy would include word-pictures describing the active lifestyle buyers have or would like to achieve.

Unmet Need in the Women's Clothing Catalog Realm—Fashionable yet casual and comfortable clothes for a mother to wear while taking care of her house and children. Something more imaginative than jeans and a sweatshirt, yet affordable, stain-resistant, and washable.

Rough Creative Concept—"MOM'S WEAR"

A catalog of unique washable clothing with elastic waists and flattering silhouettes—something Mom won't see others wearing in her town. A change from the same old jeans, these clothes might include form-fitting yet comfortable track suits, easy-to-wear casual dresses, and cropped pants with interesting styling touches. Tops will feature handsome detailing, yet be quick to recover from spilled toddler food, muddy hands, and other disasters. Price range would stay at $100 per outfit or less so that they are not out of reach for middle-income families. Layout will be done in primary colors with slice-of-life photos of Mom's busy day, surrounded by adoring kids. Some photos will show a working Mom who does a quick change into her "Mom's Wear" upon arriving home.

---

you owe responders is an explanation—either that the catalog will be published on x-date and you will send them a copy, or to apologize for the fact that it will not be published after all.

"Niches" Based on Factors Other Than Merchandise. Your challenge as the creator of a new multichannel marketing concept is to offer the consumer a range of related products that he or she does not perceive to be as readily, attractively, or conveniently available from any other source. You may achieve this on the basis of any number of attributes beyond product positioning. For instance:

- *Better selection*—Most consumers know that they can purchase cotton turtleneck tops at a local shopping center. But can they be assured that the colors and sizes they want are available no matter what the season? If you offer reasonably priced cotton turtlenecks in 25 different colors and 20 sizes, and keep them in stock for immediate delivery, your catalog/Web site may be perceived as having a "better selection."
- *Finer quality*—The consumer who buys a jacket off the rack in a midline department store is unlikely to hear about its construction and long-wearing qualities from the clerk. But if you can explain these attributes in copy—and solicit online testimonials and "star ratings" from satisfied customers who took the jackets on round-the-world trips—you may well win the customer's admiration as a source with "finer quality."

- *More affordable price*—Once again, perception is the key. It may be that a local retailer is more affordable than you are, but if the consumer perceives your product as a value, you may win the sale anyway. You can enhance the value of your product by making it easy for the consumer to obtain it: i.e., toll-free numbers, Web site with a simple interface such as Amazon's 1-Click ordering, quick turn-around, returns with no questions asked, etc.
- *Appealing presentation*—The products themselves may not be unique, but if your presentation makes them fun to buy, you may win the sale. Some catalogs and Web sites win a loyal following with homespun copy and cozy graphics. Others gain the "snob appeal" sale with slick presentation on thick paper stock, elegant gift boxes, and other touches of class.

Creating and Promoting the Catalog and Web Site

Through the multi-faceted research process described above, your creative group and the firm behind your prospective catalog and Web site may well be able to define a specific, reachable, and sizable target market. Next the creative group should join forces with merchandisers and catalog operations experts to further develop the concept. A continuous working dialogue among all of these people will help ensure that your sharply defined creative concept shines through in the merchandise, layout, copy, and even the operations of the catalog firm. Specifically, however, the direct and interactive marketing creative team is now charged with defining and developing the copy and layout of the fledgling catalog and any ads, e-mails, and other promotions that will introduce it. They may also become involved with pagination (deciding which merchandise goes on which pages—and how many pages there will be) and space allocation (which products, if any, will dominate a given page or spread). A similar investment of effort will go into the Web site presentation, including a protocol for what additional products will be "served up" to site visitors when they look at each product being offered. For example, this could be done on the basis of "this goes well with the product you've chosen," or "people who bought this item also bought these other items."

How to Do Pagination in a Print Catalog—the Hot Selling Spots

As you plan and design your print catalog, consider the best use of the prime selling spaces in your book. First is the *front cover*. Although this can be a prime selling space, many catalog marketers opt to use this first page as a "theme setter." They may show a group of merchandise items that are available for sale inside the catalog, a scene that characterizes the company and its goods, or a seasonal vignette. In any case, make sure that products shown on the front cover are readily identifiable for buying purposes. Example: a line that says "see page 5 for details on cover products."

The *back cover* is the second hot spot. It should in most cases be used for selling products with a high sales potential. Be careful that the products you choose for the back cover also characterize what's inside the catalog. If they are too different from the mainstream of merchandise in your book, prospective buyers may never make it past the front and back covers.

The *inside front cover spread* and the spread after that are next in the prime territory race, along with the *center spread* and the *inside back cover*. The *spread near the order form—if you still provide a print order form—(some catalogs no longer do so)* also carries high potential. And if you still provide a print order form, don't underestimate the power of the *order form* itself for selling merchandise, especially the add-on or impulse variety. Talk with your printer about bind-in order form designs that give you some extra selling space at an affordable cost.

For these inside hot spots, you will want to choose merchandise with excellent margins and/or top sales potential. But it is also important to consider developing a theme for each spread or section. The copywriter and designer can work together with merchandising people to find pieces that work well together. For example:

- A spread of gift suggestions with all items priced at $25 or less.
- A tabletop spread with dinnerware, glassware, linens, and accessories all in blue, yellow, and white.
- A clothing spread featuring items that work together to create a weekend wardrobe.
- A spread of items especially for children in a general giftware catalog.
- A spread of items that can be personalized.
- A spread of decorative and/or wearable items on a holiday theme such as Halloween, Thanksgiving, or Hanukkah.

How to Allocate Space for Each Product in a Print Catalog

Successful catalog firms have widely varied views on this subject. Lands' End frequently devotes a cover and inside front spread—or even more space—to one staple item like its turtleneck tops or short-sleeved pullover shirts. By contrast, many food catalogs squeeze in products with a shoe horn, just as they might appear on colorful, crowded shelves. The ultimate answer to "how much space does this product deserve?" is this: "whatever amount its sales and profit margin can support." There are exceptions to this rule, of course. Neiman-Marcus, Hammacher Schlemmer, and other upscale catalog firms may offer outlandish trips, fantasy adventures, and lavish products that require a page or more to describe—and may not sell a single unit. These products are justified because they help to create the catalog's overall aura—and because they are excellent public relations tools. At the other end of the scale, a cataloger like One Hanes Place may discover that plain white briefs sell a predictable 5,000 units whether they receive full-page treatment or a corner of a buried inside page.

In general, the most practical way to assign space is by the numbers. Use your sales history with each item to determine its relative strength. If the item or the whole catalog is new, you will need to make some decisions based on the best information you can gather. Check your competitors' space allocations for general indications. Draw upon your vendors' experience to determine the relative appeal of various products.

Consider the price point and margin of each item: for instance, it only stands to reason that a $500 home audio system has a better chance of justifying a half-page space than a $50 shower radio. If your house brand of fashionable sweater set has a three-time mark-up and a designer set sweater has only a two-time mark-up, you'd be well served to push the house sweaters with a larger space and more lengthy description. Results after your first mailing may well prove that your logical assumptions are wrong, however, and then you can make the necessary adjustments to maximize sales and profits.

You may also try out your hypotheses on your Web site with some quick product and space-allocation testing, then use the results to help shape your initial tests in print. If an item did twice as well as you projected in its first appearance, you might try allocating it more space to see if it can do even better. But test this, because some products can do perfectly fine in a small space while others only "bloom" on a half-or full-page layout.

Exhibit 12.3. Lands' End Catalog Spread

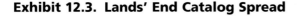

This Lands' End catalog spread illustrates several of the firm's unique strategies. First, Lands' End has devoted an entire spread to "romancing" one simple product line: Polartec 200 pullovers. Second, the firm offers a much wider range of colors and sizes than one would be likely to find in a retail store. Third, they use real people in action as models, and weave a human interest story in with their selling message.

Reprinted with permission of Lands' End, Inc.

The Print Catalog Layout and Copy Concept

While the final page line-up is in the works, the copywriter and graphic designer can be working to develop the print catalog's appearance and tone. This stage requires numerous decisions. These include:

- *Catalog size and number of pages.* Consult with merchandisers for number of products—a very general average is four to eight products per page. Check with printers to determine cost-efficient formats in the general size range you are considering: subtracting just 1/8" in size can sometimes save many thousands of dollars. Postal rates also may vary based on catalog size.
- *Paper stock.* Heavier, coated stocks bespeak an upscale offering. The thinner, grayer, and less shiny stocks are less costly and may actually be preferable if you are trying to develop a catalog that looks approachable and affordable. Recycled paper is considered a must by some target market groups today: keep this in mind when making your paper decision. Once again, consult with printers or paper salespeople for ideas on ways to save money and project the image you seek.

- *Illustrations/photography.* Some catalog firms prefer illustrations to photography. Their reasons may include saving money, developing a recognizable style, creating a "down-home" look, or carrying out a theme. Other firms swear by in-studio photography with simple backgrounds that make the product the star. Others try to use existing art from vendors to save money—but this can become costly when artwork from many sources has to be pieced together at the production stage to achieve a unified appearance. Still others use more elaborate studio photography or even location shoots in exotic locales. To make the choice for a given catalog, consider budget, the book's current or targeted image, time constraints, and product category.
- *Layout style.* Choices abound in this area as well. Catalog layouts run the gamut from the simple "rectangular picture with square copy block beside or below" layouts of a Miles Kimball book to the magazine-style looks of the Lands' End catalogs, which often feature testimonials from satisfied customers who may model the items they like best from Lands' End. Then there are the decorating books like Horchow Home that place groups of items in attractive room settings, versus Home Decorators Collection, which offers similar merchandise shown individually in simple "product-only" shots. Studying catalogs, magazines, and everything from travel posters to retail store windows may provide inspiration for layouts. Remember in all your work: the products are the stars. They should never be overpowered by "art for art's sake."
- *Copy style.* Once again, there is no clear road to success. Catalogs like L.L. Bean prosper with long, detailed copy while many other books get by with minimal description and very little copy "personality." Will you have separate copy for each item, or use common-copy lead-ins followed by individual descriptions? Will spreads or pages have headings and/or subheads? Will individual copy blocks have boldface lead-ins? Will each copy block contain a message of urgency or call to action, or will the selling message be more understated? Once again, the answers to these and other copy questions can be developed after studying catalogs, space ads, and other writing specimens you wish to emulate. In evaluating alternatives, ask yourself, "which method contributes most to the selling message of this catalog?" Another important point: make sure that products and the copy that describes them are clearly keyed to each other so that prospective buyers have no trouble matching picture with words.
- *Magalogs and advertorials.* Most catalog experts agree that the "magalog" concept seldom works in its purest form: a catalog that appears much like a magazine and just happens to sell products. But well-placed "advertorials"—short blurbs that enhance product appeal or establish the catalog's credibility in the marketplace—can prove well worth the space they require. Subjects of "advertorials" range from menus, party plans, and recipes in food and tabletop catalogs to health tips in books aimed at the needs of the over-50 consumer. Some catalogs establish a "voice" who serves as expert spokesperson.
- *Type style and type size.* In general, serif typefaces are easier to read in copy blocks. Their tiny "tails" and "fillips" are easier on the eyes than sans serif faces that are perfectly plain. Typefaces can do a great deal to reinforce the theme and

Exhibit 12.4. J. Peterman Illustration

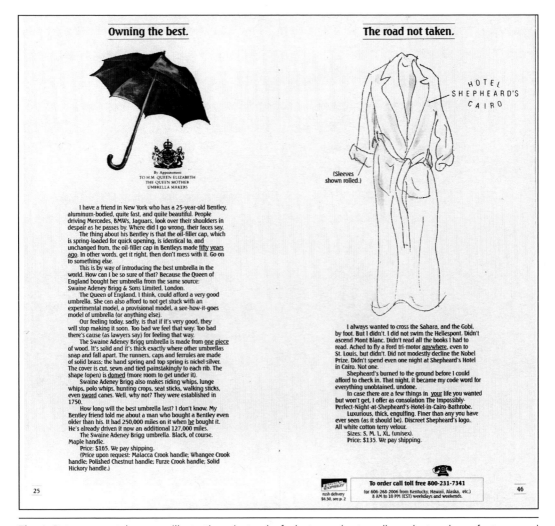

The J. Peterman catalog uses illustrations instead of photographs to sell products whose features and benefits are enlivened by a very readable, narrative copy style.

Reprinted with permission of the J. Peterman Company.

tone of a catalog: nostalgic and warm, contemporary, European or Far Eastern, classic or avante garde. Save exotic typefaces for headings and choose a more recognizable, easy-to-read face for the main copy blocks. Type smaller than 8-point size is nearly impossible for general audiences to read comfortably. If your audience includes children, or if you are appealing to people over 50, try for type no smaller than 10-point to enhance readability.

Exhibit 12.5. Williams-Sonoma

COOK'S PRIMER

How to Assemble a Cheese Tray

A cheese tray is a beautiful and delicious addition to an hors d'oeuvre selection or buffet. Why not offer a themed tasting, such as French or farmhouse cheeses, or mix favorites like Brie with less familiar cheeses, such as Manchego? Select three to six cheeses, depending upon the number of guests. Vary the flavors, textures and shapes. Cheeses are generally categorized by texture: fresh, soft-ripened, semi-soft, semi-firm and hard. Flavors vary depending upon the milk used and the aging process. Serve with thin slices of French bread or whole-grain crackers. Fruit adds color and complements the cheeses' flavor. Arrange cheeses and fruit on a tray lined with paper or fresh lemon leaves. Some suggestions: Chèvre, Coulommiers, Havarti and Roquefort; Chabis, Brie, Farmhouse and Stilton; Cheddar, St. Andre, Bucheron and Manchego.

Goat Cheese Collection
NEW Award-winning cheese maker Laura Chenel has been producing superb fresh and aged chèvre (goat cheese) in a small dairy in rural Sonoma Valley for 15 years. Having apprenticed with master cheese makers in France, she maintains the highest French standards. We offer a sampling of five of her finest cheeses: two 5-oz. logs of fresh, mild Chabis (a plain and an herb-coated); a 3-oz. aged Crottin; a 9-oz. aged Taupinière; and a 4.5-oz. jar of Cabecou marinated in herbal olive oil. Serving suggestions included. *The set* #67-1092998 **$39.00** ◉ ◆◆ *Catalog only*

Cheese Trays
In the fromageries of France, cheeses are displayed on rustic woven trays like these. Made in China of peeled willow. Large: 16˚ diam. Small: 14˚ diam. *Set of two*, one of each. #67-975417 **$12.00** ◉ *Catalog only*

Apilco Autumn Ramekins and Plates
NEW Nut-and-leaf designs enliven these classic French porcelain ramekins made by Apilco. Use them for individual soufflés, mousses and crème brûlées or to keep hors d'oeuvres near each guest. Snacks such as olives dressed with olive oil, orange zest and thyme suit these dishes well. Cocktail plates pair beautifully with the ramekins. Dishwasher, microwave and oven safe. *Sets of six* ◉
Autumn Ramekins, 6-oz. cap., 3½˚ diam. #67-1099548 **$49.00** *Catalog only*
Autumn Cocktail Plates, 6¼˚ diam. #67-1085539 **$69.00** *Catalog only*
White Ramekins #67-835264 Reg. $30.00 **Special $21.00**
White Cocktail Plates #67-1099555 Reg.$36.00 **Special $24.00**

Cheese Leaves
NEW These photographic replicas of maple leaves at their most brilliant might even fool Mother Nature. Scatter them on a cheese tray or across a buffet table for seasonal color. 7½˚ wide. *Set of 40*, 20 red and 20 yellow. #67-1058312 **$14.00** ◉

Williams-Sonoma added authority and appeal to its catalog with short Cook's Primer columns like the one on this page, "How to Assemble a Cheese Tray." The column is surrounded by related merchandise, including a goat cheese collection, trays and paper leaves for the display of cheese, and ramekins and cocktail plates.

Reprinted with permission of Williams-Sonoma, Inc.

Producing the Print Catalog

Once the page line-up and the style for the layout and copy have been approved, you may create the final, comprehensive layout. As the catalog design shapes up, make sure that one of your foremost goals is to make the catalog appealing and easy to use. Spreads should flow together in a pleasing whole, and such essentials as the order form (if you opt to include one), your return address, your Web address, and your toll-free number should be easy to find. Indeed, many catalogs today wisely display the Web address and toll-free number on every spread.

The copy should expound on the product features and their related benefits. Diagrams, close-up shots, testimonials, and product-in-use ideas will all help "activate" your catalog and make your products seem real and desirable to the prospect.

When direct mail packages—consisting of letter, brochure, order form, etc.—are developed, the copy often is created before the layout. But in most cases, catalog copy is written to fit a completed layout, since space is often at a premium. This does not mean that the copywriter should not have input on copy space; on the contrary, it is best if the writer works directly with the graphic designer to determine which products require more copy and which can be sold effectively with less.

Time was, most catalog graphic designers would "spec" copy as a matter of course—telling their writers exactly how many characters would fit a space—or at least providing the number of lines per inch and the number of characters per line or pica. In many cases today it seems that copywriters must assert themselves to obtain this information. But it is essential that they do so. Good catalog copywriters perfect the skill of writing to the space allowed. Overwriting causes costly, time-wasting rewriting and editing. With sophisticated graphic design software in common use today, the partnership between designer and copywriter is often easier to foster, since copy can be dropped right into the layout with just a few mouse clicks—and manipulated quickly and easily.

Once the layout is finalized, photography may well be taking place at the same time copy is being written. Copywriters should resist the temptation to write strictly from product description sheets or inferior product shots provided by vendors. They should insist on visiting the photography site or merchandisers' offices and spend time getting to know the products: trying on clothes, fondling fabrics, taste-testing foods, using electronic items, listening to music systems, and finding out if the new Flat Screen TV/DVD player combination is truly easy to use.

This personal experience with the product is all the more important when a catalog contains hundreds of items that are extremely similar. Witness the experience of top marketing consultant Judy Finerty when she was the copywriter for the Nestle chocolate catalog. Judy would be hard-pressed to describe the difference between a semi-sweet Swiss and a semi-sweet French chocolate unless she had tasted them both, one right after the other!

Once photography and copy are complete, and final art has been created, it is time to proofread and evaluate your work before it goes to the printer. When looking over your creative product, remember the principle of PPIPU: "perfectly plain if previously understood." Often you may become so close to a product and its presentation that you fail to notice essential missing visual or written elements—things a customer needs to know. To avoid this, have unbiased outsiders look over your photos and copy and ask them if anything seems confusing or would turn them off as prospective buyers.

In addition to proofing for typographical errors, make sure your merchandising staff and operations people have a chance for a final "once over." Have them sign off on item numbers, pricing, size ranges, color options, and special offers. Make sure that such disclaimers as "battery not included" are made where necessary. Take time to match key letters with photographs one last time:

it's amazing how many catalogs have confusing errors where copy "H" actually describes the item keyed "L."

Once you complete your paper order form, have a number of people—both catalog "regulars" and people who seldom shop by mail—attempt to fill it out and tell you where the glitches are. The order form does not have to be strictly a learn-by-doing proposition: check the competition and some of the more established direct mail marketers to see how they handle such essentials as fax ordering, postage and handling, bill to/ship to arrangements, gift wrapping and enclosure cards, personalization, charge and credit options, etc. If you are considering dropping your paper order form as more and more customers use the phone or buy online, you will be wise to test mailing catalogs with and without the order form to make sure you don't lose valuable orders from customers who still prefer to mail in their responses.

Promoting the Print Catalog

If your firm already has a database of direct response buyers, building the new business may be achieved mainly by testing the most likely database segments to find the best customers for your new catalog. In addition, you may well do some outside list prospecting and advertising in publications, online and through other means. If you are starting the catalog from scratch with no house list or database, a realistic investment plan for two or more years of prospecting "in the red" is reasonable today even for the strongest new venture.

Depending upon your financial backing and objectives, you may create magazine ads for mail order or catalog request sections as small as 1/12 page. Established firms such as Lands' End may invest in full-page ads or even double-page spreads seeking catalog prospects, but few new catalog ventures can afford such a lavish presentation.

Other ways to prospect for new catalog customers include affiliate deals or banners online, sponsored links on search engines, customer referrals, package inserts, card decks, supermarket take-ones, and public relations write-ups. Prospecting ads and flyers should carry the same look and tone as the catalog itself, and use every word to overcome inertia and gain response.

Creative Tips for the Online Catalog

While some firms use the same copy that appears in their print catalogs for their digital promotions, the majority of catalog marketers use the power of the Web to create unique presentations online. Here are some examples.

- **Home Page**—Catalog marketers tend to use their home pages to present the latest news about sales and special offers, and/or to showcase seasonal or hot-selling products. The home page should also feature both a search box and a pull-down menu of options for product offerings. Multichannel marketers often offer a "quick shopping" feature that allows customers to input the stock number of an item they've seen in the print catalog. Typically there is also a click-through for prospects to order a print catalog to be delivered to them by mail. Firms with retail stores will be wise to offer a store locator on the home page as well.
- **Relevant Pop-ups**—While many consumers claim that they hate pop-ups, and many others disable the pop-up function on their browsers, the key to a successful pop-up is relevance. Catalog site visitors may be happy to be greeted with a

Exhibit 12.6. Aerosoles

Aerosoles presents its print catalog online with some helpful enhancements. Readers simply click the lower right corner of the right-hand page to turn to the next spread. To find out more about a given product, readers click through to a page with additional facts and pictures.

Screen capture from *www.aerosoles.com*.

pop-up offering free shipping, an invitation to sign up for a sweepstakes, a special discount or other limited-time offer.

- **Print Catalog Online**—Many firms place a digital version of their current print catalog(s) on the Web site with click-throughs to more information about each product. It's easy to turn to the next spread in the catalog with a mouse click in the lower right-hand corner of the current page.
- **Product Presentation**—Instead of the themed spreads of merchandise that are typical of print catalogs, the online catalog marketer most often presents search results in a series of simple, uniform boxes. The customer then can click through to any item of special interest for a larger picture and more information.
- **Copy Style**—Online catalog copy often is presented in bullet-point form rather than paragraphs of narrative material.
- **Visual Presentation**—Print catalogs typically present only a single image of each product—sometimes with insets or detail shots. The Web offers the opportunity to show multiple images of each item, to zoom in or out, and to change the product's color with a quick mouse click. For example, shoe marketers may

Exhibit 12.7. Coldwater Creek

Coldwater Creek integrates customer reviews with many of its online product presentationas, as shown in this illustration.

Screen capture from *www.coldwatercreek.com*.

Exhibit 12.8. Pottery Barn

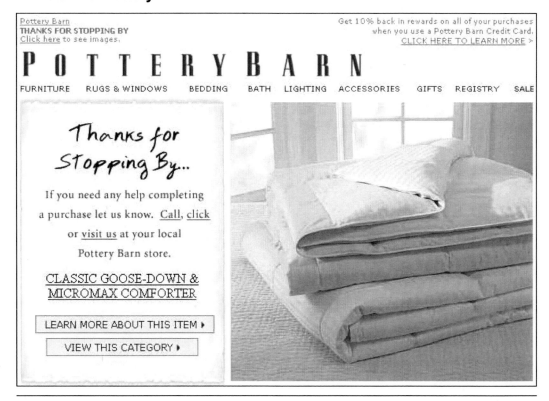

Pottery Barn recognizes active customers who visit its Web site but do not buy, and sends them e-mails like this one, offering "thanks for stopping by," and various methods of help to complete a purchase.

Reprinted from an e-mail received from Pottery Barn.

show a single product from the top, bottom, side, back and front. Ross-Simons presents product videos that feature individual jewelry items both on a plain suede stand and worn by a model.

- **Suggestive Selling**—Web marketers can use the power of suggestive selling to present additional items when a customer clicks on a product of special interest. As mentioned earlier in the chapter, these might be items that coordinate with the initial product, or items that fall under the category of "people who bought this item most often bought these items." An online marketer might even offer a discount for the combined items if bought at the same time. "Recently viewed" items might also appear at the bottom of the page or some other easy-to-see location.

- **Product Reviews**—Invite customers to rate your products and discuss their experience with the products, and then show these reviews along with the display of each product online. Over time, you'll be able to use these reviews to develop sections of "most popular" or "five star" products. Exhibit 12.7 shows an example of how Coldwater Creek integrates product reviews with product presentation.

- **Customer Service Options**—The interactive nature of the Web allows for help functions such as chat or instant messaging, voice over Internet protocol (VoIP) phone conversations, or even video conferencing. Many Web sites offer a pop-up when the customer makes a move to log off, asking if the marketer can be of help and/or reminding the customer that there are unpurchased items in their shopping cart. Some marketers even e-mail customers who leave items in the shopping cart to offer assistance or even a discount for a prompt return to purchase.

Multichannel Marketing Enhancements

There are a number of ways to amplify the effectiveness of an established catalog. Here are some that have proven profit potential.

Find Ways to Boost Average Order Size

If your average order size is $40, you are likely to be a great deal more profitable if you can boost that average order to $50, $60, or more. So why not try some promotional enhancements designed to produce add-on sales and profits? Ideas might include:

- Gift certificates that are good for x-dollars off, but only on purchases of x-dollars or more.
- Clubs for frequent buyers such as the Neiman-Marcus "In Circle®." Buyers gain points for each Neiman-Marcus charge card purchase and may store them up over time to receive gifts ranging from in-store discounts to exotic trips around the world.
- Free gift with purchase. If you are trying to boost average order size above $50 for example, offer a free item of general appeal for orders over $50. Add on more free gifts at the $100 or $150 level as well.
- Discount for volume orders. Offer ten percent off for orders over $100, for example.
- Look for order starters and impulse add-on items. Boost average order size with an appealing extra: three monogrammed golf balls for $10 in a sporting goods catalog, perhaps, or a set of potholders and mitts for $9.99 in a kitchen and tabletop book.
- Have telephone sales representatives offer callers a few daily specials after their original orders are complete. Do the same online on the customer's shopping cart screen. Daily specials may be of general appeal, or they may be keyed to the buyer's interest based on past or current purchases. Online you can make "side suggestions" for additional, related purchases every time a prospect clicks on a product.

Use Catalog Wraps for Promotions and Sale Prices

The life of an expensive color catalog can be extended by adding various four-page outer "wraps." Such a wrap might introduce a new seasonal theme, offer special values or sale prices, promote certain merchandise, or otherwise freshen and focus the mailing. This is an inexpensive way to make your catalog look new while adding a promotional flair.

Change Covers and Signatures for Seasonal Themes

To cut down on production costs yet keep your print catalog fresh through repeated re-mailings to hot buyers, rearrange the signatures (sets of pages) to put seasonal items up front for each mailing. For a Labor Day mailing, a Halloween cover might be followed by Halloween and Thanksgiving merchandise, with general and Christmas items following. For a re-mail in mid-October, you might try a catalog wrap offering Halloween and Thanksgiving items on sale, followed by a full-color Christmas cover and a rearrangement of pages so that Christmas merchandise is up front.

Consider Using a Letter

Time was, many catalogs included a letter from the company president on the inside front cover. Nowadays, few firms seem willing to give up this prime space for that theme-setting letter. In recent years, many of these messages have appeared next to the order form. Another idea: add a letter to a catalog wrap, or place a separate letter on top of the catalog and shrink-wrap the two together for mailing.

Ask for Referrals

Use otherwise wasted space on the order form or back of the Business Reply Envelope to ask customers for names and addresses of friends who might enjoy your catalog. A standard wording is as follows:

> Do you have a friend who might enjoy the (Name of Catalog) catalog? Please fill in name(s) and address(es) below.
> Follow this with no more than three blanks for names and addresses. The first few referrals are usually the best.

Use Postcards, Self-Mailers and E-mail to Supplement Catalog Mailings

A number of multichannel marketers have discovered the power of mailing timely postcards to their best buyers. For example, a postcard might offer selected buyers 15 percent off all purchases of $50 or more on the most recently mailed catalog up until a certain date. In cooperation with a vendor, catalog companies can increase sales between major catalog drops by sending out a self-mailer offering one particularly appealing high-ticket item such as a deluxe vacuum cleaner. For customers who have opted in to e-mail, offering similar price deals or product focused-messages can often increase return on investment.

How Top Multichannel Marketing Creative People Stay Fresh

As mentioned earlier in this chapter, the most stimulating part of the multichannel marketing creative person's job is positioning. The workaday job of laying out endless print or Web pages of products and writing tightly controlled blocks of formula copy can become deadly dull unless writers and graphic designers keep themselves stimulated and fresh. Here are some pointers on how to do so.

Keep an Eagle Eye on the Competition

Multichannel creative people should become frequent catalog and Web shoppers to ensure that they receive large numbers of catalogs and e-mails from many product categories. Don't attempt to analyze each catalog the minute it hits your mailbox. Rather, take time once a week or so to sit down with your pile of catalogs and leaf through them just as a consumer would. Check out the catalog's Web site and see how its presentation harmonizes with—or differs from—what you are seeing in print. If something strikes you as particularly unique or interesting, put that catalog in an active file for immediate inspiration. Most catalogs should be kept for future reference: it's extremely helpful to have a backlog of catalogs filed by product category to make the research job easier when a new catalog project comes along. To supplement this activity, surf the Web regularly using such resources as *www.catalogs.com* to see the whole range of catalogs available.

Pay Attention When Ordering from Catalogs and Online

See how much you can learn from the experience of ordering and receiving merchandise via catalog. If you order by mail, which order forms seem easiest to use? Which method of collecting money for shipping and handling seems to make the most sense? Do the firms you order from let you know how soon products will be shipped? Do they live up to those promises? If you order by phone, how knowledgeable does the telephone salesperson seem? How pleasant? How efficient? How empowered to do something special for you to make the sale or improve the relationship? How do various firms handle "specials of the day" by phone? Are there any other creative enhancements you could add to your catalog based on what you hear when ordering over the phone? If you order online, how easy is the Web site's interface? Can you locate an item using the print catalog style number, or is it hit-or-miss? Are all print catalog items available online? How does the online buying experience compare to the other methods of purchasing?

Stay in Touch with the Products

It's tempting to design and write catalogs based on specification sheets alone—after all, you can complete the job much faster that way. But there are features and benefits that can only be discovered when you touch and use the products for yourself. If a good catalog creative person is writing a spread on bath mats, you can bet his or her office is carpeted two or three mats deep with different colors, thicknesses, and shapes. Clothing writers gain inspiration by wearing samples so they can better describe soft fabrics and comfortable fit. The hands-on concept is even more important where high-tech items are concerned: you have to understand the product's attributes in use to write about it effectively.

Make Friends with the Merchandisers

If you're stumped for inspiration, talk with the merchandising people who chose these items for the catalog. Ask them what makes this watch or clock or chenille robe better than all the other ones he or she might have chosen. Better yet, tag along when the merchandiser goes on a buying trip or to a trade show. There you'll have the benefit of sales pitches from the vendors as well.

Think Like a Consumer

For every single item, imagine the target market and figure out what a member of that target audience would want to see and learn regarding this product. If possible, show the products to target market members and get their reactions. What do they like and dislike? What questions do they have? What reservations? You can play to their positive reactions and answer their objections in copy and art.

Pay Attention to Results

The best catalog creators are anxious to know the item-by-item results of each catalog that is mailed. Figuring out why item A lost sales when shown on a pink background instead of a yellow one, or why item B doubled in sales when it was shown in a product-in-use shot, will help keep your job fresh and challenging. Take an active role in space allocation based on previous results.

Don't Remain in the "Creative Box"

It's sometimes tempting to stay in the designer's or copywriter's cubicle, treating the multichannel creative function as something akin to assembly line work at an auto plant. But the creative contribution to a good catalog and Web operation can involve much more: ideas to enhance customer service, merchandising, packaging, back-order systems and reminders, and so on. Approach these creative functions as an overall marketing challenge, and it can be much more rewarding for you—and for the catalog and Web site's bottom line.

Enhance Your Understanding: Multichannel Marketing Niches

Success in the multichannel marketing world requires that each catalog/Web site/retail store combination's creator identify and develop a unique niche. You can learn more about this by gathering many catalogs in a particular field—preferably one you know something about—and also studying their Web sites and visiting their retail stores. One way to identify some of the main competitors is to purchase several special-interest publications in that field—be it English horseback riding, home computers, or golf. Then send for all the catalogs offered in these publications. You can also preview catalogs in a specific area of interest at online sites such as *www.catalogs.com or www.catalogcity.com*, and click through to appropriate Web sites to request a catalog. Or use a search engine on the Internet and enter key words that will lead you to Web sites in your chosen product category. When the print catalogs arrive, study them to see which products and product lines seem to be constant across the category, and which are unique to just one catalog. Do the same on the catalogs' companion Web sites. Study the graphic look and copy tone of each catalog and Web site: how would you characterize each? Are their target markets the same, or different? Are their pricing structures similar? What about customer service? Does there seem to be an unfilled niche in this category? If so, how would you characterize it?

Special note: The author wishes to thank Herb Krug, President of Herbert Krug & Associates, for his generosity in sharing many of these catalog creative concepts over the years.

13

Broadcast Direct Marketing

In the late 1940s and early 1950s, pioneers in direct response television (DRTV) advertising presented their commercials in the form of 15- or 30-minute "shows." These pitches were written up in the TV listings as regular programming, just as some infomercials are today. One of the star attractions at introductory direct marketing seminars is often the showing of one of these early spots, most notably the original Vitamix commercial. Working without a script, a master salesman demonstrates this versatile product while explaining how Americans need the nutrition of fresh vegetables.

In those days the TV commercials may well have been more interesting and involving than the programs. Television was a novelty, broadcast time was affordable, and there were no restrictions on how much advertising could be shown per hour of programming. Direct response historians say that on average, that original Vitamix spot sold 500 units at $34.95 every time it ran: a king's ransom circa 1950.

Fast-forward to the present, and the reality is that most every spot still must pay its own way, just as direct mail packages, catalogs, online marketing and telemarketing campaigns do. While general agencies seek awards for their "creative" (read entertaining and/or funny) television spots, direct and interactive marketers reap most of the rewards for themselves and their clients through the more concrete and enduring measures of sales and profits.

In recent years, some of America's leading brands and companies have adopted direct response techniques for at least some of their broadcast budgets. As Rick Sangerman, Senior Vice President/Account Services at A. Eicoff in Chicago notes, "DRTV has gone mainstream now, with many Fortune 500 companies using it to save money on rates." As Sangerman's colleague at A. Eicoff, Steve Miller, notes, "Because of the way that direct response television is bought, savings can be as much as 40 percent to 60 percent off the rate card." Sangerman says that these major companies have embraced "longer-length creative, generating a database, and forcing retail movement with coupons." He calls what many large companies do "Hybrid DRTV"—taking advantage of DRTV techniques and rates while continuing to evaluate campaigns using traditional general advertising measures like reach, frequency, and cost per thousand. Because of this trend, Sangerman reports that "the classic low budget gadget business now takes a total back seat to lead generation and brand DRTV. Major agencies now include DRTV as a portion of their responses to Requests for Proposal on a regular basis—as a requirement, particularly for new product introductions." Thus there is a change afoot in DRTV, as big-budget marketers continue to enter the field and strive to combine image and brand-building with a pitch that maximizes sales or leads at the same time.

While more and more major marketers add DRTV to their marketing mixes, however, only a small fraction of direct and interactive marketing companies utilize broadcast advertising as one of their top media. Television's barriers to entry are considerable: a minimal test—including production and time buys—costs $30,000 and up when done in-house, $100,000 or more when executed by a major direct and interactive marketing agency.

Even so, there are a number of traditional direct and interactive marketers with the right products and enough financial clout to use television cost-effectively. Many insurance and pharmaceutical companies promote their products for direct sale via television—or solicit leads to be followed up by mail, phone, or personal sales call. What's more, entrepreneurs frequently use the long-form infomercial medium as a main source of sales for products and services ranging from acne cures and weight loss plans to kitchenware and self-help courses.

In addition, digital, satellite, and cable television make direct response broadcast advertising a viable option for more firms each year. Digital and satellite television transmit hundreds of special interest stations with highly targeted audiences for golf, home décor, children's products, classic movies, and much more. Cable beams superstations like WTBS in Atlanta and WGN in Chicago to viewers across the country at reasonable rates. Home shopping channels provide marketers with a low-risk way to see their products sold on television. And efforts now underway may eventually open up buying opportunities via interactive television for every American home with a cable or satellite TV hook-up.

At the same, the medium of video has gained new vitality through viewing on company Web sites and the enormous reach of YouTube. Videos offer marketers a good combination of demonstration and the ability to get a detailed story across without much reading on the prospect's part.

Radio has substantial liabilities for most marketers, including its lack of visual presentation, the limited coverage area of most stations, and the fact that many radio listeners use the medium mainly as background noise. However, direct response radio does hold considerable potential for some products and services, particularly those in the executive, business-to-business, financial, and self-help realms that can be sold via all-news stations and networks, or through syndicated radio programs that encourage listener involvement—political, financial, and self-help talk shows, for example. What's more, with long-form radio time now available on many stations, this medium's attractiveness increases for many direct marketers.

Thus with present and future prospects in mind, even creative people who have not yet had occasion to do broadcast work will want to soak up as much background knowledge as they can. This chapter provides some basics. For those who want or need to know more, check the books, blogs, and articles of top direct marketing broadcast "pros," notably those at A. Eicoff and Hawthorne Direct. The late Alvin Eicoff's *Direct Marketing Through Broadcast Media* is especially valuable for its historical perspective as well as its specific how-to advice and "firing line" examples. And just as important: take time to watch and evaluate the better direct response spots you discover on TV and radio. In this way, soaking up the techniques of the masters can be enjoyable as well as instructive.

Traditional DRTV Versus General Advertising Broadcast Spots

Selling Versus Inform/Persuade/Remind

There is one basic difference that sets all direct response advertising apart from all general advertising. Direct response TV and radio spots solicit a purchase, a request for information, or some other measurable action. Most often, however, general advertising broadcast spots are strictly image and brand builders—designed to inform, persuade, or remind the consumer, but stopping short of asking for the order. A direct response spot always includes a call to specific action, asking the prospect to respond by mail or phone, or inviting them to visit a Web site or landing page. In the past, this distinction often led to the creation of direct response spots that ignored image building—even presented concepts, themes, and looks that were in direct contrast to the same firm's general advertising. Now that Integrated Marketing Communication concepts have reached wide acceptance and understanding, this is much less likely to happen. In fact, as illustrated by Rick Sangerman's comments, a significant percentage of advertisers today look at their direct response commercials as brand-building tools as well as response-generating vehicles. For best results, a direct response spot presents the same look and tone as the firm's general advertising efforts while moving along the continuum from awareness to interest to desire to *action*.

Length

A direct response spot must convince the prospect to act, so in most cases it requires more time than an image or brand-building spot. While the length of general ads on TV and radio has shrunk over the years from 60 seconds to 30, 20, 15, or even 10 seconds apiece, the majority of direct response spots still require 60 to 120 seconds to get their message across and close the sale. Today's high costs and program formats make two minutes the longest feasible commercial length with the exception of infomercials, where the advertiser purchases a full half-hour of time at "off hours" on network affiliates or cable networks.

Production Values

In the early days of direct response television, most commercials resembled an in-home version of the carnival pitchman doing his sales presentation from behind a simple table or desk. For decades, most direct response spots were made according to a few predictable formulas because they had been proven to work—and they were inexpensive and risk-free.

Cooking utensils were presented using hard-sell kitchen counter demonstrations. Ads for music collections featured "sound bites" of the various tunes combined with an on-screen "roll" that showed the name of every song. Insurance companies invited inquiries by showcasing a celebrity spokesman perched in a book-lined office.

Current research shows that the predictable forms and relatively low production values of direct response commercials hurt their credibility with an important segment of the potential audience. What's more, these simple formats did little to further the overall images of brands developed through general advertising efforts. And thus, in order to expand the customer base and add some positive image-building to their direct response ventures, many firms have upgraded the quality of their TV productions in recent years.

It is important, however, to differentiate between higher quality production and wholesale adoption of general advertising techniques. Direct response advertisers must remember to focus squarely on the product—to make the product the star. They must guard against using the quick cuts, cluttered backgrounds, dominating music, and flashy techniques that general advertisers consider their stock in trade. These "borrowed attention" devices may be all well and good for image advertisers, but they muddy the waters when a spot is expected to complete a sale in two minutes or less.

What to Sell in Traditional Direct Response TV Spots

Products That Shine in Demonstration

Television's prime benefit is that it provides an ideal medium for demonstration. Remember the classic Vegamatic commercials that showed how fruits and vegetables could be sliced, diced, and chopped, all in the wink of an eye? A more current example of demonstration is the numerous Proactiv ads for acne prevention and cure, demonstrating how celebrities and "regular people" alike go from spotted to clear using this solution. If your product comes alive when shown in use, or if the results of using the product can be actively demonstrated, television may well be a viable medium for you to explore.

Products with Wide Appeal

Most television advertising time is sold to mass marketers of toothpaste, laundry detergent, fast food, soft drinks, and other products that almost everyone needs or wants. Kitchen-related products appeal to a wide range of people, as do telephone services, insurance offers, Christmas music, online study courses, and diet plans. A look at the major advertisers using DRTV in Exhibit 13.1 shows marketers selling other near-universal products like flowers, electronics, travel services, packaged goods, hair care products, cars, and toys. If you intend to advertise on the general TV networks, make sure your product is of near-universal interest or audience waste will ensure your efforts are

Exhibit 13.1. Major Advertisers Using Direct Response Television

Major Advertisers Using Direct Response Television (provided by Rick Sangerman, A. Eicoff, Chicago)

- 1-800-Flowers
- America Online
- American Airlines
- American Express Travel
- Apple
- AT&T
- Bank of America
- Bell Atlantic
- Black and Decker
- Braun
- Bristol Myers-Squibb
- Buick
- Carnival Cruise Lines
- Century 21
- Clearwire
- Club Med
- Coca Cola
- ConAgra Foods, Inc.
- Dayton Hudson
- Direct TV

- Discover Card
- Disney
- DuPont
- Eastman Kodak
- Eli Lilly
- Epson Printers
- Estee Lauder
- Fidelity
- Fisher Price
- Ford
- Fuji
- GMC
- GM (Saturn)
- GTE
- HBO
- Helene Curtis
- Hoover
- Hyatt
- Land Rover
- Lexus

- McDonalds
- MCI
- Mercedes
- MGM/UA
- Microsoft
- Miramax
- New York Life
- Nikon
- Nissan
- Norelco
- Novartis
- Panasonic
- Pepsi
- Philips Electronics
- Porsche
- Princess Cruises
- Procter & Gamble
- Redken
- Revlon
- Reynolds
- Slim Fast

- Sony
- State Farm
- Target
- Taylor Made
- TD Ameritrade
- Texaco
- Time Life
- Toyota
- Toys-R-US
- Troybuilt
- Turtle Wax
- Upjohn
- US Healthcare
- US Army
- US Navy
- Volkswagon
- Volvo
- Walmart
- Weight Watchers

Top brands and companies have discovered the power of direct response television, as evidenced by this list of major advertisers now using the medium.

Reprinted with permission of A. Eicoff, Chicago.

not cost- effective. On the other hand, if your product is of interest to the viewers of narrow-niche cable TV channels aimed at golfers, history buffs, fashionistas, or other special-interest groups, you may well be able to succeed with DRTV on a more segmented basis.

Unique Products Not Available in This Form at Retail

Either the product or the way it is offered should be perceived as different from what the customer can get at the local department store, discount chain, or hardware store. The difference can be in price, add-ons, premiums, assortment, or other aspects the marketer can manipulate, or it can be a twist in the product itself. Often this twist can be achieved through strong demonstration. A jar of silver polish doesn't look like much sitting on the retail shelf, but when a TV spot shows how it cleans up old flatware in seconds, the TV-advertised product becomes much more attractive than the one sold at retail.

Products Appealing to Reachable and Sizable Market Segments

Cable television and syndication now allow for more effective market segmentation than could be achieved in the past. Sears, for example, might air ads for Craftsman tools on home improvement shows on HGTV. A collection of classic TV episodes on video or DVD could be sold on Nick at Nite or TV Land. Sports products and magazines find a natural audience on ESPN, while exercise videos for women may be pitched effectively during a fitness-related show on Lifetime.

Products Already Proven in Traditional Direct Response Media

Since television is a relatively expensive medium to test, many direct marketers reserve it for certain exceptional products only. Collectibles companies, for instance, advertise only a handful of their most successful general-interest products on television—those few that have potential for sales and new customer acquisition that make them worth the up-front cost of television production and time buys. Most of these firms' offerings show up only in space ads and direct mail.

Products with an Acceptable Price Range

You will notice that most products sold directly on television are in the $9.95 to $39.95 range, or have initial payments in this range. This is the "comfort level" for most consumers. If you ask more than this for a product on TV you run the risk of eliminating a big part of your audience. You may lose them for economic reasons, or because their level of trust is such that they won't lay out more than x-dollars for a product they have not yet held in their hands.

However, you may use a two-step process to sell higher-priced items via TV: obtaining leads from your TV ad and then following them up by phone, mail, or personal sales call. Firms offering everything from cars to computers to vacations have used the two-step method with positive results—especially aimed at upscale cable TV audiences. Spots for expensive fitness equipment often use this same technique—offering a comprehensive package of information in exchange for a toll-free phone call or online response. Many infomercials for high-ticket products and services do the same

Tips for Creating Traditional Direct Response TV Spots

Get Comfortable With the Medium

Writers and graphic designers who have spent most of their careers creating work for the print medium will have to switch gears to be successful in developing television spots. The time constraints of television are difficult to handle at first: it's a real challenge to compact a selling message into 60, 90, or 120 seconds, especially when 20 to 30 seconds of this time must be devoted to ordering instructions for traditional direct response spots. Repetition is imperative, both for the call to action and the ordering information, including telephone number, Web site, and/or address, price of the product, and other essentials.

Just as direct mail creative types often begin their process by immersing themselves in their "swipe files," it's an excellent idea to put together your library of top-notch television spots, recorded right off the air or linked from YouTube. Watch them over and over to get acquainted with the techniques and rhythms they represent. See how video enhances audio and vice-versa. Divide each spot into sections and note how many seconds are spent setting up the situation or problem . . . introducing the product or solution . . . explaining the benefits . . . closing the sale . . . discussing the guarantee . . . giving ordering instructions.

Consider the Classic DRTV Formats

Although you are not limited to these typical and somewhat predictable formats, one may provide the push you need to get some words and pictures onto your blank page or screen.

Problem/Solution. Many general-interest products sold via traditional direct response television solve a common household or personal problem: drudgery of housework, excess weight gain, need to quit smoking, acne problems, desire to make more money, and so on. The TV spot must grab the prospect's attention and hook him or her into the pitch.

A classic TV ad for International Correspondence Schools did this by setting up the problem of lack of money—and the solution of home study. The ad featured an attractive, young-to-middle-aged woman announcer sitting behind a desk. She began by saying,

> Do you want to make more money? Of course, we all do! And now at home
> in your spare time, you can train for a rewarding career in . . .

The announcer went on to tell how prospects could use their extra time to earn a certificate in anything from interior decorating to accounting. To find out more, they would simply call a toll-free number for more information.

John Stanphill, former Creative Director at WOL Direct, then the agency for International Correspondence Schools (ICS), attributes the spot's success to the positive twist it puts on the problem/solution format. He explains, "Instead of starting with a negative like 'I can't make ends meet,' this spot starts with the intriguing positive, 'Do you want to make more money?'" Stanphill notes that another problem/solution spot he tested, starting with the theme of "I hate my job but there's nothing I can do about it," was a major failure.

Product Demonstration. Watch the super-sharp knife cut a tomato into 20 perfect slices in a matter of seconds. See the tarnished silverware emerge from the Tarn-X dip looking better than new. Observe as the handy knitting device pops out tubes and circles of yarn in the wink of an eye, ready to make into hats, scarves, and art projects. If you have a product that looks like fun to use or makes a hard job seem easy, focus your spot on the product in use, and back up your video with an audio track that reinforces product benefits.

Parallel Structure. To emphasize the superior performance or quickness of your product in use, you may consider using a split-screen technique, or a format in which you switch back and forth between the "old way" and the "new way" of doing something. For instance, an ad might show a homemaker struggling to chop vegetables the old-fashioned way on the left side of the screen, and her counterpart on the right chopping a whole carrot in one motion with your slicer product. This technique can also help showcase a before-and-after scenario that has worked well for decades in selling weight-loss products and systems.

Testimonial. Also effective for weight-loss products is the on-screen testimonial, where a satisfied customer tells the specific benefits of the product (such as a 50-pound weight loss) and also the side benefits (better social life, spouse's renewed interest, better self-image, and so on). With patience and by asking the right questions, a skilled director can get most any "real person" subject to talk naturally and candidly about what the product has done for them, then shape the spot around the most compelling quotes.

Another interesting testimonial technique was used by *Sports Illustrated* for a pre-holiday subscription drive. Women explained how buying *SI* subscriptions cut down on the hassle of holiday shopping, and ensured that all the men on their list would be pleased with the magazine as well as the premium, a special video. Using the women personalized the offer, and helped target the pitch to a specialty audience—*SI* gift-givers—rather than the sports enthusiasts themselves.

Celebrity Spokesperson. If you are selling a parity product, one way to separate it from its competitors in the mind of the television viewer is to associate the product with a respected celebrity. That's why Bob Vila, Jessica Simpson, and other well-known individuals are called upon to sell everything from tools to exercise equipment in direct response ads. Selecting the right celebrity is crucial, and may well involve intensive market research to determine which individual has the right combination of recognition, comfort level, credibility, and respect among your target audience. Then there is the matter of compensation. With "hot" celebrities demanding $1 million or more to appear on infomercials, your firm's budget may limit the number of attractive candidates who are also financially viable.

A few words of advice on choosing your spokesperson. First, resist the urge to hire the celebrity you and your team admire most or most want to get to know: your personal perceptions are irrelevant. Note the experience of John Stanphill:

> When we decided to test Sally Struthers years ago on television for the ICS account I was continually questioned by everyone about the choice (then and for years afterward). 'Why not someone less flashy?' they said. 'Why not a male celebrity associated with education?' etc. Fortunately, we stuck to our guns and Sally's spots performed extraordinarily well—continuing to outpull more well-known celebrities for nearly a decade.
>
> Later, when we began a pre-broadcast research phase for our television creative (utilizing 'Dial Scan' methodology linked with focus groups) I saw dramatic evidence of Sally's appeal. Verbal reactions of focus group participants were generally lukewarm about Sally's presence, however the dial scan graph measurement from the same participants indicated a dramatic and positive response. Sally possessed that most intangible of qualities . . . she could get people's attention and 'sell' them.

Stanphill also speculates that Sally Struthers's unique and somewhat squeaky voice may have been a plus because people who had been waiting for an ICS spot to write down the toll-free number could easily tell when Sally came on TV. The critics' suggestions of a well-known male celebrity were way off target considering the product's best market segment: very young women without marketable job skills. At the time, this target group could relate to Ms. Struthers as "Gloria" in *All in the Family* reruns.

The second key in selecting a spokesperson is to insist that the product remains the star in all your efforts. Focus the ad on the product's benefits and use your celebrity as an enhancement to the product. Too many ads expect the product to ride on the coattails of the celebrity's sparkling personality. Third, test your ad concept with and without the celebrity spokesperson if possible. You may well find that the same pitch delivered by a top-notch (and much less expensive) unknown television announcer may yield you just as many sales or inquiries. That's why it's important to negotiate your celebrity contract with staged fees for testing and roll-out: don't obligate yourself to pay high talent fees for your entire campaign until you've had time to read results on your initial test.

Selecting the right celebrity is vital—and not always an obvious choice—as John Stanphill indicates above. Stanphill suggests the following research method to determine which celebrities might work best for specific target markets:

1. Give individuals in your target market a sheet of paper with photos only (no names) of 20 celebrities you might consider as potential endorsers for your product or service.
2. Ask the individuals to write down the names of the celebrities they recognize, and collect the sheets (don't let people collaborate).
3. Give the same people another sheet with the same pictures, but this time with the names of the celebrities identified.
4. Ask the individuals to write down which of these people they admire the most—again, no collaboration.

This simple method gives a "quick and dirty" read on both recognizability and credibility with your target segment.

Slice of Life. Although this technique is used more frequently in general advertising than it is in direct response TV, there have been successful examples. For instance, a Fingerhut ad selling towels revolved around the interaction of a husband and wife. The premise was that this family never seemed to have matched sets of towels—and the husband, especially, thought that having matching towels would be a great idea. Presented with gentle humor, the spot showed actors clothed to represent lower-middle to middle-class Americans. It offered a more human approach to selling an inexpensive towel set—as opposed to the traditional method of stacking up towels on a table with audio saying, "And that's not all—you get these matching fingertip towels too, all for the same low price of . . . "

While some of Bob Vila's tool ads have been straight demonstration spots, others have shown Bob interacting with "folks in his neighborhood" and helping them solve their home maintenance problems with products he endorses.

Romance the Benefits. Some products are difficult to demonstrate on television—but creative people can come up with exciting ways to bring them across on videotape or film. Holding up a magazine and talking about its feature articles won't inspire much enthusiasm, for example. But why not try a fast-paced montage of the best photos in recent issues, backed up by music that appeals to the magazine's target market, and enticing audio asking the provocative questions that these articles answered?

A book on the Civil War may sound dry, but it can come alive on film if a skilled cameraman pans slowly across its illustrated pages and an announcer sets the tone with a dramatic statement about how the war changed the face of America forever. For a travel magazine, a spot with sufficient budget could show readers enjoying what they've learned: dining at an out-of-the-way Paris bistro, shopping in a little-known section of London, getting a first-class airline seat for a coach fare.

Structure the Spot to Make a Sale

With no more than 120 seconds in which to sell your product or service, a highly structured format is essential. Every second should be focused on selling, yet the consumer must not feel pressured or coerced. Al Eicoff suggested a simple formula for an effective direct response TV spot: TPS. That stands for "Tease 'em, Please 'em, and Seize 'em." In his book, *Direct Marketing Through Broadcast Media*, Eicoff offered a more specific structure for a traditional direct response TV spot, inspired by the techniques of the old-time pitchmen:

> Anatomy of a Sales Presentation
>   1. Holder
>   2. Problem
>   3. Product Presentation
>   4. Solution
>   5. Turn
>   6. Guarantee

What Eicoff terms the "holder" could also be called a promise—either of a free gift, an exciting offer, a miraculous performance, or something new. Many spots are not presented in the strict problem-solution format, and thus the writer may spend more time on the product presentation. Eicoff's "turn" could also be called the move toward the close: the seller tells the price and terms, emphasizes premiums or other incentives, and calls for action. Discussing the guarantee at this point helps eliminate buyer resistance and leads into the final close. However, as John Stanphill points out, discussing explicit guarantees as part of lead generation spots is not a good idea. When seeking leads it's best to focus on "sizzle" and results, not nuts and bolts. A simpler and more general formula for a direct response spot is this, played out with examples from the classic International Correspondence Schools (ICS) spot mentioned previously:

>   1. *Attract the attention of the target group.*
>   Example: "Do you want to make more money? Of course, we all do!"
>   2. *Promise them something they want.*
>   Example: "And now at home, in your spare time, you can train for a rewarding career in . . . (various fields)."
>   3. *Support the promise.*
>   Example: The ICS ad tells how thousands of men and women have learned new and valuable skills "without ever setting foot inside a classroom." It goes on to list the various courses of study—everything from TV repair to interior decorating.
>   4. *Pitch the offer.*
>   Example: In this case, the offer is free facts for calling a toll-free number. In the case of a sales pitch, the offer would include premiums, guarantees, price, and terms.

5. *Call to action.*

Example: Give the toll-free telephone number, Web site, and/or address, and repeat it to ensure prospects have a chance to write it down. Experts say that for a traditional DRTV 120-second spot, as much as 30 seconds should be devoted to the "tag," or specific ordering information.

While these highly structured formulas still are used frequently in traditional direct response television circles, Bruce Wexler of A. Eicoff & Company notes:

> There are many DRTV spots today that don't conform to these formats. This is due, in part, to the need to do brand-building as part of certain spots. It's also due to the lack of demonstrability of certain DRTV products and services. Direct-to-consumer pharmaceutical commercials have been a hot category—spots that ask viewers to ask their doctors about a specific prescription medication. Creating a DRTV spot for this type of product requires a more creative approach, so while elements of the step-by-step processes might be used, there is a lot of room for variation.

How to Turn a Concept into a Storyboard or Script

Start creating your spot by putting ideas down on paper without regard to your format length. Write down images, words, phrases, and benefits, and then start massaging them into a unified presentation with a central theme. You may begin with an audio concept and then support it with video, or vice versa. Remember to keep your spot as simple as possible, since you need to ensure that your selling message comes across loud and clear. Don't be afraid of repetition—especially in making your offer and closing the sale. Make sure you have supplied all necessary facts a person requires to make a responsible buying decision, including all price and payment terms. Once you are satisfied with your rough copy, then you can begin timing it and adding or subtracting words to fit the 30-, 60-, 90-, or 120-second format. In doing so, keep in mind the speed and delivery style of your chosen announcer. Listen to tapes of your announcer in action to see how many words he or she can get across in each minute.

Some TV concepts are developed in storyboard form, while others are scripted. A storyboard presents a series of TV-screen images with the corresponding audio indicated below each image. A TV script presents a written description of the video portion on the left, and the actual words for the audio portion on the right. Your choice of presentation style will depend on the needs of your client or company as well as your upcoming plans for production.

Television Home Shopping

The phenomenal growth of television home shopping channels—and their integrated Web sites—is significant for direct and interactive marketers. These call-in shows represent a lucrative opportunity to sell products on TV without the time restrictions of a 120-second commercial or the high cost of an infomercial. This medium can be considered the initial step toward true interactive TV shopping. It is accessible to everyone with cable television and a phone or Internet connection. It allows for interactivity by putting customers on the air to explain what they like about products and ask questions of product designers, inventors, and celebrity endorsers. It provides entertainment for many, as the on-air salespeople become beloved personalities who keep loyal viewers coming back for more.

The creative challenge for most home shopping propositions lies in developing the overall format

Exhibit 13.2. Rough Storyboard

Client: *Ames True Temper*	Title: *"Genie" :60*	Page: *1 of 5*	A. Eicoff & Company
Product: *Water Genie*	Team: *Madsen/Zagorski*	Date: *02/19/10*	

1) OPEN ON A BEAUTIFUL PATIO/GARDEN. OUR GENIE, EQUIPPED WITH A WICKER BASKET, APPEARS OUT OF A PUFF OF SMOKE.

1) SFX: *Bwoosh!*

GENIE OC: After centuries in a lantern, I thought living in a garden would be a breeze.

2) GENIE STRUGGLES WITH A SLOSHY, FULL METAL WATERING CAN. HE BEGINS TO EMPTY IT OUT INTO THE WICKER BASKET.

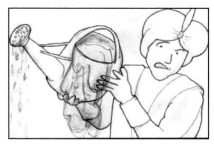

2) GENIE OC: But watering this place was alot of work!

3) CUT TO SHOT FROM INSIDE THE BASKET LOOKING UP AS GENIE DROPS SLOSHY WATERING CAN INTO THE BASKET.

3) GENIE OC: Heavy cans...

4) CUT TO MEDIUM SHOT AS GENIE FIGHTS WITH TANGLED HOSE AND STUFFS THAT INTO THE BASKET.

4) GENIE OC: Messy hoses...

Exhibit 13.2. Rough Storyboard (continued)

5) CUT BACK TO WIDE SHOT OF GENIE WITH DIRTY "SUNCAST 225' HOSE CAPACITY" CRANK HOSE REEL CART. HE CRANKS IT A COUPLE OF TIMES AND DUMPS IT INTO THE BASKET.

5) GENIE OC: And cranking? Really?

▼ TIME :14/:14

6) GENIE WAVES HIS HANDS OVER THE BASKET AND THE WATER GENIE APPEARS OUT OF THE BASKET.

SUPER: 1-800-000-0000
www.AmesWaterGenie.com
(hold throughout)

SUPER: *(logo)*

6) GENIE OC: That's why I created...

SFX: *Bwoosh!*

GENIE OC: ...the new Ames Water Genie Bottomless Watering Can.

7) CUT TO ECU OF WATER GENIE AS GENIE POINTS OUT FEATURES.

SUPER: *(logo)*

7) GENIE OC: It combines a watering can, hose, reel...

8) GENIE FLIPS PRODUCT AND CONTINUES TO POINT OUT FEATURES.

SUPER: *(logo)*

8) GENIE OC: ...and sprayer all-in-one.

Exhibit 13.2. Rough Storyboard (continued)

Client: *Ames True Temper*	Title: *"Genie" :60*	Page: *3 of 5*	A. Eicoff & Company
Product: *Water Genie*	Team: *Madsen/Zagorski*	Date: *02/19/10*	

9) PUFF OF SMOKE REVEALS GENIE WITH PRODUCT AT SPIGOT AS HE TURNS ON THE WATER.

9) SFX: *Bwoosh!*

GENIE VO: Now you'll...

10) GENIE SQUEEZES THE TRIGGER.

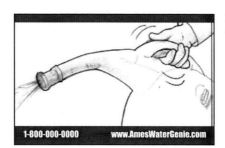

10) GENIE VO: ...never have to refill...

11) DISSOLVE TO OVERHEAD SHOT AS GENIE EASILY LIFTS WATER GENIE TO HANGING BASKET AND SQUEEZES TRIGGER.

SUPER: 1/2 THE WEIGHT OF A FULL TWO GALLON WATERING CAN

11) GENIE VO: ... or lug around a heavy can again. It's lightweight and...

12) CUT TO ECU OF NOZZLE BEING ADJUSTED.

12) GENIE VO: ...gives you a constant flow of water with an adjustable sprayer.

Exhibit 13.2. Rough Storyboard (continued)

13) CUT TO LOW SHOT OF HOSE WRAPPED AROUND PATIO FURNITURE AS GENIE FLICKS RETRACT SWITCH.

SUPER: 40' HOSE INCLUDED

13) GENIE VO: And the 40 foot hose has an automatic rewind....

14) GENIE WALKS PAST CAMERA AS HOSE RETRACTS INSIDE HOUSING.

SUPER: 40' HOSE INCLUDED

14) GENIE VO: ...vanishing magically inside....

15) CUT TO GENIE SETTING PRODUCT, NEATLY AT SPIGOT.

SUPER: 40' HOSE INCLUDED

15) GENIE VO: ...time after time.

▼ TIME   :25/:39

16) PUFF OF SMOKE REVEALS BEAUTY SHOT OF WATER GENIE.

SUPER: *(logo)*
SUPER: 2 EASY PAYMENTS OF $19.99 PLUS $11.95 S&H *(super switches out)*
SUPER: 2-YEAR LIMITED WARRANTY
LEGAL: Allow 4-6 weeks for delivery.

16) SFX: *Bwoosh!*

ANNCR VO: Call or click now to order the Water Genie. Just 2 easy payments of $19.99, plus shipping and handlling, with a 2-year warranty.

Exhibit 13.2. Rough Storyboard (continued)

17) CUT TO GENIE AS HE WATERS GARDEN.

SUPER: GARDENING TIPS DVD

LEGAL: Only available through this exclusive TV and online offer.

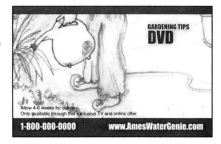

17) ANNCR VO: *Only* through this exclusive TV and online offer, get a gardening tips DVD...

18) DISSOLVE TO CU OF WATER GENIE NOZZLE.

SUPER: 2-PACK OF PLANT FOOD NUGGETS

18) ANNCR VO: ...plus a 2-pack of plant food nuggets, free.

▼ TIME :15/:54

19) CUT TO GENIE \WATERING PLANTS WITH THE WATER GENIE.

SUPER: 2 EASY PAYMENTS OF $19.99

19) GENIE OC: Get your Water Genie now before they disappear.

20) CUT TO BEAUTY SHOT.

SUPER: *(Water Genie logo)*

SUPER: *(The Home Depot logo)*

20) SFX: *Bwoosh!*

ANNCR VO: Also available at The Home Depot.

▼ TIME :06/:60

This rough storyboard for the Ames Water Genie helps both agency and client representatives envision the spot that will be created, frame by frame.

Reprinted with permission of A. Eicoff, Chicago, and Ames True Temper.

for presentation. Specific copy is not usually necessary, since part of the format normally involves ad-libs and personal commentary from the announcer. For a direct response copywriter, watching home shopping salespeople at work is both an inspiration and an education. These individuals can find scores of ways to romance the features and benefits of even the simplest product through description, demonstration, modeling, testimonials, and personal stories.

Direct and interactive marketers who are considering expanding their efforts into television can take an intermediate step by working with one or more of the home shopping channels. In this way, marketers can learn which products do best on television, and watch how the home shopping "pros" position and pitch their merchandise. What's more, with top channels like QVC and HSN frequently selling up to $1 million or more in merchandise per hour, some direct and interactive marketers may choose to form an alliance with one of these channels as their main method of promotion via broadcast media.

Infomercials

More than 60 years after the classic 15-minute Vitamix commercials aired on tiny black-and-white TV sets, long-form television spots, or "infomercials," again hold an important place in broadcast direct marketing. The deregulation of commercial limits allowed stations to sell time for long-form television commercials, beginning in the mid-1980s. Since then, infomercials for everything from car polish to hair products to exercise equipment have become a dominant part of American popular culture.

According to Bruce Wexler, however, "Many large advertisers still view infomercials negatively. While they may be intrigued by the form, they also are wary because so many marginal companies use infomercials to sell marginal products and services. Though a few Fortune 500 companies have created infomercials, most prefer short-form direct response."

While many infomercials directly generate leads and sales for products and services, some firms also use this medium for education and relationship building, or to direct customers to "key outlets" for the purchase of kitchen and sporting products and the like.

In the early days of contemporary infomercials, sets were simple and formats were predictable: mostly in the guise of a talk show with a super-enthusiastic audience and a "guest" who just happened to be selling a product. Today many infomercials still use the talk show format, but production values are improving. Costs for a simple half-hour show now run from $125,000 to $500,000 or more, experts say. And if a well-known celebrity is involved, another six-figure or even seven-figure fee may be added on top of those prices. The start-up figures pale, however, in the face of the potential rewards of a successful infomercial.

Infomercials offer a fertile field for testing of everything from the total concept and format to specifics such as order of presentation, addition or subtraction of certain "real people" testimonials, different hosts and celebrities, and so on. Focus groups and "dial scan" graph measurement technology allow marketers to test reactions to existing infomercials second by second, with separate on-screen graphs for males and females. This helps determine where weaknesses lie—and often a more effective show can be created just by re-editing existing footage.

Products that shine in demonstration and those that can benefit by enthusiastic testimonials and endorsements are good candidates for infomercials. Price is also an issue, although items selling for as much as $300 can conceivably be sold directly from television, especially if they can be purchased using split payments. Another hurdle is informational: is there enough to say about this product to keep an audience attentive for a half-hour? Testing the viability of an infomercial takes about two weekends and between 20 and 30 airings, which can be purchased for about $50,000 in most cases. Smart infomercial media buying is an art in itself, and should be entrusted to a firm with a demonstrable track record in this specialized field.

In lead generation, it's important to track cost per conversion as well as cost per lead, and eventually to compare the lifetime value of infomercial-generated customers with that of customers from other media. Conventional wisdom would say that an infomercial lead should be stronger and more committed than one generated from a 120-second spot, because the infomercial watcher gained more product information up front. However, this may not pan out in all cases: careful monitoring is essential.

Writing infomercials can be compared to scriptwriting for television or film in that it often requires intense, on-site effort for an extended period of time. This is a potentially lucrative area of specialization for direct and interactive marketing copywriters.

Videos/DVDs

Direct marketers' videos are not broadcast on television or cable—rather, they are created for a prospect's viewing on YouTube, on a marketer's Web site, or occasionally still via DVD or CD-ROM at home or office. Videos can serve the same product demonstration function as a brochure in a direct mail package, with the added dimensions of sound and motion. While "video brochures" are no longer a novelty, this medium still provides more excitement than the typical, flat product brochure. What's more, today most of your customers will have broadband access to watch your videos on the Web, and it's also easy to create your own channel on YouTube. These advancements eliminate most of the old barriers that kept prospects from watching videos: they no longer have to locate a working VCR or DVD player, insert the video, and watch it.

John Scaletta, founder and owner of Digital Studio, Inc., suggests that marketers can direct customers to the Web to view a video, and then be invited to subscribe and join their mailing list. As he says, "Video, which is the next best way to establish trust without a personal meeting, can be an essential tool to building the list. You actually build an online relationship with videos. And if you offer something valuable and deliver on the offer, customers will continue to subscribe to emails. Example: 'Enter your email address for a FREE video on '10 Trade Secrets to a Successful Email Campaign.'"

Scaletta adds that videos are highly attractive to search engines. He says, "Simply put, search engines love video because they know that that is what their users want to see. As a result, video is the best way to get to the top of search engines such as Google. Videos need to be optimized, compressed and tagged to be identified by the search engines. Similar to how a Web site needs SEO (search engine optimization), videos need VSEO (video search engine optimization).

While some viewers use their computers to view videos, Scaletta says that "smart phones are the newest preferred viewing device, and the preferred delivery is video. These users want to watch, not read."

As for length, videos no longer than four to seven minutes should serve most marketers' purposes—and some may be much shorter.

Run longer than seven minutes and you risk losing the viewers' attention—especially in today's world of 20-second news stories and three-minute "extended features" on commercial television. Scaletta notes that determining the length of the video is similar to determining the length of a direct mail letter. "The short answer is: short as possible, long enough to cover the information needed to get your idea across in a substantive, compelling and entertaining way. Remember, a targeted audience asked for it in the first place. It's no different than a person choosing a book in a library: it doesn't matter how long the book is as long as the content is good. Of course, since many people choose a book by its cover, videos require effective design, as well."

While video producers used to quote anywhere from $3,000 to $20,000 per finished minute of video, John Scaletta says that his firm creates simple videos for clients for as little as $600. If you choose to have "hard copies" of your video made in addition to posting it online or for mobile viewing, you can get 1,000 DVD copies of a video of under thirty minutes in length for about $2.00 apiece. Prices may decrease to $1.00 apiece or even less in much larger quantities.

Radio

With the rise of online music, mobile marketing, and satellite radio, it's tempting to consider traditional radio a medium on the decline. Yet according to 2010 polling by Arbitron and Edison Research, 78 percent of Americans over the age of 12 agree with the statement, "In the future, you will continue to listen to AM/FM radio as much as you do now, despite increasing advancements in technology."

Because today's radio stations are beautifully segmented by interest area and demographics, direct and interactive marketers may be able to utilize radio cost-effectively for special-interest products and local support of campaigns on television or in other media. But since radio does not offer visual demonstration possibilities, its applications are limited to those products that may be sold by means of "word pictures" and sounds. What's more, music-format stations used as background noise by their listeners are seldom effective for direct response pitches. Direct marketers require a radio format that attracts attentive listeners.

With the dominance of all-news and all-sports radio stations and other talk formats that attract businesspeople during drive time, some marketers have found radio an ideal medium for reaching affluent executives with pitches for business and personal products—mobile phone equipment and plans, computers and copiers, automobile leases, news and investment publications, investment opportunities, and the like. Since most businesspeople have mobile phones with them in their autos, they can complete direct response transactions even as they inch along the rush-hour freeway (at least in states that allow phones to be used while driving).

In addition, in recent years a strong cadre of syndicated radio talk show hosts have captured large and loyal audiences. Host/entertainers like Sean Hannity, Dave Ramsey, and Rush Limbaugh become authority figures for their listeners, and thus bring an extra dimension of credibility when they pitch products and services on their shows. Buying time on a top syndicated talk show can be costly, but the audience numbers are impressive: some boast cumulative audiences of 10 million or more in a week's time. The host's endorsement usually will cost extra: you may be wise to test your pitch with and without his/her voice-over and personal comments. Products and services generating leads on syndicated radio include foreign language learning programs, phonics and reading plans for children, financial services, and conservative newspapers and magazines.

Long-form radio formats are available as well, allowing for "radio infomercials" selling self-improvement plans, health products, and other products and services. In most cases, however, attractive time slots and affordable time for long-form radio are limited in availability except in smaller markets or on low rated stations in larger markets.

Here are a few hints for the creation of successful radio commercials:

- *Get the listener's attention up front.* Radio is largely a background medium, and even talk shows are often listened to with "one ear" while your prospect drives, cooks, works, and so on. To get the listener's attention, use a recognizable or unique voice, sound effects, stirring music that selects the audience, or an attention-getting statement at the beginning of any spots you produce.
- *Let the host do your commercial his/her way.* Unless the host of the show you're advertising on is a "shock jock" or has another personality quirk that may reflect poorly on your product, it is likely to pay off if you allow the host to use your script only as a guideline for his or her own "performance" of your spot. Also, make sure the host has the opportunity to use your product or service before the commercial is taped. Thus his or her warmth and credibility will reflect on your product, including anecdotes and personal testimonials of the product in use.
- *Use repetition to your advantage.* Because radio is a fleeting medium, it's important to give your listener enough time and warning to get a pencil and paper and write down the necessary phone number or Web site, pricing information, and so on. Experts suggest that you repeat this information as many as three to four times in a radio spot. Look for ways to achieve this repetition with good humor and grace rather than rote recitation. Dialogue between two people helps a great deal, as do jingles with the phone number clearly sung to a memorable tune.
- *Set up your long-form radio spot like a show with commercials.* Instead of hard selling throughout, create informational segments with several commercials interspersed.

This builds interest and credibility and achieves repetition of ordering information without becoming tedious.

Broadcast Production

Most direct response radio spots are simple enough to record in a local studio with voice-over talent and perhaps a few sound effects. But from storyboards or script to the finished product, television production may require a more specialized set of creative skills.

Circa 1950, a direct response "pitchman" would stand before a single camera and deliver his sales message from beginning to end. But even many of today's low-budget spots involve multiple cameras, computer graphics and animation, and other tricks of the trade. What's more, producing a quality spot is important in vying for inexpensive, available time on various channels—called remnant time. As John Stanphill explains, if a station has the option to run a spot or infomercial that is poorly produced or one with good production values, the well-produced spot will almost always get the coveted, low-cost time. This section will explain the basics of television production for direct response marketers, as well as some tips on selecting and working with a television production house.

Start with the Script and the Storyboard

In the early stages of the creative process, the function of the TV script or storyboard is to sell the commercial's concept. For production purposes, the script and storyboard become the control documents that ensure the creation of a spot that fulfills the client's expectations and stays on budget. Your storyboard renderings can help pin down such variables as background, costume, number of different shots, lighting, and camera positioning as well as details related to the presenter and other actors (see Exhibit 13.3 for an example). At this stage you should also be able to specify musical backgrounds, sound effects, and other needs for the audio portion of the spot.

Remember that simplicity is the key to success for most direct response spots: keeping the backgrounds uncluttered and the number of actors or presenters to a minimum helps retain the focus on the product you're selling.

Since production time is very expensive, having a script that details every shot including camera placement can save on costly experimentation. On the other hand, some directors prefer to leave the specifics a bit looser. What works best for you will depend on your budget and relationship with the director. Following are some of the video and audio terms commonly used as abbreviations in television scripts:

Video Terms
CUT—Move immediately to the next shot without delay
DISS—Dissolve: a slower change of scenes in which the old shot "dissolves" into the new
INT—Interior
EXT—Exterior
ECU—Extreme close-up
CU—Close-up
MCU—Medium close-up
MS or MED—Medium shot
LS—Long Shot
2-SHOT—Shot including two people
BKGRND—Background
FRGRND—Foreground
DOLLY IN/OUT—To dolly in is to move the camera toward the subject; to dolly out is to move it away from the subject
PAN—Camera moves across
TRACK—Camera moves with action
TRUCK—Move camera from side to side
ZOOM—Shot moves in or out
FADE IN/FADE OUT—Move slowly from black to the scene, or from the scene to black

Audio Terms
VO—Voice-over
ANNCR—Announcer
SFX—Sound effect
MUSIC UP—Music dominates
MUSIC UNDER—Background music
MUSIC OUT—Music stops

Exhibit 13.3. Final Storyboard

1

(MUSIC: sound design and music)
ONE: I am an artist. My car is my creation.

visual: actor #1 in large, open, empty space with a car on a lift/turntable in the background. Environment dictated by location scouting.

2

ONE/TWO: Side moldings, rear skirt, trick spoiler and chrome six spokes,

visual: Although actor #2 is depicted here, actor #1 and actor #2 will be filmed saying the same line to allow editorial freedom later. This will be repeated at certain times throughout the script.

3

ONE/TWO: all in the name of individuali-tee.

visual: actor #1 or #2 speaks to camera.

4

TWO: You may have the

visual: actor #2 speaks to camera.

5

same car...

visual: actor #2's car headlights - closeup seeing the brightness of SilverStars. This scene continues through frames 6, 7 and 8.

6

but mine looks better,

visual: panning across actor #2's SilverStars to another car with traditional halogens approaching.

7

drives better and sings a better tune.

visual: actor #2 looks over at the car that has just pulled up next to his. (perhaps at a traffic light)

8

Right down to the lights.

visual: closeup and drive away of actor #2's car. SilverStar's bright illumination demonstrated.

9

THREE: It's all about the lights.

visual: actor #3 working in a suburban family garage. Kids' props are evident (sports equipment, bike, etc.) He is working on his "weekend" vehicle - an SUV is parked next to it.

10

ONE: The brightest the whitest the

visual: actor #1 in space with car on lift/turntable. At certain times light from the vehicle's head lamps and other sources illuminate the actor.

11

oh so rightest Sylvania SilverStar.

visual: product grouping interestingly lit. Perhaps on a turntable, slowly rotating as beams of light cross the viewer's path.

12

TWO: The look of HID,

visual: actor #2 talks to camera.

Exhibit 13.3. Final Storyboard (continued)

13

like on high end imports, but nowhere near the price.

visual: night driving -actor #2. See light streaking across a downtown area, tunnel, etc.

14

THREE: And that is absolutely brilliant.

visual: actor #3 with SilverStar package in his hands - he will be installing them in his "weekend" vehicle.

15

ONE: My car is my temple.

visual: actor #1 crouches in front of the car in the empty space - the SilverStar headlights are on. (At certain points in the spot - actor #1 could interact with the car - example: deliver his line while standing on the car's hood, etc.)

16

ONE/TWO/THREE: My car is my castle. SilverStar burns crisp and white.

visual: this verbal line delivered by all 3 actors for editorial options.

17

ONE/THREE: Brightest, whitest, 100% street legal.

visual: actor #1 and #3 show the product box to camera.

18

ONE: Silver tipped,

visual: actor #1 to camera with the light bulb - possible use of lens flare, etc.

19

ONE: what a trip, you will flip

visual: actor #2 driving - night time.

20

at its beauty.
THREE: at its white hot intensity.

visual: actor #2 driving toward the camera - SilverStars shining on the view.

21

ONE: You've got a phone, you've got the number. Ask for the Star that burns so bright in the night. Forty-nine dollars and change.

(other versions: "$39.98 - 2nd set 50% off" and "$44.98 - 2nd set 50% off")
visual: product grouping interestingly illuminated. Perhaps on a turntable, slowly rotating.

22

And get a second set for half-price. S-weet.

visual: actor #1 covered off saying the entire line. Most likely use actor #1 saying only "S-weet" to get maximum time on the product grouping.

23

THREE: Sylvania does lights.

visual: actor #3 right to camera.

24

ONE/TWO: Lights are the mania at Sylvania. SilverStar burns brighter. Brighter is better. Brighter is beautiful. Brighter and whiter than that dim crowd you've been hanging with.

visual: copy to be read by actors #1 and #2. SilverStars on #2's car, he's leaning against it. Possibility of another car driving up with halogen lamps.

Exhibit 13.3. Final Storyboard (continued)

SYLVANIA SilverStar :120
"Brilliant Poetry"
page 5 of 6

A. Eicoff & Company
A Division of Ogilvy & Mather

25

1-800-000-0000
sylvania.com

ONE: Yellow is history. White hot is cool.

visual: actor #1 delivers his line while walking from a yellow-light-circle source (perhaps on the floor) to a white and bright one.

26

1-800-000-0000
sylvania.com

THREE: The better the light, the better the safety. And safe is cool, too.

visual: actor #3 talks to camera while still working on his car - perhaps a SilverStar in his hand.

27

1-800-000-0000
sylvania.com

ONE/TWO: Call now call now.

visual: said by actor #1 and #2.

28

only $49.98
2nd set 50% off
plus S&H

1-800-000-0000
sylvania.com

ONE/TWO: Get one set at 49.98. And the second set is half-off.

(other versions: "$39.98 - 2nd set 50% off" and "$44.98 - 2nd set 50% off")

29

1-800-000-0000
sylvania.com

THREE: No wallets were harmed upgrading to the look of HID.

30

1-800-000-0000
sylvania.com

ONE/TWO/THREE: Tricked out. Slammed. Tuned to the max. Your car is your princess... Your baby... Your angel of the night. And SilverStar is the window to her soul.

visual: line said by all 3 actors to allow editorial options later.

Take Advantage of the Visual TV Medium

Television is an action medium, and creatives will be wise to take advantage of its visual possibilities. Just as a feature film director can open up his production much more than the director of a stage play, the direct response television marketer should use motion to help call the prospect to action.

Adding action to a television spot need not be expensive. Even still photographs can take on a vivid effect when the camera pans across them, or when they are dissolved, one into the other. Affordable computer animation software can bring your logo alive and move your price and phone number onto the screen in interesting and unique ways. When using actors, add some movement to the script: let the actors walk from one part of the set to the other, show the product in use, or change scenes for a before-and-after effect. In all that you do, make sure that your video and audio work together: if you are saying one thing and doing another, the prospect's confusion may well cause him or her to tune out.

To sharpen your video skills, watch commercials, television shows, and feature films from the director's point of view. Watching classic films can be most helpful because the incongruity of styles, manners, and dress will help keep you on your toes to notice the director's techniques. In addition, the directors of generations past did not have as many expensive technical tricks of the trade, nor computer-generated images, at their disposal as filmmakers do today. From them, you can learn how to get a point across effectively and inexpensively.

Exhibit 13.3. Final Storyboard (continued)

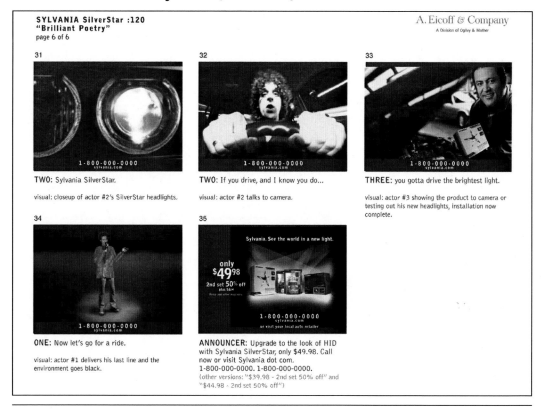

The final story board for *Sylvania's SilverStar* headlights captures all the motion and bright lights of this two-minute "Brilliant Poetry" spot.

Reprinted with permission of A. Eicoff, Chicago, and Sylvania.

Become familiar with the capabilities of computer software for video graphics and animation, but don't be seduced into overkill. The fast-paced, multi-element look of a general advertising spot may be good for image building, but a direct response spot still must sell or gain a lead in a matter of seconds. If in doubt about a flashy graphics technique, it's probably best to leave it out.

Get Bids For Your Television Production

Most broadcast experts suggest that you obtain several competitive bids for any spot you plan to produce. As a rule of thumb, *Response* magazine suggested that the cost of a short-form spot runs between $25,000 and $250,000, while the cost of a long-form spot runs between $100,000 and $800,000. In addition to comparing prices, it is important to check each production house's samples—in this case their previous direct response spots. Ask each prospective producer to show you a body of work that is comparable to the job you're planning in terms of budget, product type, generating sales versus leads, spots versus infomercials, production values, and so forth.

Make sure each firm you consider is well grounded in direct and interactive marketing—don't be swayed by an impressive set of flashy general advertising spots alone. John Stanphill notes that broadcast editors with experience in tabloid TV (*Inside Edition, Entertainment Tonight,* and similar shows) have a deep understanding of how to make a story compelling and get considerable information across in a short time frame. As he notes, "The length of a tabloid TV story used to be up to six minutes, but now it's no longer than three minutes." Editors who are used to these time constraints are great candidates for direct response broadcast production—especially for products to be sold using a hot, high-energy presentation.

To be sure that your bids are exactly comparable, give each production house the same script or storyboard, and the same instructions. Production expense categories include such items as:

- Script
- Crew and Equipment
- Art Direction, Stylist, and Props
- Make-up
- Voice-over
- Talent
- Music/Audio
- Location/Studio/Catering
- Film/Editing
- Direction
- Animation/Graphics
- Mark-up

Firms may offer you a guaranteed price or a cost-plus price. With the guaranteed price, you warrant that the commercial you wish to produce is exactly what is presented on your script or storyboard. The production house gives you a firm price for creating that spot, and agrees not to charge you more if they incur overtime or added expenses. The cost-plus price allows for more flexibility if your script or storyboards are not completely firm, or if you want the producer and director to try some different possibilities in the studio. In this case, you should ask for an overall "ball park" price, as well as a breakdown of what hourly or daily charges you will incur during production.

Experts say that the pre- and post-production periods are crucial to the success of your spot— both in terms of its quality and keeping it on budget. Careful planning on your end is the best way to keep costs to a minimum. During the "shoot" itself, indecision is very expensive, since charges for everyone from the make-up person to the high-priced talent will keep adding up while you decide what to do.

Pre-production includes the selection of costumes, props, location or studio space, music, dancing or other special talents if applicable, and personnel for everything from the on-air talent to the costumer, make-up person, camera operators, sound and lighting specialists, script person, and set designer.

Post-production focuses on the editing function, which once again may be simple or complex depending upon how tightly you plan your production, and how many customized elements you plan for various regions, seasons, or demographic groups.

Variables to Consider in Planning a TV Spot

If your budget is substantial, you may be able to plan on a celebrity presenter, original music, location shoots, and other extras for your direct response spot. But if your funds are limited, each of these factors needs to be considered very carefully.

Casting. Your producer may do your casting for you, or you may negotiate for the talent yourself. Some marketers try for a shortcut, or even massage their own egos by casting themselves, relatives, or employees in the role of the TV salesperson. However, this is seldom a good idea: to make a sale or obtain a qualified lead in 60 to 120 seconds requires the services of a trained actor or actress—preferably one with substantial on-camera selling experience. On the other hand, a good director often can develop excellent testimonials using "real people," by interviewing them and taping their natural reactions and comments, then editing the best into a spot. The time needed to assemble enough material to create such spots is difficult to estimate, however.

Music. Many direct response marketers do not require any music at all in their spots—especially those with a straightforward, "me-to-you" pitch. If music is required, you may be able to use stock tunes that your production studio can make available to you. A custom score may be less costly than you think, however. Consider contracting with a local source to develop what you need so that the music can complement the spot. Relatively few direct marketers have commissioned the creation of their own jingles, but the idea is worth considering. As direct response TV spots incorporate more image building as well as selling, having your own catchy jingle rolling around in consumers' heads may be a very powerful marketing idea.

Studio Versus Location. In general, location shooting is more expensive than using a studio. However, if you need a standard location like a homey kitchen or family room, money can be saved by renting a suitable home from its owner rather than building a set for one-time use. Direct response marketers selling exotic travel services and other such concepts will need to strongly consider budgeting funds for the customized location shots that set their products apart. On the other hand, many products to be sold direct via TV can be displayed most effectively in a simple, in-studio demonstration.

Stock Footage. Inexpensive spots may be upgraded in look with stock film footage that is quite reasonable in cost, according to John Stanphill. Stanphill recommends *www.digitaljuice.com* as a good source for the set-price purchase of such royalty-free stock footage. The firm also offers stock music and digital clip art for print production.

Film, Videotape, and Digital Formats. Film, videotape, and digital formats all have their proponents for direct response TV spots. Your own time factors, budget, and preference will help you make this decision, but here are some pros and cons to consider. Film adds depth and subtlety to a presentation because of its softness. It is considered a quality medium, and thus it may be used for TV spots by general advertisers of packaged goods. Film permits slightly less time for sound than does videotape: 58 seconds out of a 60 second spot. Although 35mm film looks better and is easier to edit than 16mm film, the less expensive 16mm version may offer a compromise for some direct marketers who need the softer, romantic look of film.

Videotape is a hot medium that gives the impression of immediacy and reality. Standard one-inch videotape provides sharp focus and good color. With good-quality lighting it can approximate the depth of a film presentation. There is also a processing technique available that gives a "film look" to videotape. Videotape is faster and less expensive to shoot than film, and may be viewed immediately, without a time lag for processing. Unlike film, videotape offers a full 60 seconds of sound for each 60 seconds of tape.

Improvements in digital video and nonlinear, random-access digital editing offer marketers enhanced ability to create the look they want—including special effects—and edit their work quickly and easily. It also allows for easy adaptation of a basic spot to fit various target markets, geographical areas, specific local dealers, seasons of the year, Web site landing pages and toll-free numbers, and so on.

John Stanphill recommends a format called 24-frame video, which he says gives a much clearer image than traditional video—more like film. He notes, "For one campaign I simultaneously shot the most important spots on both video and film so I could determine later which gave me the best combination of quality and impact."

As in so many aspects of direct and interactive marketing production, this technology is advancing rapidly. Make sure that the production houses you consider are up-to-date on their knowledge and application of cost-effective, state-of-the-art technology.

A Brand New Way to Use DRTV

by Rick Sangerman, Senior Vice President, A. Eicoff & Company

"Brand DR" is the most important trend to emerge in the DRTV business in recent years, and if this trend evolves as expected, it will be even more important in the future. By "Brand DR," I'm referring to direct response television advertising that not only contains a selling message but also helps builds the brand.

To DRTV traditionalists, such a hybrid approach may seem unworkable—anything that isn't focused on motivating viewers to buy is superfluous. In fact, branding and selling messages are not superfluous but synergistic. DRTV spots that take the time to craft the right branding provide viewers with an additional incentive to buy—it reinforces what the product stands for, motivating viewers to respond not just to the offer itself but also to the larger concepts of value, quality, service, and so on. Similarly, a product demonstration or offer that's structured with the brand in mind not only elicits a response, but also reinforces an image viewers have about the company and its products. They see an impressive demonstration and think: "The product is incredibly durable; and the company has a reputation for building products that last."

Given that DRTV spots have been around for years, why is this DRTV-branding hybrid emerging now? Let's look at three catalysts for this trend and some examples of advertisers who are making good use of it.

One of the most significant catalysts of the DRTV/branding hybrid is the growing number of blue chip advertisers in the business. While a branding message may have made no difference to a small, family-owned company selling a slicer-and-dicer, it makes a huge difference to a Fortune 500 company. In recent years, companies such as Procter & Gamble, Reynolds, Con Agra, Sears and many others have become significant DRTV advertisers. They see their DRTV spots not only as a way to generate sales and leads, but also as a way to build their brands. They recognize that a DRTV spot may reach a viewer they may miss with their other advertising; DRTV increases the number of people exposed to their brand message. They also know that a direct response commercial can reinforce that message among people who have seen their other advertising: the DRTV spot delivers the message in a different way and so provides a fresh branding "voice."

A second catalyst is an increasingly volatile economy. When industries or the entire economy experiences a downturn, companies are under increased pressure to improve their ROI. This means that advertisers must sell harder, and this motivates them to test DRTV or expand existing schedules. As a result, large corporations that previously had little or no commitment to DRTV become more active users. These big advertisers have made a huge commitment to branding, and so they want their DRTV spots to build the brand as well as sell.

The third catalyst: the growing number of products and services that can't be sold in a traditional 30-second spot. Technological advances and other factors are helping companies create products and services unlike any others—their uniqueness requires a certain amount of explanation before people are willing to buy. When Procter & Gamble introduced their unique Swiffer cleaning product, they recognized that they required additional time to explain how this multiple-purpose mop/duster/sweeper worked. Using a DRTV couponing strategy, P&G capitalized on a longer-length spot to explain their new product. But they also made sure the P&G brand remained clear and compelling throughout the spot.

In recent years, A. Eicoff & Company has had more clients than ever before emphasizing the need for their DRTV spots to deliver both a branding message and sales. Sylvania, for instance, wanted a commercial for their high-quality automobile headlights that not only generated a good response from their market but that also branded the product as hip and cutting edge. A hip hop-themed commercial accomplished this objective.

True Temper, makers of lawn and garden tools, asked Eicoff to create a spot for the Ames Water Genie, a sprinkling can attached to a hose. The purpose of the spot was to reach an audience of gardening devotees with information about this new product's benefits and generate calls about it via an 800 number, as well as drive viewers to the company's Web site. But the spot also delivered a consistent brand message—it communicated the twin themes of innovation and fun throughout the spot, using a genie as the spokesperson in the commercial. We believe that all signs point to the continued evolution and growth of the DRTV-branding trend. The days of commercials being segregated into DRTV and non-DRTV are quickly fading. Many "general" spots now have a direct response vehicle—an 800 number or a Web site. While the purpose of these spots may be to create awareness and image, they also want to elicit measurable responses from viewers. More so than ever before, companies are demanding accountability from their advertising—they want to know what they're getting for their ad dollars. A measurable response is an excellent way to measure how the ad performed.

For the DRTV-branding trend to pick up steam in the future, it's not just up to mainstream, brand-focused advertisers to embrace DRTV, but for direct response advertisers and agencies to find ways to blend these two approaches seamlessly. This may mean veering away from some traditional DRTV practices—buying some prime time networks instead of late night or weekend slots, going with a 60-second spot instead of a 120. Given the numerous benefits of the "Brand DR" approach, however, it seems likely that even the most hidebound traditionalists will be willing to adapt their approach to the new realities.

Enhance Your Understanding: Learn by Watching TV

Next time you sit down to watch some television, take your remote control in hand and "channel surf" in search of direct response spots and infomercials instead of programs. Prime time is not the best time to do this: try Sunday mornings on most any channel or weekdays on cable. Create your own diary of direct response TV viewing, including an analysis of what you've seen in terms of the length of the spots or infomercials, formats used, celebrity endorsers, and production values. Note the prices charged for products being sold outright, and the types of products where lead generation is used. Try dividing spots into segments using Eicoff's TPS or his six-part formula. How long does the toll-free number and/or Web site appear on the screen? Is it on long enough? Is there a clear offer being made, or just a pitch for "more information"? Pay attention to what appears on TV over time: which spots do you see over and over (an indication that they're working!) and which seem to vanish after the first viewing or two? What is there about the spots you've seen frequently that makes them successful? Compare the best direct response TV spots you've seen with general advertising TV spots. What are the main differences? What are the similarities? What indications (if any) do you see that the two disciplines are moving closer together, as discussed in Rick Sangerman's "Brand DR" article?

Building Long-Term Customer Value Through Back-End Marketing

In nearly all direct and interactive marketing transactions, the initial customer relationship is expensive to develop. Indeed, sophisticated marketers seldom try to break even on the first transaction with a customer. They know that finding a good prospect costs money. Turning that prospect into a customer, building a relationship, and then convincing the customer to buy again and again, are the keys to maximizing ultimate profit. Direct and interactive marketers report that their best customer database segments respond to offers at a rate five, six, or even ten times higher than that of cold-list prospects.

Many marketers have a great deal to learn in the area of back-end creative strategy. They put their finest marketing minds to work establishing a solid relationship with the customer in their front-end promotions. Then, at the turning point, when the bargain is struck but the product not yet delivered, they make the mistake of turning the customer over to the "efficiency" of an operations department. These marketers are like a wealthy suitor who wines and dines his lady love for months before proposing. Then, when she says yes, he tips his hat and rides off into the sunset alone, entrusting her to his valet as a stand-in for the wedding and the honeymoon!

Thus it's vital to know: How much does your firm or client have to pay to turn a cold-list prospect or a loose lead into a customer? And what is the long-term value of that new customer to the company? Most direct and interactive marketers expend considerable effort trying to shave the cost of bringing new customers onboard, but that's only part of the challenge. A carefully planned program of relationship building and back-end marketing can greatly improve each customer's long-term value to the firm while serving important customer service functions at the same time. Relationship building includes all efforts by the direct and interactive marketer to gain customer loyalty and advocacy, enhance personalized two-way communications, and increase "share of wallet" over time. *Back-end marketing* is the direct and interactive marketing term for the important set of tactics used to convert, keep, trade-up, and resell customers once you have their names.

In addition to the waste of identifying customers only to lose many of them before a second sale, consider the relatively small pool of potential customers available. The DMA's studies have indicated that only about half of American householders purchase even one item per year by direct mail, and only two-thirds of householders with Internet access make purchases online. DMA research shows that the key to converting more Americans to this method of shopping lies in better treatment of prospects and customers. This chapter will explain the traditional functions of back-end marketing, and then explore the broader and more strategic applications of relationship marketing.

The Functions of Back-End Marketing

The way a prospect or customer is handled on the back end is crucial to the long-term relationship. Yet in addition to pure customer service functions, back-end promotions can also be used to maximize selling opportunities and effectiveness. Some of the traditional objectives of back-end marketing are to:

- Convert a lead into a buyer.
- Cut returns and reinforce the wisdom of original purchases.
- Promote good will for the firm.
- Sell products with better profit margins than those sold by front-end marketing.
- Ensure continued sales to the new customer.
- Pay for necessary mailings, such as premium notices, by offering additional merchandise or services for sale.
- Ensure outstanding customer service.
- Collect funds owed.
- Gain subscription and club renewals.
- Retain and upgrade donors to nonprofits.
- Enhance dialogue with the customer in order to improve future recommendations and service.

The creative concepts and ideas that follow can assist in fulfilling each of these objectives.

Converting Leads into Buyers

The objective of many front-end promotions is to obtain a lead for follow-up via mail, e-mail, phone, or personal contact. These leads may come to you through direct mail, space advertising, on-line inquiries, telephone solicitation, inquiries from publicity stories, unsolicited inquiries, or customer referrals.

A quick follow-up is essential, no matter what the source of the lead. The moment the potential customer acknowledges interest in your product or service, he or she begins to "cool off." If you don't answer the lead in good time, the potential customer may not even remember asking about your offer by the time your mailing arrives.

Business-to-business author and expert Robert Bly insists marketers should respond to leads within 48 hours of receipt. Indeed, when you respond to an online request for information, it is possible to provide the promised white paper, article or brochure instantly. Bly's 48-hour deadline may be too tight for some firms to achieve if they are responding by mail, but it is imperative that you respond to a lead within a maximum of one to two weeks. Promptness is especially crucial in the case of leads that come to you by phone or online. The prospect knows exactly when you received their request—unlike mailed-in leads where the prospect may allow additional time for the foibles of the post office.

If for some reason your formal conversion package is not ready on time, communicate to your leads with a "keep warm" letter, e-mail, postcard, or phone call. Thank them and acknowledge their interest, give them a few teasers about the exciting information on the way, and let them know that the information they requested will be forthcoming soon. When you use a phone call in this way, you may also be able to gather some information to help qualify the prospect, or to serve him or her better in your response.

Keep Following Up Until a Promotion's Costs Exceed its Profits

The extent of your follow-up program should be determined by weighing the product's profit potential against the cost of continuing to promote it. If you are following up on a request for information on a $30 DVD, the cost and effort you'll want to expend will be considerably less than if you are answering leads for a $3,000 home entertainment center.

Many marketers try both one- and two-step programs on a given offer, to see which is more profitable in the long run. In the one-step approach, the marketer begins by sending a full-blown direct mail package to prospects, soliciting an immediate sale. In the two-step approach, the marketer might begin with a space ad or simple direct mail package, selling the "sizzle" of the product and inviting people to send for—or go online to ask for—more information at no obligation. Then the full-blown package would be sent only to inquiries, modified slightly to acknowledge their stated interest in the product. These modifications might include:

1. An envelope teaser stating "Here is the information you requested."
2. A revised letter thanking the person for requesting the information before launching the sales pitch.
3. Special wording on other pieces of the mail package that the lead-generation piece may have referred to, such as a premium slip, special-offer order form, and so on.

If you are selling a high-ticket item—like the $3,000 home entertainment center or an $800 online course—by means of a direct mail follow-up, one mailing package is generally not enough to maximize sales potential. Let's take the example of the $3,000 home entertainment center. You may well be able to spend hundreds of advertising dollars to convert just one sale on such an item, especially if you plan to follow up later with offers of accessories, DVDs, and other items with high margins. Thus, to stop after one follow-up package would be foolish. You can balance out the inexpensive sales you make on the first go-round with some harder-won sales generated by later efforts directed at highly qualified leads.

It is not advisable to simply re-mail the same package time and again to leads, hoping that they will eventually notice your mailing. Instead, come up with a series of mailings with varied appearances, appeals, and premium offers. You may save money through the use of standard components that you can print in quantity for use in several of the mailings. If you have obtained permission from the inquirer to send him or her e-mails, you may use this form of communication as a part of the solicitation series as well. But don't go into overkill with e-mail just because it's so inexpensive—you don't want to aggravate your inquiries to the point that they start to consider your messages "spam."

Exhibit 14.1 is an example of a possible mail-only campaign to convert leads.

Over a period of time spent selling items in a certain price/margin category, you will learn how many efforts you can make toward a list of qualified leads before the costs outweigh the rewards. In addition to possible e-mail tests, you may well want to test adding one or more phone calls as part of the conversion series to try to make the sale or at least find out why the customer is not responding. And if the customer does not end up purchasing this item, do not delete the name from your files. This may be a valuable potential customer for another offer you'll make in the near future.

A few additional points should be made about the conversion campaign described here. The reason for four-week intervals between mailings is to allow for orders to return in the mail and be noted on your records before the next mailing goes out. If you can accomplish this faster, the timing may

Exhibit 14.1. Direct Mail Conversion Campaign for Home Entertainment Center

Standard Components Checklist
1. 9" x 12" decorated outer envelope
2. #10 decorated outer envelope
3. Basic selling letter
4. 8-1/2" x 11" color brochure which can be folded down for the #10 outer envelope
5. Premium slip
6. Order form
7. Business reply envelope

Extra Components Checklist
A. Testimonial letter
B. Letter from an orchestra conductor who has tested the home entertainment center
C. Extra premium slip
D. Last-chance slip
E. Bulletin-format letter

Mailing	Timing	Contents	Mail class
#1	One week or less after receipt of lead	"Keep warm" letter with "sizzle" about package to come	First Class
#2	Two weeks or less after receipt of lead	1,3,4,5,6,7 (Outer envelope is stamped: "Here is the Information You Requested")	First Class
#3	Six weeks after receipt of lead	2,A,4,5,6,7	Standard
#4	Ten weeks after receipt of lead	1,B,4,5,6,7 (Outer envelope is stamped: "Inside: A Note to You from Famous Conductor (his or her name)")	Standard
#5	Fourteen weeks after receipt of lead	2,3,4,5,6,7,C (Outer envelope is stamped: "TWO Free Gifts: See Inside for Details"; letter has a handwritten message about the extra premium)	Standard
#6	Eighteen weeks after receipt of lead	2,E,4,5,6,7,D (Outer envelope is stamped: "Last Chance!")	Standard

be accelerated. Soliciting customers who have already responded is annoying to them, and costly for you. Initial mailings should go first class to make sure they are delivered promptly. To save money, later mailings in the conversion series may be sent by standard mail.

Another way to structure a conversion campaign is the one preferred by many distance learning schools. They make sure that the initial follow-up kit is loaded with all features and benefits that might appeal to the student: the glamour of the new career, or the chance to learn at home on one's own time schedule, for example. Then, each subsequent mailing highlights one benefit as the theme of its letter, supplemented by a brochure that covers all the positive points about the course.

To learn more about follow-up mailings, e-mails, and phone calls, send inquiries to a wide range of firms making two-step consumer and business-to-business offers. Save all of the follow-ups you receive by mail, e-mail and phone, noting the dates as they arrive. Then you will be able to reconstruct the creative approach and timing of various firms to spark ideas for your own efforts.

Reinforcing the Original Purchase

Put yourself in the place of your customer for a moment, and imagine that the product you ordered by direct response has just been delivered to your home. Better than imagining, make sure that you order products from your own firm or clients on a regular basis, as well as from major competitors. In any case, when a package arrives you open it and find the product inside. There it is: the dress or baseball glove or decor item you ordered days or weeks ago, all by itself, without the "sizzle" that was provided on the front end when you made the decision to buy it. This can be a letdown at a crucial moment when the customer needs reinforcement most.

The letdown doesn't have to occur if you, as the creative marketer, provide your customer with some materials to complement the purchase. You can do something along these lines for way less than a dollar per package, although some marketers spend considerably more to reinforce big-ticket purchases. Here are some ideas on what you could include in the package to make customers feel good about their purchases on receipt:

1. *Make the packaging attractive and appealing.* Use crisp tissue paper, elegant seals, reusable plastic storage bags, and other accoutrements that help present products with flair.

2. *Restate the reasons for buying.* Include a short letter or promotional piece that re-tells the story of the product and reminds customers of all the features and benefits that convinced them to buy it in the first place.

3. *Restate the guarantee and other terms of the offer.* Remind customers of their opportunity to put the item to use before deciding whether to keep it.

4. *Testimonials.* Include a few quotes from satisfied customers, especially those who have reordered the product many times. Each testimonial might discuss a different reason why the purchaser has found the product so useful, including ideas on various ways to put it to use.

5. *"How-to" information in easy-to-use form.* Even if it seems completely obvious how to put the product to use, remember that your customer is not as familiar with it as you are. A few step-by-step instructions, even on a simple item, will move the customer to start using the product right away. If your item is more complex, how-to information is essential. Before writing these how-tos, of course, you must have a thorough understanding of the product in use. Once you have prepared the material, share the product and instructions with some people who fit your customer profile. See if they find them understandable and usable. If they are confused at any point, your instructions need modification.

6. *Certificates and other documents that customers can save.* This could be a Certificate of Authenticity for a limited-edition collectible, a warranty statement for an appliance, or a small flyer providing an interesting historical background on the product.

7. *Clear instructions on how to return merchandise.* To make life easier both for your customer and you, tell them step-by-step how to return merchandise—and make the process as painless as possible for them so that they don't hesitate to order in the future.

8.. *A small thank-you gift.* This could be anything from a sample of skin cream to an inexpensive piece of jewelry—just a little something extra to surprise and delight the customer.

Achieving Better Margins on Sales

Because many direct and interactive marketers invest money to gain a new customer on the front end, actually going into the red on the first sale, it is essential that their back-end efforts yield a profit from that customer as soon as possible. This can be achieved in a number of productive ways. Here are several:

1. *Sell an accessory.* Nothing could be more appealing to the proud owner of a new product than something that is custom-made to enhance that prized possession. An MP3 player with headphones might come with a "ride-along" offer of small speakers to go with it. A red leather purse might be packaged along with an invitation to acquire a matching wallet and key holder. Or how about an attractive, protective cover, custom-made to fit the new e-Reader or Netbook? Such items can sell well even at hefty margins, and the profit is all the better since the offer is riding along for free with the shipment of the original purchase.

2. *Sell more, or sell better-quality items.* This tactic works best on items that are in need of quick replacement or replenishment. For instance, when you send the invoice for a magazine subscription, you can offer customers a bargain rate if they will pay for two years right away instead of just one. If you're delivering custom stationery, offer the customer a special deal on a larger quantity reorder, or a better-quality item.

3. *Send along package inserts.* Even if you offer customers something totally unrelated to the item they bought, you stand to do well if this second item is appealing to the same target market. When you have just delivered the main item the customer wanted, the timing and atmosphere for selling a second time are ideal. The customer has a good feeling about your firm, and now trusts you to deliver what you promise. Selling items of your own is one way to take advantage of this opportunity, but you may also consider allowing other direct and interactive marketers to buy package insert space in your shipments on a per-thousand or per-sale basis. It is essential, however, that you screen the package inserts that will ride along with your mailings to ensure that they are not competitive with your product line, and that they are in keeping with the image of your firm. If you sell $500 ladies' dresses, for instance, you would not want to allow a package insert for $19.99 lime green polyester slacks.

4. *Ask for referrals.* Getting a referral from a current customer won't help the margin you make on sales to him or her, but it may gain you a new customer very inexpensively. Your customers' friends are likely to be good prospects for you as well, since they probably share the same interests and socioeconomic

level. Indeed, you might offer your current customers an incentive for referring potential new customers, the so-called member-get-a-member plan. Music and book clubs give free merchandise to members who deliver friends or relatives as new, paying customers. Frequent traveler programs might provide bonus credits to their plan members who do the same. Other firms with unique product lines are able to succeed using a low-key approach, not offering any incentive other than the opportunity to share a good buying source with a like-minded friend.

Ensuring Continued Sales

After the sale and delivery of a first package to a customer, you'll need a way to keep up communications and sales. You'll want to set up a schedule of mailings (and e-mails, if you have permission to do so) to the customers on your list to keep your name on their minds and—more importantly—to keep bringing in more and bigger sales from them.

The more complete the information you can record on your database, the better a job you can do at targeting future promotions to individual customers. Send high-ticket offers to high-ticket buyers, for instance, and book offers to previous book buyers. Within these categories, high-ticket jewelry buyers might be broken down into those who prefer sapphires, amethysts, or rubies. Book buyers might be categorized as those who enjoy romance novels, the classics, or history texts.

Ever since Maxwell Sackheim and Harry Schermann started their Little Leather Library and Book-of-the-Month Club, direct and interactive marketers have been ensuring continued response by means of a front-end offer that helps win guaranteed sales on an ongoing basis. Here are some front-end offers you can make to improve the chances of regular, continuing sales from new customers.

Continuity Series. Offer the first of a series of books, movie DVDs, collectibles, food items, or how-to lessons on a front-end basis, with the promise of more to come in future mailings. You'll find that obligating customers to buy a number of items later on will probably cut the percentage of your original responses, but will also help avoid attrition as the program continues.

Testing will help you determine whether a tight or loose continuity pitch brings you the most net dollars over the life of the program. A tight continuity offer would explain very specifically to customers that they are expected to purchase x-number of items over a given period of time. A looser pitch would tell them of the existence of the additional items, but give them the option of continuing or not as they please. Loosest of all is the offer that sells the first item only, and then approaches the customer with the news that there are more items in a series that they may acquire if they so choose.

If you want to gain the greatest possible number of new customers but still have a continuity series over which to spread your cost of customer acquisition, try a loose front-end sale followed by a load-up offer, or a strong follow-up or "efforting" program on the back end.

The Load-Up Offer. The load-up offer comes after the customer has received the book, DVD, or other item he or she originally ordered. You offer the customer the opportunity to receive all of the books, DVDs, or whatever you're selling in the series, but to pay for them in convenient monthly installments over a given period of time. This cuts your shipping costs, because you'll send all of the remaining items in a single shipment. If you opt for this system, provide your customers with a coupon book so that they can make their monthly payments easily, or send them a monthly invoice/reminder by mail or e-mail. Also, test the offer to make sure you aren't stuck with too many uncollectible accounts.

The Efforting Program. This is another way to bring in additional sales from customers who were offered products on a continuity basis but with no obligation to buy. This is usually a multi-step correspondence plan. Here is how a typical efforting program might work:

1. *With the original shipment*, send the customer a selling letter, a small brochure with a picture of the next product, and an ordering device.
2. *After four weeks*, mail again to those who have not ordered the product. Send a different letter, the same or different brochure or picture, and once again an ordering device.
3. *After four more weeks*, send a more urgent message to those who have not yet responded. A telegram format with a "last chance" order form is one idea.
4. If the economics of your program allow for it, you might test adding a *telephone follow-up* after the first or second solicitation to see if it converts at acceptable levels.
5. If you have obtained permission from the customer to do so, you might add one or more *e-mail follow-ups* as well.

The number of mailings, calls, and/or e-mails in your efforting program will depend on their relative effectiveness and the price of the item you are selling. A big-ticket, high mark-up item may still yield acceptable results with a fourth or even a fifth effort, while a low-end product may merit only one or two efforts.

Negative Option. Many direct response clubs are run on a negative-option basis: customers agree to receive the monthly book, movie or music selection unless they make the effort to return a card or go online to make an alternate purchase, or direct the club to send nothing at all that month. This is a proven way to gain new customers and make them profitable over a given period. Customers are brought in under a "Four Books for $1" type of offer, with the marketer making an investment to gain the customer's name and his or her promise to make at least a minimum of future purchases. The customer agrees to buy X number of books, DVDs, or other merchandise over a specified period and also has the option to buy a number of other items via monthly mailings. The key here is to learn by testing how loose or tight the front-end offer must be to yield enough customers, at acceptable sales per customer, in the long run.

Positive Option. The positive-option program works exactly the same as the negative option, except that the customer will receive no shipment unless he/she returns a card or makes a phone call to initiate it.

Ship 'til Forbid. This is the ultimate in a continuity series: the customer gives the marketer the right to continue shipping products on a monthly, bimonthly, or other basis unless the customer expressly tells the marketer to cease. This can be a smooth way of obtaining nearly guaranteed sales, especially if customers provide their credit card numbers so that the marketer simply ships the product at regular intervals and puts the charge on the customer's account. The same can be done with "provide service 'til forbid"—for example, online services like Netflix provide ongoing movie rental opportunities to customers and bill them monthly by credit card.

Another option is to ship the item with an invoice enclosed or sent separately, but here the marketer must keep careful records to make sure an acceptable number of items is paid for before additional shipments are made. In the case of all of these offers for ensuring continued sales, it is important to make sure that the offer and follow-up sales information are worded according to legal requirements as well as sales requirements. The services of a seasoned direct mail copywriter, followed by a careful reading by a lawyer with experience in direct and interactive marketing, will avoid problems later.

Pay for Necessary Mailings with Ride-Along Offers

While many marketers have convinced their customers to receive invoices and pay bills online, there are still many millions of invoices and payment reminders sent monthly to customers by mail. Retailers are masters of the ride-along offer, sending stuffers as well as return envelopes with selling messages and tear-off coupons—called "bangtails"—with most every monthly statement to customers. Whenever you send an invoice or other communication to a customer, why not take a cue from the retailers and include some type of offer to help pay for the mailing? The premium-due notices of insurance companies, for instance, often include stuffers offering information about other policies. An invoice on a continuity program could have a brochure of seasonal merchandise "riding along" with it. Customer-service notices, order acknowledgments, and other correspondence often allow space for a selling message within the one-ounce limit for the lowest rate on first-class mail.

Ensuring Outstanding Customer Service

Simmons Research indicates 37 percent of those Americans who bought by mail in a one-year period experienced customer service problems. Many of these points fall under the heading of fulfillment and operations, but it is essential that any direct communication with customers carries a marketing orientation. Here are some examples of customer service activities you can carry on to reinforce the customer's positive impression on the back end:

1. *Acknowledge orders.* Sending an immediate order acknowledgment by e-mail (or first-class mail if the customer does not disclose an e-mail address) is vital in today's world. Customers are used to clicking the "confirm order" button and immediately seeing a confirmation e-mail appear—if you do not meet this standard, customers will be suspect . . . and you will receive a raft of customer service inquiries that would have been unnecessary if you had met your customers' expectations. As simple as text e-mail that reviews the order information, or elaborate enough to contain other offers, the acknowledgment eases customers' minds, letting them know that their purchases are on the way. If you can provide them with an estimated shipping time along with the acknowledgment, so much the better. Many marketers also send additional e-mails to let the customer know that their order has been processed, and that it has been shipped. Ideally the shipment e-mail will contain tracking information so that the customer knows when the package(s) will arrive and what carrier will bring them.
2. *Let customers know how to reach you.* Provide a specific toll-free customer service number, e-mail address, and physical address. Don't make the customer who has a problem hunt too hard to find you. He or she can shop with plenty of other direct and interactive marketers who are highly accessible and responsive, and therefore you will also have to be.

Exhibit 14.2. Amazon Order Acknowledgment

Thanks for your order, Susan K. Jones!

Want to manage your order online?
If you need to check the status of your order or make changes, please visit our home page at Amazon.com and click on Your Account at the top of any page.

Purchasing Information:

E-mail Address: sjones9200@aol.com

Billing Address:	**Shipping Address:**
Susan K. Jones	Susan K. Jones
251 Plymouth SE	251 Plymouth SE
East Grand Rapids, MI 49506	East Grand Rapids, MI 49506
United States	United States

Order Grand Total: $61.88

Get the Amazon.com Rewards Visa Card and earn **3% rewards** on your Amazon.com orders.

Order Summary:

Shipping Details : (order will arrive in 1 shipment)

Order #:	102-4188401-5027465
Shipping Method:	FREE Super Saver Shipping
Shipping Preference:	Group my items into as few shipments as possible
Subtotal of Items:	$61.88
Shipping & Handling:	$8.83
Super Saver Discount:	-$8.83

Total for this Order:	**$61.88**

Shipping estimate for these items: May 27, 2010
  2 "Brown Ram Wrought Iron Coaster Holders - Style h25"
    $11.99

    Sold by: Alien Marketing International inc.
  2 "Set of Four Fleur de Lis Thirstystone Coasters - Style ts2141"
    $18.95

    Sold by: Thirstycoasters.com

Need to print an invoice?
Visit www.amazon.com/your-account and click to view your orders. Click "View order" next to the appropriate order. You'll find a button to print an invoice on the next page

Where can I get help with reviewing or changing my orders?
To learn more about managing your orders on Amazon.com, please visit our Help pages at amazon.com/help/orders/.

Please note: This e-mail message was sent from a notification-only address that cannot accept incoming e-mail. Please do not reply to this message.

If you ever need to return an order, visit our Online Returns Center: www.amazon.com/returns

Thanks again for shopping with us.

Amazon.com
Earth's Biggest Selection

  Prefer not to receive HTML mail? Click here

Amazon.com acknowledges orders instantly once they are placed, sending an e-mail to the purchaser that recaps the order in detail.

Reprinted from an e-mail received from *www.amazon.com*.

3. *Send a letter with each shipment.* The so-called ship letter provides a perfect opportunity to thank the customer for the purchase and avoid post-purchase letdown. The ship letter should also welcome brand-new customers, and thank seasoned customers for returning with another order.

4. *Send a welcome package.* In addition to the welcoming ship letter, some firms greet first-time customers with a special package that acquaints them with the product, the firm, and the benefits of buying in this way. To help pay for the mailing, the "welcome kit" can contain buying opportunities for accessories and related products.

5. *Give the customer a "thank you" gift, or discount.* With every order over $100, you might, as an example, provide a surprise thank-you gift tucked into the package with a note. Or include another offer in the package with a very special discount for preferred customers only. Some firms establish their personalities by providing something special or free with each order. A firm in maple syrup country might tuck in a small package of maple sugar candy with every order. A cosmetics company might provide a free sample of the latest skin care treatment or eye shadow.

6. *Send a newsletter or other chatty correspondence.* Make the customer feel like a preferred member of your "family" with a newsletter in the product package announcing special offers or discounts for preferred customers only. This may be a great way to clear out small-inventory items and please your customers at the same time. Many firms send newsletters via e-mail, and feature both informative articles and product offers.

7. *Provide "preferred customers only" benefits.* These might include advance notices when sales or special values are available; a specific, extra-helpful telephone salesperson whom only your regular customers know is available; a password-protected Web site area with benefits available only to best customers; monthly discounts on various items available only to customers who are sent special coupons; quantity discounts; free gift wrapping; or some other "extra" that you offer and deliver only to persons on your present-customer list. Don't make the mistake of offering any of these extra services on the front end—at least not free or at the same discount your preferred people are getting. The service or item must be an exclusive, special-treatment one that makes customers want to continue being considered part of your firm's "inner circle."

8. *Make it simple to return goods.* Because clothing merchants traditionally have very high return rates, you might think they would shy away from telling customers directly how to send back unsatisfactory merchandise. But to get customers to buy something as personal as sized clothing by mail or online, it is essential that they feel no obligation to keep an unsatisfactory item. Thus, sellers of clothes have learned to build the cost of returns into their pricing structures, and to make it easy for their customers to accomplish a return or exchange. They may include a return-shipment label in the package and offer a step-by-step guide to returning the item. A simple form for the customer to fill out will also help, and enable you to find out the customer's reason for returning the item, which is valuable market research information.

9. *Send a thank-you note or card at year's end.* Thanks are appreciated any time

Exhibit 14.3. L. L. Bean Return Page

L. L. Bean makes it easy for customers to return merchandise, explaining everything step-by-step on this Web page and also including full information with each shipment.

Reprinted from the L. L. Bean site at *www.llbean.com*.

of year, but a letter or e-mail to preferred customers on an annual basis is a nice gesture. If you can personalize the letter so that it mentions items or categories the customer purchased, so much the better. A thank-you gift or discount for customers at certain purchase levels is a nice gesture, too.

10. *Make sure your inbound telephone functions are state-of-the-art.* Today's best marketers serve phone-in customers with database functions that streamline ordering and customer service processes and provide customers with valuable information on product availability, shipping times, gift shipments, etc. Best of the lot are the systems that can identify an individual using a customer number that appears on each catalog or mailing. Next best are systems that identify customers using their zip codes and names. It's always a good idea to "order from yourself" by mail, phone, and online, and make customer service calls regularly as a spot check to make sure customers are being treated promptly, efficiently, and with courtesy and care.

Collection Letters for Overdue Accounts

A well-written series of collection letters is a necessity for many direct and interactive marketers who send out merchandise before it is paid for. This back-end function is often neglected, put off, or given half-attention, when it can be taken care of very simply.

Keep in mind that the function of a collection letter is quite different from the function of a selling or efforting letter. In the case of collections, the customer has already committed to the product. You need not sell him or her on the product, but only on the concept of paying for it.

Begin with an invoice and a "thank you for ordering" letter. Restatement of benefits is appropriate here, to reinforce the wisdom of the purchase decision and smooth the way to a payment.

Four weeks later, start your collection series to those who have not paid. Lead off with a gentle reminder. Then in subsequent efforts, become a bit more urgent and terse with each letter, using your treasurer or accountant as the signer. Depending upon the dollar amounts involved, your collection series might range from two letters to six or more. In the final letter, take a "last chance" tone and note that you will be forced to turn the matter over to a collection agency if you do not receive payment immediately.

At this point, do turn delinquent accounts over to a good collection agency. It is not wise for your firm or client to write harsh or threatening letters to customers who may once again become valued buyers at a later date. For specific pointers and model letters for a collection series, check one of the standard business-letter reference books.

Gaining Renewals for Periodicals and Clubs

The big money in selling periodicals and club concepts by direct mail is in the renewals. The $12 or $25 paid the first time around is unlikely to cover both the cost of obtaining the name of a customer and a year's order-fulfillment activities. For each additional year for which the customer can be persuaded to remain a reader or club member, the profit of dealing with him or her improves. Thus it is worthwhile to prepare and implement an aggressive subscription- or membership-renewal program—one with four, six, or even eight steps in all.

Most renewal series begin several months before the renewal date, with a special incentive for renewing early. This might be a discount, a premium, or several free issues of a publication. On the other hand, some marketers hold off on special offers until later in a series because they have found that a good percentage of their customers will respond to a straight offer right away. The marketer can therefore save the more costly offers for the purpose of convincing the less eager segments of their customer lists to respond. Over the series of mailings, a number of formats may be used, and an extensive testing program is advised to make sure you are optimizing response and cost-effectiveness. Here are several format ideas:

- A simple, double postcard with a tear-off half for the customer to return by business reply mail. All the customer then has to do is check off "Yes," and he or she will be billed for the subscription or membership.
- A bulletin-type letter warning that the customer may lose valuable issues or membership benefits unless he or she responds in time.
- A traditional envelope mailing with a feature/benefit letter touting the exciting, specific events and articles coming up for those who renew. This mailing might also include a brochure, premium slip, and reply card.
- A contest offer, giving those who respond either "Yes" or "No" an equal opportunity to win. (Human nature tells the customer that he'll have a better chance of winning if he says "Yes," even though by law that isn't the case.)
- An "action device" tipped onto the letter, such as a sticker that looks like the cover of the magazine, to be transferred to the order form and sent back with the order.
- For membership pitches, a temporary membership card that the customer can keep until the permanent card is sent after the customer sends in the renewal.
- A wrap-around piece bound onto one of the last issues before cancellation to encourage prompt action with its built-in reply device.

Retaining and Upgrading Donors to Nonprofits

According to the Giving USA Foundation, Americans give more than $300 billion annually to charity. And although the power of personal persuasion should not be overlooked in fundraising, direct and interactive marketing offers a number of attributes that help nonprofit organizations maximize their resource development efforts.

Direct and interactive marketing methods provide:

- A cost-effective, measurable way to target and reach a large number of donors, all at the same time—not when volunteers or staff can get around to it.
- The means to develop a database that is not dependent upon the personal knowledge, special relationships, and individual biases of funds solicitors, and which is readily available for use.
- The opportunity to take advantage of sophisticated predictive modeling techniques that draw upon demographic and psychographic information as well as donor actions.
- The chance to highlight appeals for specific groups of donors based upon age and stage of life, income, special interests, wants and needs, previous donor history, etc.
- The ability to provide donors with "the whole story" about your program in written or video form—with materials that can be saved or printed out for reference or passed along.

Meeting the Needs of Donors via Direct Marketing. As Abraham Maslow explained in his book *Motivation and Personality*, each of us has a never-ending supply of needs to fulfill. Just as we sometimes satisfy these needs through the purchase and use of products and services, contributions to nonprofits can assuage our needs in various ways.

As the low-level *survival* needs of food, water, clothing, and shelter are satisfied, the human animal begins to crave *safety*, security, and the avoidance of pain. Once these basic requirements are covered, people desire *affiliation*—warm social interaction with like-minded people. Higher yet on Maslow's Hierarchy of Needs is *self-esteem*, developed by means of personal achievement, and the recognition of others. The ultimate need is for *self-actualization*—developing in all areas of life to become an independent, well-rounded person.

Direct and interactive marketers can make use of their databases, research, and demographic data to determine the "need levels" of their various donor groups, thereby providing attractive benefits to donors.

- *Survival and safety needs.* Most desirable donors have the education and money to move beyond the low levels of the Hierarchy of Needs. But even so, "fear" appeals with the theme "there but for the grace of God go I" can sometimes be effective. Donors may believe that giving to your cause somehow lessens their own chances of family tragedy, losing the power to control their own destinies, or contracting a deadly disease.
- *Affiliation.* In his book *The Membership Mystique*, the late fundraising impresario Richard P. Trenbeth quoted the observation of French philosopher Alexis de Tocqueville that Americans are inveterate "joiners" who enjoy associating with like-minded individuals. Thus many nonprofits cultivate relationships with donors by offering them membership in museum groups, symphony societies, college and university alumni groups, political action committees, and organizations devoted to animal rights. The "transaction" becomes complete when the organization provides various perquisites to its member/donors, including social, educational, and material benefits.
- *Self-esteem and self-actualization.* If a donor has basic physical and safety needs under control and already feels comfortably affiliated in home and community, he or she may well respond best to fundraising appeals that feed the need for self-esteem and self-actualization. Benefits proven to motivate such donors by developing self-esteem include those which provide praise and recognition for a job well done. Self-actualization benefits might include opportunities to do specific good toward meeting altruistic goals, and the chance to achieve immortality by leaving something important behind.

Creative Tips for Direct Response Fundraisers. Many of the proven back-end and relationship-building methods developed for profit-making ventures are used with great success by fundraisers. Here are a few specific tips that are especially helpful in creating effective fundraising solicitations:

- *Focus on the results of your work.* Don't tell donors about your wonderful new building or your dedicated staff. Tell them how you are saving lives, overcoming threats, inspiring youth to new heights.
- *Play upon human interest.* Use success stories about individuals whose lives

have been changed for the better by this nonprofit, not generalizations about how many people have been served.

- *Use the database to address donors personally.* Send customized communications to donors segmented by donation size and potential donation, specified area of interest, age and stage of life, etc.
- *Use celebrity endorsements where appropriate.* The same caveats apply here as in for-profit marketing: celebrities must be credible and likable to your target market. Ideally they would be known for their hands-on involvement with your cause—for example, former president Jimmy Carter and his wife Rosalynn, who have spent considerable time building houses for Habitat for Humanity.

Exhibit 14.4. Jimmy Carter and Habitat for Humanity

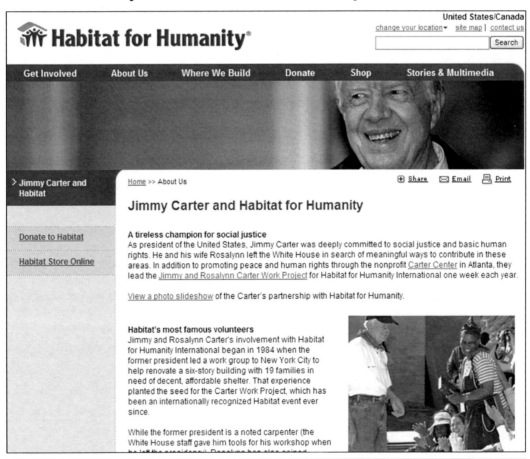

Habitat for Humanity showcases the commitment of former President Jimmy Carter on its Web page. Mr. Carter's commitment to the Habitat cause provides a powerful endorsement for potential donors and volunteers.

Reprinted from the Habitat for Humanity site at *www.habitat.org*.

- *State your position clearly.* A strong position statement is essential, because donors need to perceive a compelling and specific need before they will be motivated to respond. Thus, fundraising solicitations can and should be outspoken. They should take a definite stand, even if it may alienate some readers who are not part of the target market.
- *Ride the crest of public opinion.* Strike while the iron is hot during political campaigns and times when your issue is in the news. Your supporters may be especially likely to respond if their position is being publicly assailed, or if disaster strikes and the need for support is crucial.
- *Test involvement devices and action techniques.* Consider the full arsenal of direct marketing techniques as potential winners for your fundraising campaigns. See Chapter 10 for a host of ideas to test in direct mail.
- *Use urgency and ask for specific action.* In the fundraising arena, urgency often comes quite naturally because of a pressing problem or crying need. It is also important to ask for a specific action, including a suggested contribution amount that gently and appropriately challenges the donor to a higher level.
- *Acknowledge and thank donors promptly.* Immediate turnaround with a personal thank-you from an appropriate staff member or volunteer is essential. Fundraising expert Daryl Vogel says that organizations should "find seven ways to thank donors before asking them for more money." These ways might include thank-you notes, progress updates, e-mailed or paper newsletters, invitations to events and site visits, membership credentials, and so on.
- *Find ways to upgrade donors.* The existing donor base is the best source of future money for most all fundraising organizations and thus these donors should be cultivated carefully to maximize their lifetime values. A good database will allow the organization to guide donors along a gradual path of increasing involvement and monetary investment by suggesting manageable yearly upgrades and "holding out carrots" involving status, special events, and opportunities. Today, many organizations also spend a good deal of time educating their best donors about matching-grant opportunities, bequests, trusts, and other long-term programs.
- *Consider sales opportunities and catalogs.* In recent years, scores of cultural institutions have begun to explore merchandising opportunities aimed not only at their donors, but also at a wide range of potential customers. Museums, public broadcasting companies and individual nonprofits all have gained additional revenue—often by creating catalogs that carry the same merchandise as their on-site gift stores.

Enhance Dialogue With the Customer to Improve Future Recommendations and Service

Hugely successful online marketers including Amazon.com and Netflix.com encourage their customers to rate every purchase or rental, and to provide candid feedback to sellers and fellow customers. Such engagement methods help bond the customer to the company—and the information gained through ratings and comments help these marketers provide increasingly more relevant suggestions.

Amazon.com sends out periodic e-mails to customers inviting them to "Improve Your Recom-

Exhibit 14.5. Chicago Symphony Orchestra Store

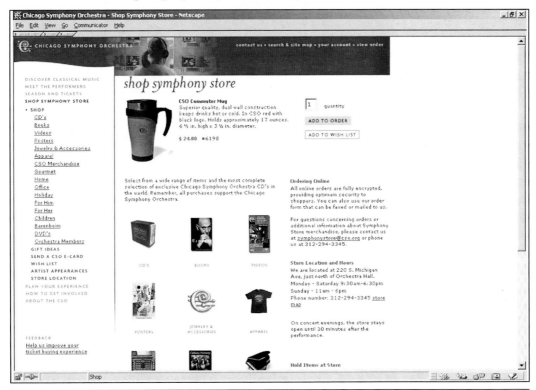

The Chicago Symphony Orchestra gains incremental revenue from patrons and others all over the world through this online store at *www.cso.org.*

Reprinted from the Chicago Symphony Orchestra site at *www.cso.org.*

mendations" on recently purchased items. Items can be rated from one star (I hate it) up to five stars (I love it). Amazon cleverly allows raters to note that "this was a gift"—in other words, the customer bought it for someone else and this item should not be used as part of the algorithm for his or her future recommendations. Like eBay, Amazon also invites customers to rate their experience with the site's affiliated vendors.

Netflix asks DVD renters to rate the movies they view and also encourages them to post detailed reviews. In addition, Netflix invites renters to "rate movies you've seen to discover movies you'll love"—including movies seen years ago, on the big screen, and through other means besides Netflix. Then when visiting the site, Netflix offers up rows of suggested titles that seem to embody the rater's interests. For instance, Netflix has presented your author with a large quantity of offerings based on a demonstrated preference for "critically acclaimed quirky comedies," "romantic movies," and "understated dramas with strong female leads."

Exhibit 14.6. Netflix Recommendations

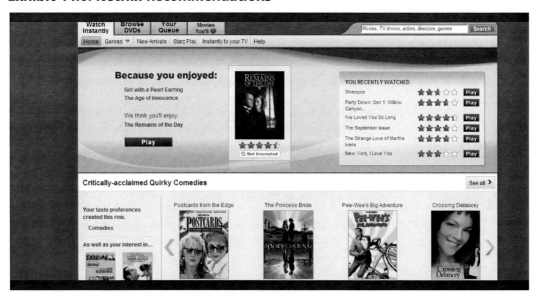

Netflix invites DVD renters to rate movies they have seen via Netflix and other sources in order to categorize customers' preferences and present them with options for upcoming rentals.

Reprinted from the Netflix site at *www.netflix.com*.

Building Long-Term Loyalty Through Relationship Marketing

In 1981, American Airlines launched its AAdvantage program as a means of cultivating customer loyalty. Other airlines soon followed American's lead, offering points toward free flights and other benefits to customers based on miles and segments flown. In the present day, most every airline, hotel chain, financial services firm, telecommunications company, and retailer boasts one or more "relationship" or "frequency" marketing programs. Many of these programs were started as defensive measures—"because the competition is doing it"—rather than as well-planned, strategic initiatives in keeping with the firm's long-terms goals. In retrospect, many firms locked into ongoing relationship marketing plans may now regret it, because their customers have come to view such programs as "parity entitlements" instead of "unique, value-added perquisites." This section will provide a framework for informed decision-making on relationship marketing, as well as some creative ideas on how to structure and administer a successful program.

Turning Customers into Advocates

A relationship marketing model from a division of Experian emphasizes the importance of moving from traditional mass marketing to what the firm calls "segment of one" marketing—meeting the individual customer's needs and thereby enhancing his or her lifetime value to the company. When the proper database is developed to do this effectively, the firm's experts argue that first-time "customers" can be turned into valuable, repeat-purchase "clients." Ultimately, the highly satisfied client may become an "advocate"—one who buys repeatedly from the firm across multiple categories, and actively refers others to become customers.

Michael LeBoeuf, author of *How to Win Customers and Keep Them for Life*, believes that clients become advocates because they feel "rewarded." As he notes, "It's the rewarded customer who tells others just how wonderful your products or services are, which, in turn, creates more customers. The rewarded customer buys, multiplies and comes back."

Marketing expert Regis McKenna asserts that "service" is the key to relationship marketing. In a world of parity products, customers need to receive exceptional "information, assurance and comfort" to remain loyal.

Direct marketing expert Jeanne Garrett points out that "meeting needs" and "providing service" need not be costly activities to the firm. Indeed, customer needs are often best met by providing tailored and timely buying opportunities. Ms. Garrett says:

> I happen to have a copy of the current *AARP—The Magazine* (from the American Association of Retired Persons—for people over age 50). As I leaf through it, I see they have maximized opportunities to deepen the customer relationship, gather information, and generate revenue by providing opportunitie to:
>
> - Sign up for their credit card
> - Sign up for group health insurance by using a personalized insert
> - Gather information regarding exercise habits by using a survey. (Obviously, this can be used for future marketing or even list rental opportunities)
> - Sign up for AARP Life Insurance
> - Sign up for AARP's Investment program and so on

Nonetheless Ms. Garrett cautions firms to "think long and hard about whether to begin a loyalty program. Do they really work? Can the cost be justified? Who should be targeted?"

Formal Loyalty Program Versus Ongoing "Customer Delights"

While many firms have already invested heavily in formal programs for "relationship building," "frequency," or "loyalty," this is not the only way to approach the strategic issues of "long-term value" and "share of wallet." In addition to or instead of such a formal program, many firms have seen the wisdom of "delighting customers" with unexpected personal service, gifts, and opportunities.

A marvelous example of "customer delight" was recounted by a car buyer who picked up his new vehicle from the dealer after leaving his trade-in a day or two before. When he turned on the new car's radio, he was surprised to hear his favorite FM station. He pushed the pre-set buttons for both FM and AM and to his *delight,* they were already programmed for the same stations he'd had on his trade-in car. The technician who performed the new car's final prep work invested a few minutes to provide this unexpected, personal service. As a creative marketer, you could create the same sense of delight in your individual customers by mail, phone, e-mail, or online by using communication, intuition, and good database information.

The "customer delight" concept helps overcome the problem of "entitlement" that has diminished the strategic effect of many formalized loyalty programs. When many of the airline frequent flyer programs raised their basic "free ticket" miles from 20,000 to 25,000, some program members became aggravated if not incensed. Keep in mind, they were still being offered something of real value absolutely free—but they perceived that something was being taken away . . . something they felt entitled to for going by the rules of the airline's structured, formalized program.

Combining "Hard" and "Soft" Benefits

Richard G. Barlow, founder of Frequency Marketing (now part of Epsilon), defines the function of relationship or "frequency" marketing as follows: "To identify, maintain and increase the yield from best customers through long-term, interactive, value-added relationships." While a formal program with rules and specific benefits and rewards may help fulfill these goals, many firms have yielded even more long-term loyalty by combining both formal and informal perquisites based on knowledge of the customer.

Barlow calls the formal offers "hard benefits"—products or services for which the customer otherwise would have to pay and which the seller pays for. He calls the informal offers "soft benefits"—something emotional and unexpected, special recognition, or insider information and opportunities. *Colloquy* (*www.colloquy.com*), the online newsletter, offers specific examples of ongoing loyalty programs as well as strategic how-tos for frequency marketers.

Effective Relationship Marketing Requires a Corporate Commitment

A Michigan-based bank introduced its own affinity credit card and offered miles toward airline travel based on customer usage. Within months, the bank pulled the program, citing "too much success" as the reason. Customers had overwhelmed the bank with their usage of the card and resulting demand for airline tickets. Rather than rejoice in their success and adjust to the demand, the bank backed away. Their initial effort to win customer loyalty did them more harm than good, as the media, customers, and non-customers alike talked about the failed program for months.

This painful anecdote underlines the importance of pre-planning and ongoing support for any relationship marketing program. Unless your firm is willing to make an ongoing commitment to the program, whatever the results may be, it is better to avoid such a dramatic undertaking. Indeed, successful relationship marketing must become a way of life for the firm and all its service, operations, and communications personnel—a facet of Customer Relationship Management (CRM) rather than an encapsulated "promotion." Experts suggest that every new relationship marketing program even include plans for a "graceful exit" if the program should ever need to end—preferably an exit that includes "farewell perquisites" for loyal customer participants.

Moving Beyond "Programs" to Serve the "Segment of One"

It is essential to recognize that relationship marketing programs cannot be "set and forgotten." The marketplace is such that new and better benefits appear almost weekly in many competitive frames. To maximize participation and profits, you must constantly monitor the success of each program facet and test new opportunities for your participants. What's more, this work must be done on a customer-by-customer basis, not on the averages. If a customer stops using your airline as the number-one choice, stops pulling your credit card "first from the wallet," or changes incentive plans on his or her phone/Internet/TV bundle, you must be aware of these changes and react with prompt, appropriate, and courteous incentives to return.

As the sophistication of databases and CRM software increases, and as companies come to a true understanding of the power of "one-to-one marketing," it is likely that formalized relationship-building programs that are open to anyone will continue to fade in importance. They are being replaced by individualized communications and opportunities based on what specific customers value and appreciate. The individual customer must become and remain the focus of all our relationship-building efforts.

As the late Betty Warden of Betty Warden Direct Marketing once said, "We've all heard of the GE Answer Center and how its *raison d'être* is customer service. Through working with GE Supply, a client of mine some years back, I was privy to attending a training session for new inside sales reps at their customer service center in Indianapolis. To stress the importance of the customer, the organization chart began with 'The Customer' on top, not the CEO as in most other places. Needless to say, that left a *very* strong impression."

Enhance Your Understanding: Cultivating the Long-Term Value of Customers

Your firm sells flowers and other gifts via mail, phone, and online services. You want to maximize the value of each new customer and gain as much "share of wallet" from each customer as possible. Outline a program that you believe will turn your new customers into repeat customers—and eventually, positive advocates for your firm and its products and services. Include your thoughts on orienting new customers, ongoing communications, privileges for customers, special offers, etc.

15

Other Consumer Direct and Interactive Marketing Media

Smart marketers today are embracing multichannel marketing: the combination of traditional, awareness-building media like network TV and big-circulation magazines with precision-targeted media such as direct mail, e-mail, sponsored search ads, social media, and mobile marketing.

For that reason, depending upon the client, budget, and marketing situation, a direct and interactive marketing creative person may be called upon to develop anything from a television spot to a mobile text message. Many direct and interactive marketers concentrate their integrated marketing plans on direct mail, space advertising, broadcast spots, catalogs, and digital media including Web sites, e-mail, and social networking. That said, there are a number of other media that may be added to the mix and stimulate a direct response from the consumer.

In most cases, a good understanding of direct and interactive marketing techniques will serve the writer and designer well as they produce work for these diverse media. In addition, the creative person should take two essential actions before beginning any assignment in a new medium: obtaining live samples through personal experience with the medium, and calling upon the vendor for advice.

Obtaining Live Samples

Whenever possible, the creative person should decoy the new medium. Ask the vendor to put your name on the mailing list for co-ops and card decks. Order products from firms known to include package inserts in their shipments. Pull the co-op Free-Standing Inserts of Valassis and other sources from your Sunday newspaper. Save the samples and coupon packs you receive in the mail from Valpak and other sources. Don't be too quick to sign up for the telephone "Do Not Call" list. Listen to the pitches of the telephone solicitors who call you, from beginning to end, absorbing their techniques. You can always decline at the end of the offer, and then see what methods they use to try to overcome your objections. Take advantage of opportunities to text offer codes to mobile marketers and see how well they respond with targeted and timely offers.

Study the samples you receive in their own environments. Which card seems to pop out of the card deck? Why? Which package insert in the group of six or eight seems to make the most impact? Of all the telemarketing pitches you listened to, which sold (or came closest to selling) you the product or service? Which companies used mobile marketing the most respectfully, and made you the most compelling offers? Begin to analyze for yourself what the success factors are in each medium. And watch for the cards and inserts and ads and mobile offers that show up month after month in these media. They may not be barn burners, but they must be effective enough to merit repeat runs. What do you think is the key to their success?

Asking the Vendor for Advice

Sales representatives who make their bread and butter from co-ops, package inserts, telemarketing, or mobile marketing can be among your best sources of advice on how to create the most effective product. Some vendors are better at this than others, so you should always take their words with a grain of salt. Many vendors offer how-to booklets, white papers, or reprints of articles that can help you pick up on the appeals and techniques that work best in each new medium.

This chapter will discuss creative approaches toward the following media: telemarketing, mobile marketing, co-ops, card decks, co-op Free-Standing Inserts, package inserts and ride-alongs, super-market take-ones, and unique ad media.

Telemarketing

Telemarketing (also known as teleservices or contact and call center marketing) can be a highly lucrative field, but it has been under fire from regulators and legislators in recent years. With both the Federal Trade Commission and the Federal Communications Commission inviting consumers to place their names on "Do Not Call" lists, and many states posting regulations of their own, prospecting by phone has become quite challenging. However, telemarketers still have the opportunity to communicate with willing consumers who are inquirers or buyers, so long as they comply with all appropriate rules and laws. What's more, most of the "Do Not Call" regulations exempt nonprofits and political organizations as well as most business-to-business calling. Before embarking on a telemarketing campaign, smart marketers will seek guidance on rules and regulations from the Direct Marketing Association, the American Teleservices Association, or a proven telemarketing expert-consultant.

Undaunted by the regulations that make telemarketing challenging, direct and interactive marketers continue to use it quite extensively. According to the Direct Marketing Association, telemarketing advertising expenditures are expected to reach $41.5 billion by 2014, with consumer sales driven by telemarketing projected at nearly $148.5 billion, and business-to-business sales driven by telemarketing projected at nearly $194.9 billion in that same year.

The boom in database marketing has allowed telemarketers to approach prospects with a great deal more selectivity than they could in the past. On one end of the continuum is the automatic dialer that calls every number with a recorded pitch. Even if such a technique pays out financially with short-term sales, it undermines the legitimate, targeted functions of telemarketing and encourages consumers to support further legislative restrictions. On the other end of the continuum is the sophisticated telemarketer who calls proven customers or well-qualified prospects with an appealing, well-tailored offer.

Telemarketing is divided into two main segments: inbound and outbound. *Inbound telemarketing* allows customers to order or make customer service inquiries. Inbound telemarketing usually involves providing toll-free numbers for customers and prospects to use. *Outbound telemarketing* takes place when the marketer calls a customer or prospect with an offer, announcement, proactive customer service message, or request for payment.

Direct marketers are divided on the effectiveness of inbound telemarketing for order taking. A minority of firms find that their telephone volume merely cannibalizes sales they would have received by mail or online. Most report a net increase in sales when the toll-free number is offered as an alternative for ordering. What's more, many customers appreciate the opportunity to speak to a human being and get clarification and reassurance about their purchases. This helps explain the popularity of "call me" features on Web sites—opportunities for the customer to ask for an immediate, helpful call from one of the company's sales representatives. (Live chat on Web sites is another feature appreciated by many customers.)

Another plus for inbound ordering is that the operators may offer callers an upgrade on their purchases, a daily special, or a telephone-only sale. This technique can increase average order size, help sell out small lots of merchandise on hand, and build the relationship with the customer. If the buyer can find out immediately from the phone rep which items are in stock and when they will be delivered, the firm reaps another positive customer relations benefit. Some firms ask a database-building question or two of customers who call them, offering an additional benefit to the call.

Most direct and interactive marketing firms now consider a well-staffed telephone customer service operation essential. The best of these operations have customers' ordering histories and current orders online so that a status report on back orders and shipments can be made in a matter of seconds. Their staffers have immediate access to the firm's Web site, and can speak to questions about items offered only on the Web. Such a customer service department also can keep a firm up to date with the pulse of the marketplace, and understanding customers' changing wants, needs, and concerns. What's more, some firms use all inbound customer service calls as an opportunity to try to "upsell" the customer after his or her problem is solved.

Outbound telemarketing is considerably more expensive than direct mail, yet for firms with offers well-suited to the medium, it can be just as profitable if not more so. The key to success lies in targeting the right prospects or customers, and developing a suitable script and approach. Although some firms consider consumer telemarketing a primary medium for following up leads and/or one-step selling to consumers, others use outbound calling only as a supplementary tool. An example of supplementary use would be calling established magazine subscribers who have not sent payment for the next year's subscription by renewal time.

The Creative Approach to Telemarketing

Effective telemarketing to consumers begins with a well-written script. Scripting is important to ensure uniformity of approach as well as split-second timing. Most consumer scripts are written verbatim, while many business-to-business scripts list only the essential points to be covered.

To prepare for scripting, the writer needs the same background material that is necessary for a direct mail package or space ad. Total familiarity with the product or service and its features and benefits is essential. The competitive environment is important, too. Consumers will know whether your offer stacks up, and may compare your offer to others they have seen. A talk with salespeople can be very helpful in clarifying typical consumer reactions and objections to this product or service. Since telephone prospects may terminate the conversation at any point, it is essential that benefits be presented in order of importance to the consumer. For the same reason, make your script concise. Avoid phrasing and superlatives that might have worked for you in direct mail. Remember that the sales representative and the prospect are having a one-on-one phone conversation, and eliminate stilted promotional language like "this amazing two-for-one offer."

It is legally imperative that the script begin by identifying the caller and the company behind the call. Telemarketing experts suggest that you load your script with two or even three offers, each keying in to a different product benefit. When framing the offer, draw upon the classic sales approach of "closers"—give the customer an either/or choice rather than a yes/no choice. Examples of this might be a one-year *or* a two year subscription . . . an appointment for a free estimate on Tuesday evening *or* Wednesday evening.

Every sales pitch draws certain standard objections from prospects. Anticipate these and have standard answers ready for sales representatives to use. For example, if the prospect objects to a product's cost, you might script in an answer that explains that the real cost is only 95 cents a day— less than the price of a can of soda from a vending machine. Then compare that small cost to the benefits of the product, and restate one or two of them briefly. To avoid wasting time with prospects who will keep objecting rather than saying no, top telemarketers suggest that you terminate the call if the sale can't be closed after you have answered two objections.

Avoid background noise. Make sure that your telemarketers are working in an area that is as soundproof as possible so that customers don't overhear a roomful of other sales representatives delivering the same "exclusive" offer.

The real test of any telemarketing script comes when it is used for practice calls. Have several experienced telephone sales representatives look over your script, suggest changes based on their experience, and then try the script on 10 or 20 prospects apiece. Then meet to determine where the "stoppers" occur in the script, and revise it until you and the sales representatives are satisfied that it is as effective as possible.

The creative person who is interested in telemarketing would be wise to spend some time as a part-time telephone sales representative. There is nothing to compare with the hands-on experience of learning what works and what doesn't when you are in the hot seat, talking to consumers on the phone.

Another must for telemarketing creatives is familiarity with Federal Trade Commission and Federal Communications Commission requirements for conducting calls and accepting requests to be placed on the firm's internal "Do Not Call" list. The Direct Marketing Association publishes a great deal of how-to material on this score, and information is also available direct from the FTC and FCC in Washington, D.C.

Mobile Marketing

Coda Research Consultancy projects that U.S. mobile e-commerce sales will reach $23.8 billion by 2015, and mobileSquared says that U.S. messaging-based advertising spending should be about $2 billion that same year. Just as impressive, more than 90 percent of Americans now use cell phones, per CTIA—The Wireless Association. eMarketer cautions, however, that this percentage may be exaggerated a bit since it counts subscriptions rather than people—and some individuals have more than one cell phone subscription.

According to the International Telecommunication Union, in a world with about 6.8 billion people, there are approximately five billion cell phone subscriptions. Third-world countries and developing nations are leading the growth in cell phone use, with hand-held devices representing the most portable and affordable option for Internet, phone, and text messaging services. Nielsen Mobile reports that Americans have texted more than they talk on the phone since 2008. And eMarketer says that by 2013, half of all mobile users in the U.S. will have Internet connectivity.

It is interesting to note that Hispanics in the United States are on the cutting edge when it comes to mobile devices. Lisa E. Phillips, senior analyst at eMarketer, says, "Hispanics cannot imagine daily life without their mobile phones and credit the technology with strengthening relationships and keeping them connected to their social world, not just friends and family. Marketers who are just turning to mobile will find a market well ahead of them." More than half of Hispanic mobile phone users are between 18 and 34 years of age, and 55.6 percent of them are male, according to eMarketer.

AERA Mobile Marketing defines mobile marketing as "Brand and/or content communication, directed to a mass audience, a targeted group, or an individual that is designed to add value and create an action or response using a mobile phone." Types of mobile marketing include Mobile Web (Internet access), Short Message Service (SMS) texting, Multimedia Messaging (MMS), Mobile Video and TV, and Mobile Applications (apps).

This unique and powerful marketing channel lets consumers instantly connect, engage and interact with content delivered to them wherever they are, whenever they want it. That said, to date mobile marketing commands only a small percentage of most direct and interactive marketing budgets. What's more, many consumers are wary about providing their cell phone numbers to companies—and firms will be wise to adhere to strict opt-in policies to avoid disgruntled consumers who complain of "message overload."

Examples of Creativity in Mobile Marketing

Two important hurdles for the mobile marketer are getting consumers to opt in to receive text messages, and providing them with compelling, unique reasons to engage with your firm via mobile device. All of this must be accomplished in a medium that allows for only 160 English characters per message. Here are a few examples of ways smart marketers have used mobile messaging to positive effect.

Jack Philbin, co-founder and president of Vibes, recounts these three successful, U.S.-based mobile campaigns:

- The Dallas Cowboys joined forces with Texas Instruments and Circuit City to offer coupons for a discount on plasma-screen televisions. While only 330 coupons were sent out to mobile devices, a total of 362 plasma TVs were sold with the program's coupon code—thus demonstrating the power of viral marketing in the mobile space.
- The Pittsburgh Penguins offered a Student Rush Club for local students interested in last-minute hockey tickets. On one occasion, a text message to 3,000 students resulted in 2,000 responses. A random drawing provided tickets to 100 of those students for the game.
- The TV show *Deal or No Deal* invited viewers to text in as program participants, at a cost of 99 cents per text. The average episode yielded $500,000 in text message revenue—more than selling another 30-second spot would garner for NBC.

Steve Snyder of Consent Media offers these two compelling examples of American mobile campaigns:

- Giant Eagle Supermarket asked people to opt in to receive mobile messages, with signs at the deli counter. The market then sent out a one-day-only offer on 2-for-1 rotisserie chickens. This measurable campaign delivered an average market basket of $30 per customer in addition to each 2-for-1 chicken purchase.
- Radio Shack initiated a mobile campaign aimed at its best customers: urban African-Americans and Hispanics. The firm was successful in bringing large

number of these customers back to the store for three weeks in a row, while the average sale stayed steady at $70.

An oft-quoted comment about Internet marketing is that it moves at the pace of "dog years"—seven years' advancement in technology and applications for every calendar year. Steve Snyder says that "Mobile years are even faster than dog years." He suggests that marketers "do something" in mobile, integrate it as part of each multichannel marketing campaign, start testing with small programs, and scale up as successful methods are identified.

For daily inspiration and updates on this dynamic field, subscribe to *Mobile Marketer*, an e-mail newsletter delivered every week day via e-mail. The Web address for sign-ups is *http://www.mobilemarketer.com/*.

Mobile Advertising in China

While mobile marketing in the United States is still in its early stages, a look at mobile marketing in China may provide a window into the future. Dr. Mary Ann McGrath of Loyola University in Chicago has made a comprehensive study of Chinese mobile advertising with her Chinese colleagues, Mars Ren and Tina Liu.

Dr. McGrath notes that there were already 700 million cell phone users in China by 2010. With no opt-in or opt-out laws or conventions in effect, she says that most mobile phone owners receive huge numbers of unsolicited text messages—many of questionable taste. Yet since the Chinese generally rely on hand-held devices instead of laptops or desktop computers—and most do not care to use voicemail—they have a habit of answering voice messages and viewing text messages immediately upon receipt.

Focus Wireless, which claims to own information on about half of China's mobile phone users, has brought some sense of propriety to the industry by establishing an internal policy prohibiting its subsidiaries from sending out messages without a mobile user's explicit permission. But even when customers opt in to receive mobile messages, Dr. McGrath suggests that they will evaluate these texts in the same way they consider promotional e-mails:

- Does it have value for me?
- Is it too frequent?

She cites an example of a firm that sent her the following three price-oriented text messages (translated here from Chinese) within a span of two weeks:

> *9/13: message "A chance to enjoy luxury at a lower price: some summer collection will be discounted by 60% this Sunday night. The only thing changed is the price."*

> *9/18: message "Say goodbye to the summer! From 9/18 to 9/28, CLEARANCE for all summer short-sleeved shirt and T-shirt! Half the price! Please help us to clear our shelves for the fall collection for you."*

> *9/26: message "This Saturday and Sunday: two-day sale! 9 new long-sleeved T-shirt, soft and warm, up to 50% off! Only for 2 days"*

Dr. McGrath observes that mobile marketers in China will be wise to develop more innovative campaigns instead of relying strictly on repetitive discount promotions like these. To that end, Dr. McGrath has seen a proliferation of popular Mobile Applications (apps) in China, such as one called

Exhibit 15.1. www.ddmap.com

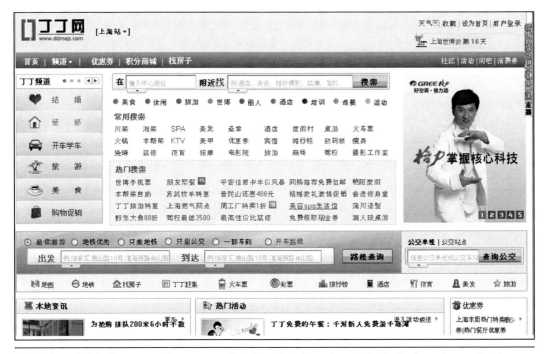

The Chinese Web site *www.ddmap.com* offers free directions via mobile device in exchange for the customer's mobile number and some demographic information. Along with the directions, patrons can receive information about businesses close to their beginning or end point.

Reprinted from *www.ddmap.com*.

"Places Directory." If you input your location, this app will show you nearby facilities such as restaurants, gyms, malls and gas stations. Currently the app accesses information from Google, but it is viewed as having the potential to add advertisements.

What's more, a service called ddmap.com provides directions for the route of your choice. After providing his or her phone number, gender, age, and interests, the user is sent a detailed path via mobile phone. At the end of the message, the user is asked whether they want to learn about available promotions around the starting point or the destination.

Co-Ops

The concept of the co-op mailing is simple: by mailing their offers together, marketers can save on postage and test a list of consumers or businesspeople at minimal cost. Many marketers find co-ops profitable, even though the medium is by nature quite cluttered and competitive.

Some firms utilize co-ops as a means of extending the reach of a successful offer—one that they are already playing out to the limit in direct mail, space, and other media. Others are able to utilize specialty co-ops targeted to specific markets like working women, sports enthusiasts, or people interested in learning more about personal finance.

Inherent in the co-op medium are certain limitations. First, even though sophisticated targeting is available through co-op vendors, the co-op comes across to the recipient as a mass medium. Because your offer arrives in a package with many others, the private and personal aspects of individual direct mail are lost. Most successful consumer co-op users, therefore, are firms that sell products with broad appeal and affordable price tags: items such as clothing and accessories, books and records, collectibles, home decor accents, family photography, checks, and photo finishing.

Today perhaps the best-known consumer direct mail co-op is the "Valpak" coupon mailing and online coupon Web site. Valpak's familiar blue envelope arrives in 45 million households and businesses in more than 115 U.S. designated market areas and Canada. Valpak pinpoints audiences using geo-demographics, and offers marketers selections based on demographics, proximity to retail shopping locations, traffic patterns, and postal carrier routes with segments as small as 10,000 names.

Another renowned direct mail co-op is the Valassis Shared-Mail Program, RedPlum (formerly known as Advo's "ShopWise.") Valassis mails its four-color, four-page RedPlum wrap weekly to about 70 million homes. It contains local and national retail ads with insertions for grocery circulars and other solo pieces. RedPlum coupons also are available online.

For more specific audiences, marketers might also consider developing their own co-op mailings, grouping sets of their own products or services in mailings aimed at segments of their own lists. What's more, Internet coupon suppliers such as CoolSavings.com, StartSampling.com and Smart-Source.com are worth a look for marketers interested in affordable co-ops that may uncover new sources of customers.

Creative Considerations for Co-Ops

Co-op pieces are more like space ads than they are like direct mail packages. In a limited format, amid a great deal of clutter, they must capture attention in a second or two and move the prospect to action. The standard Valpak co-op format is four color, and sized to fit in a #10 outer envelope. Some co-ops may accept folded pieces, which opens the possibility of modifying a direct mail flyer or a space ad to save production costs. If your piece folds, it should have one closed side on its wider dimension to make it machine insertable.

To facilitate ease of reply mailing and eliminate the need for a reply envelope, some direct marketers print their co-op pieces on high-bulk stock which is heavy enough to meet postal requirements for a Business Reply Card. This type of heavy, uncoated stock is less ideal for color photo reproduction than a coated stock would be, however.

Before creating a design, check with the co-op for its size and weight specifications. For an extra fee, you may be able to include a sample or swatch, use a slightly different size, or insert a booklet or other heavier piece. Before testing any of these special applications, however, you will do well to test the general viability of the co-op for your product or service.

An effective co-op piece is one that attracts the prospect's attention by means of striking graphics and visuals and a "grabber" headline. Use all possible means of streamlining response: post-paid reply card, Web site landing page, "send no money now," free trial period, strong guarantee, and so on. Check Chapter 11 of this book for print ad creative concepts that may also be applied to co-ops. For specifics on the types of co-ops available, check the SRDS *Direct Marketing List Source* .

Card Decks

Both consumer and business-to-business mailers have discovered the profit potential of one specific type of co-op, the card-deck mailing. This co-op style evolved from an earlier format in which postcards were printed together in bound booklets with several postcards to a page. Then the concept was simplified so that a stack of individual same-sized postcards could be mailed in a transparent or decorated plastic outer wrapper. Each mailing typically includes 30 to 100 postcard offers. Sometimes the card deck comes with an introductory piece from its sponsor, which often is a magazine or trade publication.

Some innovative card deck marketers allow for miniature four-color catalogs featuring a company's "hot seller" in their mailings, thus increasing the impact of a card deck insert. The little catalog fits right in with the postcards in the deck, but enhances the opportunity to attract new buyers because of its excellent color reproduction, attractive format, and choice of appealing products. The same piece can be used for other supplementary applications as well, such as billing statements and package inserts.

Creative Tips for Card Decks

Like other co-op mailings, card decks present a considerable challenge to the writer and artist because of space limitations and surrounding clutter. In addition, studies show that each card receives no more than one or two seconds of attention from prospects before being placed in the "discard" or "save" pile. This means that the principles of good space advertising must be observed scrupulously for card decks. For instance:

- The headlines must be short, attention-getting, and intriguing.
- The offer must be simple, specific, and hard-hitting.
- Focus on one to three main benefits only—preferably one principal benefit. Flag the benefit(s) using bold subheads or bullets.
- Strong graphics can grab the eye. Try a four-color piece in a deck that has mostly one or two-color pieces. Consider a diagonal design element or other unique "grabber." But don't design a vertical card for a horizontal deck. As direct marketing expert Bob Bly points out, your prospect may not slow down long enough to turn your card upright and make it readable.
- Use urgency and a specific call to action.
- Make your reply device as visible as possible. Try offering a toll-free number and Web site address to capitalize on impulse buyers or inquirers.

Once you have designed and written your card, make up a dummy and place it in a stack of typical cards from the co-op where you have reserved space. Rifle through the cards and see for yourself: is your piece an attention-getter, or just another candidate for the wastebasket?

Co-Op Free-Standing Inserts

On Sundays, your local newspaper probably contains one or more colorful, fold-over inserts filled with coupon offers and direct response ads, such as those of Valassis and News America Marketing (Smart Source). These inserts are primarily known as sales promotion vehicles for grocery products. But direct marketers of clothing and accessories, home decor and tabletop items, giftware, checks, and collectibles are all regular advertisers. Catalog marketers solicit new customers in this medium as well.

The co-op FSIs are the ultimate mass media, reaching tens of millions of homes via weekly newspaper inserts. Rather than try a full run in one of these co-ops, of course, the direct marketer should first schedule a test. Remnant space is readily available at attractive prices, and the sales reps of these firms are quite helpful in devising an effective testing schedule for your proposition. You may also focus your efforts on cities of a certain size, certain regions of the country, etc.

Creative Pointers for Co-Op Free-Standing Inserts

Co-op FSIs are splashy, colorful media, so you should plan on a four-color ad. When purchasing remnant space, the advertiser must be prepared to run in any configuration, with the coupon appearing left or right, top or bottom. Final art must be provided to fit each of these configurations, as the ads are slotted at the last minute. A one-half page ad is your best bet for an initial test of a product offer. Catalog marketers soliciting leads may opt for a one-fourth page slot. Ads in co-op FSIs are similar in format to space ads in magazines. As with magazine ads, the printing of a co-op FSI is in the hands of the publisher, so results may vary. FSI production specifications differ from those of magazines, so be sure to check with your sales rep for details and hints on preparation for successful printing before you create final art.

Package Inserts and Ride-Alongs

A package insert is a direct response piece that is inserted along with a shipment of product to a consumer. A ride-along is a direct response piece that accompanies a company's regular communications with a customer, such as a mailing to book or record club members.

These inserts may arrive loose, or gathered together in a folder or envelope. They may or may not be accompanied by "house offers"—similar pieces that come from the originating company. They may or may not come along with an introductory note from the sender—a piece with the theme, "We have selected these special offers because we thought they would be of interest to you, a preferred customer of the XYZ Company."

One of the positive points for package inserts is the fact that no competitive offers are allowed. In addition, the advertiser is assured that the recipients are proven direct mail buyers: in fact, since they are just receiving a purchase, they are hotter than the most recent hotline names on the sending firm's list. For this reason, and because a package insert program may be initiated rather inexpensively, some direct marketers use this method to test the viability of a list before renting it for a direct mail test.

The Creative Challenge for Package Inserts and Ride-Alongs

Like co-ops, package inserts and ride-alongs compete in a rather busy environment. They need to stand out from the competition by "calling out" to the reader with an offer and graphic look that entices him or her. An insert no larger than 5-1/2" * 8-1/2" is usually acceptable to most companies. Some inserts and ride alongs, however, must fit into a statement-sized envelope, which means they are limited to a folded size of about 3-1/2" * 6".

Within certain constraints, marketers may try various enhancements to the basic package insert, incorporating a Business Reply Envelope or Card, for example. Before developing designs, it is wise to obtain specifications, weight limitations, and costs from the sales representative. A good deal of this information is also available in SRDS's *Direct Marketing List Source*.

Supermarket Take-Ones

In thousands of the nation's supermarkets, shoppers may choose from a wide array of direct response offers displayed on a take-one rack. The rack is usually installed between the store's two exit

Exhibit 15.2. Rodale's Organic Gardening

Rodale's Organic Gardening attracted new prospects that might not be available via direct mail lists or space ads by placing this flyer in direct marketing-oriented supermarket displays.

Reprinted with permission of Rodale Press.

doors, or just inside the door near the check-out area. Perhaps the best-known purveyor of this medium is Good Neighbor®.

Supermarket take-ones are a mass medium, but some selectivity is possible. Advertisers may choose the geographic location of their take-one stores to improve their reach in the most likely target areas for a given product or service. Take-ones should be considered a supplementary medium, used in an effort to reach prospects who are not receptive to mail, space, television, or online offers. Take-one distribution is hard to control, and therefore it is difficult to predict future response based on past results.

Because the standard size for a supermarket take-one is 5-1/2″ * 8-1/2″ folded, some companies may find that they can use the same format for this purpose and for co-ops and package inserts. In general, however, supermarket pieces are printed on heavier stock than co-ops and package inserts, and almost all of the supermarket take-ones incorporate Business Reply Cards.

Unique Media for Direct Response Marketers

There are a few other media worth mentioning for consideration by marketers. Although they may be applicable only in a few select cases, they may bring incremental sales on some offers. It is wise for creative people to keep alert for unique media opportunities that may prove to have applications for various current or future clients.

Television Product Placement

With ever-increasing ad clutter on television—not to mention the ability of DVR users to eliminate ads from their viewing experience—more and more marketers are seriously exploring product placement opportunities within shows. While some product placement deals cost their sponsors millions of dollars—witness Coca-Cola and Ford's heavy involvement in the popular Fox show *American Idol*—some persistent marketers have been able to get their products in front of viewers for very little cost.

Brad Fritz, the seating unit business manager for Holland, Michigan, office furniture maker Trendway, used persistence to land a spot for his elegant Xantos executive office chair on *American Idol*. After calling every week for months, offering to provide Xantos chairs for the show's judges, Fritz hit pay dirt. For the cost of the chairs alone, Xantos appeared on each episode of *American Idol*. Then Fritz persuaded each of the judges to sign his or her chair, and he made the signed chairs available for charity drawings in New York, Los Angeles, and West Michigan. Fritz's tenacity led to the Xantos chairs' exposure to up to 33.7 million viewers per *American Idol* show, and gained him publicity worth millions to his firm as unsolicited leads poured in to Trendway headquarters.

In-Transit Television

Direct and interactive marketers may supplement their media plans for certain target markets by advertising on various in-transit television outlets. Examples include televised information on big-city hotel elevators, in malls, on public transportation platforms, on buses, and in lines at supermarkets. A company called Transit Television Network (*www.TransiTV.com*) touts the fact that it targets consumers "on the go" and works in exclusive partnerships with city, county, and state transit authorities to put its messages on buses. The company's system integrates GPS-driven information to make route location announcements interspersed with news, weather, sports, entertainment—and location-specific ads.

Viral Marketing

Internet marketers have found they can build awareness and referrals for next to nothing by implementing simple-yet-effective viral marketing programs. Like a sneeze that can spread a virus from person to person, viral marketing uses pre-existing social ties to increase brand awareness or achieve other marketing objectives like product sales—either through word of mouth or online via e-mail, text messages, or social networking sites. Here are a couple of examples:

- Visitors to Omaha Steaks one summer evening might have noticed a hot new Ford Mustang in the parking lot. The car was there as part of a joint-venture viral marketing event between Ford and Omaha Steaks. With a radio conglomerate in a nearby building, a remote broadcast was fairly easy to arrange while Omaha Steaks employees and folks from the surrounding industrial park gathered to feast on steak sandwiches and admire the new Mustang model. Some marketers might write off such an event as "too local, too small in impact"— yet when firms like Omaha Steaks take advantage of these opportunities wherever they present themselves, the long-term "word-of-mouth" effect can be powerful.
- Online grocer Peapod creates programs that have customers and employees selling memberships for them. On the back of each employee's business card is a special, individual code. When a Peapod Employee convinces a friend to sign up, buy online, and enter the code, the employee gets a financial reward. Customers can get similar referral fees when they invite friends to use Peapod. In addition, Peapod will donate a certain percentage of sales to the school of the customer's choice. The school program can be promoted at the local school level through simple flyers, meetings, and social network pages sponsored by parent-teacher organizations.

Conclusion

Understanding the various direct response media in advance of any assignment will stand the creative person in good stead. Increase your file of samples from various media, and familiarize yourself with them. By studying your samples and understanding the marketing concepts that make each medium a good bet for certain types of offers, you may soon find yourself suggesting unique ways for your firm or clients to expand their horizons in direct and interactive marketing.

Contact and Call Centers
by Mitchell Lieber, President, Lieber and Associates

CUSTOMER CONTACT

Customer contact is one-to-one individualized communications with a company representative via telephone, Web chat or e-mail. The term *contact center* encompasses both call centers that handle telephone calls only, and operations that also handle e-mails and Web chats.

Types of One-to-One Customer Contact

Type of Contact	Description
Inbound telephone calls	Via toll-free or local telephone number
Inbound e-mails	Via an e-mail address or Web form
Inbound Web chats	From a company Web site
Outbound calls	Dialed manually, by a computer or predictive dialer
Account service	Inbound and outbound calls to service and sell accounts, such as stockbroker clients or business-to-business sales reps with specific account assignments

Customer contact has a variety of business purposes. These include responding to customers with customer service, technical support, and order-taking services. Sales activities also belong under this large umbrella. Sales activities range from lead generation and lead qualification, to sales cultivation and multi-step sales, to consultative sales, up-selling and cross-selling.

HOW CUSTOMER CONTACT AFFECTS RESULTS

Companies that give the contact center little attention often sabotage their programs' results, for this area can make or break many programs. Here's why. Whether prospects contact your business to order or with questions, via chat or e-mail or phone, one thing is certain for most companies. The most personal and intimate communications a prospect or customer will have with your brand will be at the contact center. It is where the *brand promise* that underlies your advertising comes true or is proved false. Which will it be? The attention you give this area determines the answer.

Will your brand be everything the caller expects? Will reps be accessible, knowledgeable, confident, and customer focused? Or will they be difficult to reach, poorly informed, unsure or indifferent? Whether 10 percent, 20 percent, or 50 percent of your prospects or customers contact you in this personal medium, you want to win them over rather than write them off. Similarly, if you place outbound calls to prospects, you are doing so to win them over.

A DIFFERENT TYPE OF CHANNEL

There are a number of questions to ask when developing a contact center program. Can the selected organization handle the volume of calls, chats, and e-mails in or out? Will the reps be ready to respond to customers and prospects, and do so properly? If the answer is an immediate and unqualified *yes* as it almost always initially is, there's a follow up question: *Who is taking responsibility if that turns out to be inaccurate and sales are lost?* Ask that question, and *yes* may become *maybe*. Dig further, and this may become *maybe, but . . .* or *we didn't know that . . .* or *that will cost $_ more.* When conducting contact center programs, the devil is nearly always in the details.

Why? Effectiveness in the telephone channel may be trickier than in any other channel, because it is controlled differently.

Channel	Control of Message Delivery	Duplication and Distribution
Web	Agency, copywriter, Web designer	Reproduced by computers
E-mail	Agency, copywriter and designer	Reproduced by computers
Broadcast /Web TV and Radio	Producer, director and scriptwriter	Recording is played
Print Ads	Copywriter and graphic designer	Printing
Direct Mail	Copywriter and graphic designer	Printing
Telephone	Script or call guide writer	Telephone reps
Web chat /e-mail response	Template copywriter	Contact center reps

The contact center is the *only* channel in which individual human beings dynamically interpret and deliver the creative for *each individual impression.*

There is an upside to this complexity. If a program is carefully designed, it is possible to tailor communications to each prospect or customer, engendering positive feelings about the company's responsiveness. There is a downside as well. A one-size-fits-all approach sticks out like a sore thumb in this most personal of channels, as do sophisticated approaches that fail because they are over ambitious and implemented poorly or inconsistently. Which occurs is determined by a series of strategic and creative decisions. These decisions are made by program managers in the following areas:

- Purpose or goal of the call or contact
- Days and hours of operation
- In-house or outsourced
- Rep (or outsourcer) selection
- Selection of a top level manager for the program
- Method for accurately sourcing media for inbound contacts
- Database design and, if applicable, outbound calling list selection criteria
- Scripting or call guides including FAQs, and e-mail and Web chat response templates
- Rep training on the product/service, market and call guide/script/templates
- Computer system programming for script branching, data capture, and reports
- Metrics for inbound calls, e-mail, Web chat and, if applicable, outbound calls
- Regulatory compliance, especially for outbound consumer sales calls
- Use of IVRs and voice recognition on inbound telephone calls
- Monitoring calls, e-mails and Web chats, including objective evaluation criteria

While the gap between a quality and poor contact center program is often a result of design and structure, it is also seriously affected by the quality of contact center management, organization and staff, and the degree to which they are a match for your program.

CONTACT CENTER PROGRAM SUCCESS

So how does one decide what's appropriate and what won't cut it in the contact center? Experience helps a great deal. The best is experience designing, implementing *and measuring* contact center programs. The proof of the effectiveness of strategic and creative choices is usually in the numbers.

Secondarily, rely on your personal experience as a business-to-business prospect or customer, and as a consumer. What engages you in contact center programs? What turns you off? Instead of thinking about a market as an abstract mass, put yourself in each of your prospects' or customers' shoes. Would that offer appeal to you? Would you like speaking with that telephone rep? Would you answer the question if it was worded that way? What would make you interested in discussing the product or service? Simply thinking about your program through the filter of the golden rule, *do unto others as you would like done unto you*, will help make your contact center program more customer-focused, successful and profitable.

Copyright 2010 by Mitchell A. Lieber. Mitchell Lieber is president of the call center consulting firm, Lieber and Associates. He may be reached at m_lieber@lieberandassociates.com or 773-325-0608.

Common-sense Dos and Don'ts of Mobile Marketing

By Mickey Alam Khan, Editor-in-Chief, Mobile Marketer

From the noise generated by the myriad mobile conferences, blogs and publications, most brands, advertising agencies and publishers just want to know a couple of things: What's working and what's not working in mobile marketing? Here's a stab at that.

First, it's important to dispel the myth that marketers don't get mobile. They do—ask Colgate-Palmolive, Unilever, Gap, adidas, M&M/Mars, NBC, Kodak, Heineken, ESPN, McDonald's, American Airlines, Sherwin-Williams, Microsoft, AOL, MGM Grand, Johnson & Johnson, Dairy Queen, Jaguar, Skyy Vodka, Ford Motor, The Weather Channel, Discover Card, Procter & Gamble's Gillette, Brita, Jim Beam and Chase.

These aforementioned brands have run mobile campaigns, sites and applications or launched mobile commerce operations. Some of these efforts have morphed into longer-term programs that integrate mobile into overall multichannel outreach initiatives within these Fortune 500 and Fortune 1000 brands.

No doubt mobile will have to work harder to get a larger chunk of marketing budgets. But marketers surely are getting the message that mobile is where they need to be. Consumers—their customers—wouldn't expect any less, not with their newer phone models and better data plans.

KNOW YOUR AUDIENCE

This leads to the first observation about what's working in mobile marketing: *Understanding the audience and targeting* with appropriate mobile banner and video ads, sites, applications or SMS campaigns—all opted-in, not once but twice by the consumer.

This rule is not exclusive to mobile. A targeted mailer sent to a household has proven to generate sales online, in-store or via telephone. Online banners or e-mails that sync with the site audience's interests inevitably generate click-throughs and responses to calls to action.

So mobile's not any different. A relevant movie trailer banner ad on an entertainment mobile site will serve both the advertiser and consumer well. Requesting that existing customers opt-in to the marketer's mobile alert programs will also work to great advantage. Ask casino giants such as Harrah's and MGM Grand.

Not surprisingly, it is critical to research the targeted audience's mobile habits. What is it that they consume on the mobile phone? How much time do they spend on mobile? What is it that they would like to initiate elsewhere but complete on mobile or vice-versa?

Visiting a well-thought out mobile site is such a pleasure. Consider *The New York Times's* mobile site at *http:/nytimes.com*. It is hard to admit this, but the mobile site beats the wired Web site simply because the scroll-down interface is easy to navigate and the articles easy to read.

The only casualty about the mobile *New York Times* experience is the advertising. While the banner ad units are quite visible, the *Times* needs to work harder on convincing some of its current online advertisers to add mobile to their mix.

It seems almost strange to see a mobile site without ads—not ones that interrupt the experience, but ones that enhance the overall reading experience by offering a window into commercial applications.

At the risk of sounding audacious, perhaps the *Times* should offer sampling opportunities to key advertisers such as Tiffany, Macy's, Cartier and local auto dealers. And if these advertisers don't have a mobile presence, then the *Times* should work with mobile firms to mobilize their client base. Imagine the brownie points scored if mobile gains significant leads and sales for these firms.

Knowing the audience also includes knowledge of their propensity or willingness to receive permission-based communications on their phones. Mobile may not be for everyone, just like the wired Internet isn't.

But it seems quite obvious that marketers offering value through the mobile site, application, banner ad, coupon or text message will find a welcome reception. Training the customer base to expect quality in mobile marketing communications is a corollary to knowing what makes the marketer's target customer tick.

While many industry observers are waiting for a flash of light to let them know mobile is the new tableau for marketing, those already with toes in the water know where the fish are.

MOBILE WORKS FOR DATABASE AND LOYALTY MARKETING—ABSOLUTELY

One of the most astute uses of mobile—besides employing mobile advertising for branding—is the channel's ability to expand a marketer's loyalty program. And the humble foot soldier of loyalty marketing is SMS text messaging. Yes, text messaging is to mobile what e-mail is to the Internet—the choice tool for communicating one-on-one with the customer.

Marketing need not get too complicated if the goal is to convince the targeted consumer to consume the advertiser's product or service over the competitor's. SMS is the easiest way to communicate that message.

It takes some legwork to get fully SMS-enabled. The tools required are a common short code, keywords, approval of mobile campaign from wireless carriers and another channel to get the consumer to text in to opt into a program.

Marketers and retailers can use stores, direct mail, television, radio, print, online and billboards to get the consumer to opt-in—not once, but twice—to receiving coupons or alerts from the company.

Once the consumer is signed up, moderate the communications to anywhere from two messages to four messages a month, maximum. And be up-front with the opted-in consumer about the frequency of messages, company privacy policy and option to opt out at any time.

Remember, it's a land grab right now. At some point, the consumer will not agree to sign up for any more mobile loyalty programs or alerts. So it is best to start work on incorporating mobile into the company's overall loyalty program.

LEGS TO OTHER CHANNELS

Here's another point to remember: mobile's place in the multichannel context. Mobile is not an island unto itself and contrary to what its most ardent fans would like to believe, the channel's best use is in giving legs to other channels.

Mobile has the potential to drive traffic to retail stores, as has been amply proved with campaigns from restaurant chains such as Papa John's, McDonald's, Burger King, Starbucks, Jiffy Lube and countless others with a physical footprint.

The *American Idol* show on television is proof that text messaging can elect winners simply by action of keyword and short code.

Shows such as *American Idol* and *Deal or No Deal* are said to generate as much revenues for the programmers from texting as they do from advertising. Maybe it's exaggerating it a bit, but the point is that mobile brings interactivity to TV.

Now here's something that agencies don't want to hear about: actual tracking of brand commercials. Imagine a keyword and short code on spots—not just at the end of the 30-second spot, but in every frame—that invites the consumer to text in.

No, it need not turn into a direct response TV ad, but the texts could give the advertiser an idea of the consumer's engagement with the brand's TV advertising.

Ditto with radio. And it's proved to have worked. Oil change giant Jiffy Lube has gone on the record to acknowledge SMS marketing's role in driving traffic to its locations. In most cases, the SMS call to action was run first on radio spots targeted to drivers in certain areas.

What about direct mail and inserts? How about placing targeted keywords and short code on mail and inserts sent to consumers' homes and offices? Ask them to respond via text for prompt fulfillment of the desired call to action.

The examples can go on and on. Keep an open mind and a sharp eye on the consumer's needs and market trends.

WHAT NOT TO DO IN ANY CIRCUMSTANCES?

It's mostly a bunch of common sense. Don't abuse the privilege. When mobile consumers opt into receiving communications from brands, they are giving access to their most personal medium.

Err on the side of caution when sending text messages—twice a month, instead of four, for example—or make sure that the banner ad doesn't disrupt the viewing experience on mobile.

It's been said before, and bears repeating here: familiarity breeds contempt. Don't inundate the consumer with messages. Space them out and make sure each message is targeted.

Sensitivity is the watchword here. And privacy. In fact, privacy threatens to snowball into one of the biggest issues threatening online and mobile advertising.

Privacy advocacy groups and consumer watchdogs are chomping at the bit to restrain marketers from crossing a fine line. They are doing their best to convince the Federal Trade Commission of the need to regulate behavioral and location-based advertising online and on mobile.

These groups' worries, while legitimate, will affect marketing based on data and knowledge of consumer actions, even on an aggregate basis. So give no excuse to these groups or to the FTC or to the various attorneys general nationwide who want to make their name on marketing's back.

Finally, be realistic. Mobile's not a cure for what ails other channels. While it's not even realistic to call it a channel—it's a phone, TV, radio, MP3 player, video player, gaming instrument, camera, computer, e-mail tool, SMS enabler and pathway to the Internet—mobile still works best when matched with other channels.

Mobile thankfully does not enjoy the same degree of hype as the Internet did in the late 1990s. Yes, every agency, conference organizer or publisher has tacked on mobile as the new accessory to their offerings, but the venture-capital money inflow has been measured and realistic.

Those in the field know that mobile victories come hard-fought. It is their job now to communicate that mobile has its advantages and its limitations.

One of the truths is that mobile will not replace other channels, but complement them in a manner that no other channel has.

But mobile requires time to show results, and consumers need time to work out their relationship with the mobile device—is it a phone, entertainment channel, business tool, news source, video, camera, advertising vehicle or shop? All eight, as time and smart mobile marketing campaigns and programs will prove.

Mickey Alam Khan is editor-in-chief of Mobile Marketer, Mobile Commerce Daily and Luxury Daily, all based in New York. He was previously editor-in-chief of eMarketer and DM News, and also served as correspondent for Advertising Age. Reach him at mickey@napean.com.

Enhance Your Understanding:
Evaluate a Card Deck or Co-op Mailing

Get hold of an unopened card deck or co-op mailing that is targeted toward you as a consumer or businessperson. Open it as if you had just received it in the mail. First, flip through the cards or ads as any recipient would, giving each item just a second or two of attention. Decide which pieces intrigue you enough to respond and which you would reject as a consumer. Then take a closer look at each card or ad. Which elements of a good card deck or co-op—discussed in this chapter—do they exemplify? Which seem to break the rules? With a few changes in copy and art, which of your rejected pieces could have enticed you to respond?

16

Business-to-Business Direct and Interactive Marketing

Up until the U.S. recessionary period that began in 2008, business-to-business direct and interactive marketing grew much faster—both in dollars spent and revenues generated—than consumer marketing. Indeed, even during the recession, business-to-business marketing held its own better than consumer marketing, both in advertising spending and sales revenue. The reasons behind this remarkable rise are simple: as the cost of a personal sales call continues to increase, direct marketing and other forms of marketing communications become more and more attractive as pre-approach and relationship-building media. What's more, with the customization, personalization, and broad reach available on the Internet, firms can satisfy many of their customers' needs online with the immediacy buyers want and the cost-efficiency sellers crave.

According to the Direct Marketing Association, business-to-business direct marketing advertising expenditures are forecast to reach $92.1 billion in the U.S. alone by 2013—a compound annual growth of 4.9 percent over the five previous years compared with a consumer direct marketing ad spending growth rate of 4 percent.

The DMA further predicts that U.S. direct and interactive marketing-driven business-to-business sales will total $988.5 billion by 2014—a compound growth rate of 5.4 percent. It is interesting to note that the growth rate of sales tops that of advertising expenditures: a tribute to business marketers' ability to leverage inexpensive online and social media opportunities.

In addition, a study by OutFront Marketing Research for *Advertising Age* showed that ever since the mid-1990s, firms selling business-to-business have spent more than one-third of all dollars invested in marketing, including expenditures on sales force management, advertising, direct marketing, sales promotion, trade shows, and other marketing communications efforts and incentives. As for Internet marketing, the Direct Marketing Association's data estimates that business-to-business sales revenue will grow 13.1 percent per year to $56.7 billion by 2014.

Time was, firms believed they could afford to send salespeople on "fishing expeditions," making cold calls on businesses to look for likely customers. But according to Reed Business, in the current era it takes an average of 4.08 personal sales calls to close a sale, with a range by industry of 3.35 to 6.60 calls. At an average cost of $1,200 per closed sale, that makes the average cost of each individual sales call about $300. Other sources set the range in price of a single personal sales call from $100 to $500. This being the case, firms are looking for ways to cut down their sales costs, and leverage the valuable time of their highly trained sales specialists.

If direct and interactive marketing can be used to eliminate one or more of those $100-$500 sales calls, profits-per-sale to the company may improve substantially. What's more, if direct and interactive marketing can help qualify leads for the salesperson, he or she is free to pursue only the best prospects, enhancing efficiency even more. In addition, many firms have discovered that direct and interactive marketing can replace personal sales altogether for certain customer categories. Telemarketing, online marketing, and direct mailings can streamline both initial orders and reorders for small-to-medium-sized customers. Some relatively high-ticket products that used to be marketed via personal sales can now be 100 percent mail or Internet sold: for example, computers, smaller photocopiers, and office furniture and supplies. What's more, with sophisticated Extranets available to business-to-business customers online, they can manage their own accounts and inventories. This is a "win-win" situation in that it is highly cost-effective to the seller and also empowering to the buyer.

Bigger Budgets, Fresh Challenges

Business-to-business is an area of real excitement and challenge for direct and interactive marketing creatives. On the one hand today's businesspeople still receive way too many amateurish mailings in #10 outers, written by the company president and printed on limp stock. There's a challenge inherent in convincing these firms that marketing done well can increase results many times over. On the other hand, a number of sophisticated firms already have made business-to-business direct and interactive marketing the most forward-looking area of our field.

The reasons behind this business-to-business revolution are several. First, in recent years there have been remarkable improvements in list segmentation and database management for business-to-business marketers. It is now possible to target business and industrial audiences with precision, and to keep valuable information about customers and prospects accessible on the database.

Second, as business giants discover the power of direct marketing, budgets allocated for Web marketing, telemarketing, mailings, and catalogs have increased. Selling sophisticated, big-ticket customers by Internet, phone, or mail calls for exceptional creativity and customization. And when the product's price tag is in four, five, or even six figures, the dollars-per-prospect that can be allocated to direct and interactive marketing are much more substantial than in most consumer markets.

Third, business marketers have shown a remarkable openness to innovation that goes hand-in-hand with their ability to spend more per prospect than most consumer marketers can. Robust Web sites, three-dimensional packages, fulfillment packages complete with DVDs and flash drives, image-building mailings, customized trade show booths, virtual trade shows and online seminars, social media campaigns, and sophisticated public relations efforts are just a few examples of today's typical business-to-business applications.

Fourth, many firms have learned that certain customers actually prefer to have more contacts by Web, phone, and mail and less via personal sales. Direct and interactive marketing methods centered on a top-notch database allow companies to tailor contact strategies that better meet the needs and wants of their customers—often at a lower total cost than past efforts with more personal sales calls in the mix.

Fifth, the transition from industrial direct marketing to business-to-business direct marketing has broadened the field over the past few decades. Today, traditional industrial direct marketing is a subset of the overall business-to-business field, complemented by exploding growth in the sale of products and services aimed at a "nation of office workers." These newer business-to-business categories include financial services, computers and computer services, office products and services, telecommunications products and services, and business auctions and exchanges, just to name a few. What's more, the Small Office/Home Office (SOHO) revolution has put tens of thousands of new businesses in the market for everything from broadband Internet access to office furniture. These firms are often too small to be sold cost-effectively face-to-face, but there is much profit to be made in serving their needs via direct response channels.

How Business Buyers Compare with Consumer Buyers

An understanding of the business buyer's motivation is an essential starting point for direct and interactive marketing creativity. In many ways, the business direct response buyer is simply a consumer making purchase decisions from an office desk instead of a home easy chair. But there are a number of crucial differences to note—differences that will help shape the most effective creative approach for business-to-business marketing.

Similarities of Business and Consumer Buyers

When making business/industrial purchases, individuals behave the same as they do when making consumer purchases in that:

- *They are regular people* with the same problems, emotions, hopes, dreams, and fears that they exhibit on their own time.
- *They are busier than ever before in their work lives*, just as they are in their home lives. They are much less disposed to tolerate the interruption of cold calls from unknown sources than were previous generations of buyers.
- *They are subject to telemarketing and direct and e-mail clutter at the office*, just as they are at home. In self-defense, they sift out the interesting from the uninteresting with little more than a second's glance.
- *They are part of the "show me" generation*, brought up on ever-present television and video games and likely addicted to social media, smart phones, and the Internet. Pictures, demonstration videos, interactivity, and lots of color and action will draw their attention. Long, uninterrupted blocks of black-and-white copy probably will not.

How to Attract the Consumer Within the Business Buyer

Just because business buyers sit behind desks being paid to make purchase decisions, they do not become emotionless robots. To ensure that your ads, direct mail solicitations and online messages will be noticed, read, and considered, you must avoid being dull, overly serious, or prematurely fact oriented. Although business buyers need the "steak" about a product in order to sell it to management, they must first be attracted by the "sizzle" of enticing packages, easy-to-read copy, premiums, gifts, and enhancements.

Understand that business buyers are swamped with demands and don't annoy them. Save them time and money with streamlined approaches: a quick phone call or e-mail instead of a formal sales call; a highly trained customer service staff available by direct phone line at a moment's notice; a robust password-accessible Web site and/or Extranet with full information forthcoming with just a few keystrokes; a postcard instead of a phone call, a well-monitored company social network site, and so on.

Consider attention-getting promotions to cut through the clutter: entertaining and enlightening videos on a company YouTube channel, direct mail packages that stimulate involvement, use of overnight delivery service, highly relevant e-mail messages, white papers and online seminars, and so on. Read over the material in this book's general chapters on offers and formats. There are many ideas to be gleaned from consumer marketing that can be adapted for use in business-to-business direct and interactive marketing in addition to the concepts put forth in this chapter.

Differences Between Business and Consumer Buyers

Although many of the business purchaser's personal buying habits carry over to professional buying activities, there are some very specific differences that marketers should keep in mind. Here are some points to remember about business/industrial buyers:

- *They are spending someone else's money.* As a private consumer, the buyer is fairly free to purchase items on impulse, without making even a mental list of reasons to justify the expenditure. But when the same buyer makes a purchase for the company—even a purchase as simple as paper for the copy machine or replacement parts—he or she must have a rationale for the purchase based on price, service, quality, and other factors. By the same token, he or she is sometimes freer with the company's money—for example, choosing a more expensive hotel or airfare for company business than they would for personal use.

- *They are likely to go through a formal purchasing process.* Although some consumers do extensive comparison shopping, few actually go so far as to evaluate formal bids in a committee. Industrial buyers often are required to use a step-by-step purchasing process of identifying needs, establishing budgets, selecting possible vendors, sending out requests for proposal (RFPs) or getting bids, and making a group buying decision.

- *They may be "specialist types" or "purchasing types."* Lumping all business buyers together can be a big mistake. The engineer, mechanic, or other businessperson who will actually use the product is likely to be more focused on quality, ease of use, cutting-edge technology, and such personal concerns as enjoyment and status. The purchasing agent is generally interested in getting acceptable quality and service at the lowest possible price.

- *They may make decisions according to their personality styles.* Engineers and accountants tend to be analytical, CEOs tend to be driving and controlling, advertising people tend to be expressive promoters, and social workers tend to be amiable supporters.

These statements sound like stereotypes, and not everyone in a particular line of work fits the personality "norm." But the fact is that certain personality styles are attracted to specific fields of endeavor. Your knowledge of these styles and what they like and dislike can help guide decisions about both copy and design. Analytical types like charts, graphs, and lots of rational proof, for instance, while drivers/controllers want to cut to the bottom line. Promoters want to see photos of people and read human interest-type case histories, while amiables want to perceive that they are buying products that can help them be helpful to or make connections with others. For much more on this concept, read *Business-to-Business Direct Marketing* by Bernie Goldberg and Tracy Emerick.

- *They may be influenced by company politics.* Business buyers must be prepared to justify their decisions to their superiors, as well as to influencers whose positions make them anti-spending by definition: chief financial officers and rival peers, for example.

- *They may welcome contact with you as part of the job.* Even though many consumers enjoy buying by mail, phone, or online, they often complain about the volume of calls, e-mails and direct mail they receive at home. That's because buying products for personal use is a leisure activity for them, not their livelihood. But to some extent at least, the mail, e-mail, and phone contacts a purchasing agent receives are a vital part of the job. Your solicitations can help the buyer keep on top of innovations in the field, transmit news about price breaks, new products and seminars, and much more.
- *They may be making complex and costly decisions.* Although some business buying decisions are almost as simple as purchasing toothpaste at the drug store, others are highly technical. Buyers look to the seller for back-up information. They also want to be reassured that the company they are buying from is a solid, stable one to be trusted.
- *They may be insulated by a mail room and an assistant.* Depending upon the title of the person you are reaching and the size of the firm involved, your recipient's mail, phone calls, and even e-mails may go through one, two, or more layers of screening before they get to his or her desk. What's more, some large firms have altogether eliminated delivery of what they perceive as unsolicited standard mail addressed to their employees.

What is the Best Approach to the Business Buyer?

Because of these differences between the business buying mindset and the consumer buying mindset, direct and interactive marketers must adjust their strategies and appeals to maximize opportunities for success. Here are some proven ways to do so.

Use Lead Generation Programs That Sell the Sizzle First—Then the Steak. Rather than send a complex and expensive mailing package filled with statistics and facts, it is often more effective to qualify prospects first with a preliminary mailing, space ad, telephone call, or combination of these elements. Lead generation begins by getting prospects to express some level of interest in the product.

If leads are to be followed up by mail, e-mail, or phone, you can determine for yourself what makes a good lead, and gear your program to attract "tight" or "loose" leads as you prefer. Chapter 8 explains creative approaches to lead generation and follow-up. You can also use a phone call to ask some specific questions that help qualify a lead before the next mailing piece or sales call.

If leads are to be followed up by salespeople, ask the sales manager what he or she considers a good lead, and tailor the lead-generation program to suit these requirements. Some sales organizations require little more than a warm body to follow up on, while others demand a prospect prequalified right down to the credit check.

One simple way to determine a prospect's level of interest and qualifications to buy is to use check-off boxes (see Exhibit 16.1) on a mailed-in reply form. A similar format may be used with a Web response form on your Web site.

You might also ask the prospect to indicate the size of his or her business, either by number of employees or sales volume. Asking the prospect to confirm his or her title also provides valuable information for the salesperson and the database.

Exhibit 16.1. Check-Off Boxes

WHEN DO YOU INTEND TO SELECT A COLOR PHOTOCOPIER?

✝ No immediate plans—please send literature for my files

✝ Within six months to one year

✝ Less than six months from now

✝ Immediately

Please rush information

Please have a salesperson call me at_____
                        (Telephone number)

Information gathered using check-off boxes like those in Exhibit 16.1 can be used to follow up at the most likely time as indicated by the prospect, since reaching the business buyer at the time of the purchase decision is crucial. Such later follow-ups should be in addition to an immediate follow-up to the lead. Business-to-business marketers should consider customized follow-ups like this, since reaching the business buyer at the time of the purchase decision process is crucial.

For more on the nuts and bolts of operating business-to-business lead-generation programs, several books are very helpful. These include *The DMA Lead Generation Handbook* by Ruth P. Stevens (excerpted at the end of this chapter), *Successful Direct Marketing Methods* by Bob Stone and Ron Jacobs, *Profitable Direct Marketing* by Jim Kobs, and *Business-to-Business Direct Marketing* by Bernie Goldberg and Tracy Emerick.

Because Prospects Crave Plenty of Back-up Material, Give Them a Fulfillment Package Worthy to Keep on File. Once you have attracted a prospect with the "sizzle" of your initial ad, mailing, or phone call, make sure he or she receives a package from you that is substantial enough to encourage its retention. Some mailers offer their fulfillment kits in a file folder format that looks important enough to keep on hand for future reference. Others use presentation folders or binders to achieve that "keep me" look. You may be tempted to abandon elegant fulfillment packages in favor of online downloads. Downloads are a fine additional method of providing immediate information, but they do not necessarily replace the handsome materials you create as a tangible presentation of your company's capabilities and style.

Because Other Vendors May Be Bidding Against You in a Formalized Purchase Decision, You Need to Establish Your Company Image. Business buyers must justify their purchase decisions to their bosses, to financial officers, and often even to their peers within the company. All things being equal, the business buyer will probably choose an established firm with a famous name rather than a "no-name" competitor. Even if your price is lower and your product quality is superior, you'll have a hard time making the sale unless you can prove to the buyer that your company is worthy of trust. Thus building and maintaining a good company image is an important goal for most business-to-business direct and interactive marketers. There are a number of ways in which to do this—and perhaps break even or turn a profit in the promotional process. You may choose to combine several of these methods with a unified look and message.

- *The house organ/promotional newsletter.* One method of image building is to develop and mail—or more often today, e-mail—a well-designed newsletter that serves both company employees and customers. The newsletter might contain information about the firm's recent activities and promotions, focus on the functions of a different department each issue, and so forth. Customer testimonials and case histories make excellent material for such a publication, since both internal and external audiences will find them of interest. The newsletter might also cover the firm's contributions to the community and to nonprofits, fostering its image as a caring corporate citizen. General-interest feature material could also be included, as well as how-to articles related to the firm's field of endeavor.
- *The paid-subscription newsletter.* Service businesses often solicit paid subscriptions for informative newsletters that offer the firm's principals a forum in which to display their expertise. Some companies that began such newsletters as promotional vehicles have been pleasantly surprised that the publications can function as profit centers on their own. Another idea along these lines: the firm's principal might write a regular column in a trade magazine or business newspaper, or in an online newsletter, in exchange for a free or reduced-cost direct response ad in the publication.
- *Seminars—for service only or for profit.* Another way to build up your firm's image for expertise in the field is to develop informative seminars and promote them by mail and/or e-mail. Some companies offer their seminars free to qualified prospects and customers, while others charge competitive rates, hoping to break even or make money while getting out the word that this is the firm with state-of-the-art expertise. Another way to promote such seminars is to partner with a respected trade association or trade publication with a built-in audience for your information.

As for a topic, Geoff Nichols of Nichols & Associates Business Consultants suggests that "People do more to overcome painful problems than to seize opportunities." He says that finding the right topic is crucial. "People come because they have a problem and you have a solution," he notes. For best results, hold your seminar at a hotel or other public place that is centrally located with easy parking. Provide breakfast or lunch—good, free food is always a draw and having the seminar at meal time helps justify the time away from the office. Have credible outside experts speak as well as your company's salespeople—the experts' talks will serve as third-party endorsements for your product or service.

To promote your seminar beyond your present database, begin with a mailing piece targeted by geography, industry, job title, company size, and/or other parameters you deem important. Such compiled lists are readily available to purchase online through various vendors such as Dun and Bradstreet—now called simply D&B (*www.dnb.com*)—and Info USA (*www.infousa.com*). When potential attendees respond, confirm their attendance by phone or e-mail. To assure the best possible attendance, call or e-mail a day or two before the seminar date with a reminder, and again confirm the individual's intention to attend. At that point, e-mail a map and other pertinent information about parking, food provided, timing, etc. Even with this level of follow-up, experts say that only about 50 percent of confirmed attendees may actually show up at a free seminar.

A "seminar special" on your product or service may encourage attendees to become customers right away. If your product is too complex to lend itself to a specific discount offer, make sure to follow up with qualified attendees and request time for a sales consultation promptly, while the "glow" of your successful seminar remains. More and more firms are using online seminars to replace or enhance their face-to-face seminar efforts. You will find more on this later in the chapter.

- *The space advertising campaign.* Use appropriate trade and business publications to tell your story simply and clearly, with testimonials or case histories where appropriate. A series of ads with the same graphic look may be utilized to showcase different product benefits or company services. Since many narrow-niche trade publications have abandoned or cut back their print editions in favor of Web-based versions, consider advertising in these highly segmented online publications as well.

- *Mail or e-mail space ads to prospects and customers.* Business-to-business direct marketers can gain extra image mileage from their space advertising programs by mailing clippings of the ads along with a selling letter and a notation on the clipping such as, "In case you missed our ad in XYZ Magazine." Or, some firms mail their list of prospects and customers early copies of space ads as a sort of "preferred sneak preview." The same can be done with an HTML e-mail to customers and prospects, assuming you have obtained permission to e-mail them.

Because Prospects are Insulated by Mail Rooms and Secretaries, Cut Through the Clutter of Mail They Receive with Strategies to Get Your Offer on Their Desks—Then Opened and Read. In general, mail rooms and assistants are unwilling to spare the boss any piece of mail that looks as if it is important, personal, social, or valuable. Here are some ideas on how you can make your mailings secretary-proof.

- *Use "bundling" to capture attention and make a memorable connection.* It's clear that a bulky package comes across to both mail room workers and assistants as something with valuable contents that should not be discarded. Just as important, according to business-to-business guru George Cohan, is the phenomenon of "bundling." If a bulky package includes one or more items that engage any combination of hearing, touch, smell, and taste as well as sight, it provides a "layered learning" aspect that makes the solicitation more memorable. Thus in addition to items of novelty value, consider sending your prospect one or more items that engage multiple senses in relationship to your product or service.

  A campaign used by *Cuisine* magazine some years ago illustrates this concept. *Cuisine* wanted to reach a relatively small circle of media buyer prospects who might wish to advertise in the magazine. The theme of its campaign was, "If You're Not in *Cuisine*, You're Not in the Kitchen"—meaning that *Cuisine* readers were highly influenced by the magazine's ads when they chose items for their kitchens

The first of a series of mailings in this campaign was actually a shipment: a box containing a handsome crock filled with wrapped candies. Printed on the crock was the theme message, while the crock itself was an attractive piece that could be used and displayed in the prospect's home or office. Each crock was accompanied by a selling letter.

About a month later, each prospect received another selling letter along with another type of candy to fill the crock, which presumably had already been emptied by the hungry media buyer. Throughout the series, each letter was accompanied by a different food item—in an amount just sufficient to fill the crock. A series like this is likely to have prospects awaiting the next delivery—and in a positive mood to talk to the sales representative from *Cuisine* when he or she calls on the phone.

- *Send a product sample.* If your product is something that can be sampled easily, consider sending one or more samples in your mailing package. Something of obvious value—even an item as simple as a pencil, a holiday card, or color chart—will probably survive the "mail cut" and also draw the attention of the recipient. In addition, some product samples can fulfill the "bundling" concept as well: food items, industrial carpet samples, and promotional products, just to name a few.

- *Here is the information you requested.* Every lead fulfillment package should have these magic words—or something very similar—stamped or printed on the front. This wording shows the mail sorter that the boss has solicited the material inside. What's more, this phrase should trigger the recipient's memory about sending or calling for the material. You cannot count on the return address alone to spark recognition.

- *A plain outer envelope.* A fine quality, closed-faced outer envelope with an address that appears individually prepared may appear important and personal enough to make it directly onto the boss's desk. Don't ruin the illusion by using a label or an addressing mechanism that looks computerized! Another illusion-shattering problem: a standard mail indicia on a letter that is supposed to appear unique and personal. Use a meter or stamp instead, or mail first class if budgets permit. Some mailers have tried hand-addressing closed-faced outers. This appears personal and social, but it can be prohibitively expensive for high-volume mailings. A font that looks like handwriting, printed in medium-blue ink, may be a better alternative.

- *The invitation look.* Many offers can be developed in an invitation format with a squarish, top-quality outer envelope in white, buff, gray, or another neutral tone. Take a look at wedding invitations for size and paper stock ideas. Once again, a promotional look is a tip-off that the contents are not what they seem, so keep the invitation-look outer envelope plain. The mail screener may fear that he/she is tossing out the boss's invitation to an important party, and therefore will pass your mailing on.

- *Appeal to the mail screener.* A mailing addressed "To the Assistant of John Doe" meets the problem of mail screening head-on. Such a package might outline the great advantages of the seller's product to the assistant—i.e., time saving, easier to use, more attractive. It could encourage the assistant to suggest the purchase to the boss, even offering a premium geared to the assistant's interests. This should be handled discreetly, however, so that it does not appear to be a bribe. It is best simply to describe the premium, and not state in the promotional copy for whom it is meant or what should be done with it.

Because Your Prospects Must Justify Their Purchases and Deal with Office Politics, Position Yourself as a Safe Bet from Every Angle. Especially if you are pitching a high-ticket item, it may be worth your while to develop mailing packages and e-mails aimed at people with different job functions within the firm. For instance, let's say you are selling computer systems. Material mailed or e-mailed to financial officers might emphasize the money-saving qualities of the system, while marketers are told about database enhancements and ways your system gets them information faster and easier. Another idea: put the chief executive officer on your mailing list in hopes that his or her recommendation in your favor will filter down to the actual buyer of your product.

Ways to Use Direct and Interactive Marketing in Business-to-Business Communications and Sales

Some firms can use direct and interactive marketing to meet a number of business-to-business objectives. Here are several possibilities.

As an Alternative to Some or All Sales Calls for Certain Prospects and Customers

Customers who are not profitable when serviced mainly by personal sales can become profitable when serviced partly, mainly, or completely by mail, phone, e-mail and online. Many smart business-to-business marketers take the time to divide their prospect lists into groups by sales volume and potential. All of these groups receive brand-building impressions from the firm's space ads, Web site, and public relations activities. What's more, they may all take advantage of certain interactive functions on the Web site for independent management of their own accounts. In addition, they receive customized contacts according to their group in a set-up like this:

1. Smallest potential volume: Mail/e-mail only (catalogs, e-mails, newsletters, and one-shot offers)
2. Next highest level of volume: Mail/e-mail with occasional phone calls
3. Next highest level of volume: Mail/e-mail, phone, and occasional sales calls
4. Highest potential volume: Mail/e-mail, phone, and regular sales calls

A very large company could group its customers in even more categories, while a small one might have only two or three groups. The key here is strategy: nothing is left to chance. Every contact is made according to a carefully orchestrated plan, taking the customer's needs and preferences into consideration. Contact data is recorded on the database for future reference, both for tailoring communications and better serving the customer's needs.

Studies by top business-to-business expert Victor Hunter indicate that many customers today actually prefer less face-to-face contact and more communication by phone, e-mail, Web site interaction, mail, etc. His research indicates that customers often perceive they are actually being served better and receiving more personal contact when such a strategy is undertaken. Indeed, many customers have come to value having access to specific information when they want it—in a reference catalog, by phone, or online—instead of having to wait for the salesperson to arrive for a face-to-face meeting.

For Promotions to Dealers and Distributors

The first "sale" many direct and interactive marketers must make for a new campaign is to get their dealers and distributors on the bandwagon. Direct mail, phone, Web landing pages, and e-mail are excellent ways to communicate a program's goals and tactics so that field representatives know what to expect. The immediacy of e-mail adds excitement to your offer without tying up either the buyer's or the seller's time on the phone. Social media sites can build excitement about the program, invite participants to share their progress, and offer tips and updates. Sales contests and incentives can be explained by these means as well. Broadcast voicemail may also be helpful in communicating the same timely message to hundreds or even thousands of dealers/distributors at the same time. The recipient can pick up the voicemail message on his or her own time schedule. Some multi-level marketers use this voicemail technique along with or instead of e-mail to provide daily messages of inspiration and news to their "downline" associates.

For Promotions to Individual Salespeople

When a sales contest is underway, it's important to keep salespeople informed. Many marketers have had excellent results mailing to salespeople at home to get the spouse and children involved. For a successful contest, try selecting a range of awards that appeal to the family as well as the salesperson. Keep each salesperson posted on individual progress every week or so during the contest to encourage momentum building. Never make mailings to a salesperson's home and/or family members without his or her permission, however.

For Promotions to Specifiers

Often the target of a business-to-business campaign is not the product's ultimate user. Rather, target audiences such as doctors and architects make recommendations to their patients and customers. The aim of communications to specifiers is to give them the facts they need to make an informed recommendation. In addition, it is important for you to establish your firm's image, perhaps with ads in appropriate print or online trade publications, or by creating and mailing a regular newsletter or magazine with articles displaying your knowledge and expertise. An e-mail newsletter may also be welcomed by some specifiers—make sure you acquire their opt-in before sending it to them.

Tips on Business-to-Business Formats and Media

The basics of direct mail formats and catalogs are discussed in other chapters of this book. The tips offered here for business-to-business applications will provide additional idea starters.

A Letter Alone Will Often Suffice

Whereas consumer buyers usually need the reinforcement and "flash" of a brochure and other supplementary mailing inserts, the business buyer may react well to a mailing containing only a letter and a reply card, a toll-free number to call, and/or a landing page (personalized or general). This format is especially appropriate for:

1. Asking the prospect for a sales appointment
2. Introducing the sales rep who will then call the prospect by phone
3. Soliciting a lead to be followed up with free information

When a Traditional Envelope Mailing is Used, Don't Try to Combine Pieces

Often, new business-to-business marketers use "logic" to try to save money—with disastrous results. They'll try combining a brochure and letter, or incorporating a reply device as part of a brochure instead of using a separate piece. These tactics are cost-saving, but they fly in the face of direct mail experience.

A separate letter serves the personal sales function. It should be addressed by name and title if at all possible, and written in a person-to-person style. The brochure is the "leave-behind"—a demonstration piece for capabilities, features, and benefits. The reply device closes the sale, so it should be prominent, visible, and valuable looking—not buried somewhere in the brochure.

Keep the Elements of Your Mailing Program Fresh

Another money-saving ploy of some business-to-business direct marketers is to keep using a standard brochure or mailing package long after it is outdated. Remember that the mailing you send gives the prospect a first impression of your firm—an impression that may be impossible to turn around if it's unfavorable. Update your literature at regular intervals using new product shots, attention-getting graphics in keeping with your firm's overall image, and recent staff photos.

Try Solo Mailings and E-mails Even if Catalogs Are the Backbone of your Direct Mail Business-to-Business Efforts

Introducing a new product or providing extra support for top-selling or high-margin products are two applications to consider for special offers of one item or a line of related items.

Consider Self-Mailers and Postcards: They're Good for Pass-Along Readership

Many consumer direct marketers say they have a hard time making self-mailers beat the control format of a traditional envelope mailing. But self-mailers carry an extra dividend for business mailers: their pass-along value. Studies show that managers are more likely to drop a self-mailer into the inbox of a peer or subordinate than they are an envelope mailing.

Postcards are used more and more by business marketers who use them to provide the "sizzle" about an offer and then lead the prospect online to a Web site with more information, white papers available for download, videos, etc. A postcard may include a Personalized URL (PURL) that takes the prospect to a Web site that greets him or her by name and offers information tailored by industry, company size, and other factors.

In Business-to-Business Catalogs, Be Informative, Organized, and Authoritative—But Not Boring

Don't ignore good promotional language and graphics simply because you are selling a business product. Don't bog yourself down in an explanation of the features at the expense of "sizzle" about the benefits of a product. Avoid using jargon and focusing on technicalities. Nontechnical buyers may be turned off, concluding that your product is way beyond their understanding.

While only the largest consumer catalogs provide a merchandise index, this component is a must

Exhibit 16.2. New Pig Materials

The New Pig catalog illustrates the point that buying business-to-business does not have to be deadly dull. The firm uses a piggy theme in its catalog and even plays "pig theme music" while callers are on hold. In the midst of the fun, however, New Pig beautifully illustrates some of the best practices for business-to-business catalogers. These include top-notch service functions, technical assistance, and guarantees; use of case studies and testimonials; a robust Web site that exemplifies the same look and feel as the paper catalog; and even product endorsements from the "New Pig" himself!

Reprinted with permission of New Pig.

for the business customer. In addition, keeping similar products together will help your business customer make direct comparisons of costs, features and benefits.

To emphasize your firm's expertise in the field, provide testimonials and product-in-use information along with the products themselves. Adding how-tos to the copy makes your catalog presentation more lively and helps customers visualize using your products.

Make ordering easy by following these procedures:

1. Provide a phone number and customer service Web site the customer can access to expedite matters.
2. Make it clear whether the customer needs to provide a purchase order.
3. Make it clear whether a down payment is necessary or if billing can be done upon shipment.
4. Explain how long shipment takes.

All of these specifics are more important than ever in a business situation, especially when the customer is evaluating you against a competitive catalog or personal-sales representative.

Consider Card Decks

Card decks may be an inexpensive source of loose leads for business sales propositions—and loose leads can be especially valuable for business-to-business operations that can afford follow-up phone calls to qualify the prospect, then personal calls to the best prospects to clinch the sale. Card decks may be sponsored by trade publications or sent to compiled lists of individuals in certain fields of endeavor such as marketing, law, medicine, or engineering.

Airline Books May Be Good Sources of Leads

While business magazines and trade publications can be fruitful media choices for space ads, it's well worthwhile considering a test of airline magazines as well. Business travelers are a "captive audience" in the air, and they're away from the office and its multiple distractions when they read your ad. Self-improvement CDs and books, computer equipment and training plans, telecommunications products, luggage and briefcases, sales incentives, and educational products are among the many categories that have been sold successfully via airline publications.

Try Offering a Product-Centered DVD or CD-ROM

Some lead-generation programs include a DVD or CD-ROM presentation as part of the follow-up package. With the dramatic drop in the cost of reproducing such pieces, they are most often offered at no charge to qualified prospects. The cost of such a follow-up seems steep until it is compared with a $300 or $400 personal sales call. Watching a DVD or plugging in a CD-ROM may pre-sell the prospect to the extent that he or she is ready to buy when the salesperson calls by phone or in person. Some firms now offer a variety of materials for the respondent to choose from by checking off a form: a portfolio of product information, a DVD, or CD-ROM, whichever they find more intriguing and/or convenient. Or they may offer an immediate download of videos, white papers, and other information from the company Web site in exchange for some basic information from the prospect.

Harness the Power of the Fax Machine

Even in today's e-mail era, some marketers still use the fax machine as an instant response tool to follow up leads, phone conversations, and sales presentations with customized, actionable information. Fax-on-demand lets prospects call for more information from you and receive it right away on their own fax machines, as well. It is wise to create a special, faxable version of your sales literature and brochures—eliminating the heavy, dark colors that take forever to transmit and are hard to read at the recipient's end. In addition, broadcast fax can be used to communicate "personally" with thousands of customers or prospects at a time. Do keep up with changes in regulations regarding faxes, however, since restrictions on sending unsolicited faxes have been proposed and may be enacted.

Make Your E-mails Respectful and Relevant

Because e-mail is such an inexpensive medium, it is easy for business-to-business marketers to abuse. Here are some tips on developing an e-mail program that your prospects and customers will appreciate:

- **Send e-mail only to prospects and customers who have opted in to receive it**—And ask them what types of information they want to receive from you and how often they are willing to receive it. Some business and publication newsletters are welcomed by their recipients on a daily basis—but only those that are perceived to include well-researched, timely information. Most marketers will need to temper the frequency of their e-mails if the offers they contain are mainly product focused.
- **Every e-mail you send should have an opt-out opportunity at the end**—This element of e-mail etiquette also serves as a built-in edit function for you as the sender. Think about the recipient's likely reaction to the e-mail you are sending. Will they find it relevant and helpful, or just another time-waster? Will your message tempt them to opt out of receiving more messages from you?
- **Make sure that every e-mail answers the question "What's in it for me?"**—Keep the customer or prospect's wants and needs at the center of your e-mail messages. Make an offer that provides real value to the recipient: an authoritative white paper or report, fresh information on industry trends, or product-related information that is customized to their industry and needs.

Use Trade Shows to Reinforce Your Brand Image and Message

Because trade shows are costly in both time and money, savvy marketers will make sure that the image they present is in keeping with their other promotional efforts. Careful planning is essential to ensure that customers and prospects know you'll be at the show, that literature is available to suit the needs of booth personnel, and that leads are followed up promptly and appropriately.

Use direct mail and e-mail to your customer list to make them aware of your trade show presence and any speakers from your firm who will be presenting. Send an invitation to prospects as well—you can usually get the list of pre-registrants from the trade show management. Discuss the trade show line-up on social media sites—and encourage your customers and other attendees to talk about the show in advance. Work with the niche publications in your field to get pre- and post-show coverage of your new product introductions, your presentations, and any tips and trends you can provide in advance of the show.

Provide an incentive for customers to stop by—a drawing, special event, or the like. A contest or drawing will gain names for your mailing list, but there is no guarantee that the new names you receive are viable prospects. Some phone follow-up after the show will help establish your entrants' qualifications to buy or influence sales. Many firms create both a "take one" piece available to anyone who stops by, and a more complete and costly package to be kept under wraps and presented only to prospects pre-qualified by the booth worker. Instead of voluminous literature, some smart marketers now give their best prospects a flash drive containing all their relevant brochures, catalogs, and other materials in PDF form. The flash drive is much easier for prospects to transport, and it also serves the purpose of a premium with good perceived value.

Even seasoned trade show salespeople lament that they often lose or misplace business cards of "hot prospects" they were intent on following up. Prior planning again is the key. If booth workers have a simple procedure for logging in each day's prospects, follow-up can be accomplished in a smooth and organized manner. Nothing is more impressive to a prospect than returning home from a conference to find the information they requested from you already on their desk. Many trade shows today provide attendees with swipe cards that can be scanned at each booth the prospect finds interesting. The swipe card data can be used to send these prospects more information, enter them in contests, and put them on the company's mailing list.

Virtual Trade Shows

To supplement or in some cases even replace face-to-face trade shows, many marketers have now embraced Internet events of many kinds. Rather than expecting busy prospects to travel to a venue, everyone can "meet" at a URL hosted by proven companies like Cisco's WebEx, Go to Meeting, or Cvent. It is possible to set up an entire trade show that takes place online—either as a replacement for the face-to-face event, or as an option for those who choose not to attend. According to Dr. Allen Konapacki, President of the INCOMM Center for Trade Show Research in Chicago, "Only about one-third of interested people actually attend a show, so virtual shows [can potentially] reach 66 to 70 percent of the people who don't actually attend." The ultimate online trade show event is an experience that takes place in a virtual world with avatars attending in place of their human doppelgangers. Such virtual shows are offered via 6connex (*http://www.6connex.com*) for clients including Cisco, WebEx, Procter & Gamble, and Intel.

For much more information on trade show marketing, see *Trade Show and Event Marketing*, by Ruth P. Stevens.

Remember the Back End

Take advantage of available space in package inserts and invoice stuffers to sell accessories and supplies and help maintain your firm's positive image. Send along your company newsletter, if you have one. Create flyers promoting replacement parts, sales on supplies, service contracts, service checkups, or free audits of existing systems. Large business and industrial marketers who underwrite television and sports events might stuff their customer correspondence with reminders to watch upcoming shows under their firm's sponsorship. Local businesses that sponsor parades, sports teams, regional television shows, and the like can take advantage of this same stuffer concept.

Leveraging the Internet for Business-to-Business Marketing

The Internet offers a number of cost-saving, profit-building opportunities for business-to-business marketers. Some of these are supplementary to more traditional promotional methods while others are quite revolutionary. Supplementary measures include:

- Offering customers an online response mechanism for lead generation
- An e-fulfillment option for responding to leads
- Online customer service functions
- Sending a regular company newsletter or new product introduction notice via e-mail instead of or in addition to the usual paper format
- A password-protected, customized Extranet that lets buyers check order status, shipping status, and inventories with a few clicks of the mouse, and may allow for collaboration and teamwork online
- Leveraging social media to develop customer relationships, gain leads, and learn what customers and prospects are saying about your company and your products

All of these provide "win-win" solutions for buyers and sellers as they may save time, paper, and postage on both sides. What's more, when a prospective buyer visits the seller's Web site to ask for information or get a more in-depth report from a click-through on a newsletter, this provides a great opportunity to gain more of his interest and move him toward a sales call or a purchase. The following are some of the more dynamic concepts for business-to-business marketers online.

E-Commerce

Selling products online has a number of benefits to business-to-business marketers. It allows local operators to go national if they have products or services of wide appeal, and it allows national operators to gain international exposure. It provides a cost-effective way to offer almost unlimited breadth and depth of assortment without the space limitations inherent in a paper catalog format. It provides an opportunity for customers to take control of the buying process and to cost-effectively pre-sell themselves by doing online comparisons and customization. It may also expose your company and its products to new markets that would not be practical or available to serve with face-to-face or traditional direct marketing methods.

Selling effectively online, however, requires marketers to perfect their infrastructures so that they can take orders and payments electronically and deliver products swiftly, safely, and accurately, with the seamless customer service functions buyers have come to expect. Top business-to-business e-commerce marketers such as Dell (*www.dell.com*), Cisco (*www.cisco.com*), and Quill (*www.quill.com*) have set the bar high for online efficiency and service.

Webinars

While face-to-face seminars show no signs of disappearing from the business-to-business marketing horizon, buyers and sellers alike have long complained about the costly and frustrating problems inherent in such events. Logistics of travel, hotels and venues, arranging for reliable and inspiring speakers, fears of bad weather and tied-up traffic often have meeting planners losing sleep for weeks before the big event. Face-to-face meetings represent a substantial investment for promoters and attendees alike. This is a high-stakes game in which a beautifully planned seminar can nonetheless be sabotaged by freakish weather that cancels flights and ties up traffic, illness/lateness/poor performance on the part of the main speaker, or—since the recent recession began—last-minute belt-tightening on the part of attendees. What's more, even when all goes well, no-show rates of 50 to 60 percent are common for free promotional seminars offered at a specific time and place.

Many of the benefits of face-to-face seminars can be realized online with considerably less cost in time and money to both buyers and sellers. Online seminars (better known as webinars) take away most of the barriers of travel time and cost, bad weather, and time away from the office. At the participant's own computer, he or she can learn much of the same material that used to require a trip across town or across the country to acquire.

These Internet events offer much better quality control than most live events, with the help of a trusted vendor like Cisco's WebEx or its competitors. For seminars and speeches, attendees only have to invest an hour or so, and they can even multi-task while monitoring the event off their desktop. Alternately, employees can gather together in a conference room to watch and discuss a seminar as a group. Senior executives who are unlikely to take the time to travel to such an event in person may log on individually or with their employees, as well.

For best results, free online seminars hosted by vendors should not be mere commercials for the vendor's product. Featuring an outside author, expert, or other speaker as the centerpiece of the webinar will likely gain you more enthusiastic attendees. Your product information can certainly be shared during the seminar, but in the context of more general learning.

The downside of webinars is that they do not allow for the type of personal relationship building and networking inherent in face-to-face seminars. Nor do they isolate participants from their day-to-day work for a concentrated period of learning. Thus it is unlikely that online events will completely replace these traditional events—especially for senior management.

A successful online seminar does not necessarily have to include high-tech streaming video or flashy effects. Indeed, many such webinars combine a simple online Power Point presentation with an audio feed. Live seminars allow participants to feel a sense of community, participate in real-time polls and chat, and get clarification and answers to questions in real time. The seminar presentation can gain additional life and usefulness, however, if it is posted on the presenting company's Web site with streaming video and audio, for prospects and customers to view at their leisure.

A number of firms have emerged to provide turnkey services for online events and seminars at reasonable prices. Services they provide include online registration, targeted and personalized direct mail and e-mail event marketing, automated confirmations and reminders, survey capabilities, secure online fee collection, and instant reporting and data analysis. Check Cisco's WebEx (*www.webex.com*) or Cvent (*www.cvent.com*) for Web sites that tell you more about how these services work.

Communities, Auctions, and Exchanges

Business-to-business guru Victor Hunter inspires his readers and clients to "create a community of customers." He suggests that instead of the old-style model of sellers relating only one-to-one with buyers, the seller's value to the buyer increases if that seller provides a framework for a buyer community. Such a community is about more than buying products: it's about networking, sharing insights and ideas, and developing collaborations and partnerships.

Building a business community can be challenging in the offline world, but with buyers congregating online, a seller may develop a virtual community with its Web site as the hub. Or a seller may participate in what is called a "vortal"—a vertical portal that combines search engine and community features in a specific field like PlasticsNet (*www.plasticsnet.com*).

Online auctions and exchanges move past the relationship-building aspects of a community and into buying and selling. Auctions such as eBay's Business & Industrial section offer a powerful opportunity for businesses to buy or sell new or used merchandise to other businesses.

Partnerships, Sponsorships, and Affiliations

Like consumer direct and interactive marketers, many business-to-business firms have found banner advertising problematic in terms of cost and accountability. Thus they seek less risky and less costly methods of promoting their companies and Web sites online. Some of these methods include partnerships, sponsorships, and affiliations.

- *Partnerships* allow non-competitive business-to-business marketers to combine their strengths and provide each other with opportunities that would be prohibitively costly to develop alone. Even competitive firms may engage in online "coopetition"—forming joint ventures or alliances where it makes sense to do so.
- *Sponsorships* on search engines and Web sites and for online or e-mail delivered newsletters provide a way to get a company's name in front of potential buyers in a less flashy, less promotional, less financially risky manner than "screaming banner ads."
- *Affiliate agreements* allow business-to-business marketers to place banners on appropriate Web sites and pay only a percentage of resulting sales rather than less controllable cost-per-thousand or cost-per-click banner deals.

E-Fulfillment and White Papers

Customers and prospects appreciate the opportunity to download information that they want or need immediately. Offering them product literature, instruction manuals, software product trials and white papers for instant access can win their appreciation and consideration for purchases.

B2B marketing guru Bob Bly (*www.bly.com*) has introduced a book on this subject: *The White Paper Marketing Book: How to Generate More Leads and Sales by Offering Your Customers Free White Papers, Special Reports, Booklets and CDs* (RACOM Books). Bly says that, "In the 21st century, brochures have been replaced by a new, yet less understood, marketing medium, the 'white paper.'" A *white paper* is a promotional piece in the guise of an informational article or report.

Bly explains, "The white paper serves the same purpose as a brochure . . . to sell or help sell a product or service . . . but reads and looks like an article or other important piece of authoritative, objective information." Unlike a sales brochure, however, Bly notes that a white paper "must contain useful 'how-to' information that helps the reader solve a problem, or make or justify a key business decision (e.g., whether to install a new firewall or build a facility instead of leasing)."

Bly offer four quick tips for successful white paper authors:

- **Be concise.** Say what you have to say in the fewest possible words.
- **Write for scanners and skimmers.** Use heads, subheads bullets, numbers, tables, charts, and graphs.
- **Make the content relevant.** Eliminate extraneous information and facts that are interesting but not germane to the main message.
- **Use a value-added approach.** As Bly says, Americans today are "drowning in information but starved for knowledge." What your white paper can best provide is ideas, tips, guidance, wisdom, advice and solutions.

Social Media

While there is some general information about Social Media in Chapter 17, this section focuses on how business-to-business marketers can use such communities to improve brand recognition, build credibility, and stay up-to-date on what customers and prospects have to say about them and their companies.

LinkedIn is the most prominent business-to-business social network, and it has gained mainstream

Exhibit 16.3. Inside CRM White Paper

Avoid a rocky CRM rollout with this checklist.

10 Steps to a Successful CRM Implementation

By David Claus

CRM has proven its ability to enhance business performance time and time again. However, the path to effective implementation is not always easy — complexities often arise as a result of trying to align an entire company behind the concept. You can find the success that comes from leveraging customer knowledge to the fullest measure by following these 10 steps:

1. Calculate the value. Exactly how will CRM benefit your business? Strive to answer this question in terms of measurable ROI (return on investment). Don't focus too much on how the software will help customers — what will really improve your bottom line is how CRM helps your employees use customer data more effectively.

2. Work closely with key departments. Good planning is critical to your success. Use members of the call center, sales force and marketing departments as parts of your CRM planning team, because these departments can be affected to the greatest extent by a new solution. Let them tell you the business processes that need improvement. Then hammer out agreeable objectives mapped to new business processes. It's often a good strategy to place some easy ones on top of the list so you can celebrate some victories early on.

3. Budget realistically. Be a bit pessimistic when it comes to the budget to avoid the painful process of increasing cost estimates. CRM customization and integration with existing software present two big expenses. It can cost two to three times the price of software for implementation and ongoing maintenance. Make sure you factor in all of these expenses from the early stages of your CRM deployment.

DM News offers a daily white paper in cooperation with advertiser-sponsors. This example from "Inside CRM" covers "10 Steps to a Successful CRM Implementation."

Reprinted from *DM News* free-download White Paper section.

credibility with articles in *Fortune* and other major publications recommending that businesspeople create a LinkedIn profile and use it for job advancement, networking, and hiring. As John Hill, Michigan State University's director of alumni career services, says in comparing the major social media for business purposes, "LinkedIn is like the corporate office. Twitter is like the water cooler, and Facebook is like the bar. You have no idea what conversation is going to come out of the bar so I'm not going to take people interviewing me to the bar." The same would be true for carrying on business conversations.

Twitter can be used as a business-to-business reputation builder—but only if you or your company spokesperson uses Twitter as a serious information-sharing tool. Comments about what you had for breakfast, your personal or political observations and the like are better reserved for your personal Facebook account.

Michael Della Penna, co-founder and Executive Chairman of the Participatory Marketing Network, offers four main reasons why business-to-business marketers are embracing social media.

1. **"Leverage the power of the crowd to drive innovation."** Della Penna cites Salesforce.com's IdeaExchange, Oracle's solicitation of customer feedback on its homepage, and SAP's developer community of 1.7 million users. These firms are cultivating their own social media presences and using them to "interact with clients and prospects, and to generate new ideas to improve product/service offerings in real time."

2. **"Build and grow influential relationships."** Della Penna says that in the informal world of social media, marketers have an opportunity to cultivate "leading analysts, journalists, bloggers and influencers to get these people to start talking about their companies." Twitter often is used for this purpose—especially with live Twitter feeds seeking questions, comments and "re-Tweets" during events.

3. **"Become a resource."** By providing authoritative advice and answering questions, bloggers can win friends and earn a reputation for helpful advice. Della Penna notes that American Express does a good job of this with its Open Forum.

4. **"Extend the brand and bring it to life."** Della Penna cites the "fearless executives" of firms including Oracle, Cisco, IBM, Boeing, and Ernst & Young, who "have embraced social media and added a little personality to the brands they represent" while meanwhile "extending their brands' reach and influence."

Before embarking on a business-to-business social media campaign, here are some questions to consider:

- **Who is the voice of your company?** Some firms allow and even encourage many employees to blog and to label their online presences with the company name. It is wise to have some guidelines for doing so, since these unofficial "spokespeople" may inadvertently make comments that are detrimental to your firm or off-putting to customers. Other firms have an official "voice of the company" who is charged with blogging in the company's name and updating the firm's LinkedIn presence and other social media sites.
- **Can you commit to keeping up your social media presence?** Setting up a LinkedIn account and blog space is easy enough, but allocating the time and

energy to regular and meaningful updates is much more demanding. Make sure your firm's designated social media "voice" has the commitment and accountability to follow through on a regular and consistent basis.

- **Are social media important to your target market?** Rather than assuming that allocating time and money to social media make sense for your company, do some investigation to see if this investment is important to your customers and prospects. Are they regular social media participants, or do they prefer more traditional means of communication? This is likely to vary both by industry and by the age of your typical customer.
- **Are your social media messages "you oriented" to the customer?** Make sure that your social media messages are in keeping with the rest of your marketing and advertising messages. Before posting, ask yourself: does this information answer the customer's question, "What's in it for me?" Offer your customers and prospects useful facts, special deals, insider information, or learning opportunities.
- **Can you use social media for customer intelligence and customer service purposes?** Make sure you sign up for Google Alerts, Twitter Alerts, and any other services you can find that let you know when customers and prospects are commenting about you and your company via social media. This can provide you with valuable insights on customer likes, dislikes, and concerns. If you choose to, you can respond with thanks, advice, or more information—even help solve your customers' stated problems in the social media forum. Just make sure that you come across as helpful and appreciative of comments and critiques—not defensive.

The social media marketplace is changing rapidly, and top sites such as Facebook, LinkedIn and Twitter alter their rules and policies quite often. You will be wise to sign up for seminars offered by trade associations and credible vendors to be sure you stay up-to-date with best practices. Ask your business customers what social media they use and find credible as well, to make sure you are investing your time in the most productive social forums for your industry.

Copy Tips for Business-to-Business Creative People

There are several traps that are all too easy for the business-to-business writer to fall into—especially the in-house copywriter who lives and breathes the same product line for a long period of time. Here are some dos and don'ts designed to help keep your copy fresh.

1. *Don't allow yourself to become production oriented.* Keep the focus of your copy on benefits to your buyer and the ultimate user—not on the latest breakthrough of your research and development department. It may be big news to you and your company president, but that product enhancement means nothing to prospects until you tell them what's in it for them: time savings, money savings, better quality, or whatever.
2. *Don't slow down the sale with product specifications.* Granted, some of your prospects won't make a purchase decision without extensive spec sheets and technical material. But don't bog down your feature-benefit copy with too

Exhibit 16.4. Mcloone Folder with Inserts

Mcloone (La Crosse, Wisconsin) sells image-building graphics for company and product identity. The firm used this handsome folder as a fulfillment piece for leads, as an introduction to the company at trade shows, and as a leave-behind piece for sales calls. This type of folder can be customized inside with a personalized letter, modular flyers appropriate to the prospect's needs, and the sales representative's business card in slots at lower inside right.

Reprinted with permission of Mcloone.

much detail: if you do, you'll lose the buyer who is strictly results oriented. Put the specifications on a separate page or brochure panel.

3. *Make sure that buying your product looks like a safe bet for someone who believes his or her job is on the line.* Emphasize the safety and security of dealing with your stable and established company. Talk in terms of the satisfaction of the product's ultimate user. For example, tell an architect how pleased the homeowner will be with your roofing tiles or greenhouse windows—and why.

4. *Make sure both writer and graphic designer understand the product or service through and through.* Some industrial products are so complex that it's tempting to do a "surface job" of promoting them—pulling out the obvious features and benefits without coming to a full understanding of the product's innermost workings. Resist this temptation. Corner the product manager or the firm's engineer and keep asking questions until you comprehend every aspect of what you are selling. Only then will you be able to write convincingly to professionals in the field about the product's most important features and benefits.

5. *Be specific about benefits.* Don't speak in general terms about time or cost savings. Instead, use case histories and examples that put the product's attributes into perspective. Consider how much more effective it is to have a customer say, "A job that used to take me three full days was cut down to just a day and a half the first week I used my XYZ paint spray gun," rather than to have promotional literature say, "The XYZ paint spray gun saves you time and money."

6. *Copy may be long and complex, but keep it easy to read.* In a thorough presentation of a technical product, it is all the more important to use short sentences, short paragraphs, readable typefaces, and subheads.

7. *Use a good graphic designer, and maximize production values.* Don't cut the effectiveness of your carefully prepared copy with a quick and dirty printing job at your local speedy outlet. Invest in the services of an experienced graphic designer and take the time to create materials that positively reflects your firm's image and are in keeping with the "look" of your overall marketing effort.

8. *Keep reading everything you can about consumer direct and interactive marketing.* Many of the action devices, personalization techniques, offers, formats, online concepts, and production methods used first in consumer markets can be adapted to good advantage by business-to-business marketers as well.

Setting Business-to-Business Lead Qualification Criteria

by Ruth P. Stevens, President, eMarketing Strategy

One of direct marketing's most important contributions to business marketing is generating leads on behalf of salespeople. Lead generation can be defined as identifying prospective customers and qualifying their likelihood to buy, in advance of making a sales call. In other words, it's about getting prospects to raise their hands.

For salespeople, a qualified lead provided by a marketing department allows the sales rep to spend valuable time in front of a prospect who is likely to buy, instead of squandering the salesperson's skills on cold calling. In short, lead generation programs make a sales force more productive.

The most important approach to setting qualification criteria is to follow the needs of your sales force. After all, it is they who will be handling the lead and taking it to closure. They know better than anyone the nature of the sales process and what kind of buying characteristics are most likely to be workable for them. Qualification criteria will vary by company and by industry. However, as a general rule, most criteria involve the following categories:

- **Budget.** Is the purchase budgeted, and what size budget does the prospect have available? You will want to set up categories or ranges, for easier scoring. Some companies request information about the prospect company's credit history here.
- **Authority.** Does the respondent have the authority to make the purchase decision? If not, you should try to capture additional relevant contact information. Also find out what role the respondent does play, for example, influencer, user, or product specifier.
- **Need.** How important is the product or solution to the company? How deep is their pain? This criterion may be difficult to ask directly, but it can be approached by roundabout methods. "What is the problem to be solved?" "What alternative solutions are you considering?" "How many do you need?" "What product do you currently use?"
- **Time Frame**. What is their readiness to buy? When is the purchase likely to be? Depending on industry and sales cycle length, this can be broken into days, months, or even years. Also be sure to ask whether they would like to see a sales person.

Taken together, these key variables are abbreviated as BANT (budget, authority, need, and time frame), and are widely used in industrial and technology markets. Other common criteria in business marketing include:

- **Potential sales volume**. How many departments in the company might use this product? How much of, or how often, might they need the product?
- **Predisposition to buy from us.** Are they past customers of ours? Are they similar to our current customers? Would they recommend us to their colleagues? Are they willing to call us back?
- **Account characteristics**. What is the company size, whether number of employees or revenue volume? What industry is it in? Does it have a parent company?

Excerpted with the permission of the Direct Marketing Association from *The DMA Lead Generation Handbook*.

Enhance Your Understanding:
Create a Business-to-Business Catalog and Web Site

Two of the main strategic purposes for business-to-business catalogs are to:

1. Supplement a company's personal selling and/or outbound telemarketing efforts. (Example: a catalog offering mailing lists segmented from 14+ million U.S. businesses)
2. Fill a niche (market segment) with materials/supplies etc., that are not readily available via personal sales or outbound telemarketing to businesses and businesspeople. (Example: a catalog offering elegant, personalized business greeting cards)

Based upon your reading about business-to-business direct and interactive marketing, develop a positioning concept for an industrial or business-to-business catalog and Web site including:

1. Name of Catalog/Web address
2. Parent Company (if sponsored by an established firm)
3. Rationale for Catalog (e.g., supplement sales force, fill an unmet need)
4. Target Market (business type, company size, SIC codes targeted, number of employees, etc.)
5. Benefits to the Target Market
6. Product Mix—a list of at least ten products or product categories that will appear in your paper catalog and its online version
7. Any special features that will enhance the catalog's Web site scoring.

17

E-Commerce Marketing

In all the excitement surrounding the growth and development of interactive/e-commerce/digital marketing, creative people may lose sight of two important and comforting facts. First, interactive media are just that: *media* that direct marketers can approach with the same critical eye and strategic wisdom they use to create and evaluate mail, broadcast, and space ads and telemarketing campaigns. Second, unlike our general advertising cousins, traditional direct marketers were born to go online: cultivating dialogues has always been our stock in trade. Who better to close the loop on the Internet than we who have been "asking for the order" in other media for generations?

There *is* something inherently new and challenging about the Internet, however—a concept that has changed the advertising paradigm sharply and forever. Up until the proliferation of the Web, advertisers have always decided how long a message each prospect can be exposed to: 120-second broadcast spot or infomercial . . . small-space ad or double-page spread . . . postcard or jumbo spectacular mailing package. Granted, the *prospect* has always decided whether he or she would pick up on that exposure—and whether they'd read or watch the whole message or just focus on bits and pieces.

What's different with online media is that prospects aren't exposed to much of anything they don't *choose* to see or hear. They take much more control over their own experience. Our challenge is first—to get them to look at our material initially; second—to entice them to voluntarily delve deeper and deeper into our message; third—to engage them in an interactive dialogue and potential relationship and/or sale; and fourth—to intrigue them to communicate with us and return again and again.

Over the past two decades, e-commerce marketing has graduated from a high-tech medium focused mainly on young male computer geeks to a central and strategic element of most every firm's marketing plan. Scores of texts, trade books and seminars on e-business, e-commerce, Web site design, e-mail marketing and social media have cropped up in recent years, as academics and practitioners alike strive to capture and share knowledge about this rapidly advancing field.

Statistics from the Direct Marketing Association attest to the impressive growth of e-commerce marketing, during a time period where traditional media like newspapers and broadcast radio have faced daunting challenges. According to the DMA, there will be 221.1 million U.S. Internet users by 2013. Fifty-nine percent of consumers use search engines to find "deals" online, and search engine marketing commands 47 percent of U.S. spending on Internet ads. What's more, ZenithOptimedia predicts that by 2012, more than one-fifth of all U.S. marketing spending will take place on the Internet—an impressive rise from just 6.4 percent in 2006 to 20.6 percent six years later.

Even during the recent recession, online sales continued to grow—to a great extent at the expense of brick-and-mortar retail sales, according to the U.S. Department of Labor. That said, there is still plenty of room for more expansion, since online sales still accounted for less than 4 percent of total retail sales during that same period. This chapter first sets the stage for interactive/e-commerce marketing with a brief historical review.

Then it provides a framework for direct and interactive marketers' decision-making on how to maximize their opportunities online and overcome barriers to success. Finally, it offers some guidance for creative marketers on maximizing the impact of Web sites, e-mail, social media, and Web site promotion.

Interactive Media: "The Fourth Communications Revolution"

Online marketing expert Mike DeNunzio has called the interactive media phenomenon "The Fourth Communications Revolution." First there was the printing press, which meant that books and other communications could be produced in quantity—not just copied by hand. Second was radio: the first broadcast medium. Third was television: adding a picture to the broadcast message. Both radio and television are "linear" media—their messages start and stop at prescribed times and must be listened to or viewed in a set sequence (unless, of course, the listener or viewer records the program so he/she can zip through the ads, rewind, and review). With the Internet we have the fourth revolution: what DeNunzio dubs "two-way global digital communications." Not only are these new media interactive, nonlinear, and unlimited by geography, but they also are available for access at will, 24 hours a day.

In his brilliant book, *Being Digital*, Nicholas Negroponte explained this concept further by making a comparison between bits and atoms. Digital bits on computers or hand-held devices can be much more quickly and easily communicated and shared than atomic matter like newspapers, books, and magazines. Of course, communicators can turn those bits into atoms if they wish, simply by making a hard copy printout or video recording on a DVD. Radio and television are not "constrained by atoms," but they are limited by available frequencies, local boundaries, time schedules, and a host of regulations.

In the 1960s, the Internet's predecessor, Advanced Research Projects Agency Network (ARPANET), was devised as a secure way of communicating classified military information. For two decades, it was available mainly to the U.S. Department of Defense and to university researchers. Then in the 1980s, ARPANET was upgraded by the National Science Foundation with a high-speed network, which allowed for the swift linkage of millions more computers. Unlike the highly regulated radio and television media, however, what is now called the Internet has developed without ownership or government control. Essentially, the Internet is a vast "network of networks," using computers for communication.

As the Internet has exploded over the past 20-plus years, a whole new vocabulary has come into common use. We heard much about "digitization"—the process of turning information into computer bits using permutations of the numbers 1 and 0. The "Information Superhighway" was much touted in the early 1990s as a more easily understandable term for the "network of networks" that could bring us all a never-ending flow of data and pictures. Speakers warned creative direct marketers to "watch out for the potholes" on the Superhighway . . . to "avoid becoming roadkill" on the Superhighway . . . etc. In those early days the Internet seemed more like a plate of cooked spaghetti strands than a series of organized roads. The only way to navigate was to know and properly enter a site's complete "URL" (Uniform Resource Locator) or address—which often encompassed ten or more digits, including backslashes and other unfamiliar symbols. Then in the mid-1990s, user-friendly methods of navigation arose that made the Internet attractive and accessible to whole new groups of non-computer nerds. Almost overnight, e-mail was adopted by millions as a simple and inexpensive method of business and personal communication.

The World Wide Web and broadband access (nearing 90 percent in all but rural areas of the U.S. circa 2011) made pictures, motion, and sound available to the average Internet user, including current and past television shows and movies that could be downloaded to the desktop in seconds. Internet Explorer and Mozilla Firefox made it much simpler to find sites using intuition and logic. A host of search engines such as Google, Yahoo! and Bing allowed casual users to type in keywords and simplify their hunts for information and topic areas. In the 2000s, social networks like Facebook, YouTube, and Twitter provided individuals and businesses with the opportunity to share information, friendship, and support . . . provide "status updates" and locations . . . show off pictures, videos, and music . . . play games online . . . and much more. What's more, all of these online advancements showcased new advertising opportunities for direct and interactive marketers—many of which could be monitored click by click, tested and controlled with great precision, and modified in seconds.

Benefits and Barriers for Interactive Marketers

There are many positives associated with online marketing, and very few arguments against it. There are, however, a number of concerns that direct and interactive marketers should address as they develop their interactive presence.

Strengths of Interactive Media

Low cost of entry. Today many eight-year-olds and millions of college students have their own blogs, social media accounts and personal pages on the World Wide Web, so direct marketers need not fear that engaging on the Web is difficult or cost-prohibitive. A basic home page done by a professional costs anywhere from $1,000 to $75,000 and up, depending on whether you're working with your local computer guru, your advertising agency, or a specialized consulting firm. Keep in mind, however, that if you plan to sell products on your own Internet site, the initial cost may be considerably higher. Excellent operations, fulfillment, and customer service functions—all customized as necessary to fit your unique needs—must be in place before you begin accepting orders.

A small firm can look like a giant. On the Web, a cottage industry can come across with the impact of a Fortune 100 company if its site is crafted with class and flair. Interactive media provide a breakthrough opportunity for entrepreneurs who will make it their number-one channel of distribution. At the same time, a Web presence serves as an important element of the media mix—and may also be a significant sales channel—for larger firms.

The early years are a time of valuable learning. Much like the 1950s were a period of experimentation with television, the current era offers direct marketers an ideal opportunity to test and perfect techniques for interactive marketing. Even the acknowledged experts are learning something new every day as e-mail marketing, search marketing, sponsored search, social media, online video and other developing technologies offer constantly evolving opportunities for innovation.

Interactive media allow for seamless integration with other online and offline messages. Smart direct and interactive marketers take every opportunity to entice prospects and customers to their Web sites for specific offers and rewards. E-mail and mobile messaging are ideal "push" media that can highlight Web site features, offers, special sales, and other opportunities, and deliver traffic to

Exhibit 17.1. L.L. Bean E-mail, Web Site Capture, and Mailer

L.L. Bean (*www.llbean.com*) seamlessly integrated e-mail, a related Web site, and a customer mailer to promote its Book Packs in the back-to-school buying period. Each element shared the same colors, look, feel, and offer, and the e-mail and mailer arrived within days of each other.

Reprinted with permission of L.L. Bean.

the site with the ease of a click. Search engine optimization, sponsored search, and banner ads all offer online promotional opportunities for marketers.

Interactive media are outstanding for public relations and brand building. Using the same look and message as other promotional efforts, marketers can entice their prospects and customers to find out more information, have more fun, learn more about products and services, and engage in real-time dialogue with the company and with each other. As Andrew Cohen, founder of Direct Resources International noted, direct marketers traditionally have focused on the product as king. Cohen said that in the interactive world, content is king. People enjoy the medium because it allows them to delve into company history, play games, enter contests, e-mail the company with their ideas and critiques, and much more.

The spenders of the future are wired to the hilt. Today's elementary school students use computers with a casual flair that impresses their parents and amazes their grandparents. What's more, according to the Kaiser Family Foundation, 66 percent of U.S. children and teens ages 8 to 18 had a mobile phone as of 2009—and placing calls is less important to them than texting and using the phone's other features. High school students surf the Internet for research materials, chat with fellow learners all over the world, and download books online instead of trekking to the local library. Laptop computers, netbooks, or iPads are required for college students at numerous schools, and used regularly in classes. Many college professors create dedicated Web sites for each class they teach, require that homework be delivered via the Internet, ask their students to post papers online for classmates to critique, and encourage class members to contribute to wikis and blogs. Many classes and even full degrees are offered 100 percent online. The techno-savvy young people immersed in this digital world are well on their way to becoming the top consumers of goods and services—and the main buyers of business products and services as well. They're as comfortable on the Internet or using their hand-held devices to communicate and buy as their grandparents are using the TV remote control and landline telephone.

Concerns for Interactive Marketers

Strategy and planning must come before implementation. You'll still find sites—particularly in the business-to-business realm—put in place by companies that rushed to establish a "presence" without rhyme or reason. Many of these sites offer little more than an online company brochure or two—and some appear as if they've been set up and abandoned. Many more ignore the advantage of the Web's immediacy and interactivity by requiring buyers to contact them offline during regular business hours. Make sure a strategic plan is in place for the development, implementation, and refinement of your interactive media presence. Begin by asking some basic questions. For example, is your site intended to produce substantial sales or leads now? Is that realistic for your product or service? Do you want to use your site as a component in your brand-building plan? Will you build a database of visitors for cultivation via other means? Do you want to use your site to enhance your relationship with existing customers? How will your online efforts be perceived by others in your channel of distribution, and how can you avoid channel conflict?

Privacy and security concerns remain issues. With encryption programs in place to guard credit card numbers and personal information, many Web marketers feel certain that their customers can share data and buy over the Internet without fear of "invasion." Yet today's customers voice a different type of privacy concern: they want to know what information Web sites are recording about them and their visits, and how this information is being used. For this reason, smart marketers include information on their Web sites about how they collect and use information, and how they protect the privacy of their visitors and customers, and live up to those promises scrupulously. Web site owners who use surreptitious methods to scope out information about their site visitors will ultimately do damage to the perception of them and of all Internet marketers.

The ease of e-mail may lead to impropriety. Never has there been an advertising medium as flexible, immediate, and inexpensive as e-mail. Direct Marketing Association studies show e-mail to be the most cost-effective of all media in terms of return on investment (revenue per contact divided by cost per contact), for both sales and lead generation, by a very large margin. Indeed, e-mail is tempting to overuse for this very reason. But marketers who e-mail with too little care to the long-term value of their precious database of buyers and prospects may find themselves losing excellent customers—and compromising their reputations in the process. Smart marketers will offer their customers and prospects an airtight opt-in process, and get specific consent about what is to be e-mailed (newsletters, promotions, and so on) and how often it will be sent. What's more, they will offer those on their e-mail list the opportunity to opt-out at the bottom of every e-mail message.

Buying online must be fast and simple. Customers like the idea of avoiding crowded malls and buying online at their own convenience. But when the system crashes, or a customer must navigate screen after screen to complete the sale, or the customer can't determine how much shipping and handling will be without completing a long order form, or it takes minutes for the site to accept the buyer's credit card information and return confirmation, enthusiasm swiftly wanes. Make your sales sequence as quick and painless as possible. Have people test it frequently, and test it yourself to look for timewasters and bugs.

Visitors to your site may be hampered by small computer screens or slow access. Before approving your newly redesigned Web site, try using it with various browsers and computer systems. Many smart marketers keep equipment like this on hand to test their sites rather than assume all their visitors will have optimal broadband access and large computer screens.

Web sites must be advertised to attract visitors. Some visitors may happen onto your site randomly, and many will come to you via search engines if you make sure your site is optimized, and you sponsor appropriate keyword searches. But to ensure that your important prospects and customers know about your Internet site, it's incumbent upon you to promote it. Your URL (or a customized landing page) should appear on television spots, print ads, brochures and catalogs, news releases, product labels, and even trucks used for shipping your products. While advertising on some of the better-known Web browsers and search engines can be expensive, it's worth seeking out specialized Web sites that may fit your product niche and offer space for your advertising banner, sponsorship, or keyword advertising at reasonable rates or on a cost-per-click, cost-per-lead, or cost-per-sale basis.

"Cross linkages" and affiliate deals should be undertaken strategically. As a Web site proprietor, you will have the opportunity to sell or trade cross-links between your site and others. While at first this may seem a source of "found" extra revenue, such linkages should be considered using the same criteria as list rentals. Make sure the sites you link to are appropriate to your company image and philosophy. And keep in mind that when visitors click away to another site, there is no guaran-

tee that they'll eventually click back to you. As for affiliate deals, make sure that partners you allow to sell your products or services on commission are appropriate in terms of the quality and subject matter of their sites. You also need to devote time to monitoring your affiliate program or hire one of the several firms that act as go-betweens for such arrangements.

Your mistakes are magnified online. Make a mistake with a catalog or retail customer, and they might tell a few friends about the snafu. Make a mistake online, and you run the risk that your dissatisfied customer will tell thousands about your foibles via chat groups, social media, mass e-mailings, or even YouTube videos. Prompt responses and impeccable customer service are even more important online than they are with other forms of marketing.

Tips for Interactive Media

Just as most copywriters and graphic designers don't get involved in directing and filming direct response TV spots, there is no compelling need for every direct marketing creative to "do it all" in interactive media. Even so, some writers and designers will carve this out as a specialty, and most creatives will at least have the opportunity to contribute concepts, copy, and art for interactive media ventures. As an introduction, here is some general background and advice for creative people regarding Web sites, e-mail, and banner advertising.

Web Sites

Offer the choice of a "bite, snack, or meal" to site visitors. Web visitors need to be able to discern quickly what your site is about, what it offers, and how it's relevant to them. From this initial "bite," they may surf a bit deeper and enjoy a "snack"—a taste of your material that may whet their appetite for more either now or later. If they are intrigued, and if they have the time, they may settle down for a real "meal"—reading your white papers, engaging with your interactive elements, creating their own profiles, and the like. Or they may bookmark your site to visit again later, if the initial bite or snack has pleased them. Make sure each visitor can easily choose from a bite, a snack, or a meal upon visiting your site.

Chunk your information and use bullet points. Web pages of text that require scrolling down are tedious for users and may cause you to lose them altogether. Especially on the initial few click-through levels, provide information in chunks and bullet points rather than long-winded prose. You can then invite readers to click through for more in-depth information.

Offer multiple ways to search. Some site visitors will prefer to click on general-category icons and then go deeper to find the products and information they are looking for. Others will prefer to put keywords into a search function. Offer both options on your site for best results. A powerful search function is usually well worth your investment.

Plan for constant updates that entice visitors to return. Web aficionados like to "bookmark" their favorite sites and visit them often to see what's new. To ensure that your site gets frequent visits, add features that change daily, weekly, or even hourly. Depending on the topic of your site you might display a new and customized offer, quote of the day, recipe, or chance to win prizes on a regular basis. For example, Amazon.com's daily Gold Box specials give customers a reason to check the site often in search of exceptional deals. In addition, the major television networks list their daily schedules on the Internet, and many specialized sites feature late-breaking news in their field of interest.

Make your site easy to follow. According to Elias M. Awad, author of *Electronic Commerce: From Vision to Fulfillment*, customers who can't find what they are looking for on a site within a mere eight seconds will often go looking for alternatives. Some Web designers become so caught up in graphics and colors that it is difficult for visitors to follow the site's pathways. Provide a simple, descriptive menu that offers a clear and understandable path. Put a button on each page in your site that will take the visitor back to your original home page—dead-end pages make users feel backed into a corner. Use clear and consistent navigational aids such as graphics and icons, and test your site to make sure that visitors understand these elements and find them easy to use.

Understand the psychological effects of color. Visit *www.colorvoodoo.com* for helpful e-publications on the effects of colors on Web site viewers. A few instructive examples:

- *Red* attracts attention but may overwhelm other colors on the page, so use as an accent in most cases.
- *Blue* connotes trust, conservatism, and stability. Many bank Web sites are blue.
- *Green* symbolizes nature, health, and good luck to Americans. In global markets its meaning is less positive, so use with care for international sites.
- *White* means purity, cleanliness, precision, innocence, and freshness to Western audiences. Pages with a white background print easily.
- *Black* works well for fashion Web sites, but should be used with care as it connotes power, elegance, and sexuality as well as fear, unhappiness, and death.

If you're selling online, make every inch count. Successful e-commerce marketers use the lion's share of their initial home page to initiate dialogue and facilitate customer buying. Material that is not sales-related is accessible via the home page, but does not dominate that precious real estate.

Provide entertainment, interaction, and information. Studies show that consumers gain time for online pursuits by cutting down on the hours they spend watching television—or by multi-tasking while they have the TV on in the background. Make sure that what you offer them is enjoyable as well as informative, so that it beckons them back, time and again. Offer your visitors fun, games, and painless learning experiences that eventually lead to your selling message. The ideal site induces what creativity expert Mihaly Csikszentmihalyi calls the "flow" state—challenging visitors to the extent that they remain intrigued and dig deeper, but not causing them to abandon the site because it is too difficult or frustrating to use.

Use what you know about direct marketing to your advantage online. Engage site visitors in dialogue, and allow them to personalize your site to meet their preferences and needs in addition to personalization you do based on their buying history, online activity, and any third-party data you may choose to overlay. This combination of personal preference, actual consumer behavior, and demographic/psychographic information can make offering suggestions to your customers much more effective—check Amazon.com's "Improve Your Recommendations" function for an outstanding example. Select your audience by the look and tone of your site, but make sure it's in keeping with your overall brand or company image. Test offers, premiums, graphic looks, products, time of day, and so on—just as you would in the mail or on television. Make an offer, have a call to action, and an incentive to "act now."

Test everything on your site to improve your conversion rate. Internet entrepreneur Andy Jenkins used to spend much of his time, money, and effort trying to rise to the top of organic search and sponsored search listings. Then he realized that an even better leverage point was on his site itself. He claims he increased his conversion rate at *www.european-wall-tapestries.com* from 1.1 percent to nearly 4 percent through strategic testing of selling elements. His site will not win any design awards—it's busy and jam-packed with merchandise and messages—but it's highly productive. Elements Andy has successfully tested and added include:

- Featuring his free shipping and no sales tax offers
- Highlighting "we ship worldwide," including a display of flags at the bottom of the site
- Helping customers make decisions and increasing their "time on site" with sections called "most popular" and "first time tapestry shopper"
- Putting the product in context by showing tapestries in a home
- Showing the logos of a wide range of credit payment options
- Showing the logos of credibility-building organizations such as VeriSign and Alexa
- Assuring customers they can "Order Online 24 Hours a Day, 7 Days a Week, 365 Days a Year"—this may seem obvious, but adding the statement to his site increased sales
- Making an offer for customers who opt in to become members of his discount home décor club
- Showing the smiling face of a design expert and providing her name, "JoAnne"—when customers call, any one of the female call center personnel can assume the JoAnne persona
- Highlighting the 100% Money Back Guarantee and 110% Low Price Guarantee

Use landing pages and Personalized URLs (PURLs) to "pay off" specific offers made online and in other media. When a prospect clicks through to your Web site or follows up on an offer made in a space ad, postcard, or other medium by going online, send them to a specific landing page rather than your general Web site. This ensures that the prospect is greeted with the same look, feel, and offer that they saw in the original medium, thus enhancing their likelihood of continuing toward a purchase or inquiring for more information. Personalized URLs (PURLs) greet the customer or prospect by name and can provide them with an even more segmented message based on their demographics, psychographics, past buying patterns, and stated or implied preferences.

Have a mobile version of your site (and your e-mails) readily available for visitors. As more and more customers use their hand-held devices for shopping and reading messages, make sure you are ready to serve them with a seamless mobile format that can be read easily on a small screen. As Amazon.com and other firms have done, you will be wise to develop a mobile app for the iPhone and other smart phones.

Make sure your site processes orders swiftly and keeps customers informed online and via e-mail. Customers have been conditioned by the best Web sites to expect immediate and glitch-free order processing, immediate e-mail confirmation, online status checks, and e-mail updates during the fulfillment process. Be sure your site meets these standards by "ordering from yourself" regularly, and having others do so as well.

Minimize shopping cart abandonment. Studies show that on many sites, as many as 50 to 55 percent of all filled shopping carts are ultimately abandoned before purchase. Reasons may include what's called "clicker shock" at high taxes, shipping and handling charges, a clunky interface, fear that returns will be a hassle, or people who are just "window shopping" and never intended to buy. Analyze your abandoned cart information, seek feedback from your customers and prospects, and adjust your selling methods accordingly. For example, you may find that it pays to disclose the full cost, including all shipping, handling, taxes and fees, earlier in the buying process. You may also benefit by emphasizing how easy it is to return merchandise. In fact, some firms promote the fact that they allow customers to print out prepaid UPS return labels on their home computers, and arrange to have the UPS truck pick up the return package at the customer's front door.

If a known customer or prospect leaves items in their shopping cart, let those items remain there for them to re-view on their return, and provide a picture of the product in the cart—Andy Lloyd, CEO of Fluid, says the visual helps "retain that emotional connection with the product." You may also experiment with pop-ups that appear as the customer leaves your site, reminding them that there are items still in the cart, or even incentivizing them to return and buy. Another option is to send an e-mail to a known customer or prospect noting that they left items in the cart. This can be accompanied by an offer to help the customer complete his or her selection, or an incentive to do so.

Offer your customers an FAQ section and self-service options, but allow them the option to communicate with a human. A good and prominently displayed FAQ (frequently asked questions) section drawn from actual customer questions can avoid many customer service calls and e-mails. If the FAQ section fails, however, many Web sites are nearly "blind" to the visitor, without any indication of physical location, phone number, or contact names or departments. This is a mistake. Customers who become confused or have a problem on your Web site need the option to e-mail, communicate by instant message, and/or call a customer service representative for help when it is required.

Test usability with your customers and prospects. It can be very instructive to sit down with individuals who are in your target market and watch them surf your site with no prior instruction from you. You may discover stoppers, glitches, and questions that might otherwise go undetected for weeks or months. You may also engage the services of an agency or research company that can handle usability testing for you. Their experience with many sites will help them ask questions and test elements that might not occur to you.

Learn from the original masters of the medium, and stay abreast of the latest innovators. Sites like Amazon.com, Zappos.com, and eBay.com are among the top Internet pure-play companies. Get to know these groundbreaking sites, and keep abreast of how they modify their sites and add new functions. Also be sure to stay alert to the possibilities of new Web site technology and design innovations by attending online and offline seminars and trade shows, and reading online and offline trade publications and white papers, and following the Twitter feeds and blogs of top experts in the field.

E-Mail Marketing

The medium of e-mail has captured the attention of avid marketers and wary consumers alike. BI-Gresearch reports that consumers spend an average of 131.3 minutes per day with e-mail—just slightly more than they spend with television. According to Forrester Research, active users of e-mail in the United States will reach a total of 178.2 million by 2014. E-mail represents the most cost-efficient medium ever devised, with the Direct Marketing Association reporting an ROI of better than $40 per dollar invested, circa 2011. According to AMR Research, "Finely targeted e-mail marketing campaigns can garner up to seven to 12 times the response rate of comparable snail mail marketing efforts." And e-mail responses rates averaged an impressive 22 percent open rate and 5.9 percent click-through rate in late 2009, according to a study by Epsilon. But because it is so inexpensive and easy to produce and distribute, e-mail also is the easiest medium to abuse—so much so that the U.S. Congress felt compelled to pass the "Can Spam" bill which went into effect on January 1, 2004, including penalties for spammers of up to five years in prison.

Hallie Mummert of *Target Marketing* magazine lists the following benefits of e-mail for marketers:

- *Saves Money*—No paper, postage, or print production costs; no cost for media except when rented e-mail lists are used.
- *Targets Cost-Effectively*—To small or large groups.
- *Measure Response Fast*—Replies may begin within minutes of receipt and campaign results should be readable in a matter of hours or days.
- *Easy List Management*—Delete those who opt out and don't want to hear from you. (The Direct Marketing Association reported an unsubscribe rate of 0.77% in its 2010 Fact Book).
- *Integrate with Other Media*—Coordinate e-mails with mailings, Web site features, broadcast, and other campaign elements.

Tony Priore, Chief Marketing Officer at Biz360, Inc., suggests ten profitable ways that e-mail can add value to your marketing program:

1. *Branding/Awareness Building*—Reinforcing a brand name and building brand community while personalizing a message to recipient.
2. *Registration and List Building*—To grow your house file.
3. *Sampling*—Download, free trial, or product sample.
4. *E-Commerce*—Buy online or research online and buy offline.
5. *Drive Site Usage/Traffic*—Or launch a site.
6. *Up sell/Cross Sell.*
7. *Customer Communication*—Such as newsletters.
8. *Loyalty and Rewards Programs*—Points programs.
9. *New Customer Recruitment*—"Member get a member." (This could also include recruiting people to become fans of or "like" your pages on Facebook and other social media, through forwarded e-mails.)
10. *Customer Service*—Invoices, statements, order status, confirmations.

E-mail has much in common with direct mail in that lists, offers, and creative are the three key elements of leverage. Here are some of the how-tos for these essential factors for E-success.

Optimizing Your E-Mail List Strategy. Just as with direct mail, your own house list will likely work the best, with even inactives and inquiries pulling better than cold rental lists. You will be wise to keep your house list fresh by monitoring the response rates of your internal e-mail files and contacting people who have stopped clicking through to opt them in once again. But before putting e-mail names on an inactive list, check to see if they are purchasing in other ways—don't deactivate people who are buying through other channels.

To enhance that valuable house list, experts suggest that marketers collect e-mail addresses wherever they can: on the Web, at retail, when customers call in (you can record permission right there), through mailings, and so on. Offer them a benefit to giving you the e-mail address, such as shipping confirmations, tracking, high-quality niche newsletters, or periodic special offers. Reggie Brady, President of Reggie Brady Marketing Solutions, suggests that you send newly opted-in customers a welcome e-mail right away. What's more, she notes many call centers are being measured by clients on their level of success in collecting opted-in e-mail addresses.

Another way to enhance your house e-mail list is to use commercial e-mail appending and ECOA (e-mail change of address) services. Make sure that the sources you use for these services are providing you with "permission" names only—e-mail addresses of individuals who have indicated they are willing to receive promotions via this medium. You will pay only for deliverable names which are appended to your list.

Just as with direct mail, you will be wise to work with a seasoned list broker for e-mail list rental and other list services. A good broker will help make sure you are getting the type of names you specify, such as double opt-in, opt-in, recency/frequency/monetary, and selects, and that you don't pay for bounces (bad names that bounce back, which the Direct Marketing Association says average about 3.72 percent). Additional tips for renting e-mail lists include:

- Never accept physical possession of a rental e-mail list. List managers should send out the communication on your behalf.
- List owners should remind the recipients in a header on the e-mail message sent on your behalf of their relationship with the recipient.
- Any complaints or problems should be directed to the list provider, who has the established relationship with the recipient.
- Realize that despite your best efforts, some of your messages may end up in a junk-mail folder or being blocked altogether. To minimize these problems, follow the anti-spam advice provided later in this chapter.
- Monitor your response rates closely, domain by domain, such as Gmail, AOL, Hotmail, MSN, and so on, to see if you are being blocked. Some domains' filters will notify the sender when they block the mail; others do not.

Offers and Creative. According to DoubleClick, when asked what most compelled them to open an e-mail, 60 percent of respondents said the "From" line, and 35 percent said the "Subject" line. Beginning with these two elements, here are some tips for optimizing your e-mail offers and creative presentations, many of which come from e-mail expert Jeff Moriarty:

- "FROM" LINES

  ‣ Base the name on the brand your audience identifies with most readily—this could be your company name or the product name.

  ‣ Famous names like Jeff Bezos of Amazon may be effective, but in general using unknown names is not advisable.

  ‣ Don't use an e-mail address, a number, or the term "do not reply" as a "from" line.

  ‣ Once you select an ID and it works well, use it consistently for fast audience recognition.

- "SUBJECT" LINES

  ‣ Test to determine what works best for your company and product.

  ‣ Should be no longer than 50 characters.

  ‣ Need to grab attention and provide a call to action.

  ‣ Include brand or company name if they are known and trusted.

  ‣ Test putting the offer and/or benefit in the subject line.

  ‣ Use direct mail teaser strategies for subject line tests.

  ‣ Avoid being repetitive.

  ‣ Test personalization.

  ‣ Avoid elements that attract spam filters such as these words and symbols: free, !, $, win, cash, sale, limited time, percent , *, mortgage, guarantee, lots of different fonts and large fonts, ALL CAPS.

- PREVIEW PANES (windows recipients can use to screen e-mail)

  ‣ Generate interest in the top two inches of your e-mail.

  ‣ Create an immediate connection with personalization.

  ‣ Include a call to action.

  ‣ Pay-off the tease or offer in the subject line.

  ‣ Avoid text treatment that is caught in spam filters, such as those mentioned above, plus garish font colors.

- BODY AND CLOSING

  ‣ Emphasize clarity and simplicity to facilitate quick scanning.

  ‣ Test your layout for "hot spots"—Moriarty says the upper left quadrant seems to be the best place for a logo, for example.

  ‣ Don't underline things—people will think they are links.

  ‣ Test HTML versus plain text. Text loads faster and may actually outpull the flashier HTML. HTML may also become garbled depending on the e-mail program used by recipients.

  ‣ Use multiple and different calls to action throughout the e-mail, to enable immediate action at the moment the recipient is convinced.

  ‣ Close with a strong benefit and reason to take action—don't just summarize the offer.

  ‣ Offer multiple ways of responding, including a toll-free number in addition to click-through to landing pages or Web sites.

- ELEMENTS TO TRACK AND COMPARE
  - ▶ Opens
  - ▶ Clicks
  - ▶ Conversions
  - ▶ Unsubscribe (Opt-out) Rate
  - ▶ Bounce Rate
  - ▶ Time of Day/Day of Week—Moriarty says the best days to reach business people are Tuesday through Thursday between 11 A.M. and 3 P.M. their local time. The best times to reach consumers are Friday through Sunday, and in the early evenings. That said, most e-mailers have caught on to these "best times," so be aware of the clutter factor in many prospects' e-mail in boxes.

How to Avoid Having Your E-mail Messages Considered Spam. The definition of spam is very specific: it is unsolicited, commercial e-mail. The best way to avoid legal problems with spam is to make sure that you are up-front about your company name and the products you are selling, and only e-mail to customers and prospects who have explicitly opted in to receive these messages from you. In addition, you should make sure that you never use deceptive or false language in e-mails, that you provide opt-out instructions in every e-mail, and that you act on those opt-outs immediately. Your e-mails should always include a valid return e-mail address, your actual street address and, ideally, your toll-free number. Finally, you should state or link to your privacy policy in every e-mail message.

Even many marketers who are in legal compliance, however, may find their messages rejected by spam-blocking software. In addition to avoiding "spam trigger words," here are some of the best ways to avoid spam filters and improve deliverability when sending legitimate e-mail messages:

- Target and customize your e-mail messages.
- Make sure every communication has value for the recipient.
- Do not use the recipient's name in the subject line.
- Use spam content checker software such as SpamAssassin.
- Ask customers and subscribers to put your address in their e-mail address books—this is called the "white list."
- If you are blacklisted by ISPs or spam filter systems, contact them and work with them to make corrections so that you can be restored to deliverability.

Affordable E-mail Options. Even small companies can benefit by a subscription to an e-mail marketing firm like Constant Contact (www.constantcontact.com). Constant Contact plans start as low as $15 per month for unlimited e-mails, with a 60-day free trial available. Constant Contact helps subscribers organize their e-mail lists including opt-in and opt-out. It offers them options for developing personalized e-mails, newsletters, and other communications with easy-to-use templates. Constant Contact also offers full reporting software including open rate and click-through rate. Competitors to Constant Contact include VerticalResponse and iContact, among others.

Social Media

The explosive growth of social media is enough to make any marketer consider how to leverage this online phenomenon for brand-building, lead generation, and targeted selling. But social media exploration requires marketers to look at relationships and communication methods with fresh eyes. Larry Bruce of Reynolds and Reynolds says that the social media world has expanded the four Ps of marketing to the four Es:

> Product = Experience—The total brand experience
> Price = Exchange of Value—Not the cheapest, but the best overall value
> Promotion = Engagement—Not one-way communications, but conversations
> Place = Everywhere—Not just in a retail store or sitting at a computer

While there are scores of general and special-interest social media sites, the acknowledged leaders include: the general social interaction site, Facebook; the mini-blogging site, Twitter; the business site, LinkedIn; and the video sharing site, YouTube. The rules of engagement on these sites change frequently, as do their audiences and popularity—so it's vital that you stay abreast of latest developments in the social media world and adjust your strategy accordingly. With that caveat, here is some general information about several of the most prominent social media sites.

Facebook—With 150 million U.S. users at mid-2011, and a number approaching 700 million worldwide, Facebook has matured from a college student-only site to one that also boasts strong numbers among teenagers, Generation X, and Baby Boomers. Indeed, if Facebook were a country, it would be the world's third largest in terms of population, between India and the United States. For consumer marketers, creating a Facebook Fan Page offers an easy and inexpensive way to communicate with customers and prospects. What's more, it's important that you proactively create and control your own Fan Page rather than allowing a customer or competitor to do so. When you provide updates for your fans, this material will appear in their news feeds, which means that unless they have placed controls on this feature, all of their friends will be exposed to your updates as well.

Facebook ads appear to the right of users' news feeds. They are highly targetable based on demographics and keywords. The format for Facebook ads is similar to that of other sponsored search ads, except for the fact that a visual can be added as a standard feature. Facebook provides analytics including impressions, clicks, and overall spend. For privacy reasons, you can't target individuals on Facebook—you'll only see the number of potential viewers that fit the segment you designate for each ad.

Twitter—In mid-2010, there were approximately 190 million registered Twitter users, with new users signing up at the rate of 300,000 per day and an average of 65 million tweets daily. And 80 percent of Twitter updates are done on mobile devices. That said, according to Dave Marsey of Digitas, only ten percent of Twitter members are actively posting on Twitter. According to the Twitter site, there's a reason for its extremely brief, 140-character-per-message format. Twitter says, "SMS (i.e., texting on your phone) limits each message to 160 characters. Twitter takes that limit and reserves 20 characters for your username, leaving you 140 characters to play with. That's how it started and we've stuck with it!" *Tech Sanity Check* Editor-in-Chief Jason Hiner offers 11 reasons to use Twitter for your business:

1. Gain exposure for blog/site and gain potential readers.
2. Build network with transparency and trust.

Exhibit 17.2 Ross-Simons

Ross-Simons (*www.ross-simons.com*) invited opted-in customers to "like" them on Facebook in exchange for short-term and long-term opportunities and offers.

Reprinted from www.ross-simons.com.

3. Market work, products, services, etc.
4. Answer questions and ask questions.
5. Learn new things from other industry professionals.
6. Share tech tips and resources (mini blog post) and teach stuff.
7. Meet and talk with others (some business, some pleasure).
8. Conference connector (stay connected, share info, get social).
9. Seek out industry colleagues for assistance with special projects.
10. Safety—Tweet unfamiliar meeting locations and while traveling.
11. Better understand social media.

At this writing, Twitter was still at the experimental stage with sponsored Tweets, video ads, and other advertising options, and their advances in this direction bear watching and testing. In the meantime, you can use the site's short messages for promotion to your Twitter followers. Check the Wine Library example in Jerry Kaup's article at the end of this chapter for inspiration, and visit *http://business. twitter.com/twitter101/* for Twitter's advice on how to use the site for business purposes.

Linked In—As of mid-2010, LinkedIn boasted 70 million users with about half of those in the U.S. and half in other countries around the world. As a business-oriented site, it is best suited to business-to-business and career-related offers. The LinkedIn audience is well-educated, and has an average household income of more than $107K, which is higher than that of the readers of *The Wall Street Journal, Forbes,* and *Bloomberg Businessweek.*

LinkedIn offers segmentation opportunities for advertisers that include: small and medium business professionals; business decision-makers; financial service professionals; sales professionals; marketing professionals; startup professionals; corporate executives; IT professionals; and career changers. LinkedIn offers a robust how-to site for advertisers, which can be reached via a click-through at the bottom of the page at *www.linkedin.com*.

YouTube—YouTube is the world's second largest search engine (behind its owner, Google), and it boasts the world's largest video viewing audience, with 2 billion views per day.

YouTube offers several opportunities for marketers to integrate relevant advertising with videos. According to the site, its Brand Channels "provide marketers with a hub to drive and build a loyal and regular audience."

YouTube invites marketers to integrate their brands with Branded Entertainment, or to co-launch or co-create programs, events, and contests. It is also possible to use Google AdWords to target ads that will show in conjunction with YouTube videos.

As you plan for the social media presence of your company or brand, keep these basic questions in mind as posed by Alterian in its *The Little Book of Social Media*:

- What do you want to achieve through using social media? Know what success will look like for you. Alterian suggests that social media should be about listen-

Exhibit 17.3 Coldwater Creek Sale E-mail

Coldwater Creek (www.coldwatercreek.com) sends frequent e-mail offers to its opted-in customers, usually with a percentage off, sale, or other discount as the focus of the offer. In this case, the featured item information also included favorable customer reviews.

Reprinted from an e-mail received from www.coldwatercreek.com.

ing, conversations, and providing value. Be sure to build tracking and assessment into your plan.

- What should you do first? Alterian suggests that you should "secure your
  brand's online identity."
- What are the most important elements of a Social Media Marketing strategy?
  Examples could include bringing in outside ideas, generating word of mouth,
  building customer loyalty, increasing brand awareness, and reducing various
  costs.
- Who should be involved? Alterian says you should "Set the ground rules. Who
  owns your Social Media Marketing strategy?" Ground rules also include integration with other media and marketing efforts, participation, and time invested.
- What if someone says something negative about your company online? Alterian
  suggests that you find out why they are unhappy, offer to help, gather feedback,
  and take action to fix problems.
- Will you need to organize some training?
- What kind of research should you do? For example, watch the top videos, read
  leading white papers, and attend appropriate training courses, find out what your
  leading competitors are doing.

For more information about how to integrate your social media efforts with blogs and e-mail, check
the article by Jerry Kaup at the end of this chapter.

Web Site Promotion

In addition to using e-mail marketing to attract traffic to your Web site, you will be wise to test various methods of search engine optimization, sponsored search, and banner ads. Here are some pointers for each of these marketing methods.

Search Engine Optimization. When prospects visit search engines like Yahoo, Google, Bing, and
their various competitors, they use keywords and phrases to try to locate information, products, and
services. By adhering to certain rules and doing some ground work, marketers can increase the likelihood that search engines will present their sites to visitors, and that those sites will score relatively
high in the search engine rankings. Of course, the most likely way to make your site attractive to
searchers is to ensure that it is both informative and useful. But there are also some dos and don'ts
that can make a big difference. For example:

- *Set up your metatags properly.* Metatags are invisible HTML tags that can be
  seen for your site or any other site by clicking on View/Source in an Internet
  browser such as Internet Explorer or Netscape. While Google says that it ignores metatag keywords in its search rankings, the general consensus seems to
  be that having metatags will not hurt your rankings, and in some cases they may
  help. A check of major e-commerce marketers such as Coldwater Creek, Ross-
  Simons, and Eastbay shows that they use metatags—including keywords. That
  said, some prominent sites use the title and description metatags only—no keywords. Metatags include:
  - ▸ Title—What appears at the top of browser windows and on site book-
    marks

▸ Description—Should tell exactly what you do; it could be more important than the name of your site in attracting visitors

▸ Keywords—The words and phrases prospects and customers might type
into a search engine to try to locate a site like yours

Direct and interactive marketing expert Bob Bly says that your combined keywords should be no more than 1,000 characters. He notes that the fewer keywords you have, the greater effect they will have on the search engines that use
them. Don't repeat the same keyword over and over or put your competitors'
names in your keywords—search engines have long since discovered those
tricks and adjusted for them. It's a good idea to ask individuals from all parts of
your company, your agency, and even some of your better customers to submit
ideas for the keywords on your site. What's more, you should check what words
your competitors are using—especially those that seem to get better search engine rankings than you do.

• *Write copy with keywords in mind.* Copywriting for search engine optimization
is similar to other promotional writing; it's just "keyword focused." But don't
use "keyword stuffing" into every single line—simply use keywords naturally in
your copy.

• *Web spiders and crawlers can only read text.* These automated functions that
visit your site to find its keywords and subjects become befuddled by fancy programming techniques and logos. Make sure that images and logos on your site
have alternate text versions built in, and that your company name and other keywords are presented in text form on your pages.

• *Site maps help search engines find each page on your site.* A site map not only
helps your visitors locate areas of interest, but also helps search engines thoroughly account for everything on your site. On your site map, link to each page
with a keyword people would be likely to use in seeking you out.

• *Register with major search engines and free directories.* You can do this
yourself, but it can be time-consuming and must be monitored constantly. If
the budget permits, hiring a search engine optimization expert is advisable,
especially since the rules change constantly as search engines adjust to the
marketplace.

Sponsored Search. One of the hottest promotional methods for online marketers in recent years has
been sponsored search or pay-for-performance search. Google and Yahoo! Search Marketing are the
two most prominent players in this arena, with Google the leader by a wide margin. You set your
own price by choosing how much you are willing to pay for each targeted lead. The Yahoo! Advertising site offers a very basic overview of this process in three easy steps:

1. **You create an ad to appear in search results.** You choose keywords related to
   the products or services your business sells. You write a text ad to promote
   your business in search results. You decide the maximum amount you want to
   pay each time your ad is clicked.
2. **Interested customers search for what you sell.** When a searcher types one of
   your keywords into a Yahoo! search box, your ad appears. Your maximum cost-

per-click (bid) and ad quality determine where your ad is displayed in search results.

3. **When customers click your ad, they go to your Web site.** You pay only when your ad is clicked in search results—not every time it is displayed. The amount you pay is based on the maximum cost-per-click you specified.

Getting started with the rudiments of sponsored search is quick and can be inexpensive. Google offers numerous step-by-step tutorials in text and video form, as well as powerful analytics that will help you evaluate your campaigns and make adjustments as often as you like. That said, many companies focus a great deal of time and energy in developing and cultivating more advanced sponsored search campaigns using sophisticated algorithms, hundreds of keyword combinations, and narrowly targeted ads. What's more, instead of just leading prospects to their general Web sites, wise marketers create landing pages that "pay off" each specific keyword and ad combination they develop. This technique enhances relevance, which is beneficial both for your site visitors and for optimizing your ad rank in the keyword bidding process.

Sponsored search ads follow a strict, four-line format:

Line 1: A headline of up to 25 characters (with a link the prospect clicks on to get
     to your Web site or landing page)
Line 2: Up to 35 characters of ad text
Line 3: Up to 35 characters of ad text
Line 4: Display URL (your company's URL)

To see current examples of such ads for yourself, go to www.google.com or www.yahoo.com and enter a commonly purchased product in the search box. Your results will likely include sponsored search ads in the right column, and sometimes above the organic search results at top left as well.

Banner Ads. Simply put, banner ads are the billboards of the Internet. However, they have a depth and interactivity not possible with a static billboard. Like e-mails, they allow for click-through to a landing page or Web site that can result in the acquisition of a lead or completion of a sale.

In the early days of the Web, banner ads were routinely sold on a cost-per-thousand basis and touted for their brand-building attributes as well as their direct-response potential. Dwindling results soon pushed advertisers—especially those with direct marketing expertise—to seek more accountable methods of payment. Thus in recent years more and more banner ads have been placed on a cost-per-click, cost-per-lead, or cost-per-sale basis. In addition, banners can be part of an affiliate marketing program in which a site posts a banner for a partner company and collects a fee only when a sale is completed. Or two sites can agree to swap banners or links on each other's sites or sponsor each other's online newsletters.

Net Results reports that click-through rates on banner ads are enhanced when bold colors are used, when banners are placed at the top of the page, when they include animation, when they have a call to action, and when their frequency of exposure is limited.

Click-through may also be enhanced when banner ads are served based on the demographics, psychographics, and behaviors of individual Web site visitors. Interactive marketing agency Avenue A emphasized this point with an example of three different messages it served to site visitors with different demographics.

- Site visitor #1 is a married male who owns a house. He is looking to refinance his mortgage and lower his car insurance payments. He needs to pay off credit card debt and wants rate information. The site serves him a banner ad that offers the opportunity to apply for a loan.
- Site visitor #2 is a recently married female who is planning to go back to school. She travels frequently on American Airlines and needs a higher credit line. The site serves her a banner ad for an American Airlines affinity credit card.
- Site visitor #3 is male, unemployed, and bankrupt. He is not served an ad from the client bank. Instead, he is served an alternate ad for a resume service that offers guaranteed job interviews.

Practical Methods to Integrate Social Media, E-mail, and Blog Marketing

by Jerry Kaup, President, the e-mail ad agency

Three great tools for online marketing are Social Media, E-mail, and Blog Marketing. And their effectiveness is multiplied when you integrate them. Here's how to get started.

Content + Contact = Traffic X Sales

My formula above is shorthand for *Content Plus Contact Equals Traffic; Traffic Multiplies Sales.* It's a quick way to describe this single most important relationship in online marketing success: Your sales volume depends on the number of prospects you contact, and the value of the content of your message. *The key to success in online marketing is simply this: create as much valuable content as possible, and promote that valuable content to as wide an audience as possible.* By integrating social media, e-mail, and blog marketing, you'll contact more prospects and attract more traffic to your Web site or blog for your conversion-to-sales process.

Your Valuable Content Drives Action

Before I describe methods to integrate media to contact a wider audience, I want to emphasize the importance of *Valuable Content.* Prospects will only buy from you when they recognize you have the solution they seek. People are looking online for valuable content all the time! They want content that will help them solve their problems, locate products and services, meet new people, read and analyze the news, make better investments. They are looking for all types of valuable content that will help them achieve a better life. Publishing valuable content on your Web site (or blog) represents the value you offer prospects. Maximize your value and you will maximize sales.

Automate . . . Automate . . . Automate: A Word About WordPress

Content publishing tasks and the functions required to integrate media can be *automated* using WordPress. WordPress is a content management system that creates Web sites and blogs. This free software makes it fast and easy to publish all forms of content, including text, images, video, and audio. A few WordPress plug-ins and third party services will dramatically cut the time you spend integrating social media, e-mail, and blog marketing.

Integrating Media

The goal of integrating media is to quickly and easily promote your valuable content to as many prospects in your niche audience as possible.

Integrate E-mail with Social Media

Encourage your audience to share your valuable content with their friends and colleagues by including *share buttons and links* in your e-mail and e-newsletters. When they see content they think is valuable, they can easily click the share button and distribute a link to your content on their social media sites. This is a great way to increase the circulation of your messages to new prospects. Share links and tracking of this extra distribution can be found at no cost at sites like *http://www.addthis.com/* and *http://sharethis.com/*. E-mail transmission companies like My EMMA and ReachMail now offer easy ways to add share links automatically.

NOTE: You don't have to rely solely on your audience to click the share buttons. *You* can click the share buttons yourself to distribute to a wider audience on *your* social networks.

Here's how effective this method can be. We promoted a webinar to 30,000 prospects with e-mail containing share links. More than 50 percent of attendees came from individuals NOT on our e-mail lists. Most of these attendees were the result of the extra "pass along" distribution received from share links.

Integrate E-mail with Your Blog

Wouldn't it be great if each one of your e-mail or e-newsletter articles had links showing the reader additional content that is related to that article? That would be valuable to the reader, because when they find one of your articles worthwhile, they'll be encouraged to click links to easily see more of your related content. You can accomplish this automatically using a WordPress plug-in called "Yet Another Related Post."

In addition to automating "related posts," here are other functions you can automate to integrate e-mail with your blog:

- Create e-newsletter content from your new blog posts.
- Automatically send the e-newsletter on your pre-determined schedule.
- Track e-newsletter open rate and click tracking.
- Automatically create a complete e-newsletter to send to your e-mail lists outside of your subscriber list.

You can accomplish the four functions above and send your blog posts out via HTML e-mail. AWEBER.com, MailChimp.com, and FeedBurner.com offer functions that automatically converts the RSS FEED of your recent blog posts to an HTML e-mail, and sends it to all your subscribers! Of course, each article will include "related posts" links. For an example of this, see

http://associationonlinemarketing.com/automatic_enewsletters.htm

Integrating Your Blog with Social Media

While much has been discussed about Social Media Marketing, the key point is simply this: social media is a way to inform a wider niche audience of the valuable content you publish on your site. How? By distributing notices about your content on the social media sites. Each of these notices will include a link back to your Web site. This way, interested prospects can click back and get more of your valuable content.

Think of Social Media Marketing as a way to offer "samples" of your content to the widest possible audience. I'm referring to content on your Web site that your audience will consider VALUABLE, not "one-way product spin" that sounds like a kitchen-gadget TV commercial. Each of your "content samples" will include a link to more content back at your site.

Here's an example of how this works. This notice offers a "sample" of the blog article many will find valuable.

"7 Ways to Generate Targeted Niche Traffic with LinkedIn, Twitter and Your Blog Content—see http://tinyurl.com/y8qedwb"

This short promotion, or "micro blog," was distributed to social media sites via my profile on LinkedIn. Prospects interested in the topic will click the link and view the full article at my site.

I prefer to send these "sample content" promotions via LinkedIn Network Updates—NOT directly through my Twitter account. The reason: LinkedIn accounts can be set up to forward updates through to your Twitter followers, thus requiring less time and effort! Another benefit with this approach: all my LinkedIn contacts (who may not be following me on Twitter) will see this promotion via LinkedIn Network Updates.

Here's How to Do It

Immediately under and to the right of the LinkedIn Network Updates box is a check box and Twitter logo. After you enter your Update text, check that box and click the SHARE button. If you have more than one Twitter account on your LinkedIn profile, click the Twitter logo for a drop-down menu that allows you to select which of your Twitter accounts to share on.

Additional Distribution of Blog Content

New methods to automatically share your blog content over social media sites are continually being developed. Consider these four methods to reach a larger audience:

1. *Blog Share Links*—When you post articles on your blog, add social media share links to each post. Not only will some of your readers click the SHARE link and distribute your notice through their accounts, but you can also use the share link to further distribute the 140-character "Brief Notice" on your other social media sites. And when you use these share links, you can write additional introductory comments to the message that goes out to your connections or groups.

2. *LinkedIn-WordPress Integration*—You can integrate your WordPress blog with your LinkedIn account, so that each new post gets automatically updated on LinkedIn. Just add the WordPress app at LinkedIn, and your contacts will receive updates of all your blog posts.

3. *Blog Link-WordPress Integration*—Similarly, add the Blog Link app at LinkedIn, and receive blog updates from all your LinkedIn connections. When you see relevant posts, visit those blogs and comment on them to

stay connected with your network. It's a great way to maintain "top-of-mind" awareness of the value you offer.

4. *Blog-Twitter Integration*—A very successful online marketer, Gary Vaynerchuk of Wine Library TV (blog at http://tv.winelibrary.com/), describes a test he conducted to establish the value of Twitter distribution of valuable content. In this case, his valuable content was a free shipping offer for the wine he sells.

Expect GREAT Results

Gary describes this four-way test, and these results: He invested a total of $7,500 in three media to promote an offer that included a free shipping code when a wine order was placed. He took out an ad on what he describes as "a perfectly placed billboard on the New Jersey Turnpike." He sent out a direct mail piece, and he ran some radio ads.

He also Tweeted the free shipping code offer to his followers on Twitter. The main source of his followers was his blog. The Tweet contained a link back to his Web site for ordering wine.

He received 170 orders from the billboard, 240 orders from the radio, 300 orders from the direct mail, and within 48 hours, *he had 1,700 orders from his Tweet!* The orders from the Twitter promotion cost nothing in terms of media expense. The only cost was the minimal time needed to gain followers on Twitter.

Level the Playing Field with Time, Effort, Brain Power, and Creativity

Yes, it does take time and effort to execute excellent online marketing. But you'll soon discover you can effectively compete with the biggest players on the Internet. Here's my final formula for your success: You'll level the playing field and grow your business using your brain power, creativity. and the tools described here.

Enhance Your Understanding: Design a Simple Web Site

To become more conversant with interactive media, try your hand at designing a simple Web site outline for the company, product, or interest area of your choice. Keep in mind the "paradigm shift" for interactive advertisers—instead of a closed-end, linear message, you'll be developing a series of paths which site visitors may follow to delve deeper into the topics of their choice. Steve Carbone, Partner at Launchpad Advertising in New York City (formerly with Grey Direct), suggests using the two forms in Exhibit 17.4 to organize your work. His first form helps crystallize the assignment and acts as a creative strategy piece including purpose, target, content, and offer.

His second form outlines a home page with six paths or "buttons," each of which leads the way to deeper and deeper information. Your Web site may have more or less than six paths off the home page, and each path may have more or less than the six "deeper layers" on this form. Before starting your design, it's important to spend considerable time interacting with Web sites to find out for yourself what's possible, what grabs interest, and how to keep prospects coming back for more.

Exhibit 17.4. Grey Direct Strategic Elements and Navigational Layout

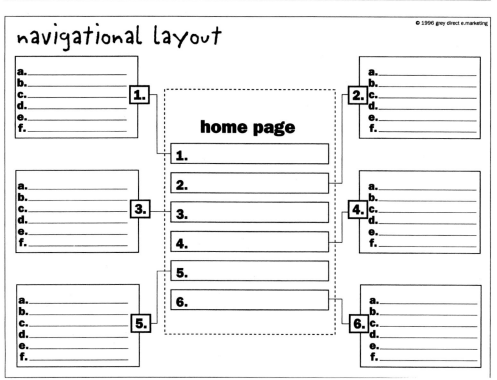

strategic elements

© 1996 grey direct e.marketing

the purpose of this form is to start the process of building a web site. key strategic and behavioral areas have been omitted and will be necessary for creative development.

1. the assignment
_____
_____

2. the purpose/objective
_____
_____
_____
_____

3. the target
current
_____
via the web
_____

4. content
_____
_____
_____
_____
_____
_____

5.offer
_____
_____
_____
_____

navigational layout

© 1996 grey direct e.marketing

a._____ b._____ c._____ d._____ e._____ f._____ **1.**

home page

a._____ b._____ c._____ d._____ e._____ f._____ **2.**

1.
2.
3.
4.
5.
6.

a._____ b._____ c._____ d._____ e._____ f._____ **3.**

a._____ b._____ c._____ d._____ e._____ f._____ **4.**

a._____ b._____ c._____ d._____ e._____ f._____ **5.**

a._____ b._____ c._____ d._____ e._____ f._____ **6.**

PART THREE

Creating and Producing the Work

18

Copywriting and Graphic Design

The popular, "retro" television show, *Mad Men*, has featured many a plotline in which a 1960s copywriter or graphic designer struggles to find just the right concept for an ad campaign. Indeed, that process can be painful—but the "eureka" or "aha" moment when the idea emerges makes it well worth the effort. In the *Mad Men* days, writers used dictaphones or scratched their ideas out on lined pads for their secretaries to decipher. Graphic designers sat at drawing boards—as memorialized by the phrase "back to the drawing board," used when an idea is completely rejected. Today, most writers and designers start with a blank computer screen, although some still rely on scratch paper or layout pads. Whatever their "weapons" of choice, these creative people must somehow turn a marketing concept into compelling copy and visuals.

Ask 20 writers and designers how they get from concept to creative product, and you'll receive as many different answers. Some creative people jump right in, writing in stream of consciousness or sketching scores of thumbnail layouts until their creative muse appears. Others do a great deal of restless stirring about, verbalizing their ideas and their midstream creative anguish in equal measure. Still others swear by a step-by-step process they use repeatedly: order card first, then brochure, then letter. Or, first write as many headlines as you can think of for an ad. Or, first put yourself in the shoes of the target customers and write down all the things they'd want to know about the product or service.

In the midst of their creative fervor, some writers cover their office walls with sticky notes, each of which contains a germ of an idea. To organize their thoughts into a direct mail package, Web page or ad, they rearrange the sticky notes again and again before putting words on paper. Graphic designers have been known to indulge in "folding fits" that look a bit like origami, using layout paper to try out a half-dozen or more brochure formats in various sizes and configurations. Visit a creative agency and you'll likely see one or more white boards covered with ideas, phrases, rough-rough layouts and bullet points—often with arrows from one idea to another and the admonition to well-meaning custodians, "Do Not Erase!" Marc Ziner, Managing Partner and Creative Director of Marketing Highway in Wilmette, Illinois, has seen his peers use all of these methods and more. As he says

> Many graphic designers work up 'thumbnails,' which are usually sketched as half-sized or quarter-sized rough layouts. Or they use layout pads or whiteboards and dry erase markers and run through a sort of brainstorm, either on their own or in a group. Some designers don't bother at all with the sketches and thumbnails. They move right to the computer and show initial

ideas that are more like finished pieces than rough ideas. The trouble is, it's relatively easy to make a mediocre idea look good on the computer, but a good idea will shine even in a rough sketch, if the viewer has imagination. That's the measure of when to use one over the other . . . who are you showing the idea to first, and what do they like to see, and can they use their imagination. I suggest that if you don't know the answer to this question, show the tightest layout and most finished copy possible.

Ziner also insists that his designers show at least three ideas to clients rather than editing down to one "make it or break it" concept. David Fideler of Concord Communications agrees. As he says, when you present what you believe is your best concept to the client, "there should be two other back-up concepts to show as well. This is the method advocated by Cameron Foote, who is the author of the two most highly respected books on how to run a graphic design business, and editor of the *Creative Business* newsletter." Some creative directors, like Kurt Dietsch, owner of Luciditi in Grand Rapids, Michigan, have been known to fill a whole room with potential concepts for a single ad or campaign theme.

Ziner believes that designers from the "old school" are more likely to go through the steps they are used to before translating their ideas to the computer. As a seasoned designer, he says, "I do both thumbnails and computer roughs because it allows me to show many ideas, in a variety of ways. Most of the time I sketch out half-size roughs because it allows more than one component or idea on a page, and sometimes that's important."

Ideally, the copywriter and graphic designer will spend a good deal of freewheeling time together at the beginning of the creative process, sharing their ideas as they develop, and working together toward a harmonious verbal and visual product. Such intense teamwork requires mutual respect, an understanding of the partner's personality and work style, and a willingness to avoid territorial squabbles in the interest of an excellent final product. In the best such copy-and-design teams, neither party remembers nor cares who wrote the winning headline or who chose the main photo for the Web page or brochure. For more on the person-to-person aspects of direct and interactive marketing creativity, check Chapter 7 of this book.

There is no one right answer as to how much copy should be included in an ad or brochure, and there is no absolute best visual for any direct or interactive marketing presentation. Decisions such as where headings, copy, and visuals should appear, what size they should be, and how they should support each other, must be worked out through this respectful interaction of copywriter and designer. While direct and interactive marketing experts assert that such teamwork offers the best chance of success for any creative advertising venture, there are situations in which the copywriter and designer work separately. In this case, one or the other must take the lead. In some instances, the copywriter may prepare rough layouts as an initial guide for the graphic designer's work. In others, the graphic designer may prepare a layout, indicating how many characters or words are available for headings, copy, and captions.

Each creative team's style will necessarily be different, but there are some common stages that most creative jobs go through. This chapter will offer an outline for the step-by-step process of copywriting and graphic design for print media. It will provide ideas on ways to evaluate and pretest copy and layout without spending undue time or money in the process. Finally, it will provide a few tips on ways to gain inspiration and fight writer's or artist's block.

Exhibit 18.1. Step-by-Step Art and Copy

	ART COMPONENT	COPY COMPONENT
STAGE 1:	Thumbnails or computer roughs	Headline(s), taglines, unique selling proposition
STAGE 2:	Full-size color layout with stock or preliminary photos for position	Headline options, subheads, key copy points
STAGE 3:	Comprehensive layout; folding dummies if applicable	Final copy

Step-by-Step Design and Copy

While time or monetary considerations sometimes dictate otherwise, the most prudent creative process for the development of art and copy includes at least three main steps, as explained by Marc Ziner.

Details of Art Components

As part of the creative process, each ad or brochure goes through various stages beginning with tiny sketches and progressing through rough layouts and finally to comprehensives. As the layout process unfolds, the creative team selects typefaces, arranges for photography or the creation of drawings to accent the layout, and determines the colors and processes that will be used to produce the work.

Once these decisions have been made and copy has been proofed and approved, the next step is the creation of production files—the computer equivalent of what used to be called "keyline and paste-up." These files typically are provided to the production house or printer in the form of a Portable Document Format (PDF). As David Fideler explains, "Creating a perfect PDF file for printing requires a certain amount of expertise, but this should be expected from any professional designer."

The Layout Process. There are several distinct layout stages, and in many cases an graphic designer will progress from one to the next without skipping over any. However, it is quite common to proceed directly from thumbnail to comprehensive layouts if the graphic designer, copywriter, and client trust each other and the job is fairly straightforward. This is also necessary when timing prohibits an extra step. What's more, with the proliferation of sophisticated computer equipment and software like Adobe InDesign, graphic designers find it faster and easier to create complex layouts—even pieces that look like finished ads—than in the days when all the work had to be done by hand.

Marc Ziner notes, "InDesign is integrated with Adobe's other products, Photoshop and Illustrator, plus Adobe Acrobat makes the whole Portable Document Format (PDF) convention work very smoothly—*if* the stars are in alignment." See Chapter 20 for more on how PDFs are used in print production.

Even though it's now very possible to do so, it is never advisable to skip directly from thumbnail sketches to production files, or even from rough layouts to production files. The comprehensive layout provides all parties involved with an opportunity to approve or correct a layout before major production expenses are incurred. Thus, the importance of the "comp" should not be underestimated.

Exhibit 18.2. Thumbnail Sketches and Rough Layout

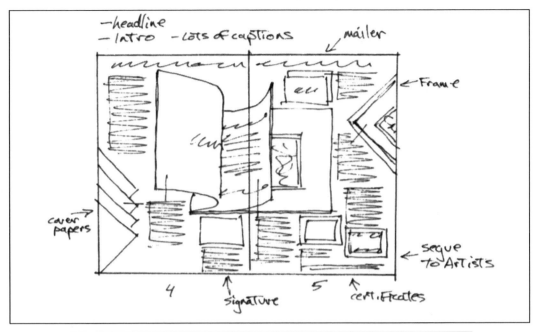

Small thumbnail layouts were the first step in planning art and copy for a 12-page brochure on the A.R.T. Card™, a product of Artagraph Reproduction Technology Incorporated. The finished product shows that numerous changes and refinements were made between thumbnail layouts and final approval.

Reprinted with permission of Artagraph Reproduction Technology Incorporated.

Thumbnail Sketches. These small sketches indicate the general shape and proportion of the piece being created, and the placement of basic elements such as headlines, photographs, borders, boxes, and so on. Thumbnails are valuable because they give the parties involved something to look at and evaluate beyond a verbal description of how the layout should be done. Because they are small and rough, they allow everyone to explore many different ideas without an undue investment of time.

Rough Layouts. Sometimes called "pencil roughs," these layouts are done to actual size, but are not exact as to color, type sizes, photograph and drawing sizes, and so forth. They help everyone involved visualize the finished product, the flow of material, and the impact of an ad or brochure done in that size. They may incorporate actual headings and subheads, if possible, since this again helps in the evaluation of flow and effectiveness. Roughs may be done by the copywriter or by the artist,

Exhibit 18.3. Half-Size Roughs

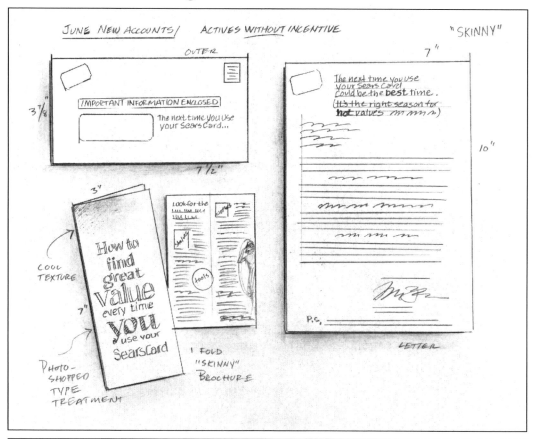

Graphic designer Marc Ziner uses half-size roughs to present basic ideas to his fellow creatives and to clients. These simple pencil roughs allow Ziner to consider and offer a wide range of possible formats and "looks" before investing the time to create comprehensive layouts on the computer.

Reprinted with permission of Marc Ziner.

or as a cooperative effort for informal presentation to the client. Roughs often are the layouts presented to fellow members of the agency or staff (account executive, product manager, etc.) to get buy-in on a concept. Marc Ziner's "half-size roughs" can serve nicely at this stage.

Comprehensive Layouts. Just as its name implies, the comprehensive layout, or "comp," covers all the bases. It measures to exact size and reflects all the folds, die cuts, and other enhancements of the proposed final product. It indicates color areas and suggests the colors that will be used, exact copy areas, the sizes of headings or photos, where borders will appear, and so on. The graphic designer will often attach color and paper samples to such a layout to indicate background hues and texture.

When created with InDesign, the layout can reflect exact type sizes and styles, with the actual copy shown in place if it is available at this point. The "comp" serves not only to help the client and artist visualize the final product, but also as a blueprint for the creation of final production files. As Marc Ziner explains, "We print comprehensive layouts out on our color printer and show them as flats or trim them out and make folding dummies." Ziner adds that in many cases, PDFs have replaced comps. He says, "Making and sharing PDFs is a surefire method for showing graphic files to clients and collaborators using Acrobat Reader." There are also collaborative spaces where agency and client representatives can work together in real time to make updates and changes to creative pieces.

Details of Copy Components

Headings and Subheads. While the graphic designer works on thumbnails and sketches various format ideas on scratch paper, the copywriter may be considering various headline concepts and secondary points for subheads. Drawing upon the approved Creative Strategy or Creative Brief, the writer noodles around with phrases and sentences—and perhaps even has the graphic designer sketch them into the thumbnails to see how they come across in a layout. Many direct marketing firms and agencies ask copywriters to provide sets of alternate headings and subheads, along with a short statement of the ad concept and the rationale behind it, before proceeding to rough copy. For an in-depth discussion of how to write headlines for direct marketing sales propositions, see Chapter 11 of this book.

Rough Copy. The rough copy stage is one which some copywriters swear by, while others polish their copy to a near-final state before showing it to anyone. Rough copy provides a general indication of copy length, the flow of ideas, tone, sentence and paragraph length, and other copy characteristics. Creative teams who use this stage as part of an approval process may share their rough copy and layouts with each other to touch base and make sure they are still on the same wavelength. Then they may show rough copy and corresponding layouts to a creative director or client representative for a general critique before final work is completed.

Final Copy. Coordinated with the graphic designer's comprehensive layout, final copy represents the copywriter's completed and fully polished efforts, ready for approval by the client and then for production. Before releasing copy for the approval and production process, successful writers work and rework their copy to ensure that it presents a compelling sales message in a way that is readable and appealing to the target market of prospects. The way in which writers polish their copy is highly individual: some take a more global view and then work down to the details, while others consider their writing sentence by sentence, then in total paragraphs, and then as part of the overall flow of the piece. An essential element of creating final copy is to distance oneself from the work

Exhibit 18.4. Potentials Unlimited

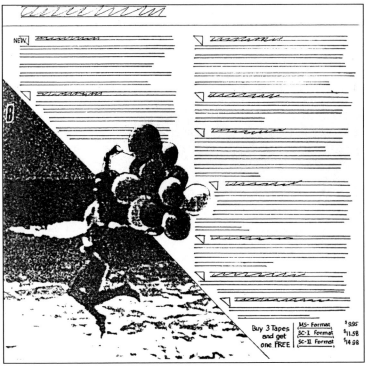

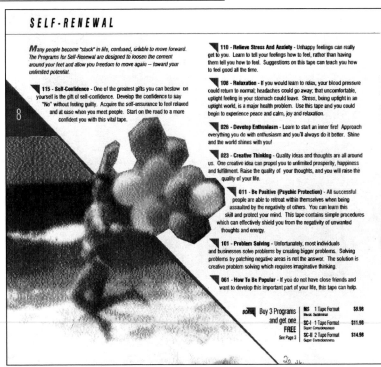

Exhibit 18.4. (Continued)

SELF-RENEWAL

Many people become "stuck" in life, confused, unable to move forward. The Programs for Self-Renewal are designed to loosen the cement around your feet and allow you freedom to move again -- toward your unlimited potential.

115 - Self-Confidence - One of the greatest gifts you can bestow on yourself is the gift of self-confidence. Develop the confidence to say "No" without feeling guilty. Acquire the self-assurance to feel relaxed and at ease when you meet people. Start on the road to a more confident you with this vital tape.

110 - Relieve Stress And Anxiety - Unhappy feelings can really get to you. Learn to tell your feelings how to feel, rather than having them tell you how to feel. Suggestions on this tape can teach you how to feel good all the time.

108 - Relaxation - If you would learn to relax, your blood pressure could return to normal; headaches could go away; that uncomfortable, uptight feeling in your stomach could leave. Stress, being uptight in an uptight world, is a major health problem. Use this tape and you could begin to experience peace and calm, joy and relaxation.

026 - Develop Enthusiasm - Learn to start an inner fire! Approach everything you do with enthusiasm and you'll always do it better. Shine and the world shines with you!

023 - Creative Thinking - Quality ideas and thoughts are all around us. One creative idea can propel you to unlimited prosperity, happiness and fulfillment. Raise the quality of your thoughts, and you will raise the quality of your life.

011 - Be Positive (Psychic Protection) - All successful people are able to retreat within themselves when being assaulted by the negativity of others. You can learn this skill and protect your mind. This tape contains simple procedures which can effectively shield you from the negativity of unwanted thoughts and energy.

101 - Problem Solving - Unfortunately, most individuals and businesses solve problems by creating bigger problems. Solving problems by patching negative areas is not the answer. The solution is creative problem solving which requires imaginative thinking.

061 - How To Be Popular - If you do not have close friends and want to develop this important part of your life, this tape can help.

BONUS Buy 3 Programs and get one **FREE** See Page 3

MS	1 Tape Format Music Subliminal	$9.98
SC-I	1 Tape Format Super Consciousness	$11.98
SC-II	2 Tape Format Super Consciousness	$14.98

Potentials Unlimited used an in-house design system for the creation of its catalog of self-hypnosis tapes and related products. Hand-drawn rough layouts (a) serve as a guide for the creation of computer-generated comprehensive layouts (b) with all art and typeset copy in place. The final, printed catalog spread (c) reflects minor changes from the comprehensive layout.

Reprinted with permission of Potentials Unlimited.

overnight—or at least for a few hours—before taking a final read-through. This cooling off period will allow the writer to spot unclear passages, inconsistencies, and even misspellings that spellchecker software can't identify.

Computers Quicken the Pace for Copy and Graphic Design

Before the widespread use of computers for layout and design, artists and writers could carve out a bit more time for a step-by-step creative process. Today, the timelines are shrinking, as Michigan-based freelance copywriter Mike Dykstra explains:

> As a general comment, I think computers have speeded up and shaved steps off the creative process described in this chapter. Rarely have I had the luxury of spending time with a product expert or consulting with friends in the agency business, for example (because of time pressures). I think projects

are initiated much later than they used to be, largely because clients feel the process shouldn't take as long using computers.

Still, computers are extremely helpful in at least one way: They very quickly allow a writer to check the length and flow of copy within the piece, before it's even submitted for client approval. Techno-savvy writers can even change copy within the layout—although they have to make sure the graphic designer is aware of any changes they've made.

How to Plan and Evaluate Art and Copy

Graphic designers and copywriters can rest assured that their clients or agency managers will critique their work with varying degrees of specificity and finesse. The best creative people, however, build in their own benchmarks for successful layouts and copy to ensure that the work they present is not only fresh and creative, but also effective as a direct and interactive marketing sales message. Here are a few basic guidelines for planning and evaluating your own layouts and copy.

Evaluating Layouts

Will the Layout Attract the Prospect? Ask yourself whether the layout presents the personality and tone that will appeal to your target market. Is it casual, sophisticated, elegant, homespun, family-oriented, hard-sell? Does the layout reflect the values and tastes of this target market by means of its visual images, type style, colors, and border treatments? Don't fall into the trap of using any trendy type styles and layout quirks currently popular with designers. You may well be "playing" to your fellow creatives at the expense of making your message accessible and readable to those in your target group.

Is the Product the Star? Even experienced graphic designers occasionally get carried away with typefaces, background colors, or special-effect shots that are gratifying to work on but in fact do very little to enhance a product. When evaluating your layout, ask yourself whether the product is the star or whether you've buried it in "art for art's sake." Ways to "star" the product include showing it as large as possible, depicting it in use, and showing it in a setting with people your target group can relate to. You may also give the product a flattering background that conjures up positive associations and contrasts in color so that the product will "pop" on the page. If your product itself is not attractive, consider focusing on the results of using it—for example, a satisfied user of a diet product who has lost 50 pounds.

What is the Point of the Layout? Try to look at the layout as a customer would. What is it that you are trying to get across? The main focus or point of the ad should be your product's prime features and benefits. What's more, the layout also needs reworking if you cannot quickly discern a point from it. A layout that tries to cover all points equally is destined to confuse or turn off the reader. Remember that your prospect is likely to give your piece only a few seconds' glance before deciding whether to read on—or to dig deeper on a Web site. Does this layout have a "grabber" of a point that will encourage the reader's involvement?

Does the Layout Look Inviting and Readable? Some printed pieces are so busy or created with such an obscure type style that reading them is literally hurtful to the eyes. Others are open, airy, and inviting. To make sure that your layouts are of the latter kind, check to see if your headings and body

Exhibit 18.5. Two-Step Process from Kurt Dietsch

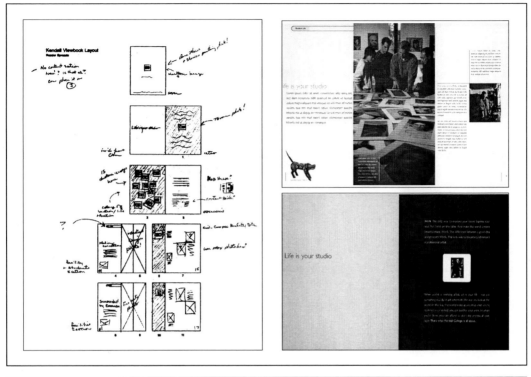

Art director Kurt Dietsch uses a two-step process to create layouts. First he develops tiny pencil thumbnails. Then, on his computer, he completes full-color comprehensive layout alternates with copy in place. After editing and client corrections, the final art is prepared for printing. Here, examples of the steps are shown for a direct mail search piece created for Kendall College of Art and Design.

Reprinted with permission.

copy are large enough to be readable (usually 8 on 9 point as a minimum for body copy). Make sure there are no stumbling blocks to the flow of the copy, such as a two-column picture that breaks up a body of related copy for no important reason. Even though relatively long copy is a typical characteristic of direct mail pieces, make sure that the copy area does not look like a sea of small print. See that the copy is broken up with subheads, small illustrations, and other visual devices.

For Space Ads: How Does the Ad Look in Its Editorial Environment? Take your comprehensive layout and place it randomly in the publication where it will run. Does it seem to blend into the background, or does it stand out? Standing out is more desirable, but the ad should shine because of its superiority and freshness—not because it seems incongruous in this publication. Ways to make an ad stand out include:

- Running a long-copy, editorial-format ad in a publication that carries mostly big picture/short copy ads.

- Running a big picture/short copy ad in a publication that normally features editorial ads.
- Running a full-page coupon ad in a publication where most direct response ads are 1/6 page or smaller and appear in the back-of-the-book direct response "ghetto."
- Using a bind-in card that pops up between the pages instead of or in addition to a clip-out coupon, toll-free number, and/or landing page.
- Running a full-color ad in a publication where this is a rarity.
- Personalizing your bound-in space ad or reply card with the reader's name and address.
- Running a short ad reversed in white out of black in a publication that has lots of black-on-white ads (be careful with this, as too much reverse copy is difficult to read—and don't reverse out the coupon, or it will be impossible to fill out).

For Direct Mail Pieces: How Does it Look in a Dummy Kit? Evaluating an unfolded layout is one thing, but seeing the piece as it will appear when folded for an envelope—and actually inserting it along with a letter and order form in the envelope—is a very valuable exercise. You can perceive the kit as your recipient will, and you may catch the little problems that could go unnoticed until it's too late: an order form that doesn't fit easily into a Business Reply Envelope, or a brochure that is too bulky when folded down for a #10 envelope.

In this same context, always fold down a brochure layout as it will appear when mailed, to be sure that the recipient's first view of the brochure is an appealing one. You probably wouldn't want the fold to cut your main front cover headline in half, for instance.

Your dummy kit serves two other purposes. First, if you create it with paper of the same weights and sizes that will go into the real kit, you can determine the weight of your kit to make sure it falls within the postal category you seek. Second, the dummy kit helps you to get proper quotes from your printer and lettershop. Your print salesperson and lettershop representative may also be able to point out cost savings on the basis of your dummy—slight modifications that will cut paper and printing costs and make inserting and addressing less expensive.

Is the Layout a Standard Size, or Is There a Good Reason for Custom Sizing? Sometimes a product calls for special treatment, an odd-sized outer envelope to give the kit a European look, for instance, or an ad that runs in three or four parts, like a checkerboard across the magazine page, to create reader interest. But unless such a special effect is part of your stated plan, you'll probably want to stick with standard sizes for envelopes, brochures, letters, and ads. This will save you money and time and allow you to take advantage of stock envelopes and standard printing configurations.

Is the Use of Color and Bleeds Appropriate for This Layout? Since the first full-color ad ran in 1937, the conventional wisdom has held that color is superior to black and white when it comes to readership and impact. A 1967 Daniel Starch research report showed that consumers' "noted" scores for half-page color ads in magazines were almost twice as high as those for half-page black and white ads. Yet in some cases, a full-color treatment just isn't necessary. And with the proliferation of color in all media, some graphic designers now find that black-and-white ads actually gain more attention because of their novelty and potential for a dramatic look. Consider as well the impact of the classic Dewars Scotch ads, in which Dewars drinkers were pictured and profiled. The individuals were shown in black and white, while only the product itself was depicted in full color. More recently, Kellogg's Rice Krispies have been promoted on television with ads that show only the package and the product in color while the parents, children, and all other surroundings are in black and white.

To determine whether color is necessary for your selling proposition, consider what the prospect needs to know and feel in order to make the buying decision. Financial service ads that rely heavily on performance percentages have little need for color enhancement. Ladies' dresses in shades of blue, orange, and yellow will probably need exacting color depiction, while men's standard white underwear may not. In some instances, a black-and-white presentation may flatter and enhance the product even more than color—in the case of elegant white bisque figurines, for example. In such an instance, you may choose to invest your budget in fine photography and excellent paper instead of color printing.

Some direct mail packages and ads gain the impact they need through the use of two-color printing. By the addition of an accent color to black, or by printing another dark color instead of black on a light-colored stock, you can achieve a multicolored look at a lower cost than with full color. Bleeds, in which color runs off the page instead of stopping at a white border, can offer a luxury look or a special impact. But because bleeds are more expensive than non-bleeds in printing (they require more paper for trimming), it is worth questioning the need for them when budgets are tight. To be sure of the differential, have your printed piece quoted for bleed and non-bleed prices. For space ads, check the magazine's rate card for bleed versus non-bleed rates.

Other Nuts-and-Bolts Considerations. Are the color combinations, typefaces, and overall graphic look pleasing and appropriate for this target market? Do they integrate well with other pieces you have done for this product and/or this company? Does the presentation make your product or service easy to order? In space ads with coupons, make sure the coupon is accessible—usually at the lower right of an ad, created for placement on the right-hand side of the page. For direct mail packages, be sure the reply form is easy to follow, well-spaced, and fits properly into the Business Reply Envelope. Put the layout away for a day if you can afford the time, and then approach it as you would if you were a prospect. Is it pleasing, easy to understand, and effective? If not, go back to the drawing board.

Evaluating Copy

There are as many different formulae for direct and interactive marketing copy effectiveness as there are copywriters, and some of the big names in the field have become famous for their "ten-point checklists" and "how-to" guides. The following is a distillation of many of these "shoulds." Rather than use a checklist of all the good and bad points of copy that are presented to you from various sources, keep the following hard-won direct and interactive marketing concepts in mind when developing and reviewing copy.

Characteristics of Effective Copy. The best copy is clean and clear, and presented in language that is simple without being simplistic. Copy great Maxwell C. Ross said that for every 100 words of copy, 70 to 80 should consist of only one syllable. Whenever possible, good copy uses the present tense and the active voice. One teacher of copywriting automatically marks points off students' work every time they use a form of the verb "to be" instead of an active verb. Good copy comes across as friendly and conversational—not patronizing or self-important. It flows well and has good transitions. It utilizes connecting phrases such as "what's more," and "in addition." Finally, it draws the reader in from the very first phrase, making reading a pleasure rather than a chore.

For an amusing and instructive check on the clarity of your copy, try pasting it into the Bull Fighter™ software at *http://fightthebull.com*. It quickly rates the copy in any document for overuse of "bull terms" or buzz words, and for clarity. Just as a benchmark, on a scale of 100 for reading ease, Bull Fighter rated newspaper comic strips at a 92 and the U.S. Internal Revenue Service Tax Code at a minus-6. Readability, percentage of passive sentences, and grade level statistics also are available in Microsoft Word's spelling and grammar function.

The "You" Approach. Some copywriters and clients fall into the trap of simply counting how many times the word "you" is used in a direct mail letter or ad. But that is not the point: it's the overall "me to you" approach that counts. Copy should be written from person to person (e.g., company president to figurine collector, or homemaker to homemaker)—not company to "target group." Make sure the copy doesn't talk only of how your product is made and what its features are. First and foremost, customers want to know what's in it for them.

As you prepare your copy, keep product benefits firmly in mind. The copy should address the prospect's wants, needs, hopes, aspirations, lifestyle, and interests. Do your best to evaluate the copy in terms of the market, not your own biases and beliefs. You may be a target for the product you're selling, but as often as not you won't be. Don't make the mistake of slanting your copy toward what pleases you and your own (non-target) type of person. This is where "infiltrating the market" can become invaluable. Find ways to spend time with typical prospects for the product or service. Learn what magazines they read, what TV programs they watch, what social networks they frequent. Catch on to their speech patterns, slang expressions, and ways of looking at the world. This hands-on research will pay big dividends in your ability to address copy to your prospects that "hits them where they live."

Copy Length. There is no reliable rule for copy length. Nothing says that a four-page letter is inherently better than a two-page letter, or vice versa. Nothing says that a 120-second spot is inherently better than a 60-second spot on direct response television: indeed, tests by The Bradford Exchange, DraftFCB, and other direct and interactive marketing firms and agencies show that shorter TV spots may actually outpull longer direct response messages.

The late copy great David Ogilvy stated firmly that long copy sells more than short copy and, in general, ads that sell direct carry much more verbiage than general advertising does. But the best advice is to write until the story is told, then revise, edit, and cut the copy until it is clear and strong. Lobby with your account executive and/or client to leave options on copy length open until you work up a rough draft of the copy; then decide whether you need more or less space than originally planned.

Another guideline is that the more complex the proposition, or the higher the price, the more explanation your customer will expect and need before buying. Therefore, for an offer of a free booklet at no obligation, your copy normally would be considerably shorter than what you would need to sell a $5,000 multi-function color printer via mail or space advertising.

Feature/Benefit/Value. It isn't enough to point out the features or characteristics of your product. It is more important to make sure the customer perceives the benefits of the product, in personal or corporate terms. In other words, you wouldn't say simply that a toaster "has low, medium, and high settings." Rather, you would say that the toaster "has low, medium, and high settings" (feature) "to toast everything from plain white bread to frozen bagels in seconds" (benefit).

The features and benefits presented should add up to a value that your prospects can perceive and which will lead them to become customers. The best way to make sure you can present meaty, benefit-oriented copy is to make sure you know the product inside and out. As the old saw goes, "sell the sizzle, not the steak." Make sure that you get across what the product will add to the customer's life. It's also vital to ensure that benefits are presented in the order of their magnitude, with the most important given first according to your customer's perceptions and not your own.

Success Stories. If possible, provide some success stories of your product in use. One graphic way to do this is via testimonials or endorsements. Testimonials and endorsements should be believable. They should be in the words of real people or representatives of organizations with expertise and credibility in your product line. They should be as specific as possible, spelling out results in dollars and cents, pounds lost, compliments received, time saved, or whatever the success story comprises. Another way to show your success story is to give proof of effectiveness. This may take the form of a notarized statement by an expert, a demonstration on television, or before-and-after shots.

The Call to Action. The goal of every component of a direct and interactive marketing campaign is to induce action: whether ordering by mail, calling, e-mailing, ordering online, or coming into a store. This action must be spurred by the copy, but without coming on too strong. Read the "call to action" copy of some direct advertising you admire, and of your competitors, to learn how they induce a response. Here are some possibilities.

- Limited quantities or limited edition
- Premium for response by x-date
- Charter subscription or membership period
- Seasonal reason, e.g., for delivery before a holiday
- Discount for "early bird" response
- Preseason discount
- Limited-time sale price
- The old "be the first on your block" pitch, presented in a fresh and subtle way that fits your target market
- Urgency based on immediate need—for donations to a nonprofit organization

Specificity. Take the copy you've written about a product and read it through, substituting some other, similar product as the subject. How much of the copy still works? If much of it works for another product, your copy has failed the specificity test. The cure for copy with this problem is to zero in on your product's unique attributes and benefits, making sure that the copy points these out in graphic, descriptive terms. Don't just say "large, economy size"; that could apply to anything from detergent to pancake mix. Say "ten pounds of seed and dried vegetable mix—enough to keep two large parrots healthy and well-fed for a month." Don't simply say, "complements any décor;" that could apply to an air freshener or a sofa. Instead, say "the classic, clean lines of this bleached pine cocktail table complement both traditional and contemporary homes."

Sales Sense. The direct response copywriter is first and foremost a personal sales representative. Copy should do everything a personal sales call does. Thus, the sales writer must anticipate objections from customers, lead them to positive responses, and then "close" the deal. Compare the copy you've written with a verbal sales presentation on the same type of product, and see how it rates.

Appearance. Work with the graphic designer to learn how your piece will come across visually. Letters should have plenty of margin space to enhance their readability. Brochures should be broken up with subheads. Strive for a paragraph length of little more than six lines whenever possible. The key is readability and appeal. The graphic designer can do a lot with typefaces, leading, illustrations, colors, and so on—but the copy itself must also draw the reader in visually.

Ease of Ordering. As a next step, let someone else read your copy—and preferably several people not directly involved in your business. Have them go through the motions to order your product and see if they have any trouble with the reply device and instructions as presented. Can they find the price? Color choices? Size of the product? Expiration date for the offer? Guarantee? Toll-free number and Web address? Mailing address to use if coupon or reply card were already removed? Ask them what they think the copy is trying to get across, and see if your benefits come back to you in some semblance of your own order of importance. Ask them which parts of the copy they find interesting, dull, easy to understand, and hard to understand. Some marketers request that their "guinea pigs" underline phrases they find remarkable in the copy—and to indicate whether their reaction to each phrase is positive or negative. Then they rework the copy until all the "stoppers" are positive ones.

Creating Words and Pictures

While there are few jobs in direct and interactive marketing as rewarding as creating a successful direct mail package, ad or TV spot, the birthing process can be long, drawn-out, and painful. Most every copywriter and graphic designer can recall a time when the flow of creative solutions to marketing problems stopped cold. But one way or the other, direct marketing "pros" are able to unblock their minds and get back on the track of creativity. Here are some ideas on what to do when writer's or artist's block strikes.

Retrace Your Steps in the Creative Process

One of the most common reasons for creative block is that the writer or designer tries to short-circuit the multi-step creative process. While there are any number of step-by-step models for creativity, they all call for an initial period of research and freewheeling "what if" games, an incubation period, a point of discovery when ideas flow fast and furious, and finally an implementation period. Chapter 2 of this book covers the steps to creative discovery in detail. If you have tried to skip from research to implementation, for instance, without taking time for incubation and the "aha" stage of discovery, your creative potential will be sorely limited.

Talk with Someone Who Knows and Loves the Product

Sometimes even after studying the psychographics, hopes, and fears of the target market and familiarizing yourself with the product, a lack of excitement will prevent you from getting anything meaningful drawn or written. In this case, it often helps to spend time with the person who created the product or service, or the individual who currently manages it. Since this person lives and breathes the product, he or she may be able to transmit enough enthusiasm, details, and specifics to get you over the hump. In addition, this is a good time to attend a focus group or ask for recordings of recent focus groups or other qualitative research to find out how consumers talk about the product, and what they like about it most.

Switch Places with Your Counterpart

If you're the graphic designer, be the copywriter for a while. If you're the writer, sit down with layout pad and start sketching. Even the most off-the-wall idea may provide the spark that gets you started, and the unfamiliarity of the other team member's job may force that idea out into the open. Marc Ziner has this to say on this score:

> I am one of those impossible graphic designers who thinks he can write. I can't help myself, and because of it, I constantly challenge my writers to do better, usually by giving them bad lines which contain the essence of a good idea. They are usually so mortified by the prospect of losing a copy battle to a graphic designer, that they do, in fact come back with better words. In any case, I am very much in favor of going head-to-head with a writer in an active brainstorming session. They can be lots of fun, and I try to never go beyond 45 minutes. I must say, however, that many of us creative types would rather spend a couple of hours ruminating by ourselves and then showing the others what we have come up with as individuals.

Ziner encourages his copywriters and graphic designers in a cross-disciplinary approach. As he explains:

> Creative people who can actually do both words and pictures, especially at this conceptual stage, are really worth more to a company than even the most expert practitioner of a single discipline. I ask copywriters and graphic designers alike to produce standard-sized (on 8-1/2″ × 11″ or 8-1/2″ × 14″ or 11″ × 17″ paper) concept roughs. The headlines may be rough, the pictures may have stick figures or Xs filling picture boxes, but call-outs explain in words what the layout may not.
>
> Standard sizes encourage collaboration and sharing of ideas without adding extra steps of reducing on a copier. I always like to see several ideas or strategic approaches in very rough form instead of one idea which is tightly rendered. This comes out of being the guy who would tightly render one idea, often to be sent back to the drawing board with a pat on the back and a reminder to set the alarm when I left that night, if you know what I mean.

Allow Yourself Some Procrastination Time

Whether it's doing the organizing that's piled up for six months in your office, taking a long lunch with a friend, or working on a completely different project, a bit of procrastination may allow your subconscious mind the necessary time and freedom to incubate the germ of an idea into a full-blown concept. Witness the experience of Eric David, then a creative director for Kaplan Thaler Group, Ltd. He came up with the idea for the AFLAC duck (the famous creature that repeats "AFLAC!" in duck-speak on numerous commercials) while walking around at lunchtime in search of a corned beef sandwich, and repeating the AFLAC company name over and over. As his colleague, Tom Amico, said in an interview, "Work hard, but take lunch."

Explain the Situation to Someone Who's Not Involved

Whether you choose to share your problem with your analyst, your spouse, your private muse, a child, or your dog, verbalize the scenario. Oftentimes in stating the problem out loud, a new clarity emerges that allows for creative solutions. If the person you're talking with asks questions, so much the better: you'll be forced to frame your thoughts in an organized way, which may gain you a new perspective on the situation.

Harness the Positive Power of Deadlines

Waiting until the eleventh hour may not be all bad: indeed, creativity expert Roger von Oech says that many of our best ideas come to us under pressure. When the adrenaline's pumping and the clock is ticking, you may find that the perfect (or at least an acceptable) creative solution pops into your head.

Plug in to a Formula

When you seem paralyzed and unable to get even a few words or lines on paper, pull out a direct mail package or ad from the old swipe file, search the Web for ideas, or reach for your favorite how-to formula (see Chapter 2 for several). By matching your current selling challenge to the structured formula at hand, you may be able to get the creative juices flowing. Or try something a little more off the wall. Ask yourself, "If this product were an animal, what kind of animal would it be? If it were a car, what brand of car would it be," and so on. By making analogies, you may find a way to express your product's strengths in new and compelling ways—or at least start getting some words and pictures recorded.

Ask for Help

Call upon your fellow creative direct and interactive marketers for a new way of looking at the problem at hand. If you cultivate such relationships, you may well be called upon to do the same for a friend who's reached a dry spell. This kind of creative generosity within a design-and-copy team, an agency, or marketing company will pay big dividends to the bottom line in the long run—so do your best to develop such a creative network in your workplace.

Lessons from Abroad: What Americans Can Learn From Overseas Direct Marketers

by Sid Liebenson, Managing Partner/Account Services, Marketing Highway

Oh, America—land of liberty, freedom . . . and direct marketing! We created the discipline, we perfected it. We own it. We do it better than anyone else. Oh yeah? This attitude comes as something of a surprise to agencies and companies from the rest of the world. Campaigns from places like Australia, Spain, Brazil, Sweden, Belgium, the United Kingdom, and India and the Philippines are now being recognized as the creative pacesetters in our field.

In fact, recent results from the Direct Marketing Association's International ECHO Awards, which recognize a combination of strategy, creative, and results, show roughly 60 percent of the winners representing non-U.S. entries. More than 80 percent of the John Caples Awards, which recognize creative solutions to direct marketing problems, have been won by non-U.S. entries in the same time period. What's more, the Cannes Lions Direct awards typically are dominated by European winners.

So why are non-U.S. campaigns winning all these awards? I'm on the board of both the ECHO Awards and the Caples Awards. Every year at the award ceremonies, I hear executives from American agencies complain that foreign marketers have an unfair advantage.

Here's what they most often cite as reasons for foreign award dominance:

- Less competition, less clutter.
- Direct marketing is newer and more novel, so response rates are higher.
- Consumers have more time to spend with direct response offers and they're not jaded.
- Lower labor costs mean lower cost per thousand for production, so foreign clients can afford creatively elaborate campaigns that U.S. clients would not want to pay for.

Some of these points may be true, but they offer much too facile an explanation for foreign award dominance. Let's consider the disadvantages that foreign direct marketers face:

- Consumers are unfamiliar with direct marketing processes and are not as comfortable responding to DM offers.
- Consumers are less trusting—they can't be sure they'll get what they ordered. They may not even trust response mechanisms like toll-free numbers.
- Little DM infrastructure—they don't have thousands of lists to choose from or much selectivity in the ones they have.
- Higher costs for DM campaigns because they don't have printers or database suppliers who understand direct marketing. They also may not have a postal service with favorable rates for advertising mail.

With all these disadvantages in mind, the sad truth we need to face is that non-U.S. campaigns are winning so many awards *not* due to comparative market advantages but because, quite often, they *are* better. So let's talk about the reasons behind the success and recognition of these non-U.S. campaigns.

1. **Strategic Thinking is a Necessity.** With smaller markets and smaller budgets, the same agency usually is charged with both awareness building and direct response. Integrated marketing is a reality, with one campaign meeting multiple objectives. In comparison, U.S. clients often have different agencies for different marketing disciplines—each focusing on its own objectives. In the U.S., overall brand strategies may not even be shared with the DM agency, so their emphasis is on tactics.

2. **Clients Are Willing to Take Chances.** In foreign countries there are fewer local "best practices" to follow, so we see clients trying to break new ground and set new standards. They need to be innovative to overcome the challenges stated above, in markets that might be unfamiliar with direct marketing. In comparison, many American direct marketers tend to avoid risk and stick with "what works." They prefer to follow "best practices" rather than to set them. They get tangled up in tactics—

a sure road to mediocrity. For an example, look in your own U.S. mailbox for the many competitive credit card offers, all focused on tried-and-true tactics like low APRs, free balance transfers, and the like. Or note how many U.S. nonprofits send nearly interchangeable packages with free address labels when seeking donations—a "best practice" perhaps, but not one that differentiates one good cause from another.

3. **A Greater Premium on Creativity.** The 40/40/20 rule for DM success (40 percent list, 40 percent offer, 20 percent creative) does not hold up without strong DM infrastructure. In the U.S., the first steps to improved ROI typically include better targeting and reduced media or production costs. Outside the U.S., the first step to improving ROI is *stronger creative*. And stronger creative is what wins awards.

So what can we U.S.-based direct marketers learn from foreign innovators? First, seek strategic partnerships to maximize budgetary impact. Second, work harder to integrate disciplines even though the infrastructure in the U.S. makes it more difficult to do so. Here are some additional lessons learned, including specific examples from foreign award winners.

Rethink the Entire Response Process. Foreign marketers are forced to do it. We Americans have to do it too, to maximize the impact of our creative. We need to rethink how we reach markets—are there new channels, new formats, new appeals to use? We need to understand how the audience deals with the medium and the message. We also need to step back and come to a full understanding of what each advertising medium can do.

Example: Twinings Herbal and Fruit Infusions

Rather than content themselves with a flat ad in women's magazines, marketers for this U.K. brand created a ride-along sample package with the headline "Pick-me-up!" The double entendre invited readers to pick up the package and to use the sample as an energizing drink. The offer lets readers send for a free trial pack of six different flavors, and also includes a coupon for immediate grocery purchase.

Be Playful! Many of the foreign award-winning entries include an element of play. Engage the audience, and make your message welcome. Make it an invitation rather than an intrusion. Let the prospect think of your company as a suitor, not a stalker. Studies show that even in the U.S., people actually like advertising, direct marketing, and even direct mail. So use this to your advantage.

Example: Citroen C5

When Citroen introduced the C5 in the Netherlands, the agency found itself saddled with a multinational creative platform that emphasized binary computer code to support its positioning and theme, "It reads the road." The agency immediately saw the need to add a more personal dimension, so they expanded the message to "It reads the road and the driver." The first mailing didn't just come from Citroen, it came from the car! The outer said, "I'd like to get to know you" and asked the respondent for his/her taste in music, favorite candy, favorite color, and driving style. In a follow-up, the C5 wrote

Exhibit 18.6. Twinings Tea

This Twinings Herbal and Fruit Infusions insert was placed as a ride-along in women's magazines in the United Kingdom. It includes a sample of the tea and a database-building offer to send away for a free packet of six different flavors.

Reprinted with permission of Sid Liebenson.

back and revealed more about itself, followed by the C5's personal invitation to the respondent to visit Holland's major auto show "for a chance to meet in person."

At that meeting, the C5 on display was outfitted with two cameras, and there was an actor behind the scenes who could see what visitors were looking at. Thus it seemed as if the car itself was specifically talking about that feature. The actor (presenting himself as the car) could also direct people to feel and touch certain parts of the interior. As an additional follow-up, the C5 gave each of its visitors a CD of their favorite kind of music.

When the C5 hit the showrooms, there was another message: "Come take me for a ride." When prospects showed up for the test drive, they got into a car of their favorite color and found a package of their favorite candy on the seat. Their favorite kind of music was playing on the sound system, too. Playful, yes. Successful? Wildly. Citroen's goal was to sell 500 cars within the first month of launch. They sold 953—92 percent over goal—plus an estimated 600 lease agreements!

Exhibit 18.7. DHL Austria

This DHL Worldwide Express package invited Austrian customers to an Asia Night event to highlight the firm's dominance as a shipper to Asia. The package engaged the recipient's senses of sight, touch, taste, and smell with very positive effects: 82 percent of those invited showed up at the event.

Reprinted with permission of Sid Liebenson.

Businesspeople Are Consumers, Too. You don't have to be dull to be taken seriously.

Example: DHLWorldwide Express

The Austrian arm of this international company sought to leverage their position as the top express carrier to Asia by sending customers a dimensional package with Asian-inspired typeface and dragon artwork. Inside, the contents were wrapped in a sheet of paper decorated with similar artwork, held closed by two chopsticks. When opened, the paper revealed a letter, plus a gift package of Asian noodles. Through the senses of sight, touch, and (if the noodles were cooked) taste and smell, the package created an experience of Asia. The letter invited key account customers to an Asia Night event, and 82 percent of them attended!

Simple Can Be Smart. Outside the U.S. they seem to have a knack for focusing on a central idea and executing it simply and well, by fully understanding the advertising medium being used.

Example: Visa Austria

Visa's objective was to activate new cardholders who had opened an account three months or more earlier, but had not yet activated the card. Unfortunately, Visa had almost no budget for an incentive premium, sweepstakes, low interest rate, or rebate offer. But they did find a way to use direct mail very well. The outer envelope showed a pot of forget-me-nots with teaser copy, "Now they start to bloom." The letter explained that the Visa card was only useful if you used it, and invited the reader to look at the enclosure, featuring the forget-me-nots photo once again. This time there were instructions to "lift here," and doing so revealed a packet of forget-me-not flower seeds. Inexpensive, playful, memorable, and possibly more effective than a more typical sweepstakes offer or rebate. With this soft approach, Visa Austria activated more than half of the targeted cardholders.

In reviewing these innovative campaigns, it might be tempting to conclude that U.S. marketers are being eclipsed by overseas creativity. But Americans aren't necessarily getting it wrong—it's just that we no longer have the high ground all to ourselves. After all, every direct marketer shares the same goals—and global strides in the field generally are built on foundations created here. So appreciate this progress—and learn from it!

Enhance Your Understanding: Features Versus Benefits

Flip through a magazine and clip a direct response ad that is selling a product—one with at least three or four paragraphs of copy. Use a pink accent marker to highlight all the features (product attributes) you can find in the copy. Then use a yellow accent marker to highlight all the benefits (advantages—statements to the prospect of "what's in it for me"). Now consider these questions.

1. Note the feature and benefit statements that go together. For example: "Made of 100 percent cotton" (feature) "that's as comfortable and soft as cashmere" (benefit). This is the most common form for feature/benefit copy. Sometimes the benefit is stated first with the feature to follow.

2. See if the product has a name that showcases its benefit—for example, the fabric described above could be called "cotton cashmere." Calling a car's air conditioning and heating system "climate control" is another example.

3. Look for features that do not have benefit statements attached. Are they missing because most readers already understand the benefit? An example of this would be automobile ads that simply list a car's features (anti-lock brakes, air conditioning, etc.) assuming that the benefits of these well-known features are implied.

4. Look for benefits without specific features attached. Is this device of "selling the sizzle and not the steak" used effectively in this ad, or would discussing the feature help provide "reasons why" justification to the reader?

19

Preparing Artwork For Printing

This chapter picks up where Chapter 18 left off: once the copy and layout have been created and approved, and it's time to prepare artwork for printing. A comprehensive layout with copy roughed in may be enough to sell a marketing concept to a client, but there are many more vital production steps that must take place before the direct mail package or ad is printed and distributed to the target audience. This process includes typography, photography and illustrations, print production, and space ad preparation.

Although many copywriters and some graphic designers complete their formal involvement at the copy and layout stage, learning the basics of production will serve any marketer well for several reasons. First, a knowledge of production helps writers and graphic designers understand the possibilities—and the limits—of the medium they are creating for. Second, creative types can make their plans more cost-effective when they know the timing and process involved in producing their work. The third reason has to do with self-interest: individuals who wish to move out of the "creative box" into overall management must fully understand the big picture—and be able to work with and supervise production operations. Fourth and final is the matter of mutual respect: the writer or graphic designer who takes the time to understand production jobs will earn more cooperation and help from artists and technicians in achieving a top-notch creative product.

Typography

Good direct marketing typography is unobtrusive. It contributes to the visual message about the product or service without calling attention to itself. Good typography catches the reader's eye with headlines, leads smoothly to the subheads, and provides easy readability in body copy.

Copywriters may contribute to the appearance and readability of their typeset copy by keeping sentences and paragraphs short, writing sufficient lead-ins and subheads to keep copy interesting, and dividing the copy story into sections. Another important function for the copywriter is writing to size: ensuring that each head, subhead, and body copy section fills the space allotted to it without running over.

In general, the layout artist or graphic designer specifies typefaces when the comprehensive layout is created. This job includes not only the selection of the face (font) and its size, but also the width of columns, use of space between lines of type (leading), and technicalities such as setting type flush left or flush right, or to wrap around an illustration or photograph. Here are some considerations for typeface selection and typesetting.

Type Styles

Serif typefaces are those that have fine lines at the top, bottom, and corners, while sans serif faces are plain and modern in appearance. Serif faces are easier to read in long copy blocks, and give a more traditional appearance. Some studies also show that serif faces lend more credibility to a presentation. They are preferred by older audiences because they are perceived as traditional. Sans serif faces give a contemporary look and are usually easy enough to read—if the lines are properly spaced or leaded. Some graphic designers do insist on using sans serif type for long copy, mainly because they prefer its appearance. A glance at the main body copy of newspapers and books, however, shows that the more readable serif typefaces are used almost without exception. Keep in mind that the exception to this rule is Web site font selection: serifs may appear muddy on the computer screen and thus sans serif type is preferred by many designers for online body copy.

There are thousands of different type styles or fonts, some used with great frequency and others reserved for special applications. Writers and graphic designers may peruse type style options in a host of books and typography annuals. There are also many computer software packages and online sources available that put hundreds of options at the designer's fingertips. While the variety is tempting, it is best to use specialty typefaces with care: they are not familiar to your reader and may draw attention away from the selling message. A good rule is to use that Asian-look typeface or the circus style one for headings or perhaps for subheads, but to select a more traditional face for body copy.

Another good rule is not to use a specialty typeface unless there is a specific reason for it, such as a *Brush Script* typeface for headings about arts and crafts products. To enhance the integration of your message, you may wish to select a typeface that fits your corporate identity, and then use that same face in almost all of your ads and mailings. Some firms opt to use a new typeface for each promotion—one that reflects the specific product or service being sold. This minimizes your ability to achieve the same integrated look across promotions and media, and thus should be considered with care. Although it is not necessary to stick with the same typeface in different sizes for all headings, subheads, and body copy, it's wise to limit your selection to one or two type styles on any one printed piece unless you're an experienced typographer. Otherwise the results may be confusing and distracting to the reader.

It has long been a rule of thumb for direct mailers that sales letters should be set in what used to be known as "typewriter type." This stems from the fact that good sales letters are intended as "one-to-one" communications—personal letters that should appear as if the sender sat down and composed them especially for each recipient. However, as the general public has become more familiar and comfortable with the appearance of computer-generated communications, this rule has been loosened quite a bit. While it is no longer necessary to limit yourself to classic pica or elite typewriter faces for letters, it is still best to stick with simple, serif faces in most cases—especially when your target customer is older. With any given typeface, you have a number of options. Most faces feature a regular type, a bold (darker and thicker) version, and a light version. There are also condensed, extended, and italic versions of most faces. In addition, you may opt to use all capital letters in certain headings or subheads, although this inhibits readability to some extent.

Type Sizes

Type sizes are expressed in "points" for height and "picas" for width. There are 72 points to an inch of height, and 6 picas to an inch of width. Another measure of height—most frequently used by newspapers—is the "agate line." There are 14 agate lines to an inch.

Generally, it is considered difficult to read any type smaller than 8 points, although in a publication that uses small type for its body copy, you might be able to succeed with 6- or 7- point type. The type sizes for promotional body copy range from 6 points to about 14 points, depending on the overall size of the piece and the impression you wish to make. Headings and subheads generally range from about 12-point up to 48-point or even 72-point type. When your target market focuses on children or senior citizens, it is wise to use larger type for body copy.

Another aspect of type size that enhances readability for prospects of all ages is leading, the amount of white space between lines of type. The larger the type, the more leading is necessary for good appearance and readability. When one point of leading is added, an 8- or 9-point type format would be expressed as "8 on 9" or "9 on 10," where the second number refers to the addition of the leading. If type is set "solid," with no leading, this is expressed as "8 on 8" or "9 on 9." Several points of leading might be added to 14-point copy for optimum readability.

It is important to note that not all 8-point type takes up the same amount of space. For instance, an 8-point typeface called Souvenir Demi Bold gets 2.68 characters to the pica, while 8-point Helvetica Condensed Bold gets 3.74 characters to the pica. This fact impacts both copywriters and graphic designers. To create the right amount of copy, writers need to know more than just that their work will be set in 8-point type. It is sometimes more helpful to ask the graphic designer to figure out how many characters will fit in a block of body copy. Graphic designers may want to experiment with various typefaces and sizes (including condensed, extended, etc.) to determine which is most readable and effective for the space available.

From Typed Copy to Final Type Style

Before computer software dominated print production, copywriters simply typed their copy according to an agreed-upon format, and turned over their hard copies or text-only disks to the graphic designer or typesetter. In recent years, however, most copywriters have become more involved in preparation for production. Writers frequently are asked to use specific word processing programs and versions that make for easy transfer to desktop publishing systems like Adobe InDesign or, less often these days, Quark Xpress or Pagemaker.

Today with the proliferation of InDesign as a design and production software tool, copywriters and graphic designers usually complete the typesetting job themselves with a minimum of cooperative effort. InDesign, and even most word processing software packages, allow creative people to try out new typefaces, sizes, italics, bold, and other modifications with a few keystrokes or mouse clicks. InDesign allows for instant modifications of leading (space between lines) and kerning (space between letters). This means that a copywriter and graphic designer can work together—either in front of the same computer screen or on a cooperative system—to touch up areas where there is too much or too little copy, to lengthen or shorten headlines, add subheads, and make other small changes that used to take days or even weeks to accomplish.

A word to the wise for both copywriters and graphic designers from Pat Klarecki, Professor of Printing Management at Ferris State University: "To save time, money and aggravation, talk about what software each of you has available and finds preferable before any work is done. For example, finished copy created in Microsoft Publisher will not flow into a professional advertising or printing workflow and will need to be entirely recreated with software that is compatible."

Photography and Illustrations

Studies show that in general, photography gets more positive attention from prospects than illustrations. If you can afford it, and if photography fits into your selling message, it is a good idea to add

Exhibit 19.1. Typefaces and Sizes

SERIF TYPE:

abcdefghijklmnopqrstuvwxyz

SANS SERIF TYPE:

abcdefghijklmnopqrstuvwxyz

1 POINT LEADING:

Language is a systematic means of communicating ideas or feelings by the use of conventionalized signs, sounds, gestures, or marks having understood meanings.

2 POINTS LEADING:

Language is a systematic means of communicating ideas or feelings by the use of conventionalized signs, sounds, gestures, or marks having understood meanings.

6 POINT:

abcdefghijklmnopqrstuvwxyz

9 POINT:

abcdefghijklmnopqrstuvwxyz

12 POINT:

abcdefghijklmnopqrstuvwxyz

20 POINT:

abcdefghijklmnopqrstuvwxyz

30 POINT:

abcdefghijklmnopqrs

48 POINT:

abcdefghijklm

72 POINT:

abcdefgh

one or more photographs to your layout plan. Generally these photos will feature the product itself or the product in use, but they may also help create an image or identify the target market.

To find a suitable photographer, ask for referrals from business associates or trade organizations. Be sure to make it clear that you are looking for an experienced product photographer, not a portraitist who specializes in family or individual "people shots." Check the work of the photographers you are referred to, and interview them to see what experience they have that qualifies them to work with your product line. Make sure the photographer has a feel for your merchandise, what you are trying to achieve, and the media in which you intend to sell. As Pat Klarecki notes, "Photos to be used on the Internet most often cannot be used in print, however, photos used for print can be used on the Internet."

In addition to a photographer, you may need to hire a photo stylist. Certain stylists specialize in working with food, clothing, or other product lines. Their expertise can be well worth the cost to ensure that hard-to-photograph products are portrayed to best advantage.

Set-ups for Photography

Experts agree that lighting is the single most important factor in successful product photography. Good lighting impacts your product's appearance in regard to color, tone, dimension, and detail, so be sure that yours is a photographer who takes proper care in this area. Backgrounds for product shots should not be chosen primarily for their artistic quality or uniqueness, but rather for the way they complement the product. In general, a background color that contrasts with the product will enhance it best. Simple, plain-colored backgrounds often are the most effective since they do not compete for attention with the product itself.

Props can be important in that they help set the tone, give lifestyle cues to prospects, and provide size relationships to the product. If a human hand is shown holding the product, for example, its relative size is easy to determine at a glance. If you need unusual props, consider working with a prop rental house. Such firms are available in most major cities.

Don't reject the concept of a product-in-use shot if you happen to be marketing an intangible service. Your in-use shot for Medicare supplement insurance policy, for example, could show a senior citizen receiving a benefit check in the mail while recuperating from illness in the hospital. Another alternative is to show the results of using the service—e.g., an expanse of beautiful, weed-free grass to promote a lawn care system.

If you choose to do photography on location, you may wish to utilize the services of a freelance location finder to line up proper interiors or exteriors for your application. Depending on the setting you require, you may be able to make a deal with a furniture store, hotel, or private homeowner for the use of their property and furnishings. The going rate for use of in-home spaces for photography is $250 per day and up in small towns; it could be more or much more in large or famous places. Use of well-known public spaces like big-city libraries and museums can be extremely expensive, so check on the cost before committing to the photography concept.

It is always a good idea to take some preliminary digital photos of any photography set-up before starting the actual photo shoot. The camera "sees" things you may have missed—and even a quick shot like this can tell you if you and the photographer are on the right track with lighting, props, and positioning.

Digital Photography

Digital photography (recording images in pixels) is now considered comparable—and in most cases superior—in quality to traditional photography. Thus most all direct marketers have embraced this technology because of its speed and the ability to transfer images directly into the artwork for a computer-produced catalog or brochure. In addition, color correction, management, and retouching can be done right on the desktop, as opposed to the traditional time-consuming and expensive retouching methods. As the technology for digital photography continues to improve, it is used more and more in the creation of promotional pieces.

What's more, as Pat Klarecki points out, variable data imaging allows for a different image to be placed with its own personalized message in each individual printed piece. "If that is the intent," he notes, "thought should be given during the photo shoot to ensure that the various photos used will all work well with the overall creative and message."

Evaluating Photography

When photography is presented to you, make sure that the shots will work effectively in the size they will appear in your printed piece. An 8″ × 10″ print, for example, comes across very differently than a two-column product shot in an ad. If cropping is necessary, check it carefully to make sure the composition of the photo is not destroyed.

Check all product shots at every stage for fidelity to your product. Remember that this photograph will provide your customer's entire perception of your product, and that if it's Kelly green in the picture, buyers will expect it to be that exact Kelly green shade when it is delivered. Pat Klarecki adds, "If the product you are selling is very color sensitive, consider working with designers, photographers, and printers who work in a 'Color Managed' workflow. Technological advances have been made that allow for nearly exact matches of color from original, to proof, to computer monitor, to finished printed product. Ask your service providers which certified standards they are following (there are several) because all providers need to share information for the same standard in order for the system to work."

Sources of Free or Inexpensive Photos

If the cost of professional, custom photography is beyond your budget, consider sources of free or inexpensive photography that has already been done. If your firm is not the manufacturer of the product you are selling, check with the manufacturers to see if they can supply product or product-in-use shots. The Reference Center of the U.S. government provides a wide variety of good, general mood-setting shots free of charge. Visit *www.usa.gov* to access this material. Try trade organizations, chambers of commerce, and other sources of free photos that may suit your needs. Keep in mind that according to Pat Klarecki, it is illegal to copy and paste a photo from the Internet and use it in a for-profit context unless you have permission from its owner.

Marc Ziner of Marketing Highway in Wilmette, Illinois, cautions that in some instances, stock photos can be even more expensive to use than original photography. PhotoDisc, Getty Images, Fotosearch and iStock are some of the current players for stock art available online.

David Fideler, Principal of Concord Communications and Design notes, "There are now a lot of services where you can get high quality images for $20, and the high-end providers (charge) in the hundreds of dollars range. While some CD-ROM collections may still be available, the trend is to just buy individual images onlines."

When to Use Illustrations

If photography does not suit your purpose, you may wish to commission the creation of line drawings or illustrations to enhance your layout. Most graphic designers should be acquainted with artists who create various types of illustrations. Some firms that use illustrations often may even keep one or more illustrators on staff, or have such individuals under contract.

In addition, you may want to subscribe to a stock illustration service—a firm that supplies you with a steady stream of non-copyrighted artwork that you can use to illustrate your brochures and ads as required. As in the case of stock photography, stock illustrations can save a good deal of time and effort—assuming you avoid choosing illustrations that appear too generic or dated. Adobe Illustrator is the most commonly used software program for computer-generated illustrations.

Preparing Art for the Printer

Prior to the InDesign revolution, keylines—also known as mechanicals, boards, or camera-ready art—were the final step of preparation for offset printing. Paste-up was the multi-step process of affixing art and type on a keyline prior to platemaking and printing.

According to Pat Klarecki, Adobe's Creative Suite (often referred to as CS4 or CS5—the number representing the version) contains a collection of programs including InDesign, PhotoShop, Illustrator, and Acrobat. These are designed to work together for ad creation. While these programs are near-miracles of efficiency and effectiveness for the graphic design profession, their mastery requires considerable time and effort. One expert reported that developing a full command of the Adobe Creative Suite may require up to 1,000 hours of effort. As with most computer software programs, an individual can learn the basics in a matter of hours. However, "the basics" are not enough to create sophisticated catalogs, brochures, and the like and produce them in a form that can be printed attractively.

According to Deborah R. Scott, former president of Copy Options, Inc., in Grand Rapids, Michigan, "With the widespread adoption of Adobe Acrobat, PDFs (Portable Document Format files) have become the standard for electronic mechanicals. When graphic artists use Acrobat to save the artwork, it doesn't matter what software program was used to create the work, nor if it was created on a PC rather than a Mac. PDF saves all the text, illustrations, and photos in a universal language, and the actual fonts chosen by the designer are embedded into the file. Using just Acrobat Reader software (easily downloaded and provided at no cost from Adobe), the client can preview the piece on his own monitor regardless of what software or hardware he has."

Mike Bloom, President of Production Plus, adds, "Electronic proofing streamlines production by using the Web and PDF to help reviewers in various locations, with different schedules, communicate and resolve their differences quickly. Individuals can mark up the same document or discuss issues in real time, capturing the discussion in an annotation. Though reviewers have the experience of marking up the document, the annotations are stored separately, resulting in an audit trail that keeps everyone in the loop." Bloom notes that while PDFs have not yet made traditional proofing and press checks obsolete—especially for ensuring exact color fidelity—"Companies that leverage this technology to streamline production will gain a competitive advantage by providing a faster, more accurate method to get from draft to approval."

Pat Klarecki cautions, "There are several ways to save a computer file as a PDF. As a rule of thumb, the more complicated the ad is with colors, photos and illustration the more difficult it is to save a 'Perfect' PDF. Failure to provide a printer with a good PDF file will cause delays and additional costs. It is best to ask your printer for file format specifications when the ad is something more than a simple black and white ad."

Check Carefully for Errors Before and During the Printing Process

Exceptional care should be taken in proofreading when a PDF of the final piece is presented for approval. Changes after the piece is handed over to the printer can be costly. Compare it to the comprehensive layout and original copy to ensure that it is accurate, line by line and word for word. Use a ruler to check each dimension of the piece. Compare the position of the panels to the comprehensive layout, remembering that a PDF may necessarily show certain panels upside down or out of sequence because of the way they will appear when printed and folded. Using a print-out to mock-up the actual piece will allow you to proof it more realistically.

Once you've determined that the copy fits and looks attractive in the layout, the next step is to check the proof for technical aspects such as proper spelling and "breaks" from line to line. Here are some of the details to check when proofing copy and art. First, avoid having type extend over illustrations: it inhibits readability. It is also important to consider the readability of body copy. Make sure that any columns of type are narrow enough for easy reading: some experts say that columns should be no more than about 40 characters in width—similar to newspaper columns. Also check to see if any paragraphs are too long and need to be broken up. Last but most important of all, proofread to ensure that the typeset version matches the approved copy, word for word. Whenever possible, have another trained individual proofread the copy as it appears in the layout, checking for spelling, grammar, and the overall sense and readability of the piece. The copywriter and graphic designer are so close to the job that they can sometimes overlook obvious mistakes. Pat Klarecki adds, "When working with PDF files or other computer files, errors in the computer code will occasionally occur. This can cause unwanted changes to the finished text or art."

If the piece is to include elements of personalization, make sure that the correct space has been indicated to accommodate the personalized fill-ins. Check that the label area—or area for computerized addressing—is sized correctly and positioned to correspond with any windows it must show through. Also ensure that any perforations, die cuts, or other special processes are indicated. Take time to check for all necessary key codes, stock numbers, and other identifying marks, and make sure that they are correct. Look carefully at the order form. Recompute amounts, shipping charges, and tax to make sure the figures are correct. Photocopy or print out the order form and fill it out as if you were the customer, making sure that each step is understandable and simple to complete.

Pat Klarecki suggests, "Ask your printer for a sample of the paper your promotion will be printed on and test it with several different types of pens and pencils to make sure it will receive your customers' information well."

Digital Workflow Replaces Traditional Separations

With the evolution to the "digital original," Deborah Scott says there has also been a revolution in every step of the production process. As she explains: "The ability to transfer artwork directly from computer to plate (CTP), has eliminated the need for traditional color separations. The process of outputting film for each color, stripping negatives, and burning plates has been consolidated into automated platemaking. For each color, computer-to-plate systems produce plates that are punched, perfectly registered to each other, and ready to be mounted on the press. The same Raster Image Processor (RIP) that outputs plates can also send those digital files to a printer that renders the proof, on Ink Jet Paper, for example. Thus clients are more commonly approving high-resolution digital proofs or computer monitor proofs rather than old-fashioned Match Prints or Chromalins."

According to Pat Klarecki, "An additional benefit of a digital workflow is the clarity and consistency of the printed image throughout the entire process. Now that the entire pre-press (and in some cases press) production process is digitized, scientists have been able to define color in absolute numeric values. This allows computer files to be adjusted so that colors will be viewed as identical, regardless of the paper, press, printer, or monitor on which they are being reproduced. Some colors are more universally tranferable to various media than others, so it is good to work with a designer and printer who fully understand a color-managed digital workflow." Yet another benefit of computer-to-plate technology is the greater clarity of the printed image. Under the old process of burning plates from negatives, there would often be dot gain in screens and fattening of serifs. Now that the printed piece is one generation closer to the digital original, typefaces are crisper and screens are more accurately reproduced. It's required some relearning for artwork preparation. Knowing screens would typically print with greater density on press, graphic artists compensated in advance by using finer screens to achieve the end result they wanted. Now that fine lines are being reproduced with greater fidelity, even typefaces with thin serifs can be used with confidence.

Evaluating and Enhancing Color

There are several things that can be done to ensure the best possible final product with your color production. First, good and sharp photography is essential. Color fidelity in photography is the first key to color fidelity in printing. Second, make sure your color images are clean and without glitches. Third, make sure your graphic designer and printer know what you are expecting in terms of color fidelity. Some customers will settle for "pleasing color" in order to save money, while others insist on absolute color fidelity at any cost. These decisions about color quality have to do with the nature of the product, its price point, and company image, among other factors. It takes a trained eye to critique and correct color before and during the printing process, but even the novice can learn to tell good color from poor color. Basic questions to ask include:

- Are the flesh tones natural?
- Is the grass green?
- Are the red roses red and the violets purple?
- Is the detail of dark-toned objects discernible, or do they disappear into mud?
- Do the whites appear white without too much yellow, pink, or blue?
- Are the details crisp?

Unless you have been trained to order specific, technical corrections on color, it is safer to comment on what appears incorrect than to instruct the experts on how to fix it. In other words, you might point out that the skin tones appear too red or yellow—then let the technicians make adjustments until the desired result is achieved.

David Fideler adds these comments: "It's possible to proof pieces on the computer screen as PDFs, but computer monitors vary wildly in terms of how they portray color—so you can only do this accurately on high end, calibrated monitors. Really, the only acceptable kind of proof is a print-out created on a SWOP-certified system (Specifications for Web Offset Printing). The best kind of proof is a SWOP-verified proof. With a SWOP-verified proof, you can be assured that everyone is seeing the same color and that it will be matched (or can be matched) when printed. Also, PMS colors may not display accurately on monitors or printed proofs; even though they can often be accurately matched, sometimes they are off wildly."

Space Ad Preparation

Since publications have varied requirements for ad production, it is wise to communicate with their advertising representatives to make sure that your ads are sized and prepared correctly. SRDS's newspaper and consumer magazine publications list considerable information on periodicals' column widths, number of columns, page dimensions, trim size, binding method, printing process, and color availability. Line drawings may be supplied as part of your camera-ready art, but photographs and drawings with shades and tones must be photographed through a screen to achieve a dot pattern. This process is known as screening. There are various types of screens, so check with each publication's advertising representative for details.

Stock Photography and Color Proofing

by David Fideler, Concord Communications and Design (www.concordcd.com)

BUYING STOCK PHOTOGRAPHY

Stock photography, or professional imagery for use in publications and marketing pieces, has been around for decades. But before the emergence of the Internet, stock photography was usually sold via printed catalogs or theme-based CDs. Both options were generally quite expensive.

Today, however, almost all stock photography is sold or licensed online through stock photography Web sites. And while expensive, high-end vendors still offer outstanding images, many alternatives exist for designers and marketers working on smaller budgets. High-quality stock photography for use in print publications or Web sites may now be easily licensed over the Web at rates ranging anywhere from $10 per image up to thousands of dollars per image.

Stock photography licensing is either *royalty-free* (RF) or *rights-managed* (RM). Royalty-free licensing is the most flexible; it allows you to use an image at any time for multiple purposes. Rights-managed licensing carries one or more kinds of limitation, including limitations on the kind of usage, the duration of usage, the size of the print run, the image size, and whether or not the usage is exclusive or nonexclusive.

Two of the largest stock photography agencies are Getty Images (www.gettyimages.com) and Corbis Images (www.corbisimages.com). Premium stock photos from these agencies typically cost several hundred dollars to license, depending on the image size and intended usage. At the other end of the spectrum are microstock agencies, like iStockphoto (www.istockphoto.com), where high-quality images, often taken by nonprofessional photographers, sell for under $20. Other stock photography agencies like Shutterstock (www.shutterstock.com) offer monthly or yearly subscription plans, or special fee packages for buying a selected number of images. Specialized vendors also exist, like Art Resource (www.artres.com), which licenses fine art images from museums around the world.

While stock photography agencies offer millions of images and provide an excellent resource for most uses, one thing to keep in mind is the danger of using stock photography for critical branding projects. If photography is going to be used to establish a significant company or product brand image, it is important to remember that most stock photography is licensed on a nonexclusive basis. Since anyone else in the world could use the same image, it could undermine the uniqueness of the brand. In such a case, it is usually best to hire a professional photographer or to commission original, unique artwork.

Typically, more expensive vendors offer higher-quality images, but that is not always the case; many images available from iStockphoto, for example, are outstanding. And no matter what vendor you use, finding just the right image often involves significant research. While it is impossible to list all stock photography Web sites and specialist vendors here, the following companies are among some of the more well-known:

Moderate to expensive:
- ▸ Corbis Images (www.corbisimages.com)
- ▸ Fotosearch (www.fotosearch.com)
- ▸ Getty Images (www.gettyimages.com)
- ▸ Jupiter Images (www.jupiterimages.com)

Very inexpensive:
- ▸ 123RF (www.123rf.com)
- ▸ Bigstock (www.bigstockphoto.com)
- ▸ dreamstime (www.dreamstime.com)
- ▸ iStockphoto (www.istockphoto.com)
- ▸ Shutterstock (www.shutterstock.com)

COLOR PROOFING—WHAT YOU SEE ISN'T ALWAYS WHAT YOU GET

One of the tricky things about print production is that different computer monitors vary widely in the way they display color. It is important to keep in mind that individuals reviewing artwork or PDFs normally will not see exactly the same colors or color saturations as other reviewers, and sometimes there will be profound differences.

Some high-end monitors like the Apple Cinema Display are extraordinarily accurate and designed for fidelity in print production, and "virtual proofing" solutions do exist. But the best way to be certain you are seeing the exact colors that will be printed is to review an accurate, hard copy color proof. One reason for this is that computer monitors and printing presses use two different models for generating colors, RGB (red, green, and blue) and CMYK (cyan, magenta, yellow, and black), respectively.

While various proofing models and systems exist for color printing, by far the most widespread is SWOP, the Specifications for Web Offset Publications, which is also the default working space in Adobe graphic design programs. Most agencies and design firms will have a SWOP-certified system available in-house to create accurate CMYK proofs, but many freelance designers do not. Accurate SWOP proofs can be supplied by your printer or ordered over the Internet. The most reliable kind of proof available is a SWOP-verified proof: it is not only created on a SWOP-certified system but the color bar is also then measured and verified for accuracy after the proof is created.

Special care must always be taken with Pantone Matching System (PMS) colors, which use an ink mixing system and are not CMYK colors. Not all PMS colors can be reproduced accurately on a computer monitor or a printed proof—and in some cases, PMS colors may appear wildly off in relation to how they will look when printed. The only way to gauge a PMS color with 100 percent accuracy is to use a printed swatch book as a reference.

Enhance Your Understanding: Field Trips and Classes

Even if print production is not part of your daily job, you will be wise to observe firsthand the many steps required to prepare and print envelopes, letters, brochures, and other promotional pieces. Ask a graphic designer for a tour of his/her studio and a hands-on explanation of how technology has changed the job in recent years. Take a class in Adobe InDesign, not necessarily aimed at becoming an expert, but rather at understanding the power of this software tool for graphic designers. Take advantage of field trips offered by trade associations—or organize your own. Visit printers of various sizes and sophistication levels and observe a graphic designer adjusting color and reproduction during a press check. Watch printed pieces being cut, folded, assembled, and addressed. These experiences will serve you well when you are charged with the development of printed pieces that can be produced in a cost-effective manner.

20

Printing and Personalization

The previous chapter outlined the steps marketers must take in order to prepare their artwork for printing. This chapter continues the step-by-step production process, covering information about printing methods and options, paper selection, press start-ups, and personalization.

Printing Methods and Options

Production personnel facing any printing challenge must consider three interdependent factors: time, quality, and cost efficiency. When told that a client wants printing done "fast, top-quality, and cheap," most print salespeople will chuckle and say, "Pick any two—you can't have all three." When sufficient time is allowed for completion of a printing job, cost efficiency and quality generally can be improved. Fast work at top quality will generally carry premium pricing, while fast work that is inexpensive will usually limit the level of quality. There are many other variables that affect quality, including choice of printing method, pre-press preparations, and paper selection. Cost-efficiency is also a function of the suitability of the printing equipment chosen for a given project. This section provides information that will allow creative marketers to optimize the time/quality/cost factors in each printing job.

Selecting a Method of Printing

Marketers should be familiar with four methods of printing, each of which may be used for some applications: offset lithography, digital printing, letterpress, and rotogravure.

Offset Lithography. Offset lithography remains the most widely used method of printing around the world. This is largely due to the fact that the interfaces between the pre-press portion of the process and the press portion have become seamless due to the use of software like Adobe InDesign. Offset lithography works on the theory that oil (ink) and water do not mix. An offset printing plate is designed to hold water like a sponge except where the image is. The image repels water but holds ink. As the press runs, the ink is transferred to a rubber blanket and then to the paper. Offset printing yields an exceptionally high quality product for medium to large quantities of print. There are two main types of offset printing presses: sheet-fed and web. The sheet-fed press prints on individual sheets of paper, one by one. It is slower than web printing, but can allow for better quality printing and color fidelity. However, sheet-fed printing is not cost-effective in higher quantity ranges (50,000 and up, generally), and you should therefore look into web printing if your quantities are this large. The web press is fed its paper from a continuous roll. There are small web presses meant for one- and two-color work (such as letters) and large presses that are as long as a railroad car. Generally, a printer prices the work done on these presses by the hours of press time used, so be sure to check what kind of press the printer's quote is based on.

Digital Printing. Digital printing is produced by simply transferring the information on a computer file to paper. According to Pat Klarecki, use of digital or direct imaging has exploded in recent years, making it the fastest-growing segment of the printing industry. As he explains:

> Pre-press workflow has become automated by PDFs and computer-to-plate digital applications, and that automation is increasingly extending into the actual printing process. Rapid technical advances in how images are produced as well as new press designs have fueled this expansion.

Klarecki notes that digital output devices can be either printers or presses. He continues:

> The 'printer' category covers the ubiquitous office copiers, faxes, inkjet and laser printers, and digital duplicators that can image on a variety of media. High-quality digital proofs used to adjust and approve color for other printing processes typically are being created with inkjet printers.
>
> Digital presses are toner based, ink jet based, or lithographic based. Advances in these three technologies yield a quality of print that is indistinguishable to the untrained eye. At the time of this writing, inkjet and lithographic digital printing will hold color more consistently from print to print than toner-based technology. Most research and development is being directed towards ink jet to allow the presses to be bigger and faster like offset lithographic presses.
>
> One of the advantages of digital printing is the ability to personalize or create numerous custom versions. There is virtually no set-up time to change a version on a digital press unlike with lithography or gravure.
>
> A disadvantage of digital printing is that it is still a relatively slow process compared to gravure and lithography. If you need more than 1,000 pieces of the exact same image, offset lithography may be a better option.

Letterpress. Although new letterpress machines are no longer being made, some publishers and printers still keep them in use because this method provides a very sharp and clear image. Although high quality is achieved, letterpress is relatively costly and time-consuming. It involves the mechanical separation of image from non-image. The print area is raised above the non-print area so that ink rollers only touch the portion that becomes the printed image.

Rotogravure or Gravure. Although experts agree that rotogravure or gravure provides a superior printed product, it is cost-effective only in very large quantities, usually several million at a minimum. Rotogravure allows for sharp detail and printing even on very light and inexpensive newsprint paper stock. It also involves the mechanical separation of image from non-image, but the process is different from letterpress. In this case, the image is sunken by etching into a copper cylinder or plate. Rotogravure/gravure is most commonly used in direct marketing by major catalog firms.

Exhibit 20.1. Kit Definition Sheet

Project				
Version/List	**Quantity**	**Final Art or Mail Date**	**Components**	**Notes**
		Size: Stock: Colors: Other: Quantity:		
		Size: Stock: Colors: Other: Quantity:		
		Size: Stock: Colors: Other: Quantity:		

What the Printer Needs to Know

To obtain an accurate quote from a printer, it is wise to supply as much detailed information as possible.

Pat Klarecki advises, "Be open to receiving questions and suggestions from your print sales professional. These are not meant to confuse you, but rather are meant to help you achieve the best results for your promotion. Remember, printers have years of experiences that if applied to your promotional needs could be very beneficial to you."

Make sure that each bidder gets the same information, so that you are comparing apples to apples when all quotes are in. This list of specifications will provide an outline for the type of information your printer will require. It is wise to develop your own quote sheet that you can use to fill out this information whenever you need to get quotes. This worksheet then can become the basis for a comprehensive purchase order once you award the job. Jerry Kaup of the e-mail ad agency suggests the format shown in Exhibit 20.1 as a simple guide for obtaining quotes on direct mail packages, also known as direct mail kits.

Print Quote Specifications

- *Quantity*—Total quantity, plus breakdowns for any versions within the main quantity for price tests, different dates, and so on. Also indicate how many over-run copies you will accept and pay for. This may range from 3 to 10 percent depending on your policy and what you can negotiate with the printer.
- *Size*—Indicate both flat size and final folded size as well as the number and type of folds necessary. Create a diagram if folds are unusual or easy to misinterpret.
- *Paper stock*—Weight, finish, color, brand name if known. If you cannot describe the paper by its specifications, attach a sample. If you plan to supply your own paper, indicate this and attach a sample.
- *Colors*—Number of colors per side (expressed as 4 over 4 for four colors on both sides of a single sheet; 4 over 2 for a four-color front and two-color back; 2 over 2, 1 over 1, etc.). Also indicate how artwork will be supplied.
- *Specified colors*—Indicate Pantone Matching System (PMS) color(s), if known.
- *Halftones*—If any halftones are to be used, indicate how many and what size they will be.
- *Bleed or non-bleed*—Or mixed bleed and non-bleed, if applicable.
- *Proofs*—Type of proof you require, and/or on-site press approval.
- *Finishing*—Type of binding, die cuts, perforations, glues, varnish, or embossing, if applicable. You will also want to discuss with the printer whether these operations will be conducted online or done separately once printing is complete.
- *Packing*—How to pack and label printed material.
- *Delivery*—Where to deliver materials, when they should arrive, and to what person's attention.

Paper Selection

While most direct marketers do not purchase their own paper for printing, this can be the most cost-effective way to proceed in several instances: when you plan to use an unusual paper stock, when you use the same paper stock again and again, or when you print an extremely large volume of material. Recurring paper shortages and dramatic paper price increases in recent years may also offer a rationale for purchasing your own paper in quantity.

Even if you plan to have your printer purchase paper for you, it is important to become involved in the process of paper evaluation and selection. Because paper accounts for 30 to 50 percent of total production costs, and an average of 50 percent of printing costs, an effective selection can positively impact your budget and enhance the appearance of your printed piece.

Before selecting paper, consider the purpose of each piece you are printing, as well as the market segment it will reach. If you are creating a throw-away flyer, an inexpensive stock will probably suit your purposes. But if you are developing a reference catalog for expensive products, you may well want to invest in a heavy, coated stock with exceptional whiteness, brightness, and opacity. When developing an entire direct mail package, be sure to coordinate your paper choices. Just as colors should be coordinated, so should paper textures, weights, and types.

Paper Attributes to Consider

The following attributes of paper will impact your decision-making process.

Weight—Paper weights are expressed in pounds, with each figure indicating the weight of a 500-sheet ream of paper. There are two sets of designations, one for "bond" stock and one for "book" stock. The standard bond paper stock is 17″ × 22″and the standard book paper stock is 25″ × 38″. Thus, a 20-pound bond paper is one in which 500 sheets of 17″ × 22″paper weigh 20 pounds (common bond papers are 16, 20, and 24 pounds). A 50-pound book paper is one in which 500 sheets of 25″ x 38″ paper weigh 50 pounds (common book papers range from 30 to 120 pounds, with those in the 50- to 100-pound range the most widely used).

Strength—The web-offset process requires especially strong paper that will not burst, tear, or break under stress. Another measure is surface strength, which evaluates whether bits of the paper are likely to shed onto the printing blanket, resulting in hickeys (blemishes) on other printed pieces.

Smoothness—In general, the smoother the paper, the better its printability. Smooth sheets allow for flatness under printing pressure, which results in better dot formation and greater fidelity to the original image.

Brightness—The brighter the paper, the more expensive it will be. Brightness is a measure of how much light the paper reflects in combination with the transparent inks printed upon it.

Gloss—Another function of light reflection. The higher the gloss, the more costly the paper.

Opacity—The more opaque the paper, the more costly it will be. Opacity is measured on a scale of 1 to 100, with 100 being completely opaque. Opacity is important because "show through" from the other side of a printed piece is distracting to the selling message, and detracts from a quality image.

Bulk—This measure of thickness is established by measuring how high a pile of a given paper stock is. High-bulk stock may increase opacity without adding weight. It is often used for business reply cards that must be sturdy enough to meet U.S. Postal Service standards.

Whiteness—Some papers tend toward pink, blue or gray, while others approach pure whiteness. A very white stock enhances color reproduction and fidelity.

Grain—This is a function of the alignment of paper fibers in a paper stock. Paper should be folded with the grain for best results.

Finish—Stocks may be coated with clay and rolled to a matte, dull, gloss, or ultragloss finish. Coated papers are good for color reproduction and fidelity, but extremely glossy papers may be difficult to read under fluorescent lights. Uncoated stocks are called vellum, antique, wove, and smooth. Their finishes are determined by the way in which they are run through the finishing rollers.

Press Start-Ups

For simple one- and two-color jobs, you may choose not to attend the press start-up, relying instead on proofs from the printer. Such proofs allow you to check one more time for typographical errors, to see that all halftones and art are in the right places, and that there are no specks or broken type to compromise the final print job. The importance, complexity, and quality of the job you are printing will impact your decision on whether to attend the press start-up in person. When color fidelity is essential, your presence at the printing plant may help ensure the quality standards you require. However, some clients put so much trust in their printing sales representatives that they allow these individuals to give press approval for millions of color brochures.

If you or your representative decides to attend the press start-up, be aware that these events seldom take place during "bankers' hours." Most color presses run 24 hours a day, and when it is time for a new job to go on press, that is when the press approval must take place. You will need to be on call for a possible middle-of-the-night summons to the printing plant to see your important, full color job go on press.

At the press start-up, the pressman will begin to run your job and bring you samples to check against your approved artwork and press proofs for fidelity. You will also want to make sure the printing is in register. Use a jeweler's magnifying glass to see if the dot pattern is crisply in line, or "hanging" over the edge. Take time to make a folding dummy from one of the proofs—it's better to catch an error in panel configuration now than after all 5 million pieces have been run. Also, production expert Jerry Kaup suggests that you do a final check on quantity, versions, perforations, glue applications, and other add-ons. As he says, "I have seen problems in each of these areas that would have gone unnoticed until too late if they were not looked for at the start-up." Once the color is approved and any other needed adjustments are made, make sure that the material that has been run up to that point is destroyed—not salvaged after you leave as part of the press run.

Personalization

The first computer letters were produced in 1952, but it has only been in the past few decades that methods of personalization have been widely used by direct marketers. Years ago, very few firms could take advantage of computer letters because of limitations of the technology and—just as important—because so few computerized lists were available on magnetic tape or disk. During the 1960s and 1970s, impact printing was introduced, followed swiftly by inkjet and laser processes.

With the range of options now available for personalization and even individualized variable data printing, most mailers can find a way to communicate more personally with their customers. The following personalization methods are presented in order from the simplest to the most sophisticated, costly, and complex.

Labels—Generated from a magnetic tape or a disk containing names of customer or prospects, labels are prepared so that they can be affixed one by one to an order form, outer envelope, or catalog. Labels commonly bear a key code in addition to the recipient's name and address. Pressure-sensitive labels allow the buyer to transfer the label from the addressing device to the reply device, thus assuring that the direct marketing company knows the original source of the name.

Word Processing—Today any personal computer can be outfitted with software that allows for the creation of personalized letters. When used in tandem with a letter-quality or near letter-quality printer, such personalized letters—prepared just as an individual letter would be—give the recipient the impression of a one-to-one message. The applications of word processing are usually limited to smaller lists for two main reasons. First, word processing is a comparatively time-consuming process. Second, while word processing and printing goes on, the personal computer and/or printer are tied up, thereby limiting other business functions.

Impact Printing—Similar to a word processor, impact printing combines the look of an individually typewritten letter with the opportunity to do fill-ins of names, addresses, and other information relevant to the recipient. Impact printing usually is done by an outside service, and is considered best for short runs with limited personalization. There is no type variation possible with impact printing.

Inkjet Printing—This computerized process for personalization improves on flexibility, but is also more costly to set up than impact printing. In this method, ink is sprayed onto a bar with a series of holes determined by a magnetic tape or disk. Inkjet printing is used mainly for mailing-address labels and letters. It is well adapted for long runs and extensive personalization, and can accommodate varied typefaces.

Laser Printing—Laser printing is more versatile and considerably faster than the personalization methods that came before it. It allows for personalization in various parts of a direct mail package—order forms, letters, brochures, and action devices all may be personalized using laser printing. This electromagnetic process allows a computer to cue charged particles as to where they should adhere, thereby producing the printed message. Laser printing allows for considerable typeface variety, including capabilities for a typeface that looks handwritten.

Who Will Do Your Personalization?

Some firms that do extensive personalization may have their own dedicated impact, inkjet, or laser printing capabilities if they use them continually—on customer service or continuity communications, for example. Today's sophisticated copiers and printers may allow for effective in-house personalization as well. Many companies, however, will seek an outside source for completion of their personalization work, be it a computer service bureau, printer, or full-service lettershop.

To select the best vendor for your job, first decide which method of personalization you prefer. Then, in dealing with prospective vendors, compare not only their prices—but also their time frames for completion of the work. A careful look at the vendor's equipment list will also help you perform a "reality check" on the firm's capabilities for quick-turnaround projects.

Variable Data Printing

Considering today's technology, the individually addressed letter and response vehicles described above are just rudimentary examples of personalization. Personalization has taken on a whole new dimension, made possible by the application of digital technology. Variable Data Printing makes it possible to incorporate relevant personal information in the printed piece. Each piece is dynamically printed—in other words, the printer must regenerate the image for every page—so every page can be different. According to Deb Scott, "Insurance companies were among the first to use data on age to generate specific rate information for the individual recipient. Automobile manufacturers took the concept further in responding to customer inquiries; in addition to pricing the options requested by the car buyer, the vehicle itself is pictured with the customized features and color combinations quoted."

The ability to customize the products pictured as well as the text in a direct marketing piece opens possibilities limited only by the creative team's imagination. As Deb Scott reports, a remarkable retail application of variable data printing took bridal registry data and used it in a mailing to the bride and groom months after their wedding. Scott explains, "The piece pictured items the couple had wanted and *didn't* receive. The concept also enabled testing multiple variables, such as format and featuring other merchandise. In one ingenious test arm that included other merchandise, the registry items were given a sale price and the whole piece was actually non-personalized to compare results when an offer was addressed to 'Dear Resident!'"

Exhibit 20.2. Toyota Postcards

These postcards are customized "on the fly" for Toyota prospects using variable data printing. They show the exact vehicle each prospect "built" online and offer incentives based on that prospect's demographics and lifestyle. They are promptly generated and mailed after a prospect's visit to the Toyota Web site.

Reprinted with permission of DME.

Exhibit 20.3. Snackinar Web Site

Xerox 1:1 Snackinar Personalized Web Site and Registration Page

Welcome Tanya Smith and
TransUnion to your
Xerox 1:1 Snackinar registration site.

Enter

If the personal information above is incorrect, please click here to register.

This site is best viewed with Microsoft Internet Explorer 6.0 or Netscape Navigator 7.0

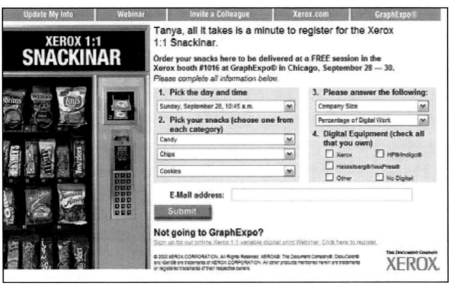

Prospects for the Xerox "Snackinar" are invited to visit their own unique URL where they are greeted with a personalized message and the opportunity to select their favorite snacks to receive at the event. While picking their choice of candy, chips, and cookies, they are also asked several database-building questions.

Reprinted with permission of Roberts Communications, Inc.

Exhibit 20.4. Snackinar Flow Chart

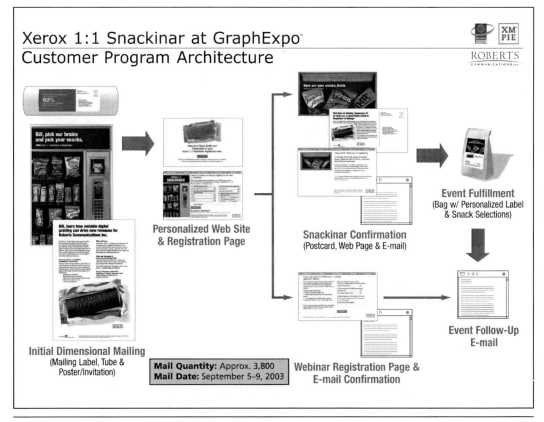

This flow chart shows how the integrated campaign for the Xerox Snackinar incorporated variable data printing techniques for direct mail, along with the Web, e-mail, and a face-to-face event.

Reprinted with permission of Roberts Communications, Inc.

Integrated Campaigns Utilizing Variable Data Printing

In the business-to-business realm, variable data printing can be used to provide highly personal and customized integrated promotions to high-potential customers and prospects. Using solutions from Xerox and XMPie and the expertise of Roberts Communications, for example, a promotion for a face-to-face seminar combines pinpoint customization with a whimsical twist. The campaign's components include the following:

1. Prospects for the seminar are mailed a personalized invitation that identifies the event as a "Snackinar." The piece shows a vending machine offering various snacks. Recipients are asked to visit a specific URL to sign up for the seminar and indicate their choice of three snacks they would like to be given when they arrive at the seminar—one each from three sets of snacks.

2. Upon arrival at the URL, the prospect finds that it is individually customized

Exhibit 20.5. Snackinar Ad

Reprinted with permission of Roberts Communications, Inc.

and greets them by name. The first questions they are asked have to do with their three "snacks of choice" for the seminar. These fun questions then lead the prospect into some database-building questions—a very clever way to prime the prospect into an "information-sharing mood."

3. Once the prospect has entered the "snacks of choice," the Web site immediately generates a visual of a vending machine with these three specific snacks peeking out of the serving tray at the bottom.

4. Using variable printing, a confirmation piece is created that carries that same image. The recipient receives a second customized mailing with details about "Snackinar" time and place, as well as the visual of the snacks they will receive upon arrival.

Enhance Your Understanding: Effective Personalization

When personalization technology first came on the scene, many creative people felt compelled to use it as often as possible. As a result consumers received letters referencing their names, addresses, buying habits, the state or town they lived in, and much more. At first, consumers may have been impressed by these seemingly "personal" communications, but the novelty wore off quickly. Today personalization must be used with more discretion, and a healthy respect for the recipient's concerns about privacy. Gather a stack of direct mail packages and catalogs and note how personalization is used in each. Does it provide convenience for the customer—an order form with the recipient's address already printed on it, for example? Does it build rapport, or seem overly intrusive in its disclosure of what the company knows about the customer? Does the personalization seem a natural and expected use, or overkill? Using the "Snackinar" example and other variable data printing concepts discussed at the end of this chapter, can you think of additional ways to use personalization effectively in multichannel marketing, for relationship building and/or selling?

Creators of the "Snackinar" report excellent response rates for this integrated campaign—making it an inspirational idea starter for marketers who want to maximize the strategic opportunities presented by variable data printing.

Print Production Planning/ Working With Suppliers

Considering that most production managers coordinate at least two or three mailings at once, and at the same time may be working on print ads, collateral materials, and the like, the importance of communication and careful scheduling is obvious. Indeed, producing direct mail is an art akin to juggling: you must keep several balls in the air at once. René Cudahy, a former Senior Vice-President at the integrated marketing agency DraftFCB, prefers a comparison to air traffic control—coordinating the actions of various vendors to keep each aspect of the job moving smoothly without "crashes" or suppliers left "circling the airport."

A day's work on a single mailing might require monitoring the arrival of lists at the service bureau, ordering outer envelopes, finalizing copy, choosing a brochure type style and format, and supervising photography. This chapter will explain how buyers of direct mail services can work best with the various suppliers who will bring their ideas to life. It will also discuss the best ways to schedule mailings, as well as the importance of a detailed production time line.

Working with Direct Mail Suppliers

All too often, direct marketing creative people wait until their ideas are cast in concrete before involving the vendors who will provide printing and production services to complete a job. It is a much better policy to invite vendor participation from the earliest stages of creative planning. Interaction among copywriter, graphic designer, production manager, and vendors will ensure the most cost-effective creative solution to the problem at hand. In addition, vendors with state-of-the-art formats and processes to share may provide ideas that increase the number of creative options to consider.

The help of knowledgeable vendors can be especially crucial if you are new to the production process—and therefore vulnerable to mistakes that may cost time, quality, and money. Many fledgling direct and interactive marketers cleverly seek out a group of dependable, experienced suppliers to rely on until they learn enough about production to proceed on their own.

Direct mail is a very complex medium for production. Lists of names must be rented from outside sources, or selected from house files. The lists must be prepared for mailing—a process that may involve a complex merge/purge, preparation for bar coding, zip code sequencing, carrier route presort and other postal presorts, and production of labels or electronic files for personalization. The preparation of pieces for mailing includes typography; art and photography; preparation of artwork for printing; paper selection and purchase; and printing. Lettershop services might include personalization as well as insertion—or personalization might take place "in line" as pieces are printed and assembled.

In some cases, each of these functions is completed by a different organization—each with its own strengths and weaknesses. The more "cooks in the broth," the more opportunities there are for vendors to point the finger in blame at others along the production line. But when vendors are included as part of a team—invited to attend everything from the initial brainstorming session to the final evaluation meeting—the chances increase for smooth and harmonious transfers from one production stage to another.

Considerations in Selecting Vendors

There are several important factors to consider in selecting vendors for direct mail applications. These include price, service, flexibility, creativity, quality, suitability, and timeliness.

Price. Price is an important consideration in any direct mail venture. The lower the cost per thousand of your package, the lower your break-even figure will be. But selecting the lowest bidder without evaluating other factors can be a mistake.

Make sure that each bidder has quoted the job using precisely the same specifications. Then compare each bidder's qualifications using the other criteria listed here. You may be better off using a supplier whose price is a bit higher, but who can provide better service, more creative ideas, or more timely delivery. Another hint: when you ask for prices, don't stop with a quotation on your original quantity for mailing. Also have each vendor bid on your projected roll-out quantities. A small vendor may be able to deliver a bargain price on a test quantity of 100,000, but may be unable to compete on roll-outs of a million or more. A large vendor whose test-quantity price seems high may be much more cost-efficient for the roll-out. In that case, you might want to negotiate with the larger vendor for a better price on the test quantity. Or consider switching vendors between test and roll-out—although this can be a dangerous proposition fraught with potential problems in the transition.

Jerry Kaup, President of the e-mail ad agency in Evanston, Illinois, suggests using quote sheets as a means of soliciting cost-saving advice from printers. He advocates including a line to the effect, "Please make any suggestions and/or possible substitutions that could cut costs but not materially affect the appearance of this job." He reports that suppliers usually come back with some helpful responses.

Service. A good vendor is available to answer any questions and to hold your hand throughout the production process. In addition to these obvious qualifications, the direct mail purchaser will want to look for subtle signs to select the right vendor for the job. Does the vendor have a thorough understanding of your business and its particular challenges? Do you feel mutual trust with the vendor? Does the vendor speak in layman's terms to you, or is your head spinning with technical language the vendor seems to think will impress you?

If you believe that a particular vendor will fit in well with your way of doing business, you can facilitate the service function by helping the vendor to understand your company and your needs. Allow the vendor to see the big picture. Take him or her on a company tour, provide examples of past successes and failures, introduce the vendor to all major decision-makers whose opinions will impact production decisions. A good vendor will relish this opportunity to gain knowledge that will help him or her serve you better. If a vendor seems too busy to soak up this vital background information, look elsewhere for the service you need.

Flexibility. Some production houses, printers, and lettershops are so tightly booked that they will schedule your job to begin at a particular hour of a particular day. If you miss that date for any reason, you may be bumped back days or even weeks in the schedule. Other vendors are more flexible—able to juggle their schedules and work your job in even if your production timetable falls behind. Still other firms can accommodate your late job—but only if you are willing to pay overtime costs for night, weekend, and holiday work.

Discuss scheduling with your vendors as soon as you become serious about using their services. Ask them what will happen if your job arrives an hour . . . a day . . . two days late or even later at their shop. Hold them to the promises they make. And a word to the wise: to avoid problems, set a production timetable that allows for a margin of error. There is nothing more unfair than to present a lettershop with a large job that is supposed to be in the mail "tomorrow" when they were expecting materials in time to allow a full week for insertion, labeling, and mailing.

Creativity. Some direct and interactive marketers don't allow their vendors to be creative. Instead, they present them with a set of very rigid specifications—right down to the weight and finish of the paper stock, or the exact positioning for personalization. Some vendors are perfectly content to function as order takers, and would not have many creative suggestions even if they were invited to provide them. On the other hand, the best vendors offer their ideas whether they are solicited or not, suggesting everything from formats and printing press configurations to ways of streamlining the preparation of artwork. Look for vendors who are full of ideas designed to save you money and time, or to add an extra flourish to the package you are designing. Their enthusiasm adds to the creative environment much more than a vendor who is strictly interested in writing down nuts and bolts like quantity, number of inserts, and mail date. For your part, be sure to ask your vendors' advice about the creative challenges you face: there may be an easy solution that can be accomplished during the process of production, printing, or lettershop activities.

Quality. Measurements of quality in direct mail must always consider the objectives of the printed piece. Some simple pieces selling items that do not require color photography may be appropriately printed on plain offset paper, utilizing stock envelopes overprinted with one-color type. Even so, there are good one-color printing jobs and poor ones. Talk to your vendor about your objectives for quality in two regards. First, discuss your needs in terms of color fidelity, quality of paper stock, uniqueness of format, extent of personalization, and so on. Then discuss quality control in relation to the production of the job itself. Look at your vendors' samples of previous jobs done in your price and quality range. How crisp is the type? How clean is the printing? Are there "hickeys" and other imperfections to mar the appearance of the job? A good vendor will understand your parameters of quality and not insist that every job be a jumbo spectacular extravaganza. At the same time, a good vendor will be just as vigilant about the quality control of a two-color, two-fold brochure on offset paper as he or she is about a glossy, four-color mailing with 12 inserts.

Suitability. When a new vendor comes to call, find out all you can about the company's suitability for your needs. Ask for an equipment list, and find out how much capacity the vendor has available for you. A lettershop may list 10 six-station inserting machines, for example, but neglect to tell you that half of them are reserved much of the time for a regular client. Ask the vendor about his or her experience with firms in your business. Find out if this particular sales rep has experience with your type of business—perhaps the company has another rep who would be better suited to consult with you. Ask for references from firms of comparable size and sophistication, and check them carefully. Find out about the stability of the vendor: does his or her firm pay their bills on time? There are few things more frustrating than learning that your printer or lettershop has gone bankrupt and shut its doors—with your job half done and inaccessible.

It is also important to find out if the vendor ever does subcontracting, and under what circumstances. Ask if you will be informed when a job requires subcontracting, and who will take responsibility for problems that may arise. Ask the vendor what his or her firm's invoices are like. Do the invoices conform to the language used on quotations? Some firms' invoices are so complex that this factor alone is enough to lose them business to companies with "user-friendly" invoices. What about up-charges? Will you be alerted in advance if additional costs are incurred? Explain to your vendors in no uncertain terms that additional charges should be discussed as soon as they become necessary. You should not accept unexplained up-charges that appear for the first time on an invoice. Ask the vendor what his or her firm's payment terms are: they may vary considerably. Some companies expect money up front from new customers, while others routinely extend Net 30 Day terms. You may be asked to submit references for a credit check: find out if this will be necessary and how long the credit check may take.

Timeliness. Part of every estimate or quote should include a statement of the time necessary to complete the job. Once again, some vendors are more flexible on time than others. Ask the vendor if the "two weeks" figure holds only if you deliver materials on a specifically scheduled date. How long would it take to complete the job if it came into the vendor's shop unannounced? What if time were of the essence and you were willing to pay for overtime and weekend work—how short could the time frame then become? The answers to these questions will help you determine how helpful this vendor will be when you are in a time crunch, or when rush jobs come up unexpectedly.

Your Responsibilities as a Buyer

Vendors have expectations for a good working relationship, just as direct mail buyers do. There are several things that you can do to ensure that you will be a preferred customer with the vendors of your choice. These include paying fairly and on time, creating a team atmosphere, limiting the number of vendors you use, giving vendors one source for authoritative information, showing appreciation for a job well done, and fostering good communication.

Payment Terms. In most cases, sales representatives are not paid commission on the jobs they expedite for you until your firm pays its bills. That means that unless you make sure your bills are paid according to agreed-upon terms, you may be compromising your sales rep's livelihood. It only stands to reason, then, that customers who pay on time will receive preferred treatment from vendors. If your vendor asks for payment terms that are more stringent than you are used to—say, Net 10 Days instead of Net 30 Days—the time to discuss other arrangements is up front rather than after the job has been billed. As a buyer of services, make it your business to know your firm's policy on paying bills. You may have to become an advocate for your best vendors to ensure that they are paid on time. If you abdicate this responsibility, you risk diluting your vendors' loyalty to you.

Another point about payments: some buyers pride themselves on squeezing the last dime out of their vendors on every single job. All vendors expect that there will be times when they need to "sharpen their pencils," even to the point of eliminating profit for their firms and commissions for themselves. But if this unprofitable situation is the case every time they deal with you, the vendor will soon move on to more fertile fields. The moral: expect your vendors to make a fair profit from your business, and you will encourage their loyalty.

Team Atmosphere. It will be in your best interest to foster a team atmosphere among your vendors and your co-workers. In addition, it may take some of the burden away from you if reps from graphic design houses, list brokerages, service bureaus, printers, and lettershops can communicate among themselves without having to go through you with every question. Cultivate vendors that you can trust, and share with them the information they need to do their jobs well. If it seems to you that a vendor is probing for proprietary information, ask why he or she needs to know. There may be a good reason. For instance, list brokers cannot do the best possible job for you without knowing what lists have worked in the past. Printers may ask when you expect to roll out with a mailing so that they may pencil it into their schedules. On the other hand, if you ever feel that your sales rep is acting as a spy, discuss it with him or her, and consider dropping the vendor. An atmosphere of mutual trust is essential for smooth direct mail production.

Limit Your Vendors. Having only one vendor for each type of application can be a mistake, but having too many vendors can be just as grave an error. Your best bet is to cultivate a manageable group of excellent vendors. Each vendor should receive enough business to make you an important client, but not so much that he or she becomes complacent or considers your account a monopoly. When impressive new vendors come onto the scene, invite them to bid competitively with your existing roster of vendors. Don't make the mistake of "jumping ship" for an untried vendor whose quote is a few cents lower on a per-thousand basis. Try new vendors cautiously, and consider other factors such as their service, timeliness, and quality before adding them to your active roster of suppliers.

Provide One Central Information Source. Vendors need one final authority who gives them their orders and deals with their concerns—not a roomful of people providing conflicting ideas with no clarification. Be sure that you—or someone in your firm—has both the responsibility and the authority to serve as the vendors' central source of information.

Show Appreciation for a Job Well Done. Buyers often assume that vendors should get all their gratification from the money they earn. Some buyers treat vendors as a Santa Claus for grown-ups—they expect the vendors to give and give without ever receiving anything in return. This may extend beyond professional service: indeed, some direct mail buyers expect lavish lunches, baseball tickets, and other "freebies" from their vendors at regular intervals. One production manager enlisted his sales representatives to show up one Saturday morning to sod his front lawn! Vendors expect to render professional service—and to pick up the tab for occasional lunches—but they all too seldom receive a simple thank-you when they go out of their way to do an exceptional job.

Smart buyers will provide praise where it is due—just as readily as they complain when there is a problem. Some firms go so far as to arrange vendor recognition parties where they thank their best suppliers for a job well done. Other buyers are thoughtful enough to write detailed letters of thanks when a sales representative provides exceptional service. These letters may become valuable testimonials that are greatly appreciated by the vendor—and help to build loyalty in the process.

Foster Good Communication. Just as you quiz prospective vendors on their records for price, service, capacity, and other factors, you should be willing to let your sales representative know what is important to your firm. Will you be buying primarily on the basis of price, or is top-notch quality the goal? Does your firm run on a predictable timetable, or should the vendor expect late materials and last-minute changes? Spend time going over previous jobs with new vendors, telling them about the challenges you have faced, and inviting them to provide ideas for improvements. After a vendor completes a job, take time to sit down and go over the finished product. Discuss how it could be improved next time around—and how your working relationship could be enhanced.

When to Let an Advertising Agency Do Your Production

A quick read through this section should convince most readers that direct mail production is a complex process. In most instances, firms that produce mailing quantities in the millions each year will reap savings of both time and money by developing their own in-house production departments to expedite this work. On the other hand, there are several reasons why you may prefer to allow an advertising agency to handle your production chores.

1. *If your mailings are small or infrequent*, you will not have much opportunity to develop clout with vendors. You may be much better off dealing with an agency or production firm that has cultivated the relationships necessary to carry out your job smoothly and on time.
2. *If you don't have trained personnel on staff*, it will be false economy to try to save an agency mark-up by keeping the work in house. People who are untrained in production can innocently make mistakes that cost you huge amounts of time and money. Until you can recruit a top-notch production staff, you will be safer using outside services for expediting.
3. *If price is not your number-one object*, you can save yourself and your staff the hassles of production by paying an agency or production firm on either a fee basis or a mark-up of services (traditionally 17.65 percent).

Scheduling and Critical Dates

Success in direct and interactive marketing has much to do with proper timing. Seasonal and competitive factors are important, as is the phasing of tests and roll-outs within your own program. Sometimes the optimum promotional schedule is fairly straightforward, as in the case of a holiday-theme product or an item tied to the Summer Olympics or the World Series. And even when there is no obvious "season" for your product or service, the dynamics of the marketplace may make it better for you to mail or promote during some weeks or months than during others.

General rules of thumb for the best and worst direct mail months are a helpful starting point for your efforts. The fall season is considered "prime time" for many direct mailers for at least two reasons. First, people head indoors as the weather cools and darkness descends earlier in the evening. They have more time for perusal of direct mail pieces and catalogs than they did in the active summer months. Second, with the holidays on the way, individuals seek gifts for friends and relatives, and home decor items for entertaining. Also good for direct mail response are the early months of the year: January through March. With the holidays over, cold weather, and early darkness, there is more time and attention available for home shopping. Keep in mind, however, that most all direct mailers are aware of this seasonality factor and mail accordingly. Clutter can be a problem during these prime periods when proven mail order buyers often receive 10 to 20 pieces of direct mail and catalogs in a single day.

Of course, these rules of thumb must be tempered with the seasonality of your own product or service. Conventional wisdom says that late spring and summer are less than optimum times to mail. But if your offer is for merchandise that is especially appealing in June—a sale on swimsuits and lightweight summer shirts, for instance—June might be a fine month for you. If you are entering the test phase of a campaign, experts agree that you should run your first test in the strongest season for your product. Then factor seasonality into your forecasts for future mailings you may choose to make in less-than-optimum time periods.

As for business and industrial mailings, factors like the year-end holidays and other vacation periods have some effect on marketing schedules. However, the seasonality factor here depends mostly on the industry in question. School supplies sold to school districts have a demand based on the school calendar. And if you are mailing to landscapers, your prime time will differ dramatically from that of snowmobile parts suppliers. But if your seasonality factor isn't so obvious, some testing to determine what months spark better lead and sales responses with the same offer could provide you with profit-building information—or at least some explanation of what may be disturbing slides in response from time to time.

If you are planning to advertise in magazines and newspapers, competitive factors should be taken into consideration. Non-seasonal propositions do best when not pitted against heavy ad schedules that ordinarily exist at holiday time. In addition, advertising readership is down in the summer, or at least attention levels suffer at this time, because many people are on vacation. So the best times for direct response space advertising are generally January through the beginning of spring, and Labor Day through Thanksgiving.

If you are selling summer products, of course, you mustn't take this warning too seriously. You can begin testing in the early spring to determine your own response curve by month or week. And if your product is Christmas-related, you may safely promote up until the time when you cannot promise delivery by Christmas (or—and perhaps more importantly—until the time when your consumer no longer believes you can deliver, even if you know you can). This time frame has widened considerably with today's low-cost shipments via FedEx and other express services.

The Critical-Date Schedule

The first step in establishing a schedule for any direct response medium is to determine the optimum date for the message to reach the prospect. In direct mail, for instance, it is not enough to schedule only up to the date your message is mailed. If you are doing a standard mailing, it may take ten days or more before all of your prospects receive the piece you've mailed. And in space advertising, don't take the cover date of the publication as a given for its arrival at the prospect's door: check out the delivery date specifically, and then choose the proper issue for the impact you seek. Then work back from the optimum delivery date to determine a schedule that will accomplish your goal. You may still be able to make a date that seems uncomfortably close, but only with a firm schedule and much vigilance. Following are some of the checklist factors in critical-date schedules for direct mail and space advertising.

Direct Mail. There are as many direct mail critical date schedules as there are firms in the business, and very little agreement about how long it takes to get certain things done. Where there are many parties involved and many levels of approval, a direct mail program may require a six-month schedule. On the other hand, firms whose approval processes are swift and whose suppliers are accommodating may be able to take a mailing campaign from the concept stage to the prospect's hands in a matter of a few weeks.

Naturally, each link in the chain of such an operation considers his or her timing to be paramount. A prototype schedule from a printer, for example, allows a month for printing but only three days for copywriting. You can imagine that the writer's optimum schedule would be quite different. We will therefore list the factors important in a mail-campaign schedule, in the basic order in which they are done. You can adjust these as needed to determine a workable schedule for your own campaign. In addition, the TargetCom Inc. form shown in Exhibit 21.1 provides one Chicago direct marketing agency's step-by-step production time lines.

Basic Critical Date Factors for Direct Mail

1. Approve marketing plan.
2. Create rough layouts and copy (this is often necessary for list owners to approve rentals to you).
3. Select and order lists, plus any overlays or other enhancements (obtaining the lists for a campaign may take several weeks, and a merge/purge may take a week or longer to complete).
4. Obtain price quotes for production work, printing, lettershop work, and other necessary services; award jobs to vendors; make vendors aware of time schedules so they can make available the proper amount of time for your job.
5. Approve rough layouts and copy, and proceed to comprehensive layouts and final copy.
6. Order envelopes; in most cases manufactured envelopes take longer to produce than other printed materials (three weeks or more).
7. Arrange for photography and have product shots and other necessary photography completed.
8. Approve final layouts and copy and proceed to finalizing artwork for printing.
9. Receive lists from broker and expedite merge/purge operation so that it can be completed in time for lettershop work.
10. Approve final art, copy, and color.
11. Send final art to printer with appropriate back-up explanations and mock-up.
12. Approve proofs from printer(s).
13. Obtain final counts by version from merge/purge data before printing commences.
14. Supervise press approvals at printer(s).
15. Send mailing instructions to lettershop, including list of all materials that will be delivered there.
16. Expedite folding and binding of printed pieces.
17. Coordinate arrival of envelopes, printed pieces, and labels or electronic files (product of list merge/purge operation) at lettershop.
18. Expedite lettershop work (addressing, materials insertion, and mailing).
19. Ascertain exact mail date (national penetration will be approximately ten days later for standard mail).

Once you have developed a critical date schedule that works for you, it is an excellent idea to set up a computer program that plugs in the optimum dates, based on the drop date for mailing. In addition, your favorite software program can help you develop a master calendar that helps keep track of all the projects you have going, all on one spread sheet or bulletin board.

Exhibit 21.1. TargetCom Direct Mail Program Development Checklist

Job Number _____   Name of Project _____

Client   _____   Date _____

Initiate	Step	Days req'd.	Task	Responsibility
	1.	2–3	Accept client input: Get every available answer to create Input Questionnaire.	AE
	2.	Included	Provide input; via strategy or input document (include postal class). Put everything in writing. Provide creative suggestions from client at this time. Also make sure you have a job number. Get logos and graphic standards from new client.	AE
	3.	1	Schedule project: Must be completed. Use schedule template, making sure that any variations from the standard timelines are made with the agreement of all team members. Account person can fill out the schedule, as long as creative department looks at it too. Do not proceed without completed schedule.	AE
	4.	1	Estimate concepts: Do this before work begins, preferably during the input session.	AD/AE
	5.	Included	Develop Creative Work Plan: Must be completed. A work plan should be done on all projects and reviewed with acct. services.	CW/AE
	6.	1	Create concepts: Must show to CD.	CW/AE
	7.	1	Create half-sized roughs: Formats, specs and production input.	AD/CW
	8.	1	Present internal roughs; and review against Creative Work Plan.	AD/CW
	9.	2	Create comps . . . B&W, spell check.	AD
	10.	1	Develop prelim, space together. Do not define window pos. at this step.	AD/PM
	11.	Included	Write creative rationale.	CW
	12.	2	Route comps, space, creative rationale, and roughs AAE Routes File Folder. All check for consistency & proof.	Team
	13.	Included	Archive concepts that are not chosen, naming them accurately.	AD
	14.	2	Create color mock-ups . . . specs, creative rationale to client, too.	AD
	15.	1–2	Write copy: As soon as comp is approved. Spell check and route to CD and AE before turning over to the AD. If appropriate to audience, reduce grade reading level	CW
	16.	2–5	Commission photography, order stock, or hand-out illustration, if applicable.	AD

Exhibit 21.1. (Continued)

Initiate	Step	Days req'd.	Task	Responsibility
	17.	2	Create Maclines.	AE
	18.	1	Update preliminary specs. Determine window size and position.	AD/PM
	19.	1	Route Maclines and updated specs. Route with original marked-up comps. AD, PM & AE to measure Maclines against specs, check postage against input document.	AAE. AD, PM, AE
	20.	1	Proof every element.	AD, PM, & AE
	21.	1–?	Submit Maclines for approval.	AE
	22.	1	Revise Maclines. If rewriting is involved, consult Copywriter.	AD/CW
	23.	Included	Route revised Maclines. Check the entire package. Not just the changes.	AAE
	24.	1	Secure final client approval. Get a copy with signature; make no further changes.	AE
	25.	1	Prepare production files:	
			A. First, print a B&W laser print with everything, including FPO visuals and laser-fill fonts in place.	AD
			B. Fill out final spec sheet & stamp FINAL.	AD/PM
			C. After approval, mark all laser-fill and mark FPOs.	AD
			D. Print a color version with all laser-fill in place.	AD
			E. Print separations, each plate, in B&W (no fill) and suppress FPOs in file.	AD
			F. Make folding dummy w/personalization, trimmed to size, with another B&W or (if requested) color print out.	AD
			G. Send final art to FTP site.	AD
	26.	1–2	Send PDFs to client or production with summary, folding Mock-up w/ personalization, actual size laser with crops and info marked FPO, and color chips for PMS colors.	AD/PM/AE
	27.	1	Final art sent to FTP site for archive. Gather all documents and art from freelancers.	AD

AD = Art Director   AE = Account Executive   AAE = Assistant Account Executive
CD = Creative Director   CW = Copywriter   PM = Production Manager
FPO = For Position Only   FTP = File Transfer Protocol

The Chicago direct marketing agency TargetCom Inc. uses this comprehensive checklist as a guide to step-by-step program development and implementation. It provides estimates of how long each task will take and which job title has responsibility for each step.

Reprinted by permission of TargetCom Inc.

Space Advertising

The critical date schedule for a space advertising campaign is simpler than for a direct mail campaign in that there is no involvement with printers, lettershops, or lists. However, a space advertising campaign has the added factor of having to meet the publication's closing dates for space reservations and materials. These dates vary considerably. Check the consumer or business Standard Rate & Data Service (SRDS) publications for magazines to determine these dates for publications in which you wish to place ads. There you will also find the specifications for the types of artwork each publication needs, so that you can direct your production people accordingly. For newspaper ads, SRDS has an online newspaper rate and data publication that provides the same helpful information.

The Importance of Vendor/Client Communications in Successful Direct Mail Production

by Deborah R. Scott, Former President, Copy Options, Inc.

From the initial conception of a mailing piece to the intact, on-time delivery to the recipients, there are a myriad of overlapping considerations. Clients are best served when creative, production, and post-production personnel work together from the beginning. Their collaboration and cooperation are key to a successful direct marketing campaign. Post-press finishing is a telling example of how those from multiple firms have overlapping interests: (1) the creative staff that conceives the piece, (2) the post-press personnel that must actually execute the binding and finishing, and (3) the lettershop or distribution service that must get the piece addressed and delivered. When those three disciplines are not in harmony, the test or roll-out as well as the campaign's profitability can be compromised. Picture this. Faced with a surprise cross-grain finishing operation, the bindery's waste factor escalates. Result: they're short. Then the lettershop finds the aspect ratio (width vs. height) isn't within U.S. Postal Services guidelines, so the mailing must drop at a higher postage rate. By contrast, when every step in the continuum is aware of the others and their constraints, the project moves smoothly to completion . . . on time and within budget for the client.

Enhance Your Understanding: New Vendors/New Ideas

No matter how busy you become in your position at an agency or company, you owe it to yourself and your employer to stay open to new applications and ideas. One way to do this is to allot time regularly for informational visits with new vendors. You'll find out about emerging technology, new formats, ways to save money, and what others in your industry are doing. Even when you feel isolated and "chained to your desk," such visits can provide you with fresh perspectives and potential breakthroughs. In addition, today there are many vendor webinars online, sponsored by companies and trade organizations. You can learn about new techniques, applications, and case histories in just a half-hour or hour spent "attending" a seminar on your computer.

Lists, Service Bureaus, the Post Office, and Lettershops

The more the creative person knows and understands about list selection, merge/purge and mailing, the more valuable he or she can be to the marketing team at large. Thus while for most creative people, their personal responsibility for a direct mail package ends when they proof their copy on final art or approve color on a press check, learning more about the nuts and bolts of production is a wise investment of time.

This chapter will explain the basics of list selection and list brokerage; list maintenance, merge/purge, and other functions of a computer service bureau; postal regulations and relations with the post office; and lettershop functions.

List Selection

No matter how excellent your product and how outstanding your offer and creative execution, your direct mail package is destined to fail if it is sent to the wrong list of new prospects. In recent years, marketers have taken full advantage of online resources and sophisticated software to hone in on the best target markets, lists, and list segments for their offers. There are four basic types of outside lists a direct mailer may use, rent, or buy. These are the firm's own customer lists, lists of other proven mail-order buyers, compiled lists, and enhanced databases.

Customer Lists—Basis for the In-House Database

Sometimes called "house lists," these files belong to the firm because they contain names and addresses of individuals who have purchased merchandise or services in the past. Customer names are the most responsive of all because these individuals have established a relationship with the firm. In the best case, a franchise has been established: these individuals want or need the company's goods or services, they are satisfied with prices and payment terms offered, and they know and trust the company.

Many marketers also keep lists of inquiries and referrals. The prospects on these lists are those who have not yet purchased a product or service. They have expressed interest through a mail, phone, fax, or e-mail response; have filled out a form online; or have been referred to the firm by an active customer. These names may prove to be more responsive than names rented from other firms, but they are generally less responsive than customer lists. Customer lists form the basis for the in-house database discussed in detail in Chapter 4. These house lists have to be maintained and cleaned on a regular basis to ensure they maintain their deliverability. Specifically, according to David Fant, President of Market Mapping Plus in Grand Rapids, MI, "Processing of a house list for in-house mailings needs to be done every 95 days to maintain USPS Automation Discount Rates."

Mail-Order/Direct Response Buyers

Lists of proven mail-order or direct response buyers are next on the hierarchy, after customer lists and inquiries/referrals. The old printed version of the Standard Rate and Data Service (SRDS) book of lists available for rental was the size of a metropolitan telephone book, attesting to the variety of mail responsive lists that are available. This information is now available online in the form of the Direct Marketing List Source. If you do not have access to SRDS information, check online—some list brokerage and list management firms allow you to preview information about the mail-responsive and e-mail responsive lists that they offer for rental, on their Web sites. See Exhibit 22.1 for an example of an online list data card. Trade publications such as those listed in Appendix A often feature ads for list brokerage and management firms you can visit online.

Firms may choose to rent the names of their buyers or inquiries for one-time use at a "per thousand" fee. When you rent such lists, you may test an "nth name" random sample of as few as 5,000 names initially, and then rent larger quantities from the list if the original test proves successful. Rental fees generally range from $70 to $100 per thousand and up, depending upon demand for the list, and the "list selects" you make. According to David Fant, "Some high-quality lists such as *Wall Street Journal* subscribers can start at around $135 per thousand with select charges added on top of the base price. When purchasing a list you are in reality renting the list's use. The list owner retains the rights to the names and addresses and typically will have you sign a rental agreement stating that you are forbidden from adding these names to your in-house database or prospect list." Many lists are offered with selections based on age, sex, income, presence of children, purchase history, geography, zip code, or other relevant factors. E-mail lists, telephone lists, and – increasingly – SMS text lists, often are available as well. David Fant adds, "You will be charged an output fee based on how you will take delivery of the names and addresses. This output fee can include e-mail delivery of a text file, disk, CD, FTP site download, or printed hard copy of the list on mailing labels."

The three classic criteria for list evaluation are recency, frequency, and monetary, known as RFM. In his FRAT model, the late direct marketing expert Robert Kestnbaum combined frequency, recency, and amount (monetary) with "type," for type of product or service purchased. Sophisticated software from firms like SPSS allow you to use mathematical models to quantify the impact of RFM or FRAT, and to predict future buying patterns of customers based on these measures. You should expect to pay more for recent, or "hotline" names—individuals who have purchased from the firm within the past three months or six months. Customers who buy often (frequency) are also especially attractive. The monetary criterion helps you zero in on customers who can afford your price range, be it $35 for a monogrammed turtleneck top or $600 for a fine-quality home music system. In addition to general direct responsiveness, a list's affinity for your type of product is very important, as Kestnbaum noted. For example, if you plan to market a line of limited-edition collector's plates, you might rent lists of individuals who buy collector's prints, jewelry, and home accessories by mail. However, you probably would not be successful in trying to rent lists of collector's plate buyers from other companies: they would turn down your rental request as being too competitive. Once you have built up your own list of collector's plate buyers, however, you might well be able to exchange names with some direct competitors.

Exhibit 22.1. Mailing List Finder

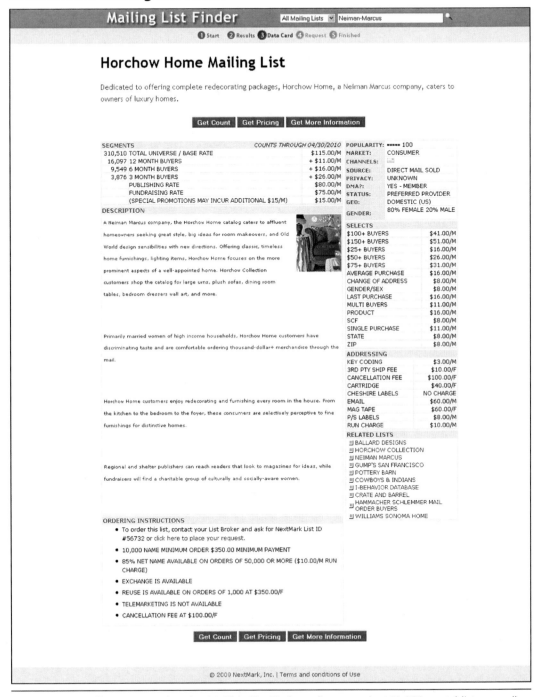

Nextmark.com offers a comprehensive Mailing List Finder online, covering 60,000 postal lists as well as e-mail lists, telephone lists and SMS texting lists as available. This is the page for the Horchow Home list.

Reprinted from www.nextmark.com.

Compiled Lists

Compiled lists are usually created from a database of information put together for purposes other than promotion. Examples might be membership lists, automobile or boat registrations, telephone directory lists, or businesses by North American Industry Classification System (NAICS) codes (formerly SIC codes). Such lists are considerably less desirable for most consumer direct mailers than are lists of proven mail-order, e-mail, or online buyers, since the names they contain are not necessarily direct responsive (only about half to two-thirds of all consumers are), and may not be qualified for your offer. Compiled lists may be used with success—particularly in business-to-business applications—if they are specific enough in content. For instance, a compiled list of college marketing professors is a worthwhile possibility for a firm selling marketing textbooks. Today, compiled business-to-business lists are available in convenient, affordable, and frequently updated online formats that allow the business marketer to play "what if" games with databases of more than 14 million firms. Then they can download names, addresses, and other information for use in mailings, e-mailings, or telephone marketing.

David Fant adds a note of caution about using compiled lists: "The quality of the list is determined by many factors. Unless you are fully aware of how the compiled list is built and how it handles duplicate entries, you can end up with many names and addresses that are either duplicated within the database itself, or that fall into an 'undeliverable' classification based on the USPS deliverability standards. A list broker can assist you in avoiding these and other pitfalls in building and selecting a mailing list."

Enhanced Databases

To refine and profile your house list or to identify the most likely segments of a compiled list, you may choose to use statistical techniques such as demographic and lifestyle overlays, predictive modeling, or regression analysis. These methods allow you to add demographics, psychographics, hobbies, and interests to your customer profiles, and to use powerful mathematical models to determine customers' likelihood of future actions. This may give you valuable ideas for cross-selling additional products and services. Techniques of this type may be too expensive to be cost-effective for small- and medium-sized firms, but for larger firms they can be invaluable in helping you gain a more robust profile of your best customers, determine what to offer them and when to offer it, and identify prospects most like them. David Fant comments: "In today's marketplace, many lists are being enhanced with lifestyle and interest information. If you want to use this type of select for your business, you don't need to do demographic or statistical analysis. Instead, simply select the lifestyle/interest enhancement you want for your business, and improve the performance of a compiled list while keeping the costs low. In addition, if you purchase a list with various demographic selects, be sure to key code each record, and when the orders come in, track who is responding. Thus you can build a mini-customer analysis for minimal additional cost."

Cooperative Databases

Because identifying fresh direct mail lists of prospects is so challenging in today's marketplace, many firms have opted to join the Abacus Cooperative, or other cooperative databases. In the case of Abacus, participating companies provide their mailing list data to Epsilon, the parent company of the Abacus Cooperative. Epsilon uses this data from multiple companies to enhance its extensive warehouse of purchasing information on both consumers and business buyers. This rich mine of data allows for sophisticated predictive modeling, which enables catalogers, retailers, consumer marketers, business-to-business marketers and non-profits that are members of the Cooperative to test lists of likely new prospects for mailings. According to Epsilon, Abacus is the world's largest cooperative database, including more than 8.6 billion consumer transactions and 4.8 billion business transactions.

List Brokerage

Some marketers choose to rent their lists directly from the owner or list manager, bypassing the function of list broker. But there are good reasons to retain the services of a knowledgeable list broker, especially if your list rental volume is substantial.

List brokers serve as advisors on list selection, and as expeditors for list rental arrangements and list delivery. The advice of a list broker customarily is free to prospective list renters. The broker is paid a commission (typically in the range of 10 to 20 percent) by the list owner whose lists are rented through the broker.

To establish a relationship with a list broker, the marketer needs to share information about the products and services being sold, present and projected volume, selling methods, and past list results. This requires a measure of trust on the part of the marketer, but the list broker's recommendations will only be as good as the background data he or she has received.

The list broker provides recommendations for rentals in the form of data cards (often presented via e-mail) carrying recent information on prospective lists. Data card information includes the list universe, average order size in dollars, and available "selects" by sex, geography, dollar amount, purchase type, and so on. The broker may also supply a rationale for each list: why it makes sense for your firm to test it for a given product or promotion. Brokers may also let you know what other firms are successfully using each list.

Smaller marketers, or those who mail infrequently, may bypass the list-brokerage function since brokers prefer to work with major mailers with frequent roll-out mailings in six- or seven-figure volume. If you fall into this group, you will find the SRDS publication on direct mail lists an invaluable source of information on lists and how to rent them. If you still believe you need the advice of a list broker, be prepared to pay him or her on an hourly or fee basis. David Fant encourages smaller mailers to consider this option before going it alone. As he says, " I make my living on small clients as do hundreds of other list brokers. It is very possible for the smaller mailer to seek out a broker who respects this type of client."

Computer Service Bureaus

Most direct marketers know the computer service bureau as a company that completes the merge/purge function. Although merge/purge is an important aspect of the service bureau's work, these firms may perform a number of other jobs for a direct marketing company, including address hygiene, postal discount processing, list maintenance, list analysis, and personalization. David Fant adds that many list brokers now have the ability to help you with customer and list analysis as well. He explains, "Since they will be assisting you with the selection of the best mailing lists, they may be a great resource to go to for customer analysis and targeting information."

In addition, the importance of proper list preparation should not be overlooked. According to the U.S. Postal Service, 17.8% of the mail has some type of error or major addressing deficiency. Missing address elements can reduce successful delivery between 50 and 60%. The cost associated with these undelivered mail pieces in a recent year was estimated at $1.8 billion and rising. In this context, here are the main preparatory steps you'll need to take for optimal mail delivery.

Merge/purge is a shorthand term representing the function of combining lists (merge) and removing duplicate names (purge). This avoids mailing multiple pieces to the same individual. Merge/purge can eliminate duplicate records within a given list as well as records that appear on more than one list. If mailings are small, or if they involve only a few lists that may not include many duplicates, the marketer may not deem it cost-effective to perform the merge/purge function. However, if mail volume is large, and if a number of lists are being tested, it becomes essential to eliminate duplicates.

When using merge/purge, it is not unusual for a mailer to eliminate 12 to 15 percent of the total names rented for a given promotion. At a mailing cost of $600 per thousand, you would save yourself up to $9,000 on each 100,000 names rented. In addition, you eliminate the prospect's aggravation at receiving two or more of the same mailing piece. David Fant suggests that you keep a close watch on the percentage of duplicates for other reasons. "The higher the duplication rate, the greater chance that the list being merge/purged will be effective since a large number of existing customers are appearing in the rented prospect list. The higher the duplication rate between your customer file and the rented file, the more the rented list looks just like your house list – and therefore should be highly responsive." Merge/purge instructions to the service bureau should include prioritization of lists. The most expensive lists should receive low priority. Less expensive lists should come next, and finally the highest priority should go to the house list—names the mailer already owns and for which no rental fee should be paid. In the merge/purge process, the computer scans high-priority names first. The computer credits each name and address to the list on which it first appears. If a name and address appears on two, three, four or more of the rented lists, the computer makes a note for its analysis report, but "purges" the output of those names. Thus the output for expensive, low-priority lists might be 80 percent or less of the input names. If the mailer or list broker has negotiated a "net down" or "net name" agreement, only the names actually mailed (within pre-agreed limits) will require a rental payment. David Fant takes a slightly different viewpoint. He advises,

> When doing a merge/purge using multiple rented files *do not* delete duplicates. Use the house list first and definitely delete current customers from the rented lists. However, when de-duping prospects from multiple rented lists, have your service bureau or lettershop create a "multi-hit" file. These are names and addresses that appear in more than one rented list. First, you have paid to use that name and address so if they appear in three different lists, you can mail them more than once. Second, these are the most *valuable* names in that they appear in multiple lists of prospective customers, which enhances the changes that they will be a highly responsive prospect. A multi-hit file can frequently double the response rate of a single-name file.

In addition to merge/purge, several other important processes involving address hygiene, postal discount processing and mail preparation may be performed at this time:

- The *CASS*™ certification process improves the accuracy of delivery point, ZIP + 4®, 5-digit ZIP™ and carrier route codes.
- The *FASTforward*® service updates addresses by identifying names and addresses for which current change-of-address orders are on file, so that mail pieces can be delivered directly to the new address rather than forwarded from the old address.

- The NCOALink® Product is a secure dataset of approximately 160 million permanent change-of-address records of individuals, families and businesses that have filed a change of address with the USPS with the past 48 months. The NCOALink service allows mailers to process mailing lists and update lists with the new addresses prior to mailing. There are two levels of NCOA service. Limited Service goes back through 18 months of registered moves and Full Service goes back 48 months. (Keep in mind that these are the movers who have actually registered their moves with the Postal Service.)
- *DMA's MPS Names* should be eliminated. These are individuals who have contacted the Direct Marketing Association Mail Preference Service (MPS) asking that they not be sent unsolicited direct mail offers. Using the MPS is required for DMA members and highly recommended for all.
- *Postal discount processing*—The net name output can be prepared to meet postal specifications and minimize your postage costs: in zip-code sequence, standard mail presort, carrier-route presort, etc. In addition, the output names can be presented in the form of labels to be affixed to envelopes or order cards, or electronically for use in various printed personalization techniques.
- *Key coding* of each name and address can be done according to the mailer's orders.
- *Intelligent Mail Barcoding* is another service being offered by the USPS. The Intelligent Mail Barcode notifies you when a mailing is inducted into the mail stream and allows for tracking of individual pieces as they travel through the postal network. This program can assist you in tracking your mailing, it helps you comply with postal regulations for move updates, and the barcode integrates address correction as well as other postal services into one very useful code.

List Maintenance

Good list maintenance helps ensure the cost effectiveness of mailing to a house list. It also increases the list's value as a rental property to other firms. As new buyer names come onto the file, a service bureau can be charged with the responsibility of recording information such as name, address, e-mail address, category (such as buyer, inquiry, referral), original order history (source, date, dollar amounts), and other variables. In addition, the service bureau can check for duplication against the current file, correct zip codes, standardize street addresses, and carrier-route code each name. There are services that will append missing e-mail addresses to lists, but these must be used carefully—it is wise to e-mail only those customers who have opted in for this form of communication. In addition, if you elect to rent your e-mail lists, those customer names need to be opted in for communications with other firms as well. When house list names are mailed or e-mailed, the service bureau can also be charged with updating promotion and order history.

David Fant laments that many companies try to do list maintenance on their own. He says, "Sadly, this is an area where someone is given the directive to enter new names and addresses into the database and given little or no supervision to see if the work is being done correctly. Thus many in-house databases are filled with duplicates and incorrect or incomplete addresses. This costs the company time and money by mailing materials to someone who doesn't exist, or who is incorrectly entered in the database. If you maintain your database in- house, look at the content of the database on a monthly basis and make sure you CASS™ certify and do an NCOA update every 95 days to ensure it will meet USPS deliverability standards. Duplicate entries, incomplete entries or entries that are typographically incorrect will increase waste and lower your deliverability rates and response.

List Analysis

At the discretion of the mailer, service bureaus can create a wide range of analysis reports that marketers may use to draw conclusions about rental lists—especially in comparison with their own house lists. For instance, *processing reports* profile each merge/purge, providing such information as gross input, percentage of customer names eliminated, percentage of duplicates eliminated, list prioritization, number of pander names eliminated, single versus multi-buyers, net output, percentage of internal duplicates, state-by-state totals, and other information. A *multi-buyer report* contains all records identified as duplications by a merge/purge. *Sales by state/sales by carrier route reports* let mailers find out which regions, states, and carrier routes perform best for certain products and offers. *Customer counts by sex, method of payment, average order size,* and many other variables can also be tracked. David Fant says that the importance of tracking cannot be overstated. He notes,

> By taking each list, including demographic segments and interests, and key coding them, you can find out who is responding to your offer. This information, when captured as a customer places an order or purchases a product or service, will allow you to refine future list needs and help improve your targeting. Look at the address area of a catalog you might have lying around. You'll notice a key code that tells the marketer exactly where your name and address came from. When you purchase from them, they ask for that code and instantly know the source of this new customer.

Personalization

Some service bureaus offer various personalization services in-house, using their own equipment. Using the service bureau to create personalized materials may save time if the firm's capacity is high enough for your application. It may also eliminate some of the expediting work necessary to transfer the merge/purge output to a printer. Mailers may prefer to have the service bureau stop short of this step, preparing the electronic list of names to be transferred to a printer or lettershop for completion.

Postal Regulations

The United States Postal Service (USPS) recognizes direct mail as a huge market, one whose volume helps keep first-class rates down for consumers. As more and more consumers receive and pay their bills online, order items online, and communicate via e-mail and text, the importance of business direct mail to the USPS grows ever stronger. Some pundits speculate that direct mail is "dead or dying," yet that is far from the case: the USPS reports that in a recent year, nearly *100 billion* pieces of advertising mail were sent in the United States.

   USPS regulations allow for a wide variety of acceptable formats and mailing rates. However, direct mailers must observe a very specific set of postal rules and regulations—rules that have been modified on a regular basis in recent years. One of the most valuable relationships for any direct mailer is an ongoing communication process with the local post office or Network Distribution Center. Postmasters and the Web site at www.usps.com can provide "how to" materials that will save considerable time in creating mailable pieces. In addition, it is essential that you understand exactly how your local postmaster enforces certain regulations that may be open to various interpretations. Indeed, a cordial relationship with the postmaster can be very helpful if a critical matter ever comes up.

You will also be wise to sign up for the USPS's *MailPro*, a free, bimonthly, mailed and online newsletter that offers the latest USPS information essential to effective mailings. It provides updated information on Domestic Mail Manual revisions, classification reform, mail processing networks, address management, technology, mailing standards, rulings, and other relevant issues, as well as feature articles about successful mailers.

Most experienced direct marketers can tell at least one horror story about a postal problem. Perhaps it was a Business Reply Card that was not quite thick enough to be sent through the mail, resulting in lost orders. Or maybe it was a first-class piece with an outer envelope just a tad too wide, resulting in a postal surcharge. One marketer prepared a direct mail package that, according to his scale, weighed a shade under the basic maximum weight for standard mail letters (currently 3.3 ounces for both "regular" standard mail and for the "enhanced carrier route" standard mail). More than a million packages were printed and prepared at the lettershop before it was discovered that according to the post office scale, the kit weighed a shade over the maximum weight. With many thousands of dollars in extra postage due, the marketer decided to have the envelopes opened, and each piece inside the package trimmed down. All of this could have been avoided if a dummy kit had been carefully prepared and weighed on the official post office scale in the first place. The bottom line is this: if in doubt, ask your postmaster. A few minutes spent on the phone or in a face-to-face visit may save you a great deal of time and money. What's more, the Postal Service has Mailpiece Design Analysts who can approve copy layouts and print specs, update with current requirements and provide artwork for Business Reply Mail and other official design related information. Go to usps.com and search for your local Mailpiece Design Analyst.

Mailing Classes

Postage rates and regulations change frequently, and therefore the most specific advice this book can provide is that you obtain current rate charts and regulatory materials from your post office. According to current USPS regulations, the basic classifications of mail are as follows: express mail, first class and priority, periodicals, standard, and nonprofit rate.

Express Mail. Marketers of high-ticket consumer items and business-to-business mailers may have strategies that justify the cost of express mail, particularly in responding to inquiries. Similar in price to commercial overnight delivery services, this mail class has the extra advantage of delivery on Sundays and holidays, 365 days a year. Express mail can be used for items weighing as much as 70 pounds. Rates are based on the weight of the addressed piece and level of service, without regard to zone. The minimum 1/2-pound rate is charged for materials mailed in the Express Mail flat rate envelope provided by the USPS, regardless of weight less than eight ounces. Express Mail is now a zone based product. There is still a Flat Rate Envelope, which is a great value for next-day delivery, but other pricing options start at 1/2 pound rates through the 70 pound maximum, and are based on eight zones from the destination across the country.

First Class Mail, Postcards, Flats, and Priority Mail. The easiest to use but most expensive regular class, first-class mail theoretically provides mail "penetration" to all parts of the continental United States within about three days. There are no special sorting requirements, although mailers may obtain a discount for bar coded first-class mail, and mail sorted in zip-code or carrier-route order. This is only practical when larger quantities of mail are involved, since the cost of presorting by zip code may outweigh the savings for small quantities. The presort option is often used by local department stores, banks, and other firms that have large numbers of customers in only a few zip codes. First-Class Mail is required for personal correspondence, handwritten or typewritten material, and bills or statements of account.

Most marketers consider first-class mail too expensive for mass mailings. In the testing phase they may use first-class mail because of its fast penetration, to obtain quick answers about the viability of their offer. First-class mail carries more immediacy than standard mail, and appears less like advertising to most consumers. First-class mail may well be used for mailings to existing customers, both for a prompt turnaround and because the volume of these customers' orders makes the more expensive mailing rate cost effective. Another reason for mailing first-class, at least periodically, is to take advantage of automatic mail forwarding and the return of undeliverable mail to the sender. This is a relatively inexpensive means of helping to keep your list clean.

Postcards. Cards that conform to USPS size and thickness restrictions can be mailed at a lower first-class rate than letters. To qualify for card rates, postcards currently must be rectangular and at least 3-1/2″ × 5″ and at least 0.007 inches thick. If they are larger than 4-1/4″ x 6″ or thicker than 0.016 inch, they are classified as a letter and charged the appropriate rate. Postcard rates also can be discounted for specific presorting work done by the mailer.

Large Envelopes (also known as "Flats"). These first-class pieces are larger than standard letter size. Currently "large envelopes" are defined as pieces that are between 6-1/8 and 12 inches high and between 11-1/2 and 15 inches long. They cannot be more than 3/4 inch thick. Large envelopes carry higher postal charges than letters, with exact postage determined by the amount of presorting work done by the mailer. First-class mail cannot be used for items weighing more than 13 ounces. The next weight class for regular mail is called *Priority Mail.* It covers items weighing between 13 ounces and 70 pounds. Priority mail delivery times are similar to those for first-class mail. Priority Mail is generally delivered anywhere in the country within two days.

Periodicals. There is a special set of rates for mailers sending out pieces that meet the post office's definition of a periodical. There are additional discounts for certain types of presort work done by the mailer. Check with your post office or online at *www.usps.com* for complete details and current rates.

Standard Mail. Most advertising direct mail is standard mail (formerly called third class mail). This category requires mailings of at least 200 pieces, addressed, sorted and marked as Standard Mail. There are content restrictions on Standard Mail that must be followed regarding personal information. The real savings for mailers are to be had in what the post office now called "automation" and "enhanced carrier route" in which a piece weighing up to 3.3 ounces can be mailed for much less than half the first-class rate for a one-ounce piece of mail. Standard Mail postage can be paid via a permit imprint, applied meter strip, or pre-canceled stamp. Actual postage rates are based on weight, presorting and entry discounts. Proper documentation in the form of a Postage Statement is also required.

Such mailings require the mailer to acquire a permit at the post office where he or she will drop the mail. There is a fee involved. In addition, the mailer must present the mail in the proper zip code and carrier route sequence, bundled, trayed or bagged according to post office regulations. There are bar coding and facing (labeling) requirements and other regulations to be followed in order to obtain the most substantial savings. Your post office and your lettershop will be able to help you conform to proper mailing procedures and your postmaster can give you current rates and application information. Work with your lettershop to determine what level of preparation on your part is likely to result in the best overall price, considering both lettershop and postal charges. Many lettershops will let you use their standard mail indicia at no additional charge.

A further point about the standard mailing permit is that firms need a separate "additional entry form" for each town from which they mail, unless they qualify for and obtain a "Company Permit." Such an indicia can save money and time, and it also allows for the preprinting of outer envelopes for use at any location. An additional benefit of the Company Permit is that its wording includes the name of the direct mail firm rather than the city of origin and/or permit number. Some mailers obtain the Company Permit strictly for this small promotional benefit.

Nonprofit Rate. Nonprofit organizations may take advantage of additional savings when they prepare mail according to standard mail-type postal regulations. A post office permit fee must be paid. Your postmaster can provide information and details about qualifications and rates.

Business Reply Envelopes and Cards

Most tests show that mailers who pay return postage for their customers get a higher level of response than those who require the consumer to pay his or her own postage. Deciding to "invest" in a stamp and locating one to use may be enough of a stopper to lose response from some individuals. For this reason, most front-end mailings are accompanied by Business Reply Envelopes or Cards. Bind-in cards or envelopes in magazines and Free-Standing Inserts provide the same opportunity for prepaid postage. To qualify for this service, the mailer must obtain a Business Reply Mail (BRM) Permit from the post office that will be receiving the incoming mail from customers. In addition, the mailer must provide postage money in the permit account to pay for incoming mail at first-class rates plus a service fee.

The amount of the service fee varies according to volume, with the best rates available to those who pay the original Business Reply fee plus a flat accounting fee. This method should be cost-effective for any mailer expecting to receive more than 600 pieces of Business Reply Mail on an annual basis. Details and current prices are available from your postmaster or at *www.usps.com*.

No matter what plan you choose for the receipt of Business Reply Mail, it is essential to keep sufficient funds in your account at the post office; otherwise your incoming mail will be held until you have properly funded the account. Besides holding up the receipt of orders or inquiries, having mail held in this manner destroys the mailer's ability to forecast on the basis of number of responses received each day. Business Reply Envelopes and Cards must be prepared according to a special set of regulations. This information is readily available at your local post office or at *www.usps.com*. Your local "Mailpiece Design Analyst" can also assist with artwork, copy and standards for business reply mail.

Lettershops

Time was, the lettershop was little more than an envelope-stuffing service, with row upon row of individuals inserting materials into envelopes by hand. In recent years, the science of preparing mail has advanced at an astonishing rate. As David Fant points out, most lettershops now perform as service bureaus as well as lettershop addressing services. Personalization is available through many lettershops, as well as variable printing where you can merge custom photos and text into your direct mail piece.

Today most mailings are prepared so that all of the pieces may be inserted by machine and the envelopes labeled or addressed and bar coded in zip-code or carrier route sequence by machine, sealed, and prepared for mailing, all with a minimum of human intervention. Some lettershops still provide hand-insertion services for mailings that are not machine insertable, and there are still cost-effective services available for smaller mailers who do not need six-station inserters and other sophisticated equipment. On the other hand, the range of lettershop services available to today's larger mailers is quite broad, and includes folding, collating, trimming, laser printing, and many more.

What to Look For in a Lettershop

To select a good lettershop, do a bit of detective work. Ask for the recommendations of other mailers whose volume and type of mailings are similar to your own. Visit the booths of lettershop services at trade shows and read their literature to learn about their capacity, specialties, and extra services. Then select several lettershops and visit their premises personally. Consider the following in evaluating each shop.

- *Neatness and organization.* The work of a lettershop is meticulous and detail oriented. Did the lettershop seem to run smoothly?
- *Equipment.* Compare the shop's printed equipment list against your own visual check. Does the firm's capacity match its promotional materials? How many machines were "down" during your visit? How many employees were standing around idle? Did the machines appear to run smoothly? Were there service people available to fix any breakdowns promptly?
- *Capabilities.* If you have need of special services, make sure this lettershop can fulfill them. For instance, most mailings have six inserts or fewer: if yours have more, the lettershop will need multi-station machines to handle them. Do you need a shop with polybag inserters, bursters or folding machines? Will you be using oversized outer envelopes? Do you need to have the lettershop affix seals, labels, or plastic cards? These are just a few examples of the special capabilities you may require from a lettershop.
- *Warehouse.* It is essential that the warehouse be clean, dry, and well organized. Are inventories stacked neatly? Would your materials stay in mint condition there until they are inserted? Ask to see how materials are recorded when they are received to ensure that your valuable printed matter is placed in inventory with care.
- *Post office arrangements and software.* Does the lettershop have a good relationship with the post office? Is there a postal official on site? If not, how far is the lettershop from the post office? Does the lettershop use the latest software for bar coding, sorting, and other functions, such as USPS's MERLIN®?
- *Customer relations.* Did the lettershop provide you with a list of the things they need to know to make your mailing run smoothly: source of materials, insertion order, codes, etc.?
- *Timing.* Find out how many shifts the lettershop runs each day. They can double or triple their available capacity for you if they are able to run second and third shifts.

Working with the Lettershop

A mailer must do four things to ensure good service from a lettershop. First, provide materials that are in good condition, packed according to the lettershop's specifications. Second, provide a complete record of what will arrive at the lettershop and how it is to be prepared. Third, keep in communication with the lettershop to make sure things proceed in a timely manner. Fourth, stay on schedule. It is not fair to expect the lettershop to make your mail date when delays in other functions lead to late arrivals of materials or lists.

Provide Materials in Good Condition. Your printer and computer service bureau will probably provide materials directly to the lettershop according to your orders. Check with the lettershop for instructions about how they prefer to receive materials: how boxes should be labeled, the preferred sizes for cartons, how materials should be stacked, and so on. Improperly boxed and shipped materials may become curled, damp, or otherwise uninsertable while in storage at the shop, and this extra care may therefore yield you savings in time and money.

The service bureau may provide labels or electronic files to the lettershop. If you are using labels, keep in mind that they may be generated in rows of one, four, or any number of other configurations. You have to know the configuration your lettershop needs for smooth machine operation. Also make sure the service bureau knows whether you want Cheshire labels, pressure-sensitive labels, or some other type of label to fit the lettershop's needs. By the same token, make sure any electronic files sent to the lettershop for addressing purposes are provided in a compatible format.

Provide Proper Documentation. If you give your lettershop a letter or form which tells what they will be receiving, how it will be marked, where it will come from, and what to do with it, your mailing will be off to a good start. The lettershop also needs the order of insertion you prefer. The following order of insertion is preferred by most mailers, because it allows the reader to see the letter first, while the reply form shows through the die-cut outer envelope, if you have one.

With outer envelope face down:
1. Letter
2. Brochure
3. Other pieces (premium slip, publisher's note, etc.)
4. Business Reply Envelope
5. Reply Form (facing backwards so label shows through outer envelope, if applicable)

Keep Communicating and Stay on Schedule. It is up to you to follow up on a daily basis and check with the lettershop to make sure things are proceeding smoothly. If they are not, you will have to prompt the printer, envelope supplier, service bureau, or other source of the problem to get things back on schedule. This is especially important because mail dates, for the most part, must remain firm. List rentals are protected only for a certain mail date, and you cannot make a casual decision to delay a mailing.

More Hints for Dealing with Lettershops

- Ask the lettershop for a hand-inserted sample of each mailing configuration in your project before machine inserting begins. Misunderstandings are much easier to correct at this point. These packages should also be weighed to make sure they meet postal regulations for the class of mail you are using.

- Get proper documentation for everything you mail through a lettershop. Postal form 3602 tells you the date your material was mailed, postage cost, number mailed, and how mailed: carrier route, five-digit presort, carrier-route presort, etc.
- Supply postage money to the post office or lettershop in plenty of time. The lettershop will not advance postage money. Make out the postage check to the U.S. Postmaster.
- Book your lettershop well in advance when big mailings are coming so that they can alert the proper authorities at the post office. This is especially important in smaller cities where million-piece mailings are rare.
- Design outer envelopes with enough tolerance left to right and top to bottom to ensure that inside pieces will be machine insertable. General guidelines: outer envelope should be at least 1/2″ wider and 1/4″ taller than the largest inserted piece.
- Graphic designers should work closely with lettershops when designing unique packages. To make sure pieces are machine insertable, certain rules must be followed. For instance, all pieces must be a minimum thickness and weight. If the outer envelope flap is deeper than 1-1/2″ to 1-3/4″, it may cause problems in inserting.

Also important: each inserted piece must have a closed side for the inserting machine to grab.

Enhance Your Understanding: Visits and Tours

Until you visit a large, bustling lettershop and tour a USPS Network Distribution Center (NDC), your understanding of the functions described in this chapter may not be complete. If you are not in charge of postal functions for your company or agency, ask those who perform these jobs to help set you up with a tour or two. In addition, local and regional direct marketing clubs often include such tours on their schedules of activities for members. While you're on tour, be observant. Ask questions about why things are done the way they are, and what other capabilities are available. Ask for a look behind the scenes in storage areas, holding areas, the postal loading dock, and so on. While you're at it, arrange for similar tours at printers of various sizes, graphic design studios, services bureaus and other key suppliers. You'll become a better-rounded marketer in the process.

The author thanks Michael K. Spaulding of the U.S. Postal Service for help in delivering accurate and up-to-date information in this chapter.

Appendix A
Periodicals, Books, and Other Resources

Print and Online Periodicals

The following are some of the periodicals that will be of interest to creative direct and interactive marketers. Many of these periodicals have robust Web sites with daily news updates, white papers, and other helpful materials, and many have multiple e-mailed newsletters to which you may subscribe. This contact information is subject to change.

Advertising Age—Published by Crain Communications, 711 Third Avenue, New York, NY 10017-4014. Weekly. (212) 210-0100. *www.adage.com*. Advertising Age has incorporated *American Demographics* into its coverage.

All About ROI: The Retailer's Guide to Cross-Channel Success. Published by North American Publishing Co., 1500 Spring Garden Street, 12th Floor, Philadelphia, PA 19130. Monthly. (215) 238-5300. *http://www.allaboutroimag.com/*

Business Publication Advertising Source—Published for online access by SRDS, 1700 Higgins Road, Des Plaines, IL 60018-5605. Updated continuously. (800) 232-0772, ext. 8020. *www.srds.com*.

Canadian Advertising Rates and Data—Published for online access by SRDS, 1700 Higgins Road, Des Plaines, IL 60018-5605. Updated continuously. *(800) 232-0772, ext. 8020. www.srds.com*.

Chief Marketer—Published by Penton Media, 11 River Bend, Dr. So., Stamford, CT 06907-0949. Bi-monthly. (866) 505-7173.

Consumer Magazine Advertising Source—Published for online access by SRDS, 1700 Higgins Road, Des Plaines, IL 60018-5605. Updated continuously. *(800) 232-0772, ext. 8020. www.srds.com*.

CRM Magazine—Published by Information Today, Inc., at 143 Old Marlton Pike, Medford, NJ 08055. Monthly. (609) 654-6266. *http://www.destinationcrm.com*

Direct Magazine Online—Published online only by PRIMEDIA Business Magazines & Media at *http://directmag.com/*.

Direct Marketing List Source—Published for online access by SRDS, 1700 Higgins Road, Des Plaines, IL 60018. Updated continuously. (800) 232-0772, ext. 8020. *www.srds.com*.

DM News—Published online and offline by Haymarket Media (646) 638-6000, *www.dmnews.com*.

Hispanic Media & Market Source—Published for online access by SRDS, 1700 Higgins Road, Des Plaines, IL 60018. Updated continuously. (800) 232-0772. *www.srds.com.*

Interactive Advertising Source—Published for online access by SRDS, 1700 Higgins Road, Des Plaines, IL 60018. Updated continuously. (800) 232-0772. *www.srds.com.*

Internet Retailer—Published by Vertical Web Media LLC, 300 South Wacker Drive, Suite 602, Chicago, IL 60606. (312) 362-0804. *www.internetretailer.com.*

Multichannel Merchant—Published by Primedia Business, P.O. Box 4949, 11 River Bend Drive South, Stamford, CT 06907-0949. 13 times yearly. (203) 358-9900. *http://multichannelmerchant.com/*

Newspaper Advertising Source—Published for online access by SRDS, 1700 Higgins Road, Des Plaines, IL 60018. Updated continuously. *(800) 232-0772, ext. 8020. www.srds.com.*

Print Media Production Source—Published for online access by SRDS, 1700 Higgins Road, Des Plaines, IL 60018. Updated continuously. *(800) 232-0772, ext. 8020. www.srds.com.*

Promo: The Magazine of Promotion Marketing—Published by Primedia Business, P.O. Box 4949, 11 River Bend Drive South, Stamford, CT 06907-0949. Monthly. (203) 358-9900. *www.promo-magazine.com.*

Radio Advertising Source—Published for online access by SRDS, 1700 Higgins Road, Des Plaines, IL 60018-5605. Updated continuously. *(800) 232-0772, ext. 8020. www.srds.com.*

Target Marketing—Published by North American Publishing Co., 1500 Spring Garden Street, 12th Floor, Philadelphia, PA 19130. Monthly. (215) 238-5300. *www.targetmarketingmag.com.*

TV & Cable Source—Published online and offline by SRDS, 1700 Higgins Road, Des Plaines, IL 60018. Updated four times a year with continuous updates online. (800) 851-7737. *www.srds.com.*

Who's Mailing What—Published by North American Publishing Co., 1500 Spring Garden Street, 12th Floor, Philadelphia, PA 19130. Monthly. (215) 238-5300.

E-mailed Newsletters

There are a host of daily, weekly, bi-weekly and monthly topical newsletters delivered by e-mail to direct and interactive marketers, and often available at no subscription cost. Here are some of the best sources to check for available newsletter subscriptions.

3D—DMA Daily Digest—To subscribe, contact *3D@the-dma.org*
B2B Online—To subscribe, visit *http://www.btobonline.com/*
eMarketer—To subscribe, visit *http://www.emarketer.com/*
Fast Company Newsletters—To subscribe, visit *http://www.fastcompany.com/newsletters*
Media Post—To subscribe, visit *http://www.mediapost.com/*
Mobile Marketer—To subscribe, visit *http://www.mobilemarketer.com/*
The Prescott Report—To subscribe, visit *http://prescottreport.com*
Tech Crunch—To subscribe, visit *http://feedburner.google.com/fb/a/mailverify?uri=TechCrunch&loc=en_US*

Books and Other Resources

The following is a brief list of some of the books and resources this author has found especially helpful in formulating and executing direct and interactive marketing creative strategies. It is by no means complete. For a good survey of the newest direct and interactive marketing books and monographs currently available, check Racom Books at *www.racombooks.com* and other online sources such as *www.amazon.com,* using keywords for the subjects that interest you. The Direct Marketing Association publishes a wide range of books, studies, monographs, and Echo Award-winning campaigns. Look for materials online at the DMA Bookstore—a subset of *www.the-dma.org.*

Books

Advertising Secrets of the Written Word: The Ultimate Resource on How to Write Powerful Advertising Copy from One of America's Top Copywriters and Mail Order Entrepreneurs by Joseph Sugarman. Published by DelStar Publishing, Las Vegas, NV.

Business-to-Business Direct Marketing by Robert W. Bly. Published by McGraw-Hill/Contemporary Books, New York, NY.

Business-to-Business Direct Marketing by Tracy Emerick and Bernard Goldberg. Published by Direct Marketing Publishers, Yardley, PA.

Business-to-Business Internet Marketing by Susan K. Jones. Published by Maximum Press, Gulf Breeze, FL.

Business-to-Business Marketing: Creating a Community of Customers by Victor L. Hunter. Published by McGraw-Hill/Contemporary Books, New York, NY.

Buying Creative Services by Bobbi Balderman. Published by McGraw-Hill/ Contemporary Books, New York, NY.

The Complete Database Marketer: Second Generation Strategies and Techniques for Tapping the Power of Your Customer Database by Arthur M. Hughes. Published by McGraw-Hill Trade, New York, NY.

Confessions of an Advertising Man by David Ogilvy. Published by Atheneum, New York, NY.

Contemporary Database Marketing: Concepts and Applications by Martin Baier, Kurtis M. Ruf, Goutam Charkraborty. Published by RACOM Communications, Chicago, IL.

The Creative Organization, edited with an introduction by Gary A. Steiner. Published by The University of Chicago Press, Chicago, IL.

The Customer Differential by Melinda Nykamp. Published by AMACOM, New York, NY.

The Direct Marketing Handbook, edited by Edward L. Nash. Published by McGraw-Hill, Inc., New York, NY.

Direct Marketing: Strategy/Planning/Execution by Edward Nash. Published by McGraw-Hill, Inc., New York, NY.

Direct Marketing Success Stories by Bob Stone. Published by NTC Business Books, Lincolnwood, IL.

Direct Marketing Through Broadcast Media by Alvin Eicoff. Published by NTC Business Books, Lincolnwood, IL.

DMA Lead Generation Handbook by Ruth P. Stevens. Published by the Direct Marketing Association, New York, NY. (Available through the DMA.)

DMA Statistical Fact Book. Published annually by the Direct Marketing Association, New York, NY. (Available through the DMA.)

Eicoff on Broadcast Direct Marketing by Alvin Eicoff. Published by NTC Business Books, Lincolnwood, IL.

The Greatest Direct Mail Sales Letters of All Time by Richard Hodgson. Published by Dartnell Corp. (an LRP Publications Company), Horsham, PA.

Handbook for Public Relations Writing by Thomas Bivins. Published by NTC Business Books, Lincolnwood, IL.

High-Performance Interactive Marketing by Christopher Ryan. Published by RACOM Communications, Chicago, IL.

How to Create Successful Catalogs, 2nd Edition, by Maxwell Sroge. Published by McGraw-Hill/Contemporary Books, New York, NY.

How to Find and Cultivate Customers Through Direct Marketing by Martin Baier. Published by McGraw-Hill/Contemporary Books, New York, NY.

How to Profit Through Catalog Marketing by Katie Muldoon. Published by NTC Publishing Group, Lincolnwood, IL.

How to Start and Operate a Mail-Order Business by Julian Simon. Published by McGraw-Hill Professional, New York, NY.

The IMC Handbook: Readings and Cases in Integrated Marketing Communications, edited by J. Steven Kelly and Susan K. Jones. Published by RACOM Communications, Chicago, IL.

Integrated Direct Marketing by Ernan Roman. Published by McGraw-Hill Trade, New York, NY.

Integrated Marketing Communications by Don E. Schultz, Stanley I. Tannenbaum, and Robert F. Lauterborn. Published by McGraw-Hill/Contemporary Books, New York, NY.

Internet Direct Mail by Stevan Roberts, Michelle Feit, and Robert W. Bly. Published by McGraw-Hill/Contemporary Books, New York, NY.

John Caples, Adman by Gordon White. Published by Crain Books, Chicago. (Out of print but may be available through amazon.com or other online sources.)

A Kick in the Seat of the Pants by Roger Von Oech. Published by Perennial Press, Saint Helens, OR.

Marketing Convergence by Susan K. Jones and Ted Spiegel. Published by RACOM Communications, Evanston, IL.

Marketing Mayhem by Herschell Gordon Lewis. Published by RACOM Communications, Evanston, IL.

My Life In Advertising & Scientific Advertising by Claude C. Hopkins. Published by McGraw-Hill/Contemporary Books, New York, NY.

The New Direct Marketing: How to Implement a Profit-Driven Database Marketing Strategy by David Shepard Associates. Published by McGraw-Hill Trade, New York, NY.

Ogilvy on Advertising by David Ogilvy. Published by Crown Publishers, Inc., New York, NY.

The 100 Greatest Advertisements—Who Wrote Them and What They Did by Julian Lewis Watkins. Published by NTC Business Books, Lincolnwood, IL. (Out of print but may be available through amazon.com or other online sources.)

The Online Copywriter's Handbook by Robert W. Bly. Published by McGraw-Hill, New York, NY.

Permission-Based E-Mail Marketing That Works! by Kim MacPherson. Published by Dearborn Trade, Chicago, IL.

Permission Marketing by Seth Godin. Published by Simon & Shuster, New York, NY.

Persuasive Online Copywriting—How to Take Your Words to the Bank by Bryan Eisenberg, Jeffrey Eisenberg, and Lisa T. Davis. Published by Wizard Academy Press, Austin, TX.

The Practical Guide to Email Marketing: Strategies and Tactics for Inbox Success by Jordan Ayan. Published by SubscriberMail LLC, Lisle, IL.

The Practical Handbook and Guide to Focus Group Research by Thomas L. Greenbaum. Published by Lexington Books, Lexington, MA.

Profitable Direct Marketing by Jim Kobs. Published by McGraw-Hill/Contemporary Books, New York, NY.

Radio Tips: 101 Tips, Tricks and Secrets to Make Your Radio Advertising More Profitable by Mark Lipsky. Published by Radio Direct, Media, PA.

Response: The Complete Guide to Profitable Direct Marketing by Lois K. Geller. Published by Oxford University Press, New York, NY.

Sales Letters that Sizzle by Herschell Gordon Lewis. Published by McGraw-Hill/Contemporary Books, New York, NY.

Successful Direct Marketing Methods by Bob Stone and Ron Jacobs. Published by McGraw-Hill Trade, New York, NY.

Successful Telemarketing, 2nd Edition, by Bob Stone and John Wyman. Published by McGraw-Hill/Contemporary Books, New York, NY.

S.U.R.E.-Fire Direct Response Marketing by Russell M. Kern. Published by McGraw-Hill, New York, NY.

A Technique for Producing Ideas by James Webb Young. Published by McGraw-Hill Trade, New York, NY.

Television Secrets for Marketing Success: How to Sell Your Product on Infomercials, Home Shopping Channels & Spot TV Commercials from the Entrepreneur Who Gave—You Blublocker® Sunglasses by Joseph Sugarman. Published by DelStar Publishing, Las Vegas, NV.

Tested Advertising Methods by John Caples. Published by Prentice-Hall, Inc., Upper Saddle River, NJ.

A Whack on the Side of the Head by Roger von Oech, Ph.D. Published by Warner Books, New York, NY.

Other Resources

Creative Whack Pack—Card game and iPhone app by Roger Von Oech. Published by United States Games Systems; game available from amazon.com and in many bookstores; app available on the iPhone.

NEWSTRACK®Advertising Classics—Cassette tapes with highlights from the writings of Leo Burnett, Rosser Reeves, Albert D. Lasker, Claude C. Hopkins, Maxwell Sackheim, Alvin Eicoff, Fairfax M. Cone, and David Ogilvy. (Out of production but may be available on amazon.com or through other online sources.)

Appendix B
Associations and Clubs

By joining one or more direct and/or interactive marketing associations, creative people come in contact with experienced professionals, and individuals who are breaking new ground in creative strategy. Conventions will expose you to cutting-edge speakers and trade shows with new ideas from vendors. Online and offline seminars by experts will yield new ideas.

Social networking as well as in-person networking with people from other agencies and firms will keep you up to date with advances they are making. Informal talks with vendors, freelancers, and consultants may make you aware of new sources of help.

As a member of one or more of these associations, you will be on mailing and e-mail lists that will enable you to receive information about conventions, services, seminars, publications, books, Web sites, and other opportunities pertaining to the direct and interactive marketing fields. You'll have the opportunity to join social networking sites and read blogs by those affiliated with these groups as well.

There is a Web site that will link you with some of the most prominent direct and interactive marketing associations that will be of interest to creative people. For U.S.-based clubs in Atlanta, Charlotte, Chicago, Cleveland, Dallas-Fort Worth, Florida, Houston, Kansas City, Long Island, Louisville, Mid-America, the Midwest, New England, New York, Northern California, the Northwest, the Ohio Valley, Philadelphia, the Rocky Mountains, Seattle, Southern California, the Southwest, St. Louis, Vermont and Wisconsin, and many more. Visit *http://www.direct marketingevents.com* and click on "Direct Marketing Organizations."

In the international realm, there are direct marketing associations in the following countries: Argentina, Australia, Austria, Belgium, Brazil, Canada, Chile, China, Croatia, Czech Republic, Denmark, Finland, France, Germany, Greece, Hong Kong, Hungary, India, Ireland, Italy, Japan, Latvia, Mexico, the Netherlands, New Zealand, Northern Ireland, Norway, Pan European, Philippines, Poland, Portugal, Romania, Russia, Singapore, Slovakia, Slovenia, South Africa, Spain, Sweden, Switzerland, Thailand, Turkey, United Kingdom and Venezuela. For a list of contacts for these groups, consult the International Direct Marketing Federation at *http://www.idmf.com* and the Federation of European Direct and Interactive Marketing at *http://www.fedma.org/*.

Code of Ethics for Direct and Interactive Marketers

Although there are some unethical operators in the direct and interactive marketing field, firms that are in the business for the "long haul" adhere to the rules of the Federal Trade Commission, Federal Communications Commission and their individual industries, such as state "Do Not Call" or "Do Not Spam" laws or state regulations on the selling of insurance. To provide guidance for their members, direct and interactive marketing organizations have established their own sets of ethics and self-regulatory rules.

For a complete list of regulations and ethics, including detailed regulations for telemarketers, contact the Direct Marketing Association in New York or visit that organization's Web site at *www.the-dma.org*. For an overview of what is considered acceptable business practice, here is the Code of Conduct of the Chicago Association of Direct Marketing (*www.cadm.org*).

CHICAGO ASSOCIATION OF DIRECT MARKETING (CADM) CODE OF CONDUCT
(Adopted by the Board of Directors on May 10, 2001)

CADM believes that proper business practices are essential to the success and growth of the direct marketing field. It is clear that both buyers and marketers gain from such proper conduct.

Regardless of the products/services, offers, terms, or media used, CADM members pledge themselves to the following guidelines:

1. Buyers have the right to expect that all visual and written depictions of a product or service, its features and benefits, are true and accurate and live up to the expectations created by the marketer.
2. Buyers have the right to expect that all purchases are sent at their request, are delivered in a timely fashion, in good condition, and have their choice of a prompt refund or replacement if not satisfied.
3. Marketers shall collect only such data about the buyer that is pertinent to an ongoing business relationship with the buyer and does not exceed accepted privacy standards.
4. Marketers may use information collected (as defined in the above statement) to facilitate the making of additional offers on the part of that marketer that may interest the buyer.
5. Marketers may offer collected information to other marketers for offers that

may be of interest to the buyer, provided that buyers are given the opportunity to inform marketers to do otherwise.

6. Buyers have the right to remedies for the failures to act ethically on the part of member firms by contacting the CADM Board to seek mediation of disputes.

7. Knowing that no set of guidelines can cover all situations, the application and/or interpretation of these principles remains the responsibility of the CADM Board.

All members of CADM pledge their adherence to these principles as a condition of their membership in the Association. Failure to follow these principles makes member firms subject to review by the CADM Board of Directors, or its appointed review committee, for possible termination of membership.

CADM PRIVACY STATEMENT

CADM recognizes the need to balance the interest of consumer's privacy rights with the interest of the direct marketing industry in ethically collecting and sharing information about consumers.

CADM and its members (hereinafter collectively referred to as "CADM") commits to a general policy of responsible use of consumer information and specifically pledges:

- CADM shall obtain personal and private information about consumers through ethical and legal means.
- CADM shall use that information strictly for its marketing and research activities.
- CADM shall maintain accurate records of consumers.
- CADM shall secure and protect consumer records.
- CADM shall comply with all regulations and laws and specifically those pertaining to the privacy rights of consumers.

Glossary

This glossary provides an overview of some of the most frequently used terms and buzzwords for writers, graphic designers, and production people in direct and interactive marketing. It is by no means complete.

A/B SPLIT—A testing method in which each copy of a newspaper, magazine, Web site, e-mail or other medium alternately carries ad "A" or ad "B."

ACTION DEVICE—A tab, sticker, or other item in or on a mailing package which makes the prospective customer "do something" that leads toward a sale. Example: stickers representing both magazines available for subscriptions and prizes available for winning, within sweepstakes packages from publishers.

AFFILIATE PROGRAM—Paying a percentage of sales revenue to a Web site that refers a purchaser to a seller.

AIDA—Attention, Interest, Desire, Action: the standard formula for the steps through which direct and interactive marketing copy should take the prospect in order to induce a response.

ART—The general term for illustrations and photography used in promotional literature; also the final material presented for printing.

BACK END—Back-end activities are those that take place after an initial order is received. This term may also indicate the customer's buying activities with the firm after an initial order. See also Front End.

BANGTAIL ENVELOPE—An envelope which serves a promotional purpose via an extra flap that holds product information, an order form, or both. Often used in credit-card statements, premium notices, and the like, where the "bangtail" promotion rides along free.

BANNER AD—A graphic display of advertising on a Web page, offering click-through to a more detailed message/offer.

BAR CODING—Vertical bars and half-bars printed in a proscribed format on the outside of a mail piece to facilitate automated processing. This saves postage for the mailer when done according to post office specifications.

BASTARD SIZE—A nonstandard size of promotional piece which requires special handling and may well cost more than an item of more usual size or configuration.

BINDERY—The facility that binds together books, magazines, or pamphlets. "Binding" means wiring with staples, sewing, or plasticizing, depending on the thickness and desired appearance of the bound piece.

BINGO CARD—Deriving its name from its resemblance to this type of game card, the bingo card is a tear-out business reply device inserted in a magazine. The reader simply circles the appropriate numbers on the card to request promotional literature or sales follow-up from advertisers in the publication.

BLACK AND WHITE—Another term for one-color printing, where black type or art on white paper is utilized.

BLEED—Where the printing on a piece goes all the way to the edge of the paper. This is accomplished by printing beyond the margins of the piece and then trimming to the margins.

BLOG—Short for "Web log"—an individual's open journal, diary or commentary about specific or general topics.

BODY COPY—The main blocks of words in a printed piece, as opposed to headings and subheads.

BOLDFACE or BOLD—A heavy-faced type.

BOUNCE BACK—An offer to a customer that comes to him or her along with the fulfillment of an order. Also a name for an offer to an "affinity" buyer, e.g., one to whom you would "bounce back" an offer on a second set of children' books after the first purchase of a set on that topic.

BROADSIDE—The name for a brochure that folds out to a flat size of 11″ × 17″ or larger. The "broadside" format lends itself to a dramatic product presentation whereby all elements of the offer may be presented on a single reading surface.

BROCHURE—Also called a circular, pamphlet, or flyer, this is the general term for a descriptive piece of literature used for promotional purposes.

BROCHUREWARE—Judgmental term for a Web site that is little more than a copy of the firm's print brochure transmitted via the Internet, and does not take advantage of the Web's depth and interactive properties.

BROWSER—A tool that enables World Wide Web users to navigate the Internet easily and to find items by topic rather than by the complex URL addressing scheme.

BULLETS—Dots or asterisks used to introduce short, declarative selling statements about a product. Also a term for the statements themselves.

BULK MAIL—See standard mail.

BUSINESS REPLY MAIL—A card or envelope with the address and indicia of the company receiving the order or inquiry. It allows the inquirer or buyer to mail the card or envelope back postage-free. The user must obtain a permit from the post office to utilize business reply, and establish an account with postage money to cover the cost of replies. Users pay the first-class postage for each reply they receive, plus a postal handling fee.

CALL OUT—Information used to describe or bring attention to a photograph, diagram or illustration in a promotional piece, usually connected to the applicable part of the visual by a line.

CAPTION—Typeset description of an illustration or photograph.

CARD DECK MAILING—A group of postcards that contain promotional information and business reply capabilities, sent to a group of people with certain characteristics (e.g., attorneys, marketing executives, physicians, etc.).

CARRIER ROUTE PRESORT—Sorting mail into a nine-digit zip-code sequence so that it is ready to be distributed to individual U.S. Postal Service carriers. This may save additional postage over five-digit zip-code sequencing.

CASH WITH ORDER—A request for payment in full when the order is placed.

CATALOG—A book or booklet whose purpose is to show merchandise, provide descriptions, and offer the said merchandise for sale via an order form, telephone, online, or retail outlets.

CD-ROM—Compact disk, read-only memory. Used by some direct marketers to deliver catalogs, lists, product information, etc., and/or to link prospects to a comprehensive Web site.

CENTER SPREAD—The middle two pages of a bound catalog, magazine, or book.

CHARACTER COUNT—The number of letters and spaces that will fill a specific area in a printed piece.

CHAT—A typed conversation over the Internet or online service between two or more people, conducted in real time.

CHESHIRE LABELS—Mailing labels prepared for use with automatic labeling machines. The machines affix the labels individually to the mailing envelope, letter, catalog, or order form.

CINEMATOGRAPHER—The individual responsible for the composition and lighting of filmed projects. For projects utilizing videotape, the title is videographer.

CLICK-THROUGH RATE (CTR)—Expressed as a percentage, this is a measure of the ratio of times an e-mail or banner ad is clicked on, to the number of e-mails sent or exposures to the ad.

CLIP ART—Illustrations, borders, and other graphics available for artists to use in design creation of artwork for printing. The cost of the clip art book, disk, or download is usually the only fee, as these designs are not copyrighted.

COATED PAPER—A smooth-finished paper that provides good photographic and printing reproduction. The paper is coated with a thin layer of clay and may be finished to a dull, matte, or glossy appearance.

CODE—Also known as a key code or source code, this is a number, series of letters, or other identifying device used to determine the source of an order or inquiry. It may appear on the order form or label, or within the return address or coupon on a space ad.

COLLATERAL MATERIALS—Printed materials used to support a sale or prospective sale, such as instruction manuals, certificates of authenticity, or warranty information.

COLOR SEPARATION—The translation of an original photograph or other piece of artwork into separate plates for four-color printing.

COMPILED LIST—As opposed to a list of buyers of a specific product or service, a compiled list does not promise any sort of past buying activity. Rather, it is a group of names gathered from directories, public records, registrations, and other sources which share one or more things in common (such as being marketing professors).

COMPREHENSIVE LAYOUT—Also called a "comp," this is a layout for a prospective printed piece that is complete enough to permit the ordering of finished illustrations, photography, and artwork for printing.

COMPUTER HOUSE—A firm that offers various computer services, including list computerization and maintenance, merge/purge operations, and computer-generated letters.

COMPUTER LETTER—A letter generated by a computer for the purpose of personalizing a name, address, previous buying record, or something else.

CONDENSED TYPE—A narrowed version of a typeface used to conserve horizontal space.

CONTINUITY PROGRAM—A program that has multiple parts, such as a series of books, records, collector's plates, or recipe cards shipped on a monthly, semi-monthly, or quarterly basis. The items are unified by a common theme and often by a common price per shipment.

CONTROL—A promotion package or ad that has been proven to perform at a certain level and that is used as the benchmark for future testing.

CONVERSION—Turning a prospect into a lead or buyer, or making a lead into a buyer.

COOKIE—Bits of code that sit in a user's browser memory to identify the visitor to the Web site. Users can disable cookies if they choose to do so. Cookies can also be embedded within a promotional e-mail's HTML to track "open" rates, forwarding, and the like.

CO-OP MAILING—Two or more (usually noncompetitive) offers combined in one envelope and sent to prospects to cut down the individual mailing, postage, and other costs. Standard Rate and Data Service publishes lists of organized co-op mailings.

COPY—A manuscript, typescript, or other written material to be used in preparing a printed piece such as a letter or brochure.

COPYRIGHT—An exclusive right that the law grants to authors and artists, or to the owners of other works.

COPYWRITER'S ROUGHS—Rough layouts prepared in pencil by a copywriter to indicate the relative sizes and positions of elements in an ad, brochure, or other piece of selling literature.

CORNER CARD—The imprint of the sender or the return address on an outer envelope or catalog, which may include the logo or slogan of the mailing firm.

COUPON—The return portion of an ad, which may involve a purchase or a request for more information.

CPM—Cost per thousand; a typical measure of cost for direct and interactive marketing promotional activities.

CREATIVE DIRECTOR—The individual responsible for an agency or company's creative product. The creative director may begin as a copywriter, graphic designer, or a combination of both.

CROP—To trim off a portion of a photograph or illustration to eliminate extraneous background and/or make it fit available space.

CUSTOMER LIST—The names owned by a particular firm. These names may be collected through outside solicitation, purchase, or compilation. Also known as a "house list" or "house file."

CUSTOMER RELATIONSHIP MANAGEMENT—Combining the skills of database management, sales, marketing, and customer service to ensure that customers receive appropriate, customized, and consistent information and treatment at every point of contact with the company—be it online or offline, on the phone, or in person.

CYBERSPACE—A more romantic term for the Internet and other online forms of communication. The word originally appeared in the novel *Neuromancer* by William Gibson.

DATA MINING—Sorting through data to identify patterns and establish relationships.

DATABASE MARKETING—An automated system used to identify customers and prospects by name, and to use quantifiable information about these people to define the best possible purchasers and prospects for a given offer or relationship-building communication at a given point in time.

DECOY—To inquire or purchase from a company with the intention of learning about its products and methods of promotion.

DECOY NAME—A "tip-off" name (a false name at your address, perhaps) inserted in a mailing list. Also known as a "seed name," or "salting the list." This assures that the mailer knows when his or her list is being used and how, and helps prevents its unauthorized use.

DEMOGRAPHICS—Social and economic information about people or groups of people, including age, income, educational level, and other quantifiable data.

DIE CUT—Special cut-out shapes on printed pieces created by using sharp steel dies to cut paper.

DIGITAL EDITING—A non-linear, random-access process that allows for swift and easy video editing and creation of customized versions.

DIGITAL PHOTOGRAPHY—Using a camera to create photographs recorded in pixels for easy transmission to the computer screen.

DIGITAL PRINTING—Enabled by digital technology, the simple transfer of information from a computer file to paper. It can be accomplished using a press, printer, copier, or fax.

DIGITAL VIDEO RECORDER—Device that records many hours of a consumer's favorite television shows automatically, whenever they are on. The consumer can watch the shows at will, and fast-forward through commercials.

DIMENSIONAL MAILING—A three-dimensional direct mail package. Also called a bulky package or bundling package.

DIRECT MAIL—The use of the postal service to send a common message to persons selected from a database or list, by zip code, or other means.

DIRECT MARKETING—Obtaining leads or selling by means of a specific message to a specific prospective buyer or inquirer.

DISPLAY TYPE—Large type in a printed piece, usually headlines or subheads.

DOMAIN NAME—A registered Web site name or address.

DO-NOT-CALL LIST—A list of phone numbers gathered and maintained by a governmental agency (usually national or state) at the behest of consumers. Companies are generally forbidden to call the numbers on this list, with certain exceptions for their own customers and prospects, and for political and non-profit entities.

DOT or DOT PATTERN—The individual elements that make up halftones. In full-color printing, dots in red, blue, yellow, and black are arranged to produce all other colors.

DOUBLE OPT-IN NAMES—A list of names of customers or prospects who have specifically indicated, and then re-confirmed (usually by return e-mail) that they are willing to receive certain types of messages from a certain company, or from the firms to which that company may rent names for direct mail or e-mail purposes.

DOUBLE-TRUCK SPREAD—A two-page spread.

DUMMY—Any "mock-up" of a printed piece used to test its appearance, weight, readability, or other properties.

DUOTONE—Two plates are combined to create a piece of art with a darker and a lighter shade of ink.

E-COMMERCE—Electronic Commerce. The process of shopping, buying, and selling goods and services online, ranging from purchase influence to ordering and payment settlement.

ENAMEL PAPER—A coated stock.

ENCRYPTION—A process of coding information so that it can be protected for transmission over the Internet. Typically used for credit card numbers and other private information.

EXTRANET—Password-protected Web sites created by firms to serve their top customers and partners.

EYEBROW—Also called "overline." A lead-in to the main heading that appears above the heading on a printed piece.

FIRST CLASS MAIL—Mail that may or may not contain individual messages, but afforded priority treatment because of the amount of postage it bears. See also Standard Mail.

FLUSH LEFT/FLUSH RIGHT—Typesetting done so that copy lines up on the left side or the right side, with the other side ragged edged.

FONT—One variety of typeface, including all its characters and symbols.

FOUR-COLOR PROCESS—Also called the full-color process, it indicates the four color plates commonly used in color printing: yellow, magenta (red), cyan (blue), and black.

FREELANCER—An independent writer, consultant, artist, or other service provider who is not employed by any one firm, but who works with various firms or agencies.

FREE-STANDING INSERT (FSI)—A promotional piece that is not constrained by the specifications of a publication, but which is inserted loosely into that publication. It allows an advertiser to "ride along" with the daily newspaper, for instance, while still printing full-color material on a good-quality paper stock.

FREQUENCY/RECENCY/AMOUNT/TYPE (FRAT)—See Recency/Frequency/Monetary.

FRONT END—The marketing activities that take place before the entering of an initial sale or lead from a prospect. See also Back End.

GANG RUN—Running several same or similar print jobs together to save money and time.

GIF—Graphical Interchange Format. A bit-mapped graphic format used on the Web; typically for smaller graphics that should look crisp and bright, such as logos and icons.

GIMMICK—A small device that may be tipped onto a direct mail letter, order form, or brochure, to call attention to the piece or dramatize the offer.

GRAPHIC ARTS—The general term for the field of printing, and for creative work on promotional materials (including art, layouts, and photography).

GUARANTEE—The marketer's promise regarding the prospective buyer's satisfaction, and the specific terms of that promise (e.g., replacement guarantee, money-back guarantee, buy-back guarantee, etc.)

HALFTONE—A plate, printed piece, or process involving the shooting of artwork through a lined screen, which breaks up the art into a dot pattern.

HARD BOUNCE—An undeliverable e-mail address that either never left the transmitting server or never reached the destination server, but rather bounced back to the sender. See also Soft Bounce.

HEADS/HEADINGS/HEADLINES—A short phrase designed to attract attention to the offer at hand and lead the reader through the body copy and subheads that follow.

HICKEYS—Marks on printed material caused by dirt or foreign matter introduced during the printing process. They may appear on all pieces or only on a few samples.

HOME PAGE—The first screen visitors see when they arrive at a World Wide Web site. It usually includes welcoming messages and links to other pages on the site and elsewhere. Also used as a term for the entire Web site.

HOTLINE NAMES—The most recent buyers on a direct mail list.

HOUSE LIST—See Customer List.

HTML—HyperText Markup Language, which can be interpreted by a browser on the World Wide Web.

HTML EDITOR—Software that assist creators of Web sites and helps them avoid learning the nuances of HTML.

HYPERLINK or HYPERTEXT—Clickable text that links one piece of information to another on the World Wide Web.

HTTP—HyperText Transfer Protocol. The language of the Internet.

INDICIA—Envelope markings substituted for stamps or other regular cancellations in bulk mailings.

INFOMERCIAL—A long-form direct response television advertisement, typically 30 minutes in length, combining product background and product-in-use demonstrations, testimonials, and selling messages.

INQUIRY—A person who has not yet purchased anything from a firm, but who has been identified via a response to an ad or other solicitation in which he/she asked for (usually free) information.

INTERNET—A worldwide "network of networks" using Internet Protocol to link computers.

INTRANET—Internet-accessible information made available only to employees and other internal participants in a company or organization.

ITALIC—Letters sloped forward instead of upright, used for emphasis or effect.

JOHNSON BOX—Named after the late Frank Johnson, the copywriter who first used it, this is a boxed-in headline or short lead-in paragraph that appears at the top of a direct mail letter.

JPEG—Joint Photographic Experts Group. A bit-mapped graphics format that is optimized for scanned photographs. They can be compressed into smaller file sizes than GIFs.

JUSTIFY—To place space between letters so that the left and right margins of all lines in copy are the same. Creates a squared-up appearance.

KEY CODE—See Code.

KEYING—The practice of coding blocks of copy to the pictures they describe by means of a letter or number.

KILL—Eliminate or delete certain copy, illustration, or whatever is so marked.

KROMECOTE—A very glossy, coated paper stock.

LABEL—A piece of paper (it may be pressure-sensitive or not) that carries the name and address (and possibly an identification code) of a prospect or previous buyer. It is affixed to an order form, letter, or outer envelope for mailing purposes.

LAID PAPER STOCK—A paper, often used for letterhead printing, which is not woven but appears to be.

LANDING PAGE—A Web page especially prepared to serve as the first "landing place" for respondents to a promotional e-mail or banner ad. It pertains specifically to the offer being made and serves as a bridge between the promotion and the firm's main Web site. May also be called a bounce page, jump page, or splash page.

LAYOUT—A rendering of a proposed printed piece, indicating positions for headings, copy, art, and borders. The term may also indicate color treatments. See also Comprehensive Layout.

LEAD—A prospect that has not yet been converted to a buyer.

LEADING—The space that appears between printed lines. Some leading is necessary for readability.

LETTERHEAD—The stationery used by a particular business, printed to identify that firm via a logo, name, and address.

LETTERPRESS—A traditional printing method in which the print area is raised above the non-print area so that ink rollers touch the portion that becomes the printed image.

LETTERSHOP—The firm that handles the labeling of order cards and envelopes and the insertion and mailing of direct mail solicitations.

LINE DRAWINGS—Solid-black-line artwork that does not require halftone reproduction.

LIST—The names and addresses of prospects, customers, or both who have something in common, whether it be previous buying habits, occupation, and/or other attributes. Also known as a file.

LIST BROKER—A professional counselor to renters of direct mail lists. The broker provides recommendations on list rental for specific propositions, and may be made privy to the results so that he or she can help plan future testing and roll-outs. The broker also helps expedite the receipt of lists, merge/purge operations, and other list-related matters.

LITHOGRAPHY—A printing process that involves the use of plates made from photographs. Offset lithography is simply called "offset" in most cases.

LOAD-UP—On continuity propositions, a system whereby the customer is sent the bulk of product at once, to save on postage and packaging costs. Generally, the customer is then asked to remit the monthly or semi-monthly fee using payment coupons from a booklet until the entire set is paid for.

LOGOTYPE—Also called logo. The trademark or signature of a company, which may simply be indicated by a certain typeface, or by artwork.

LOOSE LEAD—A loosely qualified prospect who has indicated at least minimal interest in a product or service. See also Tight Lead.

LURK—To visit a newsgroup, social media site or chat group without posting entries or making comments.

MAIL DATE—The day agreed upon between a list renter and list owner as the "drop date" for a specific mailing at the post office.

MAILER—A firm that does direct mailing (lettershop), or a carton in which products are shipped. Also a term for a direct mail piece.

MAIL-ORDER BUYER—A person with a history of frequent and recent purchases by mail, and thus a good prospect for a new mail-order proposition.

MAIL PREFERENCE SERVICE—The Direct Marketing Association provides this service to consumers who may use it to have their names eliminated from or added to direct mail lists. Both DMA-member companies and non-member companies may use this information to better serve consumers.

MASS CUSTOMIZATION—Offering products with a host of pre-developed options that allow buyers to put together what seems to be a product that's "just for them," but actually combines elements that are readily available for combination.

MERGE/PURGE—A computer process whereby lists may be merged together to facilitate zipcode sequencing and the testing of segments, and can be "purged" of duplicates, pander names, other undesirable names, or names that are to be saved for later mailing.

METATAGS—Words and phrases added to the HTML source material of a Web page to characterize its content and help search engines identify its most appropriate categories.

MOBILE MARKETING—Promotional activity designed for delivery to cell phones, smart phones and other hand-held devices, usually as a component of a multichannel marketing campaign.

MOONLIGHTER—A freelancer who is also employed regularly by a single firm.

MULTICHANNEL MARKETING—Strategic marketing using multiple marketing channels to effectively reach and influence a customer or prospect.

MULTIPLE BUYER—Also called a multi-buyer or repeat buyer. A person who has purchased more than once from a firm, on different occasions.

NEGATIVE OPTION—Used by many book and music clubs, this calls for the customer to send back a response if he or she does not want to purchase a monthly selection. The terms must be spelled out carefully and agreed to by the customer, under Federal Trade Commission regulations. See also Positive Option.

NESTING—A procedure designed to cut costs and save time in the mailing/insertion process. One piece of literature is placed inside another before insertion into an envelope, thus cutting the number of positions necessary on the inserting machine. The procedure may also be used to nest an appropriate order form with selling or other literature.

NET DOWN—The quantity of names left after a merge/purge eliminates duplicates.

NETIQUETTE—The informal rules for using the Internet with courtesy.

NEWSPRINT—A low grade of paper used chiefly for newspapers. Made from groundwood pulp and sulphite pulp and finished by machine.

NEWS RELEASE—An announcement sent to newspapers, magazines, television and radio stations, or other media with news about a person, event, product, or service. Also called a press release.

OFFER—The specified buying terms presented to the prospect, including price, payment options, delivery terms, and premiums.

OFFSET PAPER—A type of paper suited to offset lithography. It usually refers to a lower grade of offset lithography paper, as opposed to a more expensive or coated stock that might also be used for offset printing.

ONE UP—Printing one impression of a printing job at a time. Also two up, three up, four up, etc.

OPACITY—A measure of paper quality indicating the amount of "show through" from one side to the other when paper is printed on both sides.

OPT-IN NAMES—A list of names of customers or prospects who have specifically indicated that they are willing to receive certain types of messages from a certain company, or from the firms to which that company may rent names for direct mail or e-mail purposes.

OPT-OUT NAMES—A list of names of customers or prospects who have specifically indicated that they do not want to receive certain types of messages from a certain company, or from the firms to which that company may rent names for direct mail or e-mail purposes.

OUT OF REGISTER—Lack of alignment of colors that are to be printed one right over the other, resulting in "hanging" dot patterns.

OVERLINE—A phrase or heading that appears above the main headline on a brochure or other promotional piece. Also called a "kicker."

PACKAGE—The entire direct mail solicitation, typically including the outer envelope, letter, brochure, order card, Business Reply Envelope, and whatever other elements may be included.

PACKAGE INSERT—A promotional offer that is included in the shipment of a product. It may be from the firm shipping the product or, via a fee or royalty arrangement, from a different firm,. Standard Rate and Data Service publishes information on available package insert arrangements.

PACKAGE TEST—A test of a direct mail element or elements within a given package, against the control package.

PAGINATION—Determining how type will break from page to page, or how catalog products will appear from page to page.

PANDER NAMES—Names of consumers who have asked to be placed on a "do not mail" list, made available through service bureaus.

PANTONE MATCHING SYSTEM (PMS) COLORS—Standard, numbered shades and colors that are available to printers in premixed form, selected when a specific background or accent color is desired.

PASS-ALONG—The factor of additional readers for a direct mail piece or ad, obtained when the recipient passes the piece along to others. Self-mailers are considered best adapted among the direct mail formats for obtaining pass-along readers.

PDF—Portable Document Format. The current standard for electronic mechanicals. Graphic designers use Adobe Acrobat to save all the text, illustrations, and photos in a universal language. Clients then can preview and approve the piece using Acrobat Reader software.

PERSONALIZED URL—Also known as a PURL, this is a landing page that is personalized to the individual by name and often by other known information about their interests, buying patterns and the like.

PERSONALIZATION—The addition of the name and/or other individual information about a prospect or buyer to a promotion.

PICA—A measurement of lines of type. There are six picas to an inch.

PICK UP—An indication that a designated piece of copy or art will be reused without modifications.

PIGGYBACK—An offer that "rides along free" with another offer.

PLATES—Short for printing plates, which are used to separate image from non-image material during the traditional printing process.

POINT—A unit of measurement for type, with 72 points to an inch of height.

PORTAL—A Web site that serves as a gateway to a wide range of information on the Internet. It often includes a search engine.

POSITIVE OPTION—A system whereby the customer must send back a reply if he or she does want merchandise. It is used for some club appeals. See also Negative Option.

PREDICTIVE ANALYTICS—The area of data mining concerned with forecasting probabilities and trends, including what a customer is most likely to be in the market to buy next.

PREDICTIVE MODELING—A process used in predictive analytics to create a statistical model of future behavior or buying.

PREMIUM—An offer of a free item to the buyer as an incentive to purchase or try a product.

PRESS PROOF—A proof made on a regular press and used to check color before the full run is made.

PRESS RELEASE—See News Release.

PRESSURE-SENSITIVE LABELS—Also called peel-off labels.

PROGRESSIVES—Also called progs. A set of proofs that can be separated to show each color on its own, and put back together to see how the four colors combine.

PROOF—A reproduction of art and/or type used for proofreading, editing, and checking for layout errors.

PROSPECT—The name of a person who is seen as a potential buyer for a product, but who has not yet inquired or purchased from a firm.

PSYCHOGRAPHICS—Qualitative lifestyle or attitude characteristics, as opposed to quantifiable indicators like demographics.

PUBLICITY—Any form of non-paid promotion in the media.

PUBLISHER'S LETTER—Also called a "lift letter." An auxiliary letter in a mailing that keys in on a specific selling point and/or answers objections to help close the sale.

PULL MEDIA—Marketing media that draws a target audience in, such as television or a Web site.

PUSH MEDIA—Marketing media that is sent directly to members of a target audience, such as e-mail.

QR CODE—A matrix barcode (or two-dimensional code), readable by QR scanners, mobile phones with a camera, and smart phones.

REAL TIME—Conducted in the present moment, as opposed to delayed communications.

RECENCY/FREQUENCY/MONETARY (RFM)—Three criteria by which a name on a rental list is evaluated: how recent was the last purchase, how often has the individual purchased, and how large is the average order. Another version, popularized by the late Robert Kestnbaum, adds the type of merchandise to the criteria. This is known as FRAT, or Frequency/Recency/Amount/Type.

REFERRAL—Also called "friend of a friend" or "the buddy system." This is a plan whereby the seller asks customers or prospects to identify friends who are likely to be interested in the same kind of merchandise or offer. The customer may be offered a premium for doing so.

REPLY CARD—Also called "Business Reply Card" or "BRC." A postage-paid order card or inquiry card that bears the sender's address and postal indicia.

RESPONSE RATE—The percentage of orders per thousand mailed that results from a mailing or ad insertion in a publication.

REVERSE TYPE—Instead of the common dark-on-light typeface presentation, reverse type shows the type itself in a light color, presented on a dark background. It is dramatic in appearance, but more difficult to read than regular type, especially in smaller sizes.

ROI—Return on investment. Used as a financial measurement of a campaign's success.

ROLL-OUT—A scheduled mailing of the remaining names in a list universe, if a list test is successful and a possible subsequent, larger test validates the initial results.

ROP—Run of paper or run of press. A newspaper space placement that is within the regular editorial sections of the newspaper, as opposed to a free-standing insert.

ROUGH—The first draft of copy or a layout.

SANS SERIF—Type that does not have these flourishes.

SCREEN—A grid used in a special camera to create halftone prints.

SELF-MAILER—A one-piece, direct mail item that is not a catalog, but which does not come in an envelope. For best results it should incorporate all the elements of a direct mail package including letter, brochure/display, and reply device.

SERIF—A typeface featuring lines or strokes that project from each character.

SEARCH ENGINE—A Web site that allows visitors to type in words or phrases, and then returns a list of suggested site matches to facilitate visitors' research process.

SEARCH ENGINE OPTIMIZATION—The process of modifying a Web site to make it as attractive as possible to search engines.

SHARE OF WALLET—The percentage of a buyer's total expenditures in a particular product category that is spent with a certain company.

SHEET-FED PRESS—An offset press that prints on sheets of paper that are fed into the press one at a time. Usually used for smaller quantity and/or higher quality printing. See also Web Press.

SIGNATURE—A section of a catalog or book, which may be eight or more pages in length. Catalogs may be repositioned by signature to generate a new look for re-mailing.

SMS—Stands for the "short message service" commonly used for texting via mobile phones.

SKU—Stock-Keeping Unit. A firm wants to keep careful control of its SKUs to make sure it offers sufficient variety to satisfy the market without risking loss of profit by providing more than the optimum number of customer options.

SOCIAL MEDIA—Works of user-created video, audio, text or multimedia that are published and shared in a social environment, such as a blog, wiki or video hosting site.

SOFT BOUNCE—An undeliverable e-mail address that reached the destination server but could not find the specific address residing there. See also Hard Bounce.

SOLO MAILING—A solicitation for a single product or product line.

SOURCE CODE—See Code.

SPAM—Unsolicited bulk commercial e-mail sent to people with whom the sender has neither a prior business relationship nor permission to send e-mail.

SPONSORED SEARCH—A paid feature of search engines whereby advertisers bid for prominent position in a special sponsors' section that appears when specific keywords or phrases are entered.

SPLIT RUN—Two versions of an ad run in the same publication via a system whereby every other copy of the publication carries one ad and the next in line carries the other. This allows for statistically accurate testing. Same as A/B Split.

STANDARD MAIL—Mail composed of a large quantity of identical pieces, presorted and batched according to post office requirements to save the mailer money on postage. Standard mail privileges require a permit from the post office.

STANDARD RATE & DATA SERVICE (SRDS)—Chicago-area firm that publishes guides to the rates and requirements of a wide range of business and consumer media.

STET—A proofreader's word which, when applied to a word or phrase of copy that has been marked out, means "leave it as it was."

STOCK—Paper or other material used to print on.

STOCK PHOTO—Photos made available by professional photographers for non-exclusive use at a negotiable fee based on circulation and intended use.

STORYBOARDS—A series of drawings created to provide a rough idea of the visuals planned for a television spot, infomercial, or video. The corresponding audio may be displayed below each drawing.

STUFFER—An enclosure in a package, statement, newspaper, or other medium for the purpose of selling a product.

SWIPE FILE—The direct mail packages, space ads, and other samples of competitive advertising material saved by a copywriter or art director for inspiration in developing new ideas.

TEASER—Also called an envelope teaser. The copy on the outside of an envelope whose purpose is to move the reader to open it and read the offer inside. Also refers to a teaser ad: an enticing ad that encourages the reader to watch for further developments in later-running ads.

TESTING—A preliminary mailing or ad insertion that determines the relative chances of success of a given proposition in a given medium.

TEXT MINING—Deriving high-quality information from text by divining patterns and trends using statistical methods. It has been used as a method to improve the relevance and clarity of copy.

THUMBNAILS—Miniature layout sketches used to give a general idea of what a direct mail piece will look like.

TIGHT LEAD—A highly qualified prospect who has indicated strong and immediate interest in a product or service. See also Loose Lead.

TIP-ON—Something glued to a direct mail letter, order card, or other printed piece. It may be a gimmick or an action device.

TRADE PUBLICATION—A magazine intended for those involved in a specific trade or profession.

TRAFFIC BUILDER—A direct mail piece that does not have the solicitation of a direct order as its main goal, but rather is meant to bring customers into a retail store.

UNIVERSE—The total number of people who fit a certain set of characteristics. Also, the total number of people on a specific mailing list.

UP-CHARGE—A vendor's additions to the price initially quoted. Should be discussed with the customer before they are added to the bill.

UP FRONT—Getting the payment for a product or service before it is shipped.

URL—Universal/Uniform Resource Locator. An addressing scheme for World Wide Web sites.

VALIDATION—A mailing that takes place after an initial test, to verify the results before a roll-out.

VALUE BORDER—An elaborate art border resembling those on insurance policies and certificates, used on reply forms or other direct mail pieces to add the perception of worth and importance.

VIRAL MARKETING—In e-mail marketing, sending a message that is so compelling that recipients are moved to forward it to many people they know. Also applies to various other forms of word-of-mouth marketing.

VORTAL—A vertical portal that serves a specific industry, such as plastics.

WEBINAR—A seminar presented via the Web. The simplest version combines a conference call for audio with an online Power Point presentation for video. More advanced versions may include interactivity and full-motion video. Webinars are usually recorded for later online viewing at the convenience of customers and prospects.

WEB 2.0—Moving beyond one-way communications to a web where the user takes charge of his or her own web experience, including reviews and social media conversations.

WEB 3.0—The "semantic Web," where the Web can "understand itself" and becomes a guide, offering a world wide database and harnessing the power of artificial intelligence to provide customized recommendations

WEB PRESS—An offset printing press that has a rotary action and uses large rolls of paper. It is used for larger quantity printing (usually 50,000 pieces and up). See also Sheet-Fed Press.

WHITE PAPER—A short treatise aimed at educating industry customers. It should be devoid of selling messages, and should help establish the credibility of the author and the firm he or she represents.

WIKI—A collaborative Web site that can be directly edited by anyone with access to it. The most prominent example is Wikipedia.

WINDOW ENVELOPE—An envelope with a see-through area that allows for a labeled reply device and which may also serve as the address mechanism. The window is die cut, and may remain open or be covered with a see-through material.

WORLD WIDE WEB—A system for accessing Internet resources including text, graphics, sound, and video.

XML—eXtensible Markup Language. An Internet language that is more powerful than HTML and incorporates document management technology.

ZIP-CODE SEQUENCE—The arrangement of names and addresses on a list, beginning with 00000 and progressing through 99999. This provides basic sorting for standard postal bulk-rate mail. It may go further, to a nine-digit number, for carrier-route coding.

Index

Racom Communications Order Form

QUANTITY	TITLE	PRICE	AMOUNT
_____	Creative Strategy in Direct & Interactive Marketing, 4th Ed., **Susan K. Jones**	$49.95	_____
_____	The IMC Handbook, **J. Stephen Kelly/Susan K. Jones**	$49.95	_____
_____	Innovating . . . Chcago Style, **Thomas Kuczmarski, Luke Tanen, Dan Miller**	$27.95	_____
_____	The New Media Driver's License, **Richard Cole/Derek Mehraban**	$24.95	_____
_____	Aligned, **Maurice Parisien**	$24.95	_____
_____	How to Jump-Start Your Career, **Robert L. Hemmings**	$19.95	_____
_____	This Year a Pogo Stick . . . Next Year a Unicycle!, **Jim Kobs**	$19.95	_____
_____	Follow That Customer, **Egbert Jan van Bel/Ed Sander/Alan Weber**	$39.95	_____
_____	Internet Marketing, **Herschell Gordon Lewis**	$19.95	_____
_____	Reliability Rules, **Don Schultz/Reg Price**	$34.95	_____
_____	The Marketing Performance Measurement Toolkit, **David M. Raab**	$39.95	_____
_____	Successful E-Mail Marketing Strategies, **Arthur M. Hughes/Arthur Sweetser**	$49.95	_____
_____	Managing Your Business Data, **Theresa Kushner/Maria Villar**	$32.95	_____
_____	Media Strategy and Planning Workbook, **DL Dickinson**	$24.95	_____
_____	Marketing Metrics in Action, **Laura Patterson**	$24.95	_____
_____	Print Matters, **Randall Hines/Robert Lauterborn**	$27.95	_____
_____	The Business of Database Marketing, **Richard N. Tooker**	$49.95	_____
_____	Customer Churn, Retention, and Profitability, **Arthur Middleton Hughes**	$44.95	_____
_____	Data-Driven Business Models, **Alan Weber**	$49.95	_____
_____	Branding Iron, **Charlie Hughes and William Jeanes**	$27.95	_____
_____	Managing Sales Leads and Sales & Marketing 365, **James Obermayer**	$56.95	_____
_____	Creating the Marketing Experience, **Joe Marconi**	$49.95	_____
_____	Coming to Concurrence, **J. Walker Smith/Ann Clurman/Craig Wood**	$34.95	_____
_____	Brand Babble, **Don E. Schultz/Heidi F. Schultz**	$24.95	_____
_____	The New Marketing Conversation, **Donna Baier Stein/Alexandra MacAaron**	$34.95	_____
_____	Trade Show and Event Marketing, **Ruth Stevens**	$59.95	_____
_____	Accountable Marketing, **Peter J. Rosenwald**	$59.95	_____
_____	Contemporary Database Marketing, **Martin Baier/Kurtis Ruf/G. Chakraborty**	$89.95	_____
_____	Catalog Strategist's Toolkit, **Katie Muldoon**	$59.95	_____
_____	Marketing Convergence, **Susan K. Jones/Ted Spiegel**	$34.95	_____
_____	High-Performance Interactive Marketing, **Christopher Ryan**	$39.95	_____
_____	Public Relations: The Complete Guide, **Joe Marconi**	$49.95	_____
_____	The Marketer's Guide to Public Relations, **Thomas L. Harris/Patricia T. Whalen**	$39.95	_____
_____	The White Paper Marketing Handbook, **Robert W. Bly**	$39.95	_____
_____	Business-to-Business Marketing Research, **Martin Block/Tamara Block**	$69.95	_____
_____	Hot Appeals or Burnt Offerings, **Herschell Gordon Lewis**	$24.95	_____
_____	On the Art of Writing Copy, **Herschell Gordon Lewis**	$34.95	_____
_____	Open Me Now, **Herschell Gordon Lewis**	$21.95	_____
_____	Marketing Mayhem, **Herschell Gordon Lewis**	$39.95	_____
_____	Asinine Advertising, **Herschell Gordon Lewis**	$22.95	_____
_____	The Ultimate Guide To Purchasing Website, Video, Print & Other Creative Services, **Bobbi Balderman**	$18.95	_____

Name/Title_____

Company _____

Street Address _____

City/State/Zip _____

Email _____ Phone _____

Credit Card: ☐ VISA ☐ MasterCard ☐ American Express ☐ Discover
☐ Check or money order enclosed (payable to Racom Communications in US
   dollars drawn on a US bank)

Number _____ Exp. Date _____

Signature _____

Subtotal	_____
Subtotal from other side	_____
8.65% Tax	_____
Shipping & Handling	_____
$7.00 for first book; $1.00 for each additional book.	
TOTAL	_____

Racom Communications, 150 N. Michigan Ave, Suite 2800, Chicago, IL 60601, 312-494-0100, 800-247-6553, www. Racombooks.com